Studies in American Indian Art

Studies in American Indian Art

A Memorial Tribute to Norman Feder

Edited by Christian F. Feest

European Review of
Native American Studies
Distributed by University of Washington Press, Seattle and London

Studies in American Indian art: a memorial tribute to Norman Feder / edited by Christian F. Feest. Altenstadt: European Review of Native American Studies, 2001.
Includes bibliographic references.
ISBN 3-00-005871-0 (paper)

ERNAS Monographs 2
European Review of Native American Studies
Fasanenweg 4a, D-63674 Altenstadt, Germany

Publisher: Christian F. Feest
Copy Editor: Sylvia S. Kasprycki

Front cover illustration:
Portion of the pictographic painting on an undocumented bison robe. Nationalmuseet (Copenhagen), cat.no. Hd60. Redrawn by Arni Brownstone.

Back cover illustration:
Detail of a painted Hidatsa robe sketched in 1851 at Fort Berthold by Rudolph Friedrich Kurz. Tracing by Arni Brownstone.

Printed and bound in Austria (European Union)
by Adolf Holzhausens Nachfolger, Vienna
Distributed by University of Washington Press
P.O. Box 50096, Seattle, WA 94145-5096, U.S.A.

Table of Contents

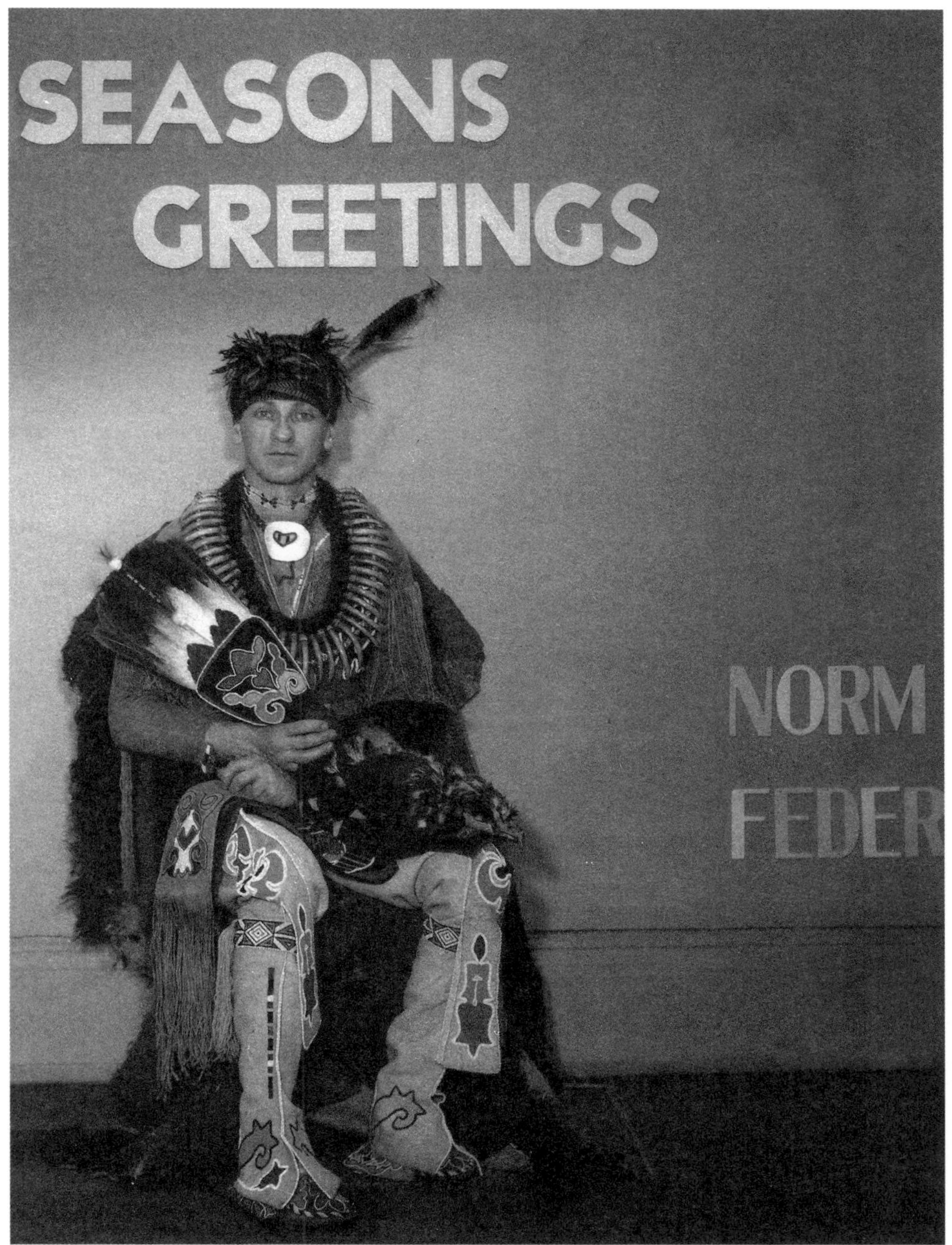

Norman Feder (1930–1995). Photograph: Samuel Cahoon.

Preface

Like few of his contemporaries, Norman Feder has helped to shape the study of American Indian art. In a mixed career spanning four decades as hobbyist craftsman, author, curator, and editor, Feder contributed to the theoretical and methodological foundation of a discipline about to emerge from the narrow interests of museum anthropologists and devoted amateurs into the public prominence of an upscale art market and of widespread appreciation. Feder entered the field without the benefit of an academic training, but with a profound firsthand knowledge of the importance of techniques for an understanding of Native American visual forms of expression. Among his lasting contributions is the explicit recognition of the historical nature of these art forms, of the resulting significance of documented collections and information contained in early drawings and photographs for a placement of artifact styles in time and space, and of the usefulness of studies of artifact types or genres in Native American art. He was also among the first to bring the resources of European museums to the attention of an American audience.

In this volume a group of American, Canadian, and European anthropologists, art historians, and collectors—friends, colleagues, and heirs—explore topics relating to Feder's far-ranging interests in Native American art and shed light on his background and his achievements. Their contributions deal with works from different regions, time periods, and traditional forms of expression of Native North America, discuss a wide spectrum of questions posed by current research, and reflect Norman Feder's direct or indirect influence on theory and methodology. Even those approaches which in their interpretations transcend the rather strict boundaries Feder had felt were imposed by the limitations inherent in the data, are clearly indebted to the foundations that he has laid.

The idea for this book was first suggested to me within weeks after Norman Feder's death by Arthur C. Einhorn. I accepted the challenge to organize a volume that in a modest manner would acknowledge the quiet importance of a modest man. My initial invitations to potential contributors were well received, and if I have to blame myself for more than the shortcomings usually inherent in editing a group of collected essays, it is that in the lapse of time some of those who had agreed to contribute, passed away themselves before they could submit their papers. Others had to drop out of the project due to a variety of reasons, but new authors were added to take their place.

Getting the book into print proved to require a much larger effort. Volumes of this kind are often regarded as unmarketable, and the indecision of various presses in this respect has contributed to a considerable delay in getting this book published. Among the several friends and colleagues who actively sought to help me in this respect, J. C. H. King deserves special mention. The ultimate decision to publish *Studies in American Indian Art: A Memorial Tribute to Norman Feder* as the second volume in the *ERNAS* monograph series was largely based upon the consideration that any further delay should be avoided. This decision would have been impossible without the generous support provided by Mary T. Hamilton, publisher of *American Indian Art Magazine*, and Roanne P. Goldfein, the magazine's editor for more than twenty years.

The book is intended to be both a tribute to Feder's seminal role in the study of American Indian art and an illustration of its interdisciplinary nature. In the long run, Norman Feder's work will continue to speak for itself. The following essays are offered as little more than personal marks of indebtedness and appreciation, in the hope that he would have liked some of them.

Christian F. Feest

Norman Feder as Hobbyist, Cultural Scientist, and Social Mover

Arthur C. Einhorn

Norman Feder was an enigmatic and eclectic product of his times. To call him merely a hobbyist would ignore the many roles he played in the general area of Native American Art. He was a hobbyist and collector to be sure, and there are many definitions of those terms, but he also was a scientist with a searching mind and an eye for detail. Broadening on this base, Norman followed the path of scientific scholarship by creating a journal to publish his findings and those of others. In that respect he became entrepreneur, publisher, and editor promoting interest in an area of art and culture long neglected by Western opinion or interest. A precocious young man, he started *American Indian Hobbyist* in 1954, when there was little general interest, but a small and growing cadre of enthusiasts whom he annealed together by means of the publication. Through those early years many professionals were added to the ranks of the readership, as were several who joined the editorial staff, including the late James H. Howard. Not so strangely the publication (renamed *American Indian Tradition* in 1960) became a catalyst for higher education, leading many of its readers and contributors into the doctoral ranks of cultural anthropology, ethnohistory, and related professions. Others, though not drawn to academia, still managed creditable publications in their own right. One could infer that Norman's pervasive influence not only inspired others, but carried the subject from shadowy museum preservation into the larger lens of public appreciation and awareness.

After his untimely death, I write about Norm with some trepidation. He was a very private person by nature, and my stepping on his buried bones may evoke an outcry from relatives or a curse from him. I hope not, as his achievements should be recognized in the broad spectrum of Native American reemergence and self-appreciation—much like Phoenix arising from the flames of destruction.

Born in Brooklyn, Norm's enculturative years were spent in a multiethnic neighborhood of the Bronx, where he absorbed appreciation for cultural diversity. He had a cherished memory of its many ethnic foods, but felt anathema for the ethnic, racial, and religious bigotry which he witnessed in that period. Though never able to draw himself, he instinctively was attracted to and appreciated art outside the Western tradition, particularly that of the Native Americans. By his own admission he once defined himself as a youthful romantic awestruck by anything Indian; a cognition which came to dominate his whole existence. Though familiar with most of New York's museums, his favorite haunt was the American Museum of Natural History with its spacious halls devoted to American Indian cultures.

During his freshman year in high school, ca. 1944–45, his parents moved to Los Angeles, where he finished high school and college (receiving his BA from the University of California, Los Angeles, in Botany). It was there the active interest in Indians blossomed as he worked with Boy Scouts and early hobbyists. Concurrently he hung around with Iron Eyes Cody, Nepo Strongheart, and other Hollywood Indians, not to mention a growing population of Indians fresh from the reservations who were relocated there under the BIA urbanization policy of the time. From those experiences he learned to treat Indian people as he treated everyone—as normal human beings. In so doing he

Arthur C. Einhorn, retired, served as Associate Professor of Anthropology at Jefferson Community College for ten years and as Chair of the Social Science Dept. at Lowville Academy for thirty years. He also taught briefly at SUNY/Buffalo while in graduate school and was adjunct Professor of graduate courses in Anthropology for St. Lawrence University, where he also codirected an Indian Education seminar for three years. His major areas of interest include the Iroquoian and Algonquian peoples and the Caribs of theWest Indies. Author's address: Box 286, Lowville, NY 13367, U.S.A.

made many good friends, which changed his entire perspective about culture and reality. Apparently while still in college in the early 1950s, there was occasion to work with hobbyist groups in Colorado, where he found the relationship between Indians and hobbyists to be rather harmonious. Years later he discovered the opposite in the East, where he diplomatically brokered a dialogue between the groups. Somewhere along the line Norman learned the intricacies of quillwork from a Sioux lady. Whether this transpired in Los Angeles or South Dakota is uncertain, but it is known that he traveled widely to visit and learn from Native craftspeople and to attend ceremonies.

The same years saw him spending considerable time at the Southwest Museum, where he met Frederick Webb Hodge and Mark R. Harrington. Whether these mentors inspired the creation of the *American Indian Hobbyist* is not known, but undoubtedly they had some influence on Norm's subsequent career. Throughout the mid-1950s, while editor of the magazine, he seems to have crisscrossed Canada and the United States viewing museum collections and making long-lasting professional contacts and friendships.

In 1958 he began to work for the Denver Art Museum, first as a clerk/typist in the Native Arts department, but quickly becoming Assistant Curator. In 1960–61 he took a leave from the Denver Art Museum to work with Frederick Dockstader at the Museum of the American Indian (Heye Foundation) in New York. It was in this period that the *Hobbyist-Tradition* apparently was sold. While with the Museum of the American Indian, Norm often held small group seminars for friends in his nearby apartment, experiences still vividly recalled by some of the participants. In the course of his work with the Heye Foundation, while researching accession records, he came to understand why so many Indians had sold their family and tribal patrimony over the years. It was simply because of despair and the desperate need for money, but more telling was the fact that many such heirlooms had lost their meaning. It was really not so different from rural Whites selling off pioneer flintlocks, swords, spinning wheels, and dry sinks, along with the family bibles, journals, and letters piled in old trunks.

Returning from New York to Denver in September 1961, Norm became Curator first of American Art, later of American Indian Art, and finally of Native Arts. During those years the Brooklyn Museum published his catalog of the Jarvis collection in 1964, he curated the important exhibition "American Indian Art Before 1850" at the Denver Art Museum in 1965, and he wrote his hefty *American Indian Art*, which was finally published in 1971. In the same year he was guest curator of a seminal exhibition of Native American art at the Whitney Museum of American Art in New York City. In the summer of 1969 he visited Europe in order to study North American and African collections and in the fall went to the Northwest Coast to collect for the Denver Art Museum.

With the money from the book and the Whitney show Norm bought property in Sidney, British Columbia, where he retreated to after leaving Denver in 1973. For the next two years he taught at Simon Fraser University in nearby Burnaby, BC. During a vacation in Phoenix in 1976, Norm had a chance encounter with Robert Ashton, then involved in publishing *American Indian Art Magazine*, who persuaded Norm to get on board as a consultant. He is first listed as a consultant in Vol. 2, No. 3, May 1977. Although Ashton was soon replaced in the publication, Norm continued as an advisor until his death.

For obscure reasons, perhaps disaffected by the growing Indian militancy and antagonism of the era, during the 1970s Norm more or less fell out of sight but for his links with *American Indian Art Magazine* and a few friends, spending his summers in Sydney and his winters in San Diego, California. As his health was deteriorating throughout the 1980s, he started disposing of books and most of his craft supplies by the 1990s. This could have been a foreboding of tragedy to come, and he was not at all well during his last few years.

Few of us can really understand another person, not even a close friend. Some of us may get near enough for a better look, but the deeper intricacies of thought and behavior usually are elusive. Norm's life and influence came upon us like a refreshing spring breeze as the nuclear era and Cold War began. His presence revitalized many people, both Indian and White, and most certainly focused attention on Native American art as equal to any other such tradition in the family of man. By itself that is an accomplishment in this busy, mad world we live in, but he did so much more. Goodbye, Norm; though most hardly knew you intimately, your passing this way will long be recorded.

Norman Feder's Double Standard

Case Studies in Critical Examination of Objects

Joyce Herold

As an accomplished scholar of material culture of North American Indians, Norman Feder operated under basic tenets that objects can be revealed to a large extent by asking a series of questions of the objects themselves and by studying verbal and nonverbal documents about the objects. He passionately supported both careful analysis and broad critical appreciation of a vast array of Native American craft-art expressions. Eclecticism within high standards of scholarship characterized Feder's influential work as Editorial Consultant of *American Indian Art Magazine*.

For his own core work, however, Norman Feder chose documented American Indian materials from the pre-1850 period. He studied and established the credentials of many rare objects and collections preserved from the times of early contact between aboriginals and invading Europeans and the following pre-reservation periods. Implicit in his specialty was preoccupation with authenticity and its frequent codependent, particularly for Feder, of traditionalism. The critique of authenticity in American Indian arts suffuses Norman Feder's writing.

This article presents an intensive test of his knowledge and evaluative skills that Feder set for himself as part of early-career graduate studies in 1969. The project played a vital role in Feder's development as a scholar: It forced him to become more self-critical and to document his opinions about objects.

Context of the Critique

Norman Feder repeatedly sought, defined, and criticized the authentic and the traditional among the myriad patterns and variations of materials, constructions, styles, and uses of Native American objects. He critiqued, that is, assessed the authenticity, quality, meaning, and importance of objects and their documentation. In a valuable body of survey articles, catalogs, and reviews, he set models for understanding the significance of early Indian materials, including the Nathan Sturges Jarvis collection (Feder 1964), pre-1850 Native American material (Feder 1965), the Malaspina expedition collection at the Museo de America in Madrid (Feder 1977a), George Catlin materials from various sources (Feder 1977b), the Berne Historical Museum collection (Feder 1978), and the John Painter collection (Feder 1994).

His remarkable visual memory was a major tool in Feder's critique of objects. A great breadth of inspections of private, commercial, and institutional collections and photographic archives had provided an incomparable personal resource and sharpened his acuity for every detail of objects. His recall of objects and images allowed self-confident questioning of attributions, as well as tracing of new object types, regional styles, and aberrant or idiosyncratic objects.

His extensive hobbyist-artist experience in Plains, California, and Northwest Coast Indian arts also served Feder well in identification and analysis of materials, cut and construction, patterning, and other formal aspects of objects. He published many artifact type profiles intended to establish process and nomencla-

Joyce Herold worked with Norman Feder in 1965–1968, studying the Denver Art Museum's American Indian basketry collection and carrying out Jicarilla Apache field research. In 1974 she became the first ethnologist at the Denver Museum of Natural History, where she continues as Curator of Ethnology. She specializes in Southwestern Indian arts, especially basketry, and has published numerous articles in *American Indian Art Magazine*, on whose editorial board she serves. Her most recent publication is "Grand Amateur Collecting in the Mid-Twentieth Century" in *Collecting Native America, 1870–1960* (1999). Herold's anthropological interests extend to tribal cultures of southern Africa and Southeast Asia, and she takes an active role with the International Council of Museums.
Author's address: Denver Museum of Natural History, 2001 Colorado Boulevard, Denver, CO 80205-5798, U.S.A.

ture in the literature, and he did not suffer lightly the misuse of terms that, in his opinion, had been clarified. Norman Feder meticulously examined attributions of culture and period by researching object-associated records, including journals of early artists and visitors on Indian frontiers, original collection inventories, museum catalog information, and the opinions of authorities. Such records "can be utilized in one form of ethnological detective work as an aid in identifying undocumented museum specimens," but they must also be relentlessly critiqued, for such sources as early paintings of Indians "are not always reliable" and museum catalog information and original collector inventories are "sometimes in error" (Feder 1977b: 72, 74, 75). He advocated the updating of museum records to show alternative object names, cultural origins, trade, materials, uses, and other key information—and generously offered his own corrections.

Although he avoided the term as artistic jargon, Norman Feder effectively practiced connoisseurship that "serves to separate authentic from false, sometimes good (expensive) from bad (cheap), and to determine an object's origins, first by region, then, if possible, by maker" (Ames 1985: 94). The imperatives of the connoisseur inform acquisition and increasingly came to attention (even to crisis) during the burgeoning buyers' interest and, hence, sellers' market for American Indian art which coincided with Feder's mature career. Monetary valuation of art objects was anathema to Feder, yet he was well aware that his scholarship and judgments heightened collector interest in scarce commodities. In fact he played a major role in triggering the precipitous 1970s rise of the Indian art market when, as an established connoisseur, he set forth "the very best American Indian art from the historic period" in his Whitney Museum catalog *Two Hundred Years of North American Indian Art* (Feder 1971).

The most basic requirement in judging objects—separating the authentic from the false—concerned Norman Feder more than it did many in the American Indian art field, because he had observed firsthand the making of replicas, reproductions, and fakes which he later saw passed off as originals. He knew the serious problems posed to records and scholarship by the "artifakes" produced increasingly from the 1970s (cf. Buffalo Bill Historical Center 1992). As in Indian projectile point collecting, which has been plagued by fakes for nearly a hundred years, artifake production, distribution, and profitability has yet to be seriously attenuated (McCoy 1993).

Feder's hobbyist experience made him particularly aware of objects that were copied or made innocently in the spirit of the genuinely Native. Early in his career he had helped build the credibility of Boy Scouts, hobbyists, students of technology, and other non-Indian artifact makers by researching and publishing the ethnographic evidence and construction details, to standards of excellence, for "rendezvous" and powwow clothing and equipment (cf. Feder 1959, 1962, 1972). Feder's authoritative "how-to" studies also assisted mid-twentieth-century Native American artisans who were reviving tradition and developing commercial arts. But Feder was appalled to see non-Indian reproductions traverse the short distance from private learning and entertainment to for-profit proliferation in trading posts and naive acceptance by museums. He reacted responsibly by exposing non-Native or non-traditional origins, which he was so uniquely qualified to recognize. In many cases he knew names of makers, their history, and favored materials, techniques, and styles.

Unlike his well-published critical judgments of early collections, Feder's evaluations of mid-twentieth-century reproductions and artifakes were usually limited to private discussions and consultations with fellow scholars and curators. One such curatorial exercise resulted in the unusually frank and informal findings and opinions presented for the first time in this essay. The manuscript, prepared for a class and for the Denver Museum of Natural History, constitutes a working paper in Norman Feder's double standard of American Indian art assessment.

A Class Project in Critical Examination of Objects

In the early summer of 1969, as part of a graduate degree program in anthropology at the University of Denver, Norman Feder undertook a "Primitive Arts and Industries" class research paper that provided an ideal vehicle for application of his already considerable knowledge of American Indian material culture. The professor, Kate Peck Kent, a redoubtable authority on Southwestern Indian textiles who had worked with Frederic Douglas at the Denver Art Museum, was one of the few American academics in the 1960s and 1970s who focused on analysis of American Indian material culture. In accepting the following project proposal from Feder, Kent took on the task of teaching a brilliant art scholar the discipline of justifying and documenting his opinions:

> "I propose to critically examine a portion of the Francis Crane collection at the Denver Museum of Natural History [including] the material currently on exhibit, and as time allows the collection of wood carvings from the Northwest Coast.
>
> "The objectives will be to determine the accuracy of the current catalog entries for each artifact, and the accuracy of the exhibit arrangement and label information. Special attention will be paid to the correctness of tribal attribution, date of manufacture, function, material, and technique.
>
> "A report will be submitted for each artifact found to be erroneously recorded, citing the literature or comparable documented specimens as justification for any suggested corrections." (This and all succeeding quotes from Project Report, Feder 1969)

A graduate classmate, Arminta Neal, curated Feder's subject, the newly-donated Mary W. A. and Francis V. Crane American Indian collection at the Denver Museum of Natural History (DMNH). The primary museum of its kind in the vast American Western Interior region between Chicago and the West Coast, the Denver Museum had heretofore concentrated on geology, mineralogy, biological sciences, and Paleoindian archaeology. The Museum had missed the great period of historic Indian collecting from 1860 to 1930 and began ethnographic work only in 1968 with the donation of the Crane American Indian collection. After it was moved to Denver from Marathon, Florida, Arminta Neal began to design the Hall of North American Indians as well as storerooms to house the collection. She planned to use outside expertise for assessment of the Crane collection's 11,600 objects and welcomed Feder's research proposal.

The uniquely miscellaneous and recent origins of the Crane American Indian collection made it an ideal subject for testing Norman Feder's expertise. In an amazing feat of modern initiative long after the closing of the Indian frontier, amateur collectors Mary W. A. and Francis V. Crane from 1951 to 1968 had assembled objects representative of Native American cultures from the Arctic to Florida and periods from early nineteenth century to contemporary times (Herold 1999). To do so, they had quietly scoured the continent for primary and secondary collections of early visitors to Indians and objects from dealers, Indian people, and other collectors. In the buyer's market of the 1950s and 1960s, before Indian art auctions were well established, the Crane Foundation was able to acquire thousands of authentic, unrestored remnants of Native life, including many master artworks. The Cranes' mission to operate a small educational, non-profit museum was realized from 1958 to 1968 in their Southeast Museum of the North American Indian.

Mary and Francis Crane also made many questionable acquisitions—wrongly or generically attributed objects, extreme variants from "type" objects, and recent non-Native creations. Despite persistent study, exhortations for honest dealing by vendors, and consultations with authorities, the Cranes failed to pinpoint all the artifakes and incorrect attributions in their collection.

Norman Feder, then Curator of Native Arts at the Denver Art Museum, later told me that he had heard of the little-known Crane American Indian collection even before it came to a rival Denver institution. He was curious to explore its reputation for inclusivity and interesting, unstudied objects, as well as for uneven authenticity and quality. His student project made the best of a degree requirement by adding the enjoyment of seeing and critiquing new objects and helping a fellow museum professional.

Feder implemented the study by focusing on about three hundred objects, a sample of the Crane collection's broad temporal and cultural range, which made up Arminta Neal's quickly executed introductory exhibit. First, Feder relied on his own knowledge and experience and noted "first impressions" of errors in the exhibit:

> "I felt that some errors would be immediately obvious and that questionable items could be noted for further checking. The usual error shows up when an object is wrongly identified on the label as to tribal origin, use, material, technique, or date of manufacture. When no labels were present in a case, all that could be noted was an object out of cultural context."

In his initial reading of the exhibit, Feder listed twenty-nine objects in error, that is, about ten percent of the exhibited objects (see Appendix, below). Included were eleven non-authentic objects, nine wrong tribal attributions, two wrong time periods, six wrong object names or uses, three wrong raw materials, and one display mistake (a few objects having multiple kinds of errors). He wrote, "undoubtedly other errors will be detected as work progresses."

Then, over several months, Feder critically examined his opinions. For each piece with an error, he noted and critiqued catalog data and searched for detailed pertinent comparisons. From the object suppliers, other contacts, and the literature Feder recorded "whatever documentation and justification I can supply on each opinion." The investigations brought to light only three mistaken first impressions, due to Feder's unfamiliarity with a particular style or a supplier's history.

Case Studies of Artifakes and Misidentifications

The eight object reports that are reproduced here test objects purchased by the Cranes from 1951 to 1968 and their original attributions and descriptions.

To convey the immediacy and informal style of the unpublished paper, the Feder format, words, and punctuation are retained as much as possible throughout. The following changes from the original report appear: Objects are rephotographed, individually in color, rather than in black-and-white *in situ* in the exhibit; DMNH accession numbers and catalog information appear under the heading "Catalog Entry" instead of an appended copy of the catalog card; names of some recently active suppliers are withheld; "First Impression" and "Note on Reliability of the Source" are transferred from separate sections to the appropriate object reports; some voluminous citations are edited; and "Later Information" additions reflect Feder's and museum research after report completion.

1. PAINTED SKIN APRON (Fig. 1)

CATALOG ENTRY: AC.10624 Skin Dance Apron. Supplied by G. B. Fenstermaker, 5/31/67. Decorated whale design. Trimmed in hoof rattles, make quite a noise.
AS REPRESENTED: No label information, but on display in case of mixed Northwest Coast materials.
FIRST IMPRESSION: Tlingit painted skin kilt—Recognized as the work of a non-Indian California hobbyist. The major identifying feature is the use of dyed pig toes on the fringes.
MY OPINION: That this specimen is a recently made fake.

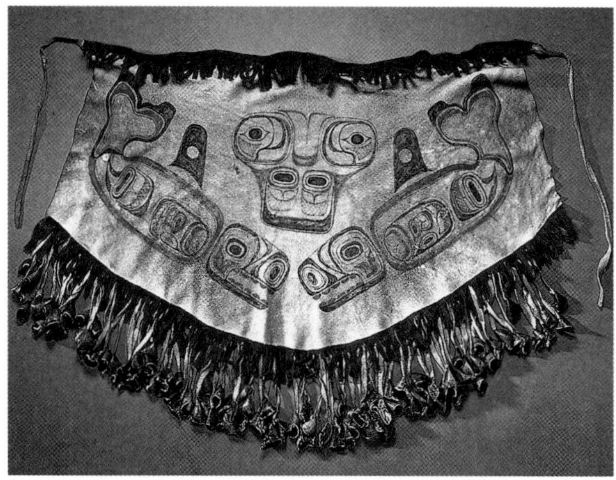

Fig. 1 Painted skin dance apron. Tlingit replica by Don Smith (Lelooska), adoptive Kwakiutl-Cherokee, before 1967. Elk hide, pig toes, felt. 105x79 cm with fringe. Denver Museum of Natural History (Denver, CO), cat.no. AC.10624. Photograph: Rick Wicker, Denver Museum of Natural History.

I recognize the animal toes attached [to] the fringes as being from pigs, rather than from deer. While still a student in Los Angeles, a dealer in Indian craft supplies, Fairchild Woodcraft of North Hollywood, California, was obtaining pig toes in quantity from a local rendering plant. He sold these to Indian craft Hobbyists as a substitute for deer toes and they had a wide distribution in the California area. As far as I know, pig toes were never used by Northwest Coast Indians.
REFERENCES: Inverarity, Robert Bruce. "Art of the Northwest Coast Indians" U. of Calif. Press; 1950. Color plate between figs. 4 & 5 (no page number). This shows a painted Tlingit apron in the Washington State museum, Cat. No. 1956. The design of the Denver Museum of Natural History specimen is an obvious copy of this illustrated piece.
NOTE ON RELIABILITY OF THE SOURCE: I did not see one piece supplied by [the source] which was made to be used within the culture of origin. The NWC material is all brand new and some faked. I would tend to be suspect of all the ethnological material he supplied.
LATER INFORMATION: In 1977 Don Smith (better known as Lelooska), adoptive Kwakiutl-Cherokee, identified the apron as his early work from the mid-1960s. Several other Lelooska "learning pieces" were supplied without identification by the same seller. Lelooska later became well known for his original Northwest Coast-style carved masks, bowls, and other objects.

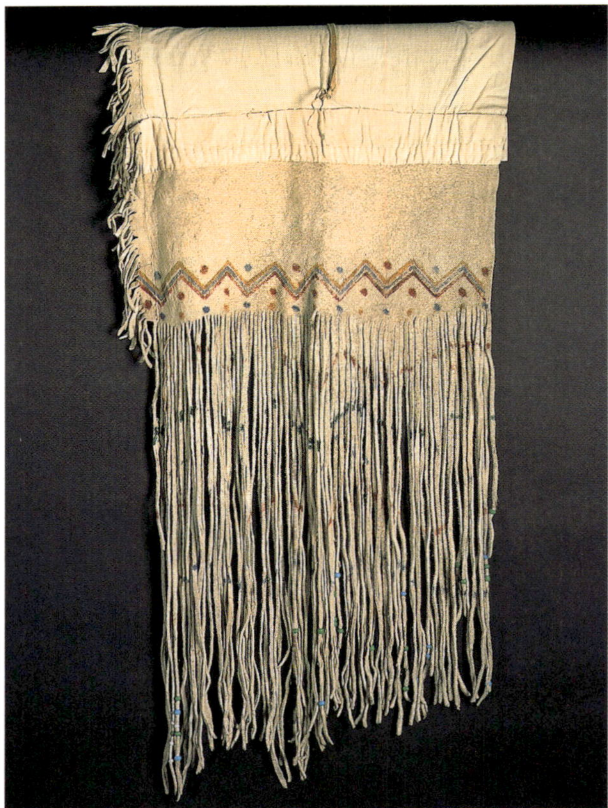

Fig. 2 Painted saddle blanket. Non-Indian or Apache, ca. 1940. Cowhide(?), cotton cloth, glass beads. 56x94 cm, fringe 61 cm. Denver Museum of Natural History (Denver, CO), cat.no. AC.3414. Photograph: Rick Wicker, Denver Museum of Natural History.

2. SADDLE BLANKET (Fig. 2)

CATALOG ENTRY: AC.3414 Saddle throw, saddle blanket. Comanche, Texas. Supplied by Pyatt 1958. Buffalo skin—painted triangular lines & dots & beads on fringes. Fringe 2 ft. long, cloth in middle 20", skin on both sides 9".

AS REPRESENTED: As a Comanche Indian saddle blanket.

FIRST IMPRESSION: Appears to be a modern fake of commercial hide and paint—not an old Indian made item.

MY OPINION: That this was most likely not made by an Indian; but that if it was Indian made that it was made very recently as a show piece by someone who [was not] familiar with traditional Comanche styles and techniques.

JUSTIFICATION: This specimen bears no relationship to any documented American Indian specimen I have ever seen in the major museum collections. I doubt that the skin is actually buffalo as indicated on the catalog card and would guess instead that it is of commercial cow skin. The painting decoration is not typical for any Plains tribe, and the paints are modern commercial paints rather than native or even old trade pigments. A few modern glass beads are strung on the fringes—to my mind the sort of thing a white man might do to give the piece an "Indian feeling."

In summary: This may have been recently made by an Indian, perhaps even by a Comanche Indian; but it does not represent a traditional type. It could have just as easily been made by a non-Indian. In any event, since it is not typical for any Indian group, it should not be exhibited. The exhibit implication is that this is a typical Comanche form of saddle blanket, which it is not.

If an Indian origin can be substantiated, I would suggest using this as an example of modern degeneration of crafts. If an Indian origin cannot be substantiated, then I would suggest placing this specimen in a study collection; but not used on display.

NOTE ON RELIABILITY OF THE SOURCE: Julian Pyatt: he has bought and sold large quantities of good material in the past, but he is a part-time dealer working out of his real estate office. Material he supplied before 1960 is probably all right, but later material (if any) should be suspect.

LATER INFORMATION: Plains Indian authority Dennis Lessard said that the blanket is made of Indian tanned hide and might be an incomplete, quickly-fashioned double saddle bag, "but that painting certainly does not look Indian." His assessment: "Maybe this is Indian made. If it is, it is Apache ... about 1940" (Lessard 1990).

3. WAR BONNET (Figs. 3a, b)

CATALOG ENTRY: AC.2891 Feather headdress. Assiniboine, Canada. Supplied by Jim Garfield, 6/28/1954. New eagle feather war bonnet, beaded band.

AS REPRESENTED: As an Assiniboine War Bonnet.

FIRST IMPRESSION: This is actually a commercial and recent bonnet of the type made by Pawnee Bill's Trading Post in Oklahoma for sale.

MY OPINION: A recently made bonnet for sale to tourists. Of the type made by Pawnee Bill's Trading Post at Pawnee, Oklahoma.

JUSTIFICATION: I cannot supply any references to support my opinion, as far as I know there are no published photos of bonnets made by Pawnee Bill's Trading Post. My opinion is based on my personal familiar-

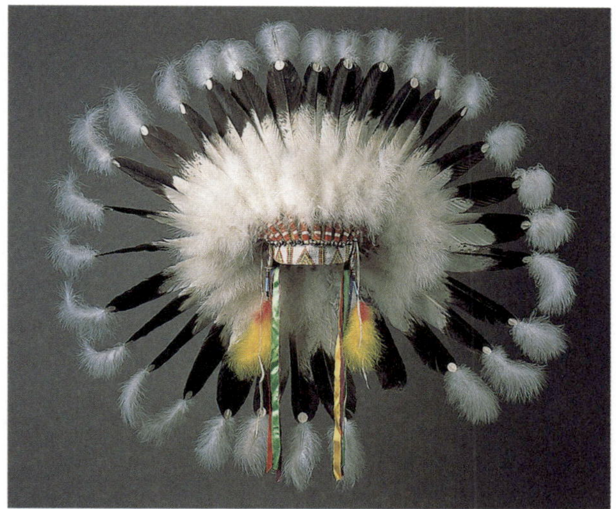

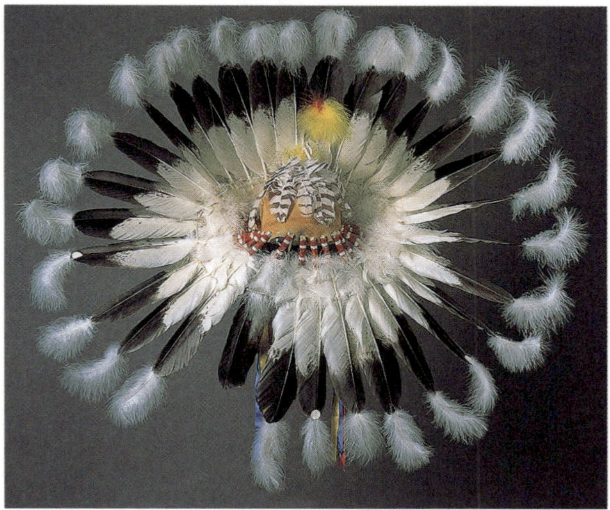

Fig. 3 War bonnet (a: front; b: back). Made by James Garfield, Assiniboine, Fort Peck Reservation, in 1954. Loom-beading, felt hat crown, eagle feathers. 112x50 cm. Denver Museum of Natural History (Denver, CO), cat.no. AC.2891. Photograph: Rick Wicker, Denver Museum of Natural History.

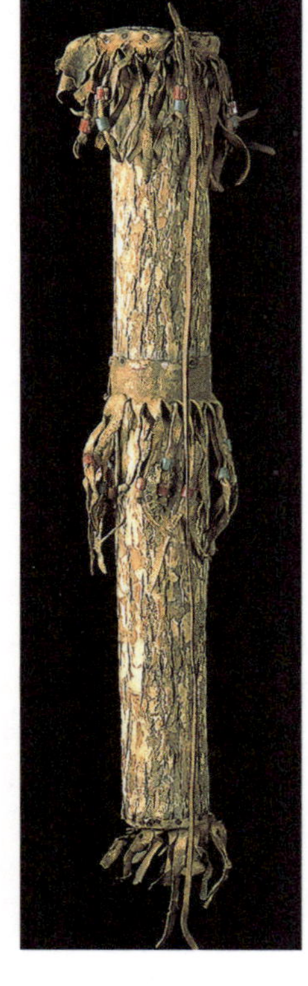

Fig. 4 Cylindrical quiver. Non-Indian(?), collected from Jerry Aaron, Six Nations Reserve, Canada, in 1966. Elm bark, rawhide, wooden beads. 75.5x28 cm. Denver Museum of Natural History (Denver, CO), cat.no. AC.10296. Photograph: Rick Wicker, Denver Museum of Natural History.

ity with the products of the Pawnee Bill's Trading Post. I have visited the retail and wholesale shops in Pawnee, Oklahoma and have seen literally hundreds of these bonnets being manufactured. They are usually made by local Indians (mostly Pawnee and Ponca) right in the shop. The loom beaded brow bands are made separately and also in quantity.

It is, however, entirely possible that an Assiniboine Indian purchased the beadwork from Pawnee Bill's Trading Post and then put the bonnet together himself.

LATER INFORMATION: Glenn Lyon of Pawnee Bill's responded in a letter of 12 December 1969: "The browband certainly appears to have been made by one of the local Indians. However, none of the Indians who bring bonnets in to us use the round white circular substance (appears to be tape) at the end of the feathers where the plume is attached. Neither do they have the two white wrapping or ties that are on the felt at the base of the feather. The side drops also appear to be different."

James Garfield, the source of the headdress, was ascertained to be an Assiniboine Tribe member from Wolf Point, Montana, who personally completed it on commission for the Cranes in 1954. Francis Crane had written requesting that Garfield put "his very best efforts to making the most beautiful that he can create" and urging use of "the finest feathers and other materials that you can secure or produce." Although neither Garfield nor the Cranes mentioned the browband, the probable scenario appears to be Feder's alternative suggestion—a Pawnee Bill's browband used on an Assiniboine-made headdress.

4. ELM BARK QUIVER (Fig. 4)

CATALOG ENTRY: AC.10296 Quiver, Elm Bark. Iroquois, Six Nations Reserve, Canada, collected from Missionary Jerry Aaron, 1966. [Supplier name withheld], 3/16/1966. Bound, trimmed with rawhide fringe (nailed on). Wooden beads on rawhide fringe.

AS REPRESENTED: An elm bark quiver from the Iroquois.
FIRST IMPRESSION: Looks fake.
MY OPINION: That this is not a typical Iroquois quiver, and was in fact a made-up piece for use as a prop.
JUSTIFICATION: The materials and techniques are not right. The folded elm bark is nailed, rather than laced together. It has commercially tanned skin as an attached fringe trim, and it has commercial wooden beads slipped over the fringes. I have never seen this type of wooden bead used on a legitimate Indian specimen.
REFERENCES: Morgan, Lewis H. "League of the Iroquois," 1922; Lyford, Carrie A., "Iroquois Crafts," no date; and Speck, Frank G., "The Iroquois," Cranbrook Institute, 1945 [with pages and quotes].
NOTE ON RELIABILITY OF THE SOURCE: [Questions the honesty of the supplier.] Try to check on the source of items labeled as "Missionary Jerry Aaron." This may be legitimate, but none of the Aaron material I saw was old.
LATER INFORMATION: The supplier described Jerry Aaron as a missionary who received this and other items from "the grand chief of the Long House, eighty years old at time of his conversion." Neither of these two persons has been further identified.

5. MASK (Fig. 5)

CATALOG ENTRY: AC.3733 Mask, Iroquois—Seneca. New York, circa 1870. Supplied by Tilton, 1959. "Snipe clan" mask, thin pointed nose, fur headgear.
AS REPRESENTED: As an authentic Seneca False Face mask of the Snipe Clan.
FIRST IMPRESSION: Fake.
MY OPINION: That this is not an authentic Iroquois False Face mask. That False Face masks were not used as clan representations.
JUSTIFICATION: Based largely on personal experience. I find that all three of the masks [AC.3733; AC.3732; AC.4393] have many features in common—all are carved of heavy wood (most likely commercial pine or Spruce); all are stained with a red dye, rather than painted; all have the backs poorly hollowed out for wearing; and all have shallow incised lines carved into the surface. Further, they do not conform to any of the standard mask types as illustrated in the literature of Iroquois masks (see Fenton, Speck, etc.)

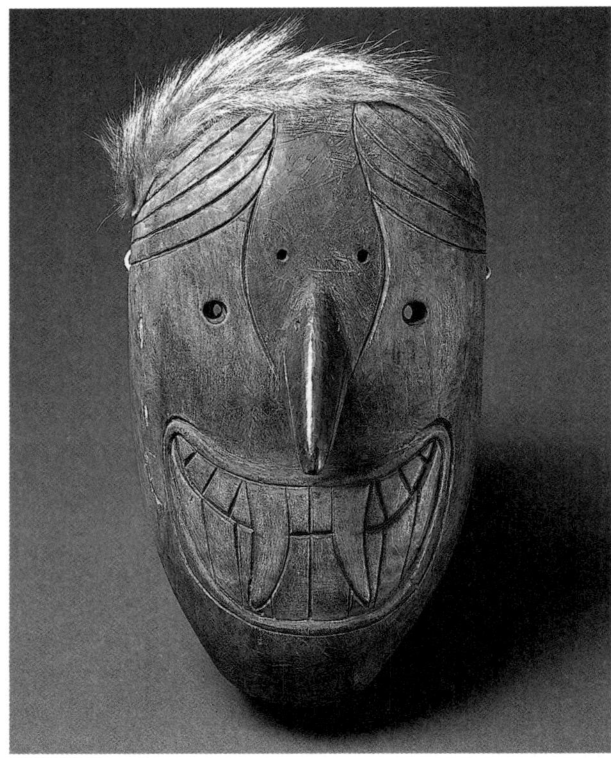

Fig. 5 Mask, Iroquois False Face-style. Made by Cliff Shongo, Seneca(?), Allegany Reservation, 1950–1960. Pine wood, fur coat fragment. 30.5x17.5 cm. Denver Museum of Natural History (Denver, CO), cat.no. AC.3733. Photograph: Rick Wicker, Denver Museum of Natural History.

I first saw masks of this type for sale at Tilton's home in Topeka, Kansas and questioned them at the time. Later saw a large group of this style of mask at the home of a dealer; Paul Summers, [address], Canyon, Texas. Mr. Summers informed me that they all came from the same source, a Chief Shongo who was supposedly a Seneca Indian living in Florida. I concluded at the time that they were all actually made by Shongo, or were made to order for him, and certainly made by someone not very familiar with Iroquois mask styles.

The information attached to Cat. No. 4393 mentions, "Coll. by Cliff Shongo (Seneca) in 1956." Attached to Cat. no. 3733 is a note which states that the wood is pine and gives a date of 1870–1880. I firmly feel that this is also a Shongo piece and more likely 1950–1960.

I would suggest writing to Shongo for more information; ... I doubt if he will admit that the masks are new, but he might. Further send photos of these three masks to Iroquois specialists Fenton, William Sturtevant, Bob Gabor, etc. to see if they feel as I do that these masks are not stylistically Iroquois.

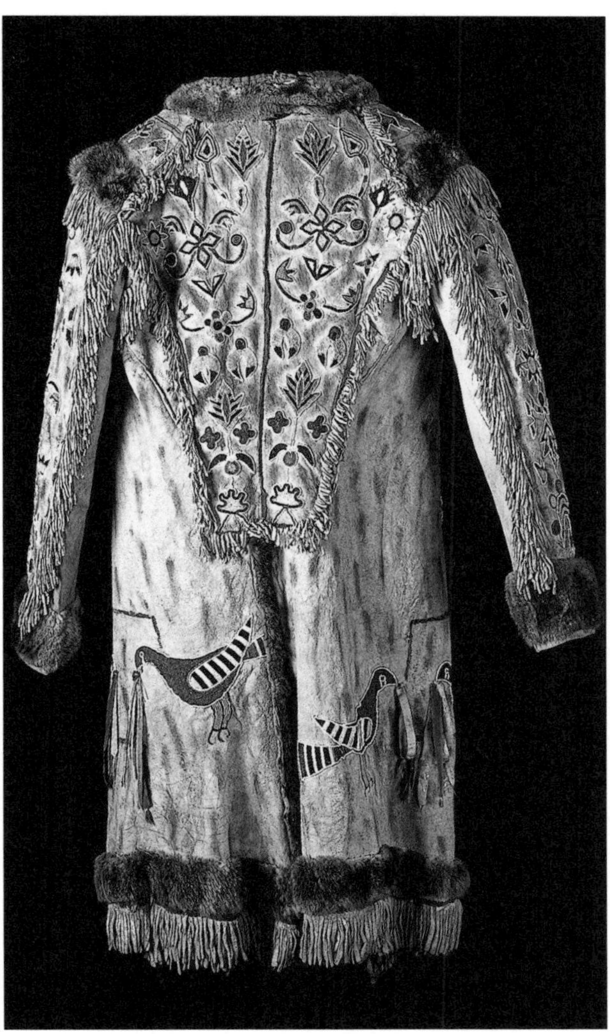

Fig. 6 Beaded and painted coat. Crow or Cree, 1860–1880. Deer skin, beaver fur. 116 cm long. Denver Museum of Natural History (Denver, CO), cat.no. AC.4248. Photograph: Rick Wicker, Denver Museum of Natural History.

NOTE ON RELIABILITY OF THE SOURCE: Willis Tilton; Topeka, Kansas. A former part-time dealer. He was always completely fair and honest, but his specialty was in books and archeological materials. He just did not know ethnological materials so that his designations are usually suspect.

LATER INFORMATION: Another note, undated and unsigned, but probably from the supplier, refers to this mask as follows: "We are dam [sic] lucky we acquired these three. Heron [sic] is by the way a fast disappearing clan. The wolves are feasting on them I guess. This was the best specimen of those that have them .... The beak has to be a dividing trunk of a tree and each portion is strong enough to withstand the knocks."

6. BEADED JACKET (Fig. 6)

CATALOG ENTRY: AC.4248 Jacket [coat]. Chippewa, Canada. Clark Estate, supplied by Kohlberg, 6/10/1959. Man's elaborately beaded coat (& painted), buckskin edged in beaver fur, fringed at bottom and along sleeves—4 large beaded birds 12" long from bottom of coat—lined with upholstery.

AS REPRESENTED: As a Chippewa beaded jacket, used on exhibit to illustrate the Woodland form of floral beadwork.

FIRST IMPRESSION: Beaded coat is Cree or Crow; not Chippewa.

MY OPINION: That this is not Woodland work, but rather from the Northern Plains. Most likely Crow, but possibly Cree.

JUSTIFICATION: It seems to be a common error among laymen to identify everything with floral beadwork motifs as from the Woodland area. Floral beadwork has a wide distribution all the way from Florida to Alaska, but floral styles vary from place to place. This jacket seems to be in the Crow floral style.

The Denver Art Museum collection has two jackets of this same general type identified as Crow. The photo files of DAM also has early (ca. 1880) photos of Crow Indians shown wearing jackets of this type.

Mr. Milford G. Chandler, a noted authority on Indian crafts, has identified this specimen as probably Crow.

REFERENCES: Wildschut, William and Ewers, John C. "Crow Indian Beadwork," Contributions from the Mus. of the Amer. Indian, Vol. 16; 1959. Fig. 22 center—Illustrates a pair of Crow moccasins with similar floral elements. Page 44—"Floral beadwork, including the conventionalized representation of leaves and stems as well as flowers, by Crow beaders cannot be differentiated from the floral beadwork of neighboring tribes with certainty in many cases. Among the Crow Indians floral patterns were used primarily in the decoration of articles of clothing and accessories, such as moccasins, leggings, vests, gauntlets and belt pouches."

Jensen, Oliver and Kerr, J. P. "American Album," Amer. Heritage Pub. Co.; 1968. Page 80—Photo of two trappers in jackets marked Crow.

NOTE ON RELIABILITY OF THE SOURCE: Kohlberg Antiques, Denver. Supplied much material including Peyote beaded dance cane. An honest dealer who knows material from the Southwest, but is not as familiar with materials from other areas.

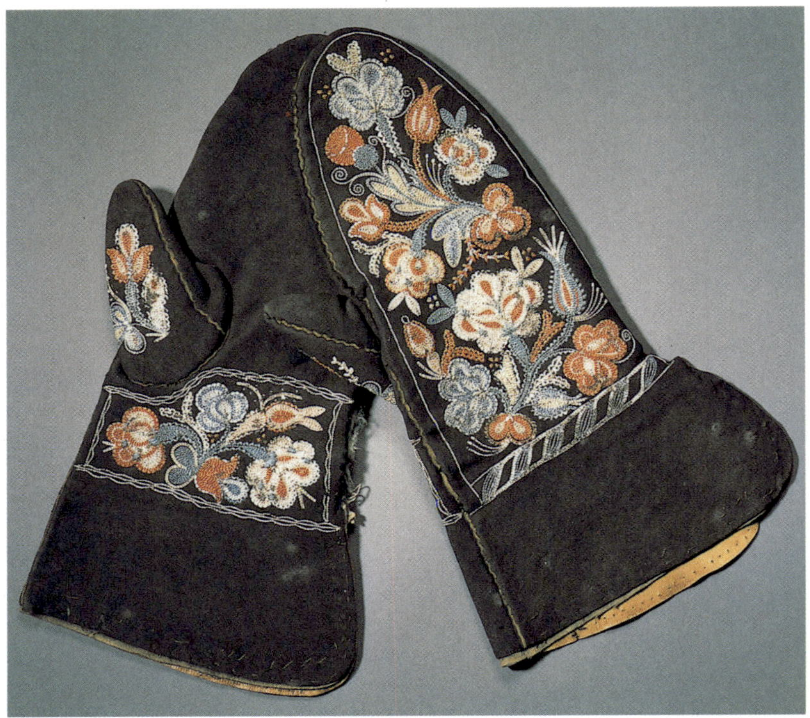

Fig. 7 Moosehair-embroidered gloves, pair. Huron, ca. 1830. Black-dyed buckskin, dyed moosehair, cotton cloth. 33x17 cm. Denver Museum of Natural History (Denver, CO), cat.no. AC.2777A,B. Photograph: Rick Wicker, Denver Museum of Natural History.

7. GLOVES (Fig. 7)

CATALOG ENTRY: AC.2777 Gloves. Huron(?), Canada. Circa 1860. Supplied by Berkeley Gallery, London, England. Fine bird quill embroidered, black suede, wool blanket lined (white man's)—tan leather cuff liner. Elaborate floral design.

AS REPRESENTED: Label states Huron ca. 1860, embroidered with fine bird quills.

FIRST IMPRESSION: Black skin gloves are decorated with moose hair embroidery and made ca. 1830.

MY OPINION: That it is actually much earlier, probably ca. 1830—but this would be difficult to substantiate. That it is embroidered with dyed moose-hair and not with bird quills.

Note: Black dyed buckskin had a wide distribution along the Northeastern portion of the Atlantic Coast and throughout the Great Lakes, and even among Lower Mississippi tribes. The usual dye was an Iron-Tannin mixture. The use of dyed buckskin died out with the introduction of commercial cloth, but probably continued among the Huron until slightly after 1850.

REFERENCES: Turner, Geoffrey "Hair Embroidery in Siberia and North America"; Occasional Papers on Technology No. 7; Pitt Rivers Museum; Oxford. Page 50—bottom paragraph, describes work on black skin in tight floral designs as from first half of 19th century. [Extensive quote.]

An entire chapter of the above monograph is devoted to an analysis of different hair types as contrasted to porcupine quills and bird quills. Turner presents a rather strong argument based on microscopic examination—that all work of the sort on these gloves is actually of moose-hair.

NOTE ON RELIABILITY OF THE SOURCE: Berkeley Galleries, London, England. Supplied the Huron black skin gloves with moose hair embroidery and a fine collection of old NWC carvings. Some of this Berkeley material is the cream of the Crane collection. Every piece I saw was old and legitimate, but the curator's comments on the catalog cards are suspect.

8. MOCCASINS (Fig. 8)

CATALOG ENTRY: AC.8399 Moccasins. Seminole. [Supplier name withheld], 2/14/66. Pair of plain moccasins.

AS REPRESENTED: No label, but in a case devoted to Seminole material.

FIRST IMPRESSION: Woodland front seam moccasins in Seminole case.

MY OPINION: That these are definitely not of Seminole manufacture, but are instead a typical Woodland front seam moccasin.

JUSTIFICATION: The same exhibit case displays a typical pair of Seminole moccasins which have a high top and crude lacing of the seams on lightly smoked buckskin. The pair in question is of heavy smoked skin, with a low top, and very fine sewn puckering of the front seam.

Moccasins of this type had a wide distribution and no comparative study has been published to my knowledge. There are slight differences in the handling of the heel seam, but I am unable to pin-point a tribe of origin. I would suggest Sauk & Fox as a possible tribal designation; but they could be Kickapoo or Potawatomi.

REFERENCES: Hatt, Gudmund "Moccasins and their Relation to Arctic Footwear" Memoir of the Amer. Anthro. Assoc. Vol. 3, No. 3; 1916. Fig. 4, Page 154—shows typical Seminole form. Described on page 153. Fig. 6, Page 154—shows the typical Woodland type. Described on page 155.

NOTE ON RELIABILITY OF THE SOURCE: He certainly supplied Crane with some fine material, but [the information supplied is questioned].

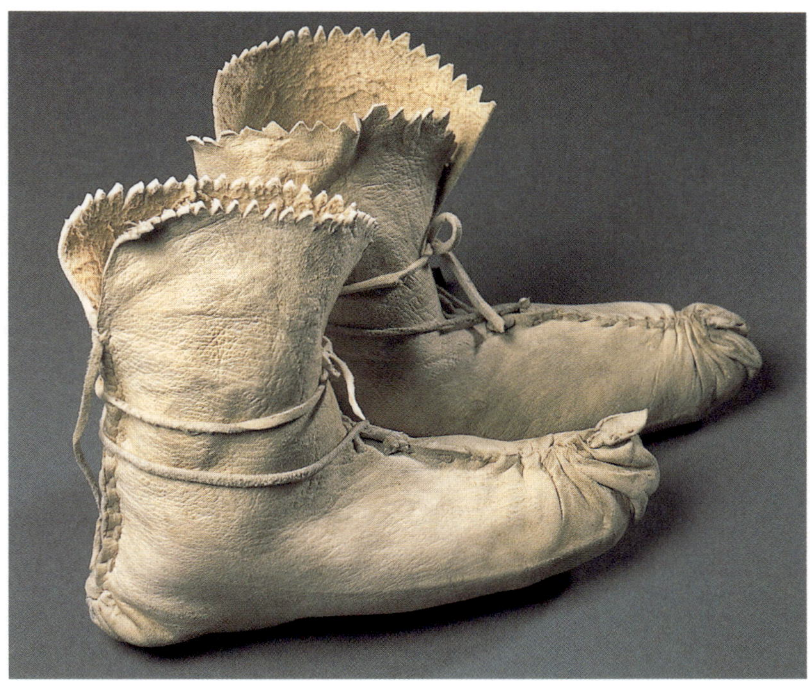

Fig. 8 Front-seam moccasins, pair. Sauk and Fox, Kickapoo, or Potawatomi, collected 1965. Smoked deerskin. 25x21 cm. Denver Museum of Natural History (Denver, CO), cat.no. AC.8399A,B. Photograph: Rick Wicker, Denver Museum of Natural History.

Summary Lessons: The Double Standard

Norman Feder's revisionist approach and purpose and his role as a critic in American Indian art studies were clear: He weighed the questionable against the authentic and the traditional by analyzing comparable materials in his experience, histories and documentation, ethnographic evidence, and material aspects of objects, in order to bring more truth to a body of Indian artifacts. Drawing together the quoted case studies and the more extensive corpus in his project report, he reflected that the lessons learned were considerably broader and deeper than he had envisaged at its beginning.

> "I found the project extremely interesting and enlightening, and in many ways a completely new experience. I have on several instances had to make similar evaluations of other Museum collections, but it was always under different circumstances. My judgments were based entirely on past experience—that is on knowledge gained from previous examination of documented collections. The main difference here was in having to justify and document my opinions. This proved my first impressions wrong in some cases ..., gave me a chance to check items I was doubtful about ..., and in general forced me to reread reference sources I have not looked at in years. I feel I have benefited quite a bit from the experience mainly in knowledge gained."

Feder then addressed how the false and erroneous became part of this particular museum collection:

> "Most of the errors I located can be traced directly to misinformation on the Crane catalog cards. Evidently Crane himself was not particularly knowledgeable about American Indian material culture and he tended, (quite naturally) to believe what the dealers told him about each piece. He also seems to have been a 'soft touch' for several dealers who were not completely honest. As a result he obtained quite a bit of material which was either brand new and represented as old; or material of doubtful Indian origin; or material from other cultures which were represented as American Indian. In many instances this does not reflect on the dishonesty of the dealer, but rather on the lack of knowledge of the dealer. I know most of the dealers who supplied materials to Crane, and so am aware of their limitations."

With marked positivism he pointed out useful directions to achieve a high standard of authentication and public education in the museum:

> "I would suggest as a first step that each piece be further researched and documented. In general, tend to disbelieve each note on each catalog card until you can verify the information with a published reference. Try to locate additional data on other collections.

"When it comes to public display of the collection, my main suggestion is that you try to utilize typical rather than atypical materials wherever possible. I would also try not to mix modern tourist production with older items made for use in the culture; but if modern items are used they should be clearly labeled as modern."

Finally, Norman Feder explained the double-standard test of traditional Indian art:

"I felt a note as to the difficulty of determining a fake from an artifact would be worth while. In general I tend to think of an authentic piece as an object made by an Indian for use within his own culture. If it was actually used, so much the better, but use is not a criterion. Using this definition it would be fairly easy to separate the artifakes from the artifacts. However, in contemporary usage we have to accept everything made by an Indian as an Indian artifact (this is the definition supplied by dealers in Indian crafts). Since many modern Indians have no traditional training in craft production it is impossible to tell their work from that of non-Indians who likewise have no traditional training in old Indian Craft techniques. The only statement that can be made then is not one of artifact versus artifake, but rather if the item in question is a traditional item made in a traditional manner."

"This leads to a great deal of confusion. For example, the recent carvings of Don 'Lelooska' Smith are traditional items and they are now made in a traditional manner, but they are misrepresented as being Northwest Coast. Likewise, the Comanche saddle blanket may possibly have been made by a Comanche Indian, but it is not a traditional item made in a traditional way.

"I tend to use the double standard: that is, the items must be both traditional and Indian made—A traditional item made in the traditional manner by an Indian trained in the tradition."

Conclusions

Norman Feder's 1969 student paper earned a grade of A. Moreover, it propelled forward a scholar-in-the-making. Feder began the project by focusing on his strength, experience in the critical examination of American Indian objects, and progressed toward a more rigorous foundation for his opinions. The case studies illuminate Norman Feder's strong reliance on the following steps in looking at each object: search of his own knowledge and experience of comparable objects; analysis of the object and documentation; testing of preliminary opinions against the pertinent authorities and literature; and conclusions about object origin, description, context, authenticity and traditionalism. The tone of the report was frank and informal, befitting a consultation, but the content did test how the practice of connoisseurship and authentication could be systematically applied to early, fine pieces as well as to later, ordinary or marginal American Indian—or supposed Indian—objects.

In practical terms, without dissembling Feder offered many clues to fakery and common misidentifications, particularly for the 1950 to 1968 period, when he moved among hobbyists, dealers, and collectors as well as museum professionals. Armed with this information and Feder's cross-sectional and general critique of its collection, the DMNH anthropology staff made the suggested corrections and over thirty years, as professional management and curation refined and utilized the Crane American Indian collection, often followed Feder's advice on attribution and selection of display objects. The specific and comparative information in his report should be helpful to other museums or collectors pursuing the critique of objects.

Most importantly, through this exercise the scholarly maturation of Norman Feder progressed: He learned to be more self-critical and to place a higher value on reasoned judgments, i.e., to temper his experience and opinions with findings of other researchers. By the end of the report period he had formalized his approach and defined the authentic and the traditional in his field. His double standard for objects—"a traditional item made in the traditional manner by an Indian trained in the tradition"—forms a foundation stone of Norman Feder's significant contributions to American Indian art studies.

Appendix

Feder noted that his preliminary check was limited by only partially completed exhibit labels. Because the listing throws light on Feder's acuity concerning common errors and recent objects, all "First Impressions" are quoted below (abridged for objects included in the text above):

1. Tlingit painted skin kilt [see above].
2. Button blanket—A recent copy of a blanket in the DAM [Denver Art Museum] collections. Not made in the running stitch technique.
3. An assortment of modern carvings made by Don Lelooska Smith, a part Cherokee commercial carver from Ariel, Washington. These include a Sun Raven Pole, an Old Woman mask, a seated male figure with imbricated basket. Other carvings in same case are not old, but may not be Lelooska's work. These include a Raven baton, a Hamatsa Raven mask, and possibly the Raven rattle held by the manikin.
4. Bark cloth pancho [sic] shirt with shell decoration—label says "Mintun" and "Periwinkle" shells. Mintun probably should read Wintun and the pancho is not Californian, nor are the shells periwinkle.
5. Typical Western Apache basket is labeled as "Yavapai."
6. Papago wood bowl is labeled as "Cheese" bowl. According to DAM Material Culture Notes on Pima bowls, only bowls with spouts or drain holes are used for cheese—others for dough.
7. Pima sash label states "made of wild cotton"—this appears to be made of commercial cotton string.
8. Apache Crown dancer kilt is actually a woman's skirt. Will Check.
9. Nez Perce bag label says made of "sisal and cotton." Check materials.
10. A Puget Sound wood working adze is displayed next to a Plains hide scraper as a hide working tool.
11. Comanche saddle throw [see above].
12. Bag labeled as Nez Perce Saddle Bag—actually not Nez Perce and not a saddle bag.
13. Crow martingale—should read "Horse Collar."
14. Blackfeet knife case—is displayed with the inner rawhide sheath outside of the case.
15. Rawhide cylinder parfleche is labeled as Blackfeet bonnet case. Not Blackfeet and not for a war bonnet.
16. Feather bonnet labeled as Assiniboine [see above].
17. Sun dance rawhide cut outs of man and of buffalo. These are recent fakes.
18. Grouping of peyote ceremonial material includes a non-peyote dance cane.
19. Quilled vest and pants labeled Arapaho—probably not Arapaho.
20. Elm bark quiver [see above].
21. Seneca mortar & pestle for sunflower seeds. Check form.
22. Iroquois mask with long thin snout [see above].
23. Pipe tomahawk labeled as French. Not French.
24. Winnebago gun stock war club is newly made.
25. Assomption [sic] sash labeled Huron. French-Canadian made.
26. Beaded coat [see above].
27. Black skin gloves [see above].
28. Woodland front seam moccasins [see above].
29. California turkey feather cape, not old. May be modern fake.

References Cited

Ames, Kenneth L.

1985 The Stuff of Everyday Life: American Decorative Arts and Household Furnishings. In: Thomas J. Schlereth (ed.), *Material Culture: A Research Guide* (Lawrence, KS: University Press of Kansas), 79–112.

Buffalo Bill Historical Center

1992 *Artifacts/Artifakes: The Proceedings of the 1984 Plains Indian Seminar.* Cody, WY: Buffalo Bill Historical Center.

Feder, Norman

1959 Modern Crow Costume. *American Indian Hobbyist* 5(7–8): 74–80.

1962 Bottom Tab Leggings. *American Indian Tradition* 8(4): 148–159.

1964 *Art of the Eastern Plains Indians: The Nathan Sturges Jarvis Collection.* New York, NY: The Brooklyn Museum.

1965 *American Indian Art Before 1850.* Denver Art Museum Quarterly (Summer1965). Denver, CO: Denver Art Museum.

1969 Project Report: Primitive Arts and Industries [class taught by Kate Peck Kent]. Unpublished student report, fall 1969, Department of Anthropology, University of Denver. On file at Denver Museum of Natural History. Department of Anthropology, Denver, CO.

1971 *Two Hundred Years of North American Indian Art.* New York, NY: Praeger Publishers.

1972 Shoshone Split Horned Bonnet. *American Indian Crafts & Culture* 6(1): 2–5.

1977a Exhibition: The Malaspina Expedition. *American Indian Art Magazine* 2(3): 40–51, 80, 82.

1977b George Catlin: Sometimes Accurate. *American Indian Art Magazine* 2(3): 72–75.

1978 Book Review: The American Indian Collection in the Berne Historical Museum. *American Indian Art Magazine* 4(1): 48–49.

1994 Book Review: American Indian Artifacts: The John Painter Collection. *American Indian Art Magazine* 19(2): 70, 72.

Herold, Joyce

1999 Grand Amateur Collecting in the Mid-Twentieth Century: The Mary W. A. and Francis V. Crane American Indian Collection. In: Shepard Krech III and Barbara Hail (eds.), *Collecting Native America, 1870–1960* (Washington, DC: Smithsonian Institution Press), 259–291.

Lessard, Dennis

1990 DMNH Department of Anthropology Collection Appraisal and Evaluation. November, 1990. Unpublished notes in object file.

McCoy, Ronald

1993 Legal Briefs: Artifakes. *American Indian Art Magazine* 19(1): 82–83.

Norman Feder at the Denver Art Museum
A Chronology, 1958–1973

Tilly Laskey

Norman Feder joined the Denver Art Museum in May 1958 as Clerk/Typist for the Native Arts Department at Chappell House. From May 1959 until June 1960, he served as Assistant Curator of Native Arts, first under Richard Conn (until September 1959) and subsequently under Royal Hassrick. Between June 1960 and September 1961, Feder took a leave of absence to work at the Museum of the American Indian (Heye Foundation), New York. When he returned to Denver in September 1961, he became Curator of American Art (until 1962), Curator of American Indian Art (1963–1966), and finally Curator of Native Arts, a position he held between 1967 and his departure from the Denver Art Museum at the end of June 1973. During a sabbatical year Norman Feder took in 1971, his predecessor and ultimate successor Richard Conn served as Acting Curator of Native Arts in his stead.

The following chronological record of Feder's activities was gleaned from the museum's *Newsletter*, *Annual Reports*, and other documents. It mainly reflects his work on exhibitions and other public aspects of museum work, rather than accessions and collection management.

1959

[Exhibitions[1] listed up to September 1959 were curated by Richard Conn. Norman Feder was the Assistant Curator during this time period, but was most likely involved in their curation. Royal Hassrick took over as curator from September 1959 to 1961.]

Africa and the Pacific (1 August 1959–indefinite).
Masterworks from the Native Arts collection; part of permanent exhibits at Chappell House.

Mistaken Ideas about Indians Explored (15 March–15 May 1959).
Misconceptions held by many regarding Indians and their customs; a technique of true and false contrasts was employed.

Albin Jake (Pawnee) (June 1959). One-man show.

Dick West (Cheyenne) (July 1959). One-man show.

Alan Houser (Chiricahua) (August 1959). One-man show.

Western Heritage (8 October 1959–20 May 1960).
Dramatizing Western American history; exhibiton included objects from the Native American collection.

1960

Primitive Theater (19 June–4 September 1960).
The drama of the Native Artist as portrayed in ceremonial ritual and dance, in mask and costume, prepared as a special feature for National Theater conferences in Denver in the summer of 1960.

[The August 1960 Denver Art Museum's *Newsletter* announces the resignation of Norman Feder; personnel notes show a leave from the museum from 15 June 1960 to 1 September 1961.]

1961

[The August 1961 *Denver Art Museum Newsletter* reports Feder's return to his post at Chappell House (as Curator of American Indian Art) after a year's service with the Heye Foundation in New York City.]

Tilly Laskey is the Curator of Exhibits at the South Dakota Art Museum at the State University Campus in Brookings, SD. She received her MS in Museum and Field Studies from the University of Colorado, Boulder in 1999. As part of her Masters Program, Laskey interned at the Denver Art Museum where she researched Norman Feder's career.
Author's address: South Dakota State Art Museum, Box 2250, SDSU, Brookings, SD 57007-0899, U.S.A.

1. Unless otherwise noted, exhibitions from 1959 to 1970 were at Chappell House. The Ponti Building noted after 1970 is the current Denver Art Museum building. Where I have specifically found documentation of Feder's curatorship, I have noted it. However, it is safe to conclude that Feder curated the shows that are listed below.

Art of the South Seas (21 September–15 October 1961). Cocurated by Norman Feder, Royal Hassrick (Assistant to the Director), and Douglas Marsh (Assistant Curator of Native Arts).

"The art of the South Seas is one of the last primitive arts to be 'discovered' in this century. It has made its debut in the western world since World War II. In this same period, the Museum has developed a collection in this field which now includes representative pieces of nearly every facet of this magical native art [...] the strange, mystical ancestor figures which are like filigrees of painted wood, the brooding house posts which are supernatural protection against evil spirits, the enormous tapas with their precise, geometric patterns, the great, carved banquet bowls, the elegantly designed, slender canoe paddles and the towering ceremonial masks. Objects from the Museum's collection of Oceanic art will be supplemented by loans from private dealers and other museums" (quoted from the Denver Art Museum's *Newsletter*).

Representational Art—American Indian Art (December 1961). Curated by Norman Feder.

Costumes and other artifacts from the permanent collection.

1962

Western Heritage (10 January 1962–11 May 1962). Cocurated by Norman Feder and Douglas Marsh.

"A documentary exhibition describing the western expansion of the United States during the 18th and 19th centuries as developed by trapper, explorer, gold miner and cattleman, this exhibition was offered to serve as visual supplement to American History courses. Some new material and a new installation will be introduced, but the content is the same as in previous years and exhibitions of the same title" (quoted from the Denver Art Museum's *Newsletter*).

Proof (January–28 February 1962). Curated by Norman Feder.

Uses American Indian artifacts and accompanying photographs to identify them in situ, showing the provenance of the work.

American Indian Seminar Series

"Norman Feder, Curator of American Indian Art, will present a series of five seminars for museum members only on April 12, April 19, April 26, May 3, and May 10. Entitled *Backgrounds of American Indian Art* it will be concerned with the contrast of tribal styles in different culture areas" (quoted from the Denver Art Museum's *Newsletter*).

Art of Africa (April–3 June 1962). Cocurated by Norman Feder and Mrs. Don Lewis, Assistant Curator.

Exhibition of the new African republics, including ancestor figures, masks, musical instruments, gold weights, and objects from the ancient site of Benin.

Indian Painting Today–Contemporary Indian Art (10 June–26 August 1962).

Material from the permanent collections is utilized in pertinent thematic displays which change every six weeks.

Ceremonial Art of the Southwest (14 June–29 July 1962). Curated by Norman Feder.

Comprehensive survey of art from the Southwest, giving insight into customs and culture of Indians of Arizona and New Mexico.

"A brilliant and informative exhibition (*Ceremonial Art of the Southwest*) assembled from the Museum's permanent collections by Curator Norman Feder coincides with correlated demonstrations and a Cooke-Daniels lecture on various aspects of this intriguing subjects. For six days, June 14–19, two members of the Navajo Nation will be on hand daily to demonstrate sandpainting. Famous for their skill, shaman Billy Norton and his son from Pinedale, AZ, will explain step by step procedures of this fascinating ritual art. This is a rare opportunity to see an esoteric form of art, the beginnings and early development of which are unknown. Made only by shamans as part of their curing ceremonies, these strangely ephemeral paintings are representations of the gods. By sprinkling powdered earth of various colors upon a smoothed surface of sand, imaginative, elongated figures of gods, animals spirits and sacred plants are created only to be destroyed at the end of the healing rites" (quoted from the Denver Art Museum's *Newsletter*).

Cooke-Daniels Memorial Lecture (18 June 1962)

To round out the activities relating to the *Ceremonial Art of the Southwest* exhibit, the distinguished Professor Kenneth E. Foster presented a lecture on "Sandpaintings and Navajo Ceremonial Art."

Masks and Mask-Makers (5 August–16 September 1962). North and South American Indians as well as African and Oceanic masks, both historic and contemporary, comprise this exhibit.

Porcupine Quill Work (September 1962). Curated by Norman Feder.

Examples of Native American quillwork from the Denver Art Museum's permanent collection. First in a series of exhibitions on American Indian decorative arts.

The American West (7 October–2 December 1962).

The story of the West is vividly portrayed through paintings, prints, art objects, and costumes recreating the drama of the Western expansion in the nineteenth century. This exhibition highlighted Plains Indian artwork.

Feather Work (9 December 1962–17 February 1963).

An unusual display of American Indian featherwork from all different tribes, including the magic symbolism of the feather of eagle and hawk, the brilliant decorative Bird Dance bustle, the elegant peyote fan, and the iridescent mallard feathers incorporated in costume and gear. All objects from Denver Art Museum's permanent collections. In the series of American Indian Decorative Arts.

1963

George Catlin Oils and Lithographs (23 February–18 March 1963).

Smithsonian Institution traveling show augmented by Denver Art Museum's permanent Native American collection hand-picked by Norman Feder. Specifically calumet pipes, prayer sticks, ribbon work blankets, buffalo robes, costumes, and war clubs depicted by Catlin in his paintings.

The Art of Africa (24 March–26 May 1963). Curated by Norman Feder.

Indian Art of the Northwest Coast (29 March–30 June 1963). Curated by Norman Feder.

Indian Art of the Northwest Coast coincided with the publication of *Indians of the Northwest Coast* by Norman Feder and Edward Malin.

Indians of the Plains (2 June–29 September 1963).

According to the Summer 1963 *Newsletter*, these two exhibitions offered an interesting contrast, presenting the cultural achievements of two very different ways of life. The sedentary, status-conscious tribes of the Northwest Coast produced enormous wood carvings and dramatic ceremonial masks, whereas the nomadic tribes of the Plains expressed themselves in art forms which were all easily packed and transported. Here one finds the decorated parfleche, the buffalo robes, the accouterments of the hunt and warfare.

Woodwork of American Indian Cultures (9 June–29 July 1963).

Carvings, masks, and other wood objects arranged geographically. In the series of American Indian Decorative Arts.

The Indian and the West (October 1963–12 January 1964).

A documentation of Western expansion in the nineteenth century offered as a special school correlation program.

The Indian's Use of Horn, Bone & Shell (15 November 1963–12 January 1964).

In the series of American Indian Decorative Arts.

1964

American Indian Metal Work (24 January–29 March 1964).

In the series of American Indian Decorative Arts.

Art of Africa (22 March–13 May 1964). Curated by Norman Feder.

Discusses the arts of Egypt, Islam, and Africa. Housed at the Schleier Gallery.

Eskimo Graphic Art (18 April–10 May 1964).

An exhibition of nearly fifty stone block and sealskin prints representing a new form of art expression for the community of Baffin Island and the Canadian Arctic. Circulated nationally by the Smithsonian Institution, it was brought to Denver Art Museum through the cooperation of the Art Department of the Denver Public Schools.

Art of the American Indian (4 June–19 July 1964).

"Numbering more than 8000 objects, the Museum's permanent collection of American Indian art is comprehensive, topflight and dramatic. Yet due to space limitations at Chappell House, it is seldom seen in full panoply. Consequently, during June and July, the spotlight will be turned on this important collection, when the Art of the American Indian takes place at the Schleier Gallery. Brilliant war-bonnets and horse trappings will be displayed on the bold warriors and hunters who dominated the Plains, great house boards, totem figures and dynamic masks will illuminate the wealthy, prestige-conscious society of the Northwest Coastal tribes and gaily painted kachina figures, precisely executed sand paintings will bring to life the social patterns of the Hopi, Zuni and Navaho peoples of the Southwest" (quoted from the Denver Art Museum's *Newsletter*).

[Chappell House was closed for the summer for recataloguing and appraisal of collection condition. *Rocky Mountain News* notes on 4 October 1964 that Chappell House reopened after being renovated by Feder.]

American Indian Art (10 October 1964–11 April 1965; presented annually since 1960).

1965

American Indian Stone Work (24 January–11 April 1965).
The sixth in a series of small exhibitions concerned with the decorative arts, this one included catlinite pipe bowls, mortars and pestles, and handsomely carved adze heads, all revealing once again the supreme artistry of American Indian craftsmen.

American Indian Art Before 1850 (2 May–19 September 1965).
"Assembled by Norman Feder, Curator of American Indian and Native Arts, this exhibit is comprised of rare, fragile, and irreplaceable art. Loans from 14 leading museums and notable private collections throughout the country, supplemented by objects from our permanent collections, make this one of the most comprehensive exhibits of early Indian material ever to be presented under one roof. The terminal date of 1850 was chosen because it precedes the development of the camera, it anticipates Colorado statehood and it marks the beginning of westward expansion brought on by the California Gold Rush. The exhibition includes material collected by such famous people as George Catlin, documentary artist in the early 1800's; Lewis Henry Morgan, one of the first anthropologists; and Stephen R. Riggs, an early missionary to the Sioux" (quoted from the Denver Art Museum's *Newsletter*).
Dr. William C. Sturtevant of Washington, DC, Chief Anthropologist of the United States Museum of Natural History, lectured in conjunction with *American Indian Art before 1850* on 19 May 1965.

Santos and Kachinas (17 July–19 September 1965).
"This exhibition explores two art forms, each a significant part of the Western tradition. Both Santos and Kachinas are in tune with the natural environment of the Southwest. Each is a dramatic expression of religious faith as developed by the Spanish American and Indian peoples of the area. Composed largely of material from the Museum's permanent collections, the Santos section will be augmented by outstanding objects on loan from the Colorado Springs Fine Arts Center and from the private collection of Dr. Nolie Mumey of Denver" (quoted from the Denver Art Museum's *Newsletter*).
This show opened with dancing by the White Buffalo Council of American Indians.

Tipis and Totem Poles (October 1965–30 April 1966).
Cocurated by Norman Feder and Philip Robinson, Associate Curator of Native Arts.
A unique and important array of American Indian arts and crafts from the Plains and the Northwest Coast Indians. The exhibition revealed how the many tribes adapted to the various environments and geographical areas in which they lived. It pointed out their basic differences and also showed the contributions made by the American Indian to our way of life today.

1966

"Norman Feder, Curator of American Indian Art, went afield with the Museum's Indian Fashion Show. In Winnipeg, he made a presentation before the Indian and Metis Conference. On this same trip, he was invited by the Minnesota State Historical Society to catalogue their collections. In return for this service, he received 34 objects, valued at $4830, which have been added to the Museum's permanent collections" (from the Denver Art Museum's *Annual Report*).

Oceanic Art (January 1966).
Objects from the permanent collection arranged geographically.

Indian Basketry (February 1966).
Part of decorative art series.

Hidden Treasure Exhibit: Native American Art (31 May–10 June 1966).
Off-site, mini exhibits used to raise funds for construction of the Ponti museum building. At Public Service Building, Denver.

Hidden Treasure Exhibit: Plains Indian Art (June–1 July 1966).
At Colorado National Bank.

American Indian Accessions (12 June–18 September 1966).
Exhibiting fifty objects donated from January to June 1966.

Crow Indian Art (July–14 September 1966).
"This exhibit reveals the Crow Indians as endowed with superior skills in beadwork and painted raw-

hide. They are brilliant colorists and their horse trappings and clothing are a-glimmer with dazzling bead patterns" (quoted from the Denver Art Museum's *Newsletter*).

American Indian Art (30 October 66–17 April 1967).
Depicted art of North American cultures of the Pacific Northwest, California, the Great Plains, Southwest, and Woodlands.

1967

"Norman Feder, Curator of Native Arts, also went afield. He served as a judge for beadwork at the Intertribal Indian Gallup Ceremonies. He attended a conference at the University of Oklahoma where the program centered on an inventory of ethnographic collections in American Museums.[2] He prepared the catalogue for the exhibition, *North American Indian Painting* for the Museum of Primitive Art, New York City. Through Mr. Feder's efforts, funds were also secured for reprinting the popular 'Indian Leaflet' series of which over a million have been sold. The American Indian Department also initiated the first in a new series called 'Material Culture Monographs.' Number one was compiled by Mr. Feder and titled *Elk Antler Roach Spreaders*" (from the Denver Art Museum's *Annual Report*).

Indians of the Plains (17 June–3 September 1967).
The most popular image of the American Indian is that of the horseback-riding nomad of the Plains. In pre-horse days there were also farmers and hunters.

North American Indian Art (30 October 1967–16 April 1968).
Distinctive arts and crafts of tribes around the United States and Canada. Emphasizing the enormous physical, linguistic, and cultural differences among tribes and regions.

Our World Heritage
The American Indian section spotlighted arts and crafts of all cultures demonstrating the universality of art in all cultures. Demonstrations by Billy Norton, Navajo sandpainter; Tony Hunt, Kwakiutl carver; Gertrude Tallbull, Cheyenne beadworker; Nellie Menard, Sioux weaver; Fred Kabotie, Hopi painter.

2. Cp. Alex F. Ricciardelli, *A Pilot Study for Inventorying Ethnological Collections* (Norman, OK: Stovall Museum of Science and History, University of Oklahoma).

1968

"Norman Feder, Curator of Native Arts, once again served as judge for the Gallup Indian Ceremonials" (from the Denver Art Museum's *Annual Report*).

The Afro-American Heritage (January–11 May 1968). Curated by Norman Feder.
Mixture of Black American artists and historic displays from the permanent collection noting cultural contributions of African art to African American art. Federally funded to promote racial understanding.

Beads and Buckskin (15 June–15 September 1968). Curated by Norman Feder.
"All across the continent the various tribes created exquisite articles of clothing and costume accessories, employing native skins, imported cloth and venetian beads acquired by trade with the white man. The Indian artisans produced leggings, moccasins, shirts, robes, headdresses, pipe bags and elegant bandoleers, all adorned with bright, glittering colored beads. The same exquisite detail of patterned glass is found on the cradles" (quoted from the Denver Art Museum's *Newsletter*). From the permanent collection.

Legacies of the American Southwest (21 September–24 December 1968).
"The American Southwest exhibits a unique fusion of traditions, a blending of the indigenous Indian, the Spanish and Mexican cultures. The exhibition dramatizes each of these traditions, explores the impact of each upon the other. The brilliant gear of the Kachina dancers, the dynamic abstraction of kiva painting, the supreme artistry of Navaho silver or Acoma pottery combine to reveal the proud lineage of the Indian peoples of the Southwest" (quoted from the Denver Art Museum's *Newsletter*).

Sponsored by the Denver Art Museum, Bill Holm lectured on "Kwakiutl Life, Dance, and Drama" at the Denver Public Library.

1969

New Accessions from the American Indian Department (March–29 May 1969).

American Indian Dress and Ornament (14 June–21 September 1969)
"One of the outstanding features of the Museum's American Indian department is the collection of

costumes, moccasins, leggings, hair ornaments, bonnets, capes and robes representing more than 50 tribes of North America. Elegant beadwork from the Creek and Ojibwa tribes, silk ribbon appliqué which adorned the blankets from the Otoe, the streaming eagle feathers of the Sioux war bonnet, the great buffalo hide robes of the Plains Indians, the handsome silver jewelry of the Navaho, the decorated basket hats of the Nootka, the distinctive button blankets from the Northwest Coast will all be included in this comprehensive display" (quoted from the Denver Art Museum's *Newsletter*).

Pueblo and Navajo Textiles (3 August–7 September 1969).

"The American Indian collections of the museum were started in 1925 by the purchase of a few Navaho rugs. Since then, the collections have steadily grown to the point were they are now one of the finest in the country. Select examples from our collections at Chappell House have been exhibited from time to time but because of lack of space we have never been able to display a major portion of the collection until this exhibition.

"The Pueblo Indians have a long tradition of weaving with native grown cotton, dating back before white contact. After the coming of the Spanish in the Southwest, sheep were introduced and wool was partially substituted for cotton in both weaving and embroidery. Sometime about 1700, the Navaho learned how to weave from the Pueblo Indians and have since developed the craft in a distinctive form by elaborating on the basic Pueblo types. Included in the exhibit are typical examples of the wide variety of Pueblo Weaving—blankets, dresses, shawls, shirts, kilts, sashes, belts, socks and leggings. Also a wide range of Navaho wearing blankets from an early period will be included, showing the development of the modern trade rugs" (quoted from the Denver Art Museum's *Newsletter*).

1970

"The past year was one of almost continual hectic activity. We closed Chappell House, after spending months carefully packing the collections for the move to our new building. Once installed in temporary quarters in the new structure, we started the installation of exhibits on the mezzanine floor. These include the sections devoted to the art of the Indians of the Pacific Northwest Coast, all of Africa and all of the South Seas. At this writing, the Mezzanine is almost completed and we are ready to start on the entire second floor which will house the remainder of the vast American Indian collections" (Norman Feder in the Denver Art Museum's *Annual Report* for 1970).

[The Denver Art Museum's new Ponti Building was slated to open October 1970, but the opening was postponed until October 1971. During the year 1970 Feder appears to have been inventorying and installing Native American exhibits.]

Traditions of the West (February–8 March 1970).

"Relives the early period of Colorado history through paintings and prints of the 19th century. Santos, one of the earliest forms of ecclesiastical art objects, unfold a culture synonymous with the Southwest" (quoted from the Denver Art Museum's *Newsletter*).

Gallery of Indian Art (October–November 1970). Curated by Norman Feder at the Heard Museum, Phoenix, AZ.

Forty-eight paintings were loaned by the Denver Art Museum to the Heard Museum.

1971

"1971, the year of the new building, has been the most significant in the Denver Art Museum's history. [...] And, naturally, most of our activities have been concerned with preparing for last October's opening. The collections were unpacked and put either on exhibition or into the new storeroom. The 50,000 volume library was also unpacked and set up in its new quarters. The Native Arts exhibitions on the Mezzanine have been completed and the American Indian cases lack only their labels.

"1971 was also a year of acclaim for the museum through the activities of its Curator, Norman Feder. In November, a major show of American Indian Art opened at the Whitney Museum of American Art in New York City. Mr. Feder selected the material for this exhibition and wrote the catalogue *Two Hundred Years of North American Indian Art* published by Praeger. Mr. Feder's magnum opus, *American Indian Art*, was also released by Abrams Publishing firm in November" (Richard Conn in the Denver Art Museum's *Annual Report* for 1971).

[The *Denver Post* of 2 July 1971 stated in an interview with Feder that he had been traveling since March to collect/assemble objects for the Whitney Museum exhibition. Various articles state that the Whitney show was cocurated by Louis Mofsie and Ida Lujan Isaacs.[3]]

[Denver Art Museum accession records for the year of 1971 were administered by Norman Feder until December, when Richard Conn's name appears as Curator.]

1972

"Richard G. Conn, Acting Curator of Native Arts during the sabbatical leave of Curator Norman Feder, extensively rearranged and reinstalled the second floor Indian Exhibitions. [...] After a year of study and travel, Norman Feder has returned to the job with new perspectives" (Director Otto Karl Bach in the Denver Art Museum's *Annual Report* for 1972).

[The *Denver Post* of 30 January 1972 noted that Richard Conn had taken over for Norman Feder for one year.]

[Denver Art Museum accession records indicate that Richard Conn was administering the Native Arts department until December of 1972, when Feder's name appears on accession records until March of 1973. Feder's and Conn's names appear concurrently from March until May 1973.]

1973

[Richard Conn will take over as Curator of Native Arts from Norman Feder on 1 October 1973 (Denver Art Museum *Newsletter*, 5 September 1973)].

"Norman Feder, who had returned from a year's sabbatical in January, succumbed to the lure of travel, research, and publication, and he left the staff in August. Here again, the museum's luck held. Richard M. Conn, who had served as Norman's substitute during his year's leave of absence, took over the Native Arts Department in early fall" (Director Otto Karl Bach in the Denver Art Museum's *Annual Report* for 1973).

"An important event in 1973 was the retirement of Norman Feder, who had been curator of the department since 1961. Mr. Feder contributed a great deal to the museum during his tenure, adding important pieces to the collection and initiating several new publications. In his retirement, he plans to continue research, to write, and to act as consultant in organizing exhibitions of native arts as he did for the Whitney Museum of American Art in 1971" (Richard Conn in the Denver Art Museum's *Annual Report* for 1973).

Fashion Shows

Feder also ran an outreach program called "Indian Fashion Shows," originally started by Frederic H. Douglas. A list of fashion shows curated by Norman Feder follows:

2 October 1961: International Conference of the Public Personnel Association, Wives Club, Denver, CO.
1962: Illinois State Museum, Springfield, IL.
27 April 1962: National Indian Youth Conference, Brigham Young University, Provo, UT.
21 June 1962: American Institute of Electrical Engineers, Brown Palace, Denver, CO.
3 April 1963: Annual Meeting of the American College of Physicians, Wives Club, Hilton Hotel, Denver, CO.
28 May 1963: American Institute of Banking, Women's Committee Cosmopolitan Hotel, Denver, CO.
17 August 1963: National Indian Youth Conference, Fort Duchesne, UT.
6 October 1963: Conference of City Managers, Ladies Program, Hilton Hotel, Denver, CO.
4 November 1963: ASBO Meeting, Ladies Activities, Denver, CO.
24–25 September 1964: Milwaukee Public Museum, Milwaukee, WI.
3 November 1965: St. Augustine Center, Chicago, IL.
12 February 1966: Indian & Metis Friendship Centre, Winnipeg, MB, Canada.
30 June 1966: Colorado Chapter, Women's Auxiliary, Denver, CO.
30 June 1966: National AIA Conference, Brown Palace, Denver, CO.
28 July 1966: Regis College, Denver, CO.
August 1966: Gallup Intertribal Ceremonial, Gallup, NM.
1966: four unknown venues.
9 October 1967: Bank Public Relations and Marketing Association Conference, Denver, CO.
1968: one unknown venue.
Summer 1968: Honolulu Academy of Fine Arts, Honolulu, HI.

3. Selected publicity for the Whitney show: *New York Times*: 16 November 1971, 21 November 1971, 28 November 1971 by Hilton Kramer. *Newsweek*: 29 November 1971. *Time Magazine*: 6 December 1971. *Village Voice*: 25 November 1971. *Wall Street Journal*: 23 December 1971. *Today's Art*: January 1972.

Norman Feder and
American Indian Art Magazine, 1977–1995

Roanne P. Goldfein

Acting as *American Indian Art Magazine's* Editorial Consultant from February 1977 until shortly before his death in 1995, Norman Feder's influence on the magazine was absolute: The magazine would never have evolved into anything like its present form without his continuous assistance and generous input. While this is of some interest to those of us currently involved in the magazine, who will always be in his debt, to most readers of this volume the more interesting point is something else: the extent to which Norm's dealings with the magazine help to illuminate particulars of the workings of his mind. Anyone who knew Norm even a little knows how seriously he valued his privacy; without violating what I know would have been his wishes, I will try to say something about how he worked with *American Indian Art Magazine* and what—over the course of seventeen years—I came to understand about this one aspect of his mind.

American Indian Art Magazine was started in 1975 by a knowledgeable but dishonorable gallery owner (subsequently imprisoned and apparently still dealing in Native American art). While his motivations might have been (and probably were) complex, the magazine was intended, at least in part, as a forum in which to show and validate the types of materials he had on hand and planned to sell. It was due to this man's knowledge (which I gather is considerable) and his charm (likewise apparently irresistible) that he managed to get various scholars, Norm included, involved in what was essentially a commercial endeavor. About two years after the magazine's inception, the original publisher wound up in prison and the current publisher, Mary Hamilton, took over. After about a year of various staff changes, I started to work at the magazine. Norm, who had been reading all materials submitted to the magazine for quite a while, continued to do so. From the outset, he responded to each article quite frankly and in considerable detail. Early on, we all made a simple decision: to keep the magazine as pretty as possible for those who use it primarily for the visuals and to keep it as factually accurate as possible for those who actually read it.

Having thus established the course of the magazine, Norm spent the next seventeen years helping for very little money and insisting, when thanked, that it was, after all, just his job. He was always unassuming; without being in the least self-denigrating, he always seemed to underestimate his input. Norm read every manuscript submitted to the magazine and some important aspects of his response never altered. He never cared to know who an author was and always preferred to read articles blind (as is the magazine's policy). He always suggested additional reviewers, generally indicating when he felt that they would likely know more than he on a particular subject (though this was rarely the case). He was always blunt and surprisingly—in the context of his bluntness—generous with other scholars. He was always willing to assume (unless it was shown to be otherwise) that another researcher might know something he did not. He was always thankful for their input and delighted by new information, particularly when it led him to revise his own thinking on a subject. In all the years that I worked with him, never did Norm respond to an article or fact personally or emotionally. He never made an exception for inaccuracy or illogic based on an author's reputation or its absence.

I think that it says much about Norm's objectivity that his good opinion of someone's research was unal-

Roanne Goldfein was Editor of *American Indian Art Magazine* from 1978 until 1999 and is still associated with the magazine in an advisory capacity.
Author's address: American Indian Art Magazine, 7314 E. Osborn Drive, Scottsdale, AZ 85251, U.S.A.

tered by personal history. One Native art specialist, for example, angry with Norm for reasons unknown to me, refused to work with *American Indian Art Magazine* for seventeen years because of Norm's association with us. Over that same period of time, Norm (though, well aware of this) never failed to include this man's name in his list of potential authors or reviewers. He was, Norm said, a good scholar; his judgment about Norm's personality did not, for Norm, figure into the equation.

Joyce Herold mentioned to me that in thinking about him recently, she realized that Norm probably had a photographic memory. She was referring to objects, saying that once Norm had seen an object anywhere in any basement of any museum in the world, he seemed to have the ability to recall it in absolute detail. While I never looked at objects with Norm, this certainly seemed to me to be the case as well. (In fact, Norm seemed to treat my absence of ability to recognize an object or photo years after having published it as some kind of odd quirk, something like a stutter, to be commented on perhaps once gently and never referred to again.)

Norm's recall of printed information was extraordinary as well. I might send him a manuscript while he was away from his home references and be told, in response to a citation from a twenty-year-old publication, to make certain that the author knew that the twenty-year-old citation was, in fact, paraphrased from another source, fifteen years prior, in such and such periodical. His recall was always sufficient so that the author or I could track down the original photo, or quotation, or object with relative ease.

I am certainly not the first to comment on the range of Norm's knowledge of Indian art. And while it may be true that I am biased or easily impressed, it is also true that in seventeen years Norm never failed to know something helpful about any manuscript on any aspect of Native art. He might literally write a seven- to ten-page letter in reference to an equally sized article that was ostensibly out of his areas of expertise, and then end by saying that I should send it to five other readers, all of whom Norm thought knew more about the subject than he did. He was utterly non-territorial about information as well, having instead a very simple interest in having misinformation corrected in print (including his own) and making correct information known (when and if available). Speculation—when not identified as such—was one of the things to make him furious; Norm felt strongly, I think, that since we could actually know so little about Indian art and had to guess about so much, misidentifying theory for fact caused irresolvable confusion. It wasn't the confusion as such that angered Norm, though, but rather the egotism so often behind it.

Norm seemed to me to have virtually no interest in common niceties. He never seemed to think that a harsh opinion should be gently phrased, for example; nor that his correction of an (impersonal) error might cause a personal response (terror, for example, or self-loathing). Until I begged him to stop after almost a decade, for example, he felt that part of his job was to go over every issue with a fine-toothed comb and tell me the seventeen or nineteen mistakes I'd let pass. He could never understand that this might be unpleasant for me when it seemed so obviously useful to him.

In the same vein, for someone who spent a great part of a lifetime involved in visual aesthetics, Norm had very little interest in niceties of language. He absolutely did not care how information was phrased, as long as it was accurate and clear and accessible to the reader. Given this disinterest on his part, his kindness to me about my editorial endeavors was always (to me) particularly touching. He was always quick to mention after reading the published version of an article, how much it had improved since his first reading of the initial draft, what wonderful changes the author and I had wrought. More than once, we had simply followed his instructions.

Niceties of language excepted, Norm was, in fact, an excellent reader and editor. I was always struck by how much he gleaned from one quick reading of a manuscript: The number of suggestions he had to offer not only about factual changes, which were ostensibly his domain, but organizational changes as well, which were ostensibly mine.

And he was, in fact, very kind. Norm was full of correction, but full of praise as well. He was an excellent teacher: brief and direct in making any suggestions, longer-winded with his praise and encouragement. He was very protective of the magazine, and quite protective of me as well in any number of ways, perhaps the most striking of which was his continuing to work when he felt quite ill, knowing that I didn't feel confident going on without him.

Norm and I met only twice and rarely spoke personally—aside from a bit of jostling, as people do upon initially meeting, to see whether they are basically on the same side of some core ethical issues or vague set of values. After some years of working together, Norm and I had developed our own sibling-like vocabulary and shorthand and never hedged our opinions with one another about matters pertaining to the magazine. He might tell me what he thought about a particular article, then tell me why I'd probably overrule him (or list the other reviewers who would disagree and why). But other than personal details given for work reasons—"I haven't answered your letters since I had a bleeding ulcer," for example, or "I'll be out of the office, having a baby"—we never spoke personally about anything.

While I felt that Norm and I had an odd kind of intimacy—since I consider the mind to be a private territory and his and mine were at least partially accessible to one another—Norm didn't, I think, consider this to be intimate, for a number of reasons, among them the fact that he was, by nature, more likely to be honest in expressing his opinions, less intellectually guarded.

Norm did much to help the magazine obtain some level of editorial integrity while he worked with us; and, in retrospect, I see that he spent a fair amount of time as well preparing me and the magazine for his absence, telling me how well I had done or would do (which was uncharacteristically personal), sending list after list of basic references that might escape my attention, talking frankly and in great detail about whom I should ask for what kind of advice, checking that I'd internalized some basic scholarly principles: not to accept attributions or documentation at face value, for example; never to assume any object's authenticity; never to be swayed by a researcher's reputation or its absence.

I hope, of course, that I did internalize the more important of Norm's lessons. No matter what manuscript comes across my desk, I am always aware of what Norm's reaction to it would have been, how he would have suggested that I proceed. And no matter how many opinions I solicit, I am always aware as well of how greatly every article we publish would benefit from Norm's touch: his knowledge and generous help. In this I am not alone: Everyone involved with *American Indian Art Magazine* is, I think, aware of working in his shadow and, to a certain extent, for his honor.

Norman Feder and American Indian Art Studies

Christian F. Feest

In 1954, when Norman Feder embarked upon an uncertain career as publisher of his journal *American Indian Hobbyist*, American Indian art studies were hardly what nearly half a century later they have come to be. Objects today regarded as outstanding examples of traditional aesthetics were then primarily displayed to the public in the anthropology halls of natural history museums as humble specimens of material culture. As auction houses and art historians largely tended to look the other way, Native American visual forms of expression were usually consigned to the intellectual and commercial flea market, rather than to the world of art. Material culture had fallen out of favor with mainstream anthropology, so that even museum anthropologists could hope for recognition only if their work was in more prestigious fields than the study of artifacts. This largely left the matter of Native American visual arts to a fairly small group of maverick scholars, private collectors, and enthusiasts like Norman Feder.

As an American Indian "hobbyist"—both in the wider sense as someone who dealt with the subject on a non-professional basis and in the narrow sense as a replicator of traditional Native crafts—Feder was at first hardly concerned with "art," but rather with "Indians." His earliest writings reported on his ethnographic observations among Apachean and Pueblo peoples of the Southwest, but increasingly also turned to other areas as well as to artifacts and how to make them.

There can be no doubt, however, that the hobbyist agenda shaped his perspective on visual material, because the replication of historical material culture necessarily contributes to an understanding not only of techniques and materials, but also of style that cannot be gained by simply looking at things. Careful analysis and observation is the major guide to successful work of this kind, and the final result will demonstrate success or failure of the research undertaken. Without having been (or having to be) trained for his undertaking, Feder realized that a familiarity with historical artifacts and illustrations, which often depict things never collected or preserved, added considerably to what could be learned from the living traditions of arts and crafts. Undoubtedly, this perspective was reinforced through his contacts with the few museum anthropologists who maintained an active interest in Native American material culture.

Like others who shared his avocation (including Richard Conn, Bill Holm, James H. Howard, and William K. Powers) and who have significantly contributed to our understanding of Native American cultures and arts, Norman Feder ultimately crossed the line between hobbyism and professionalism. That this transition occurred at the Denver Art Museum, played a decisive role in focusing his interest on "art."

Since 1925 the Denver Art Museum had been the first American museum to exhibit Native American material as works of art (followed in the early 1930s by the Brooklyn Museum). It was Frederic H. Douglas, who joined the museum in 1929 as Curator of Indian Art and served as its director from 1940 to his death in 1956, who defined the manner in which American Indian objects were recontextualized in a museum setting. Thus Douglas established a tradition of "Indian fashion shows," in which pieces from the collection were modeled by Native Americans from the area, accompanied by Douglas's interpretive commentary—a

Christian F. Feest is Professor of Anthropology at the Johann Wolfgang Goethe-Universität in Frankfurt am Main. His published work on Native American history, anthropology, and art includes *Native Arts of North America* ([2]1992), *Indians and Europe* (ed., [2]1999), *Beseelte Welten. Die Religionen der Indianer Nordamerikas* (1998), *Sitting Bull. "Der letzte Indianer"* (ed., 1999), and *Die Kulturen der nordamerikanischen Indianer* (ed., 2000).
Author's address: Institut für Historische Ethnologie, Liebigstraße 41, D-60323 Frankfurt am Main, Germany.

mode of enlivening artifacts clearly akin to hobbyism. In 1930 Douglas also initiated the popular *Indian Leaflet Series,* in which summary accounts of culture areas and specific tribes alternated with comparative discussions of artifact types. Because of the position of the Denver Art Museum as a showcase for Native American *art*, Douglas became involved in all the major exhibitions of American Indian art from the Exposition of Indian Tribal Arts (1931) through the show at the Golden Gate Exhibition in San Francisco (1939) to "Indian Art of the United States" at the Museum of Modern Art in New York (1941). After a transitional period following Douglas's death, Feder became the ideal successor to further develop the tradition defined by his predecessor.

By the time Feder joined the museum, his writings had moved to comprehensive accounts of specific artifact types based on both actual specimens and depictions. "Grizzly Claw Necklaces," for example, which names his consultant Milford Chandler as coauthor, offered a survey of the types of such necklaces in an effort to identify tribal styles, which were assumed to have existed although "very little can be stated as absolute fact" because of the paucity of data (Feder and Chandler 1961: 8). "Plains Indian Metalworking" (Feder 1962), the earliest and still the best survey of this art, documents the extent of his technical and historical knowledge. With *Elk Antler Roach Spreaders* (Feder 1968), written in the same vein, the author established a new series of publications at the Denver Art Museum, of which it remained the only issue ever published.

Feder's first publication for the Denver Art Museum (Feder and Malin 1962), a catalog to accompany a show on Northwest Coast art, is remarkable for his explicit concern with the collection history of the works illustrated. This was followed by a guide to the museum's North American Indian collection (Feder 1964a).

With *Art of the Eastern Plains Indians*, Feder (1964b) set a new trend in the North American study of Native American art. In Europe Krickeberg (1954) and others had already focused on material collected before the golden age of collecting, which especially in North America still largely defined the public perception of Native American art. In his publication of the Jarvis collection at the Brooklyn Museum, however, Feder explicitly noted the importance of such early collections for the recognition of stylistic changes, thus laying the groundwork for Native American art *history*:

> "In short, the Jarvis collection may surprise the ethnologist whose ideas of early Plains material culture have been based on more recent objects. The specimens in the Jarvis collection shed light particularly on the early development of clothing among the Eastern Sioux, and a further study of the collection will, I am sure, add immeasurably to our limited knowledge of Plains Indian culture in the first half of the nineteenth century" (Feder 1964b: 39).

In addition to supplying a historical perspective, collections with reliable data on provenance also helped to correct earlier sweeping attributions based upon a body of weakly substantiated lore, which had been developed by museum curators and collectors. (The old Museum of the American Indian was notorious for—but hardly unique in—disregarding documented evidence for provenance in favor of such made-up attributions.) Feder's discussion of Plains women's sidefold dresses, which had gone out of fashion by the mid-nineteenth century, illustrates this point (Feder 1964b: 21–23; amplified twenty years later in Feder 1984).

Equally distinctive for Feder's approach to Native art was his extensive and critical use of historical images to contextualize and supplement the surviving works. In the Jarvis catalog Peter Rindisbacher was given prominent (and perhaps somewhat too uncritical) attention; in later publications (e.g., Feder 1977) Catlin was rightly criticized as only "sometimes accurate."

American Indian Art Before 1850 (Feder 1965) took the idea of the Jarvis catalog one step further. This twenty-eight-page booklet accompanied an exhibition at the Denver Art Museum which brought together from museums and private collections in the United States ethnographic material predating the classical period of ethnographic collecting. Identifying the introduction and integration of Western materials and techniques as the major force in triggering these changes, Feder felt that 1850 marked "a moment in history when the indigenous Indian craftsmen had achieved a perfect integration of native techniques and imported trade goods," but had yet not been drawn into the negative processes resulting from "the final disintegration of Indian supremacy" (Feder 1965: [1]). Even those craftsmen who were still creating objects "strikingly similar to items which were produced in the pre-contact period" were now using aniline dyes and steel awls to create designs "radically different from those of the earlier period" (Feder 1965: [9]).

The exhibition covered North America south of the Arctic with the exception of the Southwest and California "for the simple reason that no early ethnological collections have survived from these areas" (Feder 1965: [1])—a statement which is only slightly misleading. The focus of the catalog, however, was clearly on the northeastern and southeastern Woodlands and the Plains, with only one Northwest Coast rattle and two items of Plateau clothing coming from other areas. While the arrangement of the objects in the catalog followed no clearly recognizable order, it did reflect Feder's interest in artifact types as a basis for comparison. Pipe stems, medicine bags, mirror frames, knife sheaths, wooden war clubs, garters, sashes, moccasins, etc. were illustrated in sets from three to eighteen.

Of the more than 300 objects in the exhibition, only 102 were listed and depicted in the catalog (including its front and back covers), all of them in black and white and some of them too small to show much detail. Yet the selection illustrated Feder's approach to dating based on a combination of direct evidence from artifacts and from the accompanying documentation. Since many of the early collections lack adequate data on the provenance of the artifacts, it became necessary to compare them to similar objects collected later with a documented provenance, whose comparable age can be determined by looking at the material from which they were manufactured: changing trade goods or natural resources which had become rare or unavailable through the reduction or extinction of wildlife species. To distinguish documented from attributed provenance, Feder referred to the latter as "type" or "style."

Illustrating five quilled ear pouches, e.g., Feder noted "the usual lack of documentation on early specimens. None of these are identified as to tribe," but at least one of them was known to have been collected in 1835. By referring to a sixth, similar pouch obtained by Milford Chandler among the Mesquakie of Tama (whose 1922 collection date is not given, but which is labeled as "Mesquakie (Fox), c. 1840"), a hint for the provenance of the whole group was implied (Feder 1965: [8–10]). If the Chandler piece can today be identified as an "Eastern Sioux pouch, Minnesota, 1800–1825" (Penney 1992: 66–67), it does not so much illustrate Feder's mistake, but the fact that his method combined with improved access to comparative data has indeed helped to locate poorly documented works in space and time. *American Indian Art Before 1850* provided an important step in this direction by making so many of the previously unpublished artifacts available for comparative purposes.

American Indian Art (Feder 1971a) was finished in the same year, but not published until six years later. It followed the tradition of surveys of the arts by culture area established by Vaillant (1939), Douglas and d'Harnoncourt (1941), Appleton (1950), Covarrubias (1954), and Dockstader (1961), but excluded prehistoric works. Rather surprisingly, Feder supplied only minimal information on the pieces illustrated and did not even always date them (including the works of twentieth-century painters). In a knowledgeable introduction accessible to the general reader, Feder discussed some of his favorite themes: the importance of materials and techniques, the difficulty of identifying tribal styles, factors of stability and change, and the impact of contact with Euro-Americans (described largely in the terms of "assimilation" fashionable at that time). Fifty-nine color plates and 242 black-and-white illustrations of artifacts and contextual images made this an attractive book, whose weight and size, however, were more indicative of (and contributing to) the changing public attitudes toward American Indian art than of its substantial contents. This was the time, it may be remembered, when a Northwest Coast raven rattle became the first North American Indian work of art to be sold for more than $5,000 at an auction in New York—a fact widely hailed as a major breakthrough to respectability.

That the book was finally published in 1971, may have had to do with "Two Hundred Years of North American Indian Art," the exhibition Feder guest-curated at the Whitney Museum of American Art in the same year. In its focus on sculpture it not only followed the model of Donald Collier's Chicago exhibition "Indian Art of the Americas" (1959), but also the widespread perception of "primitive art" as sculptural. In conjunction with specimens of representational painting, the exhibition (perhaps unwittingly) largely excluded the work of Native American women artists. At the same time, the emphasis on sculpture supplemented Feder's earlier exhibition on "American Indian painting" at the Museum of Primitive Art (1967). Like *American Indian Art*, with which the catalog shares the substance of the introductory section, the Whitney show strictly followed the anthropological orthodoxy of culture areas and thus separated stylistically related materials that could have profitably been shown next to one another. Thanks to Feder's ability to make a strong selection of visually attractive works based on his vast knowledge of collections (including material in European museums he visited in 1969), however, the show did have an immediate impact upon the general acceptance of Native American art.

The commercial success of his coffee-table book and the Whitney show enabled Feder to retire from the Denver Art Museum just as American Indian art studies and the interest in Native American art began to emerge from obscurity. Although he had helped pave the way for this development, Feder retreated from the limelight, irritated perhaps in part by the tremendous changes that began to affect the field. Overshadowed by a flood of new publications increasingly illustrated in full color and often tied to commercial interests, the relatively few publications of the last twenty-four years of his life revisited some of his old interests like bird quillwork, the European influence on Native art, artifaking, and the importance of early, dated collections. If Feder seemed unwilling to share his vast knowledge with an avid readership, this may have been caused by his increasing awareness of the problems posed by the limitations of the data.

> "The conclusion of this article [on sidefold dresses], if there is one, is that we should always be suspicious of anything we read and doubt any museum attribution that is not absolutely ironclad" (Feder 1984: 77).

This scepticism did not only apply to tribal attributions, but also to interpretations of meaning:

> "There is a tendency today among both anthropologists and art historians to look for hidden or deeper meanings in everything, an approach which seems completely unscientific" (Feder 1985: 49).

Such careful scrutiny had, of course, little market appeal and could not satisfy audiences who wanted to know exactly what they were seeing and what it all meant. It did, however, inform his work as editorial consultant first and briefly for *Indian America* (1976) and ultimately for *American Indian Art Magazine* (1977–1995), through which he helped to shape the growing discipline in a decisive, but almost unrecognized way.

If nothing else, Feder's sober insistence on terminological clarity based on an understanding of techniques and materials and on the importance of a critical awareness of the potentials and restrictions of the data would be a worthwhile and lasting legacy to Native American art studies for a long time to come.

References Cited

Appleton, Le Roy
1950 *Indian Art of the Americas.* New York, NY: Scribner's.

Collier, Donald
1959 *Indian Art of the Americas.* Chicago, IL: Natural History Museum.

Covarrubias, Miguel
1954 *The Eagle, the Jaguar, and the Serpent.* New York, NY: Alfred A. Knopf.

Dockstader, Frederick J.
1961 *Indian Art in America.* Greenwich, CT: New York Graphic Society.

Douglas, Frederic H. and René d'Harnoncourt
1941 *Indian Art of the United States.* New York, NY: The Museum of Modern Art.

Feder, Norman
1962 Plains Indian Metalworking. *American Indian Tradition* 8(2): 55–76, (3): 93–108.
1964a A Guide to the North American Indian Collections. *Denver Art Museum Quarterly* (Winter 1964–65): 114–131.
1964b *Art of the Eastern Plains Indians. The Nathan Sturges Jarvis Collection.* Brooklyn, NY: The Brooklyn Museum.
1965 *American Indian Art Before 1850.* Denver Art Museum Quarterly (Summer 1965). Denver, CO.
1967 *North American Indian Painting.* New York, NY: The Museum of Primitive Art.
1968 *Elk Antler Roach Spreaders.* Material Culture Monograph 1. Denver, CO.
1971a *American Indian Art.* New York, NY: Harry N. Abrams.
1971b *Two Hundred Years of North American Indian Art.* New York, NY—Washington, DC—London: Praeger Publishers.
1977 George Catlin: Sometimes Accurate. *American Indian Art Magazine* 2(3): 72–75.
1984 The Side Fold Dress. *American Indian Art Magazine* 10(1): 48–55, 75.
1985 The Jasper Grant Collection. *American Indian Art Magazine* 10(3): 46–51.

Feder, Norman and Milford G. Chandler
1961 Grizzly Claw Necklaces. *American Indian Tradition* 8(1): 7–16.

Feder, Norman and Edward Malin
1962 *Indian Art of the Northwest Coast.* Denver Art Museum Quarterly (Winter 1962). Denver, CO.

Krickeberg, Walter
1954 Ältere Ethnographica aus Nordamerika im Berliner Museum für Völkerkunde. *Baessler-Archiv*, N.F. 2: 1–280.

Penney, David W.
1992 *Art of the American Indian Frontier. The Chandler-Pohrt Collection.* Seattle, WA: University of Washington Press.

Vaillant, George C.
1939 *Indian Arts of North America.* New York, NY: Harper.

Norman Feder
A Bibliography

Compiled by Christian F. Feest[1]

Books and Articles

1954 1. Laguna Scalp Dance. *American Indian Hobbyist* 1 (September 1954): 3.
2. Navaho Feather Dance. *American Indian Hobbyist* 1 (October 1954): 9.
3. More Navaho Magic. *American Indian Hobbyist* 1 (November 1954).
4. Yei-be-chi. *American Indian Hobbyist* 1 (December 1954): 22.
5. Whistles. *American Indian Hobbyist* 1 (December 1954): 28.

1955 6. California Ethnobotany. (Mimeographed. Prepared for U.S. Department of Justice in connection with Californian Indian land claims.)
7. Bull Roarer. *American Indian Hobbyist* 1 (January 1955): 7.
8. Apache Crown Dance. *American Indian Hobbyist* 1 (January 1955): 32.
9. Basic Costume. *American Indian Hobbyist* 1 (February 1955).
10. Inter-Tribal Indian Ceremonial. *American Indian Hobbyist* 1 (March 1955).
11. Porcupine Quillwork Technique. *American Indian Hobbyist* 2 (September 1955): 3–4, (October 1955): 13–14.

1956 12. Hopi Lightning Frame Dance. *American Indian Hobbyist* 2 (January 1956): 41.
13. Ribbon Appliqué. *American Indian Hobbyist* 3 (October–November 1956): 11–26.
14. Fry Bread. *American Indian Hobbyist* 3 (December 1956): 34.

1957 15. The Jemez Buffalo Dance. *American Indian Hobbyist* 3 (January–February 1957): 48.
16. Tlingit Face Stamps. *American Indian Hobbyist* 3 (May–June 1957): 82–83.
17. Flutes. *American Indian Hobbyist* 3 (May–June 1957): 96–98.
18. (with Glenn White and Issy Umscheid) Costume of the Oklahoma Straight Dancer. *American Indian Hobbyist* 4 (September–October 1957): 3–17.
19. Old Time Sioux Costume. *American Indian Hobbyist* 4 (November–December 1957): 23–31.
20. Sioux Kettle Drum. *American Indian Hobbyist* 4 (November–December 1957): 37–38.

1958 21. Details of a Sioux Cloth Dress. *American Indian Hobbyist* 4 (January-February 1958): 50–51.
22. Oklahoma Fancy Dance Costume. *American Indian Hobbyist* 4 (January-February 1958): 52–57.
23. How to Make Hopi Yarn Anklets. *American Indian Hobbyist* 4 (March–April 1958): 70–74.
24. Embroidered Kilts. *American Indian Hobbyist* 4 (March–April 1958): 76–77.
25. Cochiti Parrot Dance. *American Indian Hobbyist* 4 (March–April 1958): 78–79.
26. Plains Hair and Roach Ornaments. *American Indian Hobbyist* 4 (May–June 1958): 83–88.
27. Hopi Butterfly Dance and Costume. *American Indian Hobbyist* 4 (May–June 1958): 90–93.
28. Oklahoma Women's Costume. *American Indian Hobbyist* 4 (May–June 1958): 96.
29. Modern Swing Bustles. *American Indian Hobbyist* 5 (November–December 1958): 28–32.
30. Gallup Ceremonials. *American Indian Hobbyist* 5 (November–December 1958): 76–77.
31. How to Make Navaho Moccasins. *American Indian Hobbyist* 5 (November–December 1958): 36–38.
32. Roach Spreaders. *American Indian Hobbyist* 5 (November–December 1958): 42–45.

1959 33. Modern Crow Costume. *American Indian Hobbyist* 5 (March–April 1959): 74–80.
34. Women's Bow-Type Hair Ornaments. *American Indian Hobbyist* 5 (March–April 1959): 86–90.
35. The Kickapoo of Coahuila. *American Indian Hobbyist* 5 (March–April 1959): 91–94.
36. Modern Oklahoma Buckskin Dress. *American Indian Hobbyist* 5 (May–June 1959): 98–104.
37. Sioux Pheasant Bustle. *American Indian Hobbyist* 5 (May–June 1959): 111–117.
38. Seminole Patchwork. *American Indian Hobbyist* 6 (September–October 1959): 1–18.
39. Mirror Boards. *American Indian Hobbyist* 6 (September–October 1959): 26–32.

1. With assistance from Ted Brasser and Tilly Laskey.

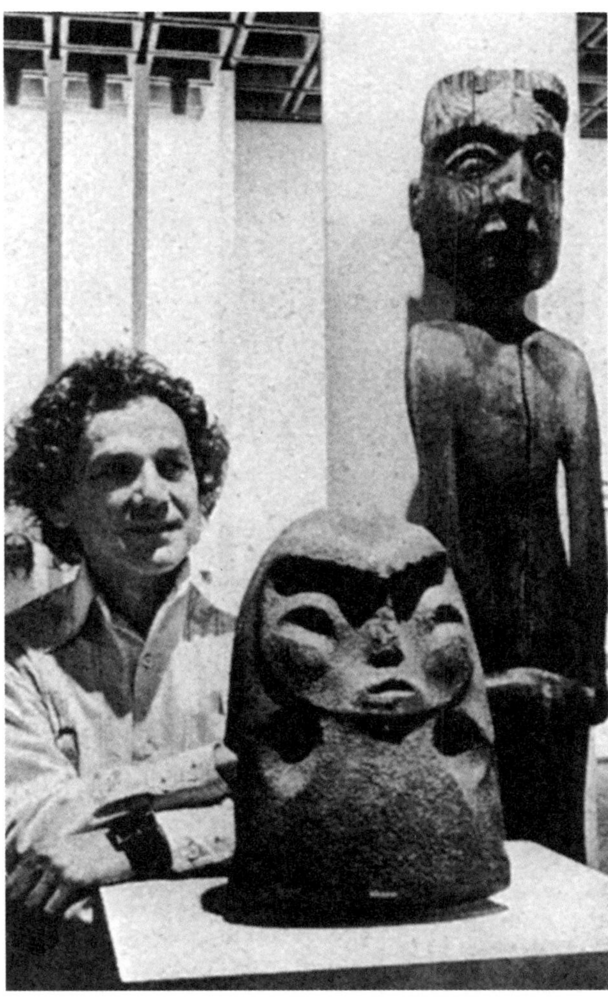

Norman Feder in his exhibition *Two Hundred Years of North American Indian Art* at the Whitney Museum of American Art, New York, 1971, with Nootka house post (back) and Bella Bella stone pile driver (front).

40. Shoshone Split Horn Bonnet. *American Indian Hobbyist* 6 (September–October 1959): 35–38.
41. Ute Bear Dance. *American Indian Hobbyist* 6 (September–October 1959): 39–42.

1960 42. Quill and Horsehair Feather Ornaments. *American Indian Tradition* 6(9–10): 109–110.

1961 43. Otter Fur Turbans. *American Indian Tradition* 7(3): 84–96.
44. (with Milford G. Chandler) Grizzly Claw Necklaces. *American Indian Tradition* 8(1): 7–16.
45. A Note on "An Unusual Beadwork Technique." *American Indian Tradition* 8(1): 41–42.

1962 46. Plains Indian Metalworking. *American Indian Tradition* 8(2): 55–76, (3): 93–108. [Reprinted in: R. D. Theisz (ed.), *Lakota Art is an American Art. Readings in Traditional and Contemporary Sioux Art* (Spearfish, SD: Black Hills State College), 87–150, 151–189.]
47. Matachines. *American Indian Tradition* 8(2): 79–82.
48. Front Seam Leggings. *American Indian Tradition* 8(3): 93–108.
49. Bottom Tab Leggings. *American Indian Tradition* 8(4): 148–159.
50. *Indian Art of the Northwest Coast. Collection Notes (Objects 1–47).* Denver Art Museum Indian Leaflet Series 148–171. Denver, CO. [Also published as:]
51. (with Edward Malin) *Indian Art of the Northwest Coast.* Denver Art Museum Quarterly (Winter 1962). Denver, CO. ["Preface" (p. 1) and "Notes on Selected Pieces from the Collection" (pp. 29–93) by Feder. Revised and reprinted in 1968.]

1964 52. Origin of the Oklahoma Forty-Nine Dance. *Ethnomusicology* 8(3): 290–294.
53. *Art of the Eastern Plains Indians. The Nathan Sturges Jarvis Collection.* Brooklyn, NY: The Brooklyn Museum.
54. Art of the Eastern Plains Indians. *The Brooklyn Museum Annual* 4: 6–41.
55. A Guide to the North American Indian Collections. *Denver Art Museum Quarterly* (Winter 1964–65): 114–131.

1965 56. *American Indian Art Before 1850.* Denver Art Museum Quarterly (Summer 1965). Denver, CO.
57. *Head and Tail Fans.* Indiancraft Pamphlet 2. Somerset, NJ: Powwow Trails.

1966 58. *Crow Indian Art.* Denver, CO: Denver Art Museum. [Exhibition brochure.]
59. Sioux Dewclaw Necklace. *Powwow Trails* 3(1–2): 12–13. [Reprinted from *American Indian Hobbyist*.]

1967 60. *North American Indian Painting.* New York, NY: The Museum of Primitive Art. [Exhibition catalog.]

1968 61. *Elk Antler Roach Spreaders.* Material Culture Monograph 1. Denver, CO: Denver Art Museum.
62. Blackfeet War Shirt. *The Singing Wire* 2(4): 6.
63. Ivory Billed Woodpecker Turbans. *The Singing Wire* 2(5): 1–8.
64. The 1965 Yuchi Green Corn Dance at Kellyville, Oklahoma. In: James H. Howard, *The Southeastern Ceremonial Complex and Its Interpretation* (Missouri Archaeological Society, Memoir 6), 165–169.
65. *The Afro-American Heritage.* Denver, CO: Denver Art Museum. [Exhibition brochure.]
66. *Legacies of the American Southwest.* Denver, CO: Denver Art Museum. [Exhibition brochure.]

1970 67. *Gallery of Indian Art.* Phoenix, AZ: The Heard Museum. [Exhibition brochure.]
68. *Traditions of the West.* Denver, CO: Denver Art Museum. [Exhibition brochure.]

1971 69. *American Indian Art.* New York, NY: Harry N. Abrams. [Abridged edition: New York, NY 1973: Harry N. Adams.]
70. *Two Hundred Years of North American Indian Art.* New York, NY—Washington, DC—London: Praeger Publishers. [Exhibition catalog.]
71. How to Obtain Help from Museums. *American Indian Crafts and Culture* 5(2): 4–7.

1972 72. Shoshone Split Horned Bonnet. *American Indian Crafts and Culture* 6(1): 2–5. [Reprint of 40, above.]

1973 73. The Art of the American Indian. *Dialogue* 6(2): 50–58. [Abridged from introduction to *Two Hundred Years of North American Indian Art* (1971).]

1974 74. Fur Garters. *Indian America* 8(7): 7–9, 45.

1977 75. The Future of Indian Art. *American Indian Art Magazine* 2(2): 26–27.

76. The Malaspina Collection. *American Indian Art Magazine* 2(3): 40–51, 80–82.

77. George Catlin: Sometimes Accurate. *American Indian Art Magazine* 2(3): 72–75.

1978 78. Pawnee Cradleboards. *American Indian Art Magazine* 3(4): 40–50.

1980 79. Plains Pictographic Painting and Quilled Rosettes. *American Indian Art Magazine* 5(2): 54–62.

80. Crow Indian Art: The Problem. *American Indian Art Magazine* 6(1): 30–31.

81. Crow Blanket Strip Rosettes. *American Indian Art Magazine* 6(1): 40–45, 88.

1983 82. Incised Relief Carving of the Halkomelem and Straits Salish. *American Indian Art Magazine* 8(2): 46–55.

1984 83. The Side Fold Dress. *American Indian Art Magazine* 10(1): 48–55, 75.

1985 84. The Jasper Grant Collection. *American Indian Art Magazine* 10(3): 46–51.

1986 85. European Influences on Plains Indian Art. In: Edwin L. Wade (ed.), *The Arts of the North American Indian* (New York, NY: Hudson Hills), 93–104.

1987 86. Bird Quillwork. *American Indian Art Magazine* 12(3): 46–57.

1992 87. How to Avoid Buying Artifakes. In: George P. Horse Capture and Suzanne G. Taylor (eds.), *Artifacts/Artifakes. The Proceedings of the 1984 Plains Indian Seminar* (Cody, WY: Buffalo Bill Historical Center), 11–15.

Book Reviews

1963 1. Paul Wingert, *Primitive Art*. *Ethnohistory* 10(1): 97–98.

1968 2. Audrey Hawthorn, *Art of the Kwakiutl Indians and Other Northwest Coast Tribes*. *American Anthropologist* 70(5): 1014–1015.

1969 3. Helga Benndorf and Arthur Speyer, *Indianer Nordamerikas 1760–1860: Aus der Sammlung Speyer*. *American Anthropologist* 71(3): 514–515.

1978 4. Adrienne L. Kaeppler, *Artificial Curiosities: An Exposition of Native Manufactures, Collected on the Three Pacific Voyages of Captain James Cook, R.N.* *American Indian Art Magazine* 3(4): 28.

5. Judy Thompson, *The North American Indian Collection*. *American Indian Art Magazine* 4(1): 48–49.

1980 6. John C. Ewers, *Indian Art in Pipestone*. *American Indian Art Magazine* 5(4): 82–83.

7. William H. Truettner, *The Natural Man Observed: A Study of George Catlin's Indian Gallery*. *American Indian Art Magazine* 5(4): 83–84.

1981 8. N. Jaye Frederickson and Sandra Gibb, *The Covenant Chain: Indian Ceremonial and Trade Silver*. *American Indian Art Magazine* 6(3): 81–82.

1982 9. Christian F. Feest, *Native Arts of North America*. *American Indian Art Magazine* 7(1): 88.

10. Peter John Powell, *People of the Sacred Mountain*. *American Indian Art Magazine* 7(4): 70–71, 74.

1994 11. John W. Painter, *American Indian Artifacts: The John Painter Collection*. *American Indian Art Magazine* 19(2): 70, 72.

Indian Leaflet Series

Norman Feder's name appears on the front of all of the *Indian Leaflets* reprinted between 1965 and 1972; no additions to Frederic H. Douglas's original material, however, were made. (But see number 50 above, for Feder's original contribution to the series.)

Material Culture Notes

Feder made definite and noted additions to some of the Denver Art Museum's *Material Culture Notes*, originally written by Frederic H. Douglas. They are as follows:

#2 A Crow Beaded Horse Collar. Revised by Norman Feder, September 1968.

#7 An Osage Yarn Bag. Revised by Norman Feder and Kate Peck Kent, July 1968.

#12 A Cheyenne Peyote Fan. Revised by Norman Feder, July 1968.

#17 Metal Jewelry of the Peyote Cult. Revised by Norman Feder, September 1968.

#20 A Jicarilla Apache Woman's Skin Dress. Revised by Norman Feder, September 1968.

#22 A Jicarilla Apache Man's Skin Leggings. Revised by Norman Feder, August 1968.

Norman Feder and the Central Coast Salish Art Style

Steven C. Brown

Norman Feder possessed a keen interest in the art forms of the Central Coast Salish First Nations, and his published work expresses this in a number of manifestations. His hefty tome of 1971, the general survey entitled *American Indian Art* (Feder 1971a), illustrates six examples of Coast Salish carving and design. Survey-type books on Northwest Coast art at that time often did not include Salish arts at all, focusing instead on the works of the northern Northwest Coast peoples, the Tlingit, Haida, and Tsimshian, and the most flamboyant artists of the southern coast, the Kwakwaka'wakw. (Norm's book also included eleven carvings or baskets attributed to the Wishram or Wasco, another seldom-represented southern coastal tradition.) Through the following decade, many publications continued to reflect the same bias (illustrating perhaps two or three Salish objects out of dozens of others), though a few printed works available in that period are worthy of note.[1] In 1975 Norm presented the paper "Coast Salish Art: A Stylistic Analysis" at the UCLA/Ethnic Arts Council of Los Angeles symposium *Traditions and New Perspectives of Northwest Coast Art*. That manuscript was in his words "completely revised" and published in the Spring 1983 issue of *American Indian Art Magazine* under the title "Incised Relief Carving of the Halkomelem and Straits Salish," which will be revisited and discussed in the next few pages.

During the aforementioned span of years, Norm lived on Land's End Road at the northern tip of the Saanich Peninsula, Vancouver Island, about twenty miles north of Victoria, British Columbia. His home was within the heart of the Halkomelem cultural region, an hour or less from a number of Coast Salish reserves and villages, and he used this proximity to advantage by visiting with First Nations artists in the area. Information resulting from those visits was included in the 1983 *American Indian Art Magazine* article.

In many ways that piece of writing reads like the oral presentation that it was originally. It has a certain spontaneity that a more polished scholarly study would not have. This aspect has, of course, its more and less positive attributes. The article contains some minor inconsistencies and a few somewhat confusing applications of terms. There are indications that the research, viewed with the power of retrospect, was a little superficial, based almost entirely on published sources (in a field with little published material). This led to some minor oversights that, under further research, disagree with some of the article's findings. Although there are these few shortcomings, it is also appropriate to declare how important and timely the article was in its day. It still retains its value as a highly visible publication that focused directly on a relatively unknown and, at the time, very under-appreciated art form.

In the years since 1983, Coast Salish arts and traditional practitioners have proliferated greatly, and the design style from the region can now be seen in a wide variety of high-profile creations in the U.S. and Canada. This expansion of the art form is due, of course, to

Steven C. Brown was drawn to the arts of the First Peoples as a young man, intrigued by artworks from the Northwest Coast. He spent over fifteen years living and working in First Nations communities from Washington State to Alaska, involved in carving and teaching projects full time. His experiences in the field inform and provide insight to his interpretive work. Brown has produced two books in association with the Seattle Art Museum, *The Spirit Within: Northwest Coast Native Art from the John H. Hauberg Collection* (1995) and *Native Visions: Evolution in Northwest Coast Art from the Eighteenth through Twentieth Century* (1998). Brown is currently Associate Curator of Native American Art at the Seattle Art Museum.
Author's address: Seattle Art Museum, 100 University Street, Seattle, WA 98101-2902, U.S.A.

1. A short list of pre-1980 publications focused on or substantially presenting Coast Salish arts should include the following: Wingert 1949, Duff 1952, Barnett 1955, Dickason 1972 (illustrates nine Salish objects or images), Suttles 1977, Calkins 1977.

the creative energy and effort of the Coast Salish artists themselves, the ones who produce the work. From a handful of pre-1983 artists working in Central Coast Salish style, the knowledge of and inspiration to do work in this tradition has passed from hand to hand, creating an ever-expanding group of artists. The awareness of Coast Salish arts among the general public has risen steadily with each new creation in the style, from imaginative serigraphs to major sculptures. The lights that have illuminated that awareness, in addition to those of the artists, also include the published discourse, which has cast a few bright beams on and in praise of this important and truly fascinating tradition. Norm's *AIAM* article is one of this group, as are a few related works that both preceded and have followed it. This list includes Calkins (1977), Kew (1980), Duffek (1986), Holm (1987), Danford (1990), and Wright (1991).

Norm based his article on historic works of the Halkomelem and Straits Salish, who created objects in a design style that is both very old and very highly developed. His position, which he uses the collection data of historic objects to support, is that only artists of the Central Coast Salish employed the design style exemplified by the most developed artworks of that region. The documentation of objects in this style collected outside of the Halkomelem/Straits area he labeled as "suspect." One such object is the fine double-ended comb acquired by George Hewitt, a member of the 1792 Vancouver expedition, at Restoration Point, Bainbridge Island, while engaged in charting Puget Sound (Wright 1991: 109, fig. 66). Who is to say, however, that it wasn't made right in that area, and not necessarily farther north in the Central Coast Salish territory? A whalebone club collected from Hartstene Island (southern Puget Sound) during a Washington State Museum expedition prior to 1923 (and since repatriated to the Squaxin Island Tribe under NAGPRA) exhibits a spare use of ovals, trigon forms, and thin incised lines to define its stylized features. The club is thought to be as old as 2,500 years (Wright 1991: 70). The notion, then, that important elements of the Central Coast Salish art tradition were more than likely present in Puget Sound and other areas for centuries prior to Euro-American contact in the region seems readily defensible.

Part of the question turns on what parameters constitute the "Central Coast Salish style." Does anything with a design on it based on circles and trigons qualify? A good look at the existing record causes one to believe that certain elements of that style were employed in widespread areas of the Northwest Coast, and that the basic elements of circles and trigons are the conceptual armature on which all historic Northwest Coast styles are based (Brown 1995: 7–11). Clearly, one must look more closely at the Central Coast Salish and other related art traditions and try to sort out the characteristics of which each is comprised.

As ever, one is also aware of how much chance and the habits of explorers, fur traders, and collectors have influenced the historical record, determining the nature of existing collections in a way that may not be truly representative of the actual distribution of object types or design styles. Trade, intermarriage, and warfare also redistribute objects in an unpredictable way, sometimes confusing the historical record. The earliest collections from the Northwest Coast were made in the areas of Nootka Sound, Dixon Entrance, and Yakutat, locations where explorers and early entrants in the fur trade encountered and traded with the First Peoples of the regions. Objects from these collections tell us a great deal about the status of First Nations arts in those times and places, but what of the locations that were seldom or not visited by the first waves of Euro-Americans to acquire Northwest Coast artifacts? The historical record is sadly skewed (and resultantly unreliable) with regard to drawing accurate, dependable conclusions about where and when design styles or artifacts were made and used. Similarly, concepts can be suggested or implied by the archaeological record, but such conclusions need also be qualified by the inconsistent source of the information. Archaeology has not been privileged to study every possible site in every area of the coast (nor has every area preserved recoverable material to begin with), so the existing record only reveals small glimpses of the overall picture.

For example, Norm cites with appropriate interest the numerous Salish-style artifacts recovered from the Ozette archaeological site on the pacific shore of Washington State. Prior to 1975, when these artifacts began to be recovered from the remains of an ancient catastrophic mudslide that inundated several houses in the village, no one had reason to include this historically Makah village in the geographic distribution of Salishan artifacts. (Exactly why and how these objects got or were made there remains unexplained, however, as Norm points out in his article; Feder 1983: 47). Now, in retrospect, we know they were there, and the view of Salishan artifact distribution has been expanded accordingly. There have been historic period and contemporary social ties (as well as warfare) between the Makah and the Straits Salish S'Klallam that may well have centuries-old antecedents. But a question remains: Where else were objects in this style made and used which have not been preserved and discovered?

In addition, certain design aspects commonly associated with the Central Coast Salish style have been employed by other Northwest Coast Nations far back in prehistory (Brown 1995: 7–11). A number of very early carved objects of antler and bone, and even wet-site-preserved wood, have survived or been excavated from certain northern coast village sites. Several important examples of such discoveries were illustrated in *Indian Art Traditions of the Northwest Coast*, a compilation of papers presented at a 1979 archaeological conference at Simon Fraser University in British Columbia (Carlson 1983). These objects exhibit characteristics more in common with Central Coast Salish design than with mature formline design of the historic period on the northern and central coasts. These locations span from Vancouver Island to Prince Rupert Harbour in northern British Columbia, suggesting that *at one very distant time*, the circle-and-trigon, strictly positive-and-negative design style was not unique to Central Coast Salish artists and may in fact have been pan-coastal.

Early examples of Nuu-chah-nulth art, in addition, especially whalebone clubs, also clearly exhibit the use of an elemental circle-and-trigon design style that is often only distinguishable from Central Coast Salish work by the characteristics of the objects so decorated. Similarly, Ozette artifacts that are not Salishan in form and use are also decorated with a very similar elemental usage of the circle-and-trigon tradition. These objects include zoomorphic designs on house screens, bent-corner containers, bone clubs, and other objects. One can conclude that the Central Coast Salish design style, as it is known from spindle whorls, combs, horn bracelets, horn rattles, and the surface of S'xwaixwei masks, is a localized stylistic development that evolved from an elemental circle-and-trigon tradition which was once widespread on the Northwest Coast. Likewise, the mature northern Northwest Coast or formline art can be seen as an evolutionary development with its roots in the original circle-and-trigon, or proto-Northwest Coast, design style. Though Norm did not appear to discuss this perspective in his 1983 article, he alluded to the possibility:

> "By the time of Captain Cook's landing at Nootka Sound—and before as evidenced at Ozette—the Westcoast [Nuu-chah-nulth] people had developed an art style and artifact inventory that was similar to, but distinct from, that of the [Coast] Salish. ... We will probably never know if the art style that we think of as typically Central Coast Salish was developed from [Nuu-chah-nulth] prototypes, or if the reverse is true ... In all likelihood, the influence passed in both directions" (Feder 1983: 47).

Nootka Sound, or specifically the Mowachaht village of Yuquot (Friendly Cove), is identified as the source of what is, in fact, perhaps the most spectacularly decorated (as well as the earliest documented) example of a Salish sheephorn rattle in existence (Museum voor Land en Volkenkunde, Rotterdam, cat.no. 34,818). Acquired on James Cook's visit to the area in 1778, the rattle is cited[2] (but not illustrated) in Norm's article as an example of the distant distribution of Central Coast Salish material culture by means of trade, marriage, or perhaps warfare. We know of its existence, however, and those of numerous other objects acquired on that largely scientific expedition, because of the twist of fate that carried Cook's ship to that location. What of the numerous other Nuu-chah-nulth villages not so heavily frequented by Euro-American fur traders in the following decades? Like their relatives at Ozette, First Peoples in those locations may have possessed similar artifacts that may have been relegated to the graves of their owners without being recorded by history. The same can be said or implied about possible artifacts in locations outside of the cultural area defined by Norm in this notably brief study.

There are some inconsistencies and oversights in Norm's article (as there may be in any preliminary type of study) that additional time and research have revealed. After listing several early objects and their dates of collection, he concluded with the following statement:

"It is likely that the Central Coast Salish *art style*

2. As indicated in Norm's endnote 3, this rattle has been illustrated in King (1981: pl. 52), Feest (1980: fig. 59), and Collins et al. (1973: fig. 341). It was also recently published in *Indianen*, the small catalog of an exhibition by the Rijksmuseum voor Volkenkunde, Leiden (Hovens 1998: 27).

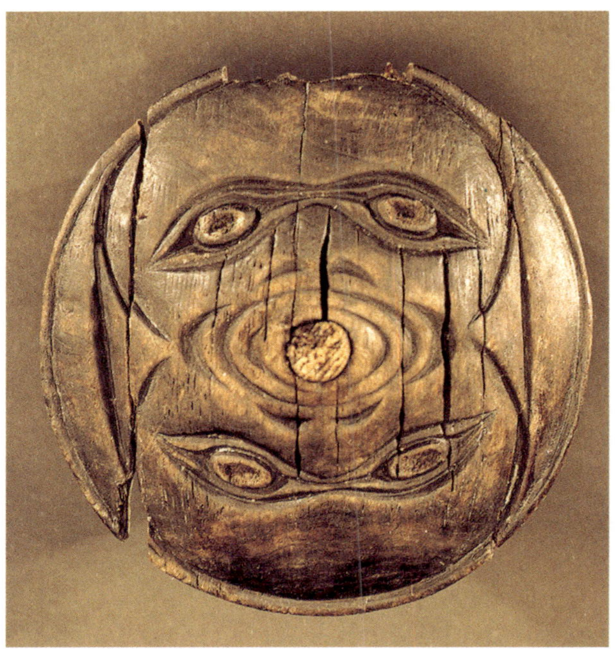

Fig. 1 Spindle whorl. Makah, Ozette village, ca. AD 1500–1700. Wood. Makah Cultural and Research Center (Neah Bay, WA). Photograph: Steven C. Brown.
A remnant of the original spindle shaft was found in the center hole of this whorl. The images seen here utilize the same carved elements and design style as Central Coast Salish carvings from the historic period. One or two spindle whorls collected within the last century feature remarkably similar overlapping face designs.

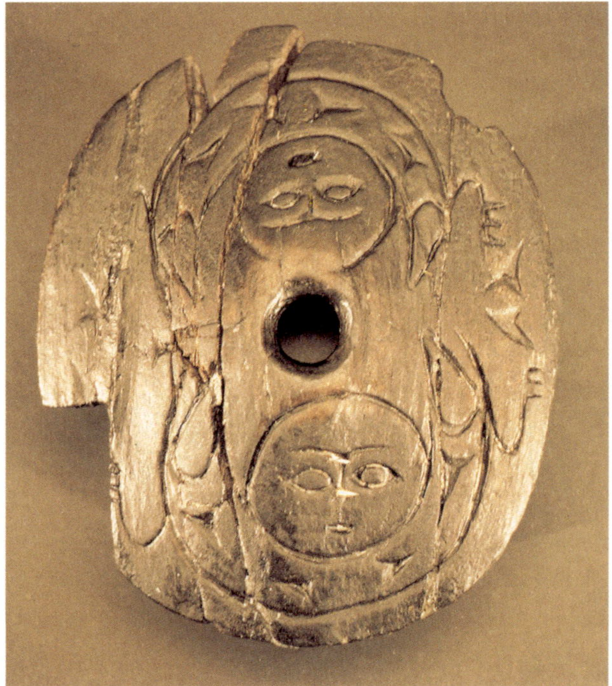

Fig. 2 Spindle whorl. Makah, Ozette village, ca. AD 1500–1700. Wood. Makah Cultural and Research Center (Neah Bay, WA). Photograph: Steven C. Brown.
The face and serpent images on this whorl are rendered in a very simple and archaic form, though employing the same essential design elements as historic examples.

began to disappear by 1830, at least for some artifact types, and that after about 1870 the few existing carvers simply copied old forms without understanding them" (Feder 1983: 52; emphasis mine).

He also wrote:

"We do know that there are no documented examples of spindle whorls with animal forms before 1861, which might indicate that this was a later *stylistic* development" (Feder 1983: 51; emphasis mine).

Just in terms of language, there is some confusion here between the words "style" or "stylistic" and "artifacts." If certain *artifact* types "began to disappear by about 1830," then that is really a different statement than the first one quoted above. The design work on those combs, bracelets, and other objects he refers to is the same as the mature Central Coast Salish style seen on spindle whorls, of which he says that there are no documented animal-form examples pre-dating 1861, and S'xwaixwei masks made well into the twentieth century. These then should have been termed a later *artifact* or *design* development, but not a "stylistic" one, because the design style is the same as of the pre-1830 objects he discussed. These inconsistencies are perhaps the result of the spontaneous approach Norm took to this article, in which he used terms that he may have intended to iron out more carefully down the road. Existing objects in fact indicate that the design style remained fairly intact well into the twentieth century and did not slide down such a steep decline as the one that Norm describes.

Norm was apparently not aware (because they had not been published prior to 1983) of two or more wooden spindle whorls from the Ozette site with human and/or animal designs beautifully relief-carved on them (Figs. 1, 2). The mudslide that inundated this site is thought to have taken place 300–500 years ago, making these the oldest known wooden whorls in existence. One of these features large human faces with the mouth used as the center hole of the whorl, not unlike the one used as the lead image to Norm's *American Indian Art Magazine* article. The two faces on the Ozette artifact are like mirror images of each other, their mouths sharing the whorl's center hole (Fig. 1). Another whorl from that site displays two human or spirit faces and two serpents or spirit creatures (Fig. 2). Additionally, a stone spindle whorl recovered archaeologically (which was illustrated in Carlson [1983: 161, fig. 8:31]), appears to be very early prehistoric. Apparently, however, the archaeological context of that site was disrupted, making accurate dating of the object impossible. The appearance of these archaeological materials certainly suggests, if not indicates, that this artifact type, with the Central Coast Salish zoomorphic design style applied to it, was in existence prior to 1861. In addition, there are spindle whorls that appear stylistically to be from at least the early nineteenth century (see Fig. 3), though these, of course, are some of the examples mentioned in the quote from Norm's article, for which no early collection dates are documented (Fig. 3 was collected in 1903).

The idiosyncrasies of historic collecting, in this case, may have created a misimpression regarding the presumed later development of zoomorphically decorated spindle whorls. Perhaps combs, bracelets, and wooden clubs (the earliest artifact types acquired) were in the possession of persons inclined to trade with early explorers. Spindle whorls of the same period may have remained back in the houses, protected as a type of creative property and not seen as a tradable commodity at the time. Michael Kew (1980), in his monograph on Central Coast Salish art, relates that C. F. Newcombe recorded information early in this century which indicates that "some spindle whorl designs were representative of personal spirit powers." As important tools employed in the creation of valuable ceremonial robes for the high-ranking families and carrying the personal power images of their owners, spindle whorls may not have been appropriate objects to trade with outsiders. Horn bracelets (the designs on which are not representative of power animals) and personal objects like combs and fish clubs may have been looked upon as more readily dispensable and thus appear in the eighteenth-century collections.

When one looks at the historical record of existing S'xwaixwei masks, it would appear that more than a few artists maintained the Central Coast Salish design style in a much more intact manner than Norm's initial assessment would suggest. In the collection of the Seattle Art Museum, donated by John Hauberg in 1985, is a fine old S'xwaixwei mask said to have been made about 1870 in Nanaimo by a carver known as Charley Jim. It shows a mastery of the adaptation of Central Coast Salish flat design to the sculptural forms of the mask (Brown 1995: 290, fig. 105). This mask may have figured in Norm's choice of post-1870 as the beginning of the tradition's decline. A large number of

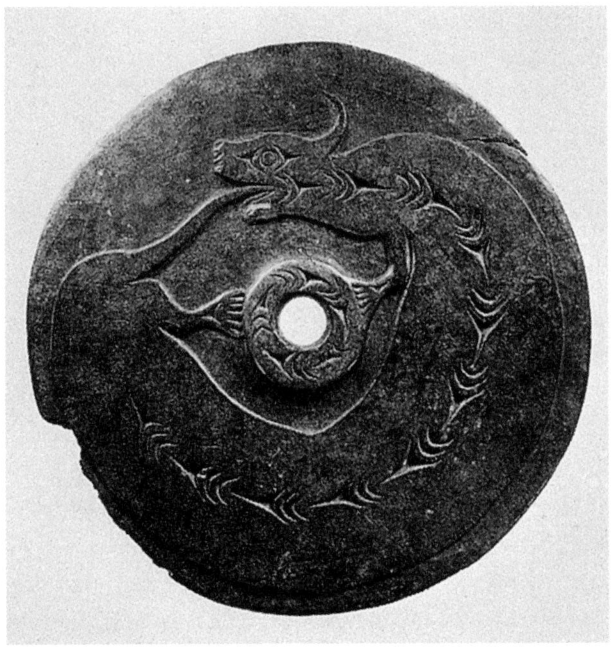

Fig. 3 Spindle whorl, Central Coast Salish. Collected by George T. Emmons among the Cowichan, 1903. National Museum of Natural History, Smithsonian Institution (Washington, DC), cat.no. 221,179-e. After Feder (1971b: 30, fig. 12).
Though collected in the early twentieth century, the design style and execution of this spindle whorl suggest that it may have been made as much as a century or more prior to its acquisition by Emmons.

S'xwaixwei masks in museum collections that were assembled after 1890 or even 1900, however, and which appear to have been carved considerably later than the Charley Jim example, exhibit the same Central Coast Salish design style in quite admirable form (Dickason 1972: 102, fig. 73). In these masks, the wings, feet, and tails of the birds (both ravens and mergansers), whose heads form the "nose" of the main image, are seen to flow about the eye sockets of the masks. Some such masks are documented as having been made deep into the twentieth century, suggesting that Norm was a little unfairly premature in writing his epitaph of the design style. Certainly a differing standard of judgment may also be at work. Along the same lines, Norm criticized the work of two contemporary Salish artists (illustrated in Macnair et al. 1980) as not reflecting the original characteristics of the tradition. In looking at one of these, a *tamanowas* staff by Rod Modeste, it is clear that the upper figure on this staff reflects the same handling of the circle-and-trigon tradition in sculpture as does the steatite pipe from pre-1833 that Norm illustrates in his article (Feder 1983: 51, fig. 8). The lower figures on that staff are more three-dimensional than many in the older tradition, and the designs incised in these exhibit some slight evolutionary development beyond the original Salish design style, and yet a direct relationship to the older work is clearly instructing the artist in his work. There are, to be sure, many examples of modern Coast Salish artists who have not represented the original Coast Salish style with such traditional accuracy, but this example is not really one of them. Today, of course, many practicing Coast Salish artists have fully mastered the traditional style of their ancestors.

In the years prior to 1983, only a handful of Native (and non-Native) artists had looked closely enough at the Central Coast Salish style of two-dimensional design to be able to replicate some of the old images and create new designs with the characteristics of the old tradition. Many artists of Coast Salish heritage elected to work in the styles of the Kwakwa̱ka̱'wakw or Haida of the northern coast, motivated largely by the familiarity of those styles among the buying public (see Danford 1990 for a well-researched discussion of this phenomenon). By 1983 Salish artists Rod Modeste, Stan Greene, and Susan Point (and perhaps others) had done silver work, woodcarving, and/or serigraphs in mature Central Coast Salish style. Nuu-chah-nulth artist Art Thompson (whose maternal grandparents were Cowichan [Central Coast Salish], living at Koksila) had carved a S'xwaixwei mask for ceremonial use that would have fit very well among the oldest of the tradition.[3] Of these, Susan Point is clearly the most prolific and inventive and is one artist who has done more to bring beautifully conceived and executed Central Coast Salish design and sculpture to the contemporary Northwest Coast art world than any other. Assisted in marketing the work by her husband, Jeff Cannell, and in producing major works by John Livingston of Victoria and a variety of apprentices from the Musqueam Band, Susan has brought Central Coast Salish art to a broad and growing public audience.

It is always difficult, of course (even for someone whose goal is to keep up with what is being done in a particular artistic area), to be aware of all that is taking place in one's field at any given moment in time. Norm, nonetheless, had made the blanket statement in his 1983 article that "present-day Salish people do not know anything about the art style or about the meanings of designs shown on older specimens" (Feder 1983: 47). In retrospect, this point can also be seen as too hastily concluded, as well as exhibiting a tone that is not so well countenanced in scholarly circles of the late 1990s. Norm was nothing if not strongly opinionated, and this aspect of his personality readily expressed itself in his written words. When asking questions about the photographs of old objects that he carried to the artists of the area, Norm was wanting to hear all about them —the design work, the identity and cultural meaning of the images, etc. Perhaps a number of obstacles, perceived as a lack of deep knowledge, stood between Norm and his informants. Newcombe's remark about spindle whorls containing images of "personal spirit powers" would place the meanings of their representations among the kinds of information that are the most guarded. What someone knows about such subjects, and what they're willing to talk about with an outsider, are sometimes two different things. Certainly though, the inherent point here that the social and cultural upheaval of the last 150 years in this region has obliterated a great deal of esoteric information from the old cultures, even among now-aged Native people, is one that often bears itself out.

In a more generous tone, Norm concluded the article by stating that "only recently have a few Central Coast Salish artists become interested in rediscovering the principles of older Central Coast Salish styles. If the trend continues, and I believe it will, the next ten years should see a revival of the older traditional Central Coast Salish art in carvings, prints, and even silver engraving using these traditional forms." The next decade did in fact produce a vast array of new practitioners and applications of the Central Coast Salish art traditions. The most prominent of these have led the rest of the coast in innovative manipulations of their First Nation's essential art style as it was practiced in the nineteenth century.

Certainly the most prominent of the new wave of Central Coast Salish artists continues to be Susan Point, a very prolific artist who has experimented widely with production techniques and color usage. (Susan has worked with media from woodblock prints and serigraphs to carved wood and silver to etched glass, cast metals, and cut aluminum; Figs. 4, 5.) She has inspired

3. Non-Native artists Duane Pasco and this writer had also produced Coast Salish-style works in wood, silver, and/or painted design prior to 1983. In 1998 Bill Holm created a Central Coast Salish-style sheephorn rattle that may be the first example made in over a century.

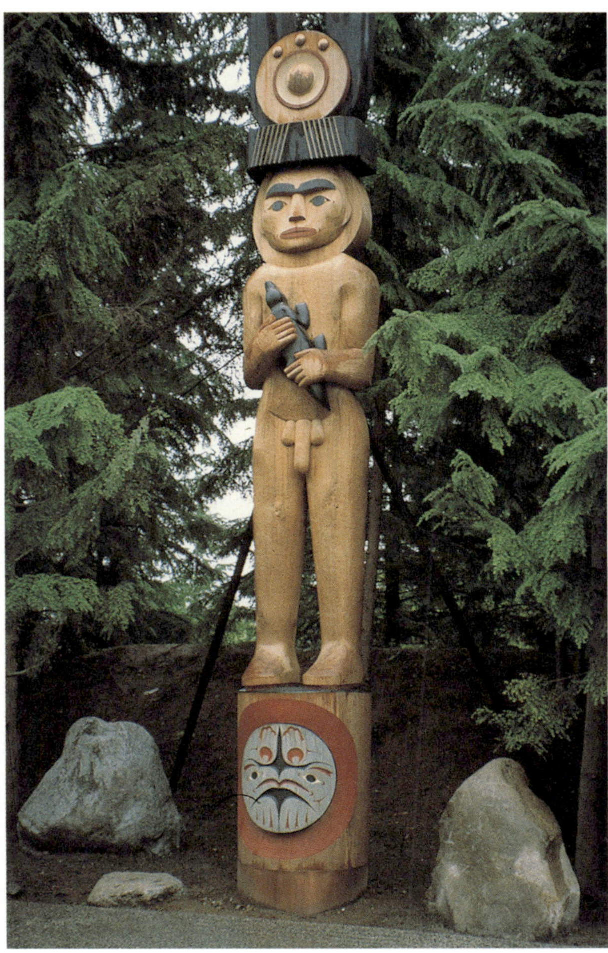

Fig. 4 Monument to Musqueam warrior Capilano by Susan Point and Musqueam apprentices, 1997. University of British Columbia Museum of Anthropology grounds (Vancouver, BC). Approximately 18 feet tall. Photograph: Steven C. Brown.
Based on a nineteenth-century monument to the Musqueam warrior Capilano, this carving was made as an interpretation of the original, rather than a duplicate or copy, by request of the Musqueam band council. This sculpture replicates the traditional Coast Salish carving style, with some additional developments from Susan's own hand.

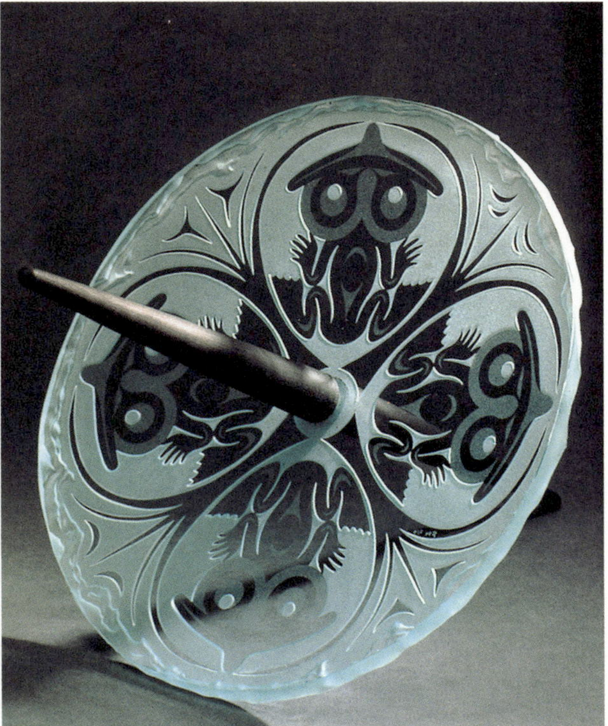

Fig. 5 Spindle whorl by Susan Point, Musqueam, 1995. Glass, wood. Diameter 16 inches. Private collection (Seattle, WA). Photograph: Paul Macapia.
Susan Point has created a large number of etched glass plates and spindle whorls (decorative, not functional), each with unique designs in the Central Coast Salish design style. This one features four frogs with water-like swirls about the outer edge.

an ever-widening group of artists from varying corners of the Salish world who have mastered the tenets and feel of the old Central Coast Salish tradition. Point's large projects include a sixteen-foot diameter spindle whorl at the Vancouver International Airport, two houseposts and a standing monument (Fig. 4) at the University of British Columbia Museum of Anthropology, and architectural features in aluminum and cast concrete for government and municipal buildings in Washington and British Columbia. Her work in etched glass, large-sized spindle whorls and plates (Fig. 5) and etched, curved-glass panels, have brought Central Coast Salish design into the realm of modern home art-furnishings and a whole new audience.

A partial list of currently producing Coast Salish artists includes Point (Musqueam), Ed Archie Noisecat (Shuswap/Stilitlimx), Maynard Johnnie, Joseph Wilson (Salish/Kwakwa̲ka̲'wakw), Manuel Salazar, and Stan Greene in British Columbia, and Marvin Oliver (Quinault-Isleta), Andy Wilbur (Skokomish), Roger Fernandes (Elwha S'Klallam), and Shaun Peterson (Puyallup-Snohomish) from Washington State. In addition, Haida artist Don Yeomans has created at least one serigraph in the Central Coast Salish style (in 1982), incorporating "non-traditional" color usage that may have inspired Salish artists to broaden their design palettes. (In addition, non-Native artist Dale Faulstich has created several Coast Salish-style designs for large wall panels installed on the exterior of the Jamestown S'Klallam Tribe's Seven Cedars Casino at Blyn, Washington.)

Like Point, Marvin Oliver has been drawn to creating monumental works employing the Coast Salish design style. The largest of these is his twenty-six foot tall bronze dorsal fin *Spirit of Our Youth,* installed on the grounds of the King County Department of Youth

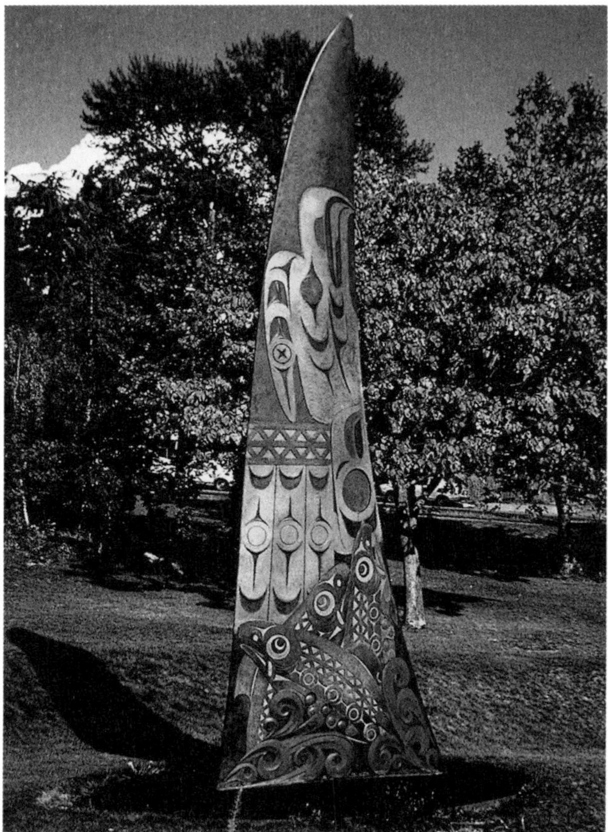

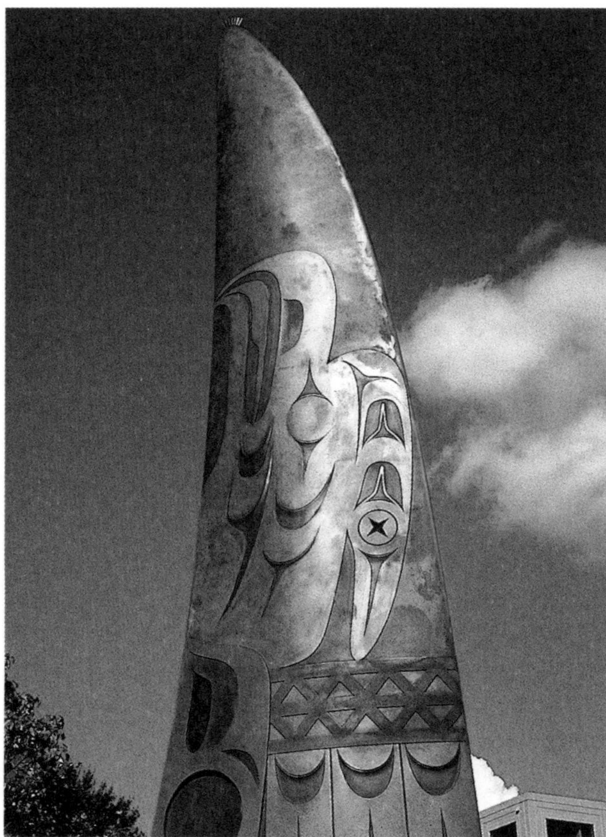

Fig. 6 a, b *Spirit of Our Youth.* Bronze dorsal fin by Marvin Oliver, Quinault/Isleta. King County Arts Commission Percent for Art Project. This twenty-six foot tall dorsal fin was installed at the King County Department of Youth Services at 13th Avenue East and East Remington Streets, Seattle, Washington, in 1994. Photographs: Steven C. Brown.

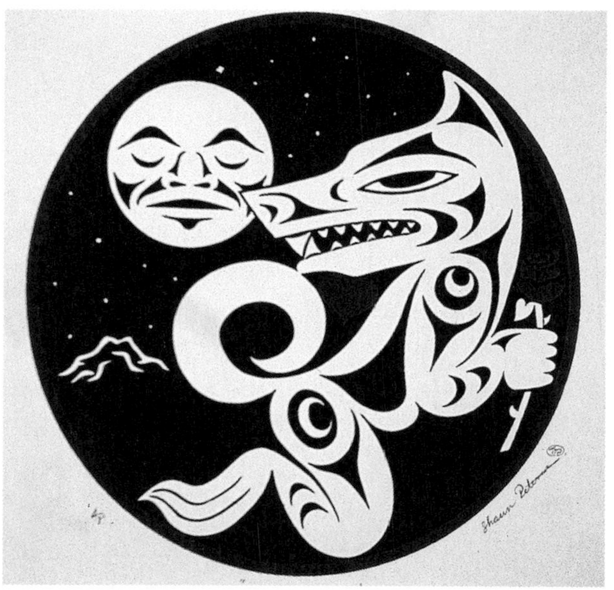

Fig. 7 *On Tenterhooks.* Serigraph by Shaun Peterson, Puyallup-Snohomish. Valentine's Day, 1999. Photograph: Steven C. Brown. A wolf is holding a rose before the full moon. Shaun is a young artist living in Tacoma, Washington, who has developed a remarkable facility with the Central Coast Salish style in recent years.

Services on south Capitol Hill in Seattle (Fig. 6). Originally carved in high-density styrofoam (primarily by his assistant Art Dunlap), then molded, cast in bronze, and mounted on an inner steel armature, the fin is surrounded by flowing ridges in the surrounding landscaping that imitate the wake of a whale in the water. A thunderbird, salmon, fish eggs, and swirling water images make up the designs, which include the inlay of a cast glass face in the wing of the thunderbird (not present at the time of this photograph).

Roger Fernandes is primarily a graphic artist who has employed images of Coast Salish design in his highly inspired and detailed pen-and-ink drawings. These have been released as hand-colored lithographs and art cards as well. Shaun Peterson is an artist in his early twenties who has taken up the Coast Salish design style in the last four years. He brings considerable talent to his work, and has become a masterful designer in a relatively short time, as evidenced by his most recent serigraph designs (Fig. 7).

Norm's predictions from the 1983 article have clearly come true.

References Cited

Barnett, Homer G.

1955 *The Coast Salish of British Columbia*. Eugene, OR: University of Oregon.

Brown, Steven C.

1995 Observations on Northwest Coast Art. In: *The Spirit Within: Northwest Coast Native Art from the John H. Hauberg Collection* (Seattle, WA: Seattle Art Museum—New York, NY: Rizzoli).

1998 *Native Visions: Evolution in Northwest Coast Art from the Eighteenth through Twentieth Century*. Seattle, WA: University of Washington Press—Seattle Art Museum.

Calkins, Harry J.

1977 Art Legacy of the Coast Salish. *Puget Soundings* April 1977: 26–29.

Carlson, Roy

1983 (ed.) *Indian Art Traditions of the Northwest Coast*. Burnaby, BC: Archaeology Press, Simon Fraser University.

Collins, Henry et al.

1973 *The Far North: 2000 Years of American Eskimo and Indian Art*. Washington, DC: The National Gallery of Art.

Danford, Joanne P.

1990 *From Periphery to Center: The Art of Susan and Krista Point*. Thunder Bay, ON: Thunder Bay Art Gallery.

Dickason, Olive Patricia

1972 *Indian Arts in Canada*. Ottawa, ON: Department of Indian Affairs and Northern Development.

Duff, Wilson

1952 *The Upper Stalo Indians of the Fraser Valley, British Columbia*. Anthropology in British Columbia, Memoirs 1(1). Vancouver, BC.

Duffek, Karen

1986 *New Visions: Serigraphs by Susan A. Point, Coast Salish Artist*. University of British Columbia Museum of Anthropology, Museum Note 15. Vancouver, BC.

Feder, Norman

1971a *American Indian Art*. New York, NY: Harry N. Abrams.

1971b *Two Hundred Years of North American Indian Art*. New York, NY—Washington, DC—London: Praeger Publishers.

1983 Incised Relief Carving of the Halkomelem and Straits Salish. *American Indian Art Magazine* 8(2): 46–55.

Feest, Christian F.

1980 *Native Arts of North America*. New York, NY—Toronto, ON: Oxford University Press.

Holm, Bill

1987 *Spirit and Ancestor. A Century of Northwest Coast Indian Art at the Burke Museum*. Thomas Burke Memorial Washington State Museum, Monograph 4. Seattle, WA: Burke Museum—University of Washington Press.

Hovens, Pieter

1998 *Indianen*. Leiden: Rijksmuseum voor Volkenkunde.

Kew, J. E. Michael

1980 *Sculpture and Engraving of the Central Coast Salish Indians*. University of British Columbia Museum of Anthropology, Museum Note 9. Vancouver, BC.

King, J. C. H.

1981 *Artificial Curiosities from the Northwest Coast of America: Native American Artifacts in the British Museum Collected on the Third Voyage of Captain James Cook and Acquired through Sir Joseph Banks*. London: British Museum Publications Ltd.

Macnair, Peter L. et al.

1980 *The Legacy: Continuing Traditions of Canadian Northwest Coast Indian Art*. Victoria, BC: British Columbia Provincial Museum.

Suttles, Wayne

1977 The "Coast Salish" of the Georgia-Puget Basin—Another Look. *Puget Soundings* April 1977: 22–25.

Wingert, Paul

1949 *American Indian Sculpture: A Study of the Northwest Coast*. New York, NY: J. J. Augustin.

Wright, Robin K.

1991 (ed.) *A Time of Gathering: Native Heritage in Washington State*. Thomas Burke Memorial Washington State Museum, Monograph 7. Seattle, WA: Burke Museum—University of Washington Press.

The Crow Ceremonial Shirt

History and Development of Styles, 1800–1900

Colin F. Taylor

Crow men's shirts worn by distinguished warriors on ceremonial occasions[1] were generally splendid and impressive. Several early explorers, such as George Catlin (1841) and Maximilian Prince of Wied (1839–1841), commented on them in some detail, and more recently, garments of this type have been recognized as prime examples of Plains Indian art. Despite this prominence, the documentary record consisting of descriptions, depictions, and actual artifacts is rather poor and fraught with problems. In addition, substantial changes in the construction and decoration of these shirts have occurred throughout the nineteenth century. The present paper attempts to summarize and discuss some of these changes in the light of the available data.

Early Descriptions of Crow Shirts

One of the earliest descriptions of the Crow ceremonial shirt comes from the trader François-Antoine Larocque, who traveled with the Crow in the summer of 1805. He describes the shirts as "composed of 3 [antelope] skins, 2 making the body and one the sleeves. The skins are joint together on the shou[l]der only & the sleeves also which are left open under the pit of the arm; The neck of one of the skins hangs on the breast and the other behind" (Larocque 1985: 215). Like the Crow leggings, which he also describes in some detail, Larocque said the shirts were ornamented with "beads, porcupine quills, horse and human hair."

Specimens and the Visual Record

An early shirt now in the Bernisches Historisches Museum (Fig. 1) is constructed in a fashion very similar to that described by Larocque. Although first noted on a list dated "St. Louis, 28 August 1838" (Thompson 1977: 147, 155–156, no. 118, fig. 83), it is probably much older than that date. Identified as "Corbeaux" (Crow), it may well have originally been in William Clark's Museum in St. Louis, which was established in 1816 and dispersed prior to Clark's death in 1838 (Ewers 1967: especially 69).

By circa 1830, however, the Crow ceremonial shirt style had considerably changed—both structurally and decoratively. Now just two skins were used in its fabrication and bighorn rather than antelope was the favored material. In 1833 the German traveler Prince Maximilian of Wied noted that the "Crow women are very skilful in various kinds of work, and their shirts and dresses of bighorn leather, embroidered and ornamented with dyed porcupine quills, are particularly handsome" (Wied 1839–1841, 1: 399–400; 1906, 22: 359–360). Maximilian further observed that these garments were often exquisitely ornamented and were popular trade (or gift) items to closely related tribes such as the Hidatsa (Fig. 2). As a result of these changes, there emerged a particularly distinctive form of ceremonial garment.[2]

In the fabrication of such garments, two bighorn

Colin Taylor has lectured and published extensively on many aspects of Plains Indian culture for over forty years. His latest publication, *With Eagle Tail*, coauthored with Hugh Dempsey (the former Associate Director of the Glenbow Museum, Calgary), concerns the life of the photographer Arnold Lupson, who spent thirty years with the Darcee, Blackfoot, and Stoney.
Author's address: 11 High Wickham, Hastings TN35 5 PB, United Kingdom.

1. My first publication on Plains ceremonial shirts was a competition entry for the *American Indian Hobbyist* (founded by Norman Feder) in 1957, primarily based on specimens in the Department of Ethnography of the British Museum, London.
2. In a recent paper, Logan and Schmittou (1998) assessed the historical circumstances surrounding the emergence of the distinctive Crow style by reference to the use of an evolutionary hypothesis by Boyd and Richerson to explain the origin and diversification of ethnic markers. In a recent article, Bill Holm (1998) concisely summarizes the possible uniqueness of Crow material culture and art.

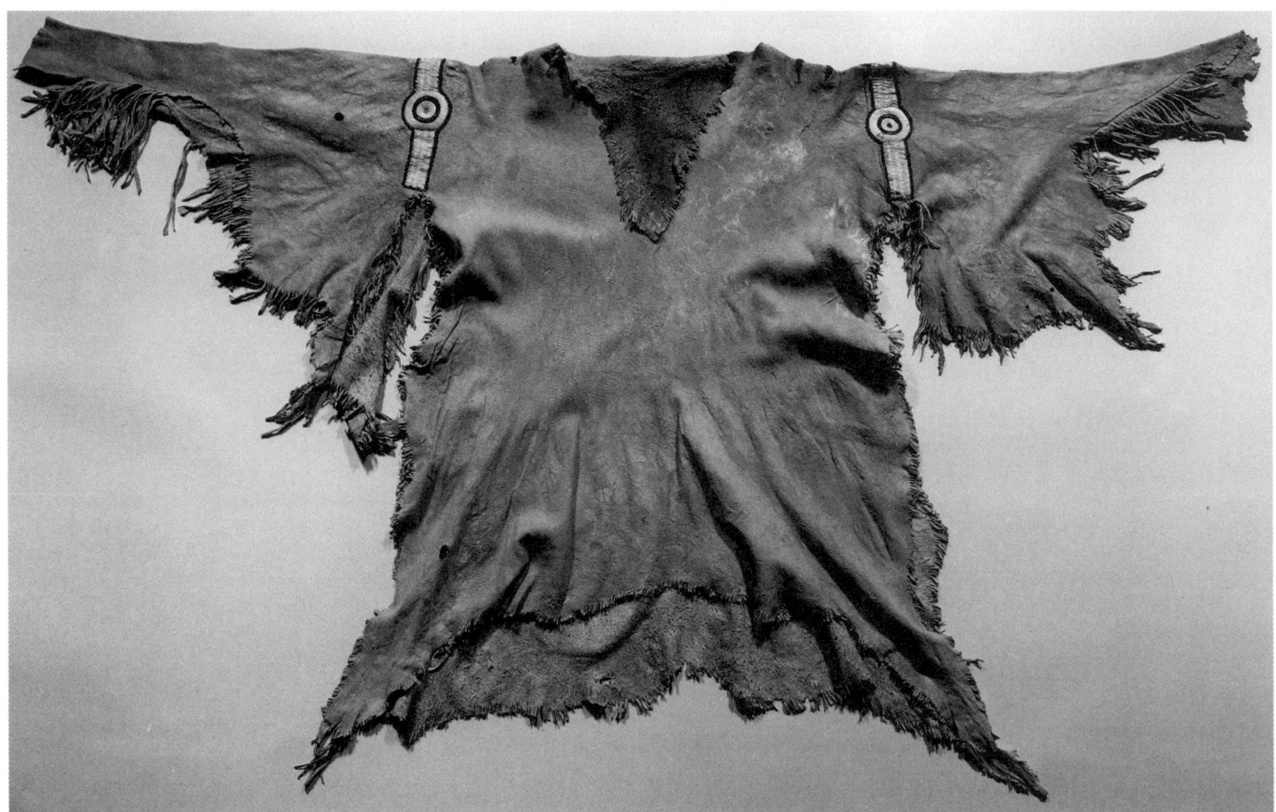

Fig. 1 Crow ("Corbeaux") shirt of three hides, two for the body and the third for the arms. Red ochre stains on the triangular flaps on both sides of the neck opening, bands of plaited quillwork and rosettes (white quills and vegetal material) edged with blue beads. Length 85 cm. Collected before 1837. Bernisches Historisches Museum (Berne), cat.no. N.A. 118 (Lorenz A. Schoch coll., possibly ex Clark Museum, St. Louis, MO). Photograph: Stefan Rebsamen.

skins were cut approximately two thirds the way up. The upper portion was folded and used to make the arms, the lower the front and back of the shirt (Fig. 3). Because a bighorn hide is very broad, there was an overlap of the sleeve with the body hide (Fig. 4). Most early Crow shirts exhibit this overlap, although shortly after 1870 many were made without it. The specific reason for this change is unknown, but it may have been caused by the increasing difficulty to obtain bighorn skins, and alternative skin types—such as antelope or deer—had a width considerably less than that of the bighorn. The terminology used in the descriptions of these ceremonial shirts is given in Fig. 5.

A shirt closely resembling that worn by Péhriska-Rúhpa (Fig. 2) is now in the collections of the British Museum, London (Fig. 6). Although not tribally iden-

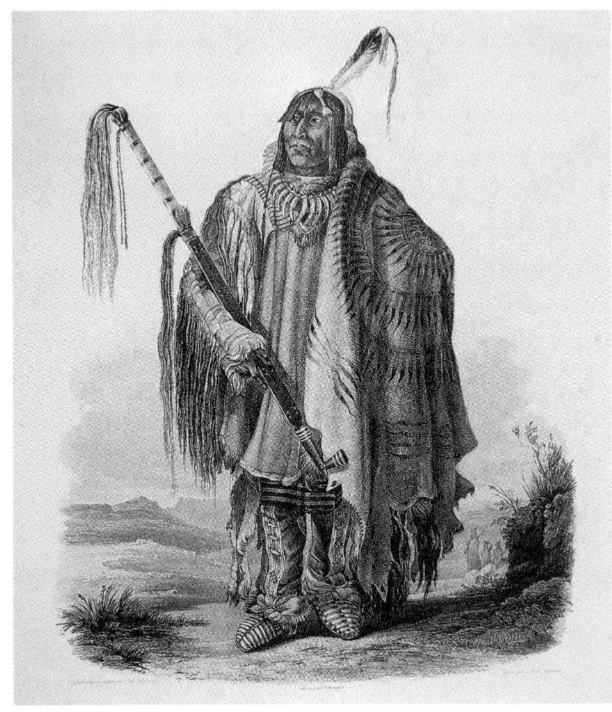

Fig. 2 Péhriska-Rúhpa (Two Ravens), a Hidatsa living among the Mandan, wearing clothing mostly obtained from the Crow. The shirt has a triangular neck flap and is decorated with plaited quillwork (yellow, blue [which would be unusual for ca. 1830], red, white). Fringing on the arms and shoulders consists of human and horse hair interspersed with strips of white weasel. Aquatint after a watercolor drawing by Karl Bodmer, 1834 (Wied 1839–1841, Atlas: pl. 17; description of colors after Goetzman et al. 1984: 318, fig. 329).

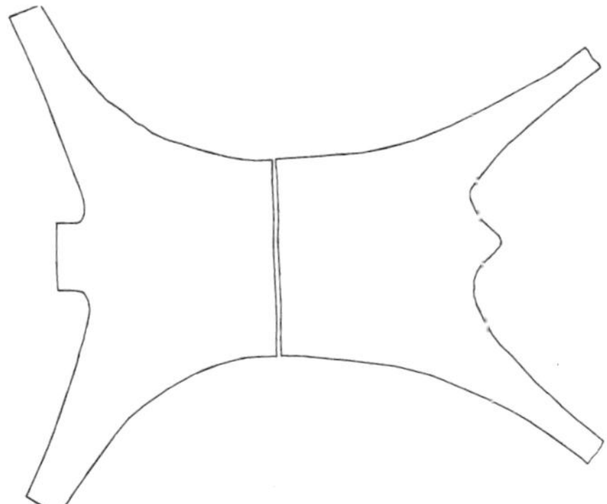

Fig. 3 Construction of the poncho-type shirt, which with some variations was widely distributed across the central and northern Plains prior to circa 1880. Drawing by Paul Ritner.

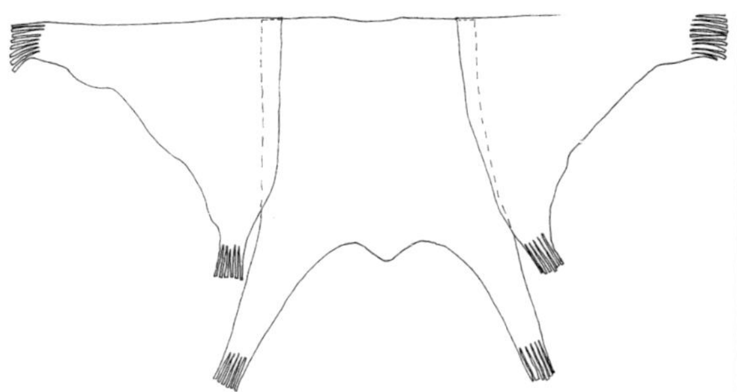

Fig. 4 Although of the poncho-type, early Crow shirts—particularly those made of bighorn skins—had an overlap of the body with the sleeve. Drawing by Paul Ritner.

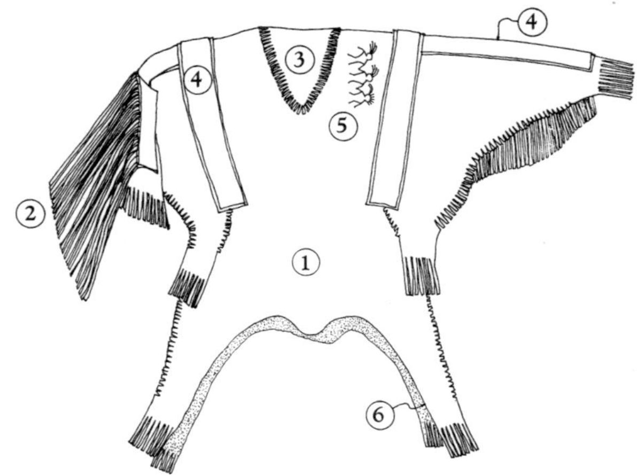

Fig. 5 Contemporary Crow terminology used to describe the ceremonial shirt, based on information obtained from Louella and Gary Johnson and Joe Medicine Crow, Lodge Grass, MT, September 1997. Drawing by Paul Ritner.

1	ceremonial shirt	*bachech'iittashte*
2	fringes	*baaannapíia*
	(a) hair	*baleiishiia*
	(b) ermine	*úute*
	(c) buckskin	*baamáxxe*
3	neck flap	*duushuíixxua*
	(a) triangular	*alapáshua dáwiia*
	(b) rectangular	*owappatchke*
4	decorative bands	*iiláshpe aanastúua*
	(a) quilled	*baaíashe*
	(b) beaded	*baanashtúua*
5	paintings/pictographs	*baachiwalátuua*
6	bighorn skin	*iisaxpúatahchee duuchisuua*
7	pony beads	*balooiisáate*
8	pipeholder's shirt	*iipchi bachech'iittashte*

tified when it was donated to the museum in 1924,[3] the construction and techniques used point to a Crow origin. It is made of two skins (probably bighorn) with broad bands of quillwork over the shoulders and narrower bands down the arms. The skin is white, hair side out, and there are long buckskin fringes along the outside edges of the shoulder and arm bands together with some interspersed yellow horsehair. Both hair and buckskin fringe have been wrapped with porcupine quills which extend some 25 mm from the point of attachment.

Crow Shirts Decorated with Plaited Quillwork

In "plaited quillwork," quills are intertwined in a criss-cross manner. While this technique limits the patterns which can be developed to diamond or triangular shapes (Fig. 7), the finished product—with yellow background and patterns in orange and white quills interspersed with a brown vegetal material[4]—is particularly attractive. The neck flaps are very similar to those on the Péhriska-Rúhpa shirt. Some 18 cm in length and of hide covered with red and green trade cloth, the edges are decorated with white pony beads in triangular patterns.

Such garments were obviously popular items in the period of ca. 1830–1860. The evidence suggests that the majority were probably made by the River Crow, who were trading extensively with the Missouri River tribes such as the Hidatsa and Mandan.[5]

3. A Mrs. Romane donated this shirt and eight other items to the British Museum in 1924 (cat.nos. 1924.10-9.1–9).
The sleeves overlap with the body hide (cp. Fig. 4). The triangular neck flap, fringing, painting, as well as the quillwork technique, patterns, and color are typical of work produced by the Crow at that time—possibly the River Crow group.

4. Previously misidentified as "maidenhair fern" by Norman Feder; for a new identification, see Bill Holm, this volume, p. 60.

5. These trade patterns are discussed at length in some previous papers (cp. particularly Taylor 1981a, 1981b, 1984b).

6. References to these neck flap shapes and their change with time are in Taylor (1981a: 51; 1987: 308–309). It is now generally agreed that triangular neck flaps were popular among the Crow prior to circa 1870, when they were displaced by the rectangular-shaped flap. Unfortunately, a recent essay by Barbara Loeb (1998) makes reference to the fact that shirts displaying triangular neck flaps "probably come from the Plateau." This is clearly an erroneous statement.

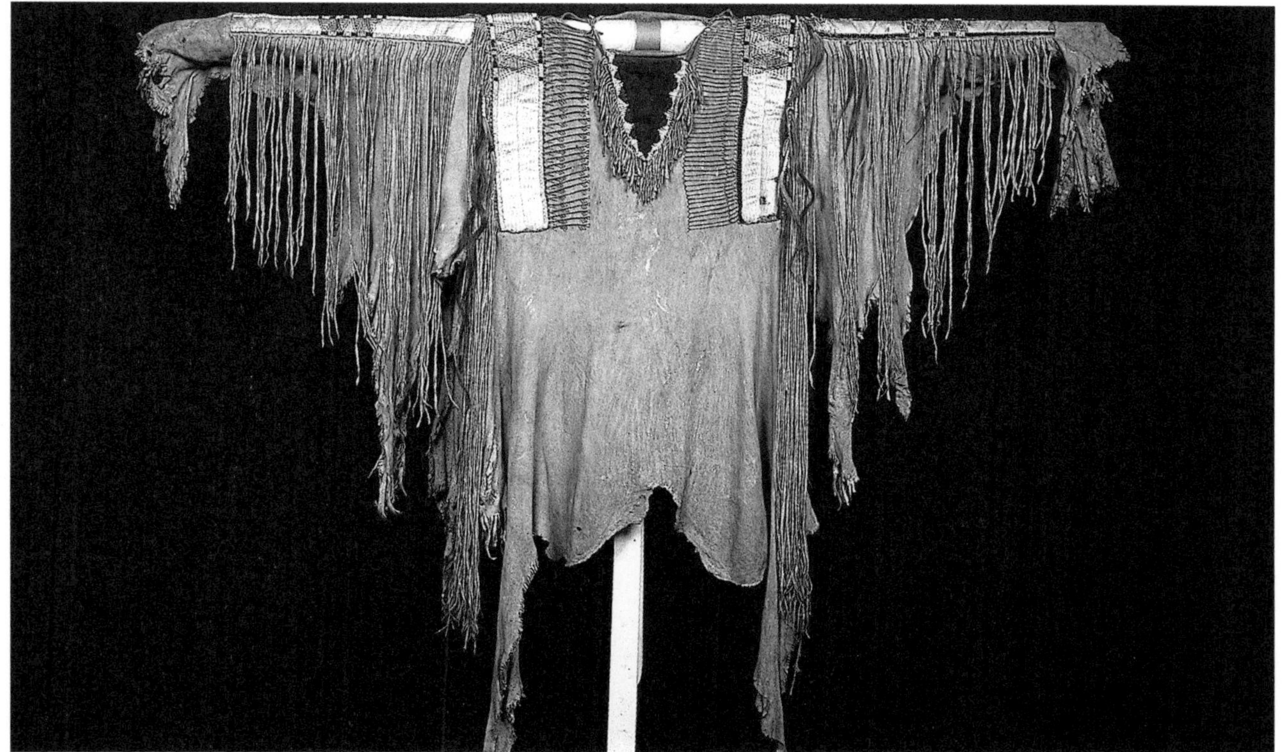

Fig. 6 Quilled shirt, almost certainly Crow and dating prior to 1850. Length 73 cm (back), 63 cm (front). Department of Ethnography, British Museum (London), cat.no. 1924.10-9.1. Photograph: C. F. Taylor. Courtesy of The Trustees of the British Museum.

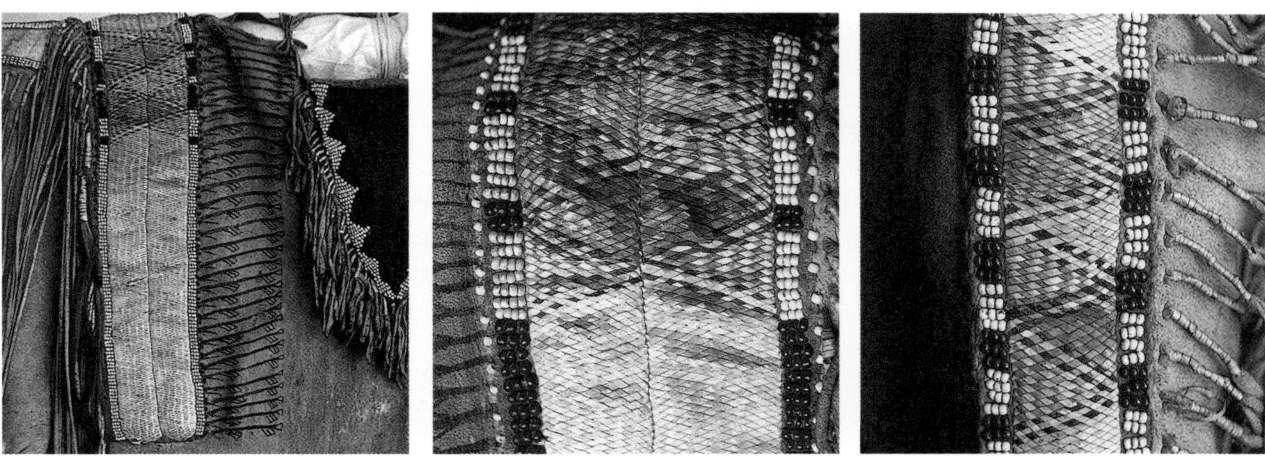

Fig. 7 Shoulder and arms bands with plaited quillwork on the shirt shown in Fig. 6. The edging in blue and white pony beads is typical of these early Crow shirts. The triangular neck flap is lined with red trade cloth edged with white and black pony beads. Photographs: C. F. Taylor. Courtesy of The Trustees of the British Museum.

Crow Shirts Decorated with Quill-Wrapped Horsehair

Although structurally similar, another early ceremonial shirt of the Crow was embellished with quillwork strips in the so-called "double-lane quill-wrapped horsehair" technique. A fine specimen of this type now in the Pitt Rivers Museum, Oxford, has already been described and other known specimens tabulated (Taylor 1981a). One which has received scant attention was recently examined in the Fort Laramie Museum (Fig. 8). This may be somewhat earlier than the *rectangular* beaded flaps suggest: Probably the original *triangular* flaps so popular on this style of shirt have been replaced with a more up-to-date style neck flap, popular from circa 1880 onwards.[6] Thus a shirt worn by the Miniconjou Sioux Scorched Lightning (Fig. 10), who was photographed by L. A. Huffman around 1880 (Brown and Felton 1955: 23), displays a rectangular

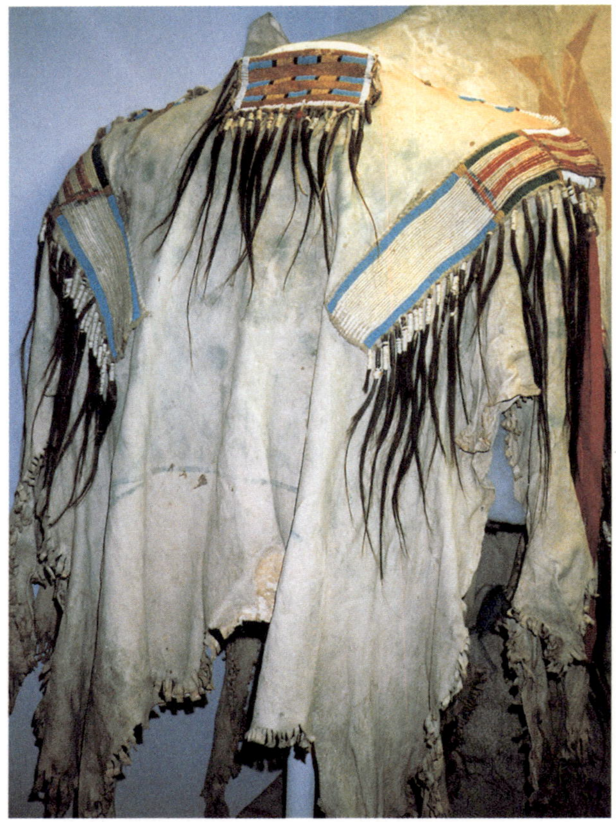

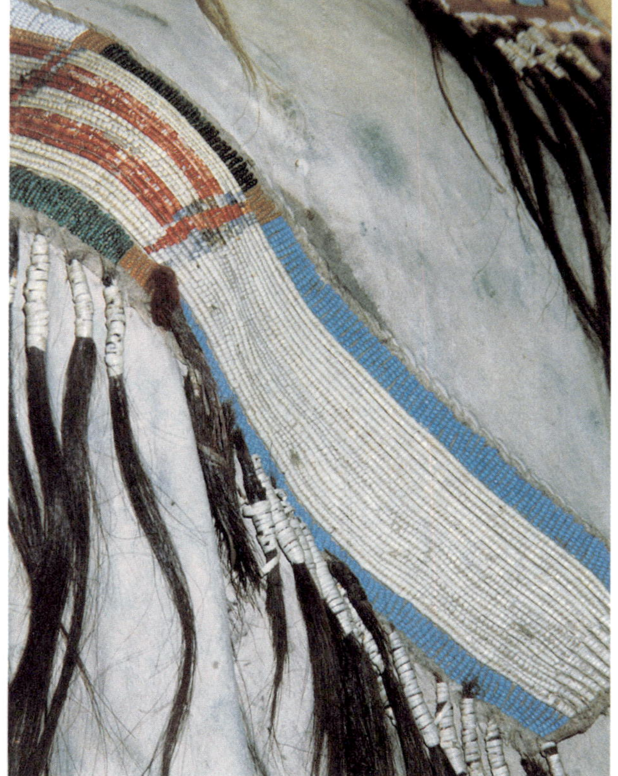

Fig. 8 Full view and detail of shirt decorated with quill-wrapped horsehair bands and fringing predominately of black human hair-locks partly wrapped with white porcupine quills. Length approximately 76 cm. No collection data, but attributed to the Mountain Crow. Fort Laramie National Historical Site (Fort Laramie, WY), cat.no. 9573. Photograph: C. F. Taylor.

neck flap. This garment (Fig. 9), almost certainly of Crow origin, provides much valuable information with regard to color, bead types, and fringing techniques.[7]

At least two members of the Crow delegation to Washington in 1873 wore quill-wrapped horsehair decorated shirts (Taylor 1981a: figs. 13 and 14). One individual was Blackfoot or He-Who-Sits-in-the-Middle-of-the-Land, who was principal chief of the Mountain Crow; the other was Old Crow, probably also a Mountain Crow. While final conclusive evidence is lacking, it seems probable that this technique was favored by the Mountain Crow, possibly being originally influenced by the Nez Perce, with whom they had extensive trade contacts (cp. Taylor 1981b, 1987).

That this style of garment was used on occasions by other tribes is shown in the famous photograph of Lakota chiefs taken at Fort Laramie in 1868; here the Miniconjou Whistling Elk is wearing a quill-wrapped horsehair shirt, his buffalo robe partially obscuring the shoulder band. We shall probably never know whether this was a gift to Whistling Elk, who made peace with the Crow in 1851 (Bray 1985: 29), or whether it had simply been loaned to him for the photographic occasion. Of related interest is the fact that at least two other members of this group—Lone Horn and Slow Bull (Fig. 11)—also appear to be wearing shirts of Crow make. A beaded shirt, almost certainly the one worn by Slow Bull, is now in a private collection (Fig. 12).[8]

By the 1870s, quilled garments were rapidly going out of fashion, particularly in the case of the less conservative River Crow. Thus, in the same 1873 Crow delegation of which He-Who-Sits-in-the-Middle-of-the-

7. This shirt is also worn by Spotted Eagle, a fellow warrior of Scorched Lightning, who was photographed by L. A. Huffman in 1880. It is thus possible that it was a studio prop. Another possibility, however, is that Scorched Lightning, a Miniconjou Sioux, or his relatives, obtained it from the Crows with whom the Miniconjou made a Peace Treaty in 1851 (cp. Bray 1985: 28–47). I am indebted to Bill Holm, whose detailed analysis leaves little doubt that the shirt shown in Fig. 9 is the same as that shown in Fig. 10.

8. This splendid garment was described in the Sotheby catalog as "An important Plateau Man's beaded and fringed hide war shirt" (Sotheby's 1996: no. 168). It was presented by General R. S. Mackenzie to General H. W. Lawton and clearly dates from circa 1865. The broad cross-like motifs in both shoulder and arm strips appear on several shirts of this type, the beadwork being in seed beads using the overlaid stitch technique; pink and blue beads predominate. It is probable that this shirt, although worn by an Oglala, is of Crow origin, as is the shirt formerly worn by the Brulé Sioux war chief Two Strike and now in the Hearst Museum of Anthropology, Berkeley, CA (cat. no. 2-18810). Bill Holm (personal communication, June 1998) and myself concur in this conclusion (cp. also the reference in Taylor 1998).

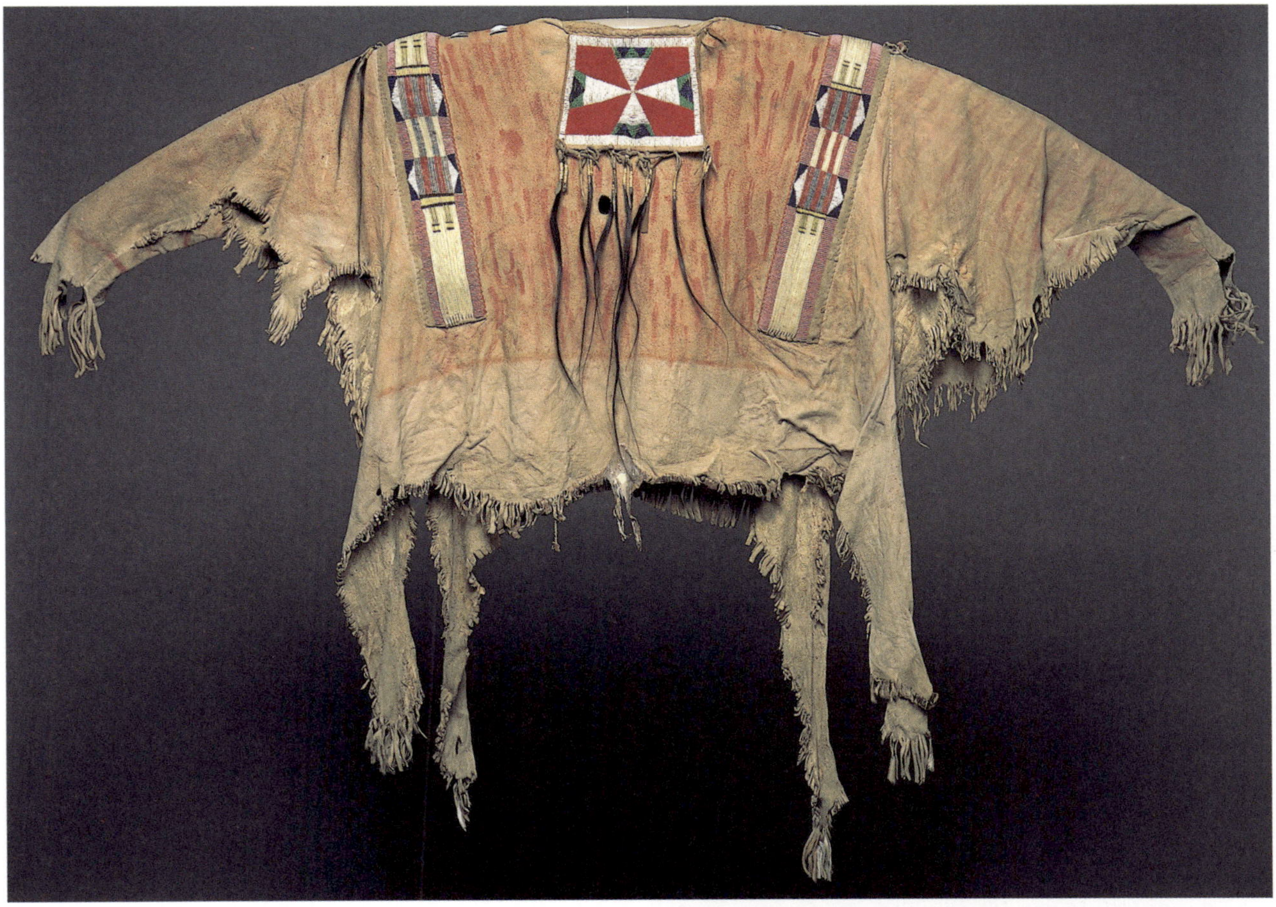

Fig. 9 Back view of shirt worn by Scorched Lightning in Fig. 10, decorated with six lanes of double-lane quill-wrapped horsehair on the sleeves and nine over the shoulders. The bands are edged with pink seed beads. Length approximately 63 cm. Photograph: Courtesy of Robert W. Musser, Boulder, CO.

Land was a member, Iron Bull, chief of the River Crow, wore a garment entirely decorated with beadwork.[9]

Such shirts were used by Crow men until the 1920s or so, when beaded waistcoats and floral designs became increasingly popular. These shirts invariably exhibited rectangular beaded neck flaps and beaded arm and shoulder bands. The beadwork in the bands became increasingly more complex and commonly consisted of "a horizontal central band flanked by triangles, or of a large hourglass form." It was further observed that those shirts made in the late years of the nineteenth century and the early years of the twentieth century show "a marked preference for the use of light blue beads as backgrounds for the arm and shoulder panel design areas. Occasionally they substituted lavender beads for those of light blue" (Wildschut and Ewers 1959: 7–8).

9. See Taylor (1984b: 43–44) for a further discussion of the differences between these Crow groups.

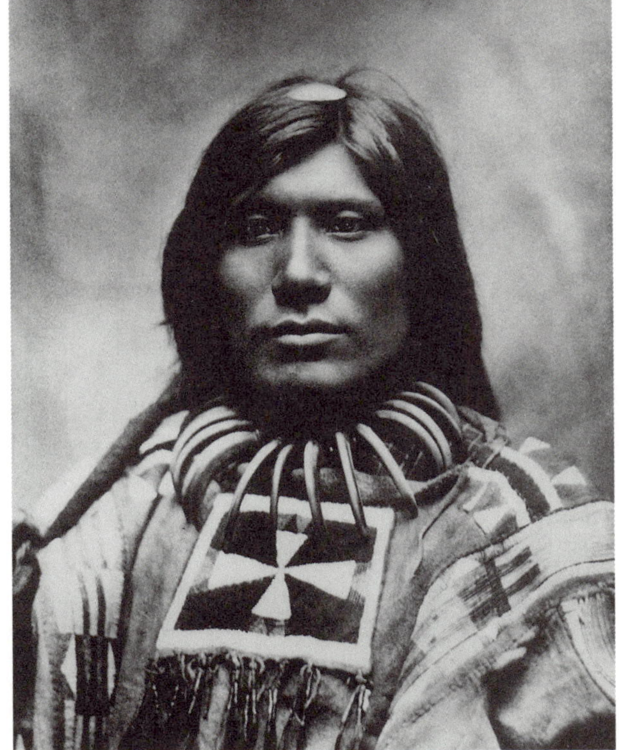

Fig. 10 Scorched Lightning, a Miniconjou Sioux, wearing a magnificent shirt attributed to the Crow and decorated with quill-wrapped horsehair with unusual rectangular neck flap. Photograph by L. A. Huffman, ca. 1880.

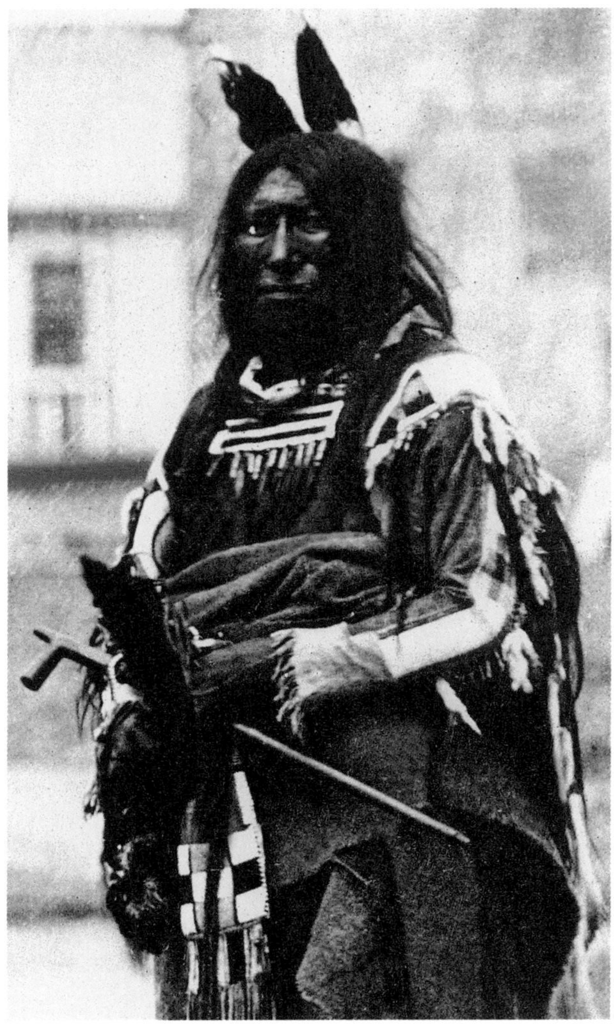

Fig. 11 Slow Bull wearing a heavily beaded Crow shirt (cp. Fig. 12). Detail from a photograph of Lakota chiefs and headmen at Fort Laramie taken in 1868 by Alexander Gardner. National Anthropological Archives, Smithsonian Institution (Washington, DC).

The patterns worked on these arm and shoulder bands were often outlined in white beads. Dennis Lessard (1984: 64, 68, fig. 8E) suggested that this feature derived from the plaited quillwork technique as did the "triangular, hour-glass, and diamond patterns ... found throughout classical Crow beadwork." A similar observation was made by John C. Ewers, who related the patterns used in the quill-wrapped horsehair bands on the shirt worn by Old Crow to those in the beadwork on the shirt worn by Long Horse (Wildschut and Ewers 1959: 7). The shoulder bands, rather than covering the seams of the shirt—as was often the case with Plains shirts—not infrequently sloped inward both on the front and back. The evidence suggests that the Crow were probably among the first of the Plains tribes to use this method of attachment.[10]

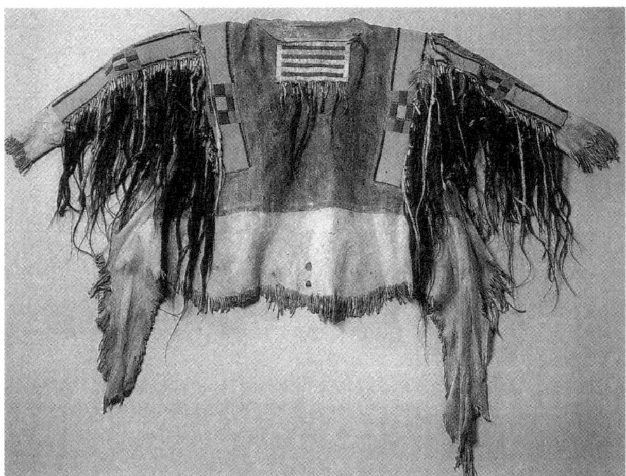

Fig. 12 Beaded and painted ceremonial shirt almost certainly of Crow make, fringed with human scalp locks. It is probably the same as the one worn by Slow Bull, a Miniconjou(?) Lakota, in Fig. 11. Length 75 cm. After Sotheby's (1996: no. 168).

Symbolism of the Shoulder and Arm Bands

While any possible symbolic meaning of the designs within the shirt bands has gone unrecorded, that relating to the symbolism of the bands themselves has been reported on in some detail. Thus the striking of an enemy, considered to be the most important of the four major coups, "entitled the shirt-wearer to attach to it the four decorated strips which were quilled in the early days and later were beaded, and which were sewn across the shoulders and to the sleeves." Wildschut (1960: 38) reported that it was a great distinction among the Crow to be able to wear a war shirt and even as late as 1927, "no Crow will publicly wear a war shirt unless he is entitled to it." There was "no hereditary right to the wearing of such a garment."[11]

10. The distribution of the various kinds of placement of shoulder and arm bands on Plains shirts has been plotted in Taylor (1984a: 40).

11. Wildschut (1960: 38) reported that since the end of intertribal wars, a new way was found by the Crow to give their ambitious youth the right to wear the decorated shirt. Thus a number of young Crows, led by an older man, offer a visiting Indian of a different tribe many presents to induce him to act as an "enemy." "This 'enemy' is given a good horse and starts out from camp in the evening. Next morning before dawn the Crows start out on the trail of this 'enemy.' The Crow who manages to overtake him and strike the first coup is entitled to wear the honors formerly earned by this act in actual combat. Four times, and on different occasions, this young man must strike the first coup, which is usually done by hitting the 'enemy' lightly with a stick or with the hand, before he is entitled to wear the decorated war shirt. This is one reason why they are valued very highly by the Crows and are scarcer among them than among other Plains Indians."

Embellishments

The fringing used on Crow shirts also changed considerably during the period of ca. 1850–1910. In the early period it invariably consisted of long buckskin thongs, generally bound with yellow quills at the point of attachment. Ingenious methods were employed to give a double-thong fringe, particularly on the finest of these garments (cp. Fig. 13). Less common was the use of a human hair fringe, probably because, unlike other tribes of the central and northern Plains, the Crow put less emphasis on hair as a war trophy. As one of Robert Lowie's informants observed: "You will never hear a Crow boast of his scalps when he recites his deeds." Lowie further reported that although the taking of a scalp was evidence of a killing, it did not rank as a deed deserving special notice (Lowie 1935: 218). Nevertheless, it is clear that the human hair fringe on Crow costume did make a symbolic statement. Thus Gray-bull, one of Lowie's informants, said that a gun-taker or coup-striker won the right to decorate his shirt with hair, while a leader of a war party could additionally put hair on his moccasins (Lowie 1935: 218). In describing the costume of the Crow war leader Deaf Bull, the artist DeCost Smith (1949: 140) observed that his tunic was of "antelope or mountain sheepskin ... The fringe was of scalp locks, or black horsehair which had the same significance ... a few locks of horsehair dyed pink, interspersed among the scalp-lock fringes, probably stood for horses captured in war."

The use of ermine—the winter coat of the weasel—

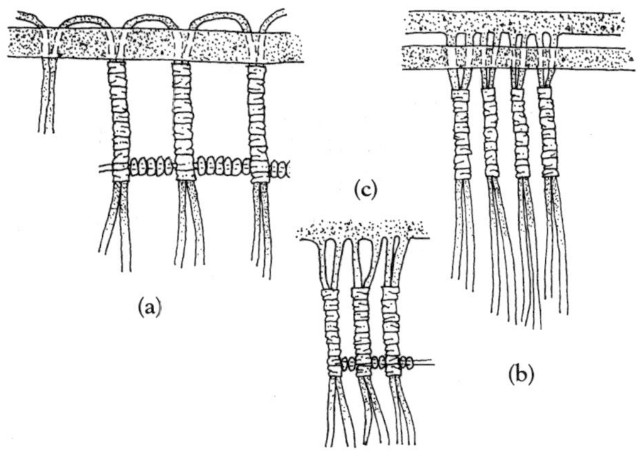

Fig. 13 Details of fringes on a Crow shirt in the Pitt Rivers Museum, Oxford (cp. Taylor 1981a: 48). (a): complex laddering technique adjacent to the outer edges of the shoulder strips with a wrapping in quills and three-bead spacing; (b): double-cut fringe thread through the hide of the arms and then quill-wrapped; (c): attenuation technique with two-bead spacing. In addition, some red commercial thread has been interspersed between the quill wrapping of the neck flap, and there is distinctive fringing (almost 100 mm long) at the cuffs. Drawing by Paul Ritner.

was limited in the first half of the nineteenth century. Maximilian noted in 1833 that "this is a very costly ornament, these little animals having become scarce" (Wied 1839–1841, 1: 564; 1906, 23: 101). Twenty years later, Edwin Denig, the American Fur Company's chief factor at Fort Union, equated the value of ten ermine skins with that of a horse among the Crow (Denig 1930: 589). Denig further observed of a "Mounted Warrior's dress" that a skin shirt and leggings "garnished with porcupine quills and trimmed with ermine" was valued at twice that of a similar outfit embellished with human hair—twenty robes or $60 and ten robes or $30, respectively (Denig 1930: 589).

While aesthetically pleasing, ermine skins may well have been important symbols of such attributes as speed, strength, cunning, and bravery, since for its size the weasel was "the most aggressive and most destructive animal on the plains" (Ewers 1977: 261).[12]

Toward the end of the nineteenth and well into the twentieth century, Crow shirts profusely embellished with ermine skins became very fashionable (Fig. 14). It seems probable that at this time such skins were actually traded to the Crow and other Plains tribes by White traders, who obtained second grade pelts via the Hudson's Bay Company.[13]

On at least one shirt known to the writer the ermine fringes have been tipped with jackrabbit ears (Fig. 15), possibly a reference to the hard-to-catch-and-

12. Reference was made by both Robert Stops and George Bull Tail (both Crow) to an individual's guardian spirit and spiritual power being derived from the weasel: "A weasel is one of the main characters that had given power" (interview with R. Stops, Crow Agency, MT, March 1969; cp. Conner 1993: 27).
Father Peter Powell reports that "a gun-snatcher trimmed his shirt with ermine skins" (Powell 1988: 20).
13. The vast quantity of second or third grade ermine skins which were obviously available for resale was made apparent to the writer on the occasion of a visit in the early 1960s to the Hudson's Bay Company in London. The (untanned) skins were in bundles of several hundred, roughly graded according to size, and could at that time be purchased for between 3d and 9d each. The Sales Manager said that sales invoices for ermine were normally for "thousands of skins" (E. G. Berry to C. F. T., July 1963). Charles Hanson of the Museum of the Fur Trade in Chadron, NE, remembered that as a youngster (about 1920), he saw bundles of ermine skins outside trading posts, such as the famous Lammer Store at Crow Agency in Montana (C. H. to C. F. T., July 1988). On the utilization of whole weasel skins in a symbolic context by the Crow, see Lowie (1919: 123) and Thomas and Ronnefeldt (1976: 111).

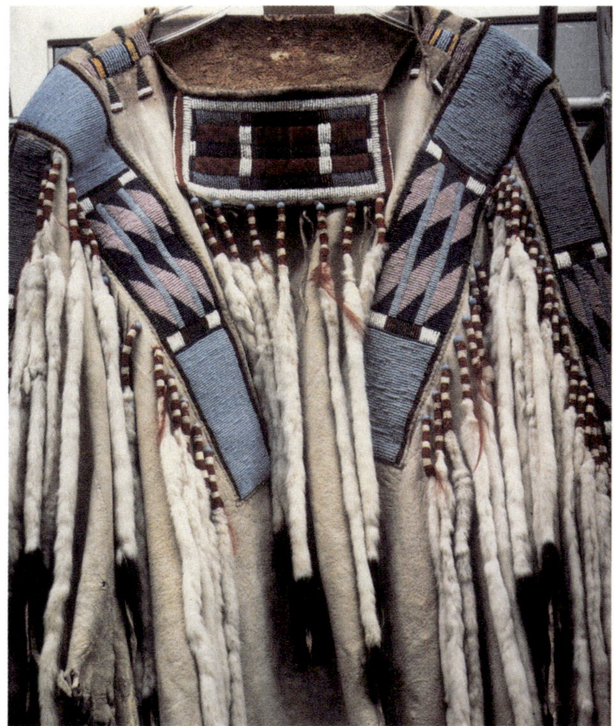

Fig. 14 Crow shirt (back view) profusely embellished with ermine tubes wrapped around a heavy cord and terminating with the black-tipped tail of the ermine or dark hair inserts. Although impressive, the fringing is far less elaborate than that exhibited on earlier Crow shirts. The beadwork pattern is somewhat unusual for shirts of this period, but the triangular elements at the shoulders are a typical Crow feature. Length 110 cm. Obtained from the Crow chief The Wet of the Pryor district by S. C. Simms in 1901 for $45. It had formerly belonged to The Wet's uncle Spotted Coyote. Field Museum of Natural History (Chicago, IL), cat.no. 69,416. Photograph: John Painter.

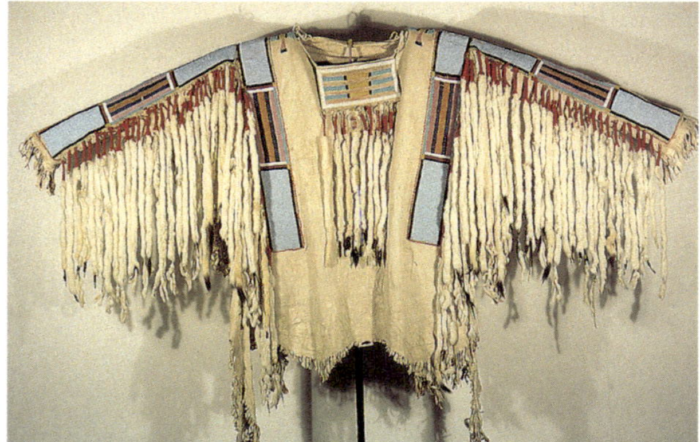

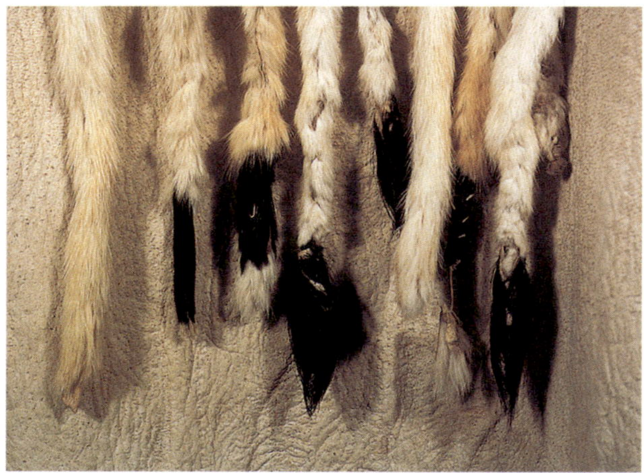

Fig. 15 Back view and detail of fine Crow shirt with ermine fringes, some of them with jackrabbit ears at the bottom. Length 80 cm. Ca. 1900. Formerly owned by Del Enterprise, Inc. (Mission, SD). Photograph: Dennis Lessard. Courtesy of Rosemary Lessard, Santa Fe, NM.

kill creature, such desirable powers being symbolically transferred to the wearer of the shirt.[14]

Painting on Shirts

Several of the earlier shirts found in collections have either the upper half or the whole body painted a very dark blue or black. Lowie relates this to the fact that returning warriors who had been victorious on the warpath always blackened their faces to symbolize the killing of an enemy, so that "with black face" is a stereotyped phrase for a victorious return. The deeds were made more permanent by painting on the ceremonial robe or shirt. Thus "the first man to capture a gun and the first coup-striker had their robe or shirt blackened all over, the second and third men had only half of their garment so decorated, and the fourth men had only the arms of their shirts painted" (Lowie 1935: 225).[15] Powell (1988: 21) surmises that a type of small

14. It was Lessard who, through his friend Gary Galante, first made reference to the possible significance of the jackrabbit in Crow symbolism (D. L. to C. F. T., April 1990). Subsequently Richard Edwards drew my attention to references by Edward S. Curtis on the use of jackrabbit parts—ears, stuffed head, tail—as symbolic attachments to Crow regalia (Curtis 1907–1930, 4: 18–20, 45, 47). Lessard was of the opinion that the eagle feather fan carried by Medicine Crow in the well-known photograph taken in 1880 (cp., e.g., Wildschut and Ewers 1959: fig. 2) has two jackrabbit ears at the base of the main feather. Jackrabbits were admired for their muscle and endurance; the naturalist Mabel Wright (1898: 148–149) reported that no other animal could run like a jackrabbit and that the swiftest horse could not overtake him. Obviously such qualities would be desired by a Crow warrior on the battlefield.

15. A special white clay, which is described in the early literature as used to *clean* buckskin (Larocque 1985: 216), also had considerable symbolic associations and was smeared on such objects as shields, robes, and headdresses. I have not, however, found a specific reference to its use on Crow ceremonial shirts. Richard Edwards suggested that "white clay was the preferred color in connection with vision quests, the sun dance, and war" and gave me numerous references in the literature to its use by the Crow (R. E. to C. F. T., September 1997). The Crow informant, Martin He-Does-It, referred to the use of white clay on a buffalo robe used during a fasting (Conner 1993: 183). Bill Holm reports that the Yakima were using white clay in the 1940s and that it exactly matches Larocque's description of "a kind of white earth resembling chalk" (B. H. to C. F. T., May 1998).

black- (or dark-)painted shirt was "an old traditional style among Crow fighting men." Ewers describes such a garment which belonged to the Crow warrior Buffalo Bull and which was collected by William Wildschut in 1922.[16] The shirt is some 32.5 cm in length and made of heavy skin, probably buffalo hide. It has no neck flap and no true sleeves. The beaded decoration is limited to narrow bands over the shoulders and two broader bands in the same color extending to the neck opening; these, in turn, are flanked by pairs of isosceles triangles with their apices touching the bands (Wildschut and Ewers 1959: 6).[17]

Other related styles have been located in various collections. Thus Powell (1988: 21) describes one in the Gallatin collection, which was attributed to Two Leggings, a River Crow chief. Although not beaded, it has a depiction of a flintlock rifle painted on the rear of the right sleeve, symbolizing a weapon captured in battle. There is also the figure of a bird (Thunderbird?) painted on the rear left shoulder of this shirt, which Powell suggests represents "Two Leggings's Supernatural Guardian, who blessed him with a share in his protecting power." Other than solid colors, it is unusual to find Crow shirts made in the reservation period embellished with pictographic images. Prior to circa 1850, both shirts and leggings were not infrequently painted with designs, which referred to guns or horses captured and exploits achieved—such as touching a live enemy. Embellishments of this kind are invariably depicted in brown or black paint (Taylor 1987: 308–311; 1994: 183–184).[18]

Ewers describes another similar garment which is painted dark blue, so embellished because the original owner, Buffalo Bull, had seen such a shirt in a vision (Wildschut 1960: 60–61). It was reported that Buffalo Bull wore this shirt into battle on many occasions and was never wounded; the protective properties of the medicine shirt were thus regarded "as very powerful" (Wildschut 1960: 61).

16. This is now in the National Museum of the American Indian (cat. no. 12/3099; cp. Wildschut and Ewers 1959: fig. 3). It is conspicuous in being partially tailored.

17. The small isosceles triangles on the shoulders of two of the shirts (National Museum of the American Indian, cat.nos. 12/3099 and 11/6486) occur on many Crow shirts. Although not exclusive to the Crow—variants of the design occur on Blackfeet men's shirts, for example—it is a definite Crow feature. According to Tim McCleary of the Little Big Horn College (Crow Agency, MT), these triangular-type designs were considered to have been given to the Crow by the Horned Toad, which has triangular and rectangular markings on its back. Such patterns were referred to as "Grandmother designs" (T. M. to C. F. T., September 1997).

18. This work is dealt with in greater detail in this volume by Arni Brownstone.

Acknowledgements

I am very appreciative of the help and interest which Louella and Gary Johnson and Joe Medicine Crow of Lodge Grass, MT, extended to me in my quest to obtain the Crow terminology relating to the ceremonial shirt, which is given in Fig. 5. Thanks also to my long-standing friend, Stu Conner of Billings, MT, who kindly took me to visit Lodge Grass in September, 1997. Once again, my thanks go to Bill Holm of Seattle, who, as always, was willing to discuss and give his opinions on several aspects of Crow material culture, which are referred to in this text. Another friend, Richard Edwards of Toledo, OH, was particularly helpful with my pursuit of the symbolism associated with white clay and the jackrabbit, the latter a topic also of some interest to our late mutual friend Dennis Lessard. The Fort Laramie garment shown in Fig. 8 was kindly made available to the writer for study purposes by Superintendent James Mack and his colleagues in September 1998.

References Cited

Bray, K. M.
1985 *Making the Oglala Hoop: Oglala Sioux Political History (1804–1877)*. English Westerners Society, American Indian Studies Series 4. London.

Brown, Mark H. and W. R. Felton
1955 *The Frontier Years: L. A. Huffman, Photographer of the Plains*. New York, NY: Henry Holt and Company.

Catlin, George
1841 *Letters and Notes on the Manners, Customs and Condition of the North American Indians*. London: Published by the author.

Conner, Stuart
1993 *Crow Conversations with Conner*. Billings, MT: Conner.

Curtis, Edward S.
1907–1930 *The North American Indian*. F. W. Hodge, ed. 20 vols. Cambridge, MA: University Press—Norwood, MA: Plimpton Press.

Denig, Edwin Thompson
1930 Indian Tribes of the Upper Missouri. J. N. B. Hewitt, ed. *Forty-sixth Annual Report of the Bureau of American Ethnology*, 375–628.

Ewers, John C.
1967 William Clark's Indian Museum in St. Louis 1816–1838. In: Walter Muir Whitehill (ed.), *A Cabinet of*

Curiosities. Five Episodes in the Evolution of American Museums (Charlottesville, VA: The University Press of Virginia), 49–72.

1977 Notes on the Weasel in Historic Plains Indian Culture. *Plains Anthropologist* 22(78/1): 213–262.

Goetzman, William et al.

1984 *Karl Bodmer's America.* [Omaha, NE—Lincoln, NE:] Joslyn Art Museum and University of Nebraska Press.

Holm, Bill

1998 Plateau and Related Crow Art. In: *Art of the Northern Plains, Plateau and Southwest* (Sale 7165, New York, NY: Sotheby's), [unpaginated, after lot 81].

Larocque, François-Antoine

1985 Yellowstone Journal. In: W. Raymond Wood and Thomas D. Thiessen (eds.), *Early Fur Trade on the Northern Plains* (Norman, OK: University of Oklahoma Press), 156–220.

Lessard, Dennis

1984 (ed.) *Crow Indian Art. Papers presented at the Crow Indian Art Symposium.* Mission, SD: Chandler Institute.

Loeb, Barbara

1998 Transmontane Beading. In: *Art of the Northern Plains, Plateau and Southwest* (Sale 7165, New York, NY: Sotheby's), [unpaginated, after lot 111].

Logan, Michael H. and Douglas A. Schmittou

1998 The Uniqueness of Crow Art. A Glimpse into the History of an Embattled People. *Montana. The Magazine of Western History* Summer 1998: 58–71.

Lowie, Robert H.

1919 *The Tobacco Society of the Crow Indians.* American Museum of Natural History, Anthropological Papers 21(2). New York, NY.

1935 *The Crow Indians.* New York, NY: Farrar & Rinehart, Inc.

Powell, Father Peter J.

1988 *To Honor the Crow People.* Chicago, IL: Foundation for the Preservation of American Indian Art and Culture, Inc.

Smith, DeCost

1949 *Red Indian Experiences.* London: George Allen & Unwin Ltd.

Sotheby's

1996 *Fine American Indian Art.* May 21, 1996. Sale number 6853. New York, NY: Sotheby's.

Taylor, Colin

1981a Costume with Quill-Wrapped Hair: Nez Perce or Crow? *American Indian Art Magazine* 6(3): 42–53.

1981b *Crow Rendezvous: The Place of the River & Mountain Crow in the Material Culture Patterns of the Plateau & Central Plains circa 1800–1870.* English Westerners Society, American Indian Studies Series 1. London.

1984a Analysis and Classification of the Plains Indian Ceremonial Shirt: John C. Ewers' Influence on a Plains Material Culture Project. In: George P. Horse Capture and Gene Ball (eds.), *Fifth Annual Plains Indian Seminar in Honor of Dr. John C. Ewers* (Cody, WY: Buffalo Bill Historical Center), 11–40.

1984b Crow Rendezvous. In: Dennis Lessard (ed.), *Crow Indian Art* (Mission, SD: Chandler Institute), 33–48.

1987 Early Nineteenth Century Crow Warrior Costume. *Jahrbuch des Museums für Völkerkunde zu Leipzig* 37: 302–319.

1994 *The Plains Indians.* London: Salamander Books Ltd.

1998 *Iho'lena. Voices from the Past: Messages for the Future. Cultural, Religious and Military Content of Plains Indian Artefacts.* Bilingual edition (English/German). Wyk auf Foehr: Verlag für Amerikanistik.

Thomas, Davis and Karin Ronnefeldt

1976 (eds.) *People of the First Man.* New York, NY: E. P. Dutton & Co., Inc.

Thompson, Judy

1977 *The North American Indian Collection. A Catalogue.* Bern: Historisches Museum.

Wied, Maximilian Prince of

1839–1841 *Reise in das innere Nord-America in den Jahren 1832–34.* 2 vols. and atlas. Koblenz: J. Hoelscher.

1906 *Travels in the Interior of North America.* In: Reuben Gold Thwaites (ed.), *Early Western Travels 1743–1846* (Cleveland, OH: The Arthur H. Clark Company), vols. 22–24.

Wildschut, William

1960 *Crow Indian Medicine Bundles.* John C. Ewers, ed. Contributions from the Museum of the American Indian, Heye Foundation 17. New York, NY.

Wildschut, William and John C. Ewers

1959 *Crow Indian Beadwork.* Contributions from the Museum of the American Indian, Heye Foundation 16. New York, NY.

Wright, Mabel Osgood

1898 *Four-Footed Americans and Their Kin.* Frank M. Chapman, ed. London: The Macmillan Company.

Quill-Wrapped Horsehair
Two Rare Quilling Techniques

Bill Holm

Like many serious hobbyists, Norm Feder was passionate in his desire to understand the character and technologies of Native American arts. More pragmatic and skeptical than most, he tested long-accepted ideas about design, materials, and techniques experientially by replicating methods and forms, partly because of this curiosity but also because he loved the objects and the processes. Norm had no degrees in either anthropology or art history and had no pretensions about it. His great knowledge was his portfolio.

He was a serious replicator, an "artifaker," in the language of those of us hobbyists who shared his passion. We were both quillwork enthusiasts and experimented with various techniques. I became particularly interested in the variations of quill-wrapped horsehair and in a fit of irresponsibility decided to make a shirt decorated with that technique. That decision led to examining and photographing every example I could find, leading eventually to the making of such a shirt (Fig. 2) and this record of their characteristics.

The Quill-Wrapped Horsehair Shirt

This very interesting variation on the Plains ceremonial shirt is receiving increasingly intense attention from scholars and collectors. It fits squarely in the Northwestern Plains ceremonial shirt tradition with the single obvious difference that the ornamental sleeve and shoulder strips are executed in an unusual porcupine quillwork technique that was used almost exclusively for such shirt adornments. This "double-bundle quill-wrapped horsehair" technique and the shirt type with

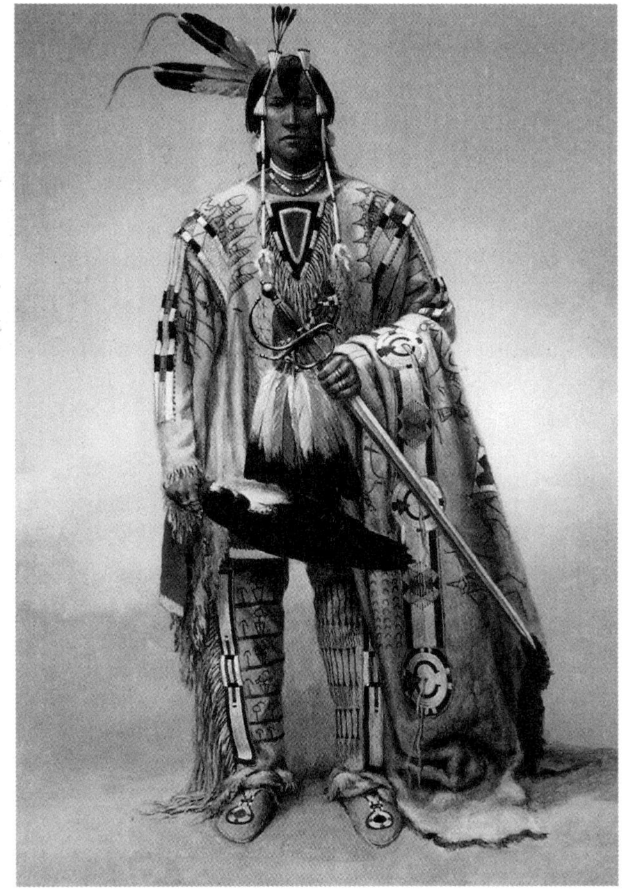

Fig. 1 A Crow warrior of the early nineteenth century wearing clothing decorated with quill-wrapped horsehair. His leggings and shirt are in the Opočno Castle collection (Fig. 4; Brownstone, this volume, figs. 4, 6). The painted buffalo robe is in the collection of the National Museum of Denmark (Brownstone, this volume, fig. 2), and the quilled moccasins are in the Bernisches Historisches Museum (Fig. 20). His early Spanish cavalry broadsword is suggested by the four pictographs of a similar sword on the shirt, one of which is visible just above the blanket strip rosette. Watercolor drawing by the author, 1998.

Bill Holm was born in 1925 in Roundup, Montana, where his lifelong interest in Plains Indian art and culture began. When his family moved to Seattle, he became involved with the Northwest Coast. His first published articles, in Norm Feder's *American Indian Hobbyist* magazine, were on Plains subjects. Since then he has published eight books and many articles. Currently Curator Emeritus in the Burke Museum and Professor Emeritus of Art History, University of Washington, he is working on a series of paintings of Indians of the Plains, Plateau, and Northwest Coast.
Author's address: 1027 N.W. 109th Street, Seattle, WA 98177, U.S.A.

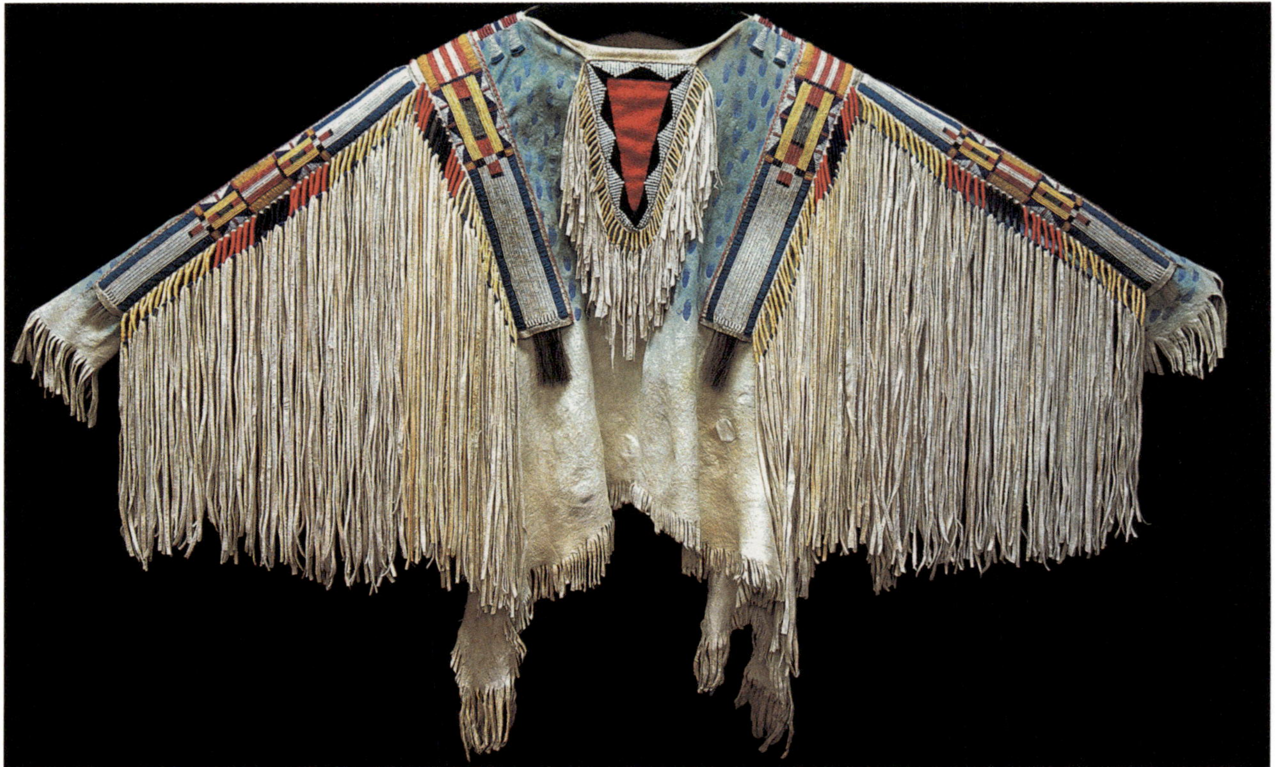

Fig. 2 Quill-wrapped horsehair shirt made in 1989 by the author.

which it is associated have been described several times in print by Colin Taylor (1981, 1984), and this paper should be regarded as supplemental to Taylor's work, with additional detail on the shirts and technique based on a much larger sample and on personal experiments with the technique, and presenting a somewhat different perspective on several points.

The quill-wrapped horsehair shirt is a variant of the short (hip-length) untrimmed two-skin binary shirt common to the northwestern Plains and eastern Plateau in the last half of the nineteenth century. It seems to have descended from the long (knee-length) shirt so familiar to us from the paintings of Karl Bodmer and George Catlin and from early shirts collected by Prince Maximilian, Lorenz Schoch, Paul Kane, and others. Short ceremonial shirts seldom appear in the early pictorial record. The only one that I know of was pictured by Bodmer, in his painting of the Yankton chief Big Soldier. On the other hand, short shirts were probably made and used for everyday wear. For example, Lewis and Clark made several specific references to "short" shirts on the Plateau (Lewis and Clark 1962: 284, 292). A typical long shirt has a three-skin (rather than two-skin) binary pattern, with the bibs or neck flaps integral with the front and back skins, whereas the usual two-skin short shirt requires separate neck flaps. Except for this and the difference in length the two shirts are almost identical in structure. Both are usually made of untrimmed skins which retain the naturally irregular configuration of the animal hides, including much of the legs and often the tails. Plains and Plateau binary shirts which have had these irregularities trimmed off have sometimes been described as "tailored." Tailoring, however, implies fitting, that is, garment construction that conforms to the three-dimensional volume of the body. Northern Athapaskan and Eskimo skin clothing was usually tailored, while traditional Plains and Plateau clothing was not. Following Dick Conn's terminology (Conn 1974: 59), I have elected to use the term "binary" for the flat, unfitted shirt style discussed in this paper.

On untrimmed skin shirts the hair on the tails and ends of the leg skins was usually left on, and many shirts also retained a thick fringe of hair along the entire lower border. Both long and short shirts were left open along the sides and under the arms at least to the elbow, with the rest of the sleeve sewn or laced closed to the wrist. A few buckskin ties under the arms and down the body held the sides loosely together. Since the full untrimmed width of the hide, along with the front legs, was used to form the poncho-like sleeves, loose folds of buckskin hung under the arms. The hides used were typically very thin—antelope and mountain sheep were favored—so these drapes of buckskin were not particularly awkward or uncomfortable. The body of the shirt also utilized the full width of the skins with the hind legs, so it too hung loosely, with the leg skins pendant at the sides.

The decorations on both short and long shirts usually include a pair of quilled or beaded bands or strips sewn down the outer edges of the arms and a similar pair sewn over the shoulders, on or near the seams joining the sleeves with the body. On earlier shirts the strips are relatively narrow and those over the shoulders quite short, actually covering the seam. On most later shirts, long or short, the strips are broader and the shoulder strips longer. They also seem to angle more inward toward the bottom, but many of them are attached nearly parallel to one another with the angle largely resulting from the draping of the shirt when worn. Fringes of buckskin, hairlocks, or ermine tubes are typically fastened along the back edges of the sleeve strips and the outer edges of the shoulder strips. Both shirt types typically have some kind of decoration on the neck flaps, which are often fringed as well. In addition to these decorations, shirts are frequently painted in solid colors, spots, lines, pictographs, symbolic designs, or combinations of these. It is primarily in the differing character of these applied decorations that shirts can be classified by tribal origin or ceremonial significance. Differences in structure have also been linked to tribal origin.

Double-Bundle Quill-Wrapped Horsehair

Before we examine the quill-wrapped horsehair shirt and its variations let us take a close look at the quillwork technique—double-bundle quill-wrapped horsehair—that is the defining characteristic of this shirt. All writers on the subject have mentioned its relative rarity. William Orchard, the first to describe it in print (although with an incorrect diagram of its construction), mentioned that, unlike single-bundle quill-wrapped horsehair work, it was only used for straight bands and never for curved work such as in rosettes (Orchard 1971: 48). However, in the same study Orchard illustrated rosettes on a fine quiver in the (then) United States National Museum, apparently collected by George

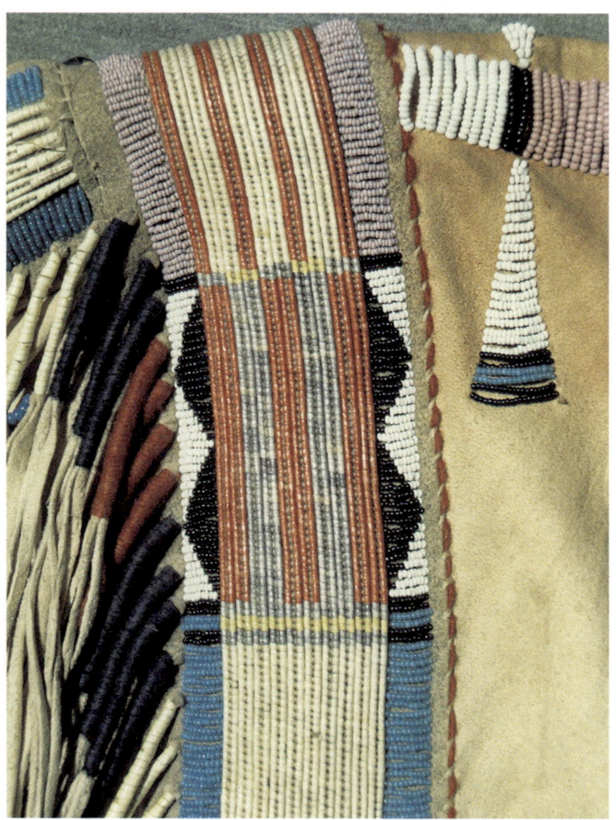

Fig. 3 Detail of a quill-wrapped horsehair shoulder strip on the shirt in Fig. 12, showing the typical ten lanes of double-bundle quillwork on the shoulder strip and six lanes on the sleeve (upper left). The design is an example of Lessard's "type A." The fringe is wrapped with yellow quills except adjacent to the patterned areas, where it is wrapped with dark blue and red yarn. The fringe is inserted through the edge of the buckskin base of the bead- and quillwork. A red yarn is enclosed in the seam attaching the strip to the shirt. A typical beaded epaulet is seen on the upper right. Collected on the Plateau. Private collection.

Catlin, done primarily in the double-bundle technique (Orchard 1971: pl. XXII). These rosettes are beautifully crafted, with very tight, perfectly executed spirals of double-bundle work, illustrating very well that such tight turns were possible. Colin Taylor mentioned these rosettes as well as a pair of moccasins with tight reversals collected by Catlin (Feder 1965: fig. 39c), but reiterated the idea that, due to the limitations of the technique, "the effort must have been very time consuming" (Taylor 1981: 44). There are, in fact, several other examples of double-bundle quill-wrapped horsehair work in which the lanes have been doubled directly back on themselves neatly and effectively. The problem was ingeniously solved by the quillworkers by simply making an extra wrap around the outer bundle between every stitch or so, effectively filling the gaps that would have resulted because of the greater cir-

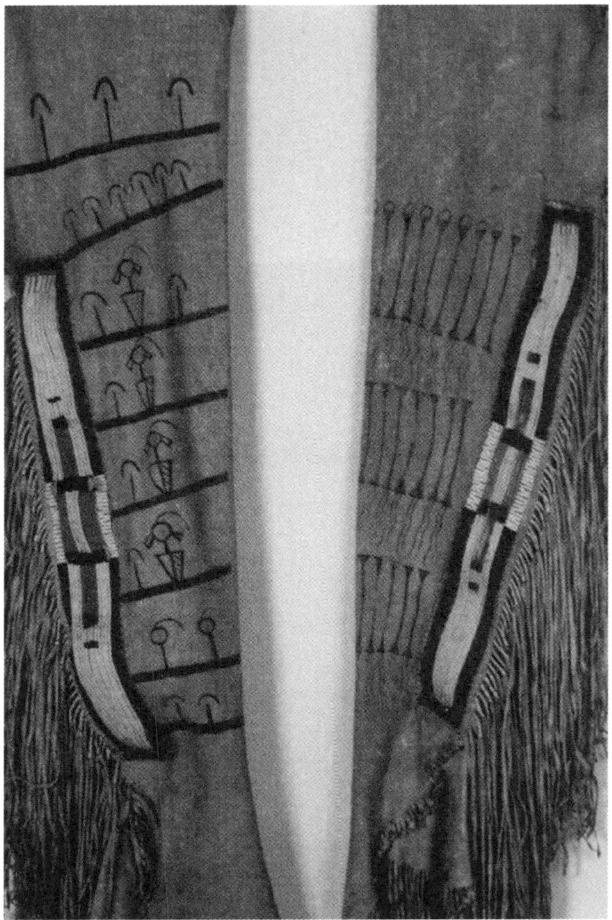

Fig. 4 Detail of a pair of leggings with quill-wrapped horsehair strips bordered with seed beads. The white and yellow areas are reversed in the two strips. The leggings were collected in Wyoming in 1905, although they certainly date from the early nineteenth century. Opočno Castle Collection (Czech Republic), cat.no. 6916. Photograph courtesy of Náprstek Museum (Prague).

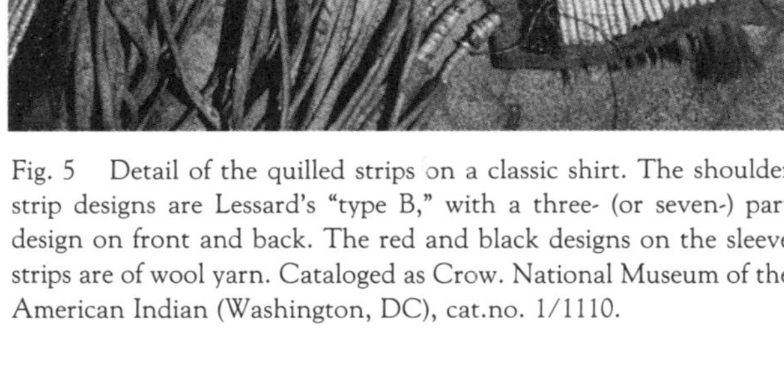

Fig. 5 Detail of the quilled strips on a classic shirt. The shoulder strip designs are Lessard's "type B," with a three- (or seven-) part design on front and back. The red and black designs on the sleeve strips are of wool yarn. Cataloged as Crow. National Museum of the American Indian (Washington, DC), cat.no. 1/1110.

cumference of the outer bundle at the bend. Nevertheless it is true that double-bundle quill wrapping is seldom found except on shirt and legging strips and single-bundle quill wrapping is essentially confined to rosettes.

Why the technique was used so rarely and then almost exclusively on shirt and legging strips is difficult to explain. It has been described as a very difficult technique, but in fact it is a relatively easy one. It uses more quill length per wrap by approximately one half than the more common two-thread, single quill, flat embroidery, and since narrower quills were commonly used in double-bundle quill wrapping there are usually more wraps per inch. Larger double bundles on strips average 5 mm (3/16 in.) in width and use approximately six wraps per centimeter (fifteen per inch). The finest example known to me, on a pair of leggings apparently collected by Catlin (NMNH,[1] cat.no. 386,514), has lanes of about 3 mm (1/8 in.) in width and eight to ten wraps per centimeter (eighteen to twenty-five per inch). The strips on the finest extant shirts approach that fineness (Fig. 3). Even though there is only one stitch per wrap, compared to two in the more common quill

1. The following abbreviations will be used for museum collections referred to in the text:

AMNH American Museum of Natural History (New York, NY)
FMNH Field Museum of Natural History (Chicago, IL)
LACMNH Los Angeles County Museum of Natural History (Los Angeles, CA)
MSHS Montana State Historical Society (Helena, MT)
NMD National Museum of Denmark (Copenhagen)
NMAI National Museum of the American Indian (Washington, DC)
NMNH National Museum of Natural History (Washington, DC)
SWM Southwest Museum (Los Angeles, CA)
UM University Museum (Philadelphia, PA)

embroidery technique, the finest set of shirt strips required in excess of 15,000 stitches, and even an average set required over 12,000. Nevertheless the technique is a fairly simple one as porcupine quillwork goes, and it does seem strange that it is so rare. In trying to replicate the technique I found that neither logic ("It must use a backstitch") nor Orchard's diagram (a running stitch) sufficed to solve the problem. Fortunately a couple of shirts and a pair of moccasins had been damaged sufficiently to show that the stitch (invisible in undamaged quillwork) was actually made just through the surface of the buckskin at a *right angle* to the lane, and then brought over the wrapped quill at a slight diagonal. Once this was learned and the mechanics of handling the hair bundles and quills worked out, the quilling proceeded at a reasonable, if not snappy pace!

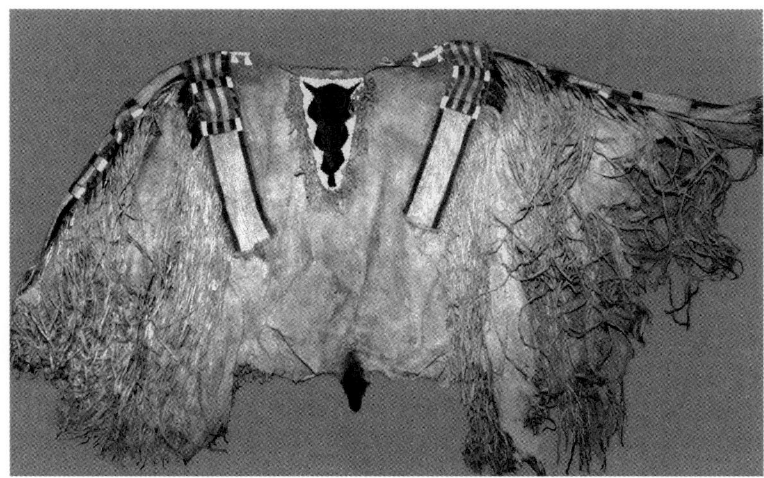

Fig. 6 Back of a quill-wrapped horsehair shirt with "type A" strips. The shoulders are painted red, and soft red spots are painted on the front and back. Red and dark blue yarn is used to wrap the fringes adjacent to the quilled designs. On shirts where the hair remains on the tail it is sometimes possible, as in this case, to identify the source of the skin. This tail exhibits the distinctive color pattern of the bighorn sheep. Collected from the Umatilla. National Museum of the American Indian, cat.no. 16/5941.

While the double-bundle quill-wrapped horsehair technique was used primarily for straight line work and only occasionally for curved lines in rosettes or "keyhole" patterns, the single-bundle technique was typically used to produce rosettes. Only one example of the use of the latter technique for straight lines is known to me, on a quilled legging strip. Here, one of the two strips has six double-bundle lanes (Fig. 4, left), while the other has four double bundles, with a single bundle on each edge (Fig. 4, right). Since the designs are nearly identical except for the reversal of the yellow and white areas, the reason for this difference in technique is not apparent.

Each lane of double-bundle quillwork usually begins and ends with a short stretch (1–2 cm) of single-bundle quilling (Fig. 3, upper left). The hair core is then divided into two equal bundles and the quilling proceeds in the double-bundle technique. This narrow row of single bundles often shows in old photographs (such as the image of Whistling Elk on Alexander Gardner's photograph of Lakota chiefs and headmen at Fort Laramie taken in 1868) and is a sure means of identifying quill-wrapped horsehair work in them, especially when the design patterns are much like early beaded strips.

At the start and finish of each lane, the horsehair bundle is inserted from front to back through a hole in the foundation strip. It is usually allowed to protrude somewhat past the end of the buckskin. The majority of strips, thirty-one of the thirty-five sets (89%), has the ends wrapped in single bundles for a short section before dividing into two bundles, as described above. In the remaining four sets, the hair bundles are divided into two from start to finish (Fig. 5). These differences seem not to be significant in relation to other differences in the shirts, so are probably representative of individual choice in technique. The finished strips are ordinarily not sewn down to the shirt across their ends.

In double-bundle work, the sewing strand of sinew is brought up between the bundles, the quill is wrapped around both bundles beyond the sinew strand and its end held back against the work, while the thread is brought over the wrapped quill and down between the two bundles. The transverse stitch is made close to the quill. The thread is then brought back up between the bundles and the quilling proceeds.

The Characteristics of Quill-Wrapped Horsehair Shirts

My tabulation of the characteristics of the shirts and strips is based on thirty-five examples. Twenty-one of these are complete, extant shirts. Another extant shirt is complete except for the neck flaps (UM, cat.no. 38,251), and another is a trade-cloth coat, open down the front and with a single neck flap (NMAI, cat.no. 9/6567). Nine are in old photographs, their present whereabouts (if they still exist) unknown. The last

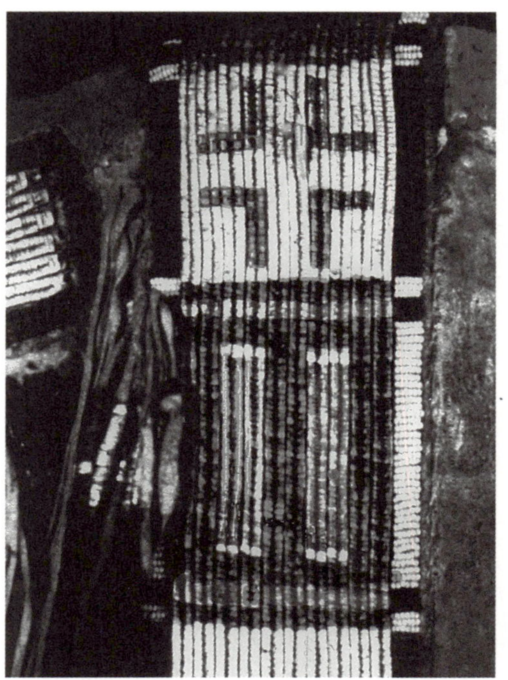

Fig. 7 Unusually elaborate design on a "type A" quill-wrapped horsehair shoulder strip. This shirt is thought to have been collected by George Catlin in the 1830s, the earliest known extant shirt. University Museum, University of Pennsylvania (Philadelphia, PA), cat.no. 38,251. Photograph by Dennis Lessard.

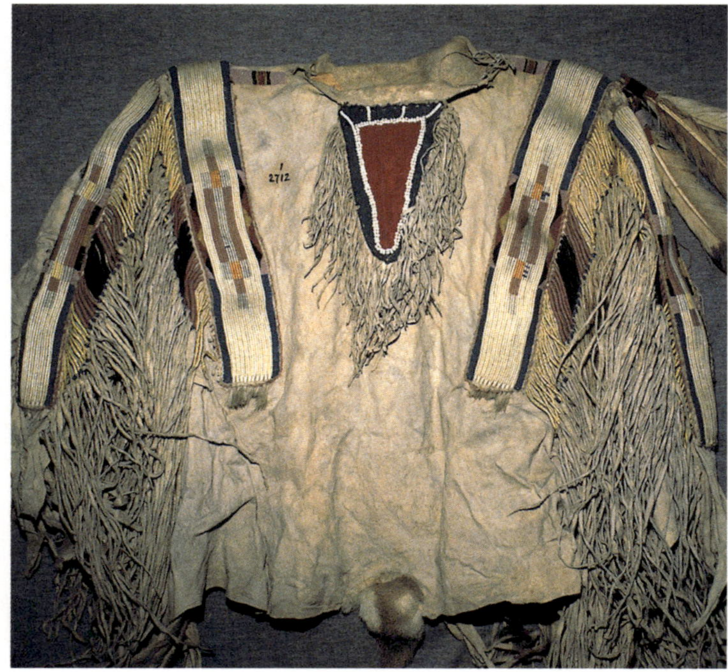

Fig. 8 Back of a quill-wrapped horsehair shirt with "type B" designs. The design blocks "float" on the background, rather than extending completely across the strip. Light blue and yellow quills and magenta yarn form the pattern, and the central bar extends beyond the block pattern, an unusual feature. Dark blue and magenta yarn wrappings on the fringes coincide with the quilled patterns. American Museum of Natural History (New York, NY), cat.no. 1/2712.

three are sets of loose strips, two of which also include the neck flaps and have been attached to reconstructed shirts. These three sets are included in the tabulation only as parts. A single sleeve strip (MSHS, cat.no. 1183) and a single neck flap of typical form (LACMNH, cat.no. P89-41) were not included in the tabulation.

The complete shirts are amazingly uniform in structure and detail. All except the coat are short, untrimmed two-skin binary shirts. Almost all have saved hair on the extremities of the leg skins and many have at least one of the tails. Four of the tails have enough hair to enable them to be recognized as bighorn sheep by their distinctive color pattern (Fig. 6). Some others are probably antelope. All of the strips tabulated are bordered laterally with single lanes of lane stitch in pony beads, seed beads, or both. Only one shirt has borders at the ends of the strips. This shirt has some other unique features and may be very early (Fig. 7). On extant shirts these lateral borders are usually blue, ranging from a light, powder blue to a medium dark, translucent color. One has pink borders, one very dark blue, two have green, and one has red borders on the sleeves. As Dennis Lessard wrote (1984: 64, 65, fig. 3), the border colors change adjacent to the blocks of design in the quillwork. Border designs are usually simple blocks, but in some examples triangles also appear. Crow-type *beaded* strips have similar borders (although seldom with triangle designs), and this feature is a part of the early historic Upper Missouri design tradition (Lessard 1984: 63).

With only a single exception (Fig. 8), the quilled block designs cross the strip from border to border, another similarity to Crow beaded shirt strips. And almost all designs are bounded at each end with a straight band, but the strips on three shirts (Fig. 9; AMNH, cat.no. 1/2312; Oregon Historical Society photograph) extend the central bar. This detail also has its beaded counterpart (Conn 1982: pl. 61). Although collected from the Nez Perce, but considered by the museum to be of Crow origin, this beaded shirt appears in several old photographs worn by three different Nez Perce and Umatilla men. It illustrates the problem of attribution so frequently addressed in recent years.

Dennis Lessard's description of the three-section block design (1984: fig. 5) as being frequently found on quill-wrapped horsehair strips is valid, but the width and complexity of some of the dividing bands gives

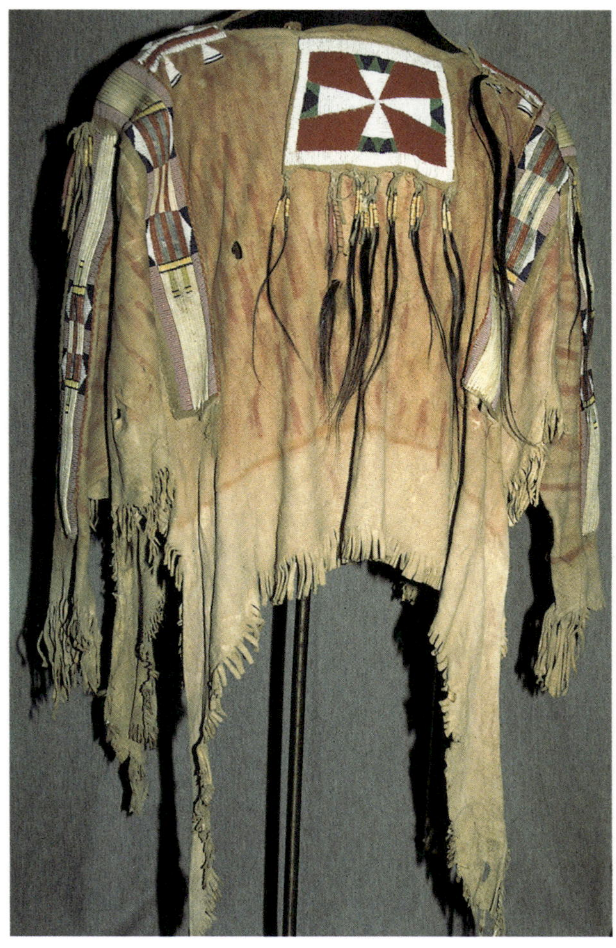

Fig. 9 Quill-wrapped horsehair shirt with unusual square neck flaps. The sleeve and shoulder strips lack fringes, but some clusters of hairlocks are attached to the shoulders. This shirt was photographed by L. A. Huffman on two Brulé Lakota men. The upper part is painted light red, with darker red stripes and streaks. An unusual feature of the quilled designs is the extension of the central bars beyond the ends of the block patterns. Private collection.

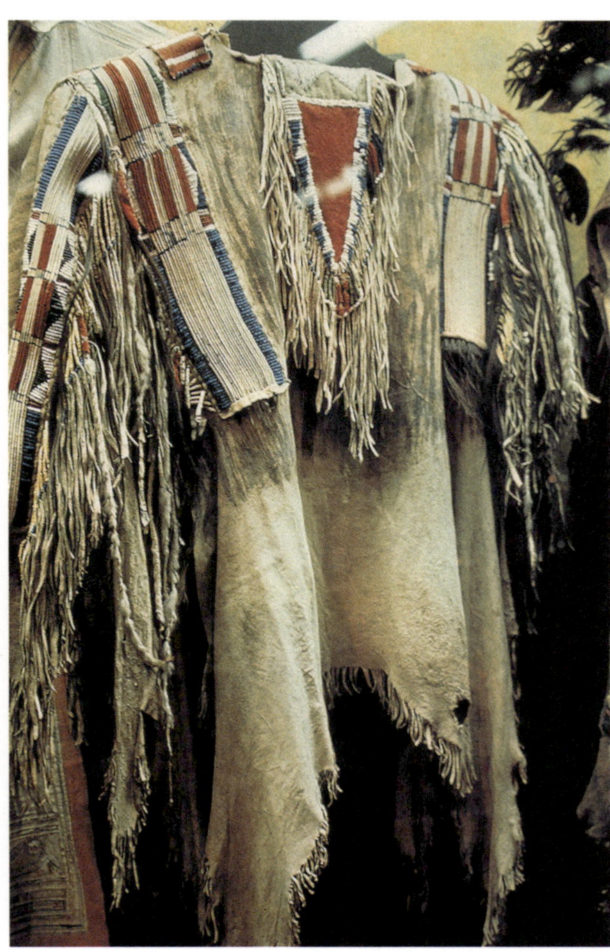

Fig. 10 Back of a quill-wrapped horsehair shirt with red yarn used in all the red bars in the design. Ermine tubes have been interspersed in the quill-wrapped buckskin fringe. The upper part of the shirt is tinted black, with darker black streaks. Pitt Rivers Museum, Oxford University (Oxford), cat.no. 1.

them the character of sections themselves, suggesting five, or even seven, divisions (Figs. 5, 12). This is particularly true of shoulder strips with single block designs (Lessard's "type A", 1984: fig. 2). The larger sample in the present study shows that the prevalence of the "type A" design layout is not quite so great as thought. Of thirty-five sets of strips surveyed, twenty-two (63%) use the "type A" pattern, as compared to eleven out of thirteen (84%) in Lessard's survey. Although the single design block is very likely an earlier style, it is probably not a reliable indicator of the relative age of any given shirt. For example, the shoulder strips on the cloth coat (NMAI, cat.no. 9/6567), which have the appearance of rather late work, are of the single block ("type A") style.

All of the extant strips examined utilize undyed white quills for the background. All but two of the shirts seen in old photographs appear also to have white background. Both exceptions, worn by Plateau men, show a medium value background with white borders. These borders were probably light or medium blue, rendered white by the highly blue-sensitive film used, and the quill background was probably yellow, judging by its similarity to the value of the wrapping on the fringes, yellow in every extant example, and by the fact that yellow was a very common background color in early Plains and Plateau quillwork. The early films typically rendered yellow as a medium to dark grey (Holm 1985).

On many examples of quill-wrapped horsehair work, materials other than porcupine quills were used for the colored element. Black was a difficult color to achieve

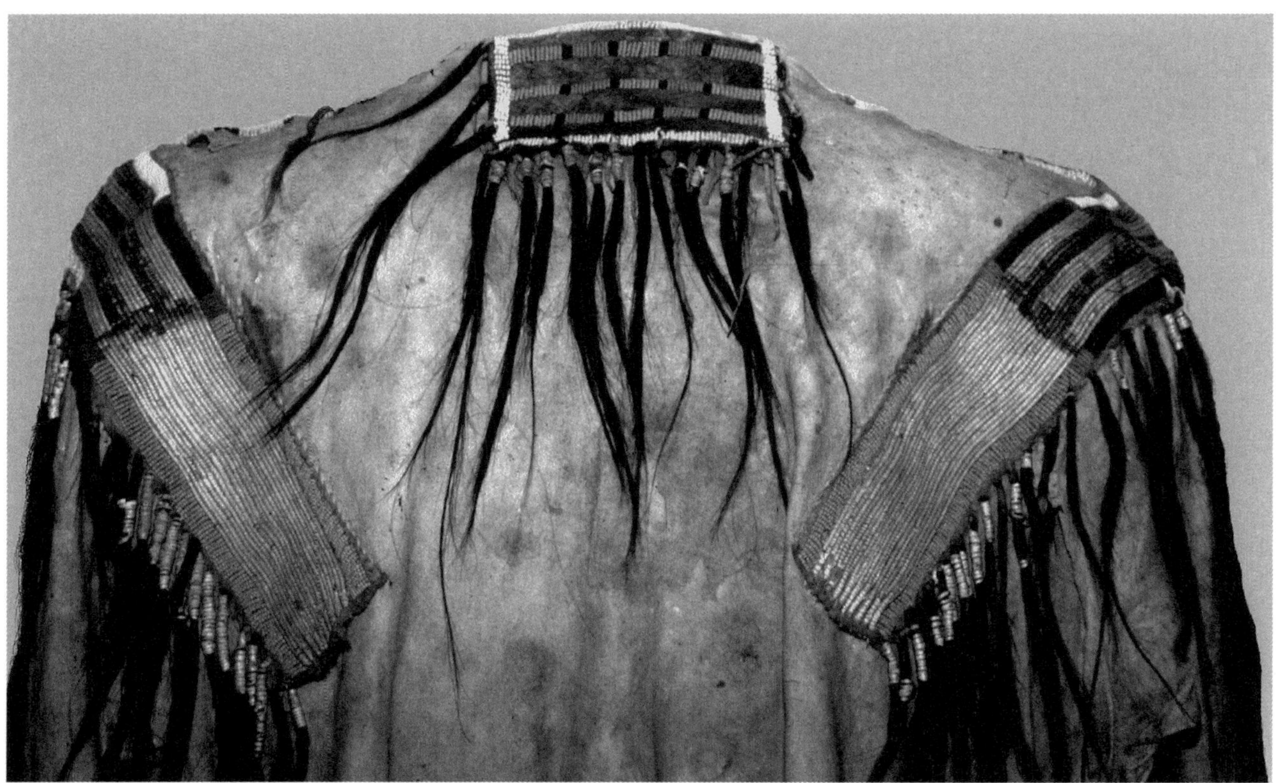

Fig. 11 Detail of a quill-wrapped horsehair shirt with square neck flaps and hairlock fringes, a usual combination. The shoulder strips are in Lessard's "type A" pattern. The buckskin is painted with pale blue spots. Fort Laramie Museum (Fort Laramie, WY), cat.no. 9573.

in dyeing quills in the early nineteenth century, and dark brown or black vegetal material was often substituted, probably the rhizome of the horsetail (*Equisetum sp.*). This material will not withstand the tension needed to pull it down between the bundles of horsehair and never appears in double-bundle quill-wrapped horsehair work. Colored yarn was also used as a substitute for quills. Seven of the extant shirts use some red or dark blue or black yarn in place of quills (Fig. 10), some only on the sleeve strips (Fig. 5). One shirt uses pale magenta yarn (Fig. 8). Another use of red yarn echoes an early quill edging technique (Fig. 20; Orchard 1971: fig. 43). Two of the shirts seen have a line of red yarn worked with this technique into the stitching joining the inner edges of the quilled strips to the shirts. Seven of the very similar shirts with multiple-quill plaited strips use the same form of decoration. Four more quill-wrapped horsehair shirts show the same red yarn line, but in simpler form, the yarn merely enclosed in the sinew stitching (Fig. 3).

The most remarkable consistency in quill-wrapped horsehair shirts is in the number of lanes in the quillwork. Of the thirty-two sets of strips in which the numbers could be reliably counted, twenty-seven (84%) have six lanes on the sleeve strips. Ten lanes on the shoulder strips is almost as typical, occurring in twenty-three of thirty-one examples (74%). The other shirts have various combinations of three to nine lanes. One shirt with five-lane quill-wrapped shoulder strips has multiple-quill sleeve strips (Batkin 1995: 27). This shirt is very unusual in being heavily punctured and having hair locks attached *inside* the shoulder strips and along the front of the sleeve strips, in addition to the usual quill-wrapped buckskin fringe along the outer edges. Another beautiful shirt with many unusual features also has a combination of three lanes of quill-wrapped horsehair on the sleeves and multiple-quill plaited strips over the shoulders (Fig. 1; Taylor 1994: 195). Of the five shoulder strips with nine lanes, all but two (SWM, cat.no. 254-L-1, and an unidentified old photo) are asymmetrical in design, apparently designed as ten-lane strips, with one edge lane omitted.

Another remarkable consistency is the relation of neck flap shape to fringe type. twenty-four (72%) of the thirty-three pairs of neck flaps are triangular. Of the shirts with triangular flaps, four have no fringe along the arm strips or over the shoulders and appear never to have had any (Fig. 9; Wardwell 1998: no. 19; Taylor

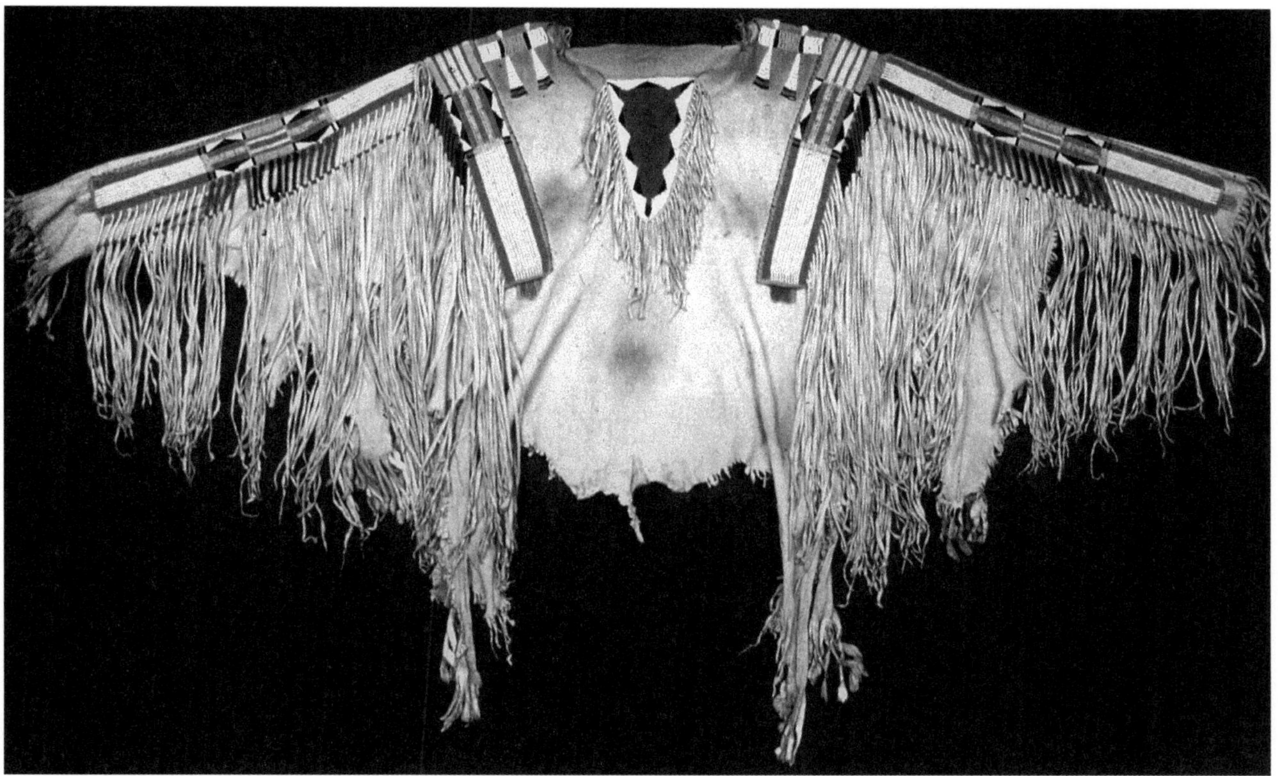

Fig. 12 Back of a classic quill-wrapped horsehair shirt with the most common construction and details. The shoulders are painted red and faint red spots are painted on front and back (see Fig. 3). Collected on the Plateau. Private collection.

1994: 195; NMAI, cat.no. 6/6845). Of the other twenty, seventeen (85%) have a fine-cut buckskin fringe, wrapped at the base with yellow quills. Some also have wrapping of contrasting yarn adjacent to design blocks. One other (Hill and Hill 1994: 83) originally had buckskin fringes, which were cut off and replaced with ermine tubes. This shirt appears worn by a Crow man in several photos taken in 1883 at a Northern Pacific Railroad "Golden Spike" ceremony in Montana (cp. Taylor 1984: fig. 14). It already had the ermine fringes attached at that time, over a century ago. All the shirts with buckskin fringes have them applied by running long, double-length skin thongs through paired holes usually in the edge of the bands (70%; Figs. 3, 5, 6) or through the shirt itself (Figs. 8, 10) in such a way that pairs of fringes come out together. A third thong is sometimes added, and each bundle wrapped with yellow quills for a distance of 3–5 cm. Only two shirts lack these quill wrappings, and it is possible that they once had them. Only two shirts with *triangular* neck flaps have *hairlock* fringes. One of these, worn by Old Crow in the 1873 Crow delegation photographs (Bush and Mitchell 1994: 46), is unusual in the horizontal band design on the bib, while that on Sits-in-the-Middle-of-the-Land's shirt, photographed at the same time, has a typically decorated triangular neck flap and the expected quill-wrapped buckskin fringes (Bush and Mitchell 1994: 42; Museum of the American Indian 1982: 33). Most triangular neck flaps are of buckskin faced with red stroud, often with a border of black and white pony beaded triangles. The "black" triangles are often formed by a dark blue stroud border on which the white beads are sewn. The fringes on the neck flaps themselves are also wrapped at the base with yellow quills, sometimes with sections of red and blue yarn wrapping.

The combination of triangular neck flaps and quill-wrapped buckskin fringe is also common on shirts with *multiple-quill plaited* strips, many of which are otherwise identical to quill-wrapped horsehair shirts (Batkin 1995: 23). Ten such shirts were photographed and measured. At least two *beaded* shirts have triangular neck flaps of exactly the same type, but one has hairlock fringes (Penney 1992: no. 86) and the other has ermine and hair fringes (private collection). Both have seemingly early-style, simple block designs on the strips; one with a "type A," three-section arrangement, and the other with a "type B," single-section of longitudinal stripes.

In contrast to the combination of triangular neck

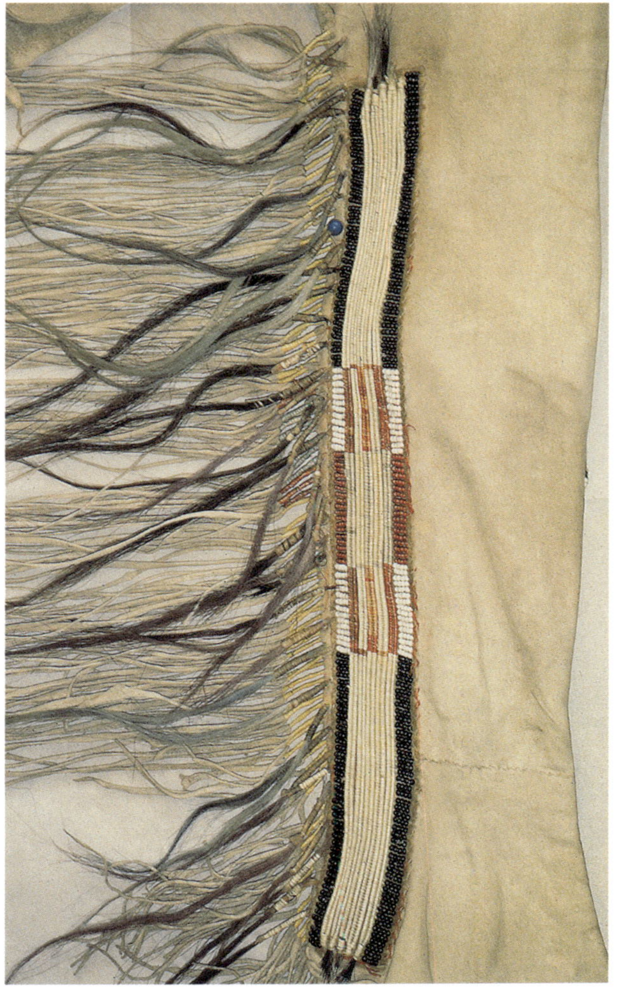

Fig. 13 Detail of a legging with quill-wrapped horsehair strip, bordered with pony beads. The pair was collected in the mid-nineteenth century, but without tribal identification. Probably Crow. National Museum of Denmark (Copenhagen), cat.no. Hd51.

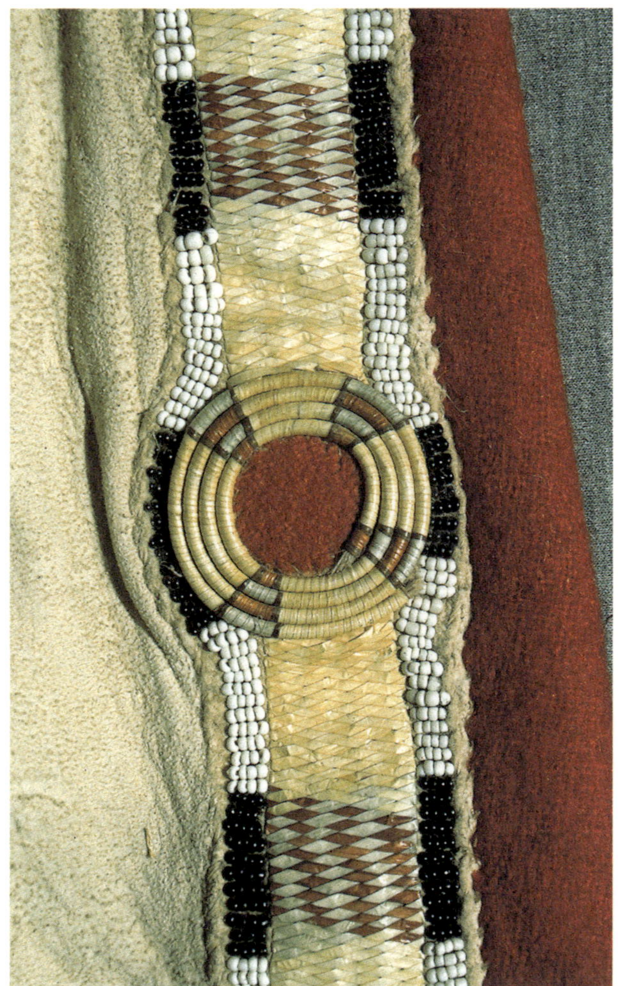

Fig. 14 Single-bundle quill-wrapped horsehair rosette in a multiple-quill plaited legging strip. Each rosette is centered with a red stroud insert. Collected by Lorenz Alphons Schoch in 1837. Attributed to the Crow. Bernisches Historisches Museum (Berne), cat.no. N.A. 9a.

flaps and buckskin fringe, shirts with square neck flaps are predominantly decorated with fringes of hair (Fig. 11), ermine, or both. Of the nine examples seen, only two have only quill-wrapped buckskin fringes. The shirt worn by "An Old Man of Waiyam" (Curtis 1911: 20) is the only one of the group showing a double rank of quill wrapping on the shoulder fringes, although it appears on at least one other old Plateau pony-beaded shirt. The technique is similar to that in netted quillwork. One other shirt (NMNH, cat.no. 200,631) combines buckskin with hair fringe.

Many (twenty of thirty-two, 63%) quill-wrapped horsehair shirts display an epaulet-like lane of beadwork covering the shoulder seam, sometimes in pony beads and often flanked by beaded isosceles triangles, another feature shared with Crow *beaded* shirts, but also found on old, clearly Plateau clothing (Figs. 2, 3, 6, 8, 11, 12). Some shirts have more elaborate epaulets combining beads with red stroud (Figs. 9, 10). When painted, quill-wrapped horsehair shirts typically have free streaks or spots of red, blue, or black, or large, soft areas of red paint, although a few are predominantly red or black on the upper half. Pictographs are rare. The Opočno Castle shirt (Fig. 1; Taylor 1994: 195) is elaborately painted with weapons, capture hands, human figures, tipis, and wounds. Another, known only from an old photograph, shows images of multiple bullet wounds, and a third (NMNH, cat.no. 200,631) has red hands painted on the back. This shirt is unusual in several other ways. It has square neck flaps, yet has quill-wrapped buckskin fringes combined with hairlocks and an unusually elaborate, asymmetrical design on the shoulder strips, which are nine lanes wide. The most unusual design is that on the Universi-

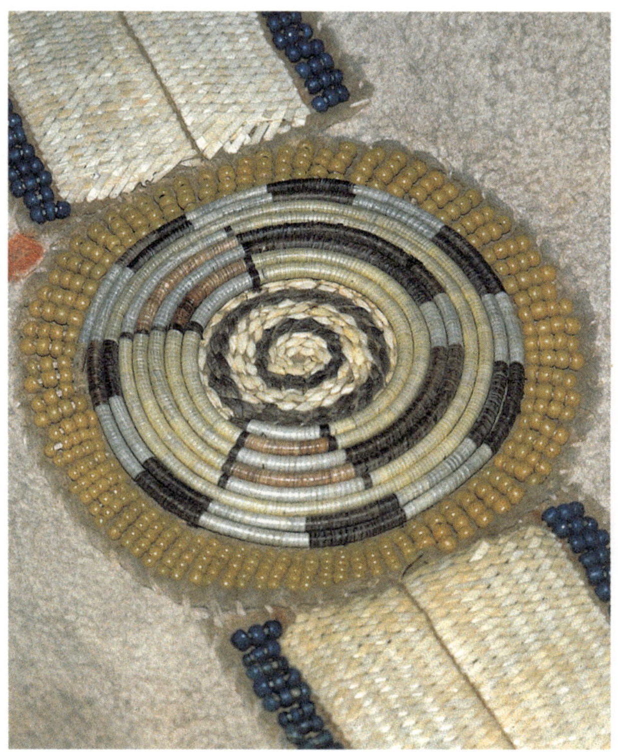

Fig. 15 Detail of a single-bundle quill-wrapped horsehair rosette in a multiple-quill plaited blanket strip on a painted buffalo robe. The center of the rosette is in single-quill linework. The dark brown color in the rosette is vegetal material. Collected by Lorenz Alphons Schoch in 1837. Schoch recorded the tribal origin as "Céré," perhaps a misreading of "Cree." Schoch never collected directly from any northern tribe and may have acquired his "Crow" objects from someone in the fur trade or even from William Clark's Indian Museum in Saint Louis, which was dispersed following Clark's death in 1838. Bernisches Historisches Museum (Berne), cat.no. N.A. 4.

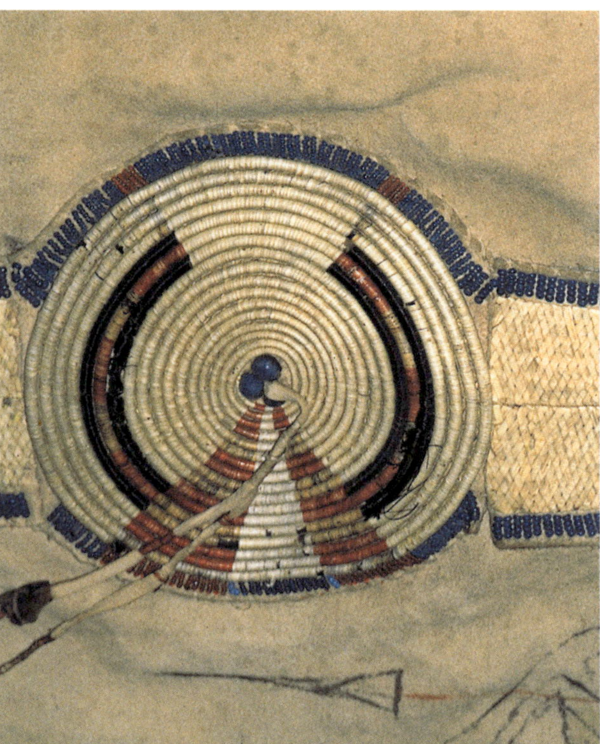

Fig. 16 Single-bundle quill-wrapped horsehair rosette in a multiple-quill plaited blanket strip on a painted buffalo robe. The black areas in the rosette are of black horsehair. The robe was collected in 1861 at Fort Benton by W. H. Schiefflin, said to be from a Cree, and given by him to his friend and traveling companion, the artist William de la Montagne Cary. National Museum of the American Indian (Washington, DC), cat.no. 1/2558.

ty Museum shirt (Fig. 7). Although it is perfectly possible to create complex designs in this technique, almost all are relatively simple arrangements of rectangular bars.

Typical Shirt Characteristics

Based on this tabulation, the most typical quill-wrapped horsehair shirt (Fig. 12) is a short, untrimmed two-skin binary shirt with shoulder strips of ten double bundles of quill-wrapped horsehair with single three-section block designs on the shoulders, and sleeve strips of six double bundles with single three-section block designs. The strips are laterally bordered with single lanes of lane-stitch beadwork with a medium blue background and block and triangle designs coinciding with color changes in the quillwork. Long buckskin fringes wrapped at the base with yellow quills are inserted along the outer edges of the shoulder strips and the rear edges of the sleeve strips. The added neck flaps are triangular, made of buckskin faced with red trade cloth bordered with white triangles of pony beads on dark

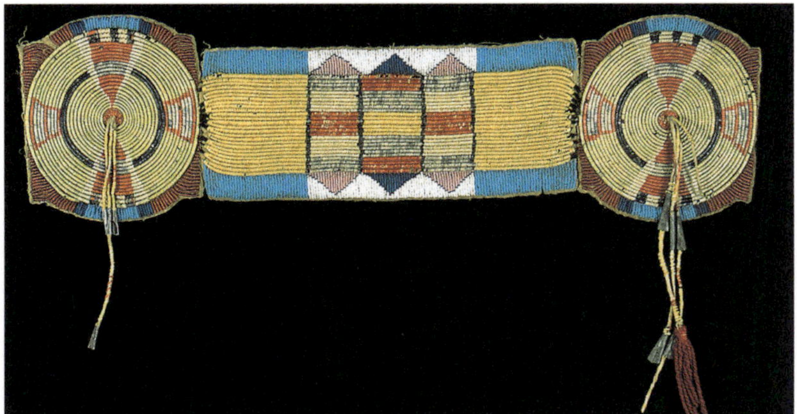

Fig. 17 Fragment of an unusual blanket strip, with rosettes of single-bundle quill-wrapped horsehair and a panel of thirteen lanes of double-bundle work. Another unusual feature is that the rosette background is light green, rather than the usual yellow. Private collections.

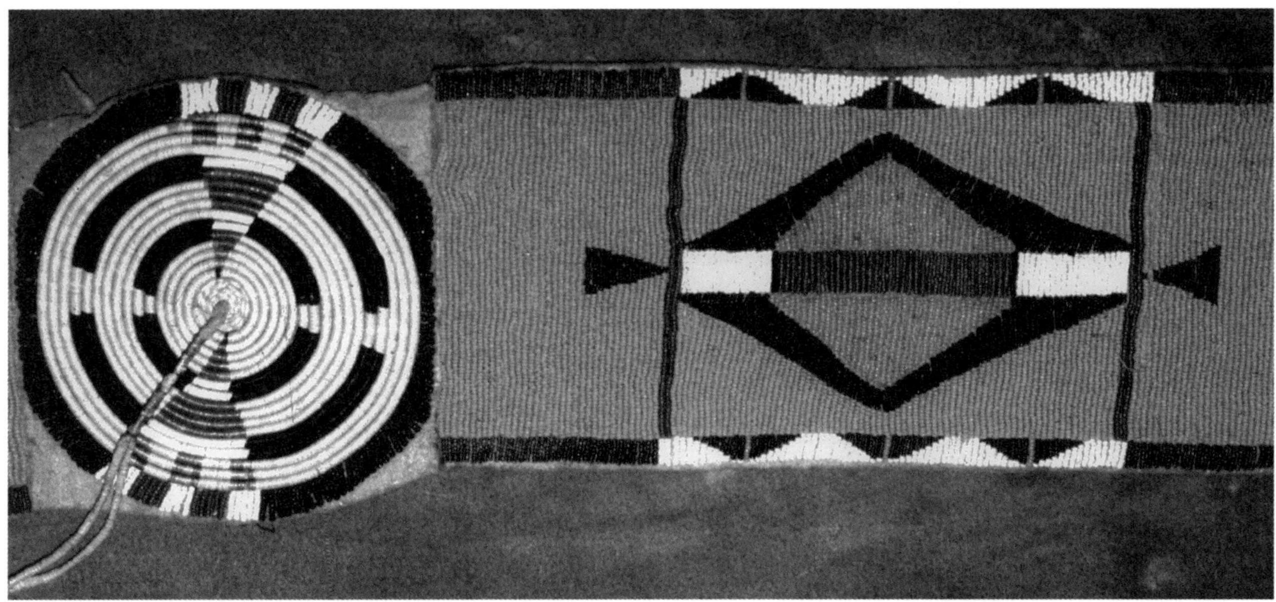

Fig. 18 Single-bundle quill-wrapped horsehair rosette on a beaded blanket strip. The black rings in the rosette are wrapped horsehair. Private collection.

blue stroud, and have a quill-wrapped fringe. Beaded lanes with appended pairs of isosceles triangles cover the shoulder seams.

Quill-Wrapped Horsehair on Other Objects

The quill-wrapped horsehair technique also appears on articles of clothing other than shirts. Five pairs of leggings with strips of double-bundle quill-wrapped horsehair technique were examined. Three of these pairs of strips are nearly identical to shirt sleeve strips in design and proportion (Figs. 4, 13). Another alternates single lanes of quillwork with lanes of pony beads (Taylor 1981: fig. 8). Several other pairs of leggings use quill-wrapped horsehair in rosettes alternated with other quill techniques (Fig. 14; Ewers 1984: 28). The quill wrapping in these rosettes is on single, rather than double bundles of hair. Typically, single-bundle quill-wrapped horsehair rosettes appear on blanket strips or legging strips, interspersed with quilled, rectangular panels in multi-quill plaiting or banded quillwork (Figs. 14, 15, 16, 17; NMD, cat.no. Hd60). Only one fragment of a blanket strip was seen with double-bundle quill-wrapped horsehair for the rectangular panels and single-bundle quill-wrapped horsehair for the rosettes (Fig. 17). Single-bundle quill-wrapped horsehair rosettes are also used on blanket strips in conjunction with beaded panels of the typical broad transmontane type (Fig. 18). These blanket strips are almost all made by beading or quilling the panels and rosettes separately and then joining them together. Commonly, red stroud inserts fill the triangular gaps where the round and rectangular parts come together.

Single-Bundle Quill-Wrapped Horsehair

The single-bundle quill-wrapped horsehair technique is very well suited to the task of quilling rosettes. Like double-bundle quill-wrapped horsehair, it has been described as a very difficult, time consuming technique. In fact it is a straightforward quilling method that, once the manipulation of the horsehair and quills is understood, proceeds fairly rapidly. As in double-bundle quill-wrapped horsehair, Orchard's diagrams (1971: figs. 26, 27) and several subsequent published descriptions (Bebbington 1982: fig. 23a; Heimbuch 1990: 66–68) are faulty. The quills are actually sewn down at every wrap, the stitch being entirely concealed by the work and only visible in damaged specimens. Single-bundle quill-wrapped horsehair is even more quill-hungry than its double-bundle counterpart, since each quill is wrapped completely around the hair core and overlaps the preceding quill by up to one-half its width. None of the hair core shows, even on the tightest turns at the center of a rosette. The stitch used is a short semi-backstitch, just through the skin surface. The quill emerges from under the hair bundle, wraps around it, overlapping the preceding quill wrap and *enclosing* the thread which

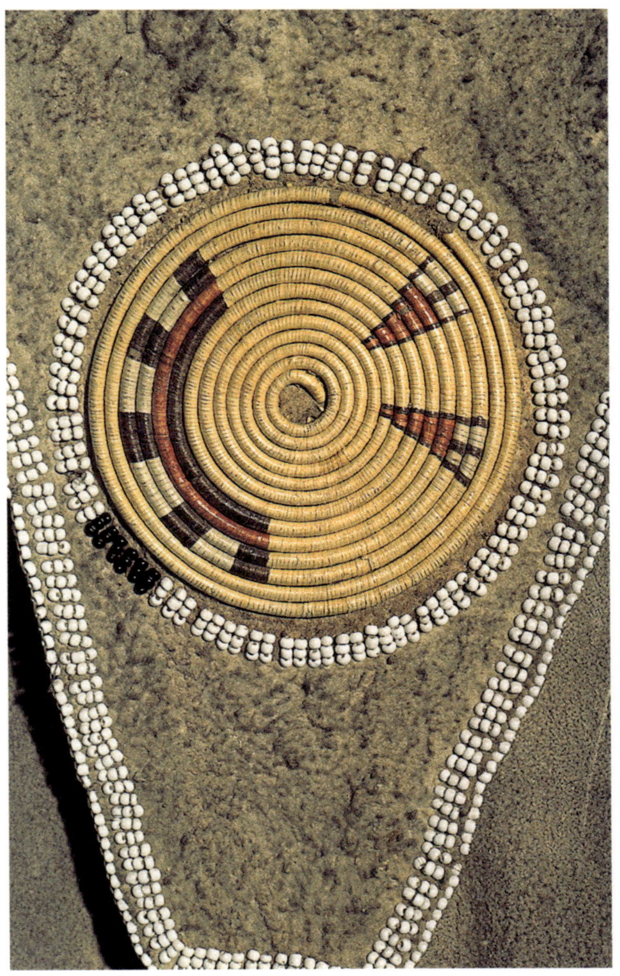

Fig. 19 Single-bundle quill-wrapped horsehair rosette on the neck flap of a Nez Perce shirt, collected before 1846 by Reverend Henry Spalding. Each of the two shirts collected by Reverend Spalding has a quilled rosette on each neck flap. Nez Perce National Historic Museum (Spalding, ID), cat.no. 8760.

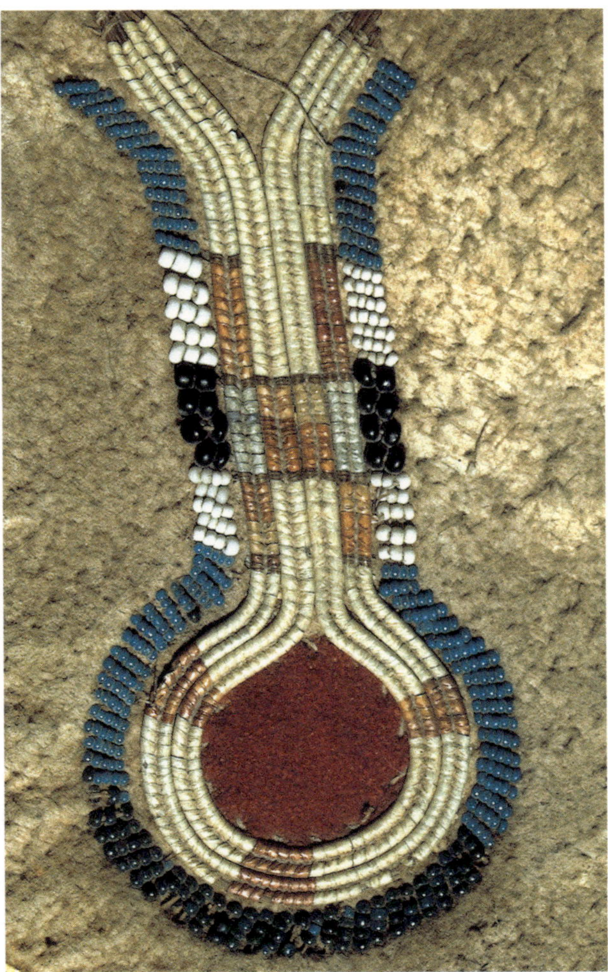

Fig. 20 Detail of double-bundle quill-wrapped horsehair "keyhole" design on a moccasin. In the center of the rosette is an insert of red stroud. The other moccasin of the pair has a dark blue stroud insert. The moccasin seam is embellished with yellow quills. Collected by Lorenz Alphons Schoch in 1837 at St. Louis. Attributed to the Crow. Bernisches Historisches Museum (Berne), cat.no. N.A. 11b.

is stretched along the underside of the hair. The quill is held back over the preceding wrap and a new stitch is made. Splicing is merely a matter of laying in a new quill under its predecessor, tightening the stitch, and wrapping the new quill over the protruding end of the previous quill. While quill-wrapped horsehair work went out of style in the nineteenth century and was apparently not made since, a related technique is still practiced among the Athapaskan peoples of the Canadian woodlands. Very narrow piping of horsehair or bird quill, wrapped with colored horsehair, porcupine quills, or embroidery thread, often borders the U-shaped aprons of moccasins (Thompson 1990: 17) or, in some cases, covers the entire apron (Thompson 1990: 33, 34). Interestingly, in single-bundle quill-wrapped horsehair work, the black areas are often formed by wrapping a strand of black horsehair several times around the bundles to the width of a quill and stitched down. This is probably due to the difficulty in the early days of obtaining a good black dye for quills.

The single-bundle technique was used almost exclusively in making rosettes, most examples being on blanket strips. Of twelve blanket strips examined with such rosettes, seven combine single-bundle quill-wrapped horsehair rosettes with beaded panels (Fig. 18), three use multiple-quill plaiting in the panels (Figs. 15, 16), and a single fragmentary example has a panel of thirteen double-bundle quill-wrapped horsehair lanes (Fig. 17). Quill-wrapped horsehair rosettes were used on other articles as well. Two fine Nez Perce shirts have single-bundle rosettes sewn to the neck flaps (Fig. 19). A Wasco shirt with three such rosettes (FMNH, cat.no. 86,492) and several pairs of moccasins were seen (Taylor

1981: fig. 5; Schulze-Thulin 1976: fig. 9). A beautiful quiver in the National Museum of Natural History (cat.no. 386,538) and believed to be from the Catlin collection is decorated with four rosettes primarily in the double-bundle technique, only very rarely used in curved-line designs (Orchard 1971: pl. XXII). However, several pairs of moccasins use the double-bundle technique to produce the well-known "keyhole" design (Fig. 20; Hill and Hill 1994: 82; Taylor 1981: fig. 15).

Some Thoughts on Origins

The question of the origin of these distinctive shirts has been the subject of some debate. Following the lead of Clark Wissler and Frederic Douglas, scholars until recently have been content to identify them as Nez Perce or more broadly as Eastern Plateau. Since there are no early descriptions of the quillwork technique and only a very meager early photographic record, this identification must have been based on the fact that the majority of shirts with collection histories were collected on the Plateau (including the Denver Art Museum shirt, which may have prompted Eric Douglas's initial interest in them), that there are a number of identified late nineteenth- or early twentieth-century photographs of Plateau men wearing them, and that there are said to be still at least four of them (some optimists claim as many as ten!) in Indian ownership on the Plateau. The record for Crow ownership is smaller, but very impressive because of the photographs of the two prominent Crow men wearing quill-wrapped horsehair shirts in Washington in 1873. There is absolutely no doubt that these shirts were worn by men of both groups; the differences of opinion revolve around the question of who designed and made them. It is probably true that many of the very closely related Crow-style beaded shirts which have been collected from or photographed on eastern Plateau people were acquired from the Crow. The preponderance and uniformity of the beadwork style and its associated shirt among the Crow themselves strongly suggests that the beaded shirts of this type were indigenous to them (Holm 1981: 68–69). The Plateau owners believe, however, that quill-wrapped horsehair shirts were made by their forebears and are a part of their own traditions. Perhaps some of those "Nez Perce" quill-wrapped horsehair shirts really were made on the Plateau, although probably influenced by Crow shirt design and aesthetics.

Appendix

Extant Shirts:

American Museum of Natural History (New York, NY), cat. no. 1/2712. Archincloss coll. Pre-1869, "Nez Perce, Idaho Territory" (Taylor 1980: fig. 13).

Dayton Museum of Natural History (Dayton, OH), cat.no. A-2436. Collected by C. O. Weaver, doctor on Pine Ridge Reservation in the 1880s.

Denver Art Museum (Denver, CO), cat.no. 1956.204 (Conn 1979: #351).

Fort Laramie Museum (Fort Laramie, WY), cat.no. 9573. Collected by John W. Barlow.

High Desert Museum, cat.no. 6.19.1. Dorothy Swayze Bounds coll. Belonged to Nez Perce Albert Moore (Horse Capture and Melton 1989: 19; Harless 1998: pl. 29).

Masco Corporation (Taylor, MI), cat.no. 8803012 (Batkin 1995: 27).

National Museum of Natural History (Washington, DC), cat.no. 200,631. Crow chief White Forehead's shirt. Collected by Emile Granier before 1898 (Taylor 1981: fig. 9).

National Museum of the American Indian (Washington, DC), cat.no. 1/1110. Collected before 1870 by H. F. Spence.
cat.no. 6/6845. Acquired from Fred Harvey.
cat.no. 9/6567. Acquired in 1919.
cat.no. 11/4243. Worn by Crow "Covers His Feet" at Last Spike ceremonies in 1883 (Taylor 1984: fig. 14; Hill and Hill 1994: 83).
cat.no. 16/5941. Collected from the Umatilla.

Opočno Castle Museum, cat.no. 6915. Collected in 1905 in Wyoming by Josef II Colloredo-Mansfeld (Taylor 1994: 195; 1998a: 56–57).

Peabody Museum, Harvard University (Cambridge, MA), cat.no. 12-54=10/84,397. Acquired in 1912 from Henry C. Wheeler. Collected from "Looking Glass" in Wyoming (Taylor 1984: fig. 12).

Pitt Rivers Museum (Oxford), cat.no. 1 (Taylor 1981: figs. 1, 10).

Southwest Museum (Los Angeles, CA), cat.no. 284-L-1.

University Museum, University of Pennsylvania (Philadelphia, PA), cat.no. 38,251. Donaldson coll., possibly collected by George Catlin in 1832.

Private collection. Collected on the Plateau (Wright 1991: #8).

Private collection. Collected from the Yakama (Wardwell 1998: fig. 19).

Private collection. Probably collected by the Earle of Dunraven in Montana in 1875. The shirt appears in an 1876 painting by Valentine Walter Bromely (*American Indian Art Magazine* 15[1]: 2).

Private collection. Collected by Walter Cooper of Bozeman, MT. Photographed by L. A. Huffman on Lakotas Spotted Eagle and Scorched Lightning before 1883 (Brown and Felton 1955: fig. 8; 1956: fig. 9).

Private collection. Collected on the Plateau.

Private collection. Nez Perce Native collection.

Photographs of Shirts:

Calfee photograph of three Crow men (Bush and Mitchell 1994: pl. 151).

Photograph of an unknown Plateau man. Oregon Historical Society.
Photograph of Martin Spedis, Wishram. Oregon Historical Society.
Photographs of David Williams, Nez Perce.
E. S. Curtis photograph of "An Old Man of Waiyam" (Curtis 1911: 20).
J. and H. Ulke photograph of Sits-in-the-Middle-of-the-Land, Crow (Hill and Hill 1994: 85; Museum of the American Indian 1982: 85; Taylor 1984: fig. 13).
J. and H. Ulke photograph of Old Crow, Crow (Taylor 1981: fig. 14; 1994: front end paper).
A. Gardner photograph of Whistling Elk, Lakota (Hiesinger 1994: 35; Taylor 1998b: figs. 22, 23).
Unidentified photograph of a shirt with wound symbols.

Unassociated Strips:

Montana State Historical Society (Helena, MT), cat.no. 1186: single strip.
Private collection. Nez Perce Native collection.
Private collection. Collected on the Crow Reservation, remade into a shirt.
Private collection. Collected on the Yakama Reservation, remade into a shirt.

Leggings:

British Museum (London), cat.no. 1924-10-9-2 (Taylor 1981: figs. 7, 8; 1984: fig. 10).
National Museum of Denmark (Copenhagen), cat.no. Hd51. Collected before 1870 (Taylor 1984: fig. 11).
National Museum of Natural History (Washington, DC), cat.no. 386,514. Collected by George Catlin in 1832.
Opočno Castle Museum, cat.no. 69̊16. Collected in 1905 in Wyoming by Josef II Colloredo-Mansfeld (Taylor 1994: 183).

Rosettes on Shirts:

Field Museum of Natural History (Chicago, IL), cat.no. 86,492: rosettes on shirt.
Nez Perce National Historic Museum (Spalding, ID), cat.nos. 8759, 8760: single-bundle rosettes on 2 shirts. Collected by Rev. Henry Spalding at Lapwai, Idaho, from Nez Perce before 1846 (Taylor 1981: fig. 6; Grafe 1997: fig. 5).

Rosettes on Blanket Strips:

Bernisches Historisches Museum (Berne), cat.no. N.A. 4. Collected by Lorenz Alphons Schoch in St. Louis in 1837 (Thompson 1977: fig. 74; Taylor 1984: fig. 7; 1994: 182–183).
Field Museum of Natural History (Chicago, IL), cat.no. 69,138. Warm Springs, collected from the Yakama in 1901 by M. L. Miller.
Jackson Hole Preserve (Jackson Hole, WY), cat.no. 168.
Masco Corporation (Taylor, MI), cat.no. 9106001 (Batkin 1995:35).
National Museum of Denmark (Copenhagen), cat.no. Hd60. Collected before 1870 (Barbeau 1960: fig. 27; Taylor 1994: 184–185).
National Museum of the American Indian (Washington, DC), cat.no. 17/6345. Collected in Fort Benton in 1861 by W. H. Schiefflin, said to be from a Cree.
Portland Art Museum (Portland, OR), cat.no. 90.33.7. Collected on the Plateau.
Private collection: 2 strips.
Private collection (Wright 1991: #15).
Private collection.

Rosettes on Legging Strips:

Bernisches Historisches Museum (Berne), cat.no. N.A 11a, b. Collected by Lorenz Alphons Schoch in St. Louis in 1837 (Thompson 1977: fig. 79; Taylor 1984: fig. 6).
Canadian Museum of Civilization (Hull, QC). Ex Speyer coll., ex Linden-Museum Stuttgart, collected before 1834 by Maximilian Prince of Wied (Benndorf and Speyer 1968: #232, pl. XIV).
University Museum, University of Pennsylvania (Philadelphia, PA), cat.no. 38,251. Donaldson coll., possibly collected by George Catlin in 1832.

Moccasins:

Bata Shoe Museum (Toronto, ON), cat.no. 0104: double-bundle "U" design.
Bernisches Historisches Museum (Berne), cat.no. N.A. 11a,b: double-bundle keyhole. Collected by Lorenz Alphons Schoch in St. Louis in 1837 (Thompson 1977: fig. 81; Taylor 1984: fig. 4).
Canadian Museum of Civilization (Hull, QC), cat.no. V-H-1: single-bundle keyhole rosette, said to be on sinew bundle. Ex Speyer coll. (Benndorf and Speyer 1968: #233, pl. VI; Brasser 1976: #98).
cat.no. V-H-3: single-bundle keyhole rosette. Ex Speyer coll. (Benndorf and Speyer 1968: #97, pl. XV; Taylor 1981: fig. 5).
Field Museum of Natural History (Chicago, IL), cat.no. 69,368: double-bundle keyhole. Collected by S. C. Simms from the Crow in 1901 (Taylor 1981: fig. 15).
Linden-Museum (Stuttgart), cat.no. 12,579: single-bundle keyhole rosette. Collected around 1823 by Duke Paul of Württemberg (Schulze-Thulin 1976: #9).
Museum für Völkerkunde (Vienna), cat.no. 14,091: single-bundle keyhole rosette. Probably collected by George Engelmann around 1840.
National Museum of Natural History (Washington, DC), cat.no. 386,530: double-bundle stripes. Collected by George Catlin in 1832 (Feder 1965: fig. 39c).
National Museum of the American Indian (Washington, DC), cat.no. 17/8027: double-bundle keyhole (Hill and Hill 1994: 84).
J. and H. Ulke photograph of Iron Bull: double-bundle keyhole (Museum of the American Indian 1982: pl. 26).

Other Objects:

National Museum of the American Indian (Washington, DC), cat.no. 10/3086: medicine bag (Orchard 1971: pl. XVII).
National Museum of Natural History (Washington, DC), cat.no. 386,538: quiver (Orchard 1971: pl. XXII).
Private collection: single rosette.

References Cited

Barbeau, Marius

1960 *Indian Days on the Western Prairies.* Ottawa, ON: National Museum of Canada.

Batkin, Jonathan

1995 (ed.) *Splendid Heritage: Masterpieces of Native American Art from the Masco Collection.* Santa Fe, NM: Wheelwright Museum of the American Indian.

Bebbington, Julia M.

1982 *Quillwork of the Plains.* Calgary, AB: Glenbow Museum.

Benndorf, Helga and Arthur Speyer

1968 *Indianer Nordamerikas.* Offenbach a.M.: Deutsches Ledermuseum.

Brasser, Ted J.

1976 *"Bo'jou, Neejee!": Profiles of Canadian Indian Art.* Ottawa, ON: National Museum of Man.

Brown, Mark and W. R. Felton

1955 *The Frontier Years.* New York, NY: Bramhall House.

1956 *Before the Barbed Wire.* New York, NY: Bramhall House.

Bush, Alfred L. and Lee Clark Mitchell

1994 *The Photograph and the American Indian.* Princeton, NJ: Princeton University Press.

Conn, Richard G.

1974 *Robes of White Shell and Sunrise.* Denver, CO: Denver Art Museum.

1979 *Native American Art.* Denver, CO: Denver Art Museum.

1982 *Circles of the World.* Denver, CO: Denver Art Museum.

Curtis, Edward S.

1911 *The North American Indian. Volume 8.* F. W. Hodge, ed. Norwood, MA: University Press and Plimpton Press.

Ewers, John C. et al.

1984 *Views of a Vanishing Frontier.* Omaha, NE: Joslyn Art Museum.

Feder, Norman

1965 *American Indian Art Before 1850.* Denver Art Museum Quarterly (Summer 1965). Denver, CO.

Grafe, Steven L.

1997 Still They Look Handsome. The Spalding-Allen Collection. *American Indian Art Magazine* 22(3): 35–43.

Harless, Susan E.

1998 (ed.) *Native Arts of the Columbia Plateau: The Doris Swayze Bounds Collection.* Seattle, WA: University of Washington Press.

Heimbuch, Jean

1990 *A Quillwork Companion: An Illustrated Guide to Techniques of Porcupine Quill Embroidery.* Liberty, UT: Eagle View Publishing Company.

Hiesinger, Ulrich W.

1994 *Indian Lives: A Photographic Record from the Civil War to Wounded Knee.* Munich—New York, NY: Prestel.

Hill, Tom and Richard W. Hill, Sr.

1994 (eds.) *Creation's Journey: Native American Identity and Belief.* Washington, DC: Smithsonian Institution Press.

Holm, Bill

1981 The Crow-Nez Perce Otterskin Bowcase-Quiver. *American Indian Art Magazine* 6(4): 60–70.

1985 Old Photos Might Not Lie, But They Fib A Lot About Color. *American Indian Art Magazine* 10(4): 44–49.

Horse Capture, George P. and Terry Melton

1989 *The Plateau.* Cody, WY: Buffalo Bill Historical Center.

Lessard, F. Dennis

1984 Classic Crow Beadwork: Upper Missouri Roots. In: Dennis Lessard (ed.), *Crow Indian Art* (Mission, SD: Chandler Institute), 61–68.

Lewis, Meriwether and William Clark

1962 *The Journals of Lewis and Clark.* New York, NY: The Heritage Press.

Museum of the American Indian

1982 *With Eagle Glance: American Indian Photographic Images: 1868 to 1921.* New York, NY: Museum of the American Indian, Heye Foundation.

Orchard, William C.

1971 *The Technique of Porcupine-Quill Decoration Among the Indians of North America.* [Reprint of 1916 ed. with additional illustrations.] Contributions from the Museum of the American Indian 4(1). New York, NY.

Penney, David W.

1992 *Art of the American Indian Frontier: The Chandler-Pohrt Collection.* Seattle, WA: University of Washington Press.

Schulze-Thulin, Axel

1976 *Indianer der Prärien und Plains.* Stuttgart: Linden-Museum.

Taylor, Colin F.

1980 Analysis and Classification of the Plains Indian Ceremonial Shirt. In: G. P. Horse Capture and G. Ball (eds.), *Fifth Annual Plains Indian Seminar. In Honor of John C. Ewers* (Cody, WY: Buffalo Bill Historical Center), 11–40.

1981 Costume Decoration with Quill-Wrapped Hair. Nez Perce or Crow? *American Indian Art Magazine* 6(3): 42–53.

1984 Crow Rendezvous. In: Dennis Lessard (ed.), *Crow Indian Art* (Mission, SD: Chandler Institute), 33–48.

1994 *The Plains Indians: A Cultural and Historical View of the North American Plains Tribes of the Pre-Reservation Period.* London: Salamander Books. (Also: Avenel, NJ: Crescent Books.)

1998a *Buckskin and Buffalo: The Artistry of the Plains Indian.* London: Salamander Books.

1998b *Iho'lena.* Wyk auf Foehr: Verlag für Amerikanistik.

Thompson, Judy

1977 *The North American Indian Collection: A Catalogue.* Bern: Bernisches Historisches Museum.

1990 *Pride of the Indian Wardrobe: Northern Athapaskan Footwear.* Toronto, ON: University of Toronto Press.

Wardwell, Allen

1998 (ed.) *Native Paths: American Indian Art from the Collection of Charles and Valerie Diker.* New York, NY: Metropolitan Museum of Art.

Wright, Robin K.

1991 (ed.) *A Time of Gathering.* Seattle, WA: Burke Museum—University of Washington Press.

Seven War-Exploit Paintings
A Search for Their Origins

Arni Brownstone

In 1851, the frontier artist Rudolph Friedrich Kurz (1937: 301) noted that in Plains Indian painting "the human form is not represented in the same manner by all nations; on the contrary, each nation has its own conventional manner." In contrast, Norman Feder (1967) rightly emphasized the difficulty for today's scholars in distinguishing between tribal pictorial styles. In tandem, these observers support the notion that the art of Plains tribes is simultaneously pulled in two directions: conservatism and insularity on the one hand, homogeneity and assimilation within a larger multicultural community on the other. Norman Feder was well aware of this dichotomy in his research into questions of tribal style. In his studies he placed special emphasis on the minutiae of visual vocabulary, the formalistic building blocks of images. These captivated his interest and inspired him to make innumerable illustrative schemata to solve the puzzle of their significance by means of the comparative method. It is with great respect for Norman Feder's formal approach to the problem of tribal style that I dedicate the following search for the cultural origins of seven Plains war-exploit paintings.

The first work in the set (Fig. 1)[1] is a war-exploit robe in the Berne Historical Museum (cat.no. N.A. 4), acquired by Lorenz Schoch in the area of St. Louis, Missouri, in 1837. In his brief description of the Schoch collection, Bushnell (1908: 3) mentioned this item along with a robe presently thought to have belonged to the Mandan chief Mato Tope. Bushnell stated that the latter painting bore the inscription "Crow I," but provided no cultural information on the painting under consideration. Several years later, however, Vatter (1927: 64) quoted museum records indicating that the Berne robe was Crow. He also believed that it shared common origins with a robe in the National Museum in Copenhagen (cat.no. Hd60), the second painting in the set (Fig. 2), which was purchased without documentation in 1861.[2] By comparing stylistic features of both paintings with the robe of the Hidatsa Two Ravens in Berlin and with Kurz's illustrations of two Hidatsa robes, Vatter (1927: 79) concluded that they must all be Hidatsa in origin. Ewers (1982: 45) studied a robe in the National Museum of the American Indian (cat.no. 1/2558), the third in the set, and found that it too was similar to the Kurz sketches (Fig. 3). However, Ewers considered the robe to be Crow, partly because it bore figures resembling those in petroglyphs in Crow country, and thought that its similarity to Kurz's sketches suggested that the Crow and Hidatsa shared a similar graphic style. Galante (1984: 55) also considered the NMAI robe to be Crow. He noted that it bore human forms resembling those on the Berne and Copenhagen robes and discovered that the distinct conical shape surmounting many of the forms was identical to that on the figure engraved on a well-documented Crow mirror frame. The documentation accompanying the NMAI robe stated that it was collected by William Schiefflin from a Cree or Blackfoot in Fort Benton, Montana, in 1861. Dorsey added to the catalog record his opinion that while the quill strip was probably made by the Nez

Arni Brownstone was born in the prairie province of Saskatchewan, Canada. After graduating from York University's Visual Arts Programme in 1974, he began working in the Anthropology Department of the Royal Ontario Museum and continues to be employed there in the position of Assistant Curator. In the intervening years his interest in painting and exhibiting his own work has shifted to the study of Plains Indian painting.
Author's address: Royal Ontario Museum, 100 Queen's Park, Toronto, Ontario, Canada M5S 2C6.

1. I produced illustrations of the paintings studied here either by tracing the originals onto plastic film and photostatically reducing the image, or by tracing from slides. I scanned the tracings into a computer graphic program where I colored, isolated, scaled, and juxtaposed details. In this way, the characteristics of the originals, including thickness of line and proportion, were carefully preserved.
2. A recent study identified chrome yellow in the Copenhagen robe, a pigment first produced commercially around 1815 (Moffat et al. 1997).

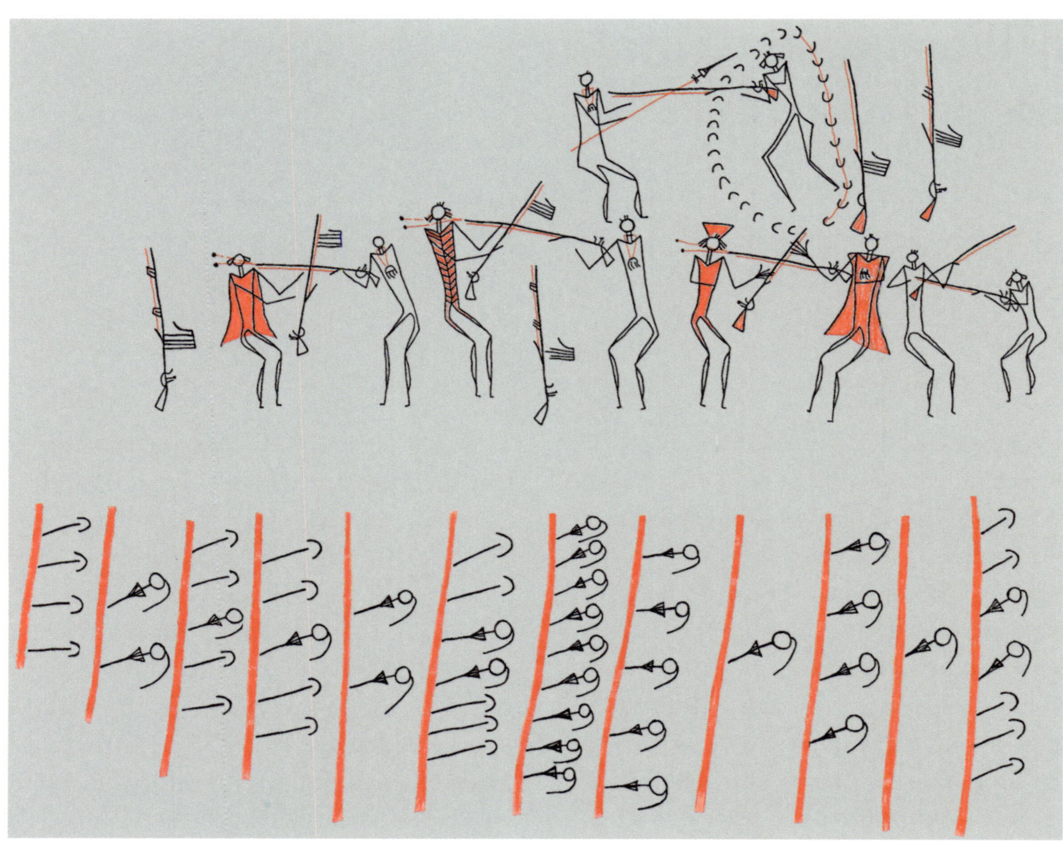

Fig. 1 Redrawing of painted bison robe, collected before 1837. Bernisches Historisches Museum (Berne), cat.no. N.A. 4 (Lorenz A. Schoch coll., possibly ex Clark Museum, St. Louis, MO).

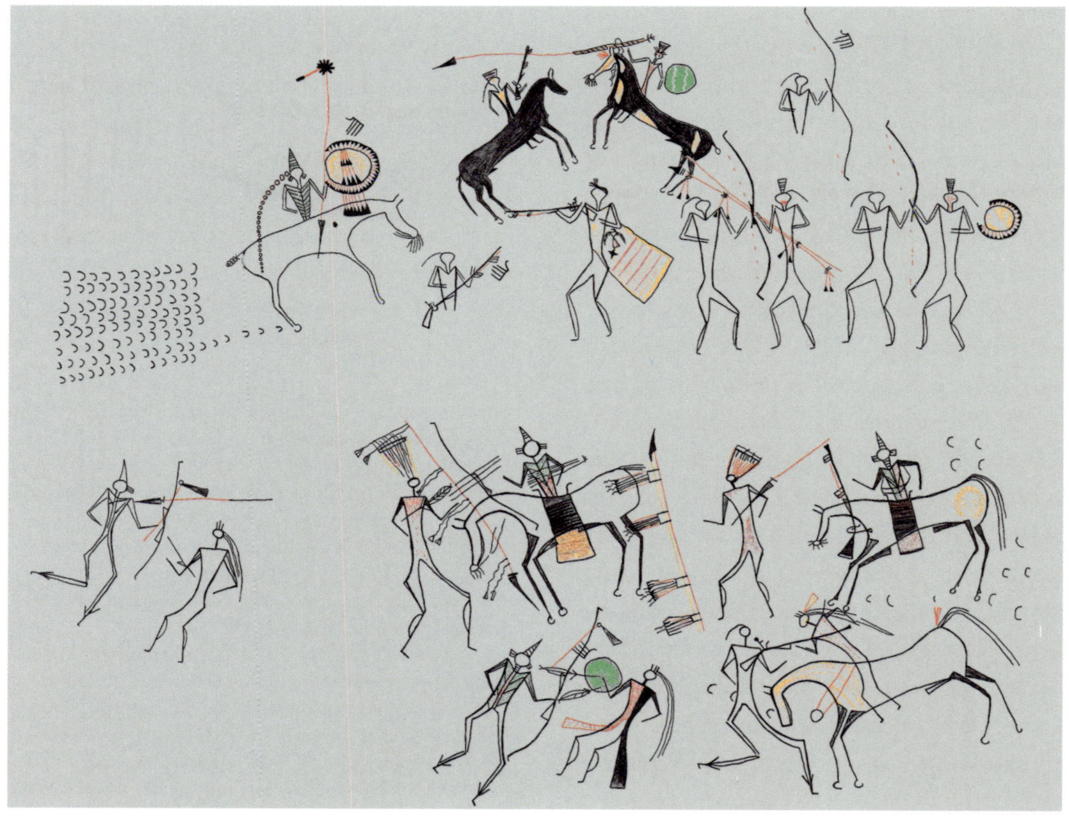

Fig. 2 Redrawing of painted bison robe, purchased without documentation in 1861. Nationalmuseet (Copenhagen), cat.no. Hd60.

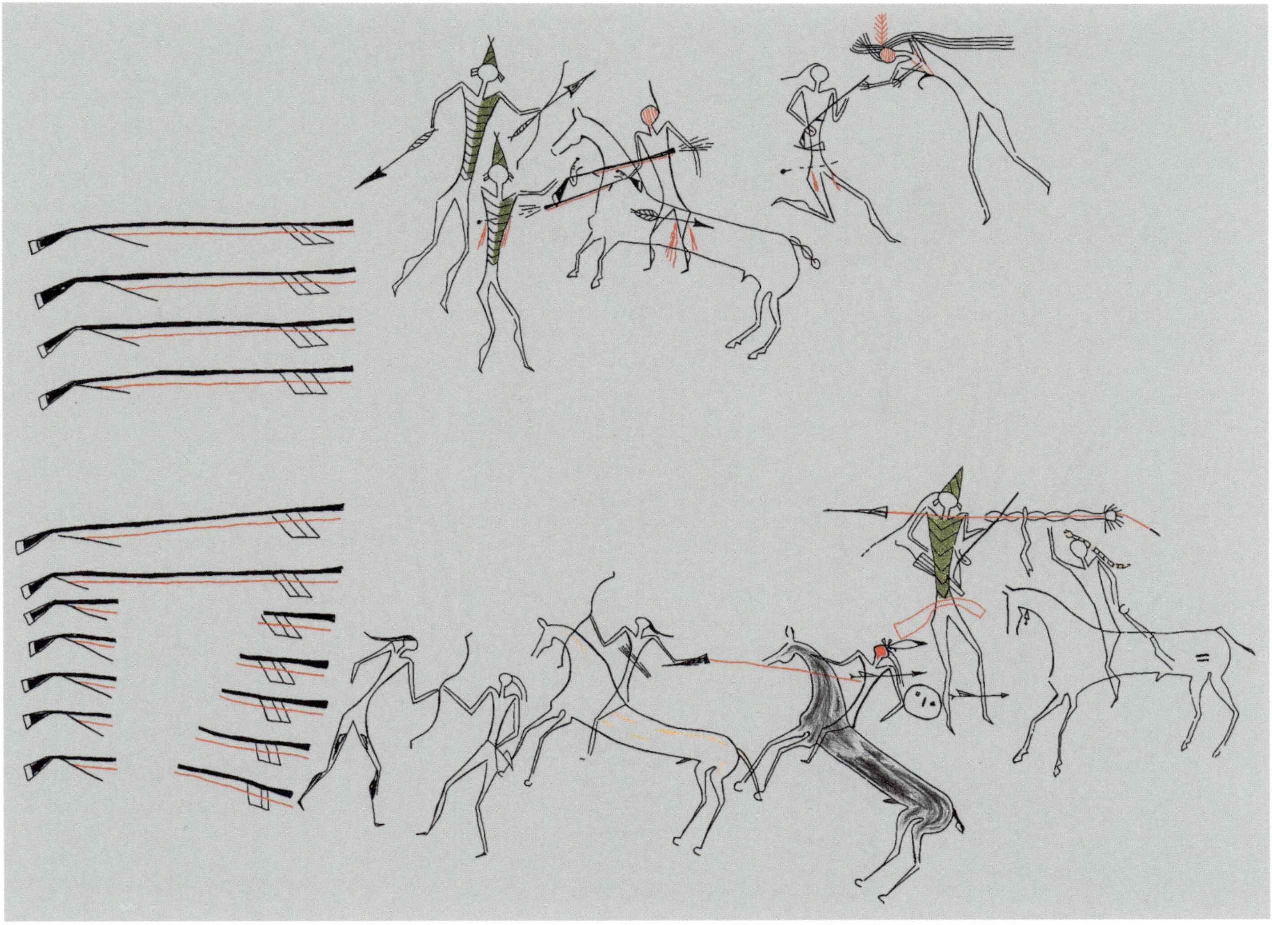

Fig. 3 Redrawing of painted bison robe, collected by William Schiefflin from a Cree or Blackfoot in Fort Benton, Montana, in 1861. National Museum of the American Indian, Smithsonian Institution (Washington, DC), cat.no. 1/2558.

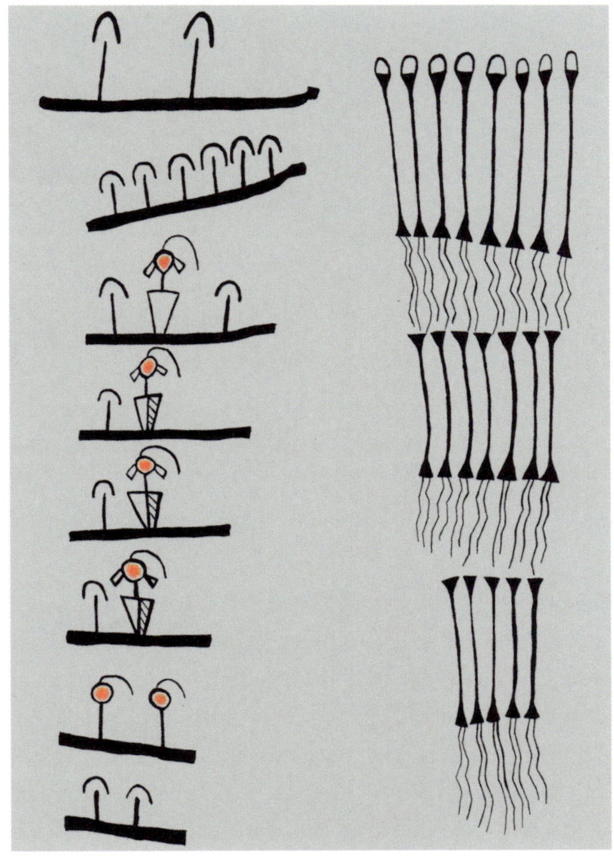

Fig. 4 Redrawing of painted leggings, collected by Josef II Colloredo-Mansfeld on his trip to Wyoming in 1905. Opočno Castle Museum, cat.no. 6916.

Perce, the painted figures and the beaded cloth triangular emblem on the flank were typical of the Crow. The Copenhagen robe is also embellished with the triangular insignia. Taylor (1987: 307) and Holm (pers. comm., 1996) concurred that triangular patches were an indication of Crow origins. However, this feature may have found wider distribution, since Cutter Woman, wife of the Blackfoot chief Crowfoot, was photographed in 1907 wearing a buffalo robe bearing such an insignia, slightly more elongated but with the typical diminutive triangles accenting each corner (Public Archives of Canada, Morris collection #497). Feder (1980) found that rosette designs such as those on the quill strips decorating the three above robes were typical of the Mandan, Hidatsa, Crow, Nez Perce, and a number of

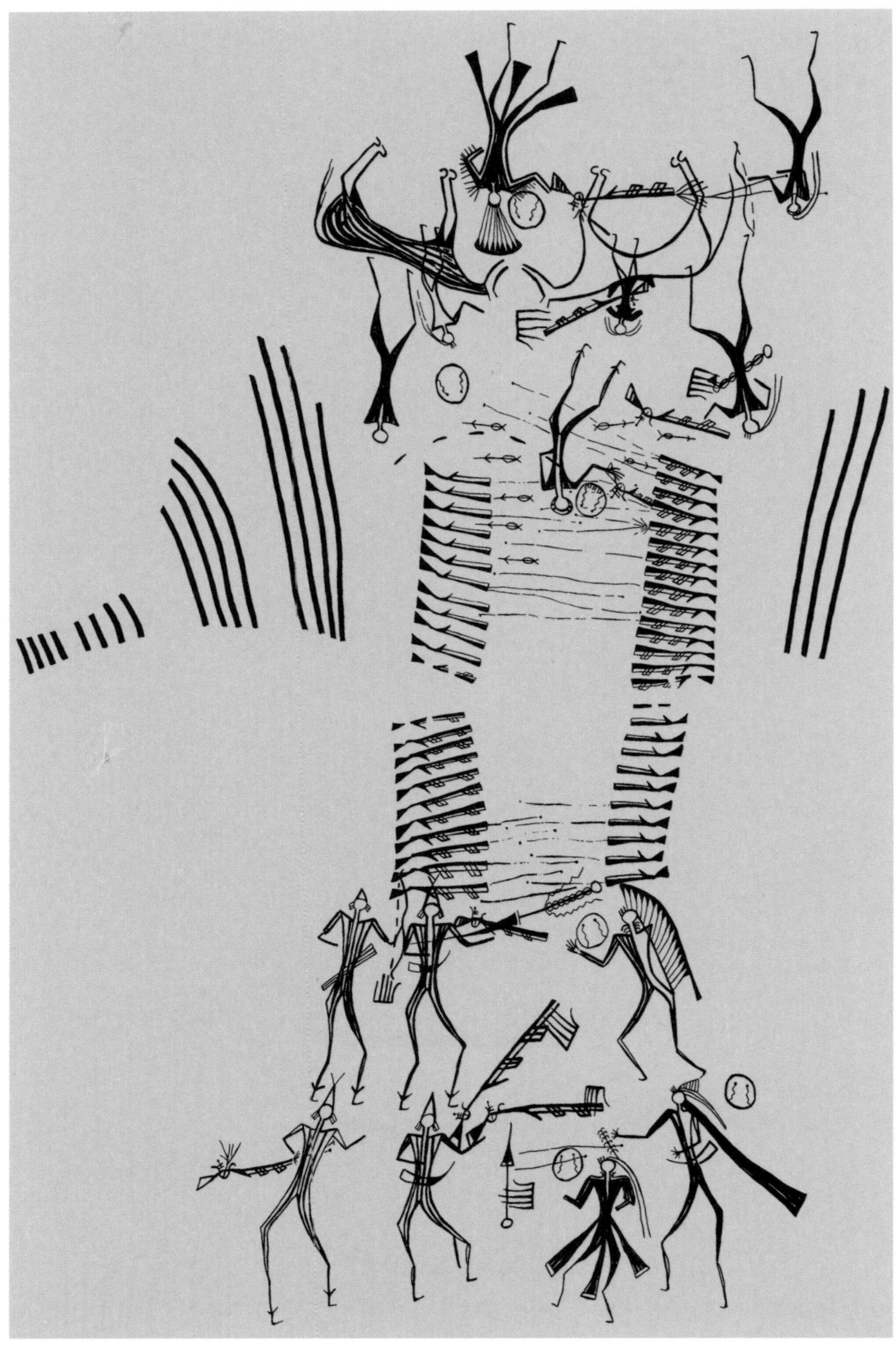

Fig. 5 Redrawing of painted shirt, acquired without documentation. National Museum of the American Indian, Smithsonian Institution (Washington, DC), cat.no. 17/6345.

neighboring Plateau and Great Basin tribes. The strips are elaborated in multiple-quill plaiting, a technique that Taylor (1987: 307) and Galante (1984: 55) associated particularly with the Crow, but that Holm (pers. comm., 1996) thought to have had a wider distribution. The quilled strips on the fourth hide painting in this study (Fig. 5), a shirt in the National Museum of the American Indian (cat.no. 17/6345), were also executed in the multiple-quill plaiting technique. Holm (1992: 49) observed that this shirt, acquired without documentation, shared a number of distinctive pictorial features with the Copenhagen and Berne robes. The shirt bears an epaulet-like feature on the shoulders which is thought by Taylor (1987: 304) to be a definite Crow feature, but by Holm to be an element shared by the Crow and Plateau tribes. Taylor (1987: 309) first published the fifth painting in the set (Fig. 4), a pair of leggings in the Opočno Castle Museum in the Czech Republic (cat.no. 6916), documented only as having been collected by Josef II Colloredo-Mansfeld on his trip to Wyoming in 1905, and noted that it bore painted figures resembling those on the three above robes. In 1991 Rolf Krusche kindly brought to my attention a shirt in the Opočno Castle Museum (cat.no. 6915), apparently with the same collection history as the leggings and displaying distinctive graphic elements characteristic of the five preceding paintings (Fig. 6). It bears multiple-quill plaiting and, like the leggings, double-lane quill-wrapped horsehair decorative strips. Taylor (1962: 60; 1981: 51) considered the latter quillwork technique to have been practiced predominantly by the Crow, specifically the Mountain Crow (Taylor 1987: 310), while Holm (1987) contended that the Nez Perce may have used this technique as extensively as the Crow. Bill Holm kindly guided me to the final hide painting in the set, a buffalo robe in a private collection with no documentation (Fig. 7).

While scholars agree that the seven paintings share enough stylistic features to indicate common origins, there is no clear consensus on who executed them. The present study is thus a contribution to the search for the creators of these works.

Kurz's observation that the human form in Plains Indian pictorials was highly subject to conventionaliza-

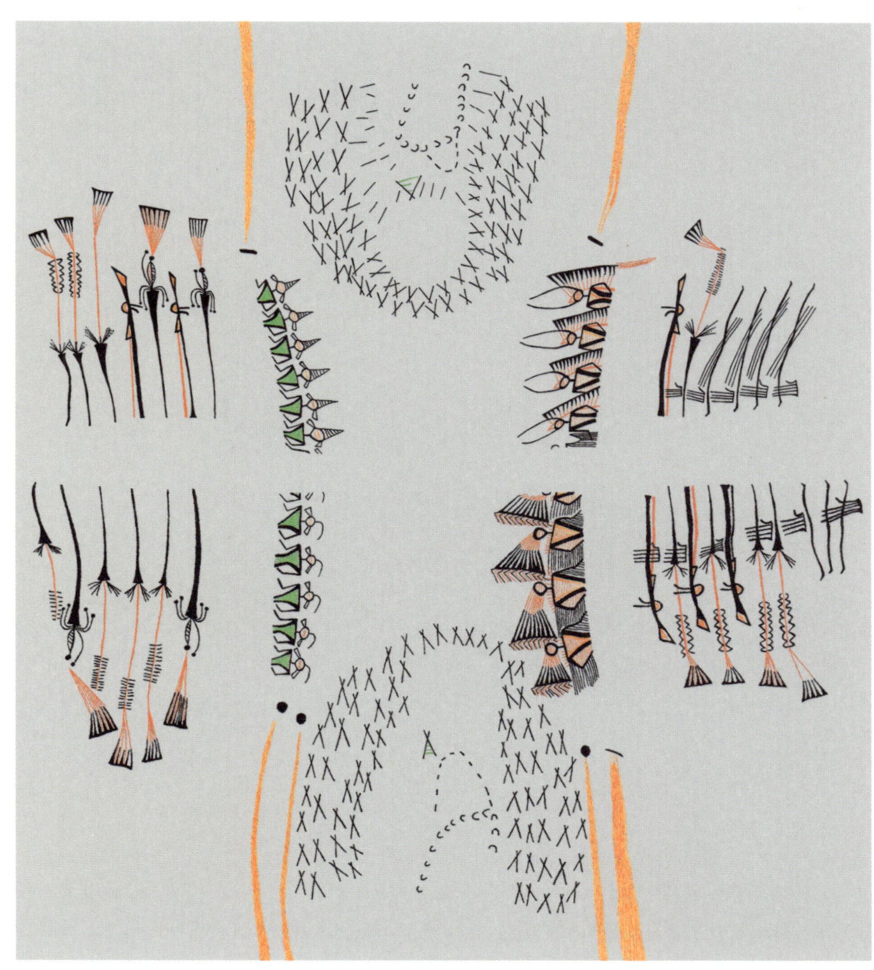

Fig. 6 Redrawing of painted shirt, collected by Josef II Colloredo-Mansfeld on his trip to Wyoming in 1905. Opočno Castle Museum, cat.no. 6915.

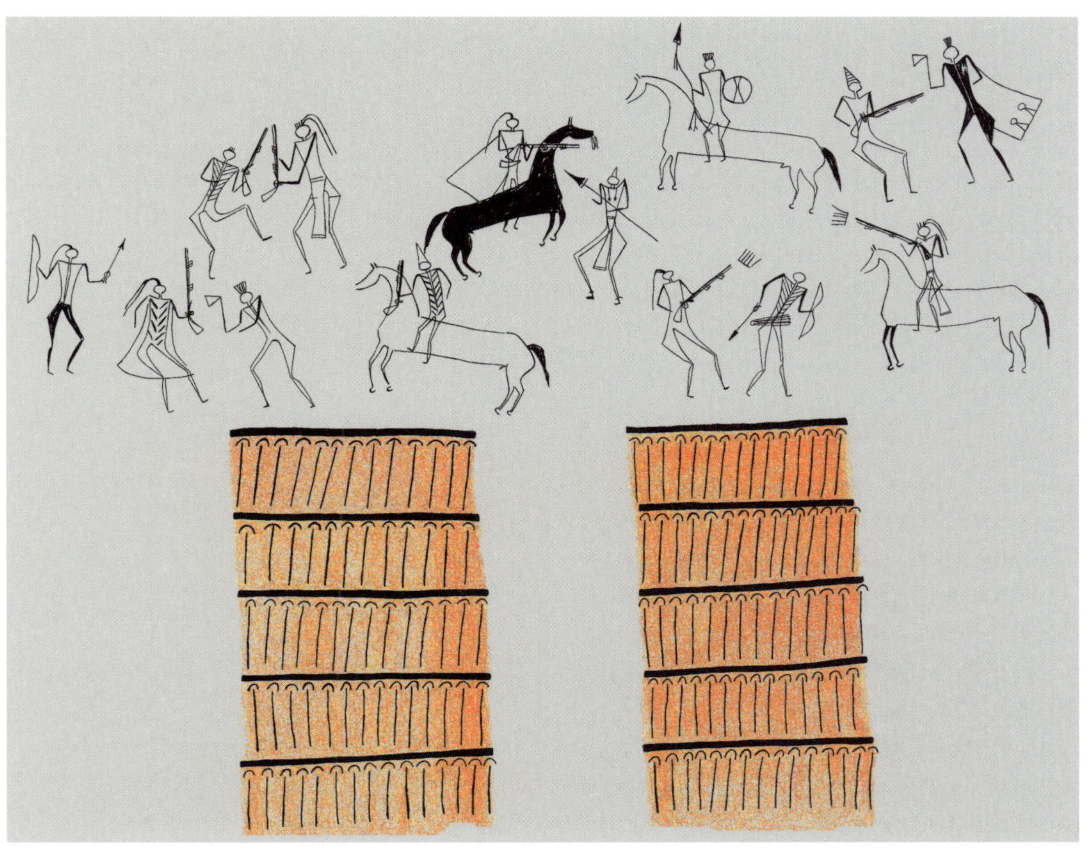

Fig. 7 Redrawing of undocumented painted bison robe. Laura Fisher collection.

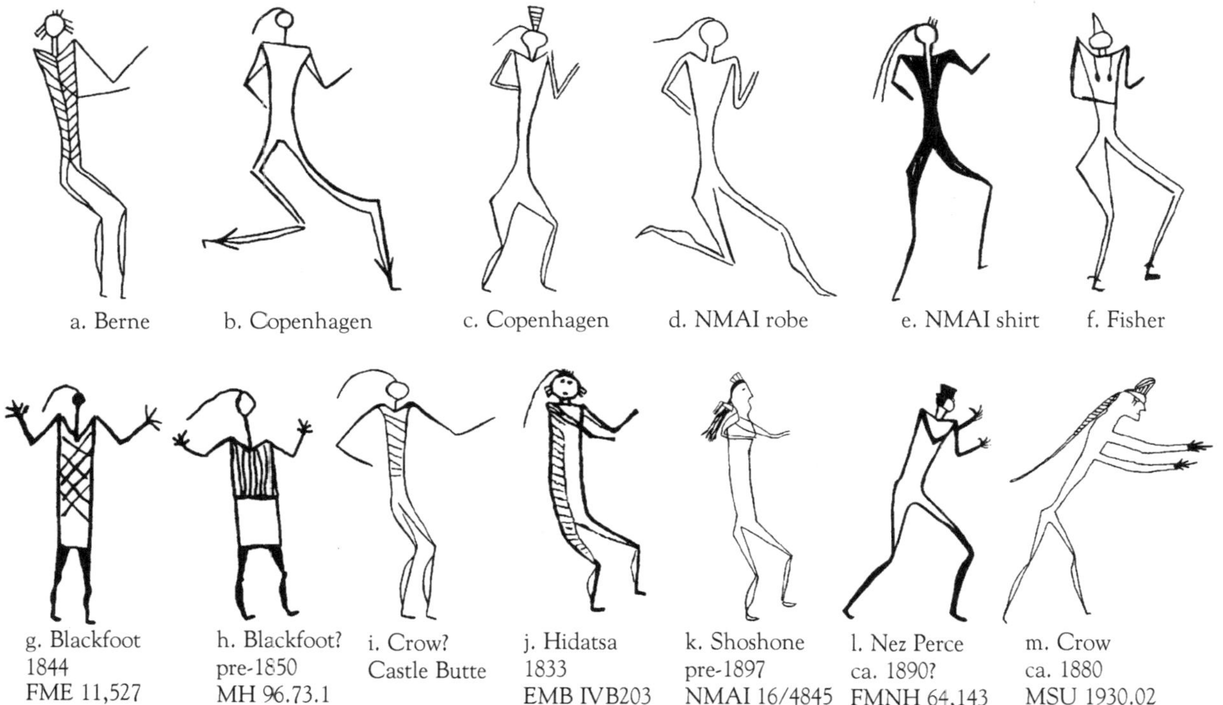

Fig. 8 Human body shapes.[3]

tion rings particularly true with regard to the assured, graceful warriors in the seven paintings (Fig. 8a–f).[4] These unique figures sometimes convey a remarkable sense of movement and at other times stand their ground, arms raised like boxers. They display a number of other distinguishing features including extreme elongation, a strong sense of line alternating between curves and angles, broad shoulders with tapering torso, V-neck shoulder lines, well-defined calf muscles, the absence of hands, and angular hip formations. Apart from those on the seven paintings, V-neck figures are almost exclusively found on painted hides thought to be Blackfoot (Brownstone 1993: 16) and rock-art sites in former Crow and Blackfoot territory (Conner and Conner 1971: 20). However, Blackfoot V-neck figures are comparatively wooden and almost always with arms uplifted and hands outstretched in "postures of epiphany" (Barry 1991: 51; Fig. 8g–h). Of the early pictorials, the warriors on a petroglyph in Crow country (Fig. 8i) and Two Ravens's robe (Fig. 8j) most closely resemble those on the seven paintings. The few comparable human figures painted in the late nineteenth century include a Shoshone figure, a figure on a Nez Perce robe, and a drawing of Medicine Crow (Fig. 8k–m).

Kurz's sketches of war-exploit robes (Fig. 9) have long been recognized as accurately reflecting the style of the paintings under study. Holm (pers. comm., 1996) pointed out the particular similarity between Kurz's figures and those on the Fisher robe. The resemblance is particularly striking between the high-stepping warrior and figures with rifles around the lower border of

3. The following abbreviations will be used for museum collections referred to in the text:

AMNH American Museum of Natural History (New York, NY)
BHM Bernisches Historisches Museum (Berne, Switzerland)
BM British Museum (London, United Kingdom)
CM Carnegie Museum (Pittsburgh, PA)
CMC Canadian Museum of Civilization (Hull, QC)
CMRE Civici Musei Reggio Emilia (Italy)
EMB Ethnologisches Museum, Berlin (Germany)
FME Folkens Museum—etnografiska (Stockholm, Sweden)
FMNH Field Museum of Natural History (Chicago, IL)
JAM Joslyn Art Museum (Omaha, NE)
LACMNH Los Angeles County Museum of Natural History (Los Angeles, CA)
MH Musée de l'Homme (Paris, France)
MMMN Manitoba Museum of Man and Nature (Winnipeg, MB)
MSU Montana State University (Bozeman, MT)
MVF Museum für Völkerkunde, Frankfurt am Main (Germany)
NMD National Museum of Denmark (Copenhagen, Denmark)
NMAI National Museum of the American Indian (Washington, DC)
NMNH National Museum of Natural History (Washington, DC)
PAC Public Archives of Canada (Ottawa, ON)
ROM Royal Ontario Museum (Toronto, ON)
SMA Snite Museum of Art (Notre Dame, IN)

4. Two figures from the Copenhagen robe are illustrated because two artists appear to have executed the painting, working on separate sides of the quill strip.

Kurz's robe (Fig. 9a), and the two warriors locked in combat in the upper left of the Fisher robe (Fig. 7). The fact that many Hidatsa believed European artists caused disease meant that Kurz had to be very circumspect in his sketching activities (1937: 76, 77, 81, 98, 116, *257*). This circumstance, coupled with the technical difficulties in delineating the details of complex war-exploit robes, and further aggravated by severe near-sightedness (Kurz 1937: 80, 163, 181), meant that Kurz probably copied figures from actual robes onto his drawings some time after the initial sittings. His note, "In so much as scenes in my [present] neighborhood have little variation, I am now attempting to perfect my first sketches and therefore am paying especial attention to details" (Kurz 1937: 89), is likely an indication that he added details, such as figures on robes, to earlier sketches. This might explain why his drawing of a robe worn by an Omaha (Fig. 9c) bears such a close resemblance to those on his Hidatsa robes (Fig. 9a–b). Despite these drawbacks, Kurz's sketches are important pieces in the puzzle of the seven paintings.

Linear patterns on human torsos have a limited tribal distribution and tend to appear on hide paintings executed before 1860. Torso designs are found on six of the seven paintings (Fig. 10a–f). For the most part they feature oblique parallel lines, often converging along the vertical axis of the chest. Elsewhere, they appear most

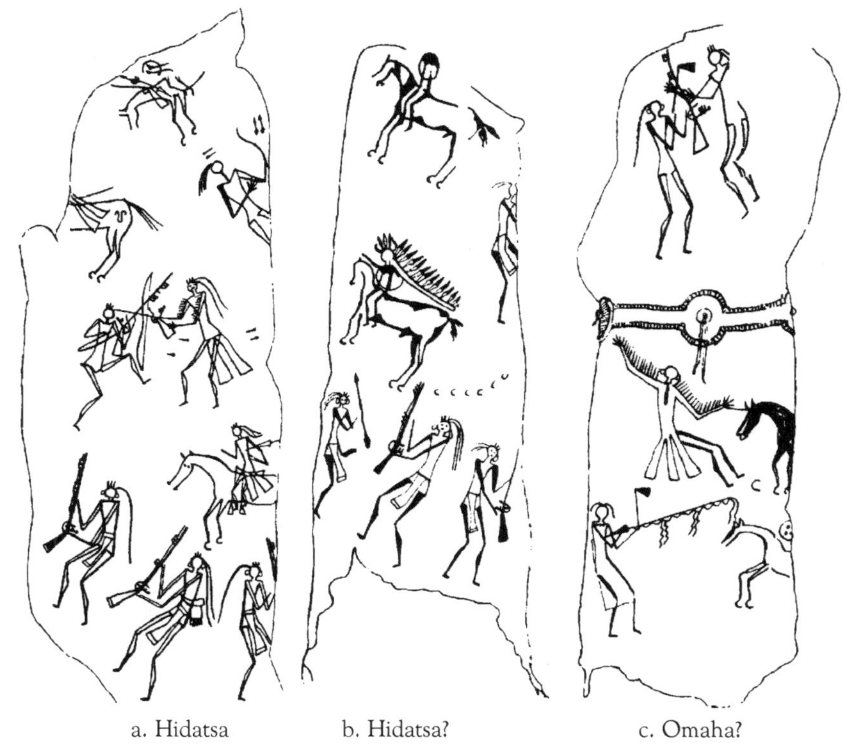

Fig. 9 Painted robes with war exploits, after drawings by Rudolph Friedrich Kurz.
a: [Fort Berthold,] "1. 8. 51." (Kurz 1937: pl. 4, bottom).
b: [Fort Berthold,] "31. 7. 51." (Kläy and Läng 1984: 150).
c: "23. 5. 51. Omahaw" (Kurz 1937: pl. 37, bottom; Kläy and Läng 1984: 149).

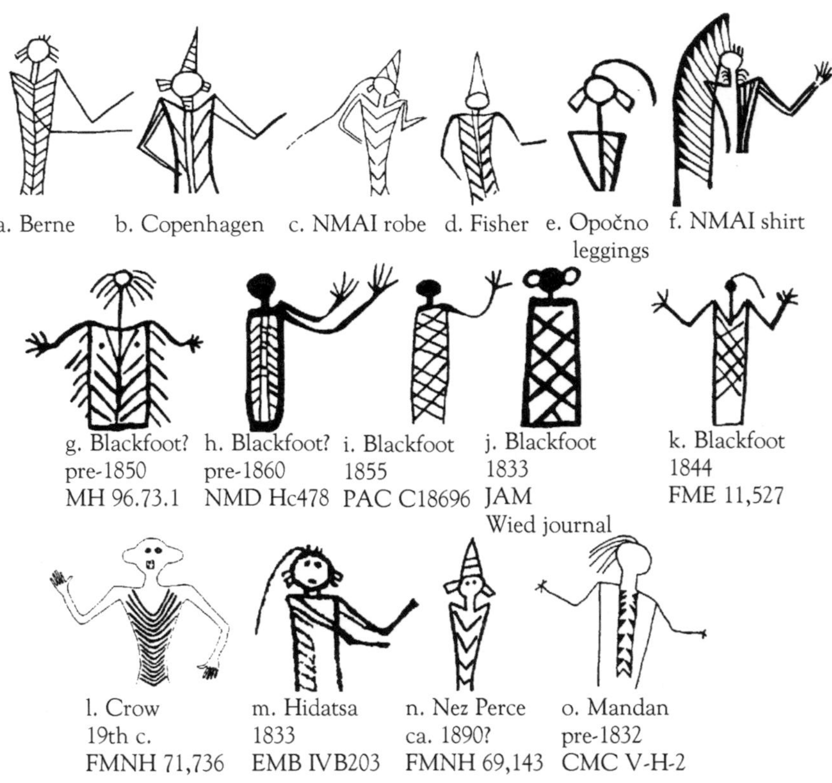

Fig. 10 Torso designs.

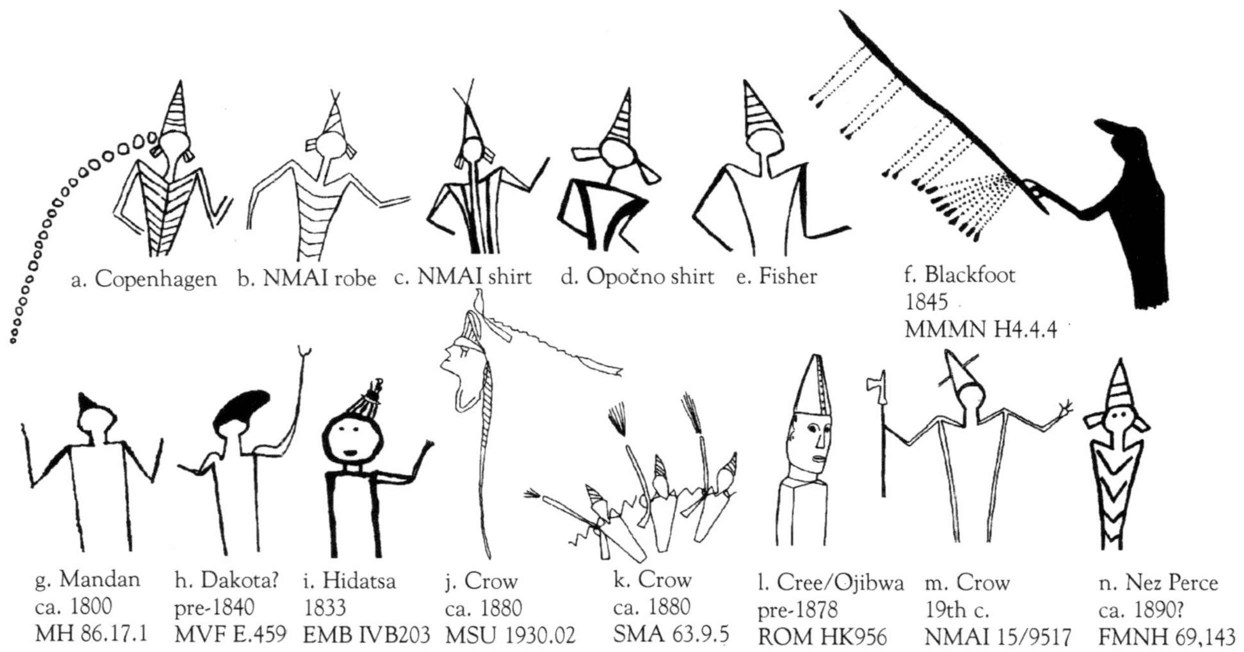

Fig. 11 Cone-shaped features on heads.

frequently on Blackfoot paintings, usually in the form of skewed crosshatching (Fig. 10g–k). Three works by the Crow, Hidatsa, and Nez Perce bear designs like those on the seven paintings (Fig. 10l–n). A few chest patterns, usually suggestive of tattoos, appear on early Mandan and Sioux paintings (Fig. 10o). Like tattoos on the Northern Plains (Light 1972; Kurz 1937: 173) and linear patterns on war shirts, torso designs on the seven paintings most probably signified war honors.

The geometrical cone shapes atop the heads of warriors are a distinctive feature common to five of the seven paintings (Fig. 11a–e). Heads surmounted by roughly conical shapes find fairly broad distribution in pictorials from both the first half of the nineteenth century (Fig. 11f–i) and the latter half (Fig. 11j). However, highly geometrical conical forms are limited to White Swan's warriors (Fig. 11k), a Plains Cree/Ojibway carved elkhorn figure (Fig. 11l),[5] a figure engraved on a Crow mirror frame (Fig. 11m), and torsos on a Nez Perce robe (Fig. 11n).

There are a number of references in the literature to hair coiled into roughly conical forms. John Macdonell (Wood and Thiessen 1985: 90) observed Assiniboines and Crees in the Red River area around 1793 with long hair coiled "like a cable on top of their heads in the form of a mitre." Around 1845 Father De Smet (1905: 590) noted that "the 'toque' among the Blackfeet is a tail, seven or eight feet long, made of horse and buffalo hair, interwoven with their own. But instead of floating behind in the ordinary way, this tail is located upon the party's forehead and stands out spirally, something like a rhinoceros horn."

Catlin's "Indian Gallery" shows an elderly Hidatsa man with hair coiled into a conical form (Truettner 1979: 93). Bodmer depicted a Hidatsa, a Crow, two Atsinas, a Blackfoot, and a Mandan (Goetzman et al. 1984: 356, 16, 239, 320, 237, 248–249; Thomas and Ronnefeldt 1976: 39, 172, 2, 128–129, 132–133) wearing very long hair massed above the forehead. Around 1845 Nicolas Point (1967: 64, 183, 130, 139, 131) painted two men presumed to be Blackfoot, a Crow, four men of unknown origins from the Northern Plains/Intermontane area, and a Gros Ventre—all with hair similarly coiled or bunched up. Kurz (1937: pls. 25, 31, 38, 41) shows three men, apparently Hidatsas, with their hair coiled up, as does Gustav Sohon's 1855

5. This figure has a hole above each ear, indicating that it may once have had projections socketed at the sides of the head. Several birchbark scrolls bear figures with conical "power projections" from the top of the head coupled with side projections, particularly in the shape of horns (Dewdney 1975: 18, 146). The horn figure was found in 1878 buried beside the Yellow Quill Trail in a box made without nails. In 1910 a Cree/Ojibway medicine man offered his opinion that the figure would once have been used by a medicine man (Morris 1985: 147). Drawing by Emil Huston.

depiction of the Peigan Chief White Bull (Nicandri 1986).

It is thus likely that the conical feature in each of the seven paintings depicts long trains of real and artificially added hair coiled or bunched up and tied above the forehead. The way a number of European artists rendered this hairdo strongly suggests that the internal striations in the conical head forms on the seven paintings depict the coiling effect.

Conically shaped hats also deserve consideration. In 1833 Bodmer portrayed the Hidatsa warrior Road-maker wearing a black (felt?) hat with a high crown encircled by a white band and with the brim turned down (Goetzman et al. 1984: 315). There is a similar Cree felt hat in the Glenbow Museum (cat.no. AP 180B), apparently dating to the same period, with two bands of brown and white weasel skins encircling the crown. The collection history states that the hat, together with a brass-studded wool jacket, was worn on the warpath to render bullets and arrows harmless. At the Ft. Laramie Council of 1867, several of the Crow delegation wore high-crowned black felt hats "Calabrian" style, like those of American generals, with a series of multicolored ribbons encircling the crown to its full height (Simonin 1966: 101; see also Campione 1995: 12; Howell 1975: 31). Kurz (1937: pls. 7, 27) portrayed traders Kipp and Culbertson on the Northern Plains in 1851 wearing Calabrese-style hats. The Ethnologisches Museum, Berlin, preserves a toque-like conical cap attributed to the Cree, which dates to about 1850 (cat.no. IVB8607). At least three Plains Crees were photographed wearing pointed caps, of both the European felt and the traditional Native tubular fur type (Silversides 1994: 78, 60, 28). Not long after 1884 Smith (1943: 21) observed that Hunkpapa and Blackfoot Sioux liked to tailor their felt stetsons by pulling them out of shape until they resembled the "pointed headgear of a clown," then scalloped the edges and tied a strip of otter skin around it. Possibly conical caps were popular among the Plains tribes because they could both accommodate and give the appearance of massive hair foretops.

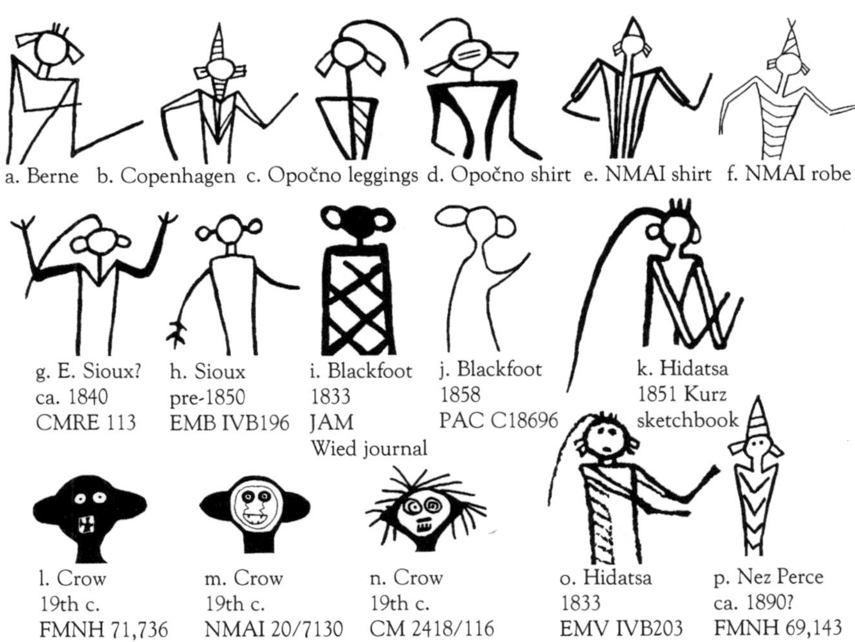

Fig. 12 Rectangular shapes at the sides of heads.

Rectangular shapes at the sides of heads, often in combination with conical foretops, are a distinctive feature of the paintings, with the exception of the Fisher robe (Fig. 12a–f). Bulbous protrusions at the sides of the head are found in other Plains pictorials (Fig. 12g–n).[6] This feature may relate to a practice that Shell Necklace described to Lowie (1922: 228), in which Crows on the warpath gathered and tied up their hair in front of each ear. Two examples display rectangular forms almost identical to those on the seven paintings (Fig. 12o–p). These rectangular shapes could represent the large shell or bead ear drops best described by Denig (1953: 35), but more likely they depict squared-off hair bangs at the sides of the head. This hair style gained considerable popularity on the Northern Plains and Plateau, judging from the pictures of Catlin (Truettner 1979: 180, 190, 194), Bodmer (Thomas and Ronnefeldt 1976: 189, 218, 222), and Kurz (1937: pls. 1, 27, 31).

The detached hand, characterized by outstretched rake-like fingers and curved-back hitchhiker-thumb, is a distinctive element in five of the seven works (Fig. 13a–f). This motif serves as a narrative device, indicat-

6. Bulbous forms at the sides of heads occur with considerable frequency on Midewewin scrolls (Dewdney 1975).

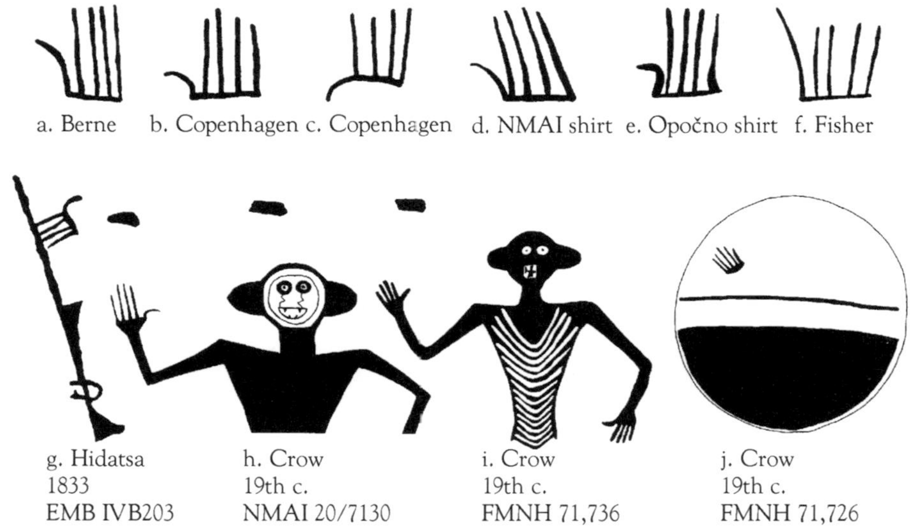

Fig. 13 Detached hands.

ing the capture of goods from the enemy. The hands on three Crow shields are similar in form only (Fig. 13h–j), while the detached hand on Two Ravens's robe (Fig. 13g), which is preceded by three footprints and is about to grasp a gun, is comparable in both form and function. Outside of these works only the Blackfoot, attested to by some twenty of their hide paintings, characteristically used a detached hand to denote the capture of objects (Brownstone 1993: 19). However, their form is unlike that of the hand motif in the seven paintings.

To my knowledge, the Field Museum Nez Perce robe (Fig. 14), together with the Fisher and Berne robes, are the only surviving examples in which the composition is split in half, isolating action scenes and tallies in separate registers.[7] Bearing in mind his tendency to overgeneralize in his illustrations of Indian pictorial paintings, Catlin (1959: frontispiece, 129, 132, 142) illustrated six split-composition robes, three of which he attributed to the Crow, two to the Blackfoot, and one to the Apache. Kurz (1937: pl. 12) illustrated one split-composition robe, apparently worn by a Hidatsa.

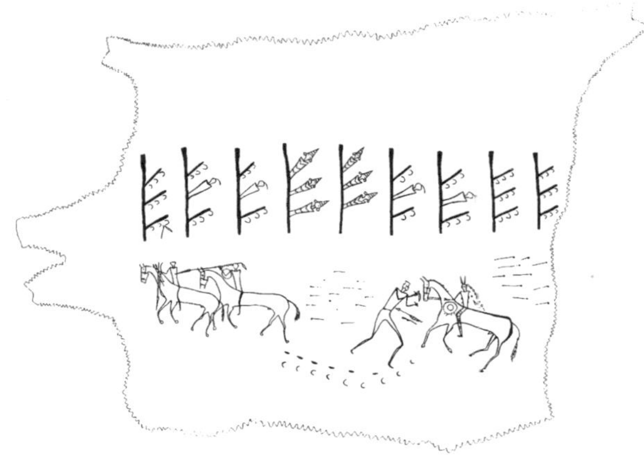

Fig. 14 Design on painted robe, Nez Perce, ca. 1890? Field Museum of Natural History (Chicago, IL), cat.no. 69,143.

The tallies or "honor charts" on the seven painted hides are of two types, termed here bar tallies and object tallies. Bar tallies are found on the Berne and Fisher robes and the Opočno leggings (Fig. 15a–c). They are characterized by rows of pin-and-cup motifs and conventionalized human torsos aligned at about ninety degrees to black or red bars. There are a limited number of bar tallies comparable to the seven paintings. Most impressive is the entire buffalo hide devoted to the honor chart of "donated treasures, through which Yellow Bear had become an honorable man" (Fig. 15d) (Peter Bolz, pers. comm., 1996). Bodmer portrayed Mato Tope with a partly visible bar tally on the left chest area of his shirt (Fig. 15e). A shirt collected by Lt. G. K. Warren bears a similar tally on the right chest area (Fig. 15f). Rudolph Kurz made a thumbnail sketch of a bar tally (Fig. 15g), and the Field Museum robe bears one as well (Fig. 15h). Gilbert Wilson collected a Mandan dress worn by Beaver and bearing a tally commemorating the war deeds of her husband, Red White Buffalo (Fig. 15i). Beaver explained that each bar plus associated pin-and-cup

7. Of all the surviving Plains Indian pictorials, the Field Museum robe is in many respects the most similar to the seven paintings. It was purchased in 1890 from Abraham Brooks, a Nez Perce scout for the U.S. Cavalry, who claimed that it had belonged to Chief Joseph. In a letter to the museum, Theodore Stern (January 1976) noted the unlikelihood that the exploits on the robe were those of the famous chief and suggested that it may even have been Brooks who painted the robe. The nature of the pigments, the scale of the figures, and the blanket-strip design suggest that it was painted around the time of acquisition, perhaps in imitation of or a throwback to earlier paintings of the type presently under study.

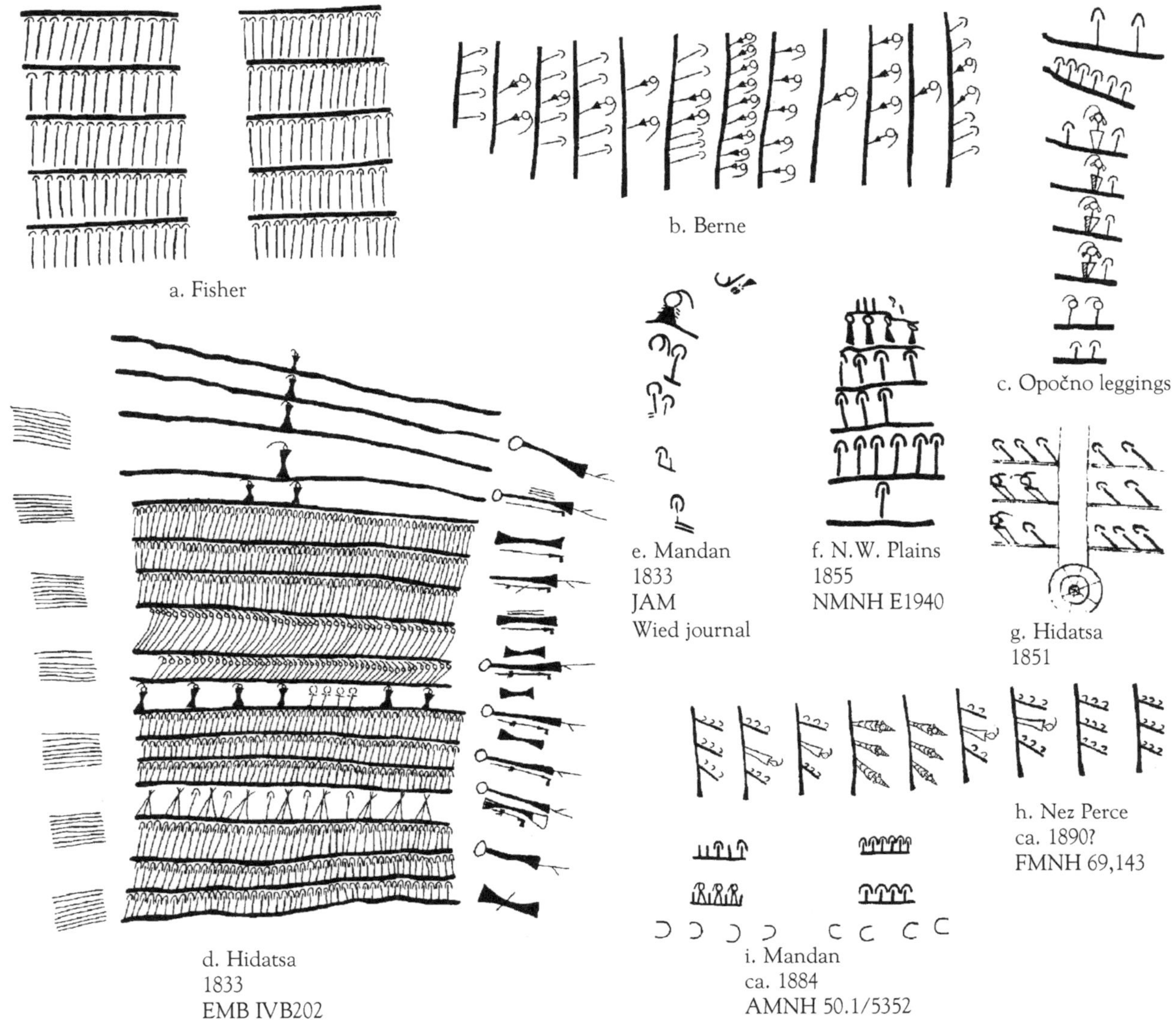

Fig. 15 Bar and object tallies.

motifs stood for a successful horse raid led by Red White Buffalo. The bar with human torsos denoted a war party led by Red White Buffalo that killed Sioux.[8] Not illustrated here are six pictures by Catlin that approximate human torso bar tallies, four of which he attributed to the Mandan.

On the seven paintings, object tallies of goods captured and perhaps given away fall into two categories: repeated guns and assorted weapons. The Opočno shirt bears a tally of the latter type, comprising rows of various weapons aligned to both sides of the sleeve strips (Fig. 16a). Similar tallies are found on a Hidatsa robe drawn by Kurz, a Crow or Nez Perce robe in the Los Angeles Museum, and a petroglyph at the Nordstrom Bowen site in Crow country (Fig. 16b–d). The

8. Taylor (1994: 183) noted that the Opočno leggings and Berne robe are likely Crow and that the pin-and-cup motif probably represented the capturing of picketed horses. In contrast, Lowie (1912: 231) noted that, according to Yellow-brow, the Crow had no special symbol for recording the cutting of a picketed horse. However, there can be no doubt that the Crow gave special recognition for "cutting the halter" (Lowie 1922: 253; Medicine Crow 1992: 45; Nabokov 1967: 34). Chief Big Moon's war exploits displayed on Panel no. 3 in the Glacier Park Hotel contained three pin-and-cup forms which, according to the explanatory label, represent sixty horses stolen (McAdams 1919: 1). In form the pin-and-cup symbol is similar to the arc and zigzag frequently used by the Blackfoot to denote a scouting mission (Brownstone 1993: 20). Wilson (1916, 22: 362) reported a Hidatsa hide scraper decorated with bored holes configured like the pin-and-cup motif. It represents a scouting mission; the number of dots in the arc stood for the number in the war party, and those forming the "pin" indicated whether he was first, second, etc., in sighting the enemy. The Hidatsa also marked scouting missions with straight bars and parallel rows of dashes (Gilman and Schneider 1987: 104), as did the Mandan (Gilbert Wilson notes for AMNH cat. no. 50.2/5352).

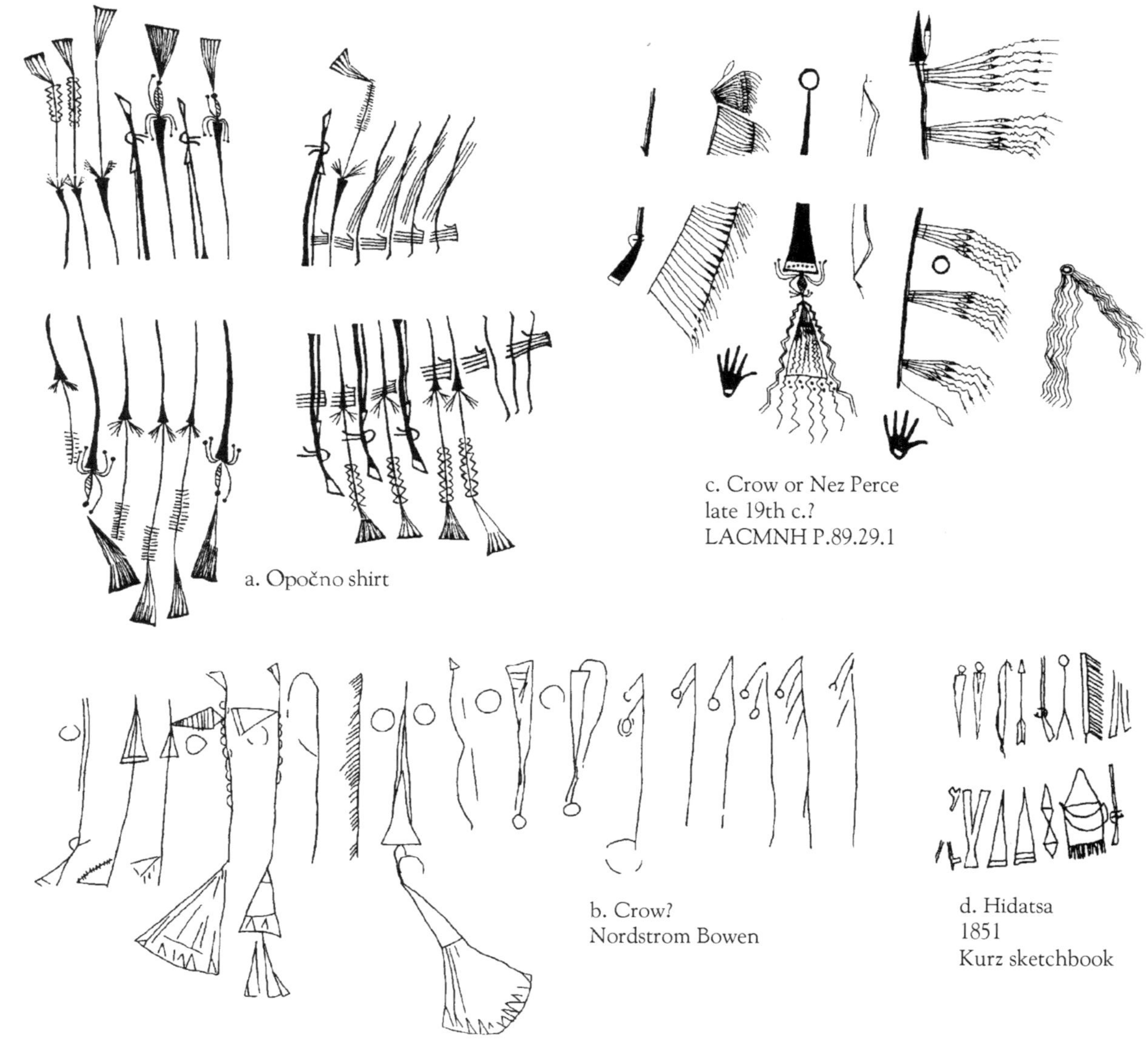

a. Opočno shirt

c. Crow or Nez Perce
late 19th c.?
LACMNH P.89.29.1

b. Crow?
Nordstrom Bowen

d. Hidatsa
1851
Kurz sketchbook

Fig. 16 Tallies: guns and other weapons.

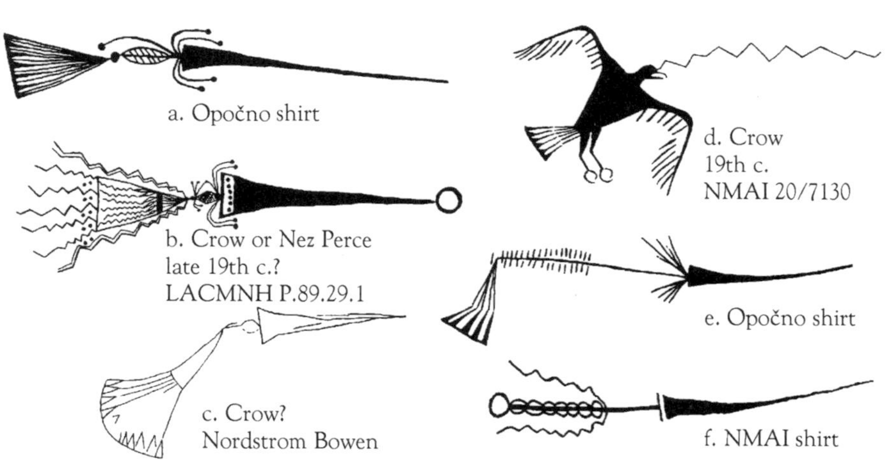

Fig. 17 Tallies: swords.

remaining comparable examples, not shown here, comprise five hide paintings devoted solely to object tallies and numerous war-exploit narrative paintings containing discrete object-tally subsections—all apparently executed by the Blackfoot (Brownstone 1993: 17).

Of particular note are the sword-like items on the Opočno shirt object tally (Fig. 17a). Comparable images are found on the Los Angeles

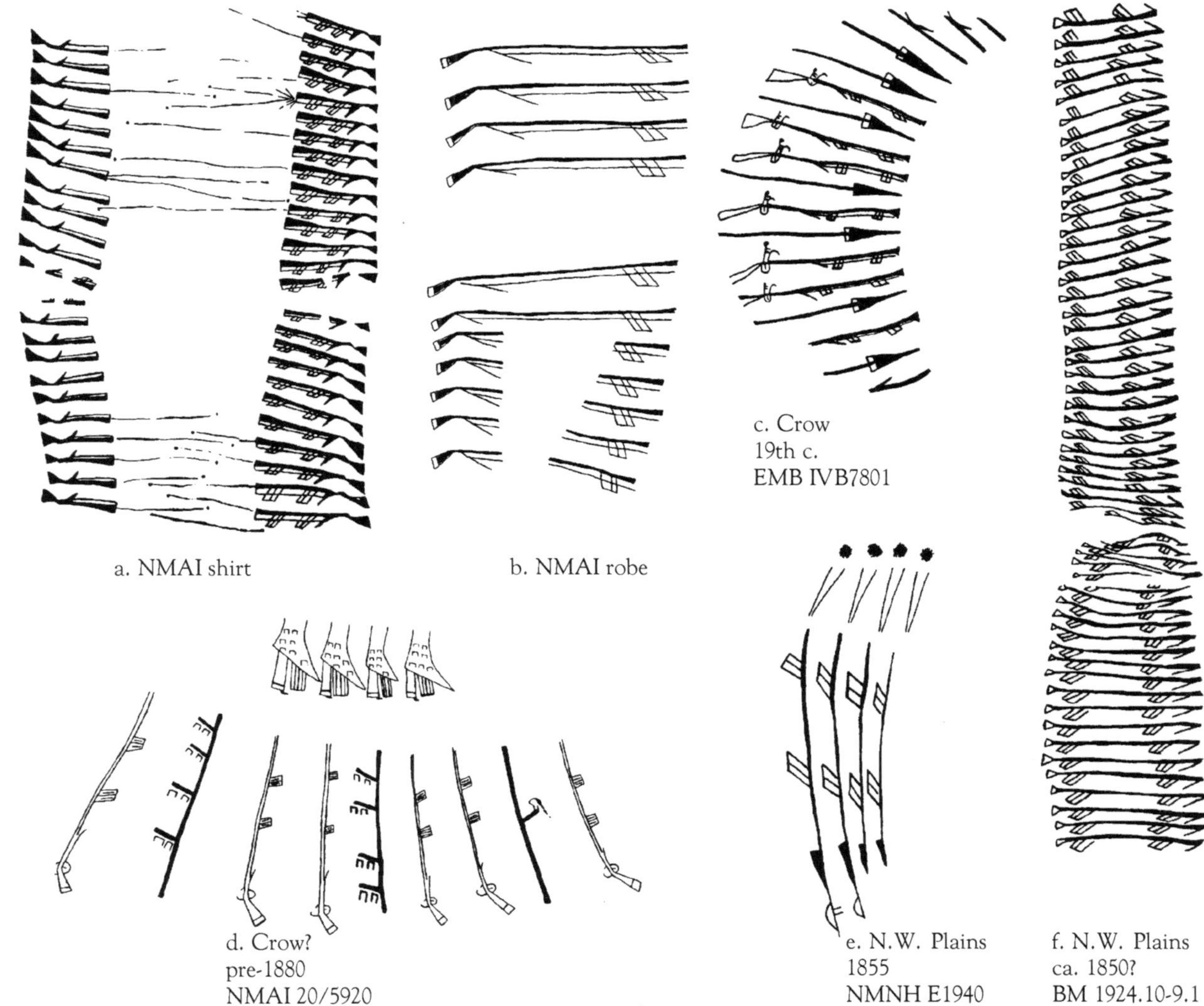

Fig. 18 Tallies: guns and lances.

robe[9] and the Nordstrom Bowen petroglyph (Fig. 17b–c). This object is composed of three segments: a triangle with internal markings at one end, an elongated triangular blade at the other end, and a sword-hilt-like configuration in between. The triangular flap-like section is also found on the Opočno lances. The internal markings in corresponding sections of the Nordstrom Bowen and Los Angeles examples, coupled with the manner of depicting feathers on the tail of the bird on a Crow shield (Fig. 17d), suggest that the triangular section represents a feather attachment. The hilt section, with its configuration of free quillons, is highly suggestive of rapiers made at least a century before the painting of the shirt.[10] The blade of this "sword" resembles the extra long spear points on the Opočno and NMAI shirts (Fig. 17e–f). Both spear points and "sword" blade points appear to be about the same size as the metal "Assiniboine" lance heads reported to have been several feet long.[11] Perhaps the hilt of the

9. The circles at the tip of the "sword" and beside the lance on the Los Angeles robe, as well as those on the Nordstrom Bowen tally, appear to be incidental to rather than a part of the adjacent objects. There is another seemingly "dissociated" circle on the flank of the horse on the upper left of the Copenhagen robe.

10. I am grateful to Bill Holm and to Cory Keeble, curator of the European arms and armor collection of the Royal Ontario Museum, for enumerating the sword-like attributes of the object in question.

11. The interpreters at the Fort Union National Historic Site termed the metal "lances, some up to three feet long" listed in Wood and Thiessen's (1985: 322) summary of goods traded on the upper Missouri around 1800, "Assiniboine" lance heads. There are several accounts indicating the presence of European swords among Northern Plains Indians. Fidler (MacGregor 1998: 82–83) observed that in 1793 the Bloods and Snakes attacked the Mountain Crow, capturing "2 guns (Spanish), 20 swords, ..." Schultz and Donaldson (1930: 2) noted that as late as the 1870s the Peigans had in their possession a Toledo blade, a shirt of mail, and a lance—all assumed to have been raided from the Spanish in the Southwest at a much earlier date.

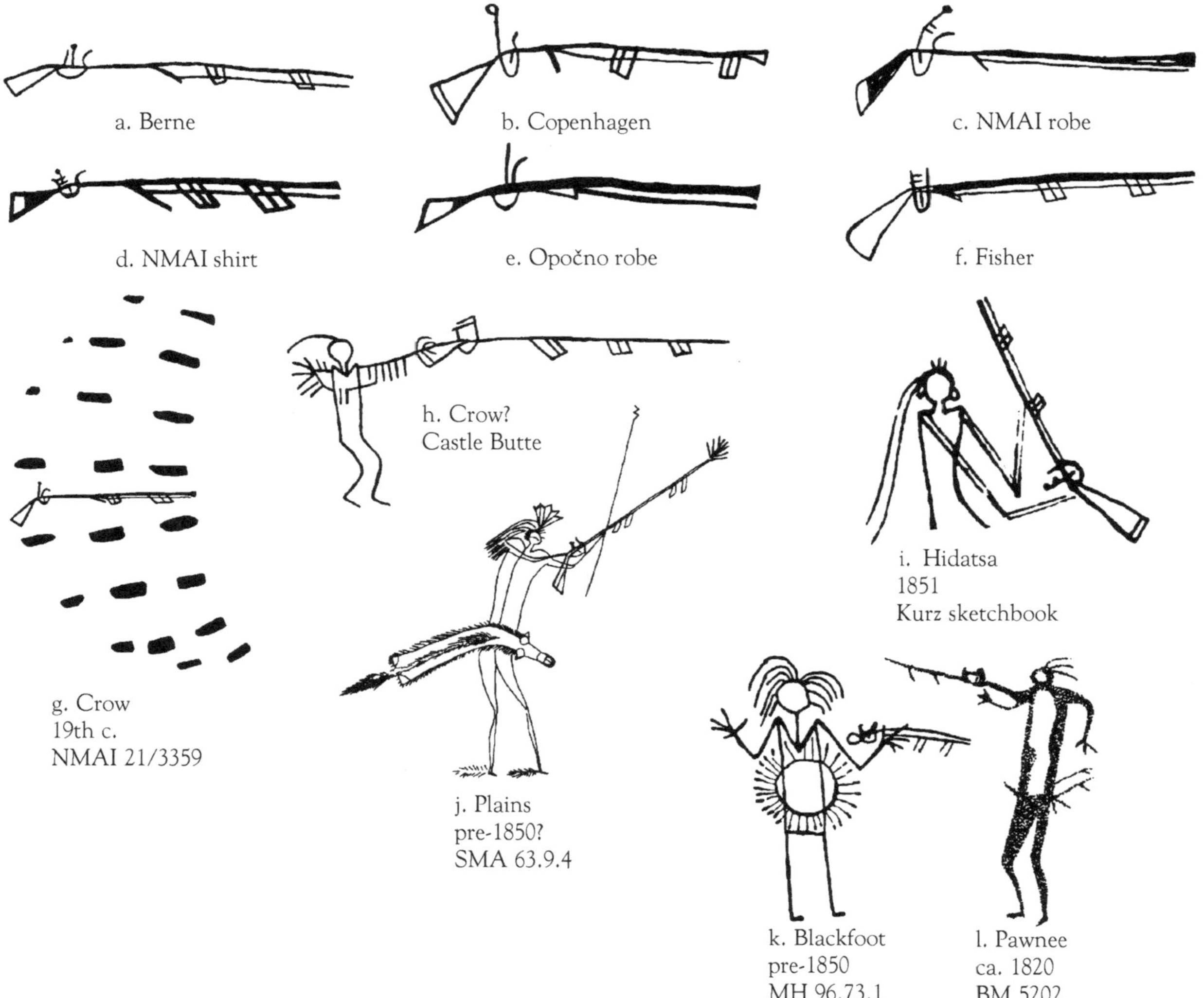

Fig. 19 Guns.

sword-like object was attached to such a spear point. This combination is not unlikely considering the practice of mounting straight sword blades onto lance shafts (Austerman 1990: 12–13) and sheathing sabers in "lance cases" (Galante 1980: 67–68).

Tallies featuring rows of guns in the seven paintings are found on the shirt and robe in the NMAI (Fig. 18a–b). Apart from these, a shield in the Berlin Museum bears a row of alternating guns and spears (Fig. 18c). Another robe in the NMAI displays a row of guns and bar tallies (Fig. 18d). Although it is undocumented, the figures wearing distinctive ceremonial regalia in the upper register are identical to a well-documented Crow drawing collected by Edwin Denig (Lessard 1984: 66). The shirt collected by Lt. Warren in 1855 has a row of guns, incompletely visible on the left chest area, opposite the pin-and-cup tally noted earlier (Fig. 18e). An undocumented shirt in the British Museum bears a long continuous row of guns aligned to the quill strip falling over the left shoulder (Fig. 18f).

Guns in the seven paintings exhibit the following distinctive features: flared barrel openings, oversized ramrods often painted red, and exaggerated rectangular shapes representing ramrod rings (Fig. 19a–f). Comparable guns are found on a Crow shield (Fig. 19g), a petroglyph in Crow country (Fig. 19h), and in Kurz's Hidatsa robes (Fig. 19i). Not illustrated here are four Crow examples that display guns of this type: a drawing executed around 1885 entitled "Crow Indians Hunting Bison" collected by Denig; a shield in the Field Museum (cat.no. 71,755); a drawing by Yellow Horse, held by the Foundation for the Preservation of

American Indian Art and Culture; and a shirt that belonged to Two Leggings (Powell 1988: 19). Catlin illustrated about thirteen hide paintings containing guns which approximate the ramrod-ring feature. He identified seven paintings as Crow, while assigning a different tribe to each of the remaining six. Several Shoshone hide paintings, apparently executed by Chief Washakie, contain guns exhibiting this feature. The practice of hanging bits of red cloth from the ramrod rings appears to be represented on several early undocumented robes and a Pawnee shield (Fig. 19j–l).[12] However, the shapes depending from the barrels differ from those on the seven paintings in that they lack the regularity and internal lines suggestive of the shape and striations of actual ramrod rings.

Having compared a number of distinctive characteristics of the seven paintings with similar features in other Plains Indian pictorials, it now remains to synthesize the data. The visual traits under discussion tend to have two aspects, one relating to form and the other to content. Massive foretops, for example, were both popular and had similar meaning to numerous tribes of the Plains. De Smet (1905: 590) noted that for the Blackfoot, the more massive the foretop, the greater was the bravery and distinction of its bearer. Kurz (1937: 88, 252; see also Wilson 1916: 129) observed that among the Hidatsa and Crow only those accredited with coups could attach false hair to there own, "coiled in a knot above the brow." Thus hair massed above the forehead was adopted by a broad community as a sign of success in warfare. However, only a few tribes graphically expressed this feature in a refined conical form.

Ramrods and ramrod rings also had a special meaning to many Plains tribes. For example, Hall (1926: 33) noted that on a war-exploit robe believed to be Teton, the lower edge of the victor's gun barrel, representing the ramrod, was painted red. Cree (Macdonnell 1985: 90) and Lakota warriors (Wied 1839–1841, 1: 359; 1906, 22: 326) used to tie pieces of wooden ramrods into their hair. Wied (1839–1841, 1: 442, 2: 202; 1906, 22: 389, 23: 357) observed in 1833 that the Assiniboine, Mandan, and Hidatsa liked to hang bits of red cloth from the ramrod rings. Many tribes associated the gun with thunder. Perhaps they also likened the glint of brass ramrod rings to lightning which flashed from the eyes of the Thunderbird. In this context it is likely that both graphic stylization and decorating with red cloth were but different ways of symbolizing a common mythological theme.[13] Again it appears that the distribution of a given form is more limited than that of its underlying content or meaning.

In addition to this quantitative aspect, there may be a qualitative dimension to the distribution of form and content. For example, the representation of captured goods by means of the object tally and detached-hand conventions appeared almost exclusively on works of the Blackfoot and the seven paintings examined here. Since the Blackfoot had no allies among the candidates presently under consideration, the artists of the seven paintings were probably their enemies. The paintings of these competing cultures are similar in terms of content but, as we saw earlier, they depart with regard to form. Similarly, the torso patterns on the seven paintings and works of the Blackfoot probably had a common meaning but differ stylistically. On the other hand, in strongly allied cultures—Crow, Hidatsa, Mandan, and Nez Perce—there is a marked convergence of formal features. The Crow were at the center of these tribes. They maintained a constant cycle of raiding and warfare with their Blackfoot neighbors to the north, and both tribes were renowned for their skill in capturing goods (Lowie 1922: 403; Wilson 1958: 2; Bonner 1965: 197; Lowie 1912: 230; Marquis 1928: 174–175; Morgan 1959: 191). The Hidatsa and the Awatixa to the east were the ancestral people of the Crow, and in many respects they remained as one tribe. At the same time, the Hidatsa and Crow have a long history of cohabitation and military cooperation with the Mandan. For much of the nineteenth century the Crow acted as middlemen in trade between the Nez Perce and Shoshone to the west and the Upper Missouri villages of the Mandan and Hidatsa. These associations clearly suggest that Crow artists executed the seven paintings. The conception of form in pictorial art as it relates to cultural identity observed by Kurz and Feder reminds us of two important additional considerations: The seven paintings preserve a marked stylistic integrity suggesting they were painted by one people, and the formal conventions typifying these works occur with greatest frequency in images of the Crow.

12. Adapted from David Williams's unpublished tracing of the Pawnee shield cover.

13. Bill Holm (pers. comm., 1998) suggested that cloth may also have been inserted in the rings to anchor the ramrod, as well as to add decoration.

References Cited

Austerman, Wayne R.

1990 Long Steel in the Buffalo Grass: The Sabre and the Plains Indian. *Man at Arms* 12(6): 11–19.

Barry, Patricia S.

1991 *Mystical Themes in Milk River Rock Art*. Edmonton, AB: University of Alberta Press.

Bonner, I. D.

1965 *The Life and Adventures of James P. Beckwourth, Mountaineer, Scout, Pioneer and Chief of the Crow Nation of Indians*. Minneapolis, MN: Ross and Haines.

Brownstone, Arni

1993 *War Paint: Blackfoot and Sarcee Painted Buffalo Robes in the Royal Ontario Museum*. Toronto, ON: Royal Ontario Museum.

Bushnell, David I.

1908 Ethnological Material from North America in Swiss Collections. *American Anthropologist* 10(1): 1–15.

Campione, Adele

1995 *Men's Hats*. San Francisco, CA: Chronicle Books.

Catlin, George

1959 *Episodes from Life Among the Indians and Last Rambles*. Marvin C. Ross, ed. Norman, OK: University of Oklahoma Press.

Conner, Stuart W. and Betty Lu Conner

1971 *Rock Art of the High Montana Plains*. Santa Barbara, CA: University of California.

Denig, Edwin Thompson

1953 *Of the Crow Nation*. Bureau of American Ethnology, Bulletin 151, Anthropological Papers 33. Washington, DC.

De Smet, Father Pierre-Jean

1905 *Life, Letters and Travels of Father De Smet, 1801-1873*. 4 vols. H. M. Chittenden and A. T. Richardson, eds. New York, NY: Harper. (Reprint: New York, NY 1969: Kraus.)

Dewdney, Selwyn

1975 *The Sacred Scrolls of the Southern Ojibway*. Toronto, ON: University of Toronto Press.

Ewers, John C.

1982 Artists' Choice. *American Indian Art Magazine* 7(2): 40–49.

Feder, Norman

1967 *North American Indian Painting*. New York, NY: The Museum of Primitive Art.

1980 Crow Blanket Strip Rosettes. *American Indian Art Magazine* 6(1): 40–45, 88.

Galante, Gary

1980 Crow Lance Cases or Sword Scabbards. *American Indian Art Magazine* 6(1): 64–73.

1984 East Meets West: Some Observations on the Crow as a Nexus of Plateau/Upper Missouri River Art. In: F. Dennis Lessard (ed.), *Crow Indian Art* (Mission, SD: Chandler Institute), 49–60.

Gilman, Carolyn and Mary Jane Schneider

1987 *The Way to Independence*. St. Paul, MN: Minnesota Historical Society Press.

Goetzman, William et al.

1984 *Karl Bodmer's America*. [Omaha, NE—Lincoln, NE:] Joslyn Art Museum and University of Nebraska Press.

Hall, H. U.

1926 A Buffalo Robe Biography. *The Museum Journal* 17(1): 5–37.

Holm, Bill

1987 The Quill-Wrapped Horsehair Shirt. In: *Annual Plains Indian Seminar* (Cody, WY: Buffalo Bill Historical Center).

1992 Four Bears' Shirt. Some Problems with the Smithsonian Catlin Collection. In: *Artifacts/Artifakes: The Proceedings of the 1984 Plains Indian Seminar* (Cody, WY: Buffalo Bill Historical Center), 43–60.

Howell, Edgar M.

1975 *United States Army Headgear 1855–1902*. Catalog of United States Army Uniforms in the Collections of the Smithsonian Institution, vol. 2. Smithsonian Studies in History and Technology 30. Washington, DC.

Kläy, Ernst J. and Hans Läng

1984 *Das romantische Leben der Indianer malerisch darzustellen ... Leben und Werk von Rudolf Friedrich Kurz (1818–1871)*. Solothurn: Aare.

Kurz, Rudolph Friedrich

1937 *Journal of Rudolph Friederich Kurz: An Account of His Experiences among Fur Traders and American Indians on the Mississippi and Upper Missouri Rivers During the Years 1846 to 1852*. J. N. B. Hewitt, ed. Bureau of American Ethnology, Bulletin 115. Washington, DC.

Lessard, F. Dennis

1984 Classic Crow Beadwork: Upper Missouri Roots. In: F. Dennis Lessard (ed.), *Crow Indian Art* (Mission, SD: Chandler Institute), 61–68.

Light, Douglas W.

1972 *Tattooing Practices of the Cree Indians*. Glenbow-Calgary Institute, Occasional Paper 6. Calgary, AB.

Lowie, Robert H

1912 *Social Life of the Crow Indians*. Anthropological Papers of the American Museum of Natural History 9(2). New York, NY.

1922 *The Material Culture of the Crow Indians*. Anthropological Papers of the American Museum of Natural History 21(3). New York, NY.

McAdams, Clark

1919 Picture Stories of the Blackfeet Indians. *Wild Life* 3(2): 1–5, 11.

Macdonnell, John

1985 The Red River. In Wood and Thiessen 1985: 77–92.

MacGregor, J. G.

1998 *Peter Fiddler: Canada's Forgotten Explorer 1769–1822*. Calgary, AB: Fifth House.

Marquis, Thomas B.

1928 (ed.) *Memoirs of a White Crow Indian (Thomas H. Leforge)*. New York, NY: Century.

Medicine Crow, Joe

1992 *From the Heart of Crow Country: The Crow Indians' Own Stories*. New York, NY: Orion Books.

Moffat, Elizabeth A., P. Jane Sirois, and Judi Miller
1997 Analysis of the Paints Used to Decorate Northern Plains Hide Artifacts during the Nineteenth and Early Twentieth Centuries. *Journal of the Canadian Association for Conservation* 22: 39–52.
Morgan, Lewis H.
1959 *The Indian Journals, 1859-62*. Ann Arbor, MI: The University of Michigan Press.
Morris, Edmund Montague
1985 *The Diaries of Edmund Montague Morris: Western Journeys 1907–1910*. Toronto, ON: Royal Ontario Museum.
Nabokov, Peter
1967 *Two Leggings: The Making of a Crow Warrior*. New York, NY: Thomas Y. Crowell.
Nicandri, David L.
1986 *Northwest Chiefs: Gustav Sohon's View of the 1855 Stevens Treaty Councils*. Tacoma, WA: Washington State Historical Society.
Point, Nicolas
1967 *Wilderness Kingdom: Indian Life in the Rocky Mountains: 1840–1847: The Journals and Paintings of Nicolas Point, S.J.* J. P. Donnelly, trsl. J. C. Ewers, ed. New York, NY: Holt, Rinehart and Winston.
Powell, Peter J.
1988 (ed.) *To Honor the Crow People: Crow Indian Art from The Goelet and Edith Gallatin Collection of American Indian Art*. Chicago, IL: Federation for the Preservation of American Indian Art and Culture.
Schultz, James Willard and Jessie Louise Donaldson
1930 *The Sun God's Children*. Cambridge, MA: The Riverside Press.
Silversides, Brock V.
1994 *The Face Pullers: Photographing Canadian Natives 1871–1939*. Saskatoon, SK: Fifth House.
Simonin, Louis L.
1966 *The Rocky Mountain West in 1867*. Wilson O. Clough, trsl. Lincoln, NE: University of Nebraska Press.
Smith, DeCost
1943 *Indian Experiences*. Caldwell, ID: Caxton Printers.
Taylor, Colin F.
1962 Early Plains Indian Quill Techniques in European Museum Collections. *Plains Anthropologist* 7(15): 58–69.
1981 Costume Decoration With Quill-Wrapped Hair: Nez Perce or Crow. *American Indian Art Magazine* 6(3): 42–53.
1987 Early Nineteenth Century Crow Warrior Costume. *Jahrbuch des Museums für Völkerkunde zu Leipzig* 37: 301–319.
1994 *The Plains Indians: A Cultural and Historical View of the North American Plains Tribes in the Pre-Reservation Period*. London: Salamander Books.
Thomas, Davis and Karin Ronnefeldt
1976 (eds.) *People of the First Man*. New York, NY: E. P. Dutton & Co., Inc.
Truettner, William H.
1979 *The Natural Man Observed: A Study of Catlin's Indian Gallery*. Washington, DC: Smithsonian Institution Press.
Vatter, Ernst
1927 Historienmalerei und heraldische Bilderschrift der nordamerikanischen Präriestämme: Beiträge zu einer ethnographischen und stilistischen Analyse. *Ipek* 1927: 46–81.
Wied, Maximilian Prince of
1839–1841 *Reise in das innere Nord-America in den Jahren 1832–34*. 2 vols and atlas. Koblenz: J. Hoelscher.
1906 *Travels in the Interior of North America*. In: Reuben Gold Thwaites (ed.), *Early Western Travels 1743–1846* (Cleveland, OH: The Arthur H. Clark Company), vols. 22–24.
Wilson, Gilbert Livingstone
1916 Papers. Minnesota Historical Society, Division of Archives and Manuscripts, St. Paul, MN.
Wilson, R. N.
1958 Red Crow and Bad Head Winter Counts. Phillip H. Godsell, ed. Unpublished manuscript, Glenbow Archives, Calgary, AB.
Wood, W. Raymond and Thomas D. Thiessen
1985 (eds.) *Early Fur Trade on the Northern Plains*. Norman, OK: University of Oklahoma Press.

The Cosmic Turtle

A Unique Representation of Cheyenne Cosmological Beliefs

Imre Nagy

This paper will introduce and analyze a remarkable material document of Cheyenne culture, which illustrates cosmological and theological concepts recorded previously only in fragmentary form.

Albert S. Gatschet, ethnologist of the Bureau of American Ethnology, collected thirteen ethnological objects in Oklahoma for the World's Columbian Exposition in 1893. All of these pieces were obtained among the Southern Cheyenne, on the North Canadian River, but none of them was described at the time, nor provided with accession information. They are now preserved in the collection of the National Museum of Natural History, Smithsonian Institution, Washington, DC.

Among these we find a painted cowhide (Fig. 1), the design of which presents a number of questions and puzzles. Although the painting contains numerous figural elements, their combination with "abstract" motifs seems unique, and the import of the composition is not apparent at first glance. The painting is applied to the flesh side of the brain-tanned hide in bright, almost unfaded colors. The broad color palette indicates that commercial paints were employed.

Although less carefully executed than the central design, the geometric border reminds us of a number of other examples with similar painted decorations. These motifs are composed of parallel lines—generally in a sequence of white-*blue*-white-*red*-white-*blue*-white—and are further embellished with diamond-shaped "feather" motifs and triangles of different sizes and proportions. One such painted robe is preserved in the collection of the National Museum of Natural History (Fig. 2). This example is exceptional in that a "feathered sun" or shield motif occupies the central position.[1]

In the unpublished field notes of James Mooney, there is a short description of a similar Arapaho woman's robe, of which his Cheyenne informant said that the rectangular border symbolizes the earth (Mooney 1902–1906).

Another example is provided by a huge, bisonhide tipi liner preserved in the collection of the American Museum of Natural History, New York (cat.no. 50.2/2641), collected by Colonel J. M. Andrews (Maurer 1992: 196, fig. 152). The perimeter is accented by blue and red parallel lines, with alternating triangles and protruding bars embellishing this border. Each of these is topped with "feather" symbols, the triangles with a single feather, while the bars have three feathers each. The entire area within the border is painted with pictographic battle scenes. Because a good number of these scenes are duplicated by various artists in well-documented Cheyenne ledgerbooks, the AMNH tipi liner can unquestionably be attributed to the Cheyenne.

This Algonquian decorative tradition is also represented by another well-documented Cheyenne robe or liner preserved in the collection of the National Museum of Natural History in Washington (Fig. 3). The robe was collected by Colonel Charles H. Heyl during his military campaigns in the West and was presented to the museum by his son in 1927. On one side it is embroidered with parallel beaded stripes in the four sacred colors of the Cheyenne Beadworkers' Guild: red, yellow, blue, and white. According to the research

Imre Nagy is an art historian and the Scientific Director of the Ferenc Móra Museum, Szeged, Hungary. He holds a Ph.D. in Ethnography (1998) and is an Assistant Professor at the English-American Institute of the Attila József University, Szeged. His research interests include Plains Indian visual art forms: ledger drawings, painted shields, tipis, and robes.

Author's address: Ferenc Móra Museum, P.O. Box 474, H-6701 Szeged, Hungary.

1. This robe was first published by Ewers (1939: pl. 13), who uncritically accepted the accession information and identified it as "Sioux."

of Alice Marriott (1956) and Winfield Coleman (1980), these stripes in four colors symbolize *név'stanevoo'o*, the Four Directions. On the reverse side of the robe we find the familiar border of parallel lines in a pattern of white-*blue*-white-*red*-white-*blue*-white. Alternating double triangles and bars decorate the inner edge of the border. The decoration on this large hide conveys the Cheyenne concept of the universe, though in a highly symbolic way. If the border painting with its alternating triangles and protruding bars symbolizes the earth, then the beaded stripes done in four colors on its reverse side show the Four Cardinal Directions, which arrange the created world into an organized whole.

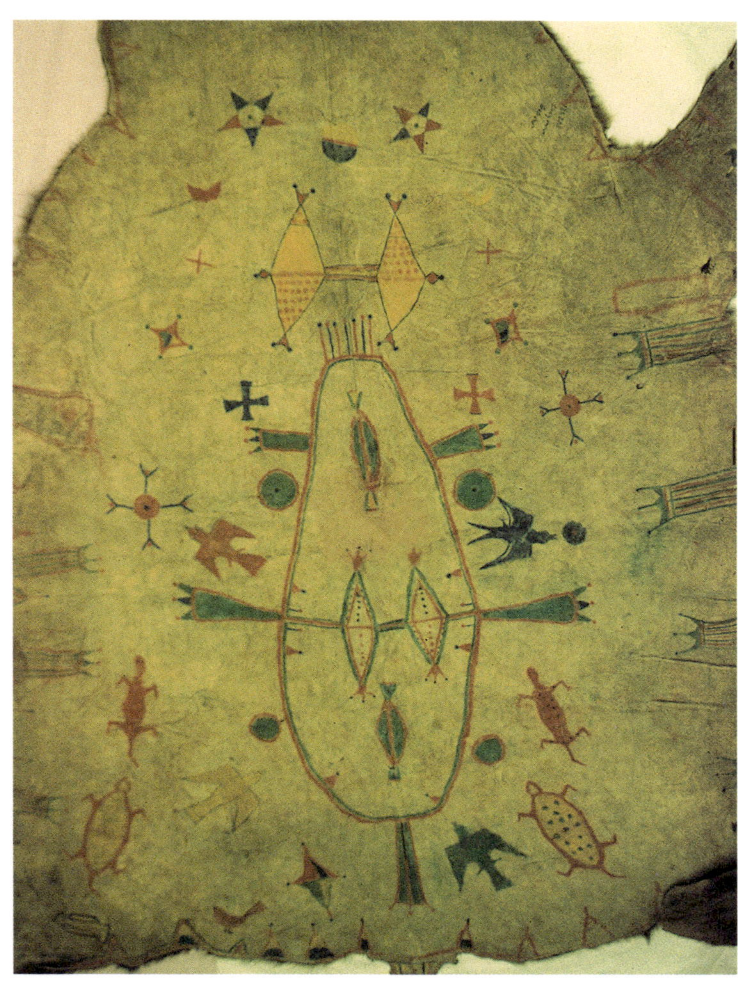

Fig. 1 Painted cowhide, Southern Cheyenne, 1893. Paint on leather. National Museum of Natural History, Smithsonian Institution (Washington, DC), cat.no. E 166,553 (collected by Albert S. Gatschet). Photograph: Imre Nagy.

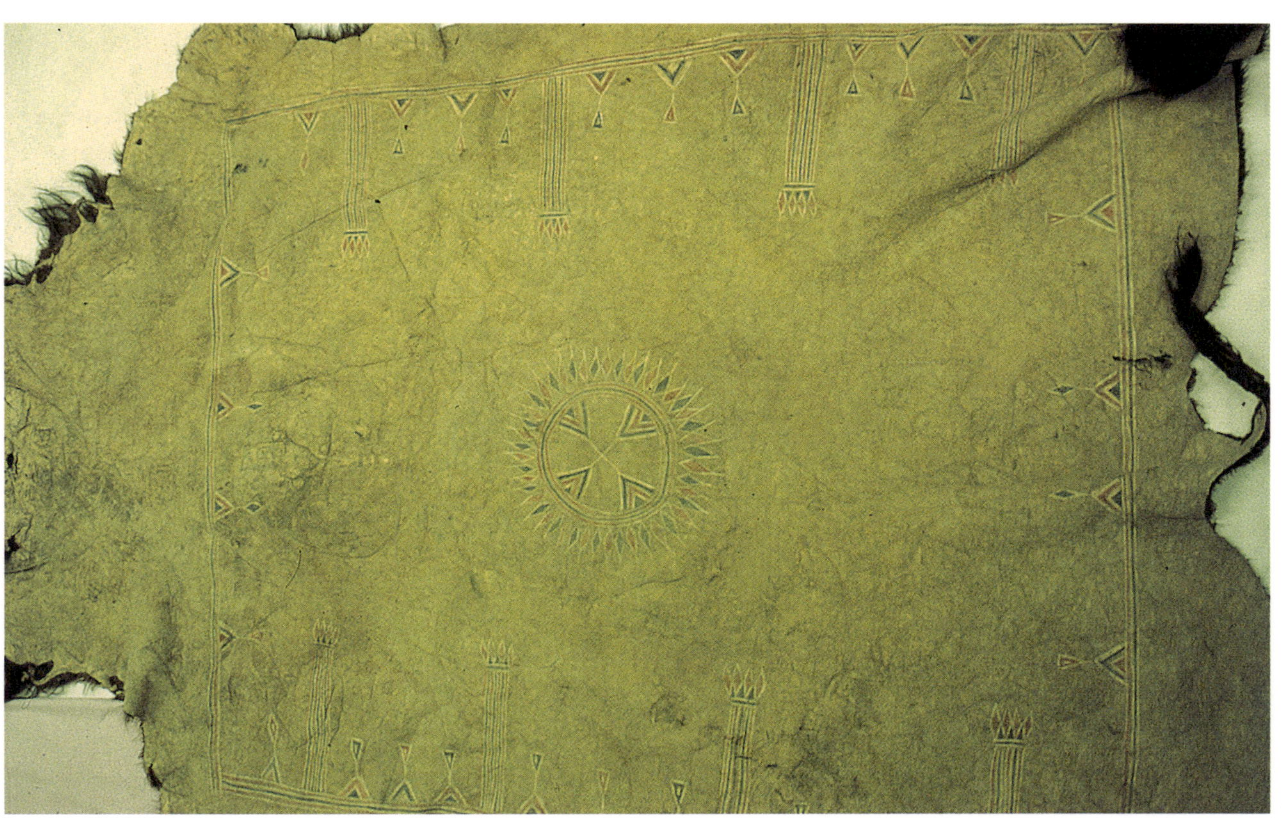

Fig. 2 Painted bisonhide, Cheyenne (originally accessioned as "Sioux"), ca. 1875. Paint on leather. National Museum of Natural History, Smithsonian Institution (Washington, DC), cat.no. E 35,101. Photograph: Imre Nagy.

Further examples illustrate the once widespread use of this Algonquian border motif. The collection of the National Museum of Natural History holds a calfskin with the same type of painted designs, attributed to the Cheyenne (cat.no. E 233,123). The Field Museum of Natural History, Chicago, has two domestic cowskins which are painted with variations of this same motif. One of these was collected from the Northern Cheyenne by S. C. Simms in 1901 at Lame Deer, Montana (cat.no. 69,889), while the other one was collected by George Dorsey probably in Oklahoma (cat.no. 96,847).

All of these examples support an attribution of the Gatschet robe to the Cheyenne. Considering this evidence, we should recognize that robes with a rectangular border of parallel lines, plus alternating triangles and protruding bars on the inner edges of the border, constitute a significant type of artifact peculiar to the Cheyenne and (rarely) the Arapaho.

A closer look at the Gatschet robe reveals that the border is not rectangular, as in the previous examples, but follows the irregular edge of the cowhide. The entire perimeter is outlined along the edge with a continuous red line, and the triangles and protruding bars (in red and green) rest on this base. The perimeter design seems to be unfinished, as only a couple of triangles are colored on the rear part of the hide.

Turning our attention to the central part of the design, we find a multitude of elements—figural and geometric—in a well-balanced composition. Geometric motifs (crosses, four- and five-pointed stars, crescents, circles, and rhomboid forms) abound, primarily on the "upper" (left) half of the hide; while zoomorphic figures (birds, salamanders, turtles, a snake, and a bee) occur on the "lower" (right) half of the cowhide.

The prominent central motif, however, resists identification. It is a huge ovoid figure outlined with red and green lines. There are five protruding elements around it, and four of these are arranged in balanced pairs. The upper pair is not connected, while the larger, lower pair is linked by red and green lines at the midpoint of the ovoid, with a pair of rhomboid figures located in between. The fifth protruding element, at the bottom of the ovoid, seems to differ slightly from the other four. All resemble the protruding bar motifs of the border decoration. At the top of the ovoid form, seven short lines are painted in alternating colors of red and dark blue. Each line has a dot of contrasting color at its tip.

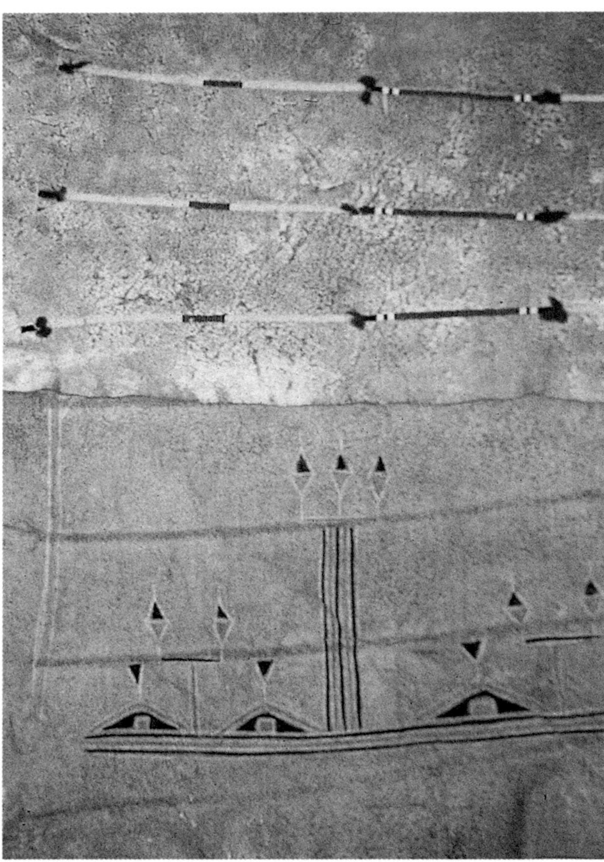

Fig. 3 Painted and beaded bisonhide, Cheyenne, ca. 1870. Painted on one side with geometric motifs and beaded on the other side in characteristic Cheyenne stripe style. National Museum of Natural History, Smithsonian Institution (Washington, DC), cat.no. E 336,826 (collected by Colonel Charles H. Heyl). Photograph: Imre Nagy.

The whole figure is so disguised that we shall need pictorial analogies to reveal its identity. The four green circles outlined in red, which surround the central ovoid, remind us of another Cheyenne composition: a shield[2] preserved in the collection of the National Museum of the American Indian, Smithsonian Institution, Washington, DC (Fig. 4). This shield's central motif is a large, horned snapping turtle. Four green circles are visible beside its legs. As we explore the possibility that the ovoid form on the Gatschet robe might also be a turtle, the Cheyenne language will provide significant clues.

The turtle has a prominent cosmological role in the Cheyenne creation myth.

2. When the shield was published for the first time (Feder 1971: color pl. 16), it was identified as Arapaho. At another time it was published as Mandan (Capps 1973: 207), and it was only after the appearance of the author's papers (Nagy 1994a, 1994b) that it received its correct attribution.

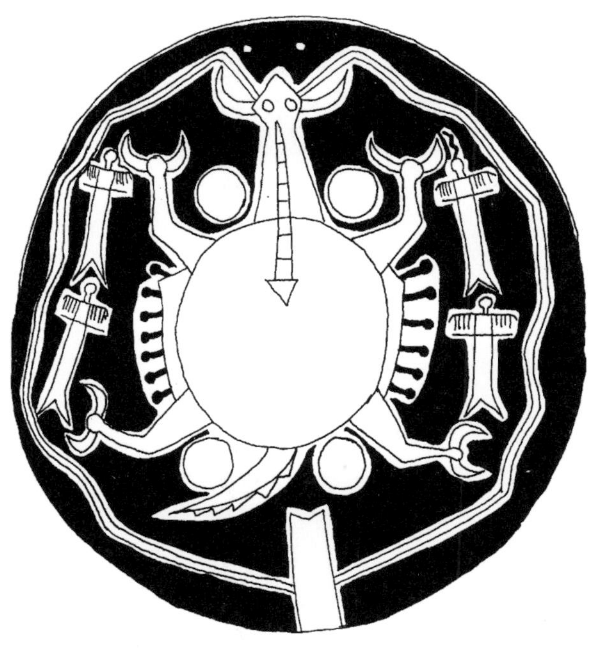

Fig. 4 Shield, Cheyenne, cataloged as Mandan/Arapaho, ca. 1850. Paint on leather, feathers. 47.5 cm diameter. National Museum of the American Indian, Smithsonian Institution (Washington, DC), cat.no. 22/8539. Drawing by the author.

"Fog, *maen enxphos*, fog (lit. the turtle hangs before), *maeno-ehos*, it is foggy (lit. the turtle hangs before) (*the Cheyenne connect turtles with the creation of the world, when it was moving about in mist*) [...]" (Petter 1915: 489, emphasis added).

Further, the Creator placed on the turtle's back that small piece of earth which had been brought up from the bottom of the cosmic sea by a little coot. Hence, Grandmother Turtle carries the earth on her back, as related by the Cheyenne elder Mary Little Bear Inkanish in 1960 (Marriott and Rachlin 1972: 41–42). Thus in Cheyenne sacred art, turtle images always have some cosmological implication.

The Mennonite missionary Rev. Rodolphe Petter added the following handwritten note to his personal copy of his *English-Cheyenne Dictionary*:

"*sovon, sovota* = south refers to 'lower region' opposed to 'high.' I believe it implies a prehistoric idea, regarding south as antipodal to *zenith*. In their ceremonies the pipe is pointed straight up and down (the latter more obliquely). Whither the four quarters correspond not to ours, but Southwest—Southeast, Northwest—Northeast. Ceremonial symbol was the turtle figure:

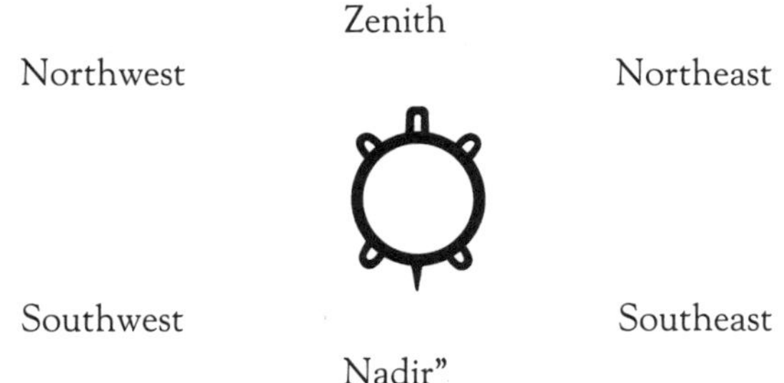

(Petter 1915: 211, copy in Montana Historical Society Library, Helena, MT).

The turtle's multivalent symbolical role as both actor in the Creation and as the foundation of the four-quartered world helps to explain the frequent use of turtle images on Cheyenne shields.

Now that we have recognized the ovoid figure on the Gatschet robe as the Cosmic Turtle floating in the mist of creation, we are also able to identify its legs and the fifth protruding element as its tail. What, then, are the short, alternating red and blue lines at its 'zenith' with small dots at their upper ends? As explained in an earlier paper, similar motifs on a Cheyenne shield (mistakenly attributed as Sioux)[3] represent *exhastoz*, or radiating cosmic power pouring down from the highest cosmic zone (Nagy 1994b: 44–45). Consequently, these short lines ending in dots in all probability represent cosmic energy, or perhaps even "breath," issuing from the mouth of the turtle.

The reptiles and amphibians on both sides of the "lower end" of the Cosmic Turtle represent the layer of the cosmic sea—the "mist" in which the turtle moved about during the time of creation. This is the abyss from which *Maheo* created the world. According to the testimony of this robe, some water creatures already existed when the four-quartered world came into existence. Grinnell (1923, 2: 111) remarks that most aquatic animals possess some mysterious power. While lizard and salamander figures appear as companions of turtles on Cheyenne shields (Nagy 1997a, 1997b), they also appear as balanced pairs with avian figures. Brightly colored lizards (and salamanders) are categorized by Cheyenne as *vé'sˀhovahne*, 'small animals,' and are used for religious or medicinal purposes (Moore 1984: 299). Turtles are also included in the same category, and their ability to live in two worlds made them powerful symbols for Cheyenne priests and shamans. Their cosmological role on the Gatschet robe might be to evoke the underwa-

3. The shield is in the Rochester Museum and Science Center (Rochester, NY), cat.no. 1953.AE 8592.

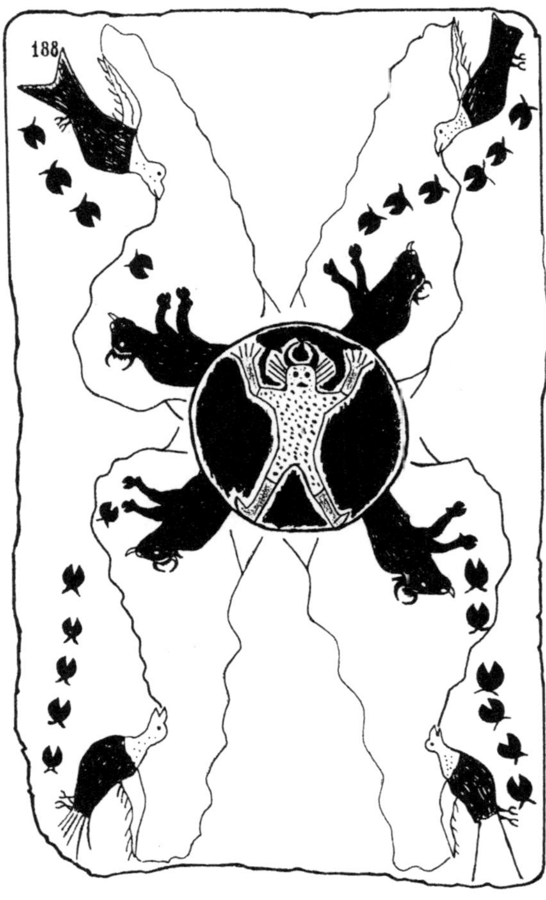

Fig. 5 Drawing on paper, Cheyenne, ca. 1870. Image from the Tie Creek Ledger, depicting a sacred cave of the bisons and four different kinds of eagles at the four corners of the world. Tracing from the original by the author.

ter monsters, called *méh'ne* (pl. *méhneo'o*) in Cheyenne. These are described as somewhat like a very large lizard with one or two horns, with their bodies often covered with hair (Grinnell 1923, 2: 87; Powell 1969, 2: 439).

The green circles beside the legs of the Cosmic Turtle represent the *vose* (pl. *vosototse*), or abodes of the *Ma'heóno*, the spirits of the Four Directions, that is, those four sacred mountains which occupy the corners of the world (Petter 1915: 721). These *vosototse* appear quite frequently in the repertoire of Cheyenne shield makers. A related example, a square flat case, shows them in the corners of the composition[4] (Torrence 1994: 117, fig. 31). Although these sacred mountains are grounded in *Vóto'ˀsto'ome*, the Middle World, they rise through *Táhtavo'ome*, the Atmosphere, up to the *Sétovo'ome*, the Nearer Sky-space (Moore 1974: fig. 3; Schlesier 1987: fig. 1).

The four differently colored bird figures are definitely connected to these prominent sacred points. Edward Red Hat, who was the renowned Keeper of the Sacred Arrows until his death in 1982, tried to identify the four types of eagles in English, but could name only the Golden Eagle and the Bald Eagle: "[...] they [i.e., the Cheyenne] have four different kind of eagles. They got names. I can't remember these two. These last two, I can't remember them. They kind of hard name. It's pretty hard for me to explain it in English" (Schukies 1993: 76). Unfortunately, the artist of the Gatschet robe failed to give us an ornithologically clear depiction of the species he intended to invoke. Their features indicate predatory birds in a general sense: eagles or hawks. John H. Moore investigated the ornithology of Cheyenne priests and religious people, and from his research we are informed that both *netseo'o*, 'eagles,' and *aénȯheo'o*, 'hawks,' belong to the category of 'great birds,' *ma'xevé'k'ˀseho*. In the genus of *netseo'o*, that is, among the eagles, we find the American Swallow-Tailed Kite (*Elanoides forficatus*), which is called *otá'tavanetse*, 'Blue Eagle,' in Cheyenne (Moore 1986: 183–185). We can positively identify the blue bird with forked tail on the Gatschet robe as a swallow-tailed kite, but we lack sufficient clues to identify the other three birds. For the Cheyenne artist, their color symbolism was much more important than their biological/natural likeness.

Before we dive into the color symbolism associated with Cheyenne cardinal points, let us consider another very important visual document of the Cheyenne religious and theological system. This image is from the so-called Tie Creek Ledger, which may date from the 1870s, and which includes some sacred images.[5] One of these depicts a spirit person—probably a Bison spirit, or one of the *Ma'heóno*—standing in the entrance of an *hesevóxe* or animal cavern (Petter 1915: 218; Schlesier 1987: 4–6). Four bisons pour out of the cave, while four eagles attack them with lightning and thunder. The image clearly shows that the eagles' tails differ from each other, while their heads display the characteristic features of the bald eagle (Fig. 5). This amazing scene from the Tie Creek Ledger supports Edward Red Hat's verbal statement and the evidence of the Gatschet robe.

We may now consider the color symbolism of the bird figures. Enumerating them from the right (north-

4. The flat case is now in the National Museum of the American Indian, Smithsonian Institution (Washington, DC), cat.no 13/5303.
5. The ledger is preserved in a private collection, and its present custodian wishes to remain anonymous. A number of scenes from it were published in Keyser (1987).

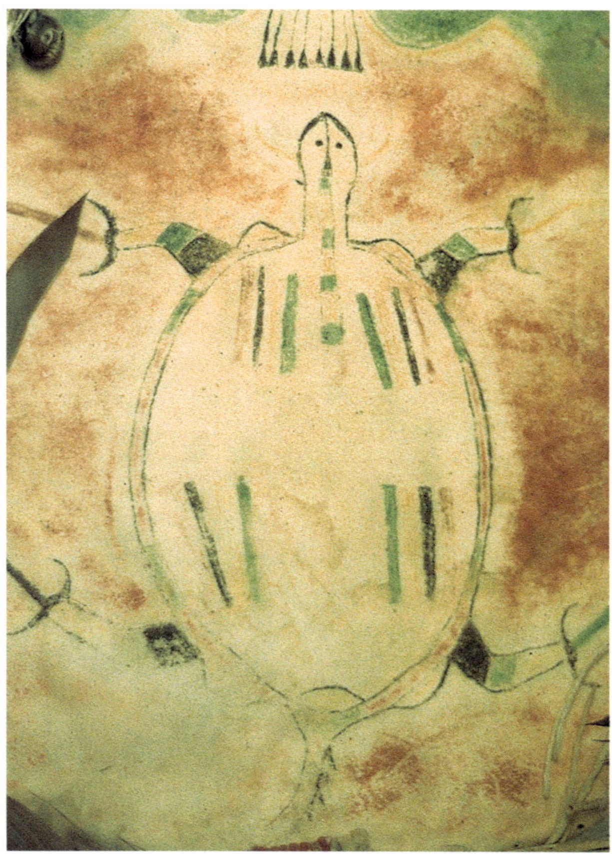

Fig. 6 Shield, Northern Cheyenne, ca. 1865. Paint on leather, feathers. 50 cm diameter. Owned by A-Crow-Split-His-Nose, one of the leaders of the Elk Soldier Society. Collected by General Ranald Mackenzie in 1876. National Museum of Natural History, Smithsonian Institution (Washington, DC), cat.no. E 151,896. Photograph: Imre Nagy.

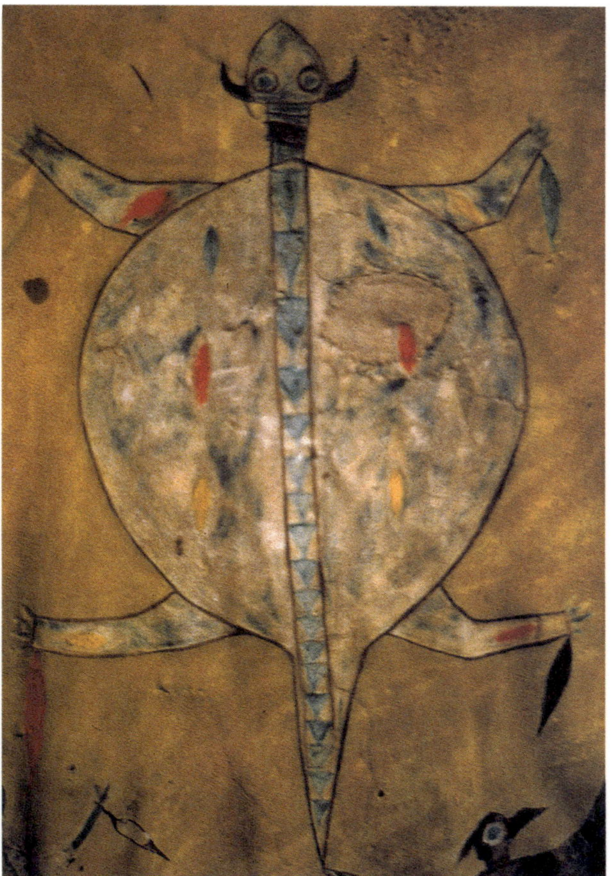

Fig. 7 Shield cover, Cheyenne, ca. 1850. Paint on leather, feathers, red trade cloth. Probably dreamed and made by Lame Bull, Cheyenne medicine man. Colorado State Historical Society (Denver, CO), cat.no. E 1850.11 (gift of Elizabeth Corse).

eastern?) foreleg in a clockwise direction—following the Sun's road, which is the Cheyenne archetype—their order is dark blue-green-yellow-red.

Two historic shields offer formal and contextual parallels to the Gatschet robe. Each has a turtle figure in its composition, and directional colors are indicated at their legs. One of these shields originally belonged to the Northern Cheyenne chief A-Crow-Cut-His-Nose, who was the leader of the Elk Soldier Society. A-Crow-Cut-His-Nose was killed during the destruction of Morning Star's village on 27 November 1876, and his shield—captured by the Shoshone scouts of General Ranald Mackenzie—is now preserved in the National Museum of Natural History (Fig. 6). It has a turtle image occupying the lower section of the composition. Wavy lines protrude from its legs, each in a different color. Their order from the right foreleg in a clockwise direction is: yellow-green-black(blue)-red.

The second shield is in the collection of the Colorado State Historical Society in Denver (Fig. 7) and, as I have pointed out elsewhere (Nagy 1997a, 1997b), in all probability was dreamed and made by the Southern Cheyenne medicine man Lame Bull. The great central motif is the figure of a snapping turtle, whose legs are decorated with colored feather symbols. Their color sequence from the right foreleg is as follows: green-black(blue)-red-yellow.

A third example, from the Northern Cheyenne, is called the "Baker shield," which allegedly was collected at Fort Keogh, Montana Territory, by Lt. Frank Baldwin. Formerly it belonged to the collection of Baker University, Old Castle Museum, Baldwin, Kansas. In 1990 it was in a private collection.

The shield—according to the evidence of its decoration—definitely originated in the Cheyenne tribe, and its probable date of origin might be ca. 1850–1860. It is exceptional among surviving Cheyenne shields in that it still has two decorated leather covers. The outermost

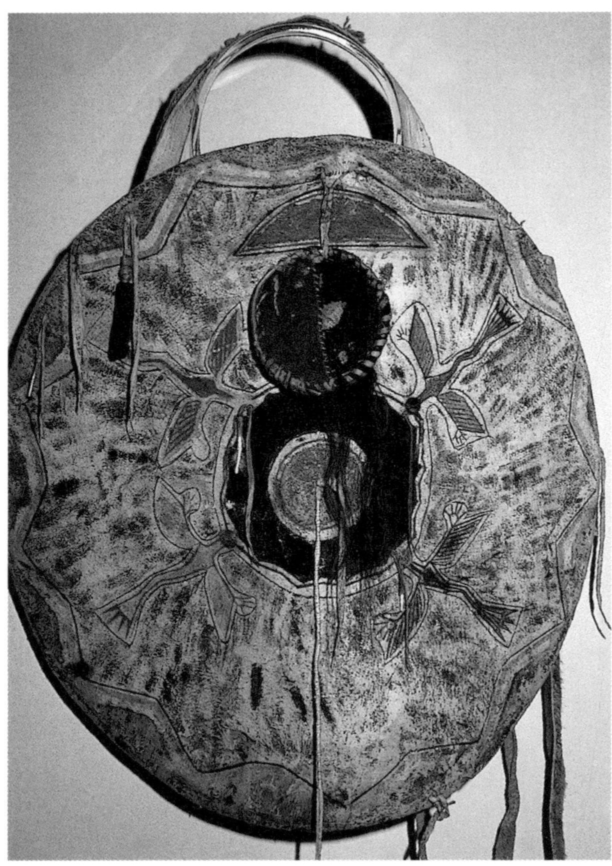

Fig. 8 Shield cover, Northern Cheyenne, ca. 1850. Paint on leather. Collected by Lt. Frank Baldwin in Montana. Private collection. Courtesy of the owner.

cover is painted at four equidistant points along the perimeter with solid dots in red, outlined with circles of blue-green. These symbolize the Four Directions—more precisely, the sacred mountains at the four corners of the world, the homes of the Listeners Under the Ground (Grinnell 1923, 2: 344). At the center of the shield cover, painted in blue-green and brownish-black, are seven circles representing the Pleiades.

The inner shield cover is an amazing example of Cheyenne visionary art (Fig. 8). At the top of the composition there is a green, downward-pointing crescent outlined with multicolored lines. A circle in the same green occupies the center of the shield and is outlined with a red line. A larger black ring with a jagged outer edge surrounds this red circle. Four figures in different colors "fly" toward this central motif. These figures are unique composite beings: They resemble birds, but they have human hands at the joints of their wings, and their heads are represented by a colored dot. If we enumerate the order of these dots in the same way as before, we get the sequence blue-green-red-yellow.

These figures are dualistic: The blue-headed figure's body is green, while the green-headed figure's body is blue; likewise, the red-headed figure's body is yellow, while the yellow-headed figure's body is red. Listing the body colors in the usual order produces the sequence green-blue-yellow-red. Directional color symbolism in Cheyenne cosmology is more related to social structure, personal visionary experiences, and paraphernalia than other symbolic entities associated with the vertical axis of the universe. Consequently, the color sequence and the qualities associated with sacred directions may have depended upon the ceremonial circumstances. Explicit cosmological information was usually communicated in Cheyenne society in the course of the major ceremonies, when the pledger learned the various prayers, songs, and rituals which incorporate different aspects of the formal cosmology (Moore 1984: 294). Our major obstacle in interpreting the design composition of the Gatschet robe is that we do not know whether it—or any antecedents—had been used in any Cheyenne ceremonies, or what purpose it may have served in traditional society.

It may help us to recognize the patterns in the directional sequence if we compare them by beginning with a single color (Fig. 9).

This arrangement reveals that the color sequences of the two shields with turtle figures are identical; but on the Lame Bull shield, the turtle "moved about in the mist." The Baker shield presents a much more complicated case, and we cannot explore its color symbolism in this paper. The color sequence of the Gatschet robe shows one anomaly: Either the blue and yellow are transposed, or we have to read the colors in counterclockwise direction to arrive at the same sequence as on the two shields.

I consider the first case more likely than the second. If we place the fork-tailed blue bird in the southwestern segment, it will occupy the direction associated with Thunder. Fork-tailed birds, swallows, and the swallow-tailed kite are associated with *Nonóma'e*, Thunder, and its direction *Onxsovota*, the Southwest. Likewise, if we place the yellow bird in the northeastern segment, it will occupy the direction associated with the rising sun, light, and morning.

We have to assume that the artist of the Gatschet robe was indulging his prerogative to withhold a portion of the truth, knowing that eventually any mechanic (or, as Claude Levi-Strauss [1966: 17] called it, any

OBJECT	(SE?)	(SW?)	(NW?)	(NE?)
Gatschet robe NMNH E 166,553	Green	Yellow	Red	Blue
Gatschet robe NMNH E 166,553 [counterclockwise]	Green	Blue	Red	Yellow
A-Crow-Cut-His-Nose shield NMNH E 151,896	Green	Black/Blue	Red	Yellow
Lame Bull shield CSHS E 1850.11	Green	Black/Blue	Red	Yellow
Baker shield (heads)	Green	Red	Yellow	Blue
Baker shield (bodies)	Green	Blue	Yellow	Red
Baker shield (heads) [counterclockwise]	Green	Blue	Yellow	Red
Baker shield (bodies) [counterclockwise]	Green	Red	Yellow	Blue

Fig. 9 Directional color patterns on Cheyenne painted artifacts, aligned on green.

bricoleur) would notice that one of the "spark plug wires" had been disconnected and be able to adjust the system so that it would function. We know nothing about the circumstances under which Gatschet collected this robe, but if we reconstruct the possible situation when an "alien White man" requested the Cheyenne artist to "paint something very sacred," or "paint something about how you imagine the creation," such caution seems understandable.

We shall now try to decipher that layer of meaning which constitutes the backbone of Cheyenne formal cosmology, and which with its associated typology of spirits is considered to be tribal, rather than personal, property (Moore 1974: 266). The six rhomboid figures pose a major challenge to the process of interpretation. It is apparent that they display a strong formal relationship to certain elements of Cheyenne parfleche designs.[6] The six rhomboids can be grouped into three dyads. The largest, yellow rhomboid figures are placed "above the head" of the Cosmic Turtle, at the zenith, between the celestial bodies. They are connected with parallel lines of red-yellow-red. Because of their position and coloring, they have to be the Spirits of the Sun and Moon. In everyday Cheyenne language, the sun is called *ése'he*, while the moon is called *taa'éese'he*, the 'night sun' (Petter 1915: 119–121; Glenmore and Leman 1984: 28). In the sacred language of the priests and religious specialists, the personified Sun was called *Hatovse* and the personified Moon *Ameonito* (Hewitt 1901: MS 893; Petter 1915: 80; Schlesier 1987: 8). Another scene from the Tie Creek Ledger shows them in this form: horned spirit figures with human bodies, standing in the circle of the sun and in the crescent of the moon, respectively (Fig. 11). The twenty-nine red dots on the left rhomboid figure correspond with the days of the lunar month—thus supporting our identification.

If we are correct in identifying the pair of yellow rhomboids at the zenith as the personified Sun and Moon, then their four smaller companions on the body of the Cosmic Turtle—that is on the created earth—cannot be anything but the Spirits of the Sacred Directions. These four also constitute a double dualism. We know from the research of John H. Moore that *Essenetahe*, the Spirit of the East, and *Onxsovota*, the Spirit of the West, constitute a pair because of their association with the Sun and Moon, respectively (Moore 1974: 150–154). On the midline of the Cosmic Turtle, two of the rhomboids are connected with parallel lines, similar to the manner in which the Sun and Moon symbols are connected at the zenith.

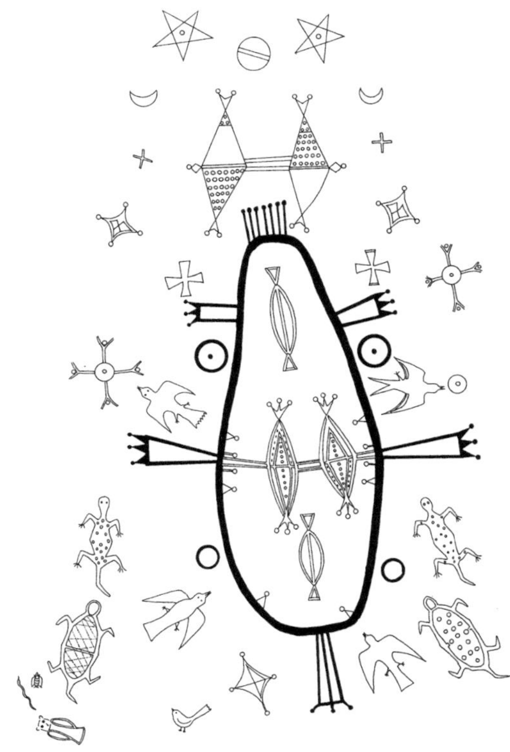

Fig. 10 Painted design on the Gatschet robe (cp. Fig. 1). Drawing by the author.

6. A marked formal analogy of these rhomboid figures with six rhomboid figures on two painted Plains Cree bison robes may indicate some common Algonquian cosmological tradition (VanStone 1991: 43, fig. 27, 49, fig. 33).

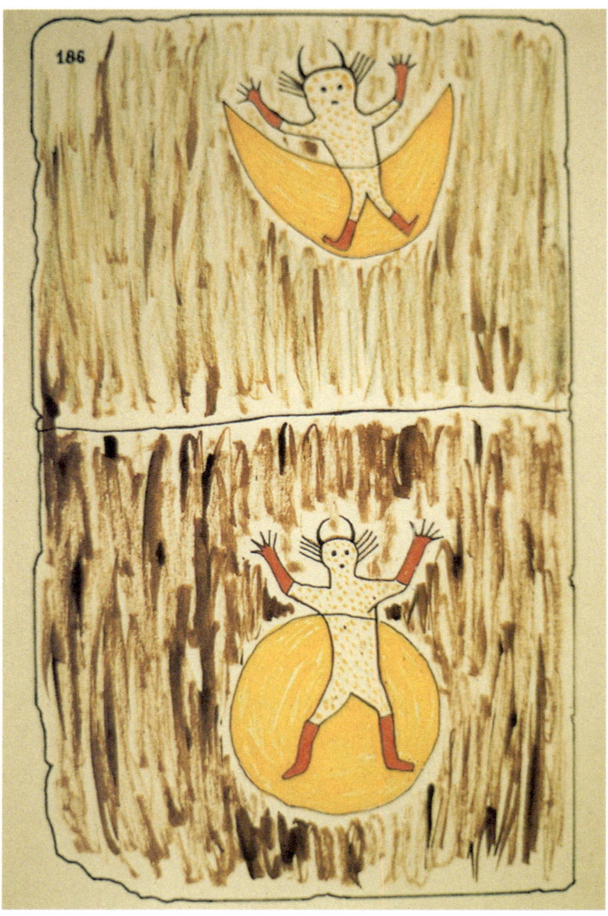

Fig. 11 Drawing on paper, Cheyenne, ca. 1870. Image from the Tie Creek Ledger, depicting the personified Sun and Moon. Tracing from the original by the author.

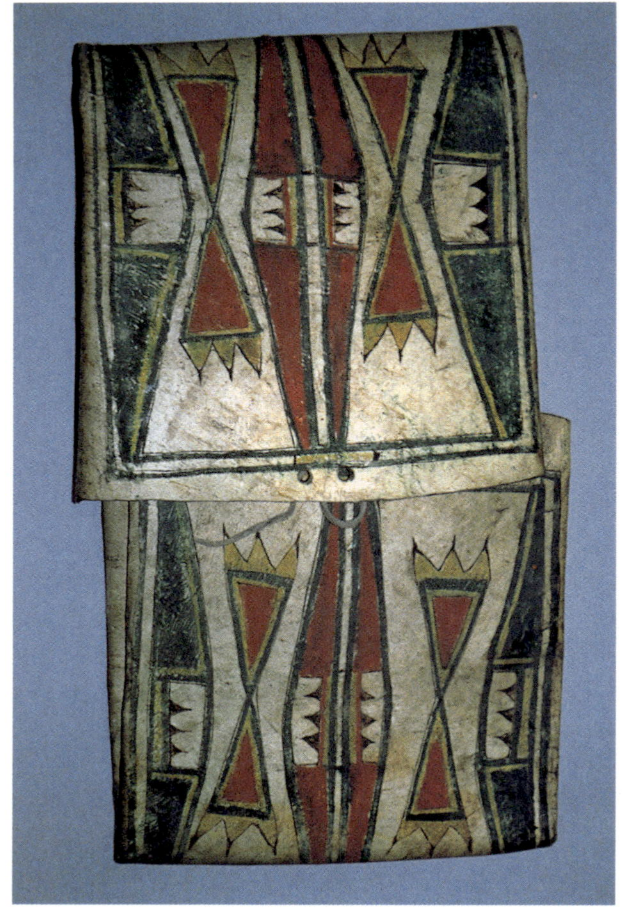

Fig. 12 Parfleche case, Cheyenne, ca. 1875. Paint on rawhide. Oklahoma Museum of Natural History (Norman, OK), cat.no. NAM 9-6-204, E/59-60/7/46.

We also know from Moore (1974: 154–159) that *Sovota*, the Spirit of the South, and *Notamota*, the Spirit of the North, are in antagonistic opposition—primarily because of the struggle between warm and cold, summer and winter. The other pair of rhomboids are not connected with each other, and they are placed at the "top" and "bottom" of the Cosmic Turtle, indicating their antagonistic opposition to each other.

One final point: Taking a closer look at the "tails" of the composite figures on the Baker shield, one can notice a formal analogy between them, the protuberances of rhomboids on the Gatschet robe, and the similar motifs on Cheyenne parfleches (Fig. 12)—all these designs may be intended to evoke the guardian spirits of the sacred directions.

Finally, we have to discuss briefly the celestial motifs. These are placed above the legs and "head" of the Cosmic Turtle, arranged in an arch-like formation. If Rodolphe Petter's diagram is applicable here, these celestial bodies occupy the northern sky dome. There is, however, a single star "below" the turtle—"down south"—which might be an important star of the southern sky. Although we know the Cheyenne names for several stars and constellations, we cannot identify any of these with the images depicted. On the other hand, the stars and crescents are balanced in corresponding pairs, which may indicate the ascendant and descendant positions of the same celestial bodies—the moon, stars, and planets. This is especially apparent in case of the crescents, where the left one is red (the color of the new moon, near the western horizon), while the right one is yellow (the color of the waning moon in the eastern sky).

The circle on the vertical axis of the hide poses another puzzle. It is bisected by a red stripe into yellow and dark blue halves. (This composition in itself is reminiscent of several Cheyenne shield designs.) This may be a pictorial image of the day and night, the brightness of sunlight and the frightening darkness of night (Moore 1974: 152). It may also be significant that this "day-and-night circle" is positioned between the yellow rhomboid symbols of the Sun and Moon.

Conclusion

Generally speaking, none of the sacred artworks of the Cheyenne attempts to depict or evoke the whole spectrum of the sacred universe. Each composition illustrates only one or two aspects/segments of the sacred realm—those territories which were revealed to the individual during visionary experiences. The Gatschet robe is an exception. It illustrates several stages of creation, several layers of the Cheyenne sacred universe, and it is a unique representation of Cheyenne theological and cosmological concepts. Without doubt, the artist of this special cosmogram was a very knowledgeable member of the traditional Cheyenne religious community. It is a loss to Cheyenne ethnography in particular, and to Native American art history in general, that he remains anonymous.

References Cited

Capps, Benjamin
1973 *The Indians*. New York, NY: Time-Life Books.

Coleman, Winfield W.
1980 The Cheyenne Women's Sewing Society. In: Gene Ball and George P. Horse Capture (eds.), *Plains Indian Design Symbology and Decoration* (Cody, WY: Buffalo Bill Historical Center), 50–69.

Ewers, John C.
1939 *Plains Indian Painting: A Description of an Aboriginal American Art*. Palo Alto, CA: Stanford University Press.

Feder, Norman
1971 *American Indian Art*. New York, NY: Harry N. Abrams.

Glenmore, Josephine Stands in Timber and Wayne Leman
1984 *Cheyenne Topical Dictionary*. Busby, MT: Cheyenne Translation Project.

Grinnell, George Bird
1923 *The Cheyenne Indians*. 2 vols. New Haven, CT: Yale University Press.

Hewitt, J. N. B.
1901 Vocabulary and Notes on [Cheyenne] Kinship Terms. Manuscript in the National Anthropological Archives, Smithsonian Institution, Washington, DC.

Keyser, James D.
1987 A Lexicon for Historic Plains Indian Rock Art: Increasing Interpretive Potential. *Plains Anthropologist* 32(115): 43–71.

Lévi-Strauss, Claude
1966 *The Savage Mind*. Chicago, IL: University of Chicago Press.

Maurer, Evan M.
1992 *Visions of the People: A Pictorial History of Plains Indian Life*. Minneapolis, MN: The Minneapolis Institute of Arts.

Marriott, Alice
1956 The Trade Guild of the Southern Cheyenne Women. *Bulletin of the Oklahoma Anthropological Society* 4: 19–27.

Marriott, Alice and Carol K. Rachlin
1972 *American Indian Mythology*. New York, NY: The New American Library.

Mooney, James
1902–1906 Cheyenne Field Notes. Manuscript in the National Anthropological Archives, Smithsonian Institution, Washington, DC.

Moore, John H.
1974 A Study of Religious Symbolism Among the Cheyenne Indians. Ph.D. dissertation, New York University. Ann Arbor, MI: University Microfilms.
1984 Cheyenne Names and Cosmology. *American Ethnologist* 11(2): 291–312.
1986 The Ornithology of Cheyenne Religionists. *Plains Anthropologist* 31(113): 177–192.

Nagy, Imre
1994a A Typology of Cheyenne Shield Designs. *Plains Anthropologist* 39(147): 5–36.
1994b Cheyenne Shields and Their Cosmological Background. *American Indian Art Magazine* 19(3): 38–47, 104.
1997a Lame Bull, the Cheyenne Medicine Man. *American Indian Art Magazine* 23(1): 70–83.
1997b "The Black Came Over the Sun ...": Lame Bull's Spiritual Oeuvre. *Irodalom- és művészettörténeti tanulmányok, Studia Historiae Literarum et Artium* 1: 59–93.

Petter, Rodolphe
1915 *English-Cheyenne Dictionary*. Kettle Falls, WA: Mennonite Mission.

Powell, Fr. Peter J.
1969 *Sweet Medicine: The Continuing Role of the Sacred Arrows, the Sun Dance, and the Sacred Buffalo Hat in the Northern Cheyenne History*. 2 vols. Norman, OK: University of Oklahoma Press.

Schlesier, Karl H.
1987 *The Wolves of Heaven: Cheyenne Shamanism, Ceremonies, and Prehistoric Origins*. Norman, OK: University of Oklahoma Press.

Schukies, Renate
1993 *Red Hat. Cheyenne Blue Sky Maker and Keeper of the Sacred Arrows*. Münster—Hamburg: LIT-Verlag.

Torrence, Gaylord
1994 *The American Indian Parfleche: A Tradition of Abstract Painting*. Seattle, WA: University of Washington Press.

VanStone, James W.
1991 *The Isaac Cowie Collection of Plains Cree Material Culture from Central Alberta*. Fieldiana, Anthropology 17. Chicago, IL.

A Piece of the Past
Alaskan Eskimo Art and the Nome Gold Rush, 1895–1915

Molly Lee

In this article I will describe private collecting as it unfolded in late-nineteenth and early-twentieth century arctic Alaska and use these data to illuminate the way people thought about collecting Native artifacts at that time. Dorothy Jean Ray's research meticulously documents the history and development of post-contact Alaskan Eskimo art, especially ivory carving, mainly from the standpoint of producer and production (Ray 1961, 1980, 1982, 1987). I want to build on her investigations by focusing on the buyers, transactions, and conduits whereby these objects were appropriated, repackaged, and recirculated in the Euro-American system of consumer goods. My consideration takes in the entire spectrum of sold and traded objects: baskets, masks, fur goods, household and hunting implements, in addition to ivory carving. Its geographical focus is the Eskimo populations from St. Michael to Point Barrow, although I will concentrate on the islands and mainland of Bering Strait. I will refer to this area as "arctic Alaska" for want of a more explicit term.

At the outset I want to hypothesize that the differences between private and institutional collecting of that period were qualitative as well as quantitative. For example, the vast array of objects amassed by Smithsonian collectors E. W. Nelson around Bering Strait (Nelson 1899) and John Murdoch in the Point Barrow vicinity (Murdoch 1892) were gathered for the purpose of scientific study. Thus they mirror turn-of-the-century anthropology's concern with taxonomy and typology. By contrast, the guiding impulse behind individual collecting was more idiosyncratic, both in aesthetic taste and object choice. Moreover, objects collected by individuals were assured more spirited, if precarious, afterlives. Far from languishing in the storehouses of the great museums, they were given as souvenirs to loved ones, incorporated into the eclectic household decor of the period, or marketed as consumables on the shelves of curio dealers or secondhand shops (Dare 1903, Lee 1991, 1992, Phillips 1998).

Early Curio Collecting in Arctic Alaska, 1816–1898

The Eskimos of arctic Alaska were skilled and sophisticated intercultural traders long before the arrival of Euro-Americans. Trade networks across Bering Strait had been in use for millennia, and European goods reached Alaska from Siberia as long as two hundred years before the Russians explored this region in the late eighteenth and early nineteenth centuries (Ray 1980). More recently, Hudson's Bay Company goods had begun to trickle south along the Arctic Coast from the mouth of the Mackenzie River (Smith 1984).

By the time of the founding of Nome in 1898, therefore, the Eskimos of Bering Strait and the Arctic Coast had been accustomed to making and selling curios to non-Natives for at least a century if not longer (Ray 1980: 166, 169). The foreigners were unanimous in their admiration of the technologically accomplished and aesthetically pleasing nature of Eskimo material culture, and it was evident that artifacts were among the Eskimos' few reliable commodities to barter for coveted trade goods.

From the beginning of the nineteenth century, non-Native enthusiasm for collecting Eskimo material culture ran high. Drill bows, ivory carvings, a hunting

Molly Lee is Curator of Ethnology and History at the University of Alaska Museum and Associate Professor of Anthropology at the University of Alaska, Fairbanks. Her research interests are in the art and culture of the circumpolar North. She is the coauthor of *Eskimo Architecture: Dwelling and Structure in the Early Historic Period* (forthcoming from the University of Alaska Press) and is at work on a book about Yup'ik Eskimo grass baskets.
Author's address: University of Alaska Museum, P.O. Box 6960, Fairbanks, AK 99775, U.S.A.s

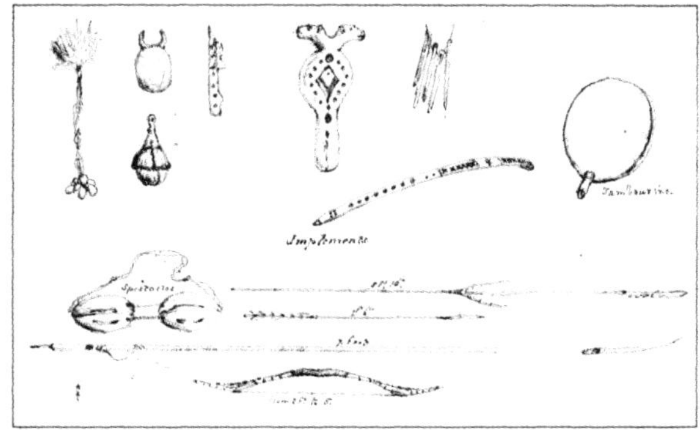

Fig. 1 A sketch of Captain Beechey's artifacts from arctic Alaska, 1826–27. After Bockstoce (1977: 24, pl. V).

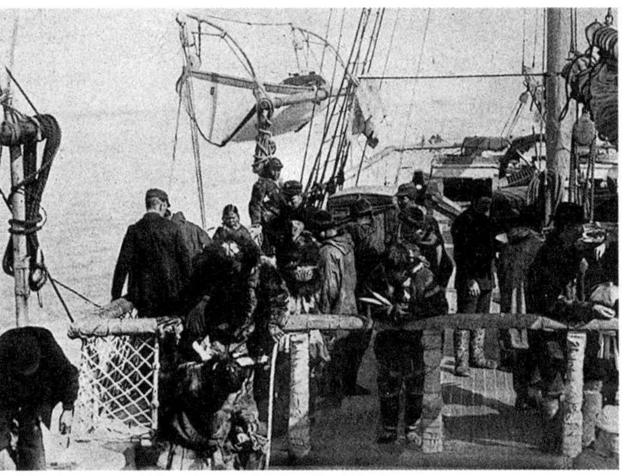

Fig. 2 Alaskan Eskimos trading aboard a U.S. revenue cutter. Courtesy of the Huntington Library (Pasadena, CA), Healy Collection 20940.

helmet, and probably more were collected by the 1816 Kotzebue expedition (Ray 1980: 169ff). In 1826–27 Frederick Beechey, the English explorer, made a sizable collection, much of it now in the Pitt Rivers Museum, Oxford (Bockstoce 1977; Fig. 1). Beechey had been ordered to make an official collection by the Lords of the Admiralty, but apparently retained the material privately for some years after. Competition for artifacts was intense among expedition members. Wrote Admiralty Mate James Wolfe: "During our stay [at Point Hope] we purchased almost everything there was in the village disposable ..." (quoted in Bockstoce 1977: 16).

In the latter half of the nineteenth century the curio trade intensified[1] in the North. In 1848 the first Yankee whaling vessel sailed through Bering Strait. From that date until the collapse of the baleen market at the turn of the century, hundreds of whalers scoured the Arctic Ocean in search of the bowhead whale. The whaling period provided the Eskimos access to a steady flow of tea, sugar, flour, whiskey, and guns and ammunition for the first time. As they had already learned, curios were among their most dependable sources for barter. Journals and accounts from the whaling period suggest that hardly a whaler sailed back through Bering Strait without an Eskimo-made memento in his sea chest. The officers and crews of the U.S. revenue cutters that patrolled the arctic waters every summer also collected curios (Fig. 2). The men were allowed to take a limited amount of trade goods north to barter with the Eskimos for cold weather clothing and curios for personal use (F. Healy 1883, M. J. Healy 1883–1884). Among others who made private collections were the school teachers and missionaries who came to the North after 1884 (Lee in press). Teachers posted to St. Lawrence Island, for example, expected to spend the first few days after arrival trading curios to the islanders, who exchanged them for the much-needed supplies the Westerners had brought along for this purpose (Doty 1898–1899).

By the 1880s Eskimos in numerous settlements from St. Michael to Barrow routinely engaged in the curio trade. The 1883 diaries of the wife and son of "Black Mike" Healy, Captain of the revenue cutter *Bear*, mention trading for artifacts at Goodnews Bay, Little Diomede and King Islands, Wales, Cape Blossom, Port Clarence, Point Hope, and Point Barrow (M. J. Healy 1883–1884). As early as 1884, the Eskimos at St. Michael "[made] their living by hunting, fishing, and selling curios in the summertime" (Wardman 1884).

As Ray (1961: 7) has noted, most Eskimo-made curios acquired before the 1890s were articles of everyday use. The Healys mention bird spears, harpoons, spear throwers, bows and arrows, boots, fish hooks, masks, labrets, pipes, and models of kayaks, umiaks, and sleds. These objects may have been aboriginal in prototype, but the demands imposed on the curio market by the whalers for several decades and the Alaska Natives' replacement of many precontact articles with those of Western manufacture make it unlikely that all examples collected in the 1880s were intended for local consumption. It is more likely that many were replicas of utilitarian articles destined all along for the market-

1. Journals and accounts from the Franklin Search years (1848–54) contain few references to curio collecting, although an unillustrated catalog of artifacts from these years tells us that the pastime continued (Snow 1858).

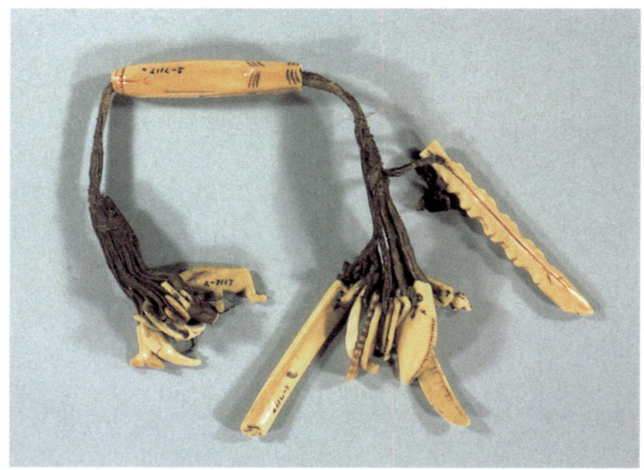

Fig. 3 Needle cases were one type of artifact made originally for local consumption and later replicated for sale to tourists. Courtesy of the Fine Arts Museum of San Francisco (San Francisco, CA), cat.no. AOA6342. Photograph: Nelson Graburn.

place (Graburn 1976, 1999). With the exception of some types of models and ivory pipes, innovations did not appear until later. In sum, by the time gold was discovered on the Seward Peninsula, the curio trade in arctic Alaska was well established. Its only limitation was the relatively small number of foreigners who traveled that far north.

The Nome Gold Rush and the Standardization of the Curio Trade

The discovery of gold at Anvil Creek in the autumn of 1898 brought cataclysmic changes to Bering Strait and, indeed, to all of arctic Alaska. Within two years, 30,000 prospectors were camped on the beaches of Nome (Fig. 4). Because the immediate vicinity was not conducive to subsistence activities, no Eskimo settlements were engulfed or displaced by the foreigners, but it wasn't long before the lure of imported goods and bootleg whiskey made Nome an irresistible magnet. The new city soon replaced St. Michael and Kotzebue Sound as the hub of intercultural trade (Ray 1987: 35). By the second year of the strike, Eskimos from King Island, Little Diomede, Wales, Shismaref, and even Siberia were summering on the Sandspit[2] west of town (Ray 1987). The intermingling of Eskimos from different localities was in keeping with the practice of summer trade fairs that had been customary since before historic contact. Such wide geographical representation undoubtedly enriched the inventory of souvenirs that were to be found in Nome.[3]

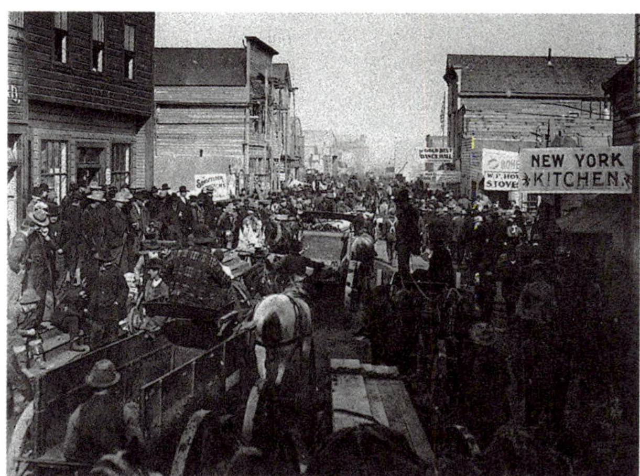

Fig. 4 Main Street, Nome, Alaska before 1905. Courtesy of the Bancroft Library, University of California (Berkeley, CA), Alaska Collection 1905.17109.200.

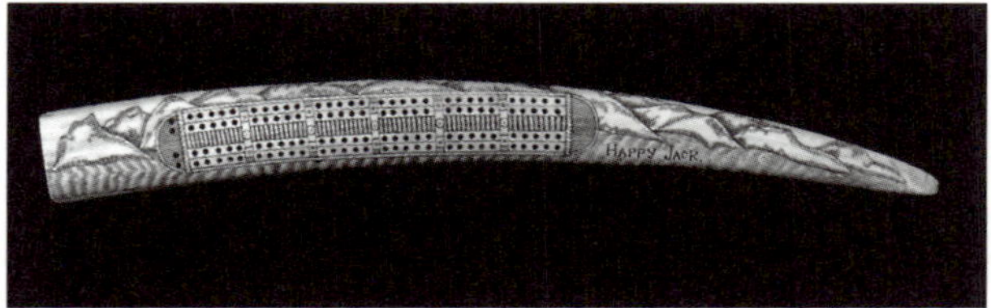

Fig. 5 Walrus tusk engraved by Eskimo artist Happy Jack. Courtesy of the University of Alaska Museum (Fairbanks, AK), cat.no. 94-9-47. Photograph: Barry McWayne.

At first, most curios sold in Nome, like those obtained elsewhere in arctic Alaska, were replicas of long-established prototypes. For example, in 1900 one man carved nothing but the ivory needle cases that once had been part of every Eskimo woman's household equipment (Ray 1961: 7; Fig. 3). However, as consumer demands became known (and probably also in response to competition), innovations proliferated. Under the tutelage of Happy Jack, ivory carvers began making cribbage boards and other new forms such as buttons, animal figurines, napkin rings, salt and pepper shakers, chess sets, and gavels (Ray 1984; Fig. 5). Also, the Eskimos quickly adapted their two-dimensional graphic skills from ivory to paper and occasionally traded drawings to non-Natives (*Nome News* 1902a). In 1902 Judge James Wickersham was presented with an extraordinary group of such drawings by

2. By 1920 the Eskimo community had fragmented along regional lines. The Diomede Islanders lived on the Sandspit and the King Islanders on the beach east of town (Ray 1961: 12).

3. Curios also reached Nome by way of the traders who supplied the remote arctic communities. They probably sold most often to the merchants.

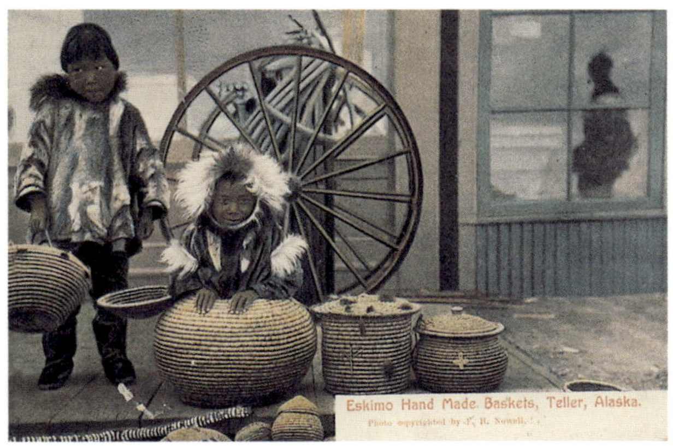

Fig. 6 "Handmade Eskimo baskets, Teller, Alaska." Portland, Oregon: Portland Post Card Co. number 90256. Photograph by F. H. Nowell, about 1900.

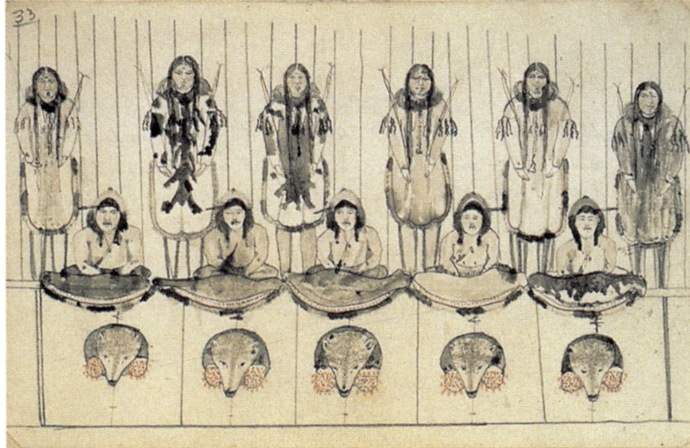

Fig. 7 Eskimo drawing by E-too-ach-in-na of Wales, Alaska, given to James Wickersham in 1902. Courtesy of the Alaska Historical Library (Juneau, AK). Photograph: Paul Gardiner.

E-too-ach-in-na, a Wales man (Wickersham 1902; Fig. 7). Archaeological material in stone, bone, and ivory was picked up or dug out of the ground around other settlements and sold (Henderson 1898: 39). Eskimo women turned their skin sewing talents to making Western-derived articles such as purses and rugs in complex geometric patterns; women also began to make coiled grass baskets, possibly introduced from Siberia (Fig. 6; Lee 1987, 1995).

Consumers

During the Gold Rush there were three main groups of curio buyers. The majority were miners, particularly those who had struck it rich. In the late summer the Eskimos did a brisk business with prospectors headed south on the last boat before freeze-up (*Nome News* 1903). Many such collections were later acquired by museums and seem to consist mainly of small amounts of carved ivory. Second were the more discriminating collectors among the permanent or semipermanent residents of arctic Alaska: civil servants, doctors, lawyers, teachers, housewives, and merchants. Usually they sought out old artifacts (or replicas of old artifact types) as illustrated here by the collection of Alice Henderson (Henderson 1898; Fig. 8). Judge Wickersham, who spent the winter of 1901–1902 in Nome, gathered a sizable collection including the drawings mentioned above, pottery lamps, a jade spoon, throwing sticks, labrets, a bow, baskets, and carved ivory (*Nome News* 1902a). Mr. Kjellman, a reindeer supervisor, had one room in his cabin crammed with curios including a string of trade beads, a caribou tooth belt, a carved ivory puppet, and a jade spoon from Siberia (Henderson 1898: 208–209). Father Barnum, a priest at St. Michael, had a sizable collection of "ancient stone implements" (Henderson 1898: 39).

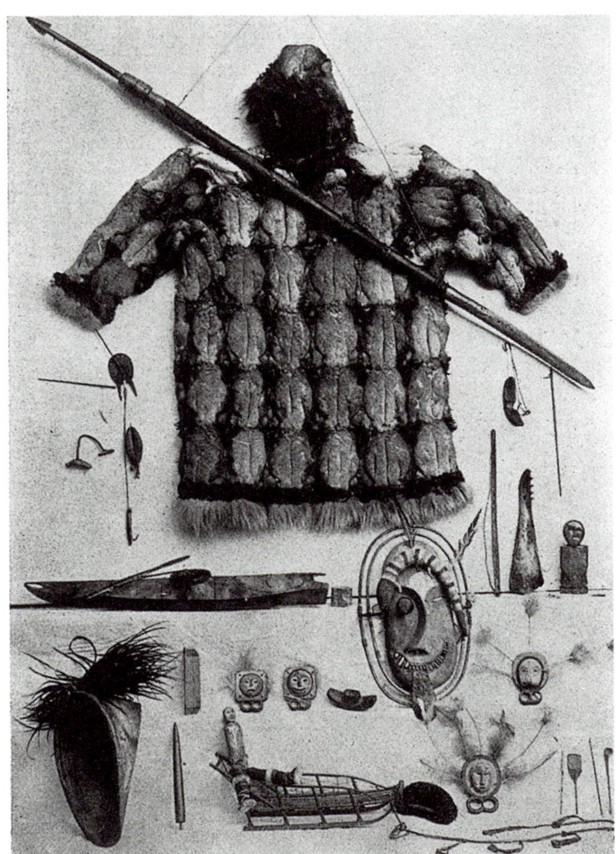

Fig. 8 Artifact collection of Alice Fletcher Henderson. Most of the artifacts are from the Central Yup'ik region of Alaska, but show types of old or replica objects that attracted tourists throughout Alaska. Photograph: Richard Veazey after Henderson (1898).

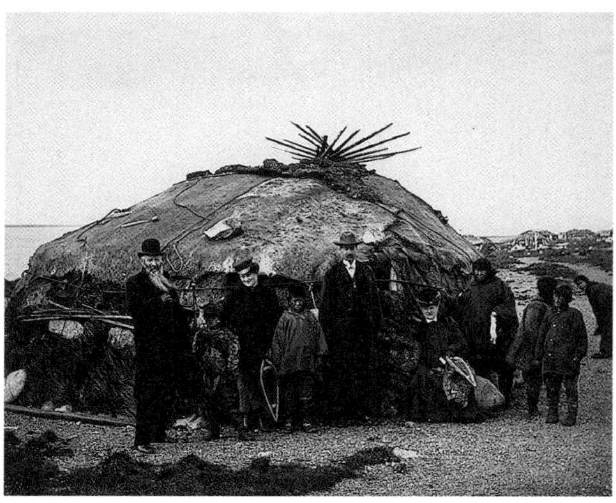

Fig. 9 Tourists in front of Uelen House. Photographed during the first tourist expedition from Nome to Siberia in 1904. Courtesy of the Bancroft Library, University of California (Berkeley, CA), Alaska Collection 1905.17109.1136.

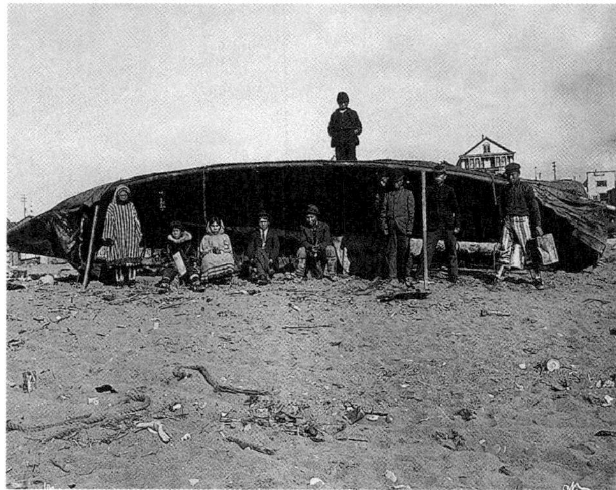

Fig. 10 "Ten Little Eskimos and their Oomiak [sic]." Courtesy of the Bancroft Library, University of California (Berkeley, CA), Alaska Collection 1905.17109.1004.

Finally, curios were bought by a small but growing number of tourists. In 1904 seventy-five Nome residents steamed across Bering Strait on the first pleasure trip to Siberia, where they bought furs, ivory, and other curios in several Siberian Eskimo settlements (Fig. 9). For those whose acquisitiveness had not been satisfied onshore, an agent of a Siberian trading company sold furs and ivory on the deck of the ship on the return voyage (*Nome News* 1904; Kunkle 1997: 115–123). The following year the first tour to Nome from the Outside was advertised. It was planned as an extension of the Inside Passage trip, which had been drawing several thousand tourists annually since the 1880s (Hinckley 1965: 70–71; Norris 1985). To get to Nome, tourists followed the same route as the Gold Rushers, traveling from Skagway to Dawson on the White Pass Railway, down the Yukon to St. Michael on paddle boats, and from there by steamer to Nome. One of the main attractions was the chance to see Native people and buy Native-made souvenirs (*Nome Nugget* 1905).

The enticement of "primitive" people was a powerful magnet at the turn of the twentieth century. "The Native people [of Alaska] are the most interesting study of ethnologists," promised an early guidebook (Scidmore 1885: 1); an analysis of guidebooks of this period suggests that hardly a traveler fails to mention them. It seems that at the outset, moreover, Native people were thought of as metonyms for Alaska, and Native artifacts as metonyms for the people who made them. This is suggested by the rapid politicization of Native artifacts. In 1869, when Secretary of State William Seward visited Alaska to stump for the Alaska Purchase, he was showered with Native artifacts wherever he went (Sessions 1890: 93).

For obtaining imports, the Eskimos still depended on trade goods. Despite Nome's boomtown atmosphere, the presence of a skilled non-Native workforce—to say nothing of rampant racism—practically eliminated job possibilities (McLain 1969: 15). So the Eskimos fell back on their accustomed inventory of meat and game (which the foreigners were too busy or too unskilled to obtain for themselves), furs, and curios.

Transactions

Collectors obtained their curios in a variety of settings, sometimes directly from the Eskimos, and at others from retail stores. Unlike in the Alaska Panhandle, where Northwest Coast Indian curio sales were handled almost exclusively by women (Collis 1890), Eskimo artifacts were sold by the artisan, whether man, woman, or child. Street vendors were the most common purveyors. By 1902 curio peddling had become common enough for the Nome City Council to consider licensing basket vendors, and in 1903 a newspaper reported that: "When one is walking about the streets ... [one] has [curios] pushed into his hands a hundred times a day by industrious Natives" (*Nome News* 1903). Women also sold curios in outlying mining camps (Sullivan 1903). More adventuresome collectors went out to the Sandspit and bought directly from the carvers and skinsewers,[4] who worked in the lea of their upturned umiaks (skin boats) (K. Nelson 1958: 71–72; Fig. 10).

Nome merchants began stocking curios very early. Stores such as Polet's Snake River Grocery, the Nome Bazaar, and the Golden Gate (Fig. 11) stocked both furs and curios. The earliest newspaper advertisement was placed by the Log Cabin Store in 1902 (*Nome News* 1902b), when merchant G. P. Groggin imported a collection of 300 Aleut baskets (Fig. 12). It was a good investment: Eleven days later only forty-five remained *(Nome News* 1902c). The date when the first shop specializing in curios opened has yet to be established. In the 1920s post-Gold Rush slump, when tourism had become vital to the local economy, curio shops were among the few that were open (K. Nelson 1958: 156).

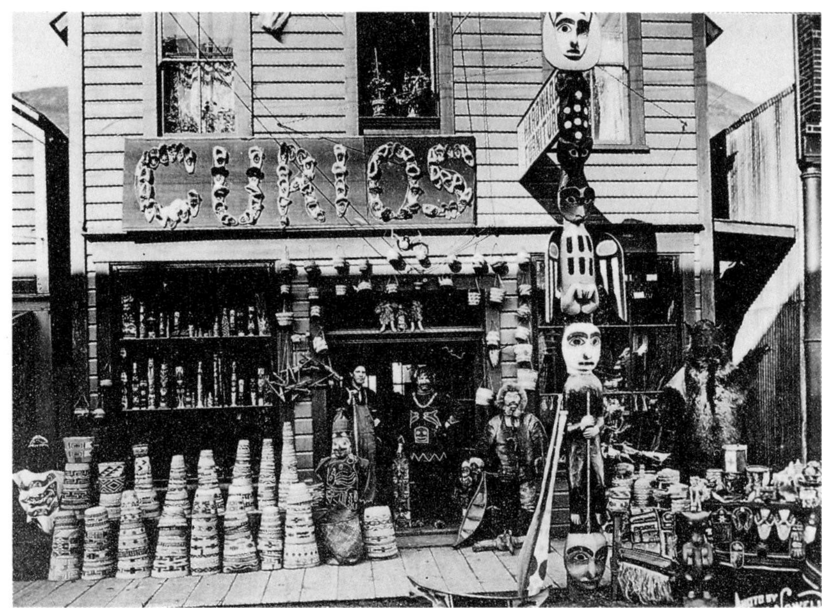

Fig. 11 Golden Gate Curio Shop, Nome. Courtesy of the Bancroft Library, University of California (Berkeley, CA), Alaska Collection 1905.17109.1947.

Cultural styles of economic exchange differed vastly between Eskimos and Westerners, and in the bargaining process the Eskimos usually came out ahead. Westerners complained that they were hard bargainers, who asked high prices, and who would not deviate from them. Curio hunters soon learned to feign indifference to a coveted object for fear it would be whisked away if they offered too little for it (Coleclaugh 1876: 8; Nowell 1911).

If Westerners found the Eskimos stubborn and impassive, the Eskimos found the Westerners inept and unbecomingly obstinate. For example, a woman newspaper reporter took a fancy to a man's labrets and when he refused to sell them kept after him until he agreed to let her cut the ivory amulets from his parka for the same price (Coleclaugh 1876: 8). Another female traveler who coveted an Eskimo child's doll pursued first the child, then her parents for two days until they capitulated: "How I did want that baby doll, but the little thing wouldn't hear of it, and when she feared I should get it went and hid her beloved, ... from the foreigner ... Only after the little thing had consented, after two day's negotiations, [did] I obtain the coveted beauty" (Henderson 1898: 49).

In the negotiations for curios both parties had a clear idea of the value of the goods, though the ideas did not always concur. In Nome, where currency was in use, curios had a dollar value. Groggin's Aleut baskets, for example, could be had for $1 to $30 in 1902. In the more remote settlements, where goods were bartered, values were often reckoned in cloth (commonly called "calico," whether silk or denim). Cloth trade was reckoned in "fathoms" (an arm's length). In 1900 a pair of mukluks was valued at four fathoms. At the same date a polar bear skin could be had for two to four sacks of flour, two to three cases of hard tack, and

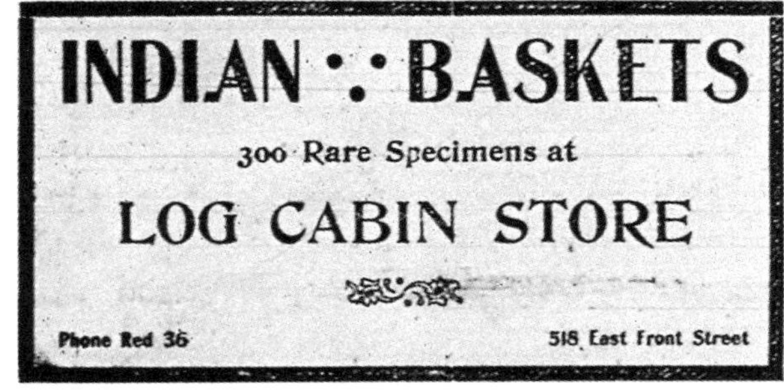

Fig. 12 Advertisement for curios at Log Cabin Store. *Nome News*, 28 July 1902: 4. Photograph: Richard Veazey.

4. Klondy Nelson, who grew up in Nome during the Gold Rush, recalled her visits to the Eskimo women on the Sandspit with great pleasure. When however, as propriety demanded, the Eskimo women returned her visit at the Nelson home, her mother was less enchanted (K. Nelson 1958: 71–72).

some cartridges. These goods amounted to $15–20; the skin was considered a bargain given that its resale value was $300 in the continental U.S. (Anonymous 1900: unpaginated).

Transmission Outside Alaska

Curios reached the Outside by numerous channels. One of the most active was through the revenue cutter personnel (Hooper 1881). It was against regulations to engage in trade for resale, but the evidence suggests that enforcement was lax. For example, "Black Mike" Healy, captain of the revenue cutter *Bear*, and his officers bought ivory in Siberia and resold it at St. Michael and probably elsewhere (F. Healy 1883), and sailors routinely supplied curios to the Alaska Commercial Company stores at Unalaska and Kodiak, to the curio shops in southeastern Alaska on their way home (Anonymous 1900, 1908), and probably to curio shops along the San Francisco waterfront (Lee 1996). It is probable, too, that crew members on the numerous steamships that traveled to Nome during the summer traded for curios in Nome and resold them in Seattle, Port Townsend, and Tacoma. Somewhat later, dealers in Nome accepted orders for Eskimo artifacts from individual collectors, museums, and specialty shops, but the earliest date remains to be established.

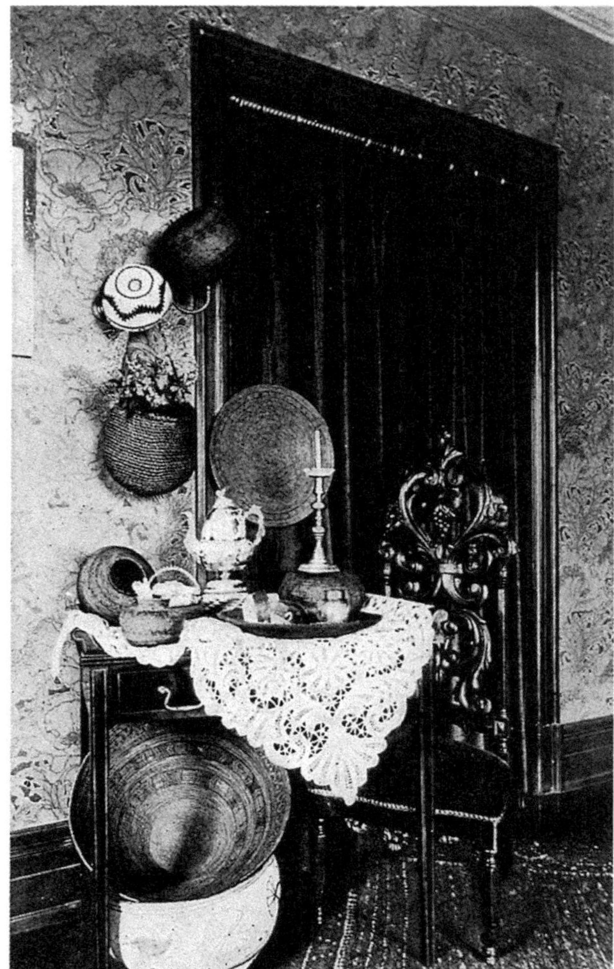

Fig. 13 Turn-of-the-century household display incorporating Native American artifacts with those of Western manufacture. From *Harper's Bazaar* 35 (1901): 471. Courtesy of the Library of Congress (Washington, DC).

Analysis and Conclusions

As this discussion makes clear, there was a pronounced upswing in Eskimo artifact collecting around the turn of the century. I want to argue here that the reasons are more complex than the purely instrumental explanation of a population explosion of potential consumers. I want to consider this fad in relation to prevailing cultural attitudes toward collecting generally and, more specifically, to the craze for Native American art collecting of which it was a part.

Ever since the seventeenth century, ownership and display of possessions have contributed increasingly to a positive self-image in Western culture (Macpherson 1962). With the marked rise in middle-class income and consumption during the Victorian era, collecting,[5] heretofore a pastime of the rich, also became a preoccupation of the bourgeoisie. The resulting culture of abundance permeated every aspect of life: the size of families, the elaboration of meals and, very significantly, the aesthetic of excess evident in interior decoration. For instance, parlors, the public spaces that communicated status and arbitrated class distinctions, were crammed with furniture whose every surface was elaborated with carving, accentuated with doilies and antimacassars, or stuffed with collections of bric-a-brac.

Among such collections were Native American artifacts (Fig. 13). Before the 1890s they were intermingled indiscriminately in the eclectic tableaux in curio cabinets or so-called "cozy corners," but increasingly thereafter they assumed predominance in display and, I would argue, in the consciousness of the growing numbers of people who collected them (Lee 1991, Phillips 1998).

5. By 1900 collecting had become a cultural phenomenon worthy of study (cf. Burk 1900).

The growing interest in Native American art was a by-product of antimodernism, a movement protesting mass production and excessive consumption that arose in America around the turn of the century (Lears 1981). It is based on the premise that the close relationship between members of small-scale societies and the fruits of their labors made for a contentment lacking in the modern industrialized West (Boris 1986). Thus the artifacts of Native Americans became a symbol of Westerners' loss of connection with their means of production and their own past. The awe and reverence that collectors used in writing about Native American artifact collecting even suggests that this activity promoted the intensity of experience that Protestant religion could no longer provide. Collecting sometimes came to serve as a substitute for organized religion (Lee 1999: 275). For instance, in 1901, one collector wrote:

> "As ... cathedrals remind the 'bookless' midieval of God so should we use Indian objects to remind us of the simplicity, religiosity and significance of the[se] first settlers of North America" (James 1901: 620).

It is evident, then, that Native American art collecting is an expression of wider cultural preoccupations, and within this framework, that Eskimo artifacts collected at the time of the Nome Gold Rush offer tantalizing insights. An image of the collection of William and Neeta Sale covering the walls of their Nome living room illustrates two key motivations of turn-of-the-century collectors, the Myth of the Vanishing Indian and the Search for Authenticity (Krug and Krug 1998: 157; Fig. 14).

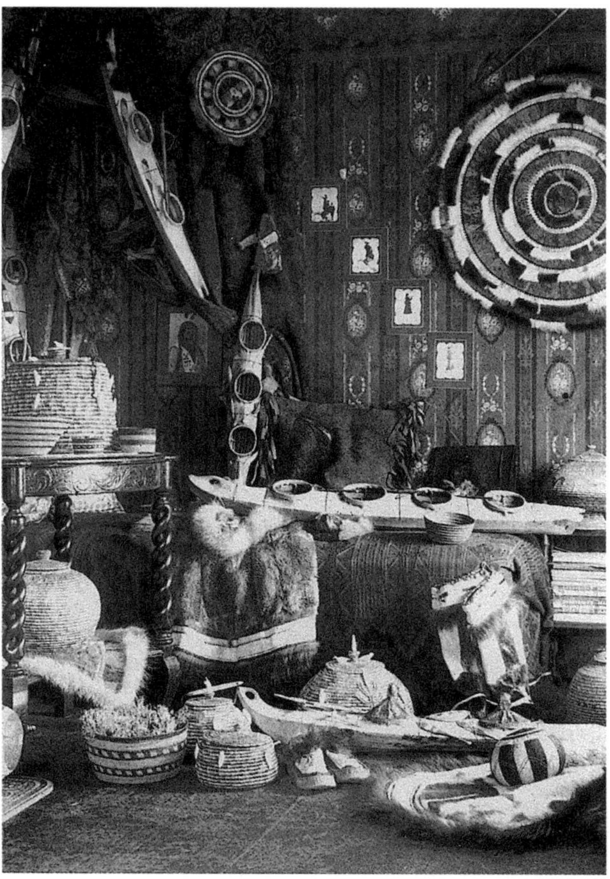

Fig. 14 William and Neeta Sale artifact collection, Nome, 1906. This collection is typical of the turn-of-the-century collections showing non-Native interest in "traditional" artifacts. Courtesy of the Alaska State Historical Library (Juneau, AK), PCA 384-25.

Some objects in the Sale collection, such as the boat models, clothing, and balls, are types associated with a precontact stage of Eskimo life. One aspect of the belief about Native people that was influential at the beginning of early-twentieth-century artifact collecting was the myth of the Vanishing Indian, the so-called "salvage" paradigm (Clifford 1987, Gordon and Herzog 1988, Herzog 1996). Lewis Henry Morgan and his followers considered small-scale societies to be earlier stages of their own. Thus the disease and degradation Native people endured as a result of Western contact could be justified as the inevitable result of evolution. Eskimos, like other Native Americans, were categorized according to this scheme. Thus "[the Eskimos] have joined the long caravansary of dead and dying peoples—not only through contact with civilization, but from natural displacement by evolution" (Bruner 1901: 338). Since their indigenous art forms were slated to become history along with them, everyone wanted a piece of the past.

Salvage-paradigm mentality led to the assumption that earlier Eskimo art forms were more authentic. A leitmotif of collecting, the search for authenticity, like the interest in Native peoples, grew out of the antimodernist protest against the mass production and industrialization of the Gilded Age. It is probably the most fundamental and unifying motivation for turn-of-the-century Native art collectors. As early as 1897, tourists to Alaska were concerned about the authenticity of Alaska Native art: "The curios are genuine," wrote an Alaskan newspaper in 1897, "and the story about the goods being shipped up from the States ... is without foundation" (*North Star* 1897).

As a concept, authenticity is flexible enough to accommodate a broad range of interpretations. Analysis of more than a hundred turn-of-the-century private collections of Alaska Native art suggests that buyers fell into three groups based in part on their definition of authenticity (Lee 1999: 269). At one end of the spectrum, souvenir buyers required only that an object be purchased from a Native person; at the other were those like the revenue cutter personnel who, because of their profession, had greater access to Alaska Natives, usually in remote localities. At this more extreme end of the spectrum, the most discriminating collectors sometimes demanded that an artifact show evidence of Native use.

The Sale collection, however, which was made by a local Nome family, falls somewhere in the middle. The artifacts read as "authentic" even though any or all may be replicas, and several—the model kayak and the coiled basket and mat—were probably not in the normal precontact inventory. Thus authenticity is a cultural construction based on the particular expectations and misapprehensions of the collector (Horner 1990).

The "salvage" paradigm and the search for authenticity affected the course of Eskimo art at the turn of the century both positively and negatively. The burst of interest in the Vanishing Eskimo and the flexible definition of authenticity undoubtedly contributed to the proliferation of art forms; but then as now, non-Native consumers' wish for a piece of the past set limits on the range of these art forms that Eskimo artists continue to strain against even today.

References Cited

Anonymous
1900 Keen Eskimo Traders. *Baltimore Sun*, 25 November.

Anonymous
1908 [Article in the] *Daily Alaska Dispatch* 139 (11 August).

Bockstoce, John R.
1977 *Eskimos of Northwest Alaska in the Early Nineteenth Century*. Pitt Rivers Museum, Monograph Series 1. Oxford.

Boris, Eileen
1986 *Art and Labor: Ruskin, Morris and the Craftsman Ideal in America*. Philadelphia, PA: Temple University Press.

Bruner, Jane Woodworth
1901 The Natives of Alaska. *Overland Monthly*, 2nd ser. 38: 338–345.

Burk, Caroline Frear
1900 The Collecting Instinct. *Pedagogical Seminary* 7: 197–207.

Clifford, James
1987 Of Other Peoples: Beyond the "Salvage" Paradigm. In: Hal Foster (ed.), *Discussions in Contemporary Culture #1* (DIA Art Foundation; Seattle, WA: Bay Press), 121–130.

Coleclaugh, Emma S.
1876 The Eskimo. *Providence Journal*, 31 May: 8.

Collis, Septima
1890 *A Woman's Trip to Alaska*. New York, NY: Cassell Publishing.

Dare, Virginia
1903 Curio Hunting of the Pacific Coast. *House Beautiful* 14(5): 260–263.

Doty, William
1898–1899 Journal of William Doty. Saint Lawrence Island Teacher Journals. Unpublished manuscript in the Alaska State Historical Library, Juneau, AK.

Gordon, Beverly (with Melanie Herzog)
1988 *American Indian Art: The Collecting Experience*. Madison, WI: The Elvehjem Museum of Art.

Graburn, Nelson H. H.
1976 *Ethnic and Tourist Arts: Cultural Expressions from the Fourth World*. Berkeley, CA: University of California Press.
1999 Epilogue: Ethnic and Tourist Arts Revisited. In: Ruth B. Phillips and Christopher B. Steiner (eds.), *Unpacking Culture* (Berkeley, CA: University of California Press), 335–355.

Healy, Fred
1883 The Journal of Fred Healy. Unpublished manuscript in the Michael A. Healy Papers, The Huntington Library, Pasadena, CA.

Healy, Mary Jane
1883–1884 The Journal of Mary Jane Healy. Unpublished manuscript in the Michael A. Healy Papers, The Huntington Library, Pasadena, CA.

Herzog, Melanie
1996 Aesthetics and Meanings: The Arts and Crafts Movement and the Revival of American Indian Basketry. In: Bert R. Denker (ed.), *The Substance of Style: Perspectives on the Arts and Crafts Movement* (Winterthur, DE: Winterthur Museum), 69–92.

Henderson, Alice Palmer
1898 *The Rainbow's End: Alaska*. Chicago, IL—New York, NY: H. S. Stone.

Hinckley, Ted C.
1965 The Inside Passage: A Popular Gilded Age Tour. *Pacific Northwest Quarterly* 56(2): 67–74.

Hooper, Calvin L.
1881 Diary. Unpublished manuscript, California Academy of Sciences Archives, San Francisco, CA.

Horner, Alice E.
1990 The Assumption of Tradition: Creating, Collecting, and Conserving Cultural Artifacts in the Cameroon Grassfields (West Africa). Ph.D. dissertation, University of California, Berkeley, CA.

James, George Wharton
1901 Indian Basketry in House Decoration. *Chautauquan* [September]: 619.

Krug, John W. and Caryl Sale Krug
1998 *One Dog Short: The Odyssey and Collection of a Family in Alaska During the Gold Rush Years*. Juneau, AK: Division of Archives, Libraries and Museums, Alaska Department of Education.

Kunkle, Jeff
1997 (ed.) *Alaska Gold: Life on the New Frontier*. San Francisco, CA: Scottwall Assoc.

Lears, C. J. Jackson
1981 *No Place of Grace: Antimodernism and the Transformation of American Culture, 1880–1920*. New York, NY: Pantheon.

Lee, Molly
1987 Alaska Eskimo Baskets: Types and Prototypes. In: Peter L. Corey (ed.), *Faces, Voices and Dreams* (Juneau, AK: Division of Alaska State Museums and the Friends of the Alaska State Museum), 44–57.
1991 Appropriating the Primitive: Turn-of-the-Century Collection and Display of "Native Alaskan Art." *Arctic Anthropology* 28(1): 6–15.
1992 Appropriating the Primitive: The Collection of Native North American Art 1880–1915, with Special Reference to Alaska. Ph.D. dissertation, University of California, Berkeley, CA.
1995 Siberian Sources of Alaskan Eskimo Coiled Basketry: Types and Prototypes. *American Indian Art Magazine* 20(4): 56–69.
1996 Context and Contact, The History and Activities of the Alaska Commercial Company, 1867–1900. In: Nelson H. H. Graburn, Molly Lee, and Jean-Loup Rousselot, *Catalogue Raisonné of the Alaska Commercial Company Collection at the Phoebe A. Hearst Museum of Anthropology* (Berkeley, CA: University of California Press), 19–39.
1999 Tourists and Taste Cultures: Collecting Alaska Native Art at the Turn of the Century. In: Ruth B. Phillips and Christopher B. Steiner (eds.), *Unpacking Culture* (Berkeley, CA: University of California Press), 267–281.
in press Zest or Zeal? Sheldon Jackson and the Commodification of Alaska Native Art. In: Shepard Krech, Jr. and Barbara Hail (eds.), *Collecting Native America, 1870–1960* (Washington, DC: Smithsonian Institution Press), 62–82.

Macpherson, C. B.
1962 *The Political Theory of Possessive Individualism*. New York, NY: Oxford University Press.

McLain, Carrie M.
1969 *Gold-rush Nome*. Portland, OR: Graphic Arts Center.

Murdoch, John
1892 Ethnological Results of the Point Barrow Expedition. *9th Annual Report of the Bureau of Ethnology for the Years 1887–1888*: 3–441.

Nelson, Edward W.
1899 The Eskimo about Bering Strait. *18th Annual Report of the Bureau of American Ethnology for the Years 1896–1897*: 3–518.

Nelson, Klondy (with Cory Ford)
1958 *Daughter of the Gold Rush*. New York, NY: Random House.

Nome News [Nome, AK]:
1902a A Curio Collection. 2 February 1902: 2.
1902b Advertisement for Log Cabin Store. 28 July 1902: 4.
1902c Advertisement for Log Cabin Store. 8 August 1902.
1903 Don't Overlook Curios. 22 September 1903: 2.
1904 Alaska's Exhibit. 19 July 1904: 2.

Nome Nugget [Nome, AK]
1905 Big Party of Tourists. 16 May 1905: 3.

Norris, Frank
1985 *Gawking at the Midnight Sun: The Tourist in Early Alaska*. Studies in History 170. Anchorage, AK: Alaska Historical Commission.

North Star [Sitka, AK]
1897 Our Tourists. 16 May 1905: 3.

Nowell, Elizabeth
1911 At Home with the Eskimos of the Far North. *Pioneer Magazine* 1(1): 7–12, 19.

Phillips, Ruth B.
1998 *Trading Identities: The Souvenir in Native North American Art from the Northeast, 1700–1900*. Seattle, WA: University of Washington Press.

Ray, Dorothy Jean
1961 *Artists of the Tundra and the Sea*. Seattle, WA: University of Washington Press.
1975 *The Eskimos of Bering Strait, 1650–1898*. Seattle, WA: University of Washington Press.
1980 Native Arts and Artifacts as Reflected in Alaska Exploration before 1867. In: Antoinette Shalkop (ed.), *Exploration in Alaska: Captain Cook Commemorative Lectures* (Anchorage, AK: Cook Inlet Historical Society), 159–174.
1982 *Setting it Free: An Exhibition of Modern Alaskan Eskimo Ivory Carving*. Fairbanks, AK: University Museum.
1984 Happy Jack: King of the Eskimo Ivory Carvers. *American Indian Art Magazine* 10(1): 32–48.
1987 Eskimo Artifacts: Collectors, Collections and Museums. In: Peter L. Corey (ed.), *Faces, Voices and Dreams* (Juneau, AK: Division of Alaska State Museums and the Friends of the Alaska State Museum), 29–43.

Scidmore, Eliza Ruhamah
1885 *Alaska: Its Southern Coast and the Sitkan Archipelago*. Boston, MA: D. Lothrop.

Sessions, Francis C.
1890 *From Yellowstone Park to Alaska*. New York, NY: Welch, Fracker.

Smith, Derek G.
1984 Mackenzie Delta Eskimo. In: David Damas (ed.), *Arctic* (Handbook of North American Indians 5, William C. Sturtevant, gen. ed.; Washington, DC: Smithsonian Institution), 347–358.

Snow, W. Parker
[1858] *A Catalogue of the Arctic Collection in the British Museum*. London: Joseph Masters.

Sullivan, May Kellogg
1903 *A Woman Who Went to Alaska*. Boston, MA: J. T. Earle.
Wardman, George
1884 *A Trip to Alaska*. Boston, MA: Lee and Shepard.
Wickersham, James
1902 Eskimo Pictures and Maps: made by E-too-ach-in-na (presented to James Wickersham at Nome by his son ... on April 4, 1902). Unpublished manuscript, Alaska Historical Library, Juneau, AK.

Reading Pictorial Imagery in Washoe Basketry

Marvin Cohodas

A photograph from about 1915 shows Washoe basket weaver Maggie Mayo James weaving a coiled willow basket, attempting to attract tourists at Lake Tahoe to purchase her basketry and beadwork curios (Fig. 1).[1] Her potential customers included not only summer vacationers visiting lakeside resorts, but also wealthy women living in summer mansions surrounding the lake who built large collections of basketry and other curios. While anthropologists stopped by to acquire collections for museum employers, at the same time soliciting information on indigenous basketry techniques and functions, dealers would pass through to collect wares for galleries in metropolitan centers. Whether perceiving their interest as "aesthetic," "touristic," or "scientific," purchasers believed they were witnessing the demise of Native American distinctiveness and chose curios to serve as relics of an unrecoverable past (Phillips 1998: 144).

Different groups of buyers would make very different purchases from among the array of objects displayed here, and there are some objects that none would purchase. The crate, bucket, and pan for water used to keep basketry materials flexible would not be purchased as they were of non-Native manufacture and non-Natives used them for relatively similar purposes as did Natives. The same discrimination applied to Maggie James's clothing and the mat on which she sat. Because anthropological inquiry of the time focused on reconstructing the past rather than describing the present, even anthropologists eschewed such "material culture," despite the fact that these objects were actually used or worn by Native peoples and in some cases essential to their lifestyle.

Although many types of curios were designed specifically for sale and therefore lacked a history of indigenous use, all classes of buyers were willing to purchase such objects if they articulated sufficient difference from Euro-American society to be useful in constructing the requisite image of the premodern Native American for parlor and museum displays. Such curios included the loom-beaded belts displayed by James, a recent development in the California-Nevada area using materials manufactured in Europe and techniques imported from the Plains. After a century of curio production in the eastern United States and Canada, beadwork had come to be metonymic for the Native American in popular thought.

In contrast, the pile of baskets supporting these belts represents items with the closest yet varied relation to precontact Native heritage. The meal brush made of soap-root leaves is perhaps unchanged and may have once been used. The truncated conical storage baskets are partially adapted for sale, displaying more elaborate decoration to attract buyers, and woven in the time-saving technique of spaced stitching to increase the quantity available for sale. In addition to "discriminating" collectors, regular collector/vacationers, casual tourists, and museum anthropologists or their agents are likely to have purchased such baskets to demonstrate indigenous technology, and the latter might also have acquired samples of basketry materials such as the willow rods visible on the basket pile and wooden box.

Marvin Cohodas received his doctorate in art history from Columbia University in 1974 and has been teaching in the Department of Fine Arts at the University of British Columbia since 1976. An accomplished basket weaver himself, Cohodas pursues research both in Native American curio basket weaving and in arts of the ancient Maya. Author's address: Department of Fine Arts, University of British Columbia, 6333 Memorial Road, Vancouver, BC, Canada V6T 1Z2.

1. A slightly earlier photograph of Maggie James at Lake Tahoe is perhaps more typical in that the photographer has arranged several baskets purchased from various weavers around one particularly "picturesque" woman (Cohodas 1990: fig. 30). While the 1915 example is less staged, it nevertheless contributes to the construction of curio-making Native American women as tourist attractions in themselves (Phillips 1998: 31–35).

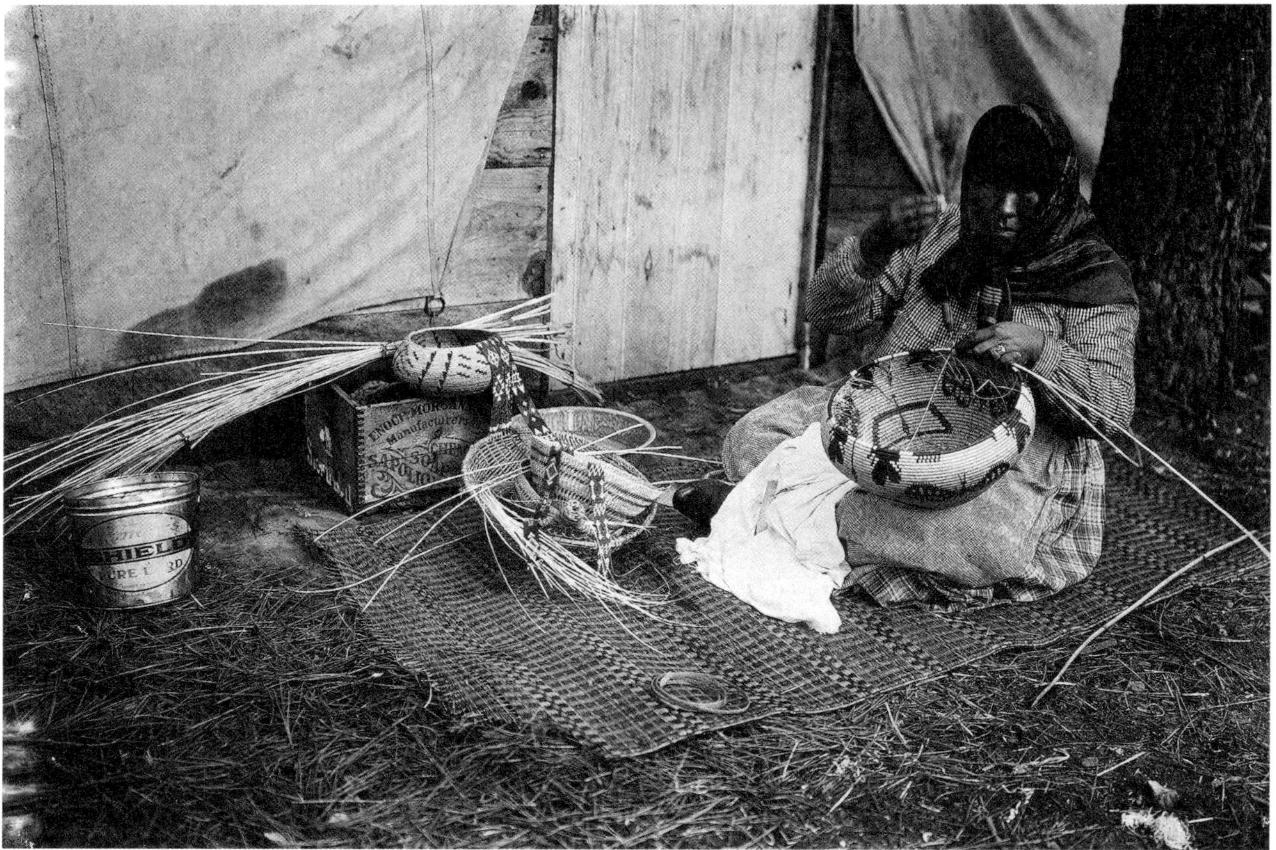

Fig. 1 Maggie James at Lake Tahoe, ca. 1915. Photographer unknown. Photo courtesy of Southwest Museum (Los Angeles, CA), photo no. 1618.

The basket on the box and that being woven mediate these extremes of long-standing indigenous practice and recent introduction. They combine increased decoration with a time-consuming weaving technique originally designed to produce watertight baskets for cooking, but now aimed at buyers willing to invest larger sums of money in what was then considered "basketry art." The incurving form of these two baskets lacked indigenous precedent or function in Washoe weaving but was instead adapted at the end of the nineteenth century from other western basket styles as a shape appropriate for eye-level display in the bourgeois home. The term *degikup* was applied to the Washoe version of this form, which was readily accepted by collectors as well as many anthropologists as the most valuable and "authentic" type of Washoe basketry product.

However, even these *degikup* were subject to varying discriminations among consumers. One of Maggie James's *degikup* is decorated entirely with geometric ornament, while the other involves pictorial imagery including arrows and butterflies. By 1915, about a decade after its introduction to Washoe basket weaving, such pictorial imagery had become common, in part because it was popular with consumers. While the authenticity of the expanded geometric arrangement was rarely questioned,[2] pictorial designs were subject to considerable debate and frequent exclusion.

Debate concerning the meaning and authenticity of pictorial imagery on baskets (as on other curio media such as clothing and pottery) touched broader issues not only of race and gender but also of nationalism and economic development at the turn of the century. As the political and economic makeup of North America changed, so too changed both the curio imagery and the ways it was interpreted by different audiences. The well-documented history of Washoe basket weaving will serve as the primary example for a discussion of such changing meanings and debates, set into a general context of Californian basketry for the curio trade.

2. An exception was C. Hart Merriam (1955: 121).

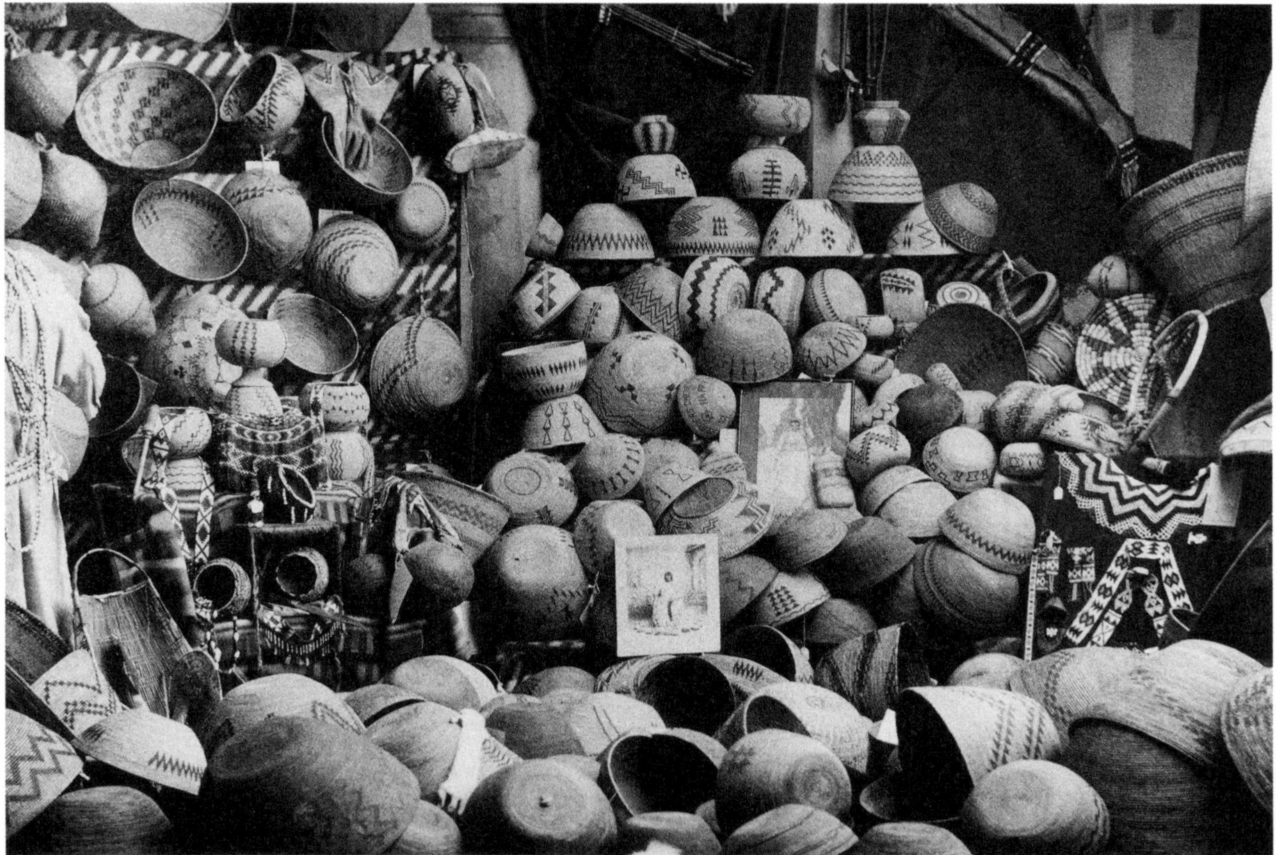

Fig. 2 Basketry display in Cohn's Emporium Company store, Carson City, Nevada, 1899. Photo courtesy of Nevada State Museum (Carson City, NV).

Pictorialism in Californian Basketry

Geometrically arranged and abstracted human figures were long used as basket weaving motifs in California. By the late nineteenth century they were joined by the "floral mode,"[3] an unrealistic combination of often quite realistic plant and bird images that swept across North America in the nineteenth century. In California and Nevada this more diverse pictorial repertoire came to include not only birds but also mammals like the horse and deer, reptiles like the snake and gila monster, humans distinguished as male or female, Native or non-Native, and architecture including forts and tipis.

Although the combination of words and images on Californian basketry has a precedent in the Chumash offering trays of the early nineteenth century,[4] the use of European letters and numbers as design motifs did not become prominent on western curio baskets until the 1890s. Combined into meaningful words and phrases including dates, this use of script even preceded adoption of the "floral mode" among groups such as the Washoe. Appearing simultaneously was another form of naturalism: the weaving of baskets in the shapes of such Euro-American household items as the cup-and-saucer, tea pot, sugar bowl, and pedestal bowl or compote server (Washburn 1984). For example, a display of predominantly Washoe baskets photographed in 1899 (Fig. 2) reveals no floral-mode decorations, but does include a basket (center) with an inscription celebrating Christmas and New Year, woven by Mrs. Cheney,[5] and a compote-shaped *degikup* (left) woven by Louisa Keyser. Such forms imitating Euro-American utensils lost popularity as Victorian taste for eclecticism waned in the early twentieth century, but they were replaced by others of exaggerated exoticism, such as the miniature cradle complete with "Indian Princess" doll.

3. The conventional term is "floral style," but in fact this combination of images was represented in many different styles as well as different techniques and media.

4. The most famous of these was made in 1822 by Juana Basilia on commission from Californian governor Sola for presentation to Mexican soldier José de la Cruz (Guy 1976: 3).

5. The inscription reads: "Merry Christmas and Happy New Year, Jan. 8, '99 and Jan. 15, '99. By Mrs. Cheney" (see Moser 1986: 68).

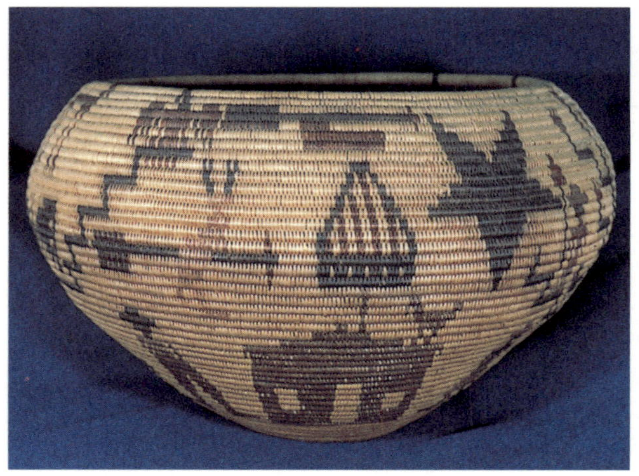

Fig. 3 Sarah Mayo coiled basket, ca. 1915–20, with scene of rabbit hunting. Private collection.

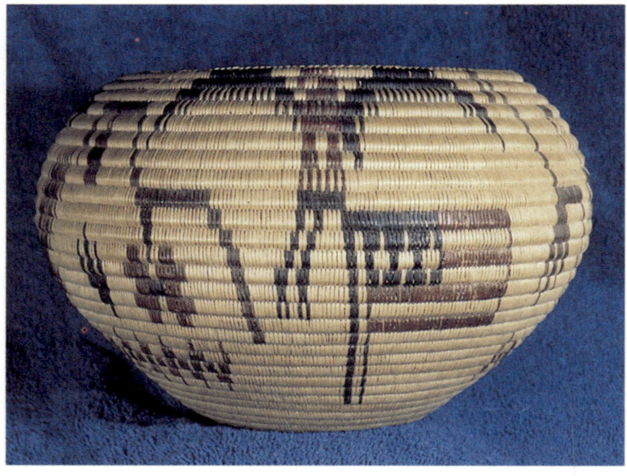

Fig. 4 Maggie James coiled basket, ca. 1915–20, with bird, butterfly, plant, and flag motifs. Private collection.

While most scholarly discussion of pictorialism in Native American curios has focused on the origin and spread of the floral mode from the northeastern Woodlands, recent analyses by David Penney (1991) and Ruth Phillips (1998) reject the passive model of "Western influence" conventionally used to explain Native adoption and diffusion of the floral mode. These authors instead highlight the active and strategic choices on the part of Native (primarily women) producers, partially aimed at reproduction of ethnic identity.

In the Far West, issues of Native agency are complicated by the importance of traders in fostering the curio trade in several media, including the national craze for basketry that was the subject of considerable popular and academic literature between 1890 and 1908. Among the Washoe, living around Carson City and Lake Tahoe on the border area of Nevada and California, the primary traders were Amy Cohn and her husband, Abe Cohn, who dedicated a portion of his Emporium Company clothing store to her curio shop. The Cohns' success depended on their patronage relationship with the innovative Washoe weaver Louisa Keyser, popularly known as Dat So La Lee. In the 1890s Keyser introduced the *degikup* shape and two-color design, both of which became standard for Washoe curio basket weaving within a decade. Keyser's engagement with pictorialism was limited to the use of imitative shape: At the start of her patronage relationship she added a pedestal to one *degikup* to create a compote shape (Fig. 2) and about two decades later wove a series of miniature cradles to hold dolls. She never experimented with the floral mode, nor did her sister-in-law and closest imitator, Scees Bryant.

In contrast, most other Washoe weavers took up floral-mode pictorial imagery. Sarah Jim Mayo, who may have introduced this mode to Washoe basketry, also greatly increased the available color palette to enhance the subtlety of her renderings (Fig. 3).[6] Mayo first introduced tree, arrow, eagle, butterfly, and horse motifs around 1905 and around 1913 added humans, the American flag, deer, rabbits, and buildings, often combined into scenes of non-Natives at "forts" and narratives of Washoe men hunting rabbit or deer. These motifs, along with the radial motif now called "whirling logs,"[7] became the standard repertoire of Washoe pictorial basketry imagery, especially in Carson Valley where Mayo lived and where they were fully taken up by Mayo's stepdaughter, Maggie Mayo James (Fig. 4). After 1915 Tootsie Dick Sam, a relative of Louisa Keyser's, adopted a limited selection of this repertoire (tree, eagle, butterfly, whirling logs; Fig. 5), and some were taken up as well by other Antelope Valley weavers including Lena Frank Dick. Pictorial imagery was also adapted to beaded basketry and remained popular among Washoe weavers into the 1930s.

Of particular significance is the fact that prominent

6. To the use of black mud-dyed bracken fern root along with the red redbud branch introduced by Louisa Keyser to Washoe coiled basket weaving, Sarah Mayo added the use of brown undyed bracken fern root and dark tan "sunburned" willow. In some baskets Mayo added willow-dyed pink and green.

7. The designation "whirling logs," derived from Navajo representation, has been applied to replace the term "swastika," an association that postdates the objects under discussion.

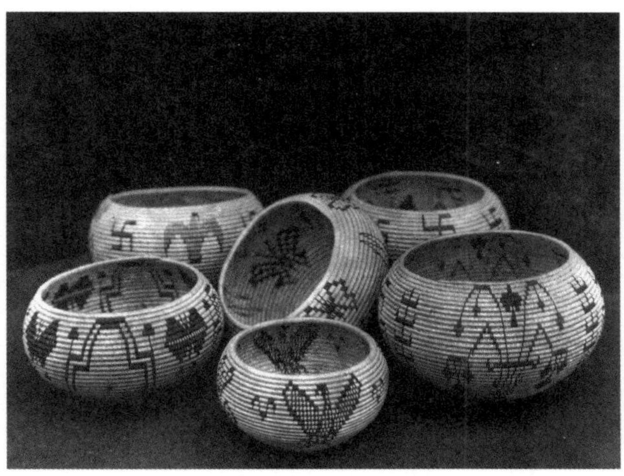

Fig. 5 Group of baskets by Tootsie Dick Sam between 1920 and 1923, photographed in 1924 by Edward Sheriff Curtis in the Cohn Emporium Company store, Carson City, Nevada. After Curtis (1926).

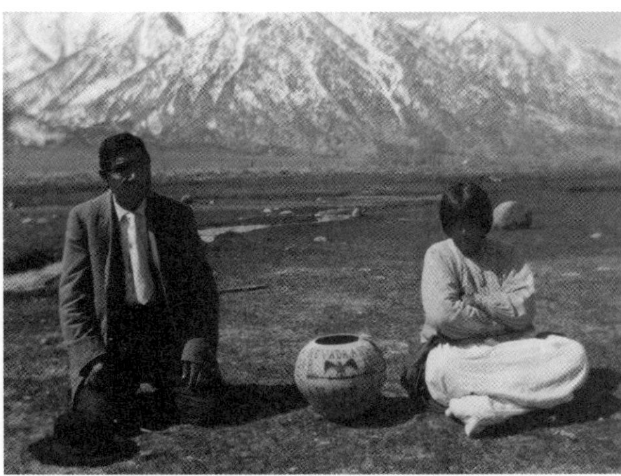

Fig. 6 Sarah Mayo and Captain Pete Mayo with the Woodrow Wilson basket. Photograph by Margaretta Dressler, 1913–14. Present location of basket unknown.

weavers like Keyser and Bryant resolutely resisted this widespread adoption of the floral mode in Washoe basketry. This refusal cannot simply be ascribed to the close patronage relationship between Amy Cohn and Louisa Keyser, even though it facilitated Cohn's strategy of increasing the value of Keyser's baskets by presenting her as the most traditional weaver (Cohodas 1992). In contrast, Tootsie Dick, also close to Louisa Keyser, enthusiastically adopted the pictorial repertoire, while Tillie Snooks, who traveled and sold baskets with Sarah Mayo and Maggie James, did not.

The contrasting lifestyles of Louisa Keyser and Sarah Mayo do appear to have influenced their diverse choices, but in a manner that belies the conventional treatment of geometric designs on baskets as "traditional" and pictorial imagery as "acculturated." In comparison to other weavers, Keyser actually followed the most altered and isolated lifestyle, generally living with her non-Native patrons in Carson City, her food provided so that she could devote full-time to weaving. On the other hand, Mayo, who innovated and inspired more pictorial designs than any other weaver, not only wove, traveled, and gathered food with other Washoe women, but was also a powerful and committed member of the Carson Valley community. Her father was Captain Jim (Henukeha), a man so respected as a political leader or "captain" that the husbands of both Sarah Mayo and her sister Agnes also became captains.[8]

Sarah Mayo's most famous political intervention was weaving a basket in 1913 for presentation to President Woodrow Wilson and Congress (Fig. 6). This basket was to accompany a petition, signed by Sarah and Captain Pete Mayo as well as Agnes and Captain Sam Pete, requesting funds to purchase homestead lands for the Washoe people, who had been relegated to the margins of non-Native settlement. The non-Native woman with whom Sarah Mayo had the closest relationship was Margaretta Dressler, who wrote out for Mayo the words she wanted woven into the design and who documented the finished product in several photographs.[9] Involving Margaretta Dressler in the project was probably a significant step in the process that led to the sale by her husband, rancher and state senator William Dressler, of the tract of land which became the Dresslerville Colony (Cohodas 1990: 170–172). The design on this basket (Cohodas 1979: figs. XX, 47–49) alternated portraits of Sarah and of her father, Captain Jim (Henukeha) with the image of an eagle grasping arrows. While eagles and arrows had been part of Mayo's weaving repertoire for nearly a decade, the form in which she combined them on this basket also suggests the presidential seal in reference to its prospective recipient. Despite the fact that Sarah Mayo's hybrid combination of text and pictorial imagery was designed to politically intervene in the campaign to improve living conditions for Washoe

8. These captains were not "chiefs" but intermediaries in dealings between Washoe and non-Native authorities. As d'Azevedo and Kavanagh demonstrate, their leadership was often contested (1974).
9. The inscription reads: "Nevada and California. Sarah, I am his daughter. Captain Jim, first chief of the Washoe Tribe. This basket is a special curio, 1913."

people and ensure their continuation as a community, such imagery has often been rejected as inauthentic and "acculturated." Early-twentieth-century definitions of "tradition" and discriminations of "authenticity" thus represent non-Native impositions that often countered the interests of Native peoples.

The meaning of Sarah Mayo's presentation basket has been understood through pictorial documentation of its production and textual documentation surrounding land negotiations of which it formed a part. It is far more difficult to interpret messages intended by weavers in other pictorial baskets, whether directed at members of their own community or designed as self-representation to the non-Native consuming society. While most interpretations of basket designs and other women's products have involved imposition of a male ritualist and symbolist discourse, an alternate view might suggest that the combination of symmetrical order and dynamic vitality in floral-mode decorations articulated abstract notions of ordered well-being. Such an approach would better account for Washoe basketry depictions of the American flag, either isolated (Maggie James) (Fig. 4) or flying from a fort (Sarah Mayo) (Fig. 7). In comparison, Herbst and Kopp (1993) suggest that Lakota women producing quill- and beadwork imbued the flag motif with positive associations of order, status, and identity that furthered Native purposes. I also wonder whether inscriptions celebrating holidays or birthdays, as well as Sarah Mayo's self-honoring message to the President, conformed to a general notion of formalized sociality—a suggestion perhaps supported by the fact that the majority of objects reproduced in basketry in the 1890s were concerned with the serving of tea, coffee, and dessert.

I do not consider it appropriate to interpret weavers' intents further. Not only is there insufficient textual or other information to offer a more specific reading, but I also believe that aboriginal peoples themselves are best situated to provide the iconographic interpretations that serve their interests.

The Floral Mode and the Domestic Sphere

While information on weavers' intended meanings is slight, there is considerable evidence for the ways in which non-Native purchasers interpreted these baskets. Ruth Phillips notes that in the Victorian and Edwardian eras (roughly 1850–1920) that saw the height of the curio trade in Native American objects, floral decoration on clothing was associated not only with Native Americans in contrast to settler societies, but also with the "folk" peoples of Europe in contrast to cosmopolitan urbanites, and with middle class women in contrast to middle class men. She notes that the bourgeois parlor, where many floral-designed curios as well as oriental fabrics would be displayed, was also decorated with Western-made floral wall papers and fabrics and that the ensemble was poetically likened to an Arcadian wilderness setting (Phillips 1998: 222). Phillips concludes that within the characteristic Victorian symbolic dualism, floral decorations could function as a sign of the feminized domestic sphere of moral and religious inculcation in contrast to the masculinized public sphere of commerce and government.

My only disagreement with Phillips is that in privileging the gendered aspect of this symbolic duality of public and private, she undervalues bourgeois men's wearing of floral patterns in the domestic space (Phillips 1998: 187). I would argue that the division between men wearing drab clothing in the public sphere and at least sometimes wearing bright floral fabrics in the domestic space is significant because it suggests that the Victorian duality of masculinized public sphere and feminized private sphere was a distorted representation. The private sphere was not the sphere of women so much as the sphere of men's leisure in contrast to the public sphere of their work. Here men ruled by a patriarchal law of premodern origin, in contrast to the representational procedures of the modern fraternal social contract in the public sphere. Essentially, the middle class domestic space represented a premodern preserve, hence it is not surprising that Victorian women decorated it with curios and crafts also associated with the premodern (Cohodas 1997).

This premodern sphere encompassed not only domestic space with its associated decorations and practices, but also ethnic constructions of Aboriginal peoples as well as non-Anglophone immigrants. Both Native Americans and immigrant laborers were at this time associated with socialism and communism, considered the greatest threats to private property and bourgeois preeminence. To counter this threat, the bourgeoisie constructed Native or "folk" "authenticity" in leisure rather than labor, which transferred the privileged forms of interaction from the economic to the symbolic (the so-called "cultural") sphere, masking exploitation with an ideology of valued difference. Taking these associations and circumstances into account, I would argue that to the Victorian bourgeoisie, floral patterns linking Aboriginal peoples, immigrant laborers, and bourgeois women with the symbolic notion of a domestic sphere were read as signs of the desired "domestication" of these groups.

Basket weavers were aware not only that the objects they made were destined for parlor or museum display, but also that they constituted a performance of ethnicity for a non-Native audience, designed in part to fulfill the dominant society's view of Native peoples' "natural" state and subordinate position. This does not mean they represented themselves as belonging to the past, but rather that they frequently limited self-representation to images, such the rabbit hunting scene woven by Sarah Mayo (Fig. 3), that could be construed as suitably different from activities of their non-Native patrons. However, Native Americans increasingly subverted the intent of all such stagings of ethnicity not only by using them to continually reproduce and assert ethnic identity in the face of assimilationist pressures, but also by turning them to political activism.

The dualistic nature of this reading, articulating contrasts of Native and non-Native, female and male, folk and modern, etc. is belied by other readings and constructions that articulate bridging relationships between Native and non-Native bourgeois practices. For example, Penney's (1991) discussion of Native males wearing drab clothing for everyday labor versus floral-decorated clothing for ethnic performance on special occasions is paralleled in the bourgeois male's contrasting public and private apparel, while hunting and camping scenes associated in curio representation with Native peoples were also valued forms of leisure-time recreation for non-Natives.

Probing such bridging practices further, Phillips reveals that Native and non-Native women shared not only the activities of sewing and embroidery but also the use of floral-mode patterns. These shared experiences with textiles were partly the outcome of several centuries of assimilationist practices. From the activity of the Lorette nuns in the seventeenth century to that of field matrons in the late nineteenth and early twentieth centuries, non-Native women had been teaching textile practices to Native women and girls as a means of instilling "civilization."

Issues of class intersect with race and gender in the framework of this textile bond between Native and non-Native women. Literature of the late nineteenth century analyzed by Phillips (1998: 220–21) constructed such needlework as a sign of bourgeois femininity, not femininity in general. Among those excluded from this textile bond were servant women who performed onerous labors in bourgeois homes: Many of these, especially in the Far West, were Native Americans. In contrast to such drudgery, the literature constructed bourgeois women's textile practice as joyful labor, a premodern Arcadian construction realized through links with romanticized views of Native American precapitalist lifestyle and filtered through the ideals of the Arts and Crafts Movement (Cohodas 1997: 21–27, 202–206). Such discursive boundaries were rarely clear in practice. For example, Washoe women served in non-Native households as well as weaving curio baskets for sale.

The issue of Native Americans as laborers versus curio-producing artisans was the subject of complex debates and overt conflict among non-Native institutions, with government assimilation programs attempting to transform Native peoples into a laboring class through residential school education,[10] and with private institutions, including museums, expositions, and the tourist industry in general, seeking to preserve them as exotic spectacles. Such strategic bourgeois constructions of Native peoples as exotic objects of leisure and entertainment appear also to have attempted in contrasting ways to control and disempower the largely non-Anglophone laboring classes in an era of unionizing and national strikes (Cohodas 1997). On the one hand, articulating an aesthetic bond with Native American artisans allowed the bourgeoisie to distance themselves from laboring classes. On the other hand, Natives, immigrants, and bourgeois women were linked through textile practices, particularly floral-mode designs, as survivors of premodern society, potentially excluded from fraternal rights of representation to subject them instead to patriarchal rule. Floral-mode decorations entered into these constructions as signs of the domestic as domesticated, linking different groups to naturalize racial and gender hierarchies, yet also providing the means by which these hierarchies were resisted.

10. Washoe girls taken to the residential schools were often prohibited from returning to their families over the summer and instead were farmed out as servants to non-Native households.

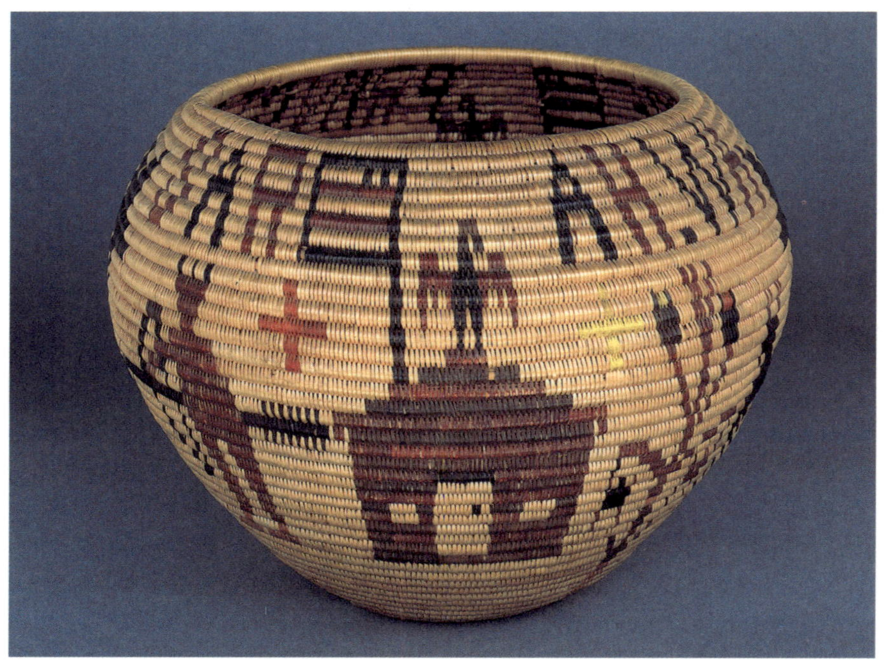

Fig. 7 Sarah Mayo basket with inscription, ca. 1914–20. Private collection.

Changing Meanings of Pictorial Basketry for Victorian Consumers

The precise readings of floral-patterned Native curios, as signs of exotic difference, bourgeois femininity, and subordination to patriarchal rule, changed as economic and political conditions altered and new ideas surfaced to compete with old ones. In order to clarify how different groups might have read and reacted differently to a pictorial basket by Sarah Mayo or Maggie James, some of these changes will be outlined.

During the 1880s and 1890s philanthropic eastern women's associations sought to end Native poverty and homelessness through assimilation into Christian agricultural society. They supported passage of the Dawes Allotment Act in 1887 which asked Natives to repudiate communal ownership of property, associated by the bourgeoisie with disruptive laboring classes, and instead embrace private ownership of land. Simultaneously, the federal government attempted destruction of tribal ties through residential schools, justifying their brutal policies with anthropological theories of social evolution. In these same years baskets came to be produced in quantity for sale as curios in the Far West, and among these appeared pictorial images as well as other representational devices such as script and imitative forms. The commercial success of these innovations suggests that they were being interpreted as evidence of the Native's advance from savagery toward civilization, as similar achievements in the eastern United States had been judged since mid-century (Phillips 1998: 54).

However, by the time Californian basketry was subjected to textual analysis, readings of representational devices as signs of progress toward civilization were being challenged by preservationists. Fearing that "assimilation" would deprive Americans of their exotic premodern Other, they decried all signs of "progress" in basketry and other curios. Arguing for the preservation of Native American distinctiveness, they countered evolutionist views of the superiority of European civilization with claims for the equal and enduring importance of all ways of life, to be appreciated in relative terms rather than judged by European standards.

Modernist nostalgia arising from alienation is frequently cited as an underlying motivation for this growing preservationist position, but we should not overlook the economic importance of a burgeoning tourist industry, nor discount the argument (made at the time) that Native Americans would be more economically successful and independent as artisans than as laborers. Nor should we underestimate the ideological importance of adopting Native Americans as a premodern heritage in the construction of a distinctive American nationalism.

Behind these changes was also an emergent elite of corporate capitalists anxious to control laboring class activism. Their rejection of hybridity as "acculturation" arose from an interest not only in preserving a pristine Native American ethnicity to constitute their premodern nationalist Other, but also in maintaining class dominance through eugenic doctrines of racial purification, enflaming fears that miscegenation led to the degradation and downfall of dominant races.[11] Hybridized curios, once favored as evidence of Natives'

11. At this time many considered Anglo-Saxons to be a race separate from and superior to other Europeans.

ability to achieve civilization, including those involving utensil imitation, script, and pictorial imagery, came to be rejected by this elite as dangerously contaminated and degraded.

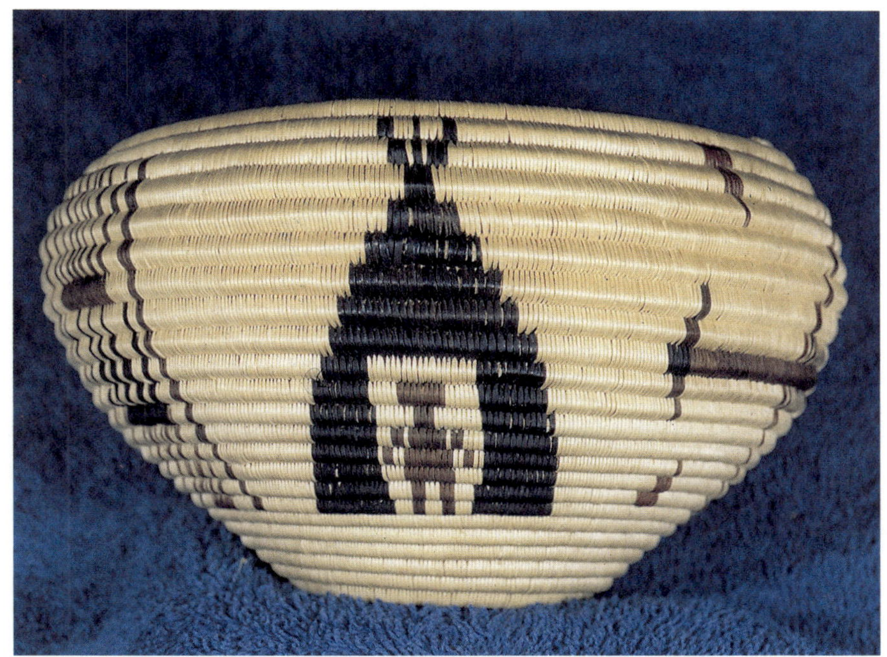

Fig. 8 Maggie James coiled basket, ca. 1915–1920, with tipi motif. Private collection.

To legitimate its recent economic supremacy through superior social status, this emerging corporate elite acquired valuable and prestigious objects that would demonstrate distinctive taste in consumption, marking out differences from the middle classes. Basket craze literature contributed to such class differentiation and elite self-construction by reducing the diversity of products to two polar categories: (1) inexpensive, quickly made objects available to any tourist as a souvenir and judged by the elite as vulgar; and (2) expensive, labor intensive objects considered to be aesthetically refined and desired by collectors both as fine art and as financial investments. Within this dichotomy, the eclecticism of the pictorial basketry mode generally relegated it to the category of tourists' vulgar souvenir, while baskets with only geometric designs appealing to modernism's formal simplicity were associated with refined elite taste for "traditional" fine arts.

However, many writers articulating a relativist position "authenticated" pictorial imagery in the floral mode by reconfiguring it from a sign of Native ability to imitate and therefore progress toward civilization, to the opposite meaning as a sign of Native peoples' "unchanging" association with nature and premodern spirituality. For Otis Tufton Mason, curator of Ethnology at the U.S. National Museum, as for George Wharton James, the leading popular writer on basketry, pictorial images demonstrated that basketry designs could encode elaborate mythological, ritual, and historical narratives.

In contrast to pictorial imagery, script and utensil shapes could not be reconfigured as premodern and were strongly rejected. Even Mason, a leading evolutionist who lauded technical and other changes in Native basket weaving as signs of "progress," characterized the use of imitative form and script as "trashy" (Mason 1904: 540). Warning prospective buyers against purchasing such "inauthentic" objects and thereby contributing to basketry's degradation, James illustrated two Californian baskets decorated with script, his caption reading "Basketry spoiled by vicious imitation" (James 1909: 192). Such vehement denunciations of script motifs suggest that they were seen not merely as vulgar or contaminated, but as a disruption of the literacy boundary that, by differentiating "primitive" from "modern" peoples, could legitimate colonialist exploitation.

While Native producers weaving for the popular, souvenir, and gift markets continued to make imitative objects like napkin rings and place mats, those aiming at the higher priced market for collectibles, and aware of discriminations made by elite consumers and their dealers, ceased using elements clearly appropriated from Euro-American design. To the consternation of some anthropologists, however, even Native weavers who specialized in producing traditionalist collectibles for the elite market continued to value the celebratory quality of script (O'Neale 1932: 158). And among the Washoe, the notoriety of Sarah Mayo's presentation basket sparked a limited fashion for the inclusion of script in floral-mode designs, including one by Sarah Mayo (Fig. 7) with the inscription "Sarah, Washoe Princess."[12]

12. In addition, Tootsie Dick Sam wove a basket with images of butterflies accompanied by the word "butterfly."

In contrast to the popular preservationist position that rejected script but accepted pictorial images as signs of the Native American as "natural man" was the stricter preservationist position that rejected all designs in the floral mode as inauthentic products of debased commercialism. This severe position was advocated by the most elite members of the industrial bourgeoisie and was promulgated as a theory of "culture" by anthropologists employed at the museums and universities they funded. While Franz Boas was crucial in formulating this approach at the American Museum of Natural History and Columbia University in New York City, Alfred Kroeber, his first student to complete a doctorate, applied it to the Far West and specifically to basketry studies during his tenure at the Department and Museum of Anthropology at Berkeley, both financed by Phoebe Apperson Hearst. Because Kroeber and his associates designed their publications as reconstructions of indigenous practices as they might have existed in precontact times, all pictorials (and some other adaptations to the curio trade) were excluded from analysis (Cohodas 1997: 232–235).

All of these categories and histories of reception appear to have influenced the way consumers read pictorial imagery in Washoe basketry. The assimilationist-philanthropic position, and the associated bond between bourgeois and Native women, is exemplified by the collaboration between Margaretta Dressler and Sarah Mayo on a basket that not only included a pictorial image with which they both identified (eagle and arrows), but also a textual motif of the type rejected as inauthentic by most collectors a decade earlier (Fig. 6). Around the same time, Maggie James attracted the attention of Edith Pope, wife of industrialist George Pope, who purchased baskets during summers spent at their estate on the south shore of Lake Tahoe, near a Washoe summer encampment (Cohodas 1990: 175). Edith Pope is remembered as having preferred James's baskets with butterfly designs (Fig. 4), which I would suggest she interpreted as an element of nature, articulating the perceived indivisibility of Washoe presence from the Arcadian splendor of her vacation surroundings. And only two years after Mayo's basket was sent to Woodrow Wilson, anthropologist Samuel Barrett, a basketry specialist who earned his doctorate at Berkeley under Kroeber, visited Lake Tahoe to make a representative Washoe collection for the Milwaukee Public Museum. He purchased several three-rod *degikup* (Barrett 1917: plate IX) which may be identified as the work of Tillie Snooks, Sarah Mayo, and Maggie James, three weavers whose baskets were regularly sold together. Although James was using pictorial designs in about half of her fine *degikup*, and Mayo in almost all of hers, Barrett's stricter position appears to have prevented him from purchasing any of these. While he acknowledged in the resulting publication that the geometric decorations of these *degikup* represented curio trade modifications (Barrett 1917: 22), Barrett apparently believed that they could be recontextualized to represent precontact authenticity in a way that the pictorial designs he excluded could not.

The variety of pictorial images would also have suggested a variety of readings to consumers. Most pictorial images in Washoe and generally in Californian basketry articulate a relationship between Native and nature that conformed to the non-threatening or domesticated aspect of the relationship to Native Americans sought by the dominant group in American society. Curio consumers may have chosen such objects to concretize their positive assessment of Western technological progress and its ability to dominate nature and colonized peoples, as well as their interest in preserving Native American difference as a premodern, nationalist Other. Diverging from this median were, on the one hand, stereotyped and often childlike images (Fig. 8) that would have legitimated the federal government's patriarchal control and, on the other hand, assertive rejections of such stereotypes that would have resonated with beliefs in Native rights of self-determination. Some of these positions would have become entrenched through Native producers' attempts to meet the diversity of taste exercised by non-Native purchasers' selections. However, the role of Native producers in resisting, altering, and in some cases originating these constructions should not be undervalued.

Conclusion

Many analyses of pictorial modes of curio decoration, including my earlier discussion of Washoe pictorial weaving (Cohodas 1982), have suffered from reductive characterizations. Closer analysis reveals that both Natives and non-Natives in this period developed lifestyles characterized by various and changing combinations of indigenous, imported, and wholly new practices and thus performed both premodern and modern identities simultaneously. Non-Natives expressed their conflicting desires for the extinction or preservation of Native difference through varied forms of consumption, including touristic souvenirs, fine art collectibles, and museum artifacts, and through varied readings as signs of progress, signs of the domestication of nature and the premodern, or warnings against miscegenation. Whether intended as submissive, assertive, or celebratory forms of auto-ethnography, consumers could read pictorial imagery as signs of progress or domestication, of difference or connection. Because this flexibility of meaning allowed floral decor and other curio forms to serve multiple agendas, conflicts between different groups and institutions were in some cases expressed as conflicts over the reading of these images.

As such conflicts of class, race, ethnicity, and gender continue to be negotiated through symbolic forms as well as political action, we can expect that these images will continue to be read and that from these readings new interpretations will emerge. For example, through current interests in transculturation and hybridity, curios once rejected as inauthentic are instead seen as marking out a history of dialogic exchange of ideas and information that must reckon with changing tastes, values, ideologies, and economic relations (Phillips 1998: 10, 73).

References Cited

Barrett, Samuel A.
1917 The Washo Indians. *Bulletin of the Public Museum of the City of Milwaukee* 2(1): 1–52.

Cohodas, Marvin
1979 *Degikup: Washoe Fancy Basketry 1895–1935.* Vancouver, BC: Fine Arts Gallery, University of British Columbia.
1982 Sarah Mayo and Her Contemporaries. *American Indian Art Magazine* 6(4): 52–59, 80.
1990 Washoe Basketweaving: An Historical Outline. In: Frank W. Porter III (ed.), *The Art of Native American Basketry: A Living Legacy* (Westport, CT: Greenwood Press), 153–186.
1992 Louisa Keyser and the Cohns: Mythmaking and Basket Making in the American West. In: Janet Catherine Berlo (ed.), *The Early Years of Native American Art History: The Politics of Scholarship and Collecting* (Seattle, WA: University of Washington Press), 88–133.
1997 *Basket Weavers for the California Curio Trade: Elizabeth and Louise Hickox.* Tucson, AZ: University of Arizona Press.

Curtis, Edward S.
1926 *The North American Indian.* Volume 15. F. W. Hodge, ed. Norwood, MA: Plimpton Press.

d'Azevedo, Warren L. and Thomas Kavanagh
1974 The Trail of the Missing Basket. *Indian Historian* 7(3): 12–13, 60, 64.

Herbst, Toby and Joel Kopp
1993 The Grandfather's Flag. In: Toby Herbst and Joel Kopp (eds.), *The Flag in American Indian Art* (Cooperstown, NY: New York State Historical Association), 15–26.

Guy, Herbert
1976 Traditional Use of Patriotic Designs in American Indian Art. *Arizona Highways* 52(7): 2–13.

James, George Wharton
1909 *Indian Basketry.* Fourth edition. S.l.: Henry Malkan. [Reprint: New York, NY 1972: Dover.]

Mason, Otis Tufton
1904 Aboriginal American Basketry: Studies in a Textile Art Without Machinery. *Annual Report of the Board of Regents of the Smithsonian Institution ... for the Year Ending June 30, 1902*: 171–548.

Merriam, C. Hart
1955 *Studies of the California Indians.* Edited by the staff of the Department of Anthropology of the University of California. Berkeley, CA: University of California Press.

Moser, Christopher L.
1986 (ed.) *Native American Basketry of Central California.* Riverside, CA: Riverside Municipal Museum.

O'Neale, Lila M.
1932 Yurok-Karok Basket Weavers. *University of California Publications in American Archaeology and Ethnology* 32 (1): 1–184.

Penney, David W.
1991 Floral Decoration and Culture Change: an Historical Interpretation of Motivation. *American Indian Culture and Research Journal* 15(1): 53–77.

Phillips, Ruth B.
1998 *Trading Identities: The Souvenir in Native North American Art from the Northeast, 1700–1900.* Seattle, WA: University of Washington Press.

Washburn, Dorothy
1984 Dealers and Collectors of Indian Baskets at the Turn of the Century in California: Their Effect on the Ethnographic Sample. *Empirical Studies of the Arts* 2(1): 51–74.

Quilled Bark from the Central Great Lakes
A Transcultural History

Ruth B. Phillips

Late twentieth-century scholarship on Native North American art has challenged and complicated the notions of authenticity, tradition, and value that informed the literature in the field during much of the twentieth century. On the one hand, the frameworks for study established by cultural evolutionist and salvage anthropology attributed the greatest value to objects thought to display the fewest influences from Western art and material culture. On the other hand, the Western beaux arts tradition has privileged Native art forms most similar to easel painting and free-standing sculpture, the genres of Western art deemed to provide the greatest freedom of expression to the artist. Together, these discourses produced a canon of Native North American art that excluded or de-emphasized many commoditized genres that were valued and sought out by nineteenth-century Western collectors. More importantly, these genres have continued to be regarded as important, authentic, and traditional within Native communities.

Among the genres marginalized in the earlier literature are the birchbark wares ornamented with porcupine quillwork produced by central and western Great Lakes peoples since the early nineteenth century—objects that were made for sale to non-Natives and that are characterized by highly innovative forms and decorative motifs.[1] The renewed interest in these objects today benefits from current academic concerns with contact histories, colonialism, and expressive culture (Thomas 1991, 1994, Pratt 1992, Clifford 1997, Mauzé 1997, Marcus and Myers 1995, Phillips and Steiner 1999), from postcolonial theorizations of hybridity and mixing (King 1986, Bhabha 1994, Lippard 1990), and from Native interventions into standard Western academic narratives (Rickard 1992, Hill and Hill 1994, Ettawageshik 1999). In this paper I will assemble a set of important nineteenth-century collections of Great Lakes quillwork in order to establish the broad outlines of its stylistic and iconographic development, and I will argue for the authenticity of the transcultural art that this history reveals. I adopt the term "transculturation" first introduced by Cuban sociologist Fernando Ortiz (1995: 102–103) in the 1940s, because its positive stress on the "creation of new cultural phenomena" better represents the complex historical processes that have been more unidimensionally conceptualized as "acculturation" (European influence) or as absolute loss of tradition. It is important to acknowledge, however, the legacy of meticulous collections-based documentation and connoisseurship to which Norman Feder's work contributed so centrally and upon which all current analyses and interpretations rest. This paper is indebted not only to Feder's foundational work on Great Lakes art, but also to research on individual collections of quilled bark from the region carried out by Christian Feest, J. C. H. King, Ted Brasser, Sylvia Kasprycki and others. I hope that this initial attempt at synthesis will act as a spur to further work both within Native communities and in archival and museum collections.

The fact that quilled bark fancy wares are included in most of the important collections made in the Great Lakes from the 1830s to the late nineteenth century

Ruth B. Phillips is Director of the Museum of Anthropology and Professor of Art History and Anthropology at the University of British Columbia. She has worked in the areas of African and Native American art, focusing in recent years on the art of Northeastern and Great Lakes peoples. Her recent books are *Trading Identities: The Souvenir in Native North American Art from the Northeast, 1700–1900* (1998), *Native North American Art*, written with Janet Catherine Berlo (1998), and *Unpacking Culture: Art and Commodity in Colonial and Postcolonial Worlds*, coedited with Christopher B. Steiner (1999). Author's address: Museum of Anthropology, University of British Columbia, 6393 NW Marine Drive, Vancouver, BC, Canada V6T 1Z2.

1. Great Lakes quillwork was, for example, omitted from the most widely distributed surveys of Native American art published before 1980, such as LaFarge et al. [1931], Douglas and d'Harnoncourt (1941), Dockstader (1961), and (Feder (1971a, 1971b).

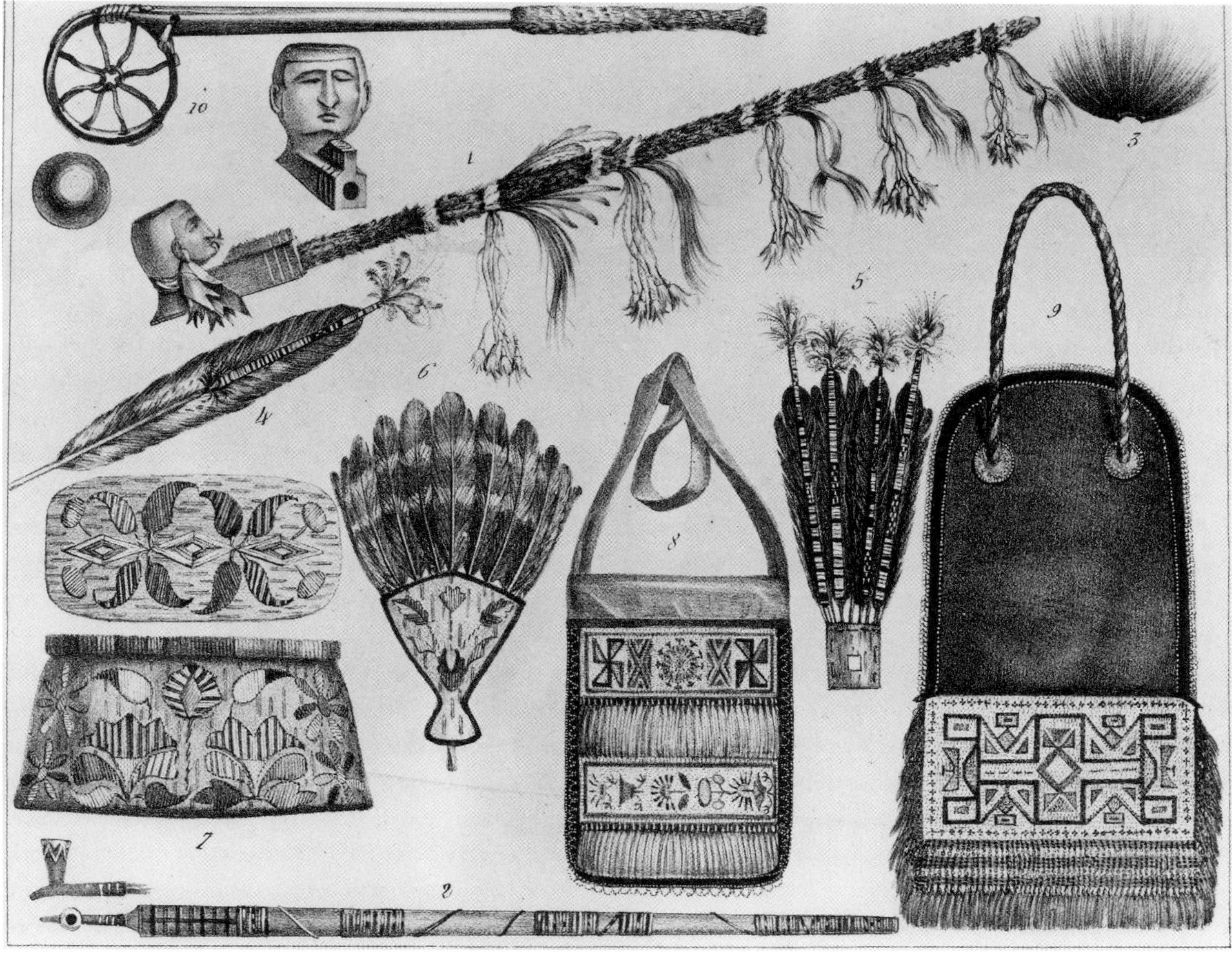

Fig. 1 "Ornements, calumets, boîtes, etc. ... des Indiens de l'Amérique du Nord." Lithograph by Ludewig in Castelnau (1842: pl. 33). Photograph: The Library of Congress (Washington, DC).

strongly suggests that the original collectors did not regard such made-for-sale objects as less authentic than the ritual implements and dress accouterments later defined as traditional. In Francis de Castelnau's 1842 *Vues et souvenirs de l'Amerique du Nord*, for example, a quilled container and fan are included among pouches and pipes under the heading "Weapons and Utensils" (Fig. 1). Other influential intellectuals and early anthropologists who collected and/or published quilled bark include Henry Rowe Schoolcraft, Prince Maximilian of Wied, and Lewis Henry Morgan. Examples of quilled bark were also prominent among the gifts given to high-ranking visitors to North America, such as the Prince of Wales, heir to Queen Victoria, Lord Elgin, Governor General of Canada, and Father Purbrick, overseer of the English Jesuit missions in North America. Although the relative ease with which the movements of such personages can be documented makes it easier to establish provenances and dates for their collections, these research possibilities have not yet been fully exploited.

The Early Development of Quilled Bark Wares

Great Lakes fancy bark wares are rooted in both aboriginal and Victorian visual traditions. The earliest fancy wares adopt the forms of two precontact Native containers made of folded and sewn birchbark. The box-like *makak* is a lidded storage container with high, inward slanting sides. A shallower bowl form, the *onakan*, has flared sides and a high curved end and was a second important prototype. Both types are represented in the largest extant collection of early nineteenth-century bark containers made by Giacomo Costantino Beltrami in the western Great Lakes in 1823 and now in the Museo Civico "E. Caffi" in

Bergamo, Italy. As suggested by this collection, at the time of contact the surfaces of bark containers were either left plain or were decorated with geometric sgrafitto designs formed by scraping away the dark outer layer of bark (Vigorelli 1987). Porcupine quills, sometimes dyed, occur only on the rims of bowls where they are interwoven with spruce root wrapping to form decorative geometric patterns. The second source for the Great Lakes fancy wares of bark and quillwork, Victorian home crafts and mass-produced wares, will be discussed in more detail below.

The earliest documented extant bark containers whose sides display quilled designs date to the early 1820s.[2] The idea of embroidering the surface of the bark was almost certainly introduced through contact with the quilled bark wares made by the Mi'qmak and Maliseet of Nova Scotia and New Brunswick (Whitehead 1982) or the moosehair-embroidered bark objects made first by French Canadian nuns and then by the Huron-Wendat in Quebec (Phillips 1998: 103–134). Both of these curio productions were enormously popular with the many British military and government officials who stopped at Halifax, Quebec, and Montreal on their way to postings in the central Great Lakes from 1760 through the 1820s. These transient Europeans probably took examples of moosehair or quilled bark objects with them on their journeys west. Odawas and other central Great Lakes peoples trading into Montreal and Quebec would also have seen examples on their own travels. The trading networks in which they participated may well have carried occasional pieces into central Great Lakes trading posts.[3] After 1814, with the reestablishment of peace in the central Great Lakes following the War of 1812, a greatly expanded market for Indian curiosities opened up in this region to serve the increasing numbers of Euro-North Americans who were pouring into the region as soldiers, administrators, settlers, and missionaries.[4]

Military Officers and Government Officials as Consumers

A terminus post quem for the commercial production of quilled bark wares of about 1815 is suggested by the fact that none of the many curiosity collections made by soldiers who served in the War of 1812 contains examples of these wares, although they do contain examples of moosehair embroidery on bark.[5] Yet within five or six years of the war's end, military travel diaries began to mention a trade in fancy bark work produced in the central and western Great Lakes. Major Joseph Delafield, for example, participated in a British army survey of the southern boundary of present-day Ontario. He was, on the evidence of his diary, an avid collector of curiosities, and he mentions bark wares in several entries of 1820. While visiting in the Detroit area, Delafield (1943: 328) noted "the rage for Indian curiosities amongst strangers that visit the upper country" and the high prices asked in the shops. At the Ojibwa village of Portaganasing on Drummond Island west of Manitoulin Island he ordered some of the "bark baskets used by them as curiosities" (Delafield 1943: 311). A local acquaintance, a Mrs. Solomon, also gave him "a plate of Seneca [sweet] grass handsomely braided by an Indian and a little Indian mat to add to my stock of curiosities" (Delafield 1943: 318).

That Delafield's purchases were probably ornamented with quillwork is suggested by the clear distinction made in contemporary writings between the unadorned bark containers used in the large-scale maple sugar trade and the smaller, decorated ones made as curios. In 1820 the young Henry Schoolcraft (1966: 122) saw Native people selling curiosities including "bark baskets filled with maple sugar, called mokeocks" at Michilimackinac. His travel book includes a plate showing a *makak* ornamented with a simple quilled geometric design. Thomas McKenney (1827: 194), who, accompanied by Schoolcraft, made a visit to the area seven years later, noted that only "the smaller

2. They are absent from earlier Revolutionary War period collections made in the central Great Lakes, such as those of Colonel Arendt De Peyster (Armour and Widder 1978) and Lieut. Andrew Foster (now, respectively, in the King's Regiment Collection, Merseyside County Museum, Liverpool, and the National Museum of the American Indian, Washington, DC). Both were stationed at Fort Michilimackinac, which was regularly frequented by the Odawa of Arbre Croche, who were among the earliest producers of quilled bark objects.

3. This trade may have been the source of the moosehair-embroidered bark basket illustrated by Beltrami (1828, 2: pl. III, fig. 4), although he could also have acquired it from another collector.

4. A curio trade was reported in the region by Nicolas Perrot as early as the late seventeenth century, probably in decorated Native clothing accessories and small carved objects (Blair 1911, 1: 76).

5. Quill-embroidered bark wares do not appear in the collection made by Colonel Jasper Grant in the vicinity of Detroit—Amherstburg, Ontario between 1806–09, now in the National Museum of Ireland (Phillips 1984). It is particularly striking that Beltrami's large collection, made in Minnesota, contains no quill-worked bark, although he did illustrate a bark basket embroidered in moosehair, identified as "colored grasses" (see note 3).

ones are ornamented with porcupine's quills, died [sic] red, yellow, and green. They hold from two to a dozen table spoons full of sugar, and are made for presents or for sale to the curious. The larger ones, also of birch bark, are not ornamented, and contain from ten to thirty pounds of sugar." De Castelnau illustrated a quill-embellished *makak* as well as a fan with a quilled bark handle in his 1842 travel book, and he notes the vividness of the colors achieved by Native women. Museum collections have yielded several dozen extant examples of these miniature *makaks* dating to the first half of the nineteenth century, some of which are still filled with maple sugar.

The Settler Market

The exploration and boundary surveying that brought Delafield, Schoolcraft, and McKenney into the central Great Lakes accompanied the opening up of southern Ontario and the Old Northwest to the intensive White settlement that followed the termination of more than fifty years of intermittent warfare along the U.S.-Canada border and the final defeat of Native efforts to prevent further White occupation. Settlement brought exploitative trade practices and massive land appropriations that increased the economic importance of art commodity production for Native people. It also brought an expanded consumer group and increased exposure to Euro-North American art and material culture.

Catherine Parr Traill, who in the 1830s settled near Peterborough, Ontario, southeast of Toronto, took a lively interest in the neighboring Ojibwa of Rice Lake, with whom she had regular contacts. Like other settlers she bought from them both the utilitarian baskets and containers needed for household and farming tasks and more decorative wares to brighten her house. Traill (1836: 168–69) wrote that, "when ornamented and wrought in patterns with dyed quills, I can assure you, they are by no means inelegant," and also noted Native women's skilled use of dyes. "Our parlor," she reported, "is ornamented with several very pretty specimens of their ingenuity in this way, which answer the purpose of note and letter-cases, flower-stands and work-baskets." The decoration on Traill's bark wares probably resembled that displayed on a shallow, open basket mounted on a pedestal base and ornamented with quilled flowers and geometric motifs that was made at Rice Lake about 1833.[6]

Great Lakes Floral Style

Early contact-period two-dimensional art from the Great Lakes consists both of dense geometric patterns applied to hide with quillwork and painting and an elegantly linear graphic style used to represent human and animal forms. The floral motifs that occur in Great Lakes quilled bark are entirely new. Although they are almost certainly conceptually linked both to Huron-Wendat and Euro-North American floral iconography, they resemble neither in their specific renderings of plants and blossoms. Traill's memoir of her early years in the "backwoods of Canada" gives us a precious insight into the formative period of this new floral art. She records the admiration of a group of local Ojibwa women for her husband's "gay chintz dressing-gown" and their expressed desire to own it. Although she "resolutely refused to part with it," all the women of the family "by turns came to look at 'gown'" (Traill 1836: 169). In the light of this anecdote the stylistic affinities of floral chintz with the bold, stylized floral motifs of early central Great Lakes quilled bark cannot appear coincidental, for many such encounters must have occurred during the first half of the nineteenth century. The stylizations of Great Lakes quillwork are, however, more extreme than those found in European textiles of the period. Great Lakes Native floral and leaf shapes are large, geometricized, and often simplified almost to the point of abstraction. The non-naturalistic patterning of the flowers with bold stripes of red or black and white is directly linked to geometric patterns found on eighteenth-century appliqué quillwork on hide (cp. Fig. 1).

In these early examples of quilled bark the visual sensibility of the artists seems to strain against the naturalism of the Western textile tradition (mediated, in fabrics like chintz, through India). Their floral designs retain many of the compositional and coloristic traits of earlier Ojibwa and Odawa painted and quilled geometric design. Significantly, in many examples of central Great Lakes quilled bark, motifs are arranged either along a strict axis of bilateral symmetry or in a quadri-partite composition. Such differences may con-

6. Royal Ontario Museum (Toronto, ON), cat.no. 958.76.1 (illustrated in Phillips 1998: fig. 5.12). The basket is lined with newspaper displaying the date 1833.

tain clues to the distinctive cosmology and world view that, I would argue, Great Lakes quillwork continues to express, for such spatial regimentations of floral forms appear to translate into the new medium of floral representation the four directional quadrants of Woodlands and Plains cosmology that are expressed in the ancient, sacred, and abstract motifs of the equal-armed cross and the quartered circle. The carryover of design principles suggests not only a consistent approach to space, but also the common source of women's artistry in contemplative and visionary experience which is evidenced by more recent ethnographic sources (Landes 1938: 9).

The central Great Lakes was a classic contact zone during the first half of the nineteenth century. In arguing for the transcultural genesis of Great Lakes floral art during this period it is also important to recall the connotations of immortality and the divine that floral images carried for European women (Phillips 1998: 155–196). Although the specific meanings of the new floral motifs were not identical for Native quillworkers and Euro-North American consumers, the two groups shared a belief in a spiritually empowered natural world that made their separate arts mutually translatable, but that has become obscured by the secularizing force of modernity. Traill, for example, was a serious student of natural history for whom "the cycles of growth and the transitoriness of flowers became metaphors for human destiny, underlining the fragility of life but also offering proof of a caring providence" (Berger 1983: 36).

With the exception of the more naturalistic floral style that developed among the Odawa of northwestern Michigan (discussed further below), this more stylized and geometricized mode of representation remained remarkably consistent across the central Great Lakes from the 1820s until at least the 1880s. Flowers, leaves, and heart motifs executed in this style occur on a basket presented by the daughter of Henry Schoolcraft and his Ojibwa wife to friends in Philadelphia in 1836 or 1837,[7] on miniature maple sugar *makaks* bought in northwestern Michigan during these years, as well as on a bark basket in the collection of Prince Maximilian of Wied that can be attributed to the 1830s.[8] The heart motif also occurs among the geometric designs on a wall pocket collected in Canada by General Frederick Markham between 1834 and 1840 (Fig. 2). The collections made by Lord and Lady Elgin and Lewis

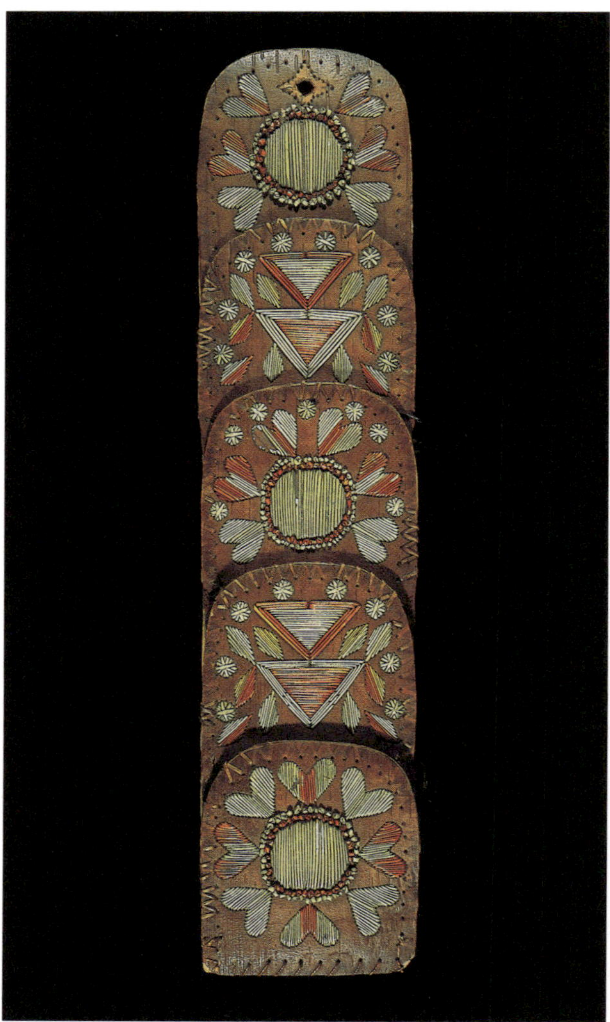

Fig. 2 Wall pocket, Cree. Length 48 cm. Collected by General Frederick Markham 1834–40. Glenbow Museum (Calgary, AB), cat.no. AP 3198. Photograph: Glenbow Museum.

Henry Morgan a little over decade later are almost exactly contemporary and also exhibit the familiar style of ornamentation. Morgan collected a number of quilled items, including a purse and several boxes, on a trip to Marquette, Michigan in 1855 (Fig. 3).[9] The Elgin collection was formed during Lord Elgin's term as Governor-General of Canada between 1847 and

7. University Museum, University of Pennsylvania (Philadelphia, PA), cat.no. NA 7788 (illustrated in Phillips 1998: fig. 5.8).

8. Linden-Museum (Stuttgart), cat.no. 36,050 (illustrated in Phillips 1998: pl. 18).

9. Morgan's collection is now in the Rochester Museum and Science Center (Rochester, NY). The bark wares, which include a purse (cat.no. 70.89.108), a *makak* (cat.no. 70.89.109), and three boxes (cat.nos. 70.89.110ab, 70.89.112ab, and 70.89.107ab), must have been acquired during his trip from Rochester via Toronto, St. Mary, and Mackinaw to Marquette, Michigan in July–August 1855. See Morgan Field Notes, Vol. II, University of Rochester Rare Books and Manuscripts Collection.

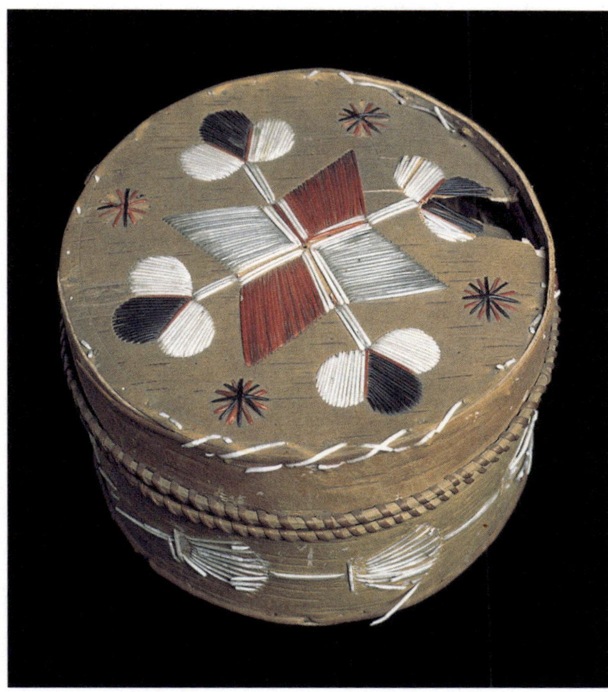

Fig. 3 Quilled bark box. Collected by Lewis Henry Morgan in 1855. Rochester Museum and Science Center (Rochester, NY), cat.no. 70-89-110. Photograph: Rochester Museum.

1854. His central Great Lakes pieces could well have been presented to him during his trips to Port Sarnia and Sault St. Marie in 1850.[10] Though not specifically mentioned in the newspaper reports, gifts of quillwork would almost certainly have been included in the presentations commonly made to a Governor-General on such an occasion.

Missionaries and the Promotion of Quillwork

It is no accident that many of the early Great Lakes centers of decorative bark production were closely associated with the new Christian missions that began to spread throughout the region after the War of 1812, some sixty years after the British conquest of New France had forced the departure of the French Catholic missionaries. Many of these new missionaries actively promoted the production of quilled bark objects and other kinds of commercial wares in the communities they served, both as a form of economic development and as a fund-raising strategy. The standard elements of the "missionary shows" held to raise money for missions included heart-warming (or -rending) speeches and a display and sale of Native-made goods whose skilled artisanship was intended to testify to the "industriousness" and worthiness of the Native people. The floral and geometric decoration of quilled bark wares seems to have provided particularly persuasive evidence of the "natural goodness" of Indians because they were held to furnish proof of an inherent love of nature and also to manifest the abandonment of "pagan" images in favor of "civilized" decoration.

A typical example of the role missionaries played in art commodity development occurs in the autobiography of Egerton Ryerson, a prominent Canadian educator, who served in his youth as a Methodist missionary to the Ojibwa in the same region of southern Ontario where Catherine Parr Traill settled five years later. In 1826–27, while with the Mississauga at Port Credit, Ontario, he reported that some of the money needed to build a church had been provided out of the proceeds of what was obviously an already established commodity trade in bark baskets and other items. "The squaws came forward," Ryerson (1883: 60) wrote, "to subscribe from shillings to dollars, the proceeds of what they might earn and sell in baskets, mats, moccasins, & etc." Following the standard pattern, Ryerson (1883: 66) remarks on the good character of Ojibwa women and their industrious production of handicrafts, their generosity, and their inventiveness. He also reproduces a letter from a fellow missionary written from New York City which includes a request to "encourage the Indian sisters to make a quantity of fancy trinkets, we could sell them to advantage here" (Ryerson 1883: 77–78).

Such conditions of display, sale, and performance, many times repeated, constructed a context within which the meanings of the bark wares were read. In the 1860s, for example, the Reverend Edward Wilson journeyed to England with Chief Buhkwujjenene of the Garden River Ojibwa to raise money for a school. "Nearly every night," Wilson (1886: 109–110) recounts, "there was a meeting, and often we had two or three

10. According to Sherry Brydon's research, this appears to have been the only trip made by Lord Elgin to Great Lakes Indian communities. He wrote in a letter to Lady Elgin of 28 August 1850: "Yesterday was spent at Port Sarnia where there were great doings and all went off very well. I received addresses, attended a marriage, visited an Indian settlement, partook of a great feast, in short had a regular field day of it" (National Archives of Canada, Reel A-401). Some of the objects could also have been acquired on other occasions, such as visits from Native leaders who came to present petitions. Chief Shingwaconse of Garden River, e.g., visited Lord Elgin at Toronto in 1847 and Montreal in 1849. The Elgin quilled bark objects are now in the Eugene and Clare V. Thaw Collection at the Fenimore Art Museum (Cooperstown, NY).

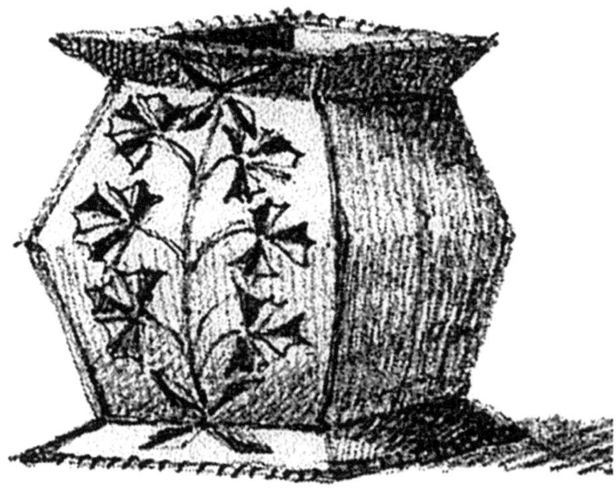

Fig. 4 Paul Kane sketch of quilled container, Manitoulin Island, 1845. Royal Ontario Museum (Toronto, ON), cat.no. 946.15.42. After Rogers (1969).

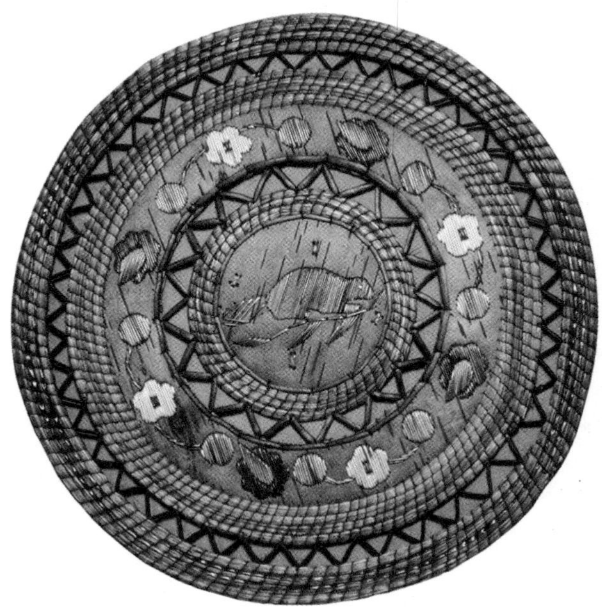

Fig. 5 Sweetgrass and birchbark mat. Purbrick collection, Stonyhurst College, on loan to the British Museum (London), loan no. 79.40.

engagements in the course of a day." "Meetings," he wrote, "were all much of the same character—money collected, and photographs and articles of birchbark sold." Wilson's account reports the way that he and Chief Buhkwujjenene carefully orchestrated the Chief's appearance: "Several likenesses were taken—representing him as a Christian Chief in his ordinary dress; and as a Chief of former days in feathers and Indian costume" (Wilson 1886: 100). These photographs were sold alongside the birchbark articles. The alternating glimpses of the savage and the civilized man exactly parallel the combination of exotic materials with familiar forms and ornamental designs that are comprised by the bark objects themselves. A similar equation of meaning is suggested by a quilled box sent to the Andover-Newton Theological Seminary near Boston. Glued inside its lid is a letter that begins, "An Indian Basket. Ko-ko-pi-nai-gun. From Mssrs Bartwell and Hale, missionaries to the Chippeway Indians near La. Superior. Aug 5th 1831," and goes on to give a description of a missionary service at Mackinac prior to the missionaries' departure to serve "the poor benighted Chippeways."[11] Pious missionary text and aboriginal flower-decorated bark basket are brought into alignment by a physical overlay, literally constructing the significations the piece of barkwork was intended to have for Boston viewers.

Catholic missionaries, who had been expelled from the Odawa region of northwestern Michigan after the defeat of the French in 1760, returned to the area in 1825, establishing a mission among the Odawa at Arbre Croche on Lake Michigan. Other Catholic missions were reestablished in the Great Lakes including one at Wikwemikong, on Manitoulin Island, to which the Michigan Odawa began moving in the 1820s and in larger numbers after 1836. As Paul Kane's sketch of a quilled bark container, made on Manitoulin Island in 1845 (and later incorporated into his painting of "Caw-Kee-Kee-Keesh-E-Ko," a Saulteaux woman[12]) testifies, the Odawa brought the art of making quilled bark fancy wares with them (Fig. 4). When Major Samuel Strickland (1970: 76) visited Manitoulin in the mid-nineteenth century, his daughter was presented with "a pretty bark-basket worked with colored quills" by women of the Nogun family at Gore Bay.

One of the earliest and most splendid collections of nineteenth-century Great Lakes quillwork on bark is today in the Museum für Völkerkunde in Vienna. Thanks to the research of Christian Feest and Sylvia Kasprycki (Feest 1968, Kasprycki and Krpata 1989, Feest and Kasprycki 1993), the dates and provenances of many of the objects have been recovered. Important

11. Peabody Essex Museum (Salem, MA), cat.no. E53,440, transferred from Andover Newton Theological School (illustrated in Monroe et al. 1997: 215 and Phillips 1998: fig. 5.18).

12. The container is now in the Royal Ontario Museum (Toronto, ON), cat.no. 912.1.30 (illustrated in Phillips 1998: fig. 5.27).

parts of this collection were originally acquired through Bavarians and Austrians connected to Catholic missions in the Great Lakes.[13] The core of the collection, which also includes a wide range of other Odawa and Menominee objects, was assembled by Martin Pitzer, a Bavarian church painter who was attached to the Arbre Croche mission in 1851 (Pitzer 1854; Feest 1968: 28; Feest and Kasprycki 1993: 17). In 1854 Pitzer toured a collection of central Great Lakes objects around Bavaria and Austria, among which quilled bark items were prominently featured, to raise money for the establishment of Odawa mission schools. In the descriptions Pitzer provided in the exhibition pamphlet, as in the examples of missionary shows previously cited, quickness and skill in fine craft is consistently cited as primary evidence of the Odawas' worthiness and suitability for conversion. "The works presented here made of birchbark," Pitzer (1854: 10) wrote,

> "through their ornamentation of white feathers, porcupine quills, etc., together with their way of producing glowing colors and mixing colors out of boiled rocks, roots, and herbs without any knowledge of chemistry, and of applying them to rushes to make mats, etc., unmistakably reveal their sharp intelligence and patience at monotonous work, which makes one wish to do the utmost to furnish them with schools as the means to achieve a better lot."[14]

The most celebrated assemblage in Pitzer's collection is a set of altar furnishings comprised of a tabernacle and six candleholders made of wood covered with birchbark panels exquisitely embroidered in quillwork.[15] Made in 1846 for the Arbre Croche church, they were replaced six years later, according to Pitzer (1854: 11), by "a more beautiful altar from the city of Detroit," which the artist painted and gilded with the help of Odawa assistants. The floral motifs with which the original birchbark altar was decorated were, for Pitzer, a further example of the inventive and imitative impulses of Odawa artists—"these flowers show how this people in their simplicity will mobilize any kind of thing to ornament their altars," he notes, presumably referring to the mixed media used which included edge-bindings of silk and cloth ribbon and appliques of paper. "Every little ribbon or scrap, for which they would have had to trade dearly in maple sugar to the merchants, was used to form a flower according to its color or allowed to flutter to their particular delight" (Pitzer 1854: 12). Pitzer's remarks about the pleasure taken in the kinetic aspects of the altar assemblage—the "fluttering" of the ribbons—recall the use of similar materials by Woodlands peoples on offering poles and calumet pipes and suggest a continuity in the aesthetics of ritual.

Another large collection connected to Catholic missionary activity was made by Father Edward Purbrick between 1877 and 1879, probably during visits to Wikwemikong, Manitoulin Island, and the Garden River Ojibwa that were part of a tour of inspection of the English Jesuit missions in Canada. He presented his collection to the small museum at Stonyhurst College, an English Jesuit school, and it is now on loan to the British Museum. The collection includes canoe models, a model wigwam, a lady's purse, baskets of various shapes and sizes, table mats, a wall rack, and napkin rings (Fig. 5). All are ornamented in the familiar bold, rather geometricized floral style, and many of the pieces also incorporate braided and coiled sweetgrass either as decorative edging or as the basic fabric of the objects.

Regional Styles, Individual Innovations

Because the Pitzer collection was made over a three-year period (1851–1853) in one region, it offers the possibility of identifying the styles current among the Odawa of the northwestern lower Michigan peninsula at that time. Many of the pieces, and particularly the altar furnishings, display a more naturalistic and less geometricized floral style than was being employed elsewhere. On the Arbre Croche altar, for example, the foliage is freer and more asymmetrical, and the flowers are more uniform in color. Other pieces in the Pitzer

13. One of the most important collections of quilled bark now in Vienna was assembled by Johann Georg Schwarz and includes examples made by several different central Great Lakes peoples acquired during his activities in North America as fur trader in 1820–21. Schwarz acted as American consul in Vienna (1827–48), and as secretary of a missionary society, the Leopoldinen-Stiftung, he acquired the collection of Bishop Résé of Detroit and other North American artifacts (Kasprycki and Krpata 1989; Feest and Kasprycki 1993: 16–17). Bark and quillwork objects from the Vienna collection have been published in Feest (1968), Harbor Springs Historical Commission (1983), and Phillips (1998).

14. I follow Kasprycki's translation in the latter part of this passage (1998: 338).

15. Museum für Völkerkunde (Vienna), cat.nos. 131,684–131,690, 131,693 (illustrated in Feest 1968: pl. 6; 1980: 157).

collection display the more geometricized stylizations, striped overlays and decorative alternations of color that appear in the earlier Rice Lake and other Ojibwa examples. A distinct stylistic variation related to a particular European model coexists with the style in general use since the 1820s in the central Great Lakes.

Perhaps the richest information about the styles of named individuals within a single community is offered by the collection of quilled bark wares presented to the Prince of Wales during his visit to the Rice Lake Ojibwa in 1860. This visit, the first to Canada by a member of the royal family, was greatly anticipated and carefully reported in the press. The Prince's brief stop at Rice Lake was described in the *New York Times*:

> "Friday, September 7, 1860 [Rice Lake, Ontario]. On the north side of the lake a sort of arch had been erected by the Missisage [Mississauga Ojibwa] tribe of Indians, who stood on the landing place and fired guns as the Prince approached, and endeavored to play 'God Save the Queen' with their brass band, as their chief, named Pandosh, who is one hundred years old, presented an address to H.R.H., signed with both his English name and Indian totem. Then a number of birch-bark baskets, filled with Indian work, and having labels with the names of the squaws who had made them, were given to the Prince, and in the midst of a parting volley, the royal train moved away."

On the Prince's return these quilled bark baskets and other gifts were installed in the Swiss Cottage Museum set up for Queen Victoria's children at her summer home, Osborne House, on the Isle of Wight. Most still have tags with the makers' names carefully inscribed, some written on quill-edged rectangles of birchbark—Catherine Muskrat, Polly Soper, Mrs. John, Hannah McCue, Sarah Taunchy. Many of the paper tags are written in the same hand, possibly that of a missionary or other non-Native person. Unfortunately, however, over time some of the tags have been separated from the bark wares so that only certain makers can be definitely identified.

Most of the bark containers are of the classic *makak* type, and most display stylized floral designs very similar to those seen on wares from the 1830s. There is also, however, one example that translates elements of a more ancient iconography into the new medium of quillwork on bark. Although Polly Soper's box displays striped leaf-forms on its lid, its sides are worked in rows of geometric hourglass forms and zigzag lines—very old Great Lakes patterns used in clothing, carving, and other contexts and that may also sometimes represent the powerful Thunderbird *manito* (Phillips 1984).[16] Similar motifs, executed in the older sgrafitto technique, can be seen on a *makak* collected in Minnesota in 1823 by Beltrami.[17] Another carryover of pre-contact quilling techniques unusual for quilled bark wares is the handle, which is worked in the techniques used on quilled clothing accessories dating to the early contact period. The Prince of Wales's collection also, however, contains bark wares of a radically innovative kind, such as a briefcase in a contemporary Victorian leather style that is fashioned of bark and embroidered with naturalistic floral motifs.[18]

A number of the makers of the Prince's gifts were artists of established reputation whose individual styles were admired in their own time. As Brydon has discovered, their names appear in the prize lists of the Ontario Provicial Exhibition. In 1848, for example, Polly Soper and Margaret Anderson, both of whom presented quilled bark to the Prince, each won several times in the "Indian Prizes" category.[19] It is clear from this precious evidence that the anonymity which surrounds nineteenth-century quillwork today is an artifact of an ethnographic typological discourse and not of the original Victorian climate of reception.

Picturing Identity and Belief

A smaller number of quilled bark pieces from the first half of the nineteenth century display human and animal figures. One of the earliest datable pieces is a small maple sugar *makak* collected among the Miami about 1820–30.[20] One side shows two canoes with figures wearing feathered headdresses, while the other shows an encampment scene. Both of these vignettes were commonly represented in European depictions of Indians as well as in early aboriginal souvenirs produced in other media. Another undocumented *makak* that can be stylistically related to these early pieces displays two

16. Reproduced in Phillips (1998: pl. 25).
17. See, for example, Vigorelli (1987: 13, fig. 32).
18. Illustrated in Phillips (1998: fig. 5.15).
19. *The Cobourg Star* for 11 October 1848. Lord Elgin could have acquired quilled bark when he visited the same fair.
20. Museum für Völkerkunde (Vienna), cat.no. 11,997 (collected by Johann Georg Schwarz).

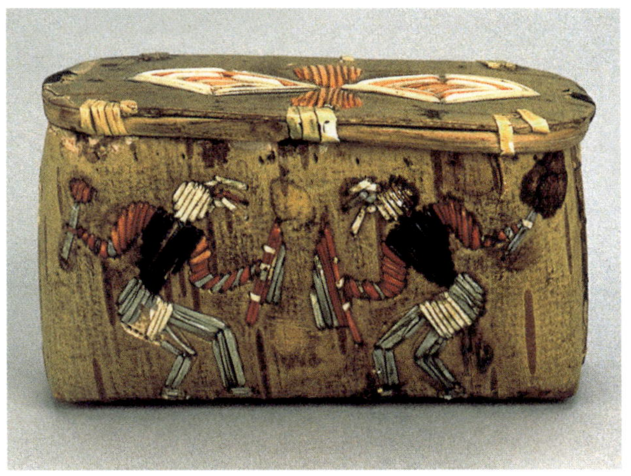

Fig. 6 Quilled *makak* with dancing warriors, attributed to the Menominee. Length 9 cm. Canadian Museum of Civilization (Hull, QC), cat.no. III-N-37a,b (ex A. Speyer collection). Photograph: Canadian Museum of Civilization, photo no. S99-4753.

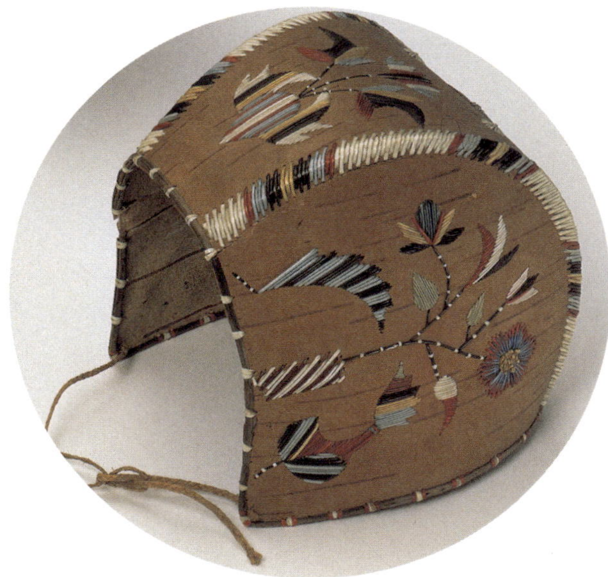

Fig. 7 Baby bonnet. Eugene and Clare Thaw collection, cat.no. T259 (ex Lord Elgin collection), on permenant loan at the Fenimore Art Museum, New York State Historical Association (Cooperstown, NY). Photograph: John Bigelow Taylor.

dancing men holding a club and dance staff[21] (Fig. 6). Such images offer a kind of self-portraiture at the same time that they exploit the Western interest in exotic spectacles. A few other early *makaks* display individual bird or animal forms, such as American eagles and a pig,[22] but most are ornamented with floral and geometric motifs.

Perhaps the most elaborate extant example of pictorial quillwork on souvenir art is a box attributable to the 1830s from the collection of Prince Maximilian of Wied (Schulze-Thulin 1982: 244).[23] Its side panels display repeated scenes of encampments, Indians hunting from canoes, fish, beavers, beaver lodges, and otters. The lid of the box is crowded with two scenes of men fighting with tomahawks and more Indians paddling canoes. Amidst this busy array stand three ladies in high-crowned European bonnets and hooped skirts. This complex imagery is of great interest both for its combination of specifically Great Lakes themes (the long-tailed animal and the beaver lodges) with the more standard iconography of Indianness and also for its notable lack of narrative unity. The absence of groundlines, landscape details, and other devices familiar in moosehair embroidery relates the Stuttgart box, rather, to the older compositional structures found in eighteenth-century Great Lakes quilled hide and in nineteenth-century Mide scrolls.

A wall pocket collected by General Markham in Canada between 1834 and 1840, now in the Royal Ontario Museum, displays similarly elaborate and unusual pictorial quillwork.[24] Stylistic and iconographic details such as the depiction of the profile faces, the tomahawks, and bows and arrows link the Markham wall pocket to the Wied box and lead to the conclusion that the latter can also be dated to the 1830s.[25] The images of a buffalo, horses, and tipis on the Markham wall pocket further suggest a western Great Lakes association for both pieces. The Markham wall pocket and the Stuttgart box are also linked by their unusual edging technique; bundled, unflattened porcupine quills are tacked down with individual colored and flattened quills. This technique, which imitates exactly the edging common on Huron-Wendat moosehair embroidered bark wares, is found on only a very few examples of Great Lakes quilled barkwork. Such a borrowing is most likely to have occurred during the early development of quilled bark, when makers had not yet developed their own conventions of

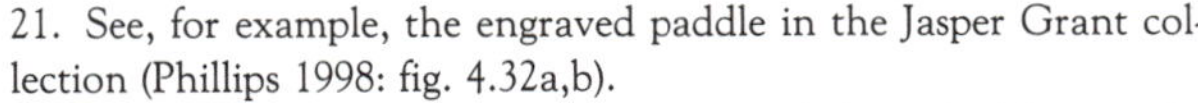

21. See, for example, the engraved paddle in the Jasper Grant collection (Phillips 1998: fig. 4.32a,b).

22. Eagles appear on two other miniature *makaks* in the Museum für Völkerkunde (Vienna), collected by Martin Pitzer in the early 1850s (cat.nos. 131,740, 131,742ab); a pig appears on an example also in Vienna in the Johann Georg Schwarz collection, probably acquired by Bishop Résé in the 1830s (cat.no. 11,996).

23. Linden-Museum (Stuttgart), cat.no. 36,054 (illustrated in Phillips 1998: pl. 18).

24. Royal Ontario Museum (Toronto, ON), cat.no. 992.39.21 (June Bedford collection).

25. Although Prince Maximilian did not visit the Great Lakes, the piece could either have been presented as a gift or acquired by him at a more distant trading post.

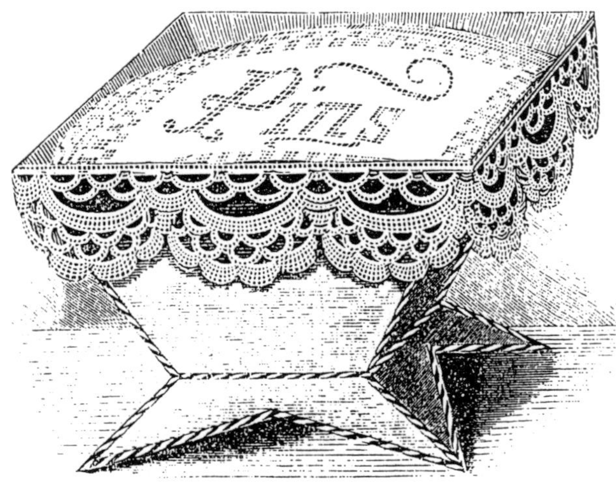

Fig. 8 Toilet Cushion and Box. Illustration from *Englishwoman's Domestic Magazine* 5(2) (June 1856), 64.

manufacture. One of the small number of pieces edged in this way was collected at Michilimackinac,[26] and this major crossroads of trade may well be where Great Lakes quillworkers came into contact with Huron wares.

Two other unusual pieces of pictorial quillwork, a model wigwam and a basket in the shape of a frame house, both complete with human figures and foliage, are found in the Elgin and Purbrick collections. These pieces display the growing mastery of European pictorial conventions among Great Lakes artists during the middle decades of the nineteenth century. In both the Elgin wigwam[27] and the Purbrick house-basket,[28] the figures are arranged against implied groundlines, and the repetitive rhythms of pictography seen on the Stuttgart and Toronto pieces are replaced with coherent illusionistic scenes. There is also a notable iconological shift. Whereas the works I have attributed to the 1830s can be read as strong statements of Great Lakes cosmological and socio-political principles according to which animals and humans share space in reciprocal and balanced relationships, the Elgin wigwam and the Purbrick house depict, respectively, a romantic and an assimilationist ideal of Native domestic life.

The scenes depicted on the Elgin wigwam, a hunter shooting a bird amid stylized foliage and, on the opposite side, a woman and a man with a rifle, participate in a romantic tradition of the depiction of the Indian as natural man and nomadic hunter closely related to the iconography of contemporary Huron-Wendat moosehair embroidery. The Purbrick house-basket depicts not this "traditional" lifestyle but rather the new ideal of the Indian as farmer—the frame house of the settlement, complete with curtained windows, a cultivated garden, and the little woman at the door—disarmingly conveying the Western ideal of domesticity that was being preached intensively to aboriginal people during the last decades of the nineteenth century. The wigwam is a unique piece, although versions of the house-basket have continued to be produced by Odawa quillworkers up to the present. All these examples of pictorial iconography are, however, exceptions to the predominant tradition of floral imagery.

The Victorian Culture of Novelty

Experimentation with the forms of bark objects is even more striking than is innovation in surface design. The Vienna collection displays a particularly great variety of object shapes, ranging from the traditional *makak* to different styles of covered containers, ladies' handbags, fan handles, and needlework accessories. Pitzer (1854: 23) commented that the Odawa were in the habit of copying new and strange objects whenever they were encountered without necessarily knowing their intended uses, "out of a pure *addiction to imitation*" ["Nachahmungssucht"—the emphasis is mine]. His observation accords with numerous examples already noted of Native artists' relish in virtuosity and their desire to push the limits of the medium. During the Victorian era Great Lakes women imitated the calling card trays, watch pockets, and boot-shaped pincushions made in other media by Huron-Wendat and Iroquois women, they copied in birchbark the forms of Euro-North American trunks, and made whole suites of doll's furniture. The Elgin collection contains an exquisite quilled bark baby's bonnet (Fig. 7), and the Purbrick collection a full-sized embroidered birchbark cap with peaked bill. These objects convey a sense of the individual quillworker's joy in her medium, her desire to challenge herself and, perhaps, a tricksterish urge to astound her audience.

This inventiveness also clearly responds to the cult of the novelty that was part of Victorian commodity culture in general and of Victorian women's culture in

26. I am grateful to Christian Feest for pointing out the significance of this piece, a box in Vienna, cat.no. 11,994, identified by its collector, Johann Georg Schwarz, as "Chippewa, Michillimackinac" (cp. Feest 1968: 47).

27. Fenimore Art Museum (Cooperstown, NY), Thaw collection, cat. no. T258 (illustrated in Phillips 1998: pl. 19).

28. British Museum (London), Stonyhurst loan no. 79-3 (illustrated in Phillips 1998: pl. 20).

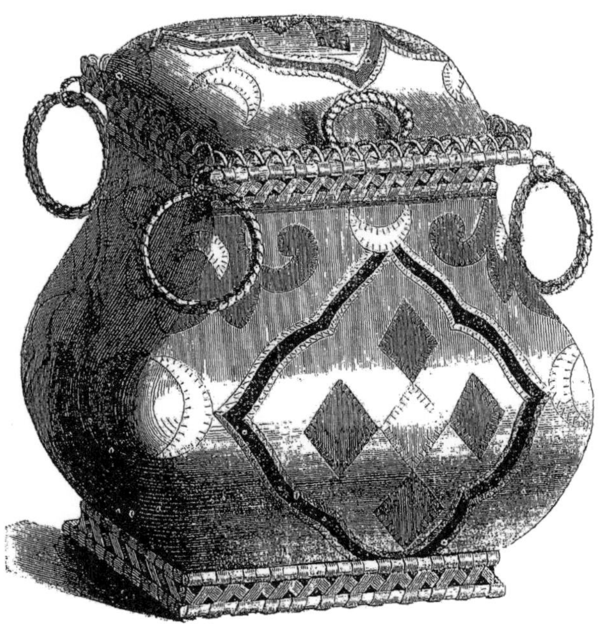

Fig. 9 Wastepaper basket. Illustration from *Englishwoman's Domestic Magazine* 11(72) (April 1866), 57. Photograph: Cambridge University Library.

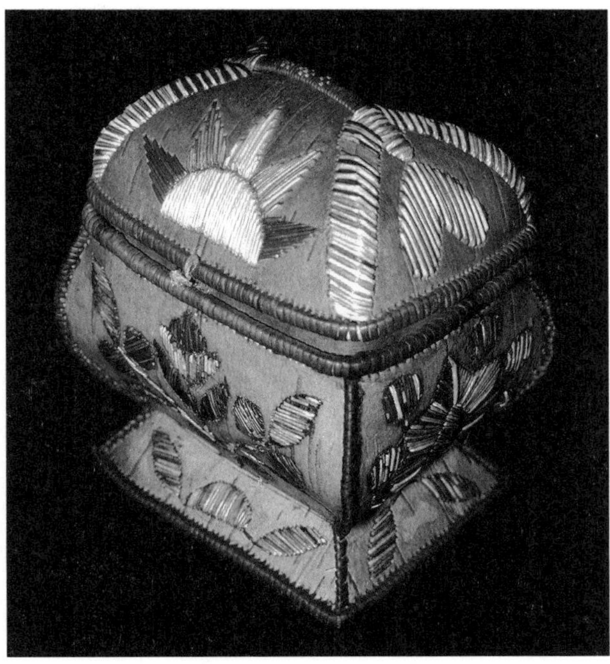

Fig. 10 Quilled bark box, Odawa, Arbre Croche, Michigan. Height 15.4 cm. Museum für Völkerkunde (Vienna), cat.no. 11,992 (Johann Georg Schwarz coll., 1828–48).

particular. Inventive and witty forms for domestic ornaments were a feature of the "home crafts" European women settlers had brought with them to North America since the late eighteenth century. With the advent of weekly mass-circulation women's magazines in the 1850s the instructions and printed patterns for making a dizzying array of container forms and parlor ornaments multiplied tremendously. As we have seen, Native women would have had many ways of seeing both Victorian-made examples and patterns through their contacts with settlers and missionaries. The 1833 Rice Lake pedestal basket discussed earlier in this essay, for example, remained current for decades; it resembles the form of a cloth-covered cardboard container for which instructions appeared in an 1856 number of the *Englishwoman's Domestic Magazine* (Fig. 8). The curving volumes of a container in Vienna (collected about 30 years earlier) recall an 1866 pattern for a wastepaper basket made of cloth covered wicker to "resemble a Chinese *potiche*" (Figs. 9, 10). The commodified material culture of Native women was clearly in a dialogic relationship with the domestic arts of non-Native women during the Victorian era. The precise dynamics of invention and imitation provide a fruitful area for further research.

Margaret Boyd: Quillwork and Political Empowerment

The making and sale of quilled bark, like other art commodities, meant economic empowerment and, at times, survival for many communities. It could also support directly political agendas. Despite the appearance of acquiescence in the assimilationist project that barkware production signalled in missionary shows and other contexts, Native people also used the economic power and respect that derived from successful commodity production to support their own projects of resistance. A particularly dramatic instance of such intersecting roles is contained in the life of Margaret Boyd, the sister of the prominent Odawa leader Chief Andrew Blackbird, and one of the most famous Odawa quillworkers of the third quarter of the nineteenth century. During her life Margaret Boyd saw almost all the ancestral lands of her people melt away through enforced transfers, which were frequently fraudulent. In the 1870s the towns of Petoskey and Harbor Springs (near Arbre Croche) became the heart of an extremely popular vacation area, and a familiar pattern developed in which income from the production of art commodities became a vital replacement for the lost yields of the land. Frances Pailthorp, the daughter of a prominent local judge who took a strong interest in Odawa quillwork, has left us a simple but vivid capsule sketch. "Margaret Boyd hated the white people," Pailthorp wrote, "she told father that she wished she could poison all the streams and get rid of them." In 1877, as Pailthorp recounted, Boyd took positive action.

> "[She] went to Washington to tell the President how her people here were being mistreated. The Indians made her a beautiful canoe about three foot long covered with quill wild flowers to give to the president. When she got to Chicago she had a chance to sell it for $50 so she sold it and bought clothes to go to see the president in. They told her in Chicago they would take all she made. She got $25 to $50 for them. No dealer here could afford her work."[29]

Boyd, in fact, financed not only a proper Victorian wardrobe, but also her whole trip east by selling her quillwork at railway stations along the way. This historical episode is a particularly dramatic example of the way in which the art of quilling bark, like other art commodity productions, has been a means of negotiating cultural and economic survival during a period of almost overwhelming pressure for acculturation.

As we have seen, Great Lakes quilled bark wares were radically innovative in relation to earlier styles of bark containers, and they were produced almost exclusively for sale to non-Native consumers. As we have also seen, the transcultural aspects of quilled bark wares—the often fanciful, hybrid forms and the new forms of floral and pictorial imagery—were not problematic for prominent Victorian collectors, although the interest and value of these features has been obscured by a penumbra of alleged "inauthenticity" during much of the twentieth century. My argument in this paper has been that the transcultural features of quilled bark constitute material evidence of important cultural negotiations. They reflect carefully devised artistic strategies of self-presentation and cultural preservation by means of which their makers asserted unique histories and cultural identities at the same time that they displayed the up-to-date, modern taste and the demonstration of skill and industriousness demanded of them by the historical moment. As such, quilled bark wares and other similar genres should be regarded as more rather than less "authentic" examples of Great Lakes art of the nineteenth century.

29. Manuscript memoir headed "Chief Blackbird," Frances Pailthorp papers, Little Traverse Bay Historical Society (Petoskey, MI).

References Cited

Armour, David A. and Keith R. Widder
1978 *At the Crossroads: Michilimackinac During the American Revolution*. Mackinac Island, MI: Mackinac Island State Park Commission.

Beltrami, J. C. [Giacomo Costantino]
1828 *A Pilgrimage in Europe and America, leading to the Discovery of the Sources of the Mississippi and Bloody River*. 2 vols. London: Hunt and Clarke.

Berger, Carl
1983 *Science, God, and Nature in Victorian Canada*. Toronto, ON: University of Toronto Press.

Bhabha, Homi
1994 *The Location of Culture*. London: Routledge.

Blair, Emma H.
1911 (ed.) *The Indian Tribes of the Upper Mississippi Valley and Region of the Great Lakes, as Described by Nicolas Perrot, French Royal Commissioner of Canada; Morrell Marston, American Army Officer; and Thomas Forsyth, United States Agent at Fort Armstrong*. 2 vols. Cleveland, OH: Arthur H. Clark Co.

Clifford, James
1997 *Routes: Travel and Translation*. Cambridge, MA: Harvard University Press.

Castelnau, Francis de
1842 *Vues et souvenirs de l'Amerique du Nord*. Paris: A. Bertrand.

Delafield, Joseph
1943 *The Unfortified Boundary: A Diary of the First Survey of the Canadian Boundary Line from St. Regis to the Lake of the Woods*. New York, NY: privately printed.

Dockstader, Frederick J.
1961 *Indian Art in America: The Arts and Crafts of the North American Indian*. New York, NY: Promontory Press.

Douglas, Frederic H. and Rene d'Harnoncourt
1941 *Indian Art of the United States*. New York, NY: The Museum of Modern Art.

Ettawageshik, Frank
1999 My Father's Business. In Phillips and Steiner 1999: 26–29.

Feder, Norman
1971a *American Indian Art*. New York, NY: Abrams.
1971b *Two Hundred Years of North American Indian Art*. New York, NY: Praeger Publishers.

Feest, Christian F.
1968 *Indianer Nordamerikas*. Wien: Museum für Völkerkunde.
1980 *Native Arts of North America*. London: Thames and Hudson.

Feest, Christian F. and Sylvia S. Kasprycki
1993 *Über/Lebenskunst nordamerikanischer Indianer*. Wien: Museum für Völkerkunde.
Harbor Springs Historical Commission
1983 *Ottawa Quillwork on Birchbark*. Harbor Springs, MI: Harbor Springs Historical Commission.
Hill, Tom and Richard W. Hill, Sr.
1994 (eds.) *Creation's Journey: Native American Identity and Belief*. Washington, DC: National Museum of the American Indian.
Kasprycki, Sylvia S.
1998 The Native American Collection of Friderik Baraga: The Missionary as Ethnographic Collector. *Etnolog* 8(59): 331–355.
Kasprycki, Sylvia S. and Margit Krpata
1989 Hildesheim—Detroit—Wien. Bischof Rese als Sammler indianischer Ethnographica. *Hildesheimer Heimatkalender* 1989: 49–53.
King, J. C. H.
1986 Tradition in Native American Art. In: Edwin L. Wade (ed.), *The Arts of the North American Indian: Native Traditions in Evolution* (New York, NY: Hudson Hills Press), 65–92.
LaFarge, Oliver et al.
1970 *Introduction to American Indian Art*. [1931] Glorieta, NM: The Rio Grande Press.
Landes, Ruth
1938 *The Ojibwa Woman*. Columbia University Contributions to Anthropology 31. New York, NY: Columbia University Press.
Lippard, Lucy
1990 *Mixed Blessings: New Art in a Multicultural America*. New York, NY: Pantheon.
Marcus, George and Fred Myers
1995 (eds.) *The Traffic in Culture: Refiguring Art and Anthropology*. Berkeley, CA: University of California Press.
Mauzé, Marie
1997 (ed.) *Present is Past: Some Uses of Tradition in Native Societies*. Lanham, MD: University Press of America.
McKenney, Thomas L.
1827 *Sketches of a Tour to the Lakes, of the Character and Customs of the Chippeway Indians and of Incidents Connected with the Treaty of Fond du Lac*. Baltimore, MD: Fielding Lucas, Jun'r.
Monroe, Dan L. et al.
1997 *Gifts of the Spirit. Works by Nineteenth-Century & Contemporary Native American Artists*. Peabody Essex Museum Collections 132. Salem, MA: Peabody Essex Museum.
Ortiz, Fernando
1995 *Cuban Counterpoint: Tobbacco and Sugar*. Harriet de Onis, trsl. Durham, NC: Duke University Press.
Phillips, Ruth B.
1984 *Patterns of Power: The Jasper Grant Collection and Great Lakes Indian Art of the Early Nineteenth Century*. Kleinburg, ON: The McMichael Canadian Collection.
1998 *Trading Identities: The Souvenir in Native North American Art from the Northeast, 1700–1900*. Seattle, WA: University of Washington Press.
Phillips, Ruth B. and Christopher B. Steiner
1999 (eds.) *Unpacking Culture: Art and Commodity in Colonial and Postcolonial Worlds*. Berkeley, CA: University of California Press.
Pitzer, Martin
1854 *Verzeichnis der Gegenstände und Arbeiten eines Indianer-Stammes im nördlichsten Amerika nebst einer Charakteristik desselben*. München: J. G. Weiss'sche Universitäts-Buchdruckerei.
Pratt, Mary Louise
1992 *Imperial Eyes: Travel Writing and Transculturation*. New York, NY: Routledge.
Rickard, Jolene
1992 Cew Ete Haw I Tih: The Bird That Carries Language Back to Another. In: Lucy Lippard (ed.), *Partial Recall: Photographs of Native North Americans* (New York, NY: The New Press), 105–111.
Rogers, Edward S.
1969 (ed.) *Paul Kane Sketch Pad*. Toronto, ON: Charles J. Musson, Ltd.
Ryerson, Egerton
1883 *The Story of My Life: Being Reminiscences of Sixty Years' Public Service in Canada*. J. G. Hodgins, ed. Toronto, ON: William Briggs.
Schoolcraft, Henry
1966 *Travels through the Northwestern Regions of the United States*. [1821] Ann Arbor, MI: University Microfilms, Inc.
Schulze-Thulin, Axel
1982 Amerika. In: Friedrich Kussmaul (ed.), *Ferne Völker, frühe Zeiten. Kunstwerke aus dem Linden-Museum Stuttgart* (2 vol., Recklinghausen: Aurel Bongers), 1: 223–320.
Strickland, Samuel
1970 *Twenty-Seven Years in Canada West or the Experience of an Early Settler*. [1853] Edmonton, AB: M. G. Hurtig, Ltd.
Thomas, Nicholas
1991 *Entangled Objects: Exchange, Material Culture, and Colonialism in the Pacific*. Cambridge, MA: Harvard University Press.
1994 *Colonialism's Culture: Anthropology, Travel and Government*. Princeton, NJ: Princeton University Press.
Traill, Catherine Parr
1836 *The Backwoods of Canada, being Letters from the Wife of an Emigrant Officer*. London: Charles Knight.
Vigorelli, Leonardo
1987 *Gli oggetti Indiani raccolti da G. Costantino Beltrami*. Bergamo: Civico Museo "E. Caffi."
Wilson, Rev. Edward F.
1886 *Missionary Work Among the Ojebway Indians*. London: Society for Promoting Christian Knowledge.
Whitehead, Ruth Holmes
1982 *Micmac Quillwork: Micmac Indian Techniques of Porcupine Quill Decoration, 1600–1950*. Halifax, NS: Nova Scotia Museum.

California Feather Blankets

Objects of Wealth and Status in Two Nineteenth-Century Worlds

Sally McLendon

The Indian peoples of north-central California were fishers, hunters, and gatherers of an unusual sort. They had denser populations than usually thought possible for peoples who rely on hunting and gathering for their subsistence (Bennyhoff 1977). They lived in large, permanent winter towns, accumulated wealth, and marked rank and status differences in a variety of ways, including the use of dramatically beautiful objects: elaborate shell necklaces (Hudson 1984), feather and bead belts (Uhle 1886, Vatter 1925, Kroeber 1929, 1932, McKern 1922, Driver 1936, Bates 1981, 1982a, 1983, Feest 1984), feather and bead encrusted baskets (Kroeber 1929, 1932, McKern 1922, Driver 1936, Bates 1983, Hudson 1984), and remarkable feather blankets (Uhle 1886, Willoughby 1922, Vatter 1925, Kroeber 1929, 1932, Feest 1980, Bates 1983).

The complexity and elaborateness of these societies was difficult to appreciate at the beginning of the twentieth century when professional anthropological research was initiated by Alfred L. Kroeber and his students and colleagues through interviewing knowledgeable elderly members of these groups. These authorities recalled their societies as they were when they were young, before the profound changes brought about by the loss of lands, the loss of population through epidemics, disease, and attacks from settlers and gold miners, and the adoption of Euro-American material culture. This invaluable ethnographic record can be surprisingly enriched and supplemented through the careful and systematic study of museum collections which preserve examples of the material culture of wealth and status, collected in the early nineteenth century (Bates 1981, 1983, Hudson 1984, McLendon 1981).

During the first half of the nineteenth century at least fifteen remarkable thick, soft, incredibly light, beautiful, downy feather blankets are known to have been collected. Fourteen survive at the end of the twentieth century.[1] Seven are in museums in the United States, seven in Europe (Feest, pers. comm. 1980). None are documented as to the particular Native group that made and used them. Only the collector and approximate

Sally McLendon is Professor of Anthropology and Linguistics at Hunter College and the Graduate School of the City University of New York. The recipient of Guggenheim, Woodrow Wilson, and Smithsonian Fellowships, she has carried out linguistic and ethnographic fieldwork with California Indian peoples, especially Pomoan peoples, since 1959 and has been studying museum collections in Europe and North America since 1979. She has been a consultant for several museum exhibitions and is senior curator of the national traveling exhibition "Pomo Basketweavers, their Baskets, and the Art Market."
Author's address: Department of Anthropology, Hunter College, CUNY, 695 Park Avenue, New York, NY 10021, U.S.A.

1. I first encountered these remarkable objects in 1980 when, as a Smithsonian Fellow at the National Museum of Natural History of the Smithsonian Institution, I opened a deep metal drawer in the attic and found it full of the most amazingly beautiful, soft feather textile, of a sort I had never before seen. On top of the textile was an envelope containing a long letter from a Mrs. Charles Goodwin to the former Curator of Anthropology, Otis T. Mason. It described the feather blankets her father, Captain William Dane Phelps, had acquired in California in the early 1840s from John Sutter. Mesmerized by this beautiful, unfamiliar textile and the fragment of history that accompanied it, I determined to learn more about California feather blankets. William C. Sturtevant, Curator of North American Ethnology at the National Museum of Natural History, volunteered to ask Christian Feest, then Curator of North American Ethnology at the Museum für Völkerkunde, Vienna, if he knew of any others. Feest generously produced a list of all fourteen feather blankets then known, including one which had been lost, the museums they were in, the names of their collectors, their collection dates (when known), and the three major articles published about them (Uhle 1886, Willoughby 1922, Vatter 1925). This study would not have been possible without that guide. As time and travel opportunities permitted, I studied all the known feather blankets, except for the two at the Museum of Anthropology and Ethnology in St. Petersburg, of which William C. Sturtevant kindly secured photographs and catalog data. I looked for documentation for each blanket in its museum and at libraries and archives nearby. The award of an NEH travel to collections grant in 1986, combined with a sabbatical year spent in Oxford, England, at the then Institute of Social Anthropology, made it possible to study the blankets in Belfast, Frankfurt, and Dresden (then part of the German Democratic Republic and not simple to get to), and to pursue rare travel accounts and documents in the Bodleian Library, the British Library, the Pitt Rivers Library, and the Library, Rhodes

date of collection are known for the best documented blankets. For some, not even this is known.[2]

Feather blankets were objects of wealth and status in the Native societies that produced and used them. Among the tribes speaking the Wappo language north of San Francisco Bay (from just above Sonoma and Napa in the south along either side of the Napa River to Cloverdale and Middletown in the north), the "wealthy had expensive capes of goose- or duck-down feathers" (Driver 1936: 188). Among the Bay Miwok-speaking people of Wi-pa (i.e., Wai-pa, also recorded as Guapen or Guaypemne) on Sherman Island in the Delta, "the wife of the chief used to wear a feather blanket which was very rich and handsome" made of snow goose and mallard (Merriam 1967: 367). Feather blankets were given to Mariano Vallejo by Succara, chief of the Satiyomi, as part of an exchange of valuables in the conclusion of a peace treaty between them (see p. 137 below).

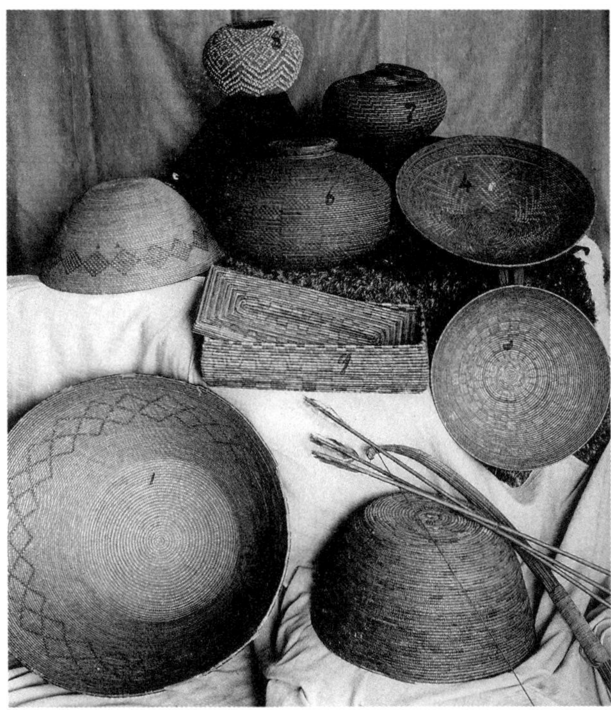

Fig. 1 A bow, arrows, baskets and, in right rear under three baskets, a corner of a feather blanket, given by William Alden Gale to his friend Joseph Eaton around 1821, on his return from his first trip to California. Photograph sent by Joseph Eaton's daughters, Catherine and Lucy Eaton, to Otis T. Mason in 1899. National Anthropological Archives, Smithsonian Institution (Washington, DC), neg.no. 81-6505.

Feather blankets were equally valued by the arriving Europeans and Americans, who made gifts of such objects to each other to mark their own wealth and status. Some of the known blankets are documented as such gifts. Captain William Dane Phelps (1871: 258; cp. Fig. 2) reported that he received feather blankets as well as baskets and other valuables as gifts from Captain Sutter and Mr. Sinclair when he visited them in 1841. Ferdinand von Wrangell gave a feather blanket and other objects of wealth and status (which he no doubt received as presents when he visited Bodega Bay and Fort Ross) to his father-in-law, Baron Rossillon (cp. Fig. 15). William Alden Gale gave a feather blanket and many baskets to his friend Joseph Eaton on his return from his first trip to California and the South Seas around 1821 (Fig. 1). The use of feather blankets as gifts in this manner inadvertently obscured the identity of the makers of these stunning textiles. Feather blankets can be repositioned in more precise contexts of collection, however, by combining accounts of blankets by early nineteenth-century visitors with early twentieth-century ethnographic accounts of the tribes that made such blankets and the careful study of the blankets themselves.

House. I will always be in the debt of the many librarians in these institutions that made this research possible. As patterns emerged, I gave papers on this research at the California Indian Conference, University of California, Berkeley in 1989 and at the American Indian Workshop held in Frankfurt, Germany in 1997.
In January 1999 I put all my notes, photographs, xeroxes of early accounts, and drafts of the paper in a suitcase and went away for a month to finish writing the research up. The second night away the car was broken into and the suitcase with all its contents stolen. Fortunately my packing had not been totally thorough. Some photographs survived, as well as some xeroxes and a few notes. Many friends and colleagues helped me reconstruct a great deal of what was lost. Susan Haskell of the Peabody Museum, Harvard University, kindly allowed me to restudy the three feather blankets there on very short notice. Adrienne Kaeppler and Jane Walsh of the National Museum of Natural History, Smithsonian Institution, reminded me that I had sent them xeroxes of materials and papers of which they gave me back copies. Jane Walsh also gave me pictures she had taken of the blanket in Copenhagen. Christian Feest gave me catalog data for European blankets, Margaret Hardin of the Los Angeles County Museum sent me drafts of the paper I had written on their blanket, and Craig Bates generously sent me notes and slides he had taken of the Petersburg blankets on a recent trip. Glenn Farris sent me once again his unpublished paper. William C. Sturtevant helped me track down many arcane references again. I can never thank them enough.

2. When these blankets have been attributed to specific ethnographic groups, they have been attributed to the Maidu, on the basis of an article by Willoughby (1922). Maidu is an ambiguous term. It is used to refer to tribes living in the high mountain meadows between Lassen Peak and the present town of Quincy, generally 4,000 feet or more above sea level, who spoke a language called Maidu (sometimes called Northern Maidu). It is also used to refer to a family of languages to which the language called Maidu belongs, which is also called Maiduan. The family includes the distinct languages Nisenan and Konkow, unfortunately called "dialects" by Kroeber (1925). The peoples who spoke the language called Maidu did not make feather blankets (Dixon 1905: 148). Only speakers of Konkow and Nisenan who lived in the Sacramento Valley made feather blankets. Speakers of these two languages who lived in the foothills also did not make feather blankets (Wilson and Towne 1978: 390–391).

Eyewitness Accounts

1. Georg Heinrich Freiherr von Langsdorff, Spring 1806

California feather blankets were first described at the beginning of the nineteenth century by Georg Heinrich Freiherr von Langsdorff, a young Hessian physician and naturalist in the Russian service. Langsdorff arrived in San Francisco Bay at the end of March 1806 on the first Russian ship to visit California, the *Neva*. He had spent the preceding three years as naturalist and physician on the first Russian circumnavigation of the world, under the command of Captain Adam Johann von Krusenstern. In Kamchatka Chamberlain Nikolai von Rezanoff separated from Krusenstern to visit the Russian settlements in North America and invited Langsdorff to accompany him as physician. From Sitka they sailed to California on the *Neva* to search for supplies for the Russian colony in Alaska. While Rezanoff negotiated with the Spanish authorities, Langsdorff carefully observed the Spanish settlements, missions, Native peoples, and fauna and flora for six weeks. Rezanoff and Langsdorff, with some of the ship's officers, made expeditions north of San Francisco Bay to Bodega Bay and were impressed with the possibilities for colonization (Duflot de Mofras 1937: 3). Rezanoff returned to Sitka determined to both establish permanent trade relations with California and acquire territory along the coast north of San Francisco Bay for "an agricultural and trading establishment" (Bancroft 1886, 4: 78). In 1809 Ivan A. Kuskoff spent six months in Bodega Bay hunting sea lions and sea otters and establishing friendly relations with the tribes speaking Coast Miwok around the bay (who apparently welcomed the possibility of playing the Russians off against the Spanish further south). In 1811 he returned to continue both operations and in 1812 established the Russian colony of Fort Ross a bit to the north of Bodega Bay. It would be an important presence in this part of the world and a source for collections until it was sold to John Sutter in 1841 (Bancroft 1886, 4: 78).

Upon Langsdorff's return to Europe he published in his native German a three-volume account of his observations during these voyages (Langsdorff 1812). It was translated into English a year later (Langsdorff 1813–1814). While describing the clothing of the Indian converts of Mission San Francisco Langsdorff remarked:

> "They also make for themselves garments of the feathers of several kinds of water-fowl, particularly ducks and geese. These they bind closely together in a string-like fashion, which strings are afterwards joined tight, making a dress of a feather-fur appearance. Both sides are alike, and it is so warm that it would be an excellent protection against the cold of even a more northerly clime" (Langsdorff 1813–1814, 2: 56).[3]

The fourteen known feather blankets show that Langsdorff's description was amazingly accurate. He must have actually seen such blankets and possibly even seen one being made.

Captain James Cook's landmark accounts of his three voyages, published quickly after each of his trips, set a pattern for mariners on long voyages of exploration to the Pacific and the west coast of North America. They also created an audience of eager readers. Commanders of subsequent voyages organized by nations for exploration, and sometimes for trade, read the previous accounts and published their own, frequently comparing their experiences to their predecessors'. Few of those who visited California, however, mentioned feather blankets.

Partly this is surely due to lack of contact with Native peoples, especially women, and especially outside the mission context. Women were the usual wearers of feather blankets (except among tribes speaking the Patwin language, apparently; cp. Kroeber 1932: 271). Since women traditionally avoided contact with strangers, leaving diplomatic relations to the men, a European or American in a port for a few days or a week might never see any Native women, even if the visitor went beyond the mission context to areas where unconverted Native peoples still lived.

Partly this may have been due to the season of their visit. Feather blankets were primarily worn in the winter and thus would not have been seen in the summer. Partly it also reflected the locations commonly visited: the Spanish presidios and Franciscan missions along the coast south of San Francisco Bay to San Diego. Feather blankets were associated with the Native peoples living north of San Francisco Bay and along the Sacramento River. These peoples were among the last to be contacted and proselytized by the Spanish and so were less like-

3. "Sie bereiten auch wohl eine Kleidung aus den Federn der vielen Wasservögel, besonders der Enten und Gänse, die sie fest und dicht eine neben der andern um eine Schnur festbinden und mehrere solche Schnüre nachher so an einander reihen, daß dadurch eine Art von Federpelz entsteht, der sich auf beiden Seiten der innern sowohl als der äußern, völlig gleich und so warm ist, dass er auch selbst in einem nördlichen Klima mit Vortheil getragen werden könnte" (Langsdorff 1812, 2: 141).

ly to be encountered by foreigners. When Langsdorff visited the mission at San Francisco, significant numbers of converts from north of the Bay area had only just arrived the preceding year, and there were not yet converts from the Sacramento River area (Milliken 1995).

2. Captain Auguste Duhaut-Cilly, Autumn 1827

The few mentions of feather blankets by visitors after Langsdorff are all from people who had occasion to spend time north of San Francisco Bay or along the Sacramento River, especially in the cooler rainy season, and to have contact with unconverted Native peoples. The earliest of these was the commander of the French commercial ship *Héro*, Auguste Bernard Duhaut-Cilly, who was accompanied by Paolo Emilio Botta as naturalist. From January 1827 to September 1828 they traveled up and down the California coast trading (Duhaut-Cilly 1834–1835). Duhaut-Cilly and Botta visited the Russian establishment at Fort Ross and the recently founded twenty-first mission at Sonoma, Mission San Francisco Solano. At Sonoma they saw unconverted Native families from the surrounding area who had been hired to harvest the mission crops at the end of August. Duhaut-Cilly (1834–1835, 1: 110) noted that while the men who came to harvest wore almost nothing, the women wore rabbitskin blankets. In a later section describing Native peoples Duhaut-Cilly remarked:

> "They make for themselves, however, cloaks of rabbit skins or bird feathers, skillfully worked and decorated with bands of varied colors."[4]

Rabbitskin blankets were not decorated with bands of colors, but all the known feather blankets are made of at least two, and sometimes three, different colors of feathers arranged in vertical bands. None of the other early descriptions of feather blankets mention this feature, although the surviving blankets show that it was a quite visible and universal characteristic.

3. John Work, Winter 1832–1833

Five years later, in 1832, a Hudson's Bay Company party of hunters and trappers under the leadership of John Work entered California and worked their way down the east side of the Sacramento River, hunting and trapping as they went (Maloney 1945). By 9 December 1832 they had crossed Butte Creek and moved "11 miles S.S.W. down the fork to the end of the [Marysville] butte" (Maloney 1945: 21). The large River Patwin-speaking town of Koru (present-day Colusa) was somewhat to the northwest on the opposite side of the river. Several Valley Nisenan towns were to the east along the Feather River. The party camped there for five days in the rain, watching the water rise around them. On 11 December, the third day, Work reports:

> "A party of 26 Indians visited the camp today, their camp is not far off, they were very civil to one of the men who passed their huts [i.e., temporary shelters]. Some of them had blankets made of feathers and rabbit skins about their shoulders and a few of them had themselves covered from the neck to the knees with long grass or straw ..." (Maloney 1945: 21).

These people must have been from one of the Patwin-speaking tribes in this area. Their appearance matches Kroeber's (1932: 271) description: "A man fishing would put a feather or rabbit fur blanket over one shoulder, covering himself to the hips." The people who visited Work's party were clearly temporarily camping there to have access to hunting or fishing resources: Work refers to the permanent Native houses as 'house,' saving the term 'hut' for the temporary shelters made while camping.

Work's party passed the worst of the rainy season on the Marysville [formerly Sutter] Buttes. The Buttes are a huge, massive, volcanic outcropping with three principle peaks—called North, South, and East Butte—surrounded by many lower peaks lying between and around them. They are the most impressive landmark along this part of the Sacramento Valley, rising abruptly from the level floor of the valley between the Sacramento River on the west and the Feather River on the east. They are the only consistently dry land in the rainy season for miles around. As the rivers rose and flooded during the rainy season, Work remarked on 5 February 1833, "we are now nearly on an island as the butte is surround[ed] nearly with water" (Maloney 1945: 29).

At the end of February, when the waters began to subside, the Hudson's Bay Company party moved east to the Feather River. Along the lower Feather River the Native tribes spoke Valley Nisenan, while along the upper reaches they spoke another, distinct language, Konkow. It is not clear from Work's account whose territory they were in. On Sunday, 24 February 1833, they began to

4. "Ils se font cependant des manteaux de peaux de lapin ou de plumes d'oiseaux, artistement travaillés et bariolés de bandes de diverses couleurs" (Duhaut-Cilly 1834–1835, 1: 168; translation S. McL.).

work their way up the Feather River toward the mountains and higher ground. That night Work observed:

"The Indians are very numerous here [space in original] in about 1½ hours march after we started this morning we passed four villages with 40 to 50 houses in each and there is another large village a little way ahead of us. The country must be rich in resources for food or so many people could not subsist ... We find them employed fishing ... —they are also seen out in the plains when overflowed [sic] with nets set for wildfowl, they have stuffed skins of geese as decoys, they must take a good many of these at times, as their only clothing, a small square blanket which barely covers their body from the shoulders down to the buttocks are [sic] made of feathers" (Maloney 1945: 32).

4. John Sutter, 1839

Near the end of his life the famous Swiss settler and entrepreneur John Sutter claimed in his autobiography:

"I gave names to many of the streams in California. ... The term Feather River, *Rio de las Plumas*, I selected because the Indians at the river decorated themselves profusely with feathers and because there were piles of feathers lying about everywhere from which the Indians made blankets. The geese in this district flew in such dense flocks that one rifle shot would frequently bring down two or three. I have never seen such a profitable hunting ground for geese, ducks, etc." (Gudde 1936: 70).

The John Work diary makes clear that Sutter, who arrived in California in 1839 and settled on the Sacramento River, was not the first to name the Feather River. The Hudson's Bay Company men were already calling it the Feather River in 1832. This name appears to have been first given the river in Spanish by Captain Luis Arguello almost twenty years earlier, in 1820, no doubt for the same reasons Sutter did (McGowan 1961).

5. Captain Edward Belcher, 1837

In late October 1837, while visiting San Francisco Bay, the English Captain Edward Belcher decided to explore the navigable limits of the Sacramento (Belcher 1843: 118–119). He took several crew members with him in six small vessels with a Native guide, who had formerly been in one of the missions. About halfway up they were joined by two other Indian men who had passes from General Vallejo to "absent themselves from mission San José, in order to make treaties with the natives or wild Indians" (Belcher 1843: 120) and agreed to accompany Belcher as interpreters. On 30 October they reached the fork of the Feather River with the Sacramento. The people of the town at the fork, which was called Wallock [Wolok], had hidden at their approach and refused to emerge and have contact with Belcher and his men. Belcher's party turned around at this point and retraced their course down the river.

Belcher described the Sacramento Valley as flat, with "scattered eminences" upon which the tribes who inhabited the valley built their towns. These eminences

"consisted of a rounded pile, raised about fifteen feet at the apex above the surrounding level; the space from which the earth is removed forming a ditch to carry off the superfluous water ... Our pilot termed them Rancherias, ... and assured us that each was the separate property of a distinct tribe" (Belcher 1843: 124).

According to Belcher,

"the pilot, a native, converted and retained by the mission, informed us that the banks [of the Sacramento] throughout our whole route were once thickly studded with these Rancherias and with natives to possess them" (Belcher 1843: 128).

Belcher and his party found many of these town sites abandoned and some covered with bones, as a result of a terrible epidemic in the summer of 1833.[5]

Belcher (1843: 125) reports that his pilot named most of the towns below Wallock [Wolok] "Onē̄ē-shăn-á-tē̄ē" ("from among us, of our side" in the Nisenan language). Lower down the Sacramento Belcher visited the Rancheria of one of the two men who had volunteered to join the exploration as interpreters, which he says they also called "Onē̄ē-shăn-á-tē̄ē." There,

"some of the women were clad in cloaks made from the skins of a slate-coloured duck we had not yet seen (either now or in 1827 [when Belcher had visited San Francisco on the *Blossom* under the command of Captain Frederick Beechey]) which presented a very neat appearance" (Belcher 1843: 126).

5. This epidemic may have been malaria. It may in fact have been introduced by John Work's party, who came down with fever and ague during the summer of 1832 on their way to California from the Columbia River and became sick with the same symptoms again the following summer in California (Cook 1955: 308).

Belcher was not impressed by the Native peoples of California, so the blankets must have been neat indeed.

6. Mariano Vallejo's Treaty with Succara, 1837

Mission San Francisco Solano, established in 1823, was secularized in 1833, along with the rest of the missions in California. Mariano Vallejo was sent to Sonoma to divest the mission of its property and took advantage of the assignment to enrich himself. In 1834 he was granted the Petaluma Rancho, and in 1836 he was made Commandante-General of Alta California (Farris [1989]: 3). At least three campaigns against the Satiyomi are described in Vallejo's reminiscences (Vallejo n.d., vol. 3, cited in Farris [1989]). The second campaign was concluded by a formal peace treaty signed between Vallejo and Tucumin Succara, the Chief of the Satiyomi. It had eleven provisions as to the behavior to be followed in the future by each side. Vallejo would deliver weekly to Succara eight steers and two cows, while Succara would "contract to hand over every new moon at the plaza in Sonoma two bears of regular size which would be considered strong enough to fight with savage bulls," etc. (Farris [1989]: 8).

> They then exchanged gifts. Vallejo records that "my gifts consisted of tobacco, chopped and in leaf, glass beads of all colors, red handkerchiefs and blankets; the gifts of Succara consisted of fish nets, blankets of bird feathers, dried fish, deer hides, stag [elk?] hides, and six young girls; I kept for the use of my people the deer and stag hides and delivered to [Chief] Solano [Vallejo's main Native ally] the girls, the feather blankets, the fish nets and the dried fish ..."[6]

Thus even if records documented from which tribe a blanket was collected, the blanket might well not have been made by that group.

7. Captain William Dane Phelps, 1841

From 1840 to 1842 an American sea captain, William Dane Phelps, in command of the Bryant and Sturgis trading ship *Alert*, was up and down the California coast trading various manufactured goods for hides and tallow. He kept a lively and detailed journal in which he recounted his experiences and impressions of the land and residents (Busch 1983). In early February of 1841, a few days after Phelps arrived in San Francisco Bay on his second trip up the coast, John Sutter came to trade. He spent the night with Phelps and invited him to visit his settlement on the Sacramento, which Phelps reports had "about 20 white men & 250 Indians, with which he traps Beaver & Otter & is also engaged in agricultural pursuits" (Busch 1983: 107). A little more than a month later, on 14 March, Sutter's boat brought "a large quantity of Beaver Skins" as part of the trade they had no doubt agreed to in February (Busch 1983: 139).

At the end of February Captain Phelps wrote his wife that he would send her his journal up to that point and some specimens of bows and arrows and baskets on another Bryant and Sturgis ship, the *Monsoon*, which would soon be returning to Boston. He then added to the journal more general descriptions of California and its Native peoples and says:

> "They also make ... blankets of feathers, one of which I obtained from the Sacramento which exhibits much ingenuity and I should think a great deal of labor" (Busch 1983: 145).

Since Phelps had not yet visited the Sacramento, it is highly likely that the blanket was received from Sutter, perhaps as a gift. Unfortunately Phelps collected three blankets, so it is not possible to identify the one that he refers to here.

At the end of July 1841 (not the season for seeing feather blankets in use, unfortunately), Phelps went up the Sacramento in the *Alert*'s pinnace (a light, single-masted sailing vessel) to visit Captain Sutter at "New Helvetia," his settlement at the junction of the American River and the Sacramento (Busch 1983: 190). Here Sutter had built a fortified establishment subsequently known as "Sutter's Fort," which later was to become the site of the town of Sacramento, now the capital of California. On 1 August, returning from an elk hunt at the mouth of the Feather River, Phelps and his companions "stopped at a settlement of Secumnes consisting of about 40 persons" on the north side of the American River (Busch 1983: 207; see Wilson and Towne 1978: 388; town #44 on Fig. 3). There, Phelps reports,

> "I saw a string o[n] stretch of about 500 feet in length into which the feathers of the wild duck

6. "... mis regalos consistian de tabaco picado y en rama[?], avalorios [sic] de todos colores, frezados y pañuelos colorados; los regalos de Succara se componian de redes para pescar, frezados de pluma de aves, pescado seco, cueros de venado, cueros deciero y seis jovenes muchachas; guardé para el uso de mi gente los cueros de venado y de ciervo y entregué a Solano las muchachas, las frezadas de pluma, las redes de pescar y el pescado seco ..." (Vallejo n.d., 3: 303, cited by Farris [1989]; translation S. McL.).

were closely worked, part of it white and part black. This was to form a blanket or at least the warp of one. The labour of making one of these blankets is immense. Captain Sutter presented me with one which he assumed occupied six females four months in the making" (Busch 1983: 207).

In 1871 Phelps published his memoirs, entitled *Fore & Aft*, in which he recalled that on his first visit to New Helvetia in 1841, as he was leaving

"my good friends, Captain Sutter and Mr. Sinclair had collected a great many beautiful articles of Indian manufacture, such as fine woven ornamental baskets, feather blankets, bows, arrows, etc., which they kindly forced me to accept; as I was their first visitor from the sea, they said I was entitled to them" (Phelps 1871: 258; Fig. 2).[7]

Phelps made a second trip to Sutter's establishment, New Helvetia, at the end of March 1842. Like Work's party he found

"the plains which were dry when I was last up here, now are covered so as to resemble a sea while the little hills and detached clumps of trees resemble islands in the distance" (Busch 1983: 277).

This was the right time of year to see feather blankets in use, but Phelps does not mention them, and he was a generally good observer. Perhaps he did not see very many Native women, or perhaps feather blankets were already less worn then a decade earlier when Work commented on them.

8. The U.S. Exploring Expedition, 1841

In August of 1841, a week after Phelps returned from his first visit to Sutter, the United States Exploring Expedition ship, the *Vincennes*, under the command of Lt. Ringgold, anchored in San Francisco Bay. The hospitable, gregarious Phelps went immediately to pay his respects and offer assistance, since these Americans were strangers on the coast. He spent the next several days with the officers, supplying them with fresh meat, dining and partying with them, and giving them assistance. When Ringgold heard of his recent experiences on the Sacramento, Phelps notes that Ringgold

"was much pleased with my account of the Sacramento and intends to explore it as far up as possible, feels much interested in Capt. Sutter's settlement and said he would certainly visit him even were it a hundred miles out of his way" (Busch 1983: 219–220).

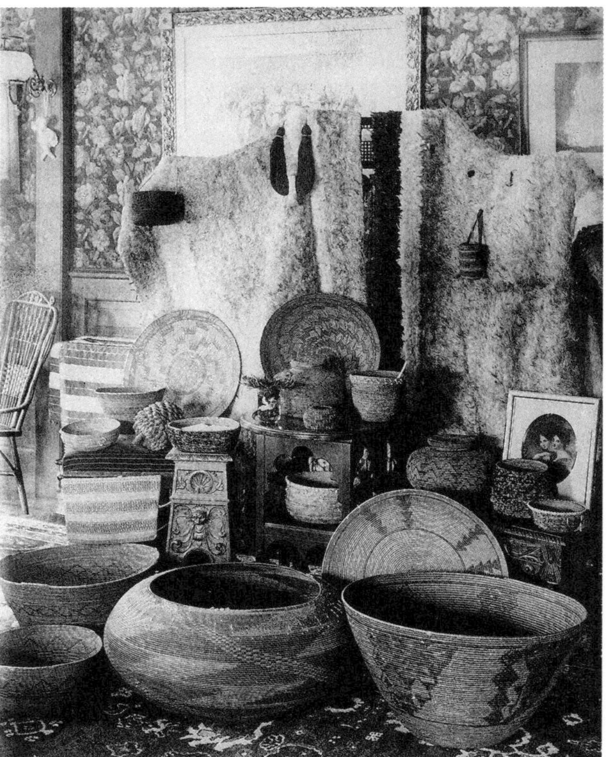

Fig. 2 Collection made by William Dane Phelps, captain of the *Alert*, during a hide and tallow trading voyage, 1840–1843. Two California feather blankets (PMH, cat.no. 98238 on left, cat.no. 98240 on right) hang in back. California baskets in foreground, a Hawaiian necklace hangs on the blanket on the left. Photograph sent by Mrs. Charles Goodwin to Otis T. Mason, 26 March 1901. National Anthropological Archives, Smithsonian Institution (Washington, DC), neg.no. 81-6504.

On 20 August 1841 Ringgold left with seven boats, over sixty officers and men, including the naturalist Charles Pickering and Lt. Budd, and provisions for six weeks. It took them three days to get to Sutter's establishment on the American River. There Sutter entertained them as he had Phelps, even to having a group of boys put on traditional dances for them in the evening.

From Sutter's, Lt. Ringgold and his men continued up the Sacramento. On 28 August Pickering reports that they passed

"the remnant of a platform of poles with cordage, at the water's edge, erected apparently for the taking of salmon" (Pickering 1848: 104),

which Lt. Wilkes in his *Narrative* identified as part of a former fish weir (Wilkes 1845, 5: 185). The next day Pickering reports they

7. Phelp's daughter, Mrs. Charles Goodwin, later took a photo of his collection which shows two of the feather blankets and the baskets (Fig. 2). Some of the baskets are Chumash and from Southern California, but many others are clearly from the Sacramento River area and therefore probably the ones Sutter and Sinclair gave him.

"had our first interview with the Sacramento tribes. Several men made their appearance on the [western] bank, armed with bows and arrows and some ... javelins, and kept pace with the boats in silence. For quivers they used the skins of quadrupeds, such as the fox, lynx, and cub-bear, suspended at the side, or sometimes carried in the hand" (Pickering 1848: 104).

A bit later they landed on the western bank and encountered three seated men, who were soon joined by others. Pickering recounts:

"After awhile the natives invited us to the village which was visible in the distance with some of the inhabitants perched upon the roofs. The houses ... were partly subterraneous, being built over a large roundish pit, three or four feet in depth. The roof [was] firm and covered with earth ... We observed ... in one of the houses, a blanket or *cloak*, made of the feathers and down of water-fowl; very similar to one seen in the Straits of De Fuca" (Pickering 1848: 105).

These people on the west bank would have been speakers of Valley Patwin, probably from the town of Saaka, which had one of the two important fish weirs on the river, as discussed below (Kroeber 1932; cp. Fig. 3).

The next day Ringgold's party passed the most significant landmark along the winding Sacramento—now called the Marysville Buttes. A day later, toward sunset, they came to another town with an active fish weir. At this point Pickering's account describes the party as "several miles above the Butes" (Pickering 1848: 105). In fact, the Sacramento becomes extremely winding at this point and doubles back and forth (cp. Fig. 3). Therefore, although the boats had gone no doubt "several miles," they were not that far away from the Buttes as the crow flies. This second town must have been the important Valley Patwin-speaking town of Koru. Here the party turned around and returned down the river.

Charles Willoughby (1922) in his seminal article on California feather blankets identified the three feather blankets he then knew about as Maidu, based on his reading of Wilkes's narrative of Lt. Ringgold's trip up the Sacramento River (Wilkes 1845, 5: 187; cp. note 2). Willoughby knew that the U.S. Exploring Expedition had collected a beautiful feather blanket still preserved in Washington[8] (NMNH, cat.no. 2119; Fig. 24), and he apparently assumed that that blanket had been collected where a blanket was seen.

A careful reading of Wilkes's narrative—which is extracted from Pickering's own eyewitness account (partly published in his *The Races of Man* [1848: 105]) combined with extracts of the eyewitness accounts from the journals of the other officers (all of whom were required to keep journals and turn them over to Wilkes at the end of the voyage)—makes clear that the party was not sufficiently far north to be encountering towns where Maidu was spoken. The Marysville Buttes (referred to by the Exploring Expedition as "Prairie Bute") is the major easily identifiable landmark on this part of the Sacramento. It is on the east side of the Sacramento, opposite the middle of the territory held by tribes speaking the River Patwin language (Kroeber 1932; cp. Fig. 3). The Buttes were passed the day *after* the party visited the first town where a feather blanket was seen (Wilkes 1845: 187; Pickering 1848: 105).

Pickering reports that both the first and second towns visited were on the *west* bank of the Sacramento. Only towns speaking River Patwin were located on the west bank (Kroeber 1932; cp. Fig. 3). The remains of a fishing platform/fish weir had been observed earlier on the day that the party visited the first town where they saw the feather blanket, while the party turned back at a second, active fish weir at approximately the latitude of contemporary Colusa (located near the site of the River Patwin-speaking town Koru). Kroeber (1932) records two traditional fish weir sites for tribes speaking River Patwin who lived along the Sacramento River. The most southerly one was located at Saaka below the contemporary town of Grimes (Kroeber 1932; cp. Fig. 3). The second fish weir was to the north, near the town of Koru, right where the Exploring Expedition saw it!

Willoughby was apparently also misled by Dixon's monograph *The Northern Maidu* (1905). The Northern Maidu were the tribes speaking the northern Maidu

8. The following abbreviations will be used for museum collections referred to in the text:

AMNH	American Museum of Natural History (New York, NY)
DAM	Denver Art Museum (Denver, CO)
EMB	Ethnologisches Museum [formerly: Museum für Völkerkunde] (Berlin, Germany)
LACMNH	Los Angeles County Museum of Natural History (Los Angeles, CA)
MAE	Muzei Antropologii i Etnografii (St. Petersburg, Russia)
MVF	Museum für Völkerkunde (Frankfurt am Main, Germany)
NMD	National Museum of Denmark (Copenhagen, Denmark)
NMNH	National Museum of Natural History (Washington, DC)
PMH	Peabody Museum, Harvard University (Cambridge, MA)
SMVD	Staatliches Museum für Völkerkunde (Dresden, Germany)
UMB	Ulster Museum (Belfast, Northern Ireland)

language, or Maidu proper, but in fact the monograph discusses the material culture, subsistence, and religious practices of tribes speaking the three related Maiduan languages: northern Maidu or Maidu proper, Konkow, and Nisenan (Kroeber 1925: 392). In the actual discussions Dixon usually makes clear which groups he is referring to, if one reads carefully, but the title of the book is misleading. Dixon says, for example:

> "The making of robes and blankets from strips of rabbit and wildcat skins, or of the skin of geese and crows, was also an important branch of the weaving-art as practiced by the Maidu [i.e., speakers of Maiduan languages]. The fur blankets were more common in the mountain region, it would seem, the bird-skin in the Sacramento Valley" (Dixon 1905: 148).

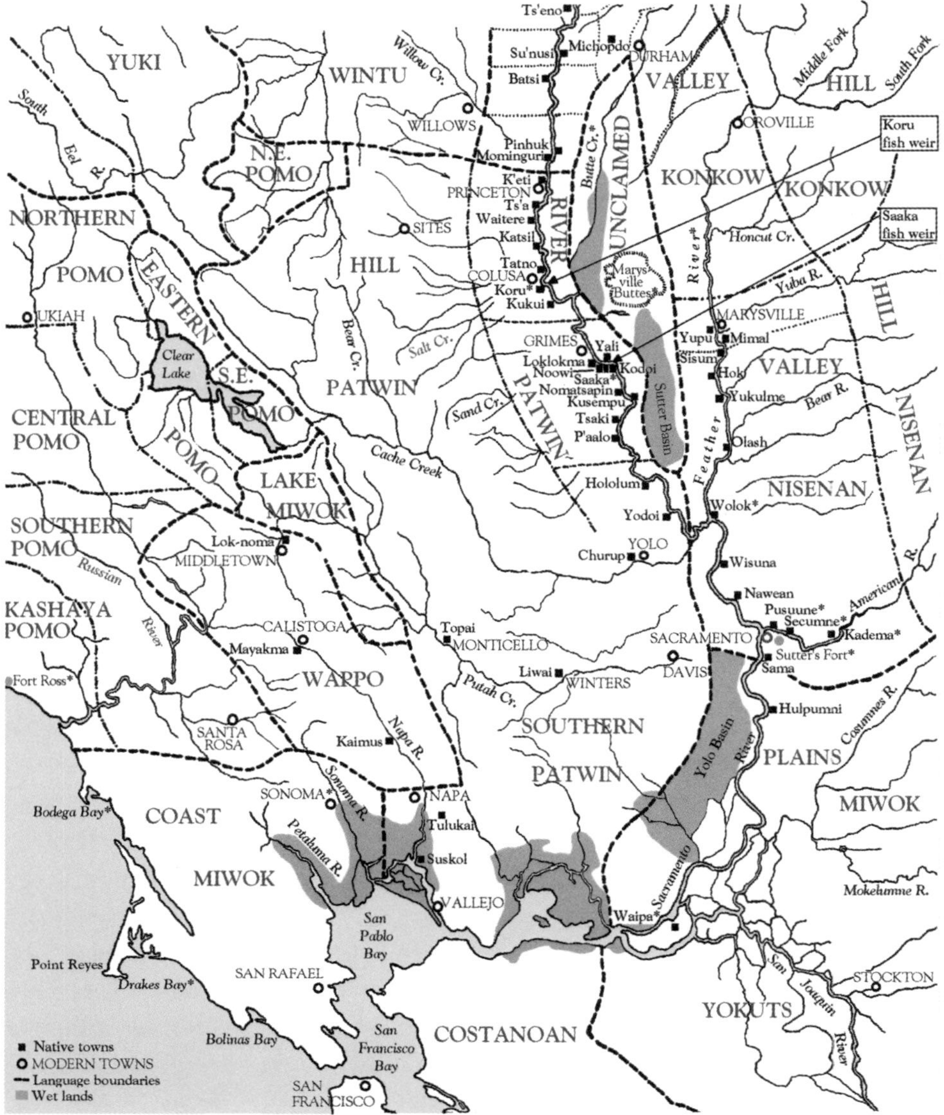

Fig. 3 Map showing the towns of the feather blanket-making tribes in the Pacific Flyway in central California and the boundaries of the several languages spoken in this area: Coast Miwok, Wappo, Patwin, Southern Patwin, Bay Miwok, Plains Miwok, Northern Miwok, Valley Nisenan, and Valley Konkow. Based on map in Kroeber (1932), redrawn by Christian F. Feest. * indicates places mentioned in the text.

Alfred L. Kroeber agrees, explaining that

> "in the Sacramento Valley water birds are more numerous than rabbits, and the blankets were usually of feathers" (Kroeber 1925: 416).

The Northern Maidu or Maidu proper did not live in the Sacramento Valley.

Work's account (Maloney 1945) shows that both rabbitskin and feather blankets were used in the Sacramento Valley, where only Konkow, Nisenan, and River Patwin were spoken. But feather blankets are unlikely, except as trade items, further east in the mountain meadows, where Maidu proper was spoken, or even in the foothills, where Hill Konkow and Hill Nisenan were spoken.

The U.S. Exploring Expedition collected two feather blankets (Jane Walsh, pers. comm.). One, which Willoughby knew about, is in pristine, brand-new condition and preserved in Washington (NMNH, cat.no. 2119; Fig. 24). The other, which Willoughby did not know of, is now in Copenhagen and shows a great deal of ethnographic wear (NMD, cat.no. Hd.78; Fig. 26 and discussion on p. 156 below). Willoughby apparently assumed that the Exploring Expedition had collected a blanket where they saw it, which is, of course, possible.

However, there is no evidence that either of the blankets were collected at Saaka, where a blanket was seen. Since Phelps and Voznesenski report that Sutter gave them blankets, there is every reason to expect that he would have treated the famous Exploring Expedition of the United States at least as well. However, if the blanket seen at Saaka was collected, it would undoubtably be the badly worn blanket now in Copenhagen.

9. Ivan Gavrilovich Voznesenski, 1841

On 20 February 1841 another significant visitor to California, the Russian scientist Ivan Gavrilovich Voznesenski, went to visit Sutter on the Sacramento for a month. Voznesenski had been sent to California by the Russian Academy of Sciences in St. Petersburg to systematically collect information and objects from the Native peoples in and near the Russian colonies on the Northwest Coast and in California, as well as to make zoological and botanical collections. Sutter helped Voznesenski make important collections now in the MAE in St. Petersburg, including at least one feather blanket (Okladnikova 1985: 135–136). Many items in his collections from California are strikingly similar to items collected by Phelps and by the members of the U.S. Exploring Expedition (Bates 1983: 39–41), who both visited Sutter.

Voznesenski kept a diary of his travels and numbered lists of all the objects he collected. These lists specified where he collected something and often from whom. Unfortunately they have never been published and are only available in small bits and pieces quoted in articles by various Russian scholars (e.g., Liapunova 1967, Okladnikova 1985).

Voznesenski left California for Sitka in September 1841 and continued his collecting activities on the Northwest Coast and in Siberia for several more years, returning home to Russia only in 1849 (Liapunova 1967). In St. Petersburg Voznesenski spent the rest of his life at the ethnographic museum, arranging collections and exhibits and often even collecting admissions. For lack of exhibit space, most of his ethnographic collections remained in storage throughout the rest of his life. He "compiled lists of the ethnographical materials brought back" (Liapunova 1967: 26). But he seems never to have had the time to actually systematically catalog his collections and make sure that the objects were securely connected to the lists he had made. Or perhaps it did not seem important, since he knew to which object an entry on a list referred. But it didn't matter, since Voznesenski apparently had a phenomenal memory and had arranged all the collections on exhibit and in storage, so he could always find whatever was wanted.

After Voznesenski died in 1871, however, no one else on the museum staff could find anything, and a need for a formal cataloging system became apparent. Gradually a system of cataloging the items was organized where every object was assigned to a numbered collection within the major geographical areas (America, Pacific, etc.) and then sequentially numbered within each collection. The lower numbered collections seem to have been numbered earlier and the higher numbered ones only later. Thus Kinzahlov in his "History of the American Collections in the MAE, Leningrad" (1983) refers to a "Kolosh" [Tlingit] collection, No. 91, which was donated to the museum by Alphonse Pinart in 1873. A great deal (but not all) of Voznesenski's California collections made in 1840 and 1841, over thirty years earlier, and some things not collected by Voznesenski, are cataloged together as collection No. 570. Thus new acquisitions after 1871 were probably cataloged as they were received. Older collections were cataloged probably when the staff could find the time, using whatever documentation could be found. Unfortunately, some of the objects Voznesenski collected, such as at least one feather blanket, appear not to have been cataloged as his, and the information on the lists as to where and from whom Voznesenski collected something was not tightly associated with the object. Thus two California feather blankets, at least one of which was probably collected by Voznesenski, are in the MAE in St. Petersburg, but until 1983 they were identified as coming from the Northwest Coast and as collected by Captain James Cook on his third voyage (Kaeppler 1983).

The Peoples Who Made Feather Blankets

During the first three decades of the twentieth century, descriptions of duck and goose feather blankets were provided by a number of elderly knowledgeable California Indian people. They were members of tribes whose territories had been located north of San Francisco Bay and in the Sacramento-San Joaquin Delta region of California and along the Sacramento River and its tributaries, who today are known by the names of the languages they spoke as Patwin and Southern Patwin or Suisun (Kroeber 1932: 282), Wappo (Driver 1936: 188), Bay Miwok (Merriam 1967: 367), Plains and Northern Miwok (Barrett and Gifford 1933: 221), and Valley Nisenan and Valley Konkow (Dixon 1905: 148; Kroeber 1929: 260).

The Sacramento-San Joaquin Delta was the "largest watered flatland in the Pacific Flyway," "the winter quarters for a large share of the ducks and geese" who annually migrated along the flyway until unbridled development destroyed most of their habitat (Linduska 1964: 236). Some idea of what the Delta and the Sacramento River Valley were like is given by Captain William Phelps, who collected three feather blankets in 1841. In San Francisco Bay in the winter of 1841 Phelps

> "found Ducks & Geese by the acre. The plains were alive with them and upon firing at them ... they would rise in immense bodies with a clang that could be heard at a long distance" (Busch 1983: 120).

Long, large nets were used by the Native peoples in the Bay area, the Delta, and the Sacramento River basin to harvest ducks and geese in the winter for food. Again in February of 1841 Captain Phelps

> "observe[d] the Indians catching ducks between [Point Quentin] and a little island which lies near it. They construct large nets of strips of hide or of flags and repair to places [that] are the resort of their game which is usually rivers or headlands off which there is an island or a mud bank. They fix a long pole in each bank and secure one end of the net to the pole opposite to where they hide themselves. A dozen or two of artificial ducks to serve as decoy (made of bullrushes in a very ingenious manner) are then sent afloat under the net and between the poles and the Indians, having a line fast to the other end of the net passed through a hole in the upper [part] of the pole near them, wait in concealment for their game. When the birds approach they suddenly extend the net across the river by pulling the lines and intercept [sic] them in their flight when they fall stunned into the bag of the net and are thus easily taken" (Busch 1983: 118).

The Construction of Blankets

All the blankets are rectangles. Their manufacture among the groups on the Sacramento and American Rivers speaking the Nisenan language was described in 1925 by Tom Cleanso to Alfred Kroeber and his students, Anna Gayton and L. S. Freeland (Kroeber et al. 1925, 1929). Cleanso, an elderly speaker of Valley Nisenan, was the consultant for the field-methods class which Kroeber was teaching. Freeland's notes are the fullest, but each of the three anthropologists recorded some details not noted by the others. Cleanso was apparently very shy and soft-spoken and must have been speaking more rapidly than the three anthropologists could write.[9]

Cleanso was blind when interviewed. He had been born on the north side of the American River at the town of Kadema, eight miles north of the modern town of Sacramento, not far from the Valley Nisenan-speaking town of Pusuune where his father was born. Cleanso must have been born in the 1850s or 1860s, since he was already elderly (and blind) when C. Hart Merriam consulted him twenty-six years earlier, in 1903 (Merriam 1967).

According to Cleanso, "duck feather blankets" were called *chi'i* (Freeland in Kroeber et al. 1925) or *ch'i* (Kroeber in Kroeber et al. 1925) in Valley Nisenan. Men normally made them for women, working inside, in the winter, with women helping. However, Cleanso also remembered an aunt making such a blanket (Gayton in Kroeber et al. 1925). Women wore the blankets in the winter.

Cleanso remembered that "duck feather blankets" were woven on two poles, "4' high," planted in the ground the desired width apart (Freeland in Kroeber et al. 1925). Kroeber (Kroeber et al. 1925) recorded that "small feathers were pulled off, wrapped/worked into a long cord, stretched on [a] vertical frame [made by the 2 poles]; [the cord was a] double string = 2 ply." Freeland (Kroeber et al. 1925) specified: "The twine is made double, i.e., two strings are wound together as feathers are put in." Gayton (Kroeber et al. 1925) recorded: "Had string wrapped around [by] duck feathers, Had two poles upright in ground/ [and this string was] wrapped back and forth [a quick sketch shows horizontally] around these & then up and down." Freeland (Kroeber et al. 1925) expands and clarifies Gayton's shorthand description: "Vertical strings are made just long enough to reach up to top when wound [twined through the horizontally wrapped feathered rope], put in every 2 inches and tied when finished," and includes a detailed diagram (cp. Fig. 4).

A similar procedure is described by Driver (1936) for the tribes speaking Wappo around and north of Sonoma in the coast range of mountains:

9. Cleanso had earlier described the manufacture of these blankets to Merriam, but Merriam seems to have confused the description of the manufacture of feather blankets with that of feather dance skirts.

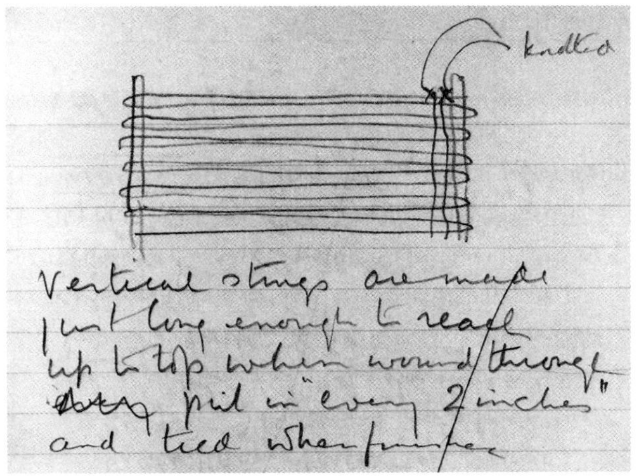

Fig. 4 Sketch by L. S. Freeland, 1925, showing how members of the Nisenan-speaking Kadema and Pusuune tribes on the American River constructed feather blankets. Bancroft Library, University of California (Berkeley, CA), neg.no. 990339.

> "*Feather cape.*—Informants not clear on manufacture. Made on same ... loom of 2 upright poles in ground as was rabbitskin blanket. Pairs of hemp strings, twisted, stretched between poles to form horizontal warp. Down feathers of goose or duck twisted in this 2-ply warp probably as by Maidu [Dixon 1905: 151–152], and tied with third short string. Warp thus made fastened together with hemp weft" (Driver 1936: 191).[10]

None of these descriptions mentions the heavier three-sided braided cord, dyed red in all the known blankets, which the vertical twining strings are looped around (cp. Fig. 18). Since Freeland describes (and sketches) the vertical strings as twined from the lower edge of the horizontally wrapped feathered cord upwards and tied off at the top, this three-sided braided cord must have been on the bottom, below the horizontally wrapped feathered cords (cp. Figs. 4 and 18). Thus blankets were woven upside down from the way they were worn.

None of the anthropologists specify what is clear from the blankets, that each vertical string was in fact doubled so that a loop was created in the middle of the string. This looped string was placed around the initial three-sided cord and the two loose ends of the string pulled through the loop around the three-sided braided cord, so that the two ends of each string were of equal length. Each pair of strings was then wrapped vertically over each horizontal row of feathered cord, and then around each other between each row of feathered cord, so as to encompass each feathered row, catching it firmly to produce a beautiful, soft, thick, incredibly light, but warm, down fabric.

10. The blankets show that many of the descriptions of the manufacture of feather blankets in the ethnographic literature are inaccurate. Dixon (1905: 148), for example, says that feather blankets were made from cut strips of bird skin which on drying curled or rolled, leaving the feather side out, and then were often twisted with a fibre cord for extra strength to make the feathered warp for a blanket. None of the extant blankets are made from cut strips of bird skin.

The Evidence of the Surviving Blankets

All the known blankets consist of horizontal feathered ropes held together by vertical pairs of hemp strings twined around the horizontal feathered ropes as Cleanso described. The vertical pairs of hemp strings are always looped over a two-string, three-sided braided cord, which is always dyed red (cp. Figs. 18, 23). The vertical pairs of hemp strings are always knotted off along the opposite side from the three-sided braided cord, but the type of knot varies from blanket to blanket. The horizontal feathered ropes in all the blankets begin in the center of the blanket where they are tied to the three-sided braided cord. Changes in the color of the feather bands always take place at least six to twelve inches in from one of the side edges, so it is difficult to detect where one color stops and another begins. The blanket fabric therefore appears seamless, without beginning or end (cp. Fig. 21).

Some of the blankets are brand new. Their feathers show no signs of wear and are very fresh and brillantly colored even after roughly 150 years of museum storage. Others show varying degrees of wear, ranging from essentially worn out (as the Dawson blanket in the LACMNH) to only slightly worn. The areas of wear are similar in all blankets: (1) an area at the top center, just below the three-sided braided cord; (2) symmetrically paired areas on the two ends of the upper edge where the wearer would have grasped the blanket to hold it around her; and (3) a large area in the lower center back. Clearly the blanket was worn with the braided cord around the neck and hanging down the front, so that the blanket wore in the center back where it rubbed on the neck and shoulders (cp. Fig. 26). The two ends of the upper edge and adjacent areas of the vertical sides of the blanket were gripped with the hands to hold it around the body, producing wear marks (cp. Fig. 19). The Berlin blanket also shows wear along the bottom ends where the blanket may have rubbed on the ground when the wearer bent over or sat. Or perhaps the owner of this blanket also wore it reversed (cp. Fig. 20). The wearers must have frequently sat down in the blankets, since many show wear in the lower center back. The Dawson blanket in the LACMNH has in fact been "sat out": The vertical weft cords have broken leaving the feathered cords hanging loosely, if at all, in this area.

These feathered ropes are always of at least two and sometimes three colors, producing blankets with horizontal bands of different colors. The blankets vary most dramatically in their color. There seem to be five possibilities:

(1) dark black/brown iridescent purple/blue feathers with a pair of pure white bands six to eight inches in from both the top and the bottom edges;
(2) pale beige feathers with a similar pair of white bands a few inches in from both top and bottom edges;
(3) darker, grayer feathers with a similar pair of white bands;
(4) a combination of all three colors: dark bands of iridescent black/brown feathers on the outside, followed by a pair of pure white bands, surrounding a central pale beige field;
(5) dark bands of iridescent black/brown feathers on the outside, with a large, totally white center, rather than white bands.

Different colors of blankets are correlated with different collection dates (when these are known). All but the Dawson blanket now in the LACMNH have a distinctive pair of horizontal white stripes woven of snow-goose contour feathers some six to eight inches from both the top and bottom edges.

An analysis of the feathers in five of the blankets in the United States—the three in the PMH, one at the AMNH, and one at the NMNH—carried out by Roxie Laybourne of the Department of Birds of the Smithsonian Institution's National Museum of Natural History (pers. comm. 1989), reveals that the blankets' makers were highly selective. Only specific types of feathers from three birds were used in the three color combinations found in the blankets studied.

The pure white contour feathers of the snow goose formed the three blankets at the Peabody Museum. The soft, downy, light beige breast feathers of the Canada goose (combined with some pale beige, vermiculated side feathers of the mallard duck) were used in the two-color beige and white blanket collected by Captain Phelps in 1841 (PMH, cat. no. 98238; Fig. 11). The dark speculum feathers of the mallard—of which there are a scant eight per wing—which are a beautifully iridescent brownish-black, reflecting sometimes purple, sometimes blue-green iridescence, or sometimes both, were used in another two-color blanket at the Peabody Museum (PMH, cat.no. 84680; Figs. 5–6) collected by William Alden Gale prior to 1819 and probably around 1812. All four types of feathers were combined in the three-color blankets at the AMNH (neg.no. 39537; Fig. 14), the NMNH (cat.no. 2119; Figs. 24–25), and the third blanket collected by Captain Phelps (PMH, cat. no. 98240). Hundreds, if not thousands of birds were thus required to produce a single blanket.

Grouping the blankets by their color types reveals interesting patterns in their collection dates and the periods in which their collectors were in California.

1. Two-Color Black and White Blankets

Three blankets are woven of the black/brown iridescent purple/blue speculum feathers of the mallard, stripped off the shaft and wrapped around paired cords, with two white bands of feathers, identified as snow goose breast feathers for the Gale blanket. Only one has any collection data.

1.1 The Gale Blanket in Cambridge

The two-color black and white blanket collected by the Boston businessman William Alden Gale is the only blanket of this type with documentation (PMH, cat.no. 84680; Fig. 5). Gale collected it on his first trip to California prior to 1819 and probably prior to 1812. He gave it to a Boston friend, Joseph Eaton, around 1821 (Willoughby 1922: 434).

Gale left Boston, aged nineteen, in July of 1809 on the *Albatross* as clerk to the captain, Nathan Winship. A year later, when the ship anchored off the southern Farallon Islands opposite the entrance to San Francisco Bay, Gale was left in charge of seven men to hunt seals on the Farallons while the *Albatross* went south to hunt sea otter and then north to the Russian colony on Norfolk Sound for repairs and to contract for the services of fifty Kodiak Island hunters with thirty baidarkas. By early December, when the *Albatross* brought some of these hunters to join them, Gale and the other seven had already taken 30,000 seal skins. For six months the

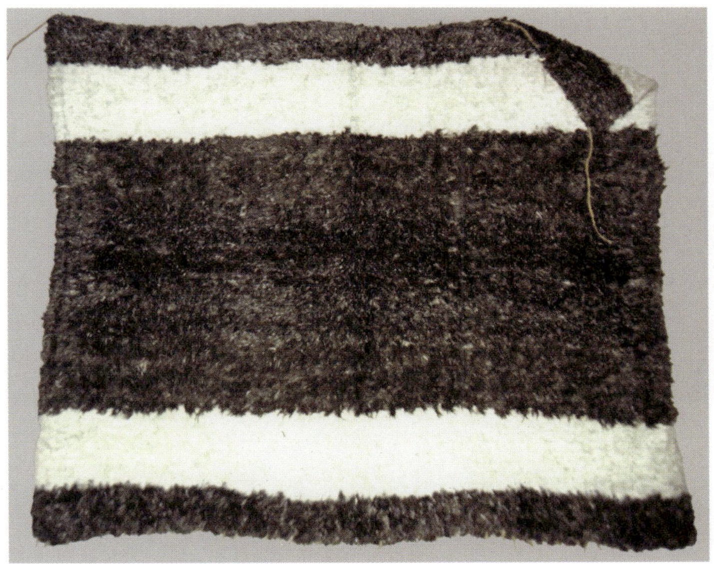

Fig. 5 Two-color black and white Gale Blanket (PMH, cat.no. 84680); ca. 141 x 126 cm. (Willoughby 1922: 434). Collected in California before 1819 and probably before 1812. Photograph: Sally McLendon.

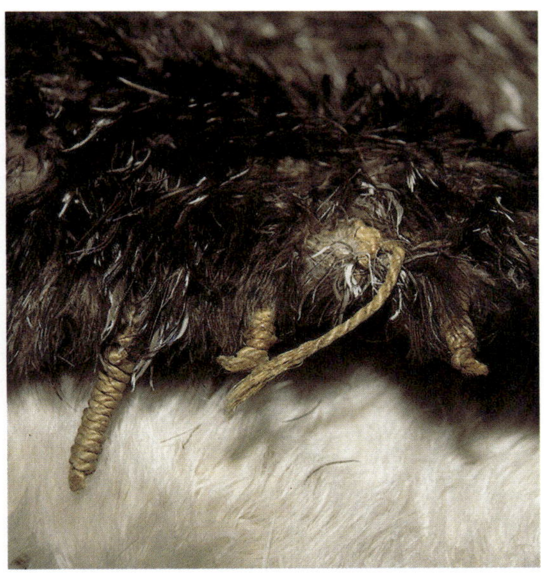

Fig. 6 Close-up of distinctive cone-shaped knot, lower-left, on bottom of Gale blanket. Photograph: Sally McLendon.

Albatross shuttled between the south where hunters had been left on the Santa Barbara Channel Islands and Drakes Bay, in Coast Miwok territory, bringing supplies and dropping off and picking up hunters (Bancroft 1886, 4: 93–94).

After returning the Kodiak Islanders to the Russian settlements in the North, the *Albatross* sailed in October 1811 for Honolulu and then China. She returned to California to Drakes Bay and the Farallons in August of 1812, then returned to the Hawaiian Islands where the ship and its crew were blockaded for nearly three years during the War of 1812 with England. It is not clear if they returned to California again before returning to Boston. According to Beardsley,

> "between 1807 and 1818 Drake's Bay or Bodega Bay (including Tomales Bay) were hide-out anchorages for two or three ships a year, while their Aleut or Northwest Coast Indian hunters were sent overland across the Marin peninsula to San Francisco Bay, thus detouring the small Spanish garrison at San Francisco" (Beardsley 1954: 18).

During this period the Spanish records contain references to observations of canoes (i.e., baidarkas?) and "Russian Indians" in Bodega Bay, Drakes Bay around Pt. Reyes on the north end, and in San Pablo Bay (at the northern end of San Francisco Bay) between Pt. Bonita and San Antonio Creek (Bancroft 1886, 4: 95n30), that is, along the western and southern edges of the Marin peninsula where Coast Miwok was spoken. Speakers of Coast Miwok from towns in this area had just begun to be incorporated into Mission San Francisco in some numbers in 1806 when Langsdorff visited, and a large number of the Native peoples of this area were still living in their own towns independent of the missions while Gale was in the area. It seems likely that the blanket Gale gave Joseph

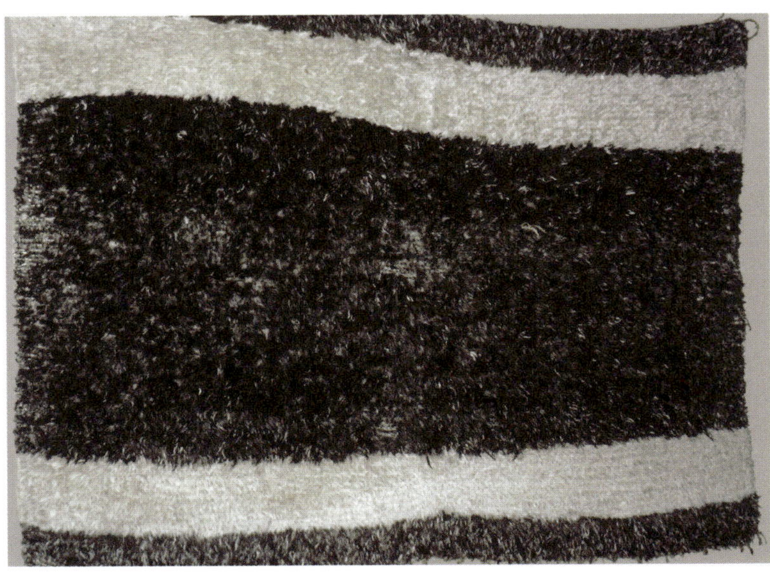

Fig. 7 Two-color black and white undocumented blanket in St. Petersburg (MAE, cat.no. 2520-9). Photograph: Brian Bibby.

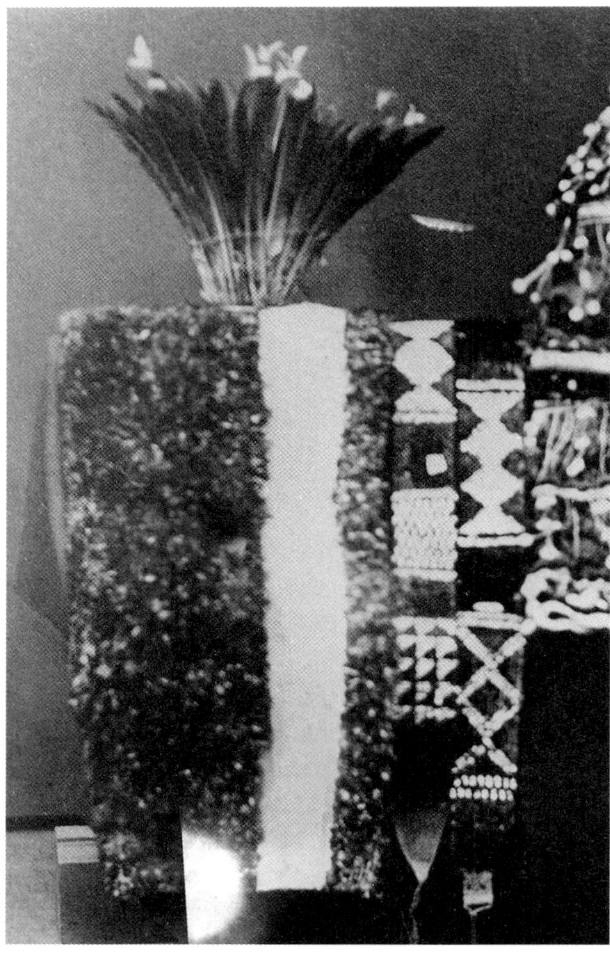

Fig. 8 1873 photograph of objects from Fort Ross in the Museum of Ethnography of the Imperial Academy in St. Petersburg, now the MAE. On the left, a quarter of a feather blanket (MAE 2520-9). A feather headdress (MAE 570-4) sits on top of the blanket. Two rare bead and feather belts (MAE 570-11 and 570-12) are draped to the right of the blanket. In the upper right corner, an elaborate Kodiak Island gutskin garment. Photograph: Santa Barbara Museum of Natural History, Department of Anthropology print, Heizer Photo FP-9.

Eaton was made by one of the Coast Miwok-speaking groups in this area or among groups speaking Bay Miwok further inland to the east (cp. Fig. 3).

Canoes and "Russian Indians" or "fishermen" were also seen around San Mateo, San Bruno, and in the estuaries near San José along the southern part of San Francisco Bay. The Native peoples living in this area spoke one of several Costanoan languages. However, all the peoples on the southern side of San Francisco Bay had been successfully proselytized by the missionaries, and most of them now lived at Mission San Francisco, Mission Santa Clara, or Mission San José rather than in their own towns (Milliken 1995). It seems less likely that Gale would have visited these missions, since hunting seals and sea otters on the Farallons was in direct violation of Spanish law. However, a letter from Gale preserved in the Bancroft Library asking for the return of a Kodiak Islander captured by the Spanish suggests that there was at least some contact with the Spanish authorities in San Francisco during this period.

The Gale blanket is a beautiful, pristine blanket in perfect condition (PMH, cat. no. 84680; Figs. 5–6). It is unique in the long cone-shaped knots that tie off each pair of weft cords at the bottom. The lack of any signs of wear and its clean, brilliant feather colors indicate that it was brand new when collected. It is possible that Gale received this blanket as a gift.

1.2 The Black and White Blanket in St. Petersburg

The second blanket known of this type is found in the MAE in St. Petersburg, where it carries the number 2520-9 (Fig. 7). Together with the second California feather blanket in the MAE (cat.no. 2520-8), it was for most of the twentieth century cataloged as from the Northwest Coast and collected by Captain James Cook on his third voyage around the world (Rozina 1978: 10). After the publication of Kaeppler's *Cook Voyage Artifacts* (1978) containing a black-and-white photograph of this blanket, Jonathan Batkin and Richard Conn recognized that blanket 2520-9 was strikingly similar to a California blanket in the Denver Art Museum (FMA-1-Ex/1952.299) originally acquired by Captain William Phelps (although they in fact differ in feather color [Kaeppler 1983]; cp. Fig. 11 for a blanket which is identical in color and was also collected by Captain Phelps.)

Earlier, in the 1950s, the California anthropologist Robert Heizer had discovered in the Photothèque of the Musée de l'Homme in Paris a set of photographs taken of objects in the Museum of Ethnography of the Imperial Academy in St. Petersburg in 1873, the predecessor of the MAE. One photograph shows part of blanket 2520-9, parts of two California feather belts (MAE cat.nos. 570-11, 570-12), a California feather headdress (MAE cat. no. 570-4), plus a Kodiak Island gutskin coat (Fig. 8). The original photograph can no longer be found in the Photothèque. The back of Heizer's copy of the photograph carries a typed label reading:

> "Heizer Photo FP-9, print 1: 'Copy of photo of Russian pcs. from Fort Ross.'"

It is not clear if this attribution was on the original photo. Heizer's notes describe the photo as "an old photographic print in the Photothèque of the Musée de l'Homme (classed under 'Etats-Unis, Region du Pacifique, Californie, #44-130-12') shows 5 objects in the 'Museum of the Imperial Academy, St. Petersburg.' 4 pieces are from Fort Ross, the 5th is from Kodiak Island. Photo is dated 1873 & has no scale" (Heizer n.d.).

Kodiak Islanders were at Fort Ross as seal and sea otter hunters during most of the period of the Russian settlement there, so the fifth object, the gutskin coat, could have been collected at Fort Ross as well. The grouping of California objects in this photograph suggests that it was known in the nineteenth century that 2520-9 was from California, not the Northwest Coast.

The other California objects shown in the photograph are cataloged as part of Collection 570, which in principle contains objects collected by Voznesenski. It is possible, therefore, that Voznesenski collected the blanket as well. However, so far documentation has been found only of the fact that Voznesenski collected a feather blanket from the Sacramento with Sutter's help (Okladnikova 1985: 135–136). It is possible that the headdress and feather belts were not collected by Voznesenski either, but were erroneously cataloged as part of Collection 570 of Voznesenski-collected material. The Geographical Society and the Admiralty are known to have transferred their early collections to the MAE. Okladnikova (1985: 121–122) reports that in lists of objects given by the Geographical Society and the Admiralty Department relating to the Indians of northern California compiled by F. F. Russov in 1875–1879, No. 16 is a feather "kover" ('rug, carpet'). Such a feather blanket could have been collected by a number of Russian visitors to California. Changes in staff, disassociation of documentation, and the natural tendency of museum personnel to try to improve their records might have led to an erroneous reclassification. It is to be hoped that the translation of Voznesenski's field notes from California that is currently in preparation will be completed soon and will help to clear up the documentation for these blankets.

I have not yet had the opportunity to study this blanket. According to Travis Hudson it measures 178 by 126 cm (Hudson and Bates [1984]: 136a). Photographs suggest that it is extremely similar to the Gale blanket in the PMH and the third blanket in Dresden. It does not seem to show signs of wear, so perhaps like the other two it was acquired when brand new. An identification as coming from Fort Ross would suggest it was collected in the same area where Gale spent time in 1810–1811 and that two-color, black and white feather blankets might have been characteristic of the Coast Miwok peoples of Marin County.[11]

The source of the photograph from Paris is not identified. It was very likely taken or acquired by Alphonse Pinart, a French anthropologist, collector, and major contributor to the Musée de l'Homme. Pinart donated a Kolosh (i.e., Tlingit) collection to the Museum of Ethnography in St. Petersburg (coll. no. 91) in 1873, the year the photograph was taken (Kinzhalov 1983: 316). The other photos from this group in the Photothèque illustrate Northwest Coast objects, including Pinart's donation. Pinart was sent to Russia in 1873 by Hubert Howe Bancroft to look for Russian records on California for his multi-volume *History of California* (Shur and Gibson 1973: 38, 58n8, cited in Hudson and Bates [1984]: 17a–17b).

1.3 The Uraga Blanket in Dresden

The blanket in Dresden, cat.no. 161, is in pristine condition and equally as beautiful as the Gale blanket (Fig. 9). It differs from the Gale and St. Petersburg blankets in the several dangles composed of red, white, and black trade beads, arranged on one (presumably the outer) side (Fig. 10). These are reminiscent of the red woodpecker scalps on the Phelps three-color blanket in Cambridge, which probably was a gift from Sutter.

The Uraga blanket is described in the 1875 inventory of the ethnographic collection of the Royal Historical Museum of Dresden as Mexican. The entry reads:[12]

"F. Mexican Objects. "General Uraga Mexican envoy, to King Friedrich August II.

11. Feather blankets are not documented for the Kashaya Pomo in whose territory Fort Ross was located, and the territory in which they live does not have a great deal of the ideal habitat for the ducks and geese used in blankets, like that found around the mouths and lower reaches of the Petaluma and Sonoma Rivers or further inland in the Delta and along the Sacramento. Isabel Kelly (1978: 414–425) does not mention them for the Coast Miwok either, but a "birdfeather jacket" was seen in the late eighteenth century at Bodega Bay (Beardsley 1954: 18).

12. "F. Mexikanische Gegenstände. "General Uraga mex. Gesandter, an König Friedrich August II.

"1. Ein indianischer Überwurf aus sorgfältig aneinander gereihten kleinen Federn gebildet, derselbe soll aus der Zeit vor der spanischen Eroberung Mexicos herrühren, ist aber jedenfalls wenigstens einem altmexikanischen Kleidungsstück nachgebildet. Ein ähnlicher, jedoch etwas kleinerer mexikanischer Überwurf befindet sich im mexikanischen Museum" (Anonymous 1875: 101, from Feest, pers. comm. 2000).

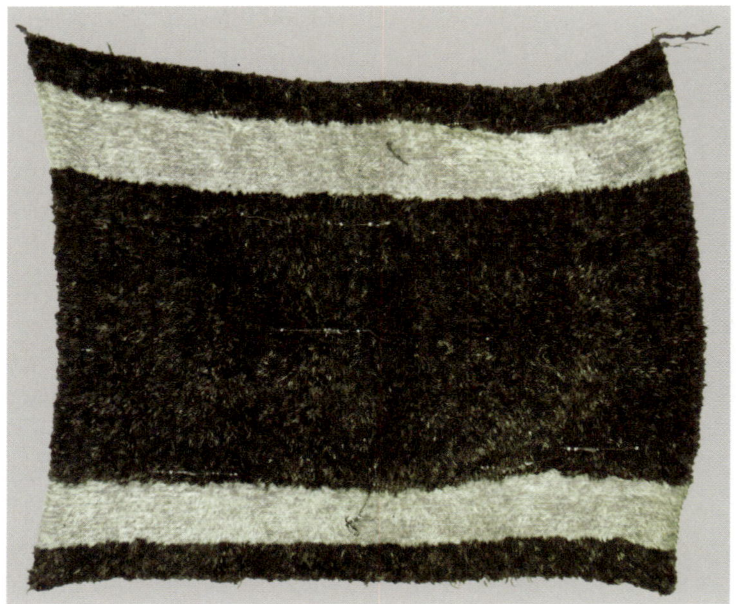

Fig. 9 Two-color black and white feather blanket (SMVD, cat.no. 161), ca. 135 x 108 cm, a gift from General José López Uraga to King Friedrich August II of Saxony, probably in 1854. Photograph: Christian F. Feest (1966).

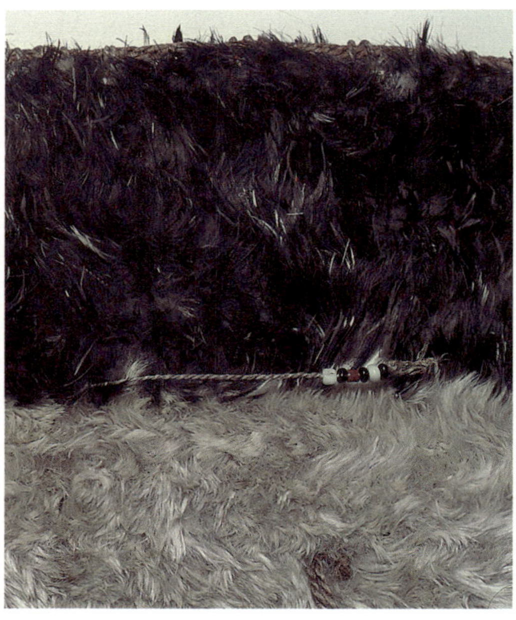

Fig. 10 Detail of López Uraga blanket (SMVD, cat.no. 161), showing glass bead decoration. Photograph: Christian F. Feest (1966).

> An Indian mantle made from small feathers carefully lined up next to each other, which is said to date from the time before the Spanish conquest of Mexico, but is, in any case, at least copied from an ancient Mexican garment. A similar, but somewhat smaller Mexican mantle is found in the Mexican museum."

The smaller Mexican mantle in the Mexican museum is possibly the one mentioned by the collector of the Los Angeles County Museum blanket, Nicholas Dawson (1933: 56), who saw it in the "museum of Aztec antiquities in the City of Mexico" in 1842. The Mexican museum is undoubtedly the National Museum of Mexico, founded in 1825, but incorporating antiquities previously housed in the university and codices and documents from the Boturini Collection. In the same year of its founding, the museum requested the governors of all the Mexican provinces to provide collections for exhibit. By 1840, in addition to Aztec and other Mexican antiquities, the museum included "various dresses, arms, and utensils from both the Californias" (Calderón de la Barca 1966: 340). It is unclear whether the exhibit included a California feather blanket or whether Aztec featherwork was confused with California blankets.

There is no accession date for the blanket, which is identified as part of a small Mexican collection of fourteen pieces, including nine Mexican costume wax figurines, a quechquemetl, a rebozo, a shawl, an idol, and the feather blanket (Feest, pers. comm. 2000).

General Uraga was actually General José López Uraga, a hero of the Mexican-American War and the War of Reform and a potential presidential candidate in the early 1850s. In 1854, during the final presidency of Santa Anna, López Uraga was sent by his competitors as minister to the Court of the King of Prussia, to remove him from Mexico. He subsequently was a general in the War of Intervention (against the French invasion) under Benito Juarez, then in 1864 switched sides and became a supporter of Maximilian and Carlotta. He escorted Carlotta into exile and became an exile from Mexico himself, living in San Francisco in the 1880s until his death in 1885.

The Bancroft Library acquired the papers of López Uraga after his death, and these contain some correspondence from his days as Mexican minister to Prussia. They include a letter in French giving him an appointment with her Majesty, Queen Marie, on 4 January 1855 at 1:30 (by then she was the widow of King Friedrich August II) and an undated letter, also in French, signed "Jean, Duc de Saxe" and therefore probably from 1854 or early 1855, since King Friedrich August died on 9 August 1854, when his brother Johann (Jean in French) succeeded him. The signature on the letter suggests he had not yet assumed the throne at the time he wrote. In his letter Jean, Duke of Saxony, thanks López Uraga for

> "thinking of a conversation that you had with my daughter Sidonie and satisfying her curiosity by

Fig. 11 Two-color beige and white Phelps blanket (PMH, cat.no. 98238), ca. 166 x 116 cm. Collected on the Sacramento River, probably a gift from John Sutter. Photograph: Sally McLendon.

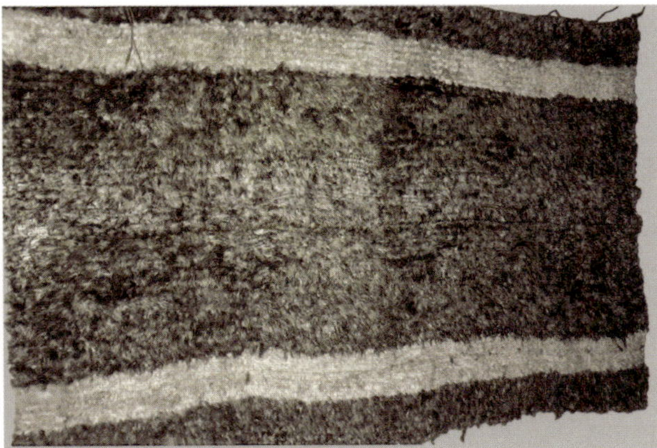

Fig. 12 Two-color grey and white undocumented blanket in St. Petersburg (MAE, cat.no. 2520-8). Possibly collected by I. G. Voznesenski at John Sutter's establishment on the Sacramento River. Possibly an example of the "slate-coloured" duck feather "cloak" seen by Belcher in 1837. Photograph: Brian Bibby.

sending her the charming little figurines representing the costumes and customs of your country."[13]

López Uraga must have visited Dresden and King Friedrich August II, presumably bringing the blanket and other presents, met and talked with the Duke and his daughter, then sent the Duke's daughter the wax figurines, which were quite admired at that period. López Uraga had apparently brought several sets of Mexican wax figures with him, since there is another thank-you letter from a recipient of a set in Berlin. It is not clear why López Uraga wanted to visit, and give presents, particularly an unusual California feather blanket, to the King of Saxony. Perhaps he also gave presents to the King of Prussia, and the goal was to secure the friendship and potential support of these German-speaking kingdoms in case of another invasion of Mexico by the United States or another European power.

It is not clear how López Uraga came into possession of the blanket. The Mexican government could have provided items for gifts, but this seems unlikely given the considerable problems it faced at this period. López Uraga probably brought it with him from Mexico and thus must have anticipated that it could serve as a gift to someone significant. It is also not clear how the blanket came to be in Mexico. Several California baskets from Chumash-speaking peoples found their way to Mexico, where they were subsequently recognized as Californian (Nuttall 1924). There must have been many more California objects that were taken to Mexico.

Nicholas Dawson's claim to have seen a feather blanket identical to his on exhibit in the National Museum in Mexico City and the Dresden inventory's comparison of the Dresden blanket to a smaller one in the "Mexican Museum" suggests that at least one other California blanket was taken to Mexico.

2. *Two-Color Beige and White Blankets*

2.1 The Phelps Two-Color Blanket in Cambridge and 2.2 The Phelps Blanket in Denver

Both two-color beige and white blankets known today were collected by Captain William Dane Phelps in California in 1841 (Fig. 11). At least one and probably both

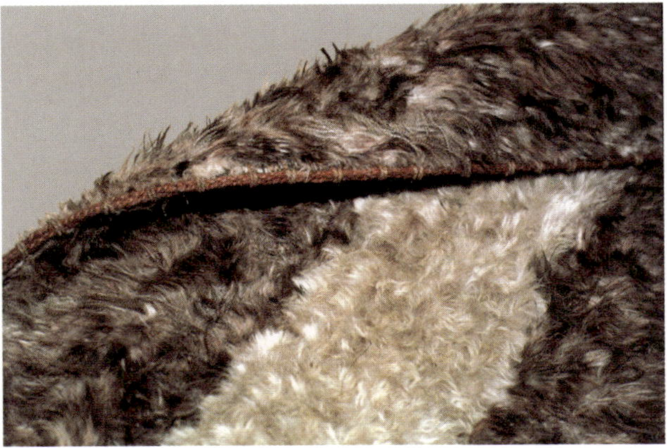

Fig. 13 Close-up of two-color grey and white undocumented blanket (MAE 2520-8) showing greyish feathers. Possibly an example of the "slate-grey" blankets seen by Belcher in 1837. Photograph: Brian Bibby.

13. "... penser à une conversation que vous avez eu avec ma fille Sidonie et à satisfaire sa curiosité en lui envoyant les charmantes petites figurines representante les costumes et usages de Votre pays" (López Uraga [1844–1883, Box 1]).

blankets were acquired as presents from John Sutter, either during Phelps's first visit to Sutter's establishment in July 1841, or earlier when Sutter visited Phelps in San Francisco Bay to trade and Phelps then reported to his wife that he had a feather blanket from the Sacramento. These blankets thus represent a type of blanket associated with the Sacramento River. Since they don't include the black feathers Phelps saw being combined into a rope with white feathers at Secumne on the American River, they are unlikely to come from this southern part of the territory where Nisenan was spoken. They could come from Nisenan- or Konkow-speaking tribes on the Feather River further to the north or from Plains Miwok-speaking tribes south of the American River.

Both blankets were given to the PMH in 1927 by Mrs. Charles Goodwin, Captain Phelps's daughter, in memory of her father. The blankets were cataloged as cat.nos. 98238 and 98239. The smaller blanket, 98239, was exchanged with the DAM in 1952, where it is cataloged as FMA-1-Ex 1952.299. The two-color beige and white blanket still in Cambridge (PMH, cat.no. 98238) shows no signs of wear. It is another brand-new blanket, possibly commissioned by Sutter for Captain Phelps.

3. *Two-Color Gray and White Blanket*

What seems to be the only two-color gray and white blanket is the second feather blanket in St. Petersburg (MAE, cat.no. 2520-8; Figs. 12–13). I have not been able to examine it, but color slides indicate that the feathers combined with the white bands are gray, not beige. According to Travis Hudson it measures 178 by 126 cm. Its coloration strikingly matches Belcher's description of seeing women wearing "cloaks made from the skins of a slate-coloured duck, which present a very neat appearance" (Belcher 1843: 126). So this presently undocumented blanket is likely to come from the Sacramento River as well. The only Russian known to have collected on the Sacramento was Voznesenski. Thus this is likely to be the feather blanket Voznesenski reports that he secured on the Sacramento in the winter of 1841 with Sutter's help. The blanket's feathers have not been identified, but Jess Bill, a member of a recent delegation to the MAE, part of whose family were Patwin speakers from the Colusa area, thought it might be female mallard or widgeon (Bates, pers. comm. 2000).

4. *Three-Color Black, White, and Beige Blankets*

Half of the known blankets are of the three-color type. Three are in museums in the United States and four in Europe. All were collected between 1830 and 1841.

4.1 The Hooton Blanket in New York

Possibly the earliest collected blanket of this group is that now in New York (AMNH, neg.no. 39537; Fig. 14). As Willoughby (1922: 437) recorded,

> "it was purchased from Mr. W. A. Hooton of Brooklyn, New York, in 1914, in whose family it had been since 1830, 'at which time it was purchased either in Mexico or California'."

Museum documentation shows that Mr. Hooton approached the museum offering to sell his blanket, but did not provide the name of the relative who had acquired it. In 1922, eight years after its acquisition, Willoughby noted that the blanket was "somewhat soiled and shows wear." Since Willoughby wrote, the blanket has apparently been exhibited for long periods of time in a sunlit space. The feathers are now very brittle, the white feathers are badly yellowed, and the blanket is very dusty. (Only the Deppe blanket in Berlin, but recently returned from Leipzig, is its equal in the brittleness of the feathers and the dust.) Beneath this later accretion, there are signs of substantial Native wear.

4.2 The Wrangell Blanket in Frankfurt

The next earliest collected blanket is that acquired by Baron Ferdinand von Wrangell, the Governor General of the Russian American Fur Company from 1831 to 1836, during a visit to Fort Ross and Bodega Bay in California in 1833, almost two decades after Gale probably collected his blanket (Figs. 15–16). Wrangell presented the blanket to his father-in-law, the Baron Rossillon, Etatsrat (coucillor) of Reval, and he in turn presented it with other objects given him by Wrangell to the Senckenbergische Naturforschende Gesellschaft in 1834, which transferred its entire ethnographic collection to the Historical Museum of the City of Frankfurt in 1877. When the Museum für Völkerkunde in Frankfurt was established in 1904, the blanket was transferred there, retaining the Senckenberg catalog number E.175. It is a beautiful blanket, in pristine condition. It

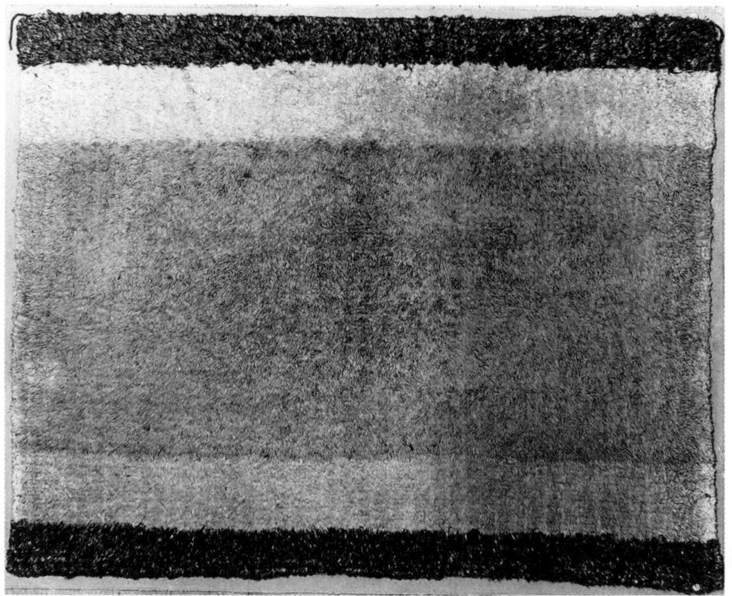

Fig. 14 Three-color feather blanket (AMNH, neg.no. 39537) purchased in either Mexico or California before 1830 by a member of the family of Mr. A. W. Hooton of Brooklyn, NY. Photograph: Courtesy of the American Museum of Natural History (New York, NY).

shows a slight sign of wear at the upper edge on one side that could have been produced by wearing. There does not seem to be a matching area of wear on the opposite side. The blanket was probably a present to Wrangell.

The ends of the top three-sided braided cord have been cut off. On one side the remaining braided cord is approximately 12 cm long and has ten early small, thickish, white trade beads attached to the last third of the cord with a different finer, reddish-brown thread. On the opposite side, approximately 20 cm remain with sixteen beads attached to the last two thirds of the cord (Fig. 16). The bead decoration is surely an additional sign of wealth and status.

According to Vatter (1925: 78), the Rossillon donation included a group of nine objects collected by Wrangell on his trip to California, consisting of "a feather belt, a feather blanket, a feather headdress, two earrings, and four baskets."[14]

The catalog information for all but the earrings is as follows:

"1. Belt of a Tajon (i.e, an Indian elder or chief) in New Albion (E. 168, Abb. 12, 13).
"2. A blanket made out of feathers from New Albion (E.175, Abb. 17).
"3. A headdress made of feathers of a Tajon in New Albion (E.169, Abb. 20).
"4. Four watertight baskets, woven of vines and rushes; from New Albion (E.172, Abb. 25)."[15]

The first three objects are very similar to those shown in the 1873 photograph that Heizer found in the Musée de l'Homme in Paris of the two-color black and white MAE blanket 2520-9 with two feather and bead belts and a headdress. Such a combination of objects of wealth and status seems to have been a recurring presentation to prominent Russian visitors.

The identification of these objects as from "Neu-Albion," a term used by the Russians for the Marin peninsula where they had established their base, which was not favored by other nationalities, suggests that the objects came from this area.

4.3 The Deppe Blanket in Berlin

One of the most extensive and interesting of the early nineteenth-century collections from California in Europe is that acquired in 1837 by the king of Prussia from a German traveler to America, Ferdinand Deppe, which included a feather blanket (Figs. 17–20).

According to Bankmann (1999), Deppe initially went to Mexico in 1824 in the employ of Count Sachs, to collect natural history specimens for the royal collections. Deppe subsequently went into business in Mexico, and after spending a few years there collecting and trading, became the "supercargo" or trading master on ships belonging to the German merchant Henry Virmond. Virmond was based in Acapulco and Mexico City, but did a large business in California even before he visited for the first time in 1828 (Bancroft 1886, 5: 764).

The "supercargo" or trading master was central to the success of maritime trading enterprises on the California coast. These could be phenomenally profitable for their backers, but were also extremely risky. A good supercargo made the difference between profitability

14. "... einem Federgürtel, einem Federmantel, einer Federkrone, zwei Ohrgehängen und vier Körben" (Vatter 1925: 78).
15. "1. 'Gürtel eines Tajon (d.i. indianischen Aeltesten oder Häuptlings) in Neu-Albion' (E. 168, Abb. 12, 13).
"2. 'Eine aus Federn verfertigte Decke aus Neu-Albion' (E.175, Abb. 17).
"3. 'Aus Federn bestehender Kopfputz eines Tajon in Neu-Albion' (E.169, Abb. 20).
"4. 'Vier wasserdichte Körbe, aus Schlingpflanzen und Binsen geflochten; aus Neu-Albion' (E.172, Abb. 25)" (Vatter 1925: 78).

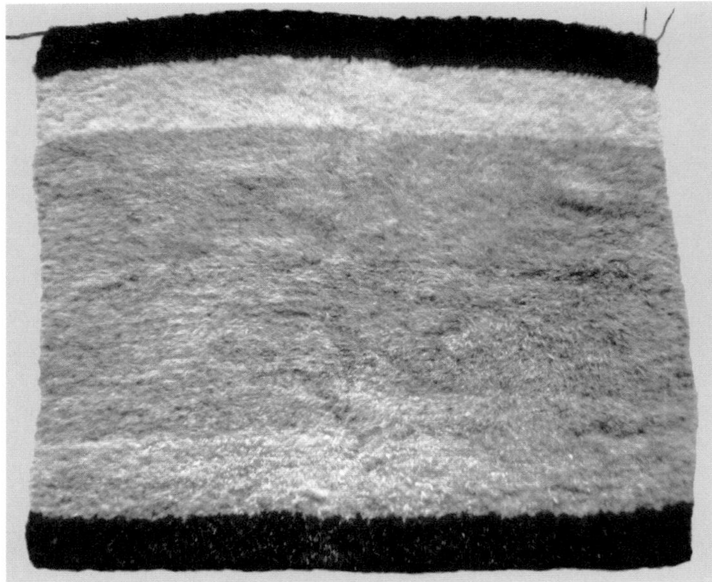

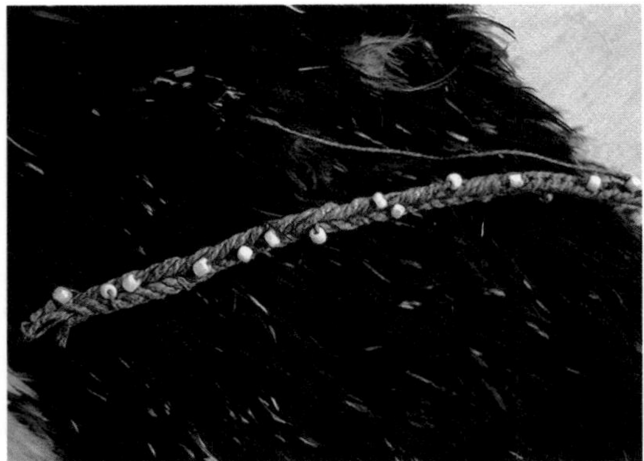

Fig. 16 Close-up of Wrangell blanket (MVF, cat.no. E. 175) showing the sixteen beads attached to the top three-sided braided cord. Photograph: Sally McLendon.

Fig. 15 Three-color feather blanket (MVF, cat.no. E.175) collected by Baron Ferdinand von Wrangell, Governor General of the Russian American Fur Company, on a visit to the Russian establishments at Fort Ross and Bodega Bay in 1833. 143 x 115 cm. Photograph: Sally McLendon.

and loss and usually worked for a percentage of the profits. A supercargo had to be shrewd but honest, a hard bargainer and compulsive record keeper, but able to maintain long-term cordial friendships with his customers, the priest missionaries at the twenty-one Franciscan missions, and the formerly Spanish, now Mexican, administrative officials and military personnel and their families. Ferdinand Deppe seems to have been friends with them all and, in fact, probably acquired some or all of his ethnographic collection through those friendships. He was also good friends with two of the most successful American supercargos on the California coast in the 1820s and 1830s, although they were his competitors—William Alden Gale, who collected a two-color black and white feather blanket on his first trip to California in 1809–1819, and his protegé, Alfred Robinson. Gale and Robinson, like Deppe, were both involved in the lucrative hide and tallow trade, which Gale had in fact been instrumental in opening.

Robinson in his autobiography *Life in California* (1846) describes making a trip with Deppe overland to Mission San José in 1832 to see Indian dancing there during a religious celebration because of Deppe's interest in learning more about California Indians. It provides a sense of the conditions under which he may have made his collections.

After mass and a lavish meal the festivities began. According to Robinson,

> "at a signal from their 'Capitan,' or chief, several Indians presented themselves at the corner of one of the streets of the 'Rancheria' and gradually approached towards us. They were dressed with feathers and painted with red and black paint ... There were several women amongst them. Soon they formed a circle, and commenced ... dancing ... fixed to one spot they beat time with their feet to the singing of half a dozen persons who were seated upon the ground. When these had performed their part, they retired to an encampment beyond the building and another party appeared, painted and adorned rather differently from the former, whose mode of dancing, also, was quite dissimilar" (Robinson 1846: 114–115).

These dancers were no doubt from different tribes, hence their difference in dress and dance style. The dancing was followed by a fight between a bear and a bull after which Robinson and Deppe

> "walked to the encampment, where the Indians were dancing in groups, as we had seen them at the Mission. Around the large space which they occupied were little booths, displaying a variety of ornaments, seeds, and fruit. All was hilarity and good feeling ... At sundown the bells were rung—rockets were let off —guns were fired; and long after supper, at a late hour of the night, we could hear from our beds the continued shouts of the multitude" (Robinson 1846: 115).

Perhaps on this very trip Deppe collected the fine feather dance headdress now in the British Museum, which is identified as from San José, as well as the six yellow-

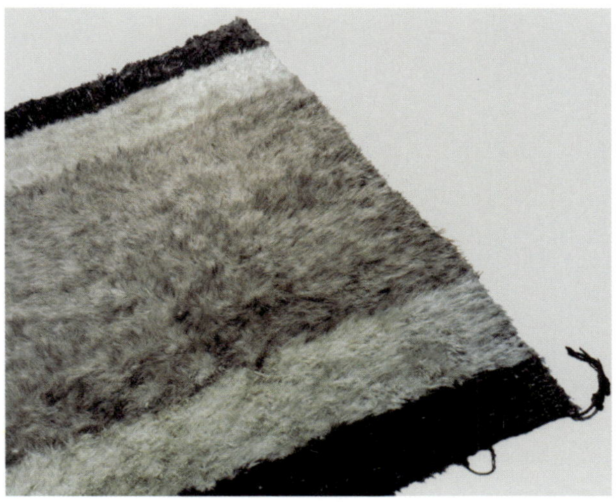

Fig. 17 A third of the Deppe blanket (EMB, cat.no. IV B 182) showing the difference in the widths of the upper and lower dark and white bands. Photograph: Lynn M. Schneider.

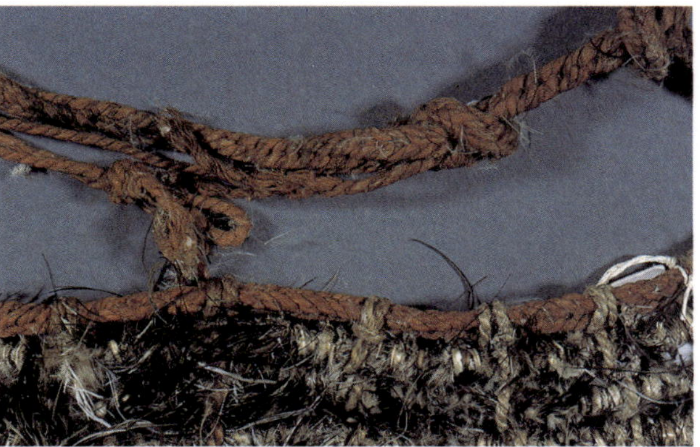

Fig. 18 Detail of Deppe blanket (EMB, cat.no. IV B 182) showing the reddened, three-sided braided cord at the top. Six of the undyed vertical weft strings are visible looped around it at regular intervals. The horizontal feathered warp cords below are badly worn, exposing the construction. Each horizontal warp is twined around by a pair of vertical weft strings which alternate being forward or behind. Photograph: Lynn M. Schneider.

hammer dance headbands and the three pairs of bone and shell ear plugs, also identified as from San José, that are still in Berlin (EMB).

Deppe visited San José again in 1833 and probably later. There were converts from feather blanket-making tribes on the Sacramento River at San José by this time; the two Sacramento River Natives whom Belcher picked up on his trip up the Sacramento in 1837 carried passes authorizing them to leave Mission San José (Belcher 1843: 120). Possibly Deppe acquired his blanket from a Sacramento Valley convert on one of those visits.

On 1 May 1836 Alfred Robinson wrote his employers that

> "I have embarked in the Alert Boxes containing specimens of Natural History ... to be embarked in Boston the first opportunity for Hamburgh
>
> "The Owner is a particular friend of Mr. Gale & undoubtedly ere this you may have the pleasure of his acquaintance—he having left this Coast in January last to return to his country via Los Estados Unidos de Norte in company with Baron Merryhoff & Ladd
>
> "Respecting the freight the House in Hamburgh will satisfy all expenses & it is the request of Mr. Deppe that the cases may not be opened in Custom House if possible to avoid it" (Ogden 1944: 319).

So some of Deppe's collections were sent to Hamburg via Boston in 1836, although Bancroft (1886, 5: 779) reports that Deppe took his collections back to Germany with him on the *Rasselas*.

Deppe's California collection as it has now been identified was not a random, haphazardly made one. It is quite systematic, containing examples of ceremonial dance dress, a man's hunting outfit, baskets, ear ornaments, and a feather blanket. It is second only to Voznesenski's 1841 collection in importance.

The baskets and the feather blanket for most of the twentieth century were not documented as collected by Deppe, although Krickeberg (1914: 716) and others (McLendon [1991]) suspected Deppe might have collected the blanket. Quite recently Ulf Bankmann discovered a handwritten addition to a price list of natural history specimens being sold by Deppe's brother, Wilhelm Deppe, in 1830. The addition is entitled "Sammlung seltner californischer Pracht-Kleidungsstücke aller Art, und geschnitzte Knochen Arbeiten, zusammen 20 Nummern" [Collection of rare California splendid clothing of all kinds, and engraved bone work, altogether 20 numbers] (Bankmann 1998 cited in 1999: 572). It seems unlikely that Deppe had collected all of this material by 1830. In fact, it is not clear that he was working in California by 1830. Hinrich Lichtenstein, in a paper on the ornithology of California based on Deppe's collections, reported that Deppe "... in the last 6 years has constantly moved between Acapulco and Monterey in the trading business ..." (Lichtenstein 1839: 418).

This would mean Deppe began working along the coasts of California in 1831. The great historian of California, Hubert Howe Bancroft, gave the following summary of Deppe's career in California:

> "Deppe (Ferdinand), 1832, German supercargo of Virmond's vessels, often in Cal. '32–6; perhaps

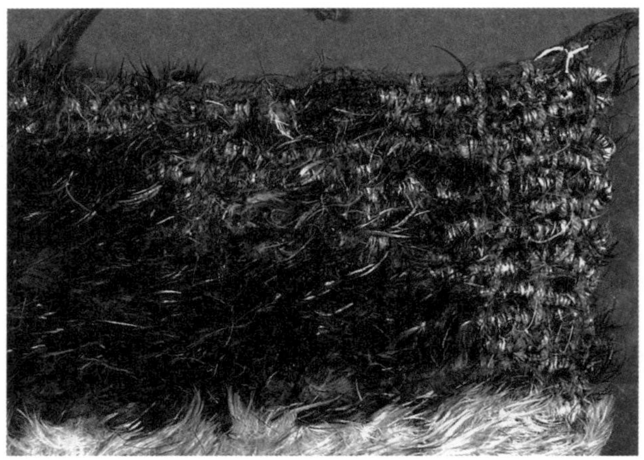

Fig. 19 Close-up of Deppe blanket (EMB, cat. no. IV B 182) showing wear at an upper corner of the outer band of dark mallard speculum feathers. The wearer would have gripped here to hold the blanket close around her. Less worn mallard speculum feathers are visible in lower left of band. Photograph: Lynn M. Schneider.

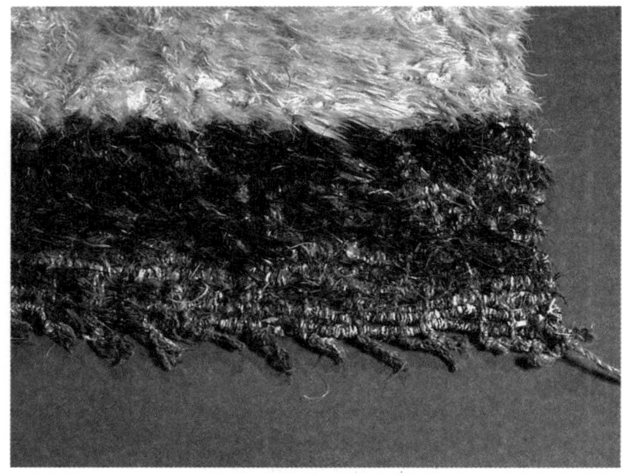

Fig. 20 Close-up of Deppe blanket (EMB, cat.no. IV B 182) showing wear at lower corner of the outer band of dark mallard speculum feathers. These corners would have dragged on the ground when bending over or sitting. Photograph by Lynn M. Schneider.

> from '29–'30. ... Said to have made a drawing of S. Gabriel in '35 ... Also a naturalist devoting his spare time to the collection of birds, plants and shells. Sailed with the Rasselas '36 ..." (Bancroft 1886, 5: 779).

Since the addition of ethnographic materials has been inserted in the price list, it could actually be from a later date and erroneously inserted in the 1830 price list. In any case the addition shows that the baskets and feather blanket were part of Deppe's collection (Bolz and Sanner 1999: 133).

The blanket has had a stressful history. It was part of the collection of the EMB that was found by the Soviets at the end of World War II in storage outside Berlin. The collection was taken to Moscow, where it was kept for several years (and recataloged), then transferred to the Museum für Völkerkunde in Leipzig in what was then the German Democratic Republic (East Germany). When the Berlin Wall came down and the two Germanies were reunited, the collection was returned to Berlin (Bolz and Davis 2000).

The blanket unfortunately returned in an extremely fragile condition. The feathers are dirty and very brittle. Only the blanket in the AMNH approaches the Deppe blanket in fragility. It is clear, however, that the Deppe blanket must have seen a good deal of traditional use before Deppe acquired it. The feathers on the two top ends have been worn away by gripping, so that mostly the quills are left, revealing the construction technique of horizontal feathered ropes held together by vertical strings twined around the feathered ropes (Figs. 18, 19).

The Deppe blanket is unusual in that the dark bands of mallard speculum on the outer edges and the following bands of white feathers are of uneven width. The bottom two bands are much narrower than the top ones (Fig. 17).

4.4 The Thomson Blanket in Belfast

Another blanket of the three-color type is in Belfast, Northern Ireland (UMB, cat.no. 1910:188), the gift of Gordon Augustus Thomson, a world traveler (Fig. 22). Museum records indicate that the blanket arrived in the museum in 1834. I have reconstructed Thomson's itinerary based on unpublished documents preserved in the museum (cp. Glover 1978: 10–11) and on information in Hawaiian newspapers of the 1830s. These establish that Thomson was in California only briefly, from 1 to circa 13 July 1839, and that he in fact went to California on the *Clementine*, the same ship that brought Captain John A. Sutter to California, stopping at Sitka on the way.

Thomson came with a letter of introduction from John Jones, the American consul in Hawaii, to the governor and General Mariano Vallejo, the military chief of Upper California. The letter describes Thomson as well-educated in the sciences and says he came in search of specimens (Bancroft 1886, 5: 747; Bancroft Library, Vallejo Papers).

Vallejo was based in Sonoma, at the edge of the territory where Coast Miwok was spoken. A different language, Wappo, was spoken by tribes just to the north, while a third language, Patwin, was spoken by tribes to the east. Speakers of all three languages made and used feather blankets. Vallejo in fact received feather blankets in his exchange of gifts with the Sotiyomi chief Succara. So Vallejo would seem to have been a likely source of the blanket Thomson collected, and his blanket is likely to have come from a tribe near Sonoma that spoke one of these three languages. The basket Thomson collected at the same time is stylistically like those made by Patwin-speaking tribes (Glover 1978: 19, 60, #58).

The blanket shows signs of wear and is puckered in places as if it had gotten wet and shrunk. This could have happened after Thomson acquired it, but the blanket had surely be worn a good deal before Thomson came to own it.

Roxie Laybourne of the NMNH tentatively identified the feathers, based on an examination of color slides, as mallard speculum for the blackish borders, duck down for the white bands, and pintail or hooded merganser for the central area of dark brown feathers (Fig. 23). This might suggest that it is a subtype of the three-color blanket, and that it is unlikely to have been collected from any of the tribes that were the sources of the other three-color blankets. Perhaps it was produced by speakers of Wappo, and perhaps it is even one of the feather blankets given by Succara to Vallejo in conclusion of their treaty and then worn by some of Solano's people for two years until Thomson arrived looking for specimens.

4.5 The Three-Color Phelps Blanket in Cambridge

Another three-color blanket is now in the PMH (cat. no. 98240; Fig. 21; cp. Fig. 2; ca. 155 x 126 cm). It was collected by William Dane Phelps, the Boston sea captain in the service of Bryant and Sturgis, who spent the winter of 1841 in San Francisco Bay and who worked for the same company as William Alden Gale and his protegé, Alfred Robinson. The blanket is in pristine condition, beautiful, and must have been acquired brand new. It differs from the other blankets in having two vertical rows of woodpecker scalps placed symmetrically on either side of the blanket on the beige central panel. Originally there were probably six scalps on either side. Five survive on one side, four on the other.

Phelps collected three feather blankets, only one of which was three-color. The other two were two-color beige and white blankets. His three-color blanket is the

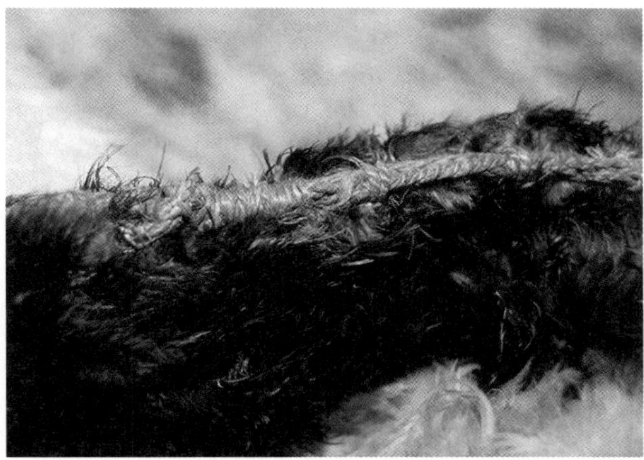

Fig. 21 Close-up of top three-sided braided cord on Phelps blanket (PMH, cat.no. 98240) showing attachment of the beginning of the horizontal feathered rope in the center of the blanket. Photograph: Sally McLendon.

only blanket that would fit with his description of seeing a

> "string on stretch of about 500 feet in length into which the feathers of the wild duck were closely worked, part of it white and part black. This was to form a feather blanket or at least the warp of one" (Busch 1983: 207).

According to Tom Cleanso (Kroeber et al. 1925, 1929), feather blankets were normally woven by men, with women helping, in the winter, yet Phelps saw women working on this string in July of 1841 in a town only few miles from Cleanso's town of Kabema. Perhaps they had been asked to make a blanket out of season so that Sutter could give it to Phelps when he left, and they were rushing to complete the task. Certainly blanket no. 98240 is strikingly similar to the three-color blankets collected by the U.S. Exploring Expedition apparently just a few weeks after Phelps was given his blankets by Sutter. It is likely that they all came from the same group, perhaps the Nisenan-speaking tribe at the town of Seku (Secumnes in Plains Miwok) near the mouth of the American River, where Phelps saw the feathered rope being made.

4.6–7 The U.S. Exploring Expedition Blankets

In 1841 the U.S. Exploring Expedition collected two three-color feather blankets on the Sacramento River. One is in beautiful, pristine condition and must have been acquired brand new (NMNH, cat.no. 2119; Fig. 24). The other is now in Copenhagen (NMD, cat.no. Hd.37; Fig. 26), to where it was exchanged by the

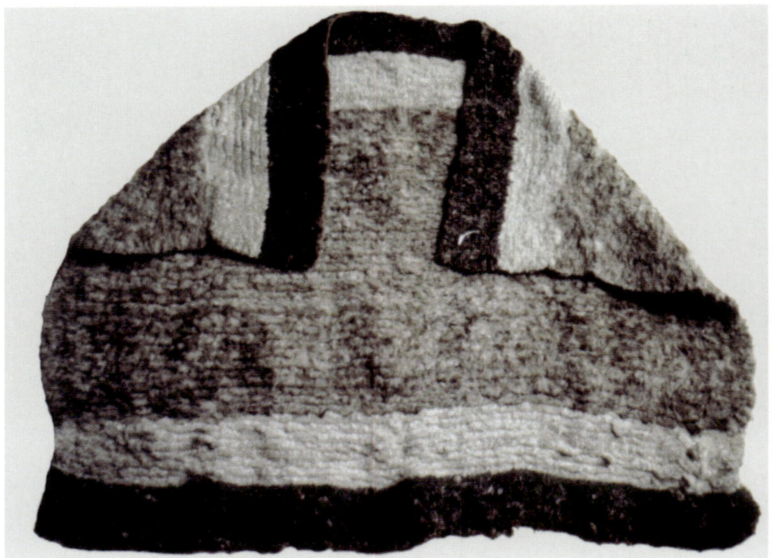

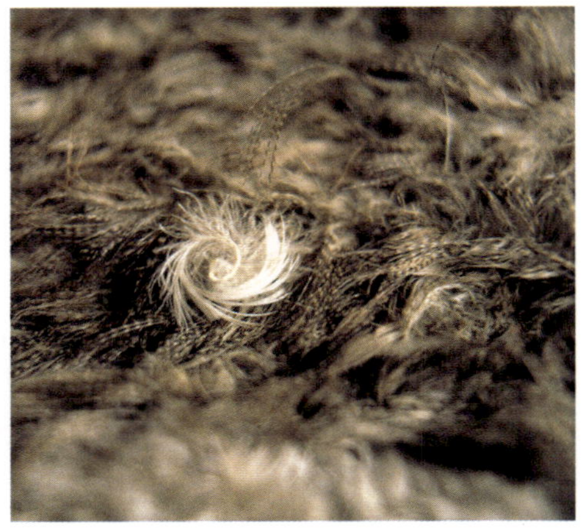

Fig. 23 Close-up of central band of Thomson blanket (UMB, cat.no. 1910:188) showing the dark brown feathers that are probably pintail or hooded merganser. Photograph: Sally McLendon.

Fig. 22 Three-color feather blanket (UMB, cat.no. 1910:188), folded as it would appear when worn. Collected by William Augustus Thomson between 1 and 13 July 1839, possibly through General Mariano Vallejo in or near the present town of Sonoma, CA. 160 x 119 cm (Glover 1978: 21). Photograph: Sally McLendon.

Smithsonian Institution in 1867. It shows clear signs of extended use, in areas similar to those showing wear on the Dawson blanket at the LACMNH and the Deppe blanket in the EMB.

The documentation of both blankets has become much confused. The blanket now in the NMNH has the number 2119. A blanket exchanged to the NMD (then the Royal Ethnological Museum of Denmark) from the Smithsonian Institution's National Museum was cataloged in Denmark as also having the original catalog number 2119 and coming from the "Ex[ploring] Ex[pedition] Capt. Wilkes." But this blanket is a Northwest Coast down blanket, not the California blanket. The California blanket is identified as collected at Neah Bay by James G. Swan. Since Swan is famous for his Northwest Coast collections and is not known to have ever collected in California, it appears that the documentation for these two American blankets became switched at some point.

The Exploring Expedition visited two Patwin-speaking towns on the Sacramento River, Saaka and Koru. They saw a feather blanket in a semi-subterranean house at Saaka, which C. C. Willoughby (1922) assumed they collected. Jess Bill, who is descended from people from Koru, remarked upon seeing the feather blankets in St. Petersburg that as a child, older relatives had told him that they had slept on feather blankets when they themselves were young (Craig Bates, pers. comm. 2000). The blanket the U.S. Exploring Expedition saw was most likely an older, worn blanket being used for sleeping. If the Exploring Expedition collected the blanket seen at Saaka, it is undoubtably the worn blanket now in Copenhagen.

However, it seems just as likely that one or both blankets were presents from John Sutter, with whom the members of the Exploring Expedition stayed twice. Sutter surely gave them presents similar to the ones he gave Voznesenski and Phelps.[16] If the Copenhagen blanket was collected at Saaka, it was made by Patwin-speaking peoples. If both blankets come from Sutter, they could be from Nisenan speakers on the American River, where Phelps saw the black and white feathered string for a blanket.

One interesting question is why did Sutter give Phelps feather blankets of two different colors, but the U.S. Exploring Expedition only one color, and why did Voznesenski, who visited first, possibly got still another type of blanket (grey and white), rather than a three-color blanket? The most plausible explanation seems to be that blankets of different color combinations came from different groups, and hence slightly different color combinations differentiated groups. Since all sources agree that a feather blanket took a great deal of time and labor to make, a single tribe would be unlikely to want to supply Sutter with blankets in the quantity that he needed to treat all his foreign visitors as royally as he treated Voznesenski and Phelps.

Sutter is known to have established relationships

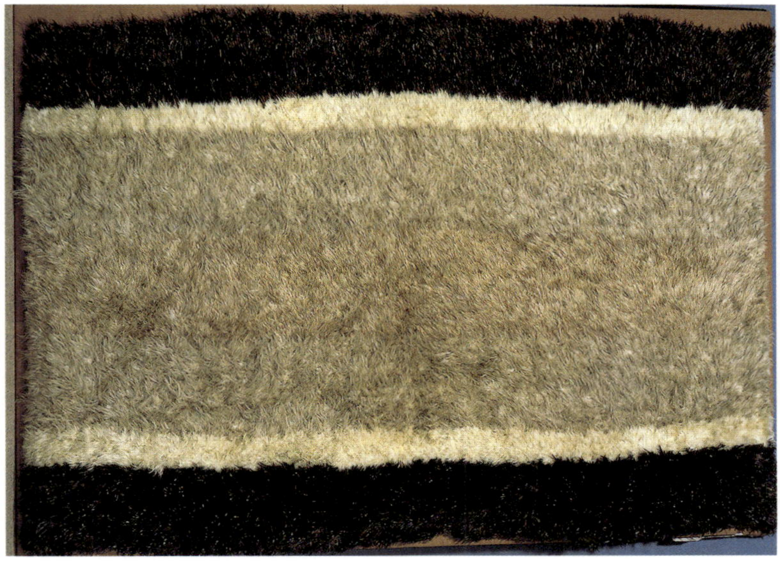

Fig. 24 Three-color feather blanket (NMNH, cat.no. 2119) collected in California by the U.S. Exploring Expedition. Probably a gift from John A. Sutter, Summer 1841. 162 x 110 cm. Photograph: Vic Krantz.

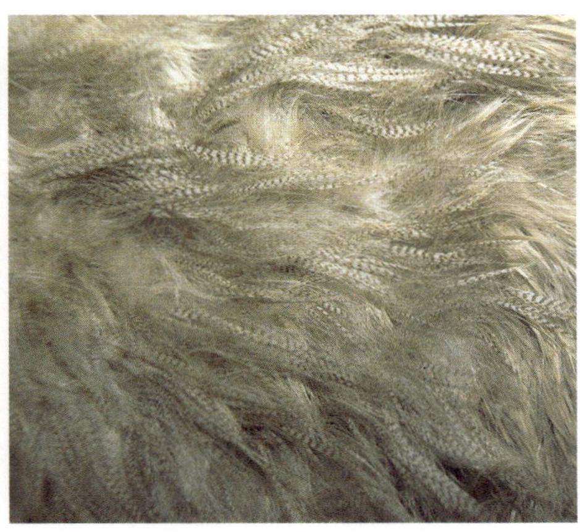

Fig. 25 Close-up of U.S. Exploring Expedition blanket (NMNH, cat.no. 2119) showing one of a pair of beige-colored bands that frame a central band of Canada goose. These framing bands are probably wood duck flank feathers, with some mallard flank feathers mixed in. In the center a loose feather illustrates how tightly the feathers were wrapped around the paired strings. Photograph: Sally McLendon.

with the chiefs of the many tribes living in or near the area where he settled. He also employed many members of these different tribes.

Presumably he canvased his neighbors for a feather blanket and a Moki cloak when Voznesenski came to visit, then did the same thing for Phelps and the U.S. Exploring Expedition. Perhaps the Exploring Expedition got the worn cape now in Copenhagen because Sutter's Indian neighbors were all out of new blankets, and since blankets were normally made in the winter, there was not sufficient supply of feathers and time to make a new one.

The pristine blanket in the NMNH supports this hypothesis. Although basically a three-color blanket, the central beige field is actually composed of three stripes of almost identical beige color, but of different feathers. In 1975 Roxie Laybourne, S. Olson, and J. P. Angle of the Department of Ornithology of the NMNH examined the feathers of this blanket and determined that the "center stripe is Canada Goose breast (light brown with lighter tips) and down, with some Mallard (finely vermiculated) feathers tied in." They determined that "the broad brownish-yellow stripes of vermiculated feathers on either side of the center stripe are mostly Wood duck flank feathers, with some mallard flank feathers mixed in (Fig. 25). These feathers have become faded with age ... Since a large portion of the blanket consists of Wood duck feathers and Wood duck are exclusively fresh water inhabitants (preferring the lower, slow-moving parts of rivers), it is probable that the feathers originated inland in the Sacramento Valley" (Laybourne, Olson, and Angle [1975]). Wood ducks are resident in California on a year-round basis, as are mallards. Canada geese, however, are winter visitors. If Sutter commissioned a blanket for the U.S. Exploring Expedition in August of 1841, but the individuals making it did not have sufficient goose feathers, they would not have been able to get more until at least November of the following winter. It seems logical that they would substitute a feather close in color to Canada goose from birds then available: wood ducks and mallards.

16. The U.S. Exploring Expedition records do not identify Sutter as the source of any collections. Yet both Voznesenski and the Exploring Expedition collected the feathered cape or cloak of the Moki or Kuksuyu, which are the oldest known examples of this type of dress (Bates 1982b: 16). According to Craig Bates, "cloaks of this type show great diversity, each individual making them differently," yet the Voznesenski-collected cloak and the U.S. Exploring Expedition-collected cloak "are so similar as to suspect manufacture by one individual" (Bates 1982b: 17). Voznesenski's fieldnotes indicate that he collected his cloak on the Sacramento River while visiting Sutter (Okladnikova 1985; these fieldnotes were unfortunately not available to Bates in 1982). The simplest explanation for the surprising similarity in the two cloaks is that Sutter had the same individual make both cloaks, and they were both made to be used as presents, not for traditional use. It is likely that other objects such as ear plugs, baskets, and the feather blankets, which are similar or identical between the Voznesenski, Phelps, and U.S. Exploring Expedition collections, were also acquired from Sutter.

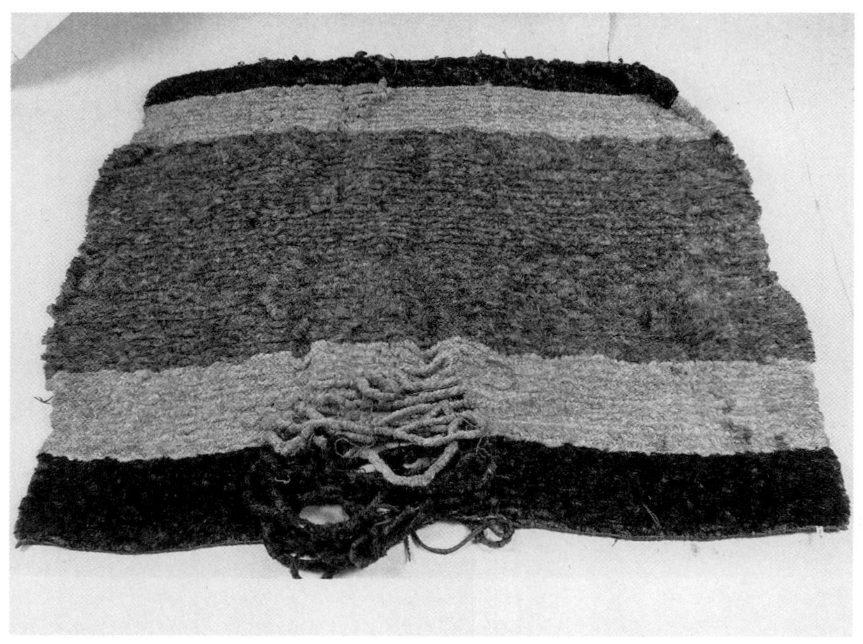

Fig. 26 Three-color feather blanket now in the NMD (cat.no. Hd.37), collected by the U.S. Exploring Expedition. 136 x 106 cm. Photograph by Jane Walsh.

5. Two-Color Black and White Blanket without White Stripes

In 1994 a Texan, Mary Jane Ramsey, presented a California feather blanket to the LACMNH (cat.no. F.A. 3349. 94-1). It had been collected in California by her ancestor, Nicholas "Cheyenne" Dawson, as a young man of twenty-two. Dawson had run away from his home in Pennsylvania at the age of nineteen to "see part of the world" (Dawson 1933: 48). Three years later he arrived in California with the first overland emigrant train, the Bartleson train. Dawson composed a narrative of his adventures for his Texas family in 1894, "fifty-three years after the occurrences of the principle events narrated ..., mostly from memory, but with an anxiety to say only the truth" (Dawson 1933: frontispiece). While describing his return from California, traveling in steerage from Vera Cruz to New Orleans, he casually mentions that he slept "in the hold on my feather blanket [which] had been my bed since I purchased it in Santa Cruz, California in '42 ... in the old mission of Santa Cruz, from a trapper, for two or three dollars in whisky" (Dawson 1933: 56). Thus Dawson, like the collectors of the other blankets, did not collect the blanket directly from its Native maker or owner and provided no information as to the precise California Indian people who produced it.

Dawson hypothesized that it was made "after the fashion of the Aztec Indians, because afterwards, when I visited the museum of Aztec antiquities in the City of Mexico, I found one exactly like it" (Dawson 1933: 56). The Aztecs did not make blankets exactly like California blankets, although they did do splendid featherwork, and if Dawson saw a blanket "exactly like" his, there must have been still another, now missing, California blanket in Mexico (see "Missing blankets," below).

The Dawson blanket measures 142 by 96.5 cm. Its feathers have not yet been identified, but the blanket clearly differs from the others in its color patterning, although it is identical in construction. The Dawson blanket is unique in having no pair of white stripes a few inches from the outer edges. Instead, the entire center of the blanket appears to be made of white, possibly snow goose feathers, with dark brownish-black feathers at the outer edge. Both types of feathers are very worn, often so that only the bare quills remain, but the blackish-brown feathers are most likely the same mallard speculum feathers that are used on the outer edges of most of the other blankets. If the feathers are mallard speculum and snow goose, the Dawson blanket might be an example of the "rich" snow goose and mallard blanket the wife of the chief wore at Waipa, where Bay Miwok was spoken (Merriam 1967: 367).

Although Dawson says he used his blanket as a mattress for two years after buying it, the major pattern of wear could only have come from being worn. The Dawson blanket is worn especially thin in the center at the top next to the braided cord where the blanket would have hung on the nape of the neck and towards the bottom of the center where the blanket would have been sat on in sitting. It is in fact completely "sat out" at this point. The Dawson blanket is also particularly worn at two spots on the upper ends where a wearer would have grasped the blanket in hugging it around herself. The blanket was already badly worn when Dawson acquired it and perhaps had even been discarded as worn out before the trapper acquired it, unlike many of the other blankets which appear to have been acquired brand new (McLendon 1995).

Missing Blankets

1. The Vischer Blanket in Basle[17]

There was once a feather blanket in the Museum der Kulturen in Basle, donated in 1844 to the city of Basle as part of the American collections of Lukas Vischer (1780–1840). Accessioned as IV.1:8, "ein Federmantel/manto de un Capitan apache de la baja California $52," the blanket is the first item on a short list of artifacts acquired in Mexico, but ultimately "partly from the North American coastal regions, partly from the South Sea islands," which also included a Yaqui fiddle. When the collection, which is best known for its Mexican antiquities, was finally cataloged in the 1890s, the blanket was apparently no longer in existence. It was explicitly listed as missing in the course of a revision of the collection in 1920.

Lukas Vischer was the son of a family active in the Basle silk ribbon business. He moved to the United States in 1823, where he traveled widely and began to collect ethnographic artifacts, an activity he continued during his sojourn of ten years in Mexico, from 1828 to 1837 (Anders et al. 1967). He is not known to have traveled outside the central highlands of Mexico, and if the feather blanket was indeed from California, it must have been obtained in trade. The reference, however, is unspecific enough to allow the possibility that the "feather mantle" was a pelican feather blanket made from whole pelican skins by the Seri and other peoples of Baja California. The attribution of the piece to an "Apache captain" is a reflection of Mexican usage of the time to designate all "uncivilized" Indians of the northern frontier by the generic term "Apache."

It is tempting to link the blanket in the Lukas Vischer collection to the activities of Edward Vischer, who was another employee of Virmond, first in Acapulco on the west coast of Mexico, and then from 1842 on in California (Bancroft 1886, 5: 764). If Edward was Lukas's source, Baja California is indeed the more likely provenience of the feather mantle, since Lukas died two years before Edward moved to California.

2. The Feather Blanket in the Mexican Museum

The feather textile that Nicholas Dawson saw in the National Museum of Mexico in 1842, which is probably also referred to in the 1875 descripton of the Uraga blanket in Dresden (cp. pages 147–149), may be still another California feather blanket.

17. The section on the Vischer blanket was revised and partly rewritten by the editor.

Conclusion

California feather blankets, though now widely distributed in museums in the United States and Europe, actually were collected by a small number of people who often knew each other, most of whom were in the fur trade or the hide and tallow trade. Most came to California trying to make their fortunes, but they shared a nineteenth-century compulsion to collect. Although they rarely learned very much about the Native peoples of California, they valued the same beautiful objects that marked wealth and status in Native societies. As a result, their collections provide an important window on the Native societies they collected from.

References Cited

Anders, Ferdinand, Margarete Pfister-Burkhalter, and Christian F. Feest

1967 *Lukas Vischer (1780–1840). Künstler—Reisender—Sammler.* Niedersächsisches Landesmuseum, Völkerkundliche Abhandlungen 2. Hannover.

Anonymous

1875 Inventarium der ethnographischen Sammlung des königl. historischen Museum zu Dresden. Manuscript in the archives of the Staatliches Museum für Völkerkunde, Dresden.

Bancroft, Hubert H.

1886 *The History of California.* 7 vols. San Francisco, CA: The History Company.

Bankmann, Ulf

1999 Zwischen Pazifik und Lietzensee: Ferdinand Deppe, Gärtner und Sammler für die Berliner Museen. *Mitteilungen des Vereins für die Geschichte Berlins* 95(4): 566–577.

Barrett, S. A. and E. W. Gifford

1933 Miwok Material Culture. *Bulletin of the Milwaukee Public Museum* 2(4): 117–376.

Bates, Craig D.

1981 Feather Belts of Central California. *American Indian Art Magazine* 7(1): 46–53, 86.

1982a Wealth and Power: Feathered Regalia of Central California. In: Douglas Ewing (ed.), *Pleasing the Spirits* (New York, NY: Ghylen Press), 32–47.

1982b *Feathered Regalia of Central California: Wealth and Power.* Occasional Papers of the Redding Museum 2. Redding, CA: Redding Museum and Art Center.

1983 The California Collection of I. G. Voznesenski. *American Indian Art Magazine* 8(3): 36–41, 79.

Beardsley, Richard K.

1954 Temporal and Areal Relationships in Central California Archaeology, Part I. *Reports of the University of California Archaeological Survey* 24: 1–62.

Belcher, Sir Edward

1843 *Narrative of a Voyage Round the World Performed in Her Majesty's Ship Sulphur, during the years 1836–1842 ...* Vol. I. London: Henry Colburn.

Bennyhoff, James A.

1977 The Ethnohistory of the Plains Miwok. *Center for Archaeological Research at Davis Publication* 2. Davis, CA.

Bolz, Peter and Ann Leslie Davis

2000 From the Kunstkammer to the Museum für Völkerkunde: The Eventful History of the Early North American Indian Collection in Berlin. *American Indian Art Magazine* 25(2): 34–45, 81.

Bolz, Peter and Hans-Ulrich Sanner

1999 *Native American Art: The Collections of the Ethnological Museum Berlin*. Berlin: G-und-H Verlag.

Busch, Briton Cooper

1983 (ed.) *Alta California, 1840–1842: The Journal and Observations of William Dane Phelps*. Glendale, CA: The Arthur H. Clark Company.

Calderón de la Barca, Fanny

1966 *Life in Mexico: The Letters of Fanny Calderón de la Barca*. [1843] Howard T. Fisher and Marion Hall Fisher, eds. New York, NY: Doubleday and Company.

Cook, Sherburne F.

1955 The Epidemic of 1830–1833 in California and Oregon. *University of California Publications in American Archaeology and Ethnology* 43(3): 303–326.

Dawson, Nicholas

1933 *Narrative of Nicholas "Cheyenne" Dawson ...* San Francisco, CA: Grabhorn Press.

Dixon, Roland B.

1905 The Northern Maidu. *Bulletin of the American Museum of Natural History* 17(3): 119–346.

Driver, Harold E.

1936 Wappo Ethnography. *University of California Publications in American Archaeology and Ethnology* 36(3): 179–220.

Duflot de Mofras, Eugène

1937 *Duflot de Mofras' Travels on the Pacific Coast ...* [1844] Vol. II. Marguerite Eyer Wilbur, trsl. and ed. Santa Ana, CA: The Fine Arts Press.

Duhaut-Cilly, August Bernard

1834–1835 *Voyage autour du monde, principalement à la Californie et aux îles Sandwich, pendant les années 1826, 1827, 1828, et 1829*. Paris: A. Bertrand.

Farris, Glenn

[1989] A Peace Treaty between Mariano Vallejo and Satiyomi Chief Succara. Paper presented at the Fifth California Indian Conference, Humboldt State University, Arcata, CA, October 13.

Feest, Christian F.

1980 *Native Arts of North America*. New York, NY—Toronto, ON: Oxford University Press.

1984 Review of *Pleasing the Spirits*. *American Indian Art Magazine* 9(2): 69–72.

Glover, Winifred

1978 *In the Land of the Brave. The North American Indian Collection in the Ulster Museum, Belfast*. Belfast: Blackstaff Press.

Gudde, Edwin G.

1936 (ed.) *Sutter's Own Story: The Life of General John Augustus Sutter and the History of New Helvetia in the Sacramento Valley*. New York, NY: G. P. Putnam's Sons.

Heizer, Robert F.

n.d. Notebook labeled "Ethnographic Pieces." [1950s] Robert F. Heizer Collection of notes on objects in the Musée de l'Homme, Anthropology Department, Santa Barbara Museum of Natural History.

Hudson, Travis

1984 Early Russian-Collected California Ethnographic Objects in European Museums. *American Indian Art Magazine* 9(4): 30–37.

Hudson, Travis and Craig D. Bates

[1984] People from the Water: Indian Art and Culture from Russian California. Unpublished manuscript.

Kaeppler, Adrienne L.

1978 (ed.) *Cook Voyage Artifacts in Leningrad, Berne, and Florence Museums*. Bernice P. Bishop Museum Special Publications 66. Honolulu, HI: Bishop Museum Press.

1983 A Further Note on the Cook Voyage Collection in Leningrad. *The Journal of the Polynesian Society* 92(1): 93–98.

Kelly, Isabel

1978 Coast Miwok. In: Robert F. Heizer (ed.), *California* (William C. Sturtevant, gen. ed., Handbook of North American Indians 8. Washington, DC: Smithsonian Institution), 414–425.

Kinzhalov, R.V.

1983 History of the American Collections in the Museum of Anthropology and Ethnography, Leningrad. In: Henry N. Michael and James W. VanStone (eds.), *Cultures of the Bering Sea Region: Papers from an International Symposium* (New York, NY: IREX), 311–324.

Krickeberg, Walter

1914 Einige Neuerwerbungen der nordamerikanischen Sammlung des Königlichen Museums für Völkerkunde. *Zeitschrift für Ethnologie* 46(4–5): 678–745.

Kroeber, Alfred L.

1925 *Handbook of the Indians of California*. Bureau of American Ethnology Bulletin 78. Washington, DC.

1929 The Valley Nisenan. *University of California Publications in American Archaeology and Ethnology* 24(4): 253–290.

1932 The Patwin and their Neighbors. *University of California Publications in American Archaeology and Ethnology* 29(4): 253–423.

Kroeber, A. L., A. H. Gayton, and L. S. Freeland

1925, 1929 Southern Nisenan Ethnographic Notes and

Vocabularies, 5 notebooks. Manuscript CU 23.1 No. 120, Bancroft Library, University of California, Berkeley, CA.

Langsdorff, Georg H. von

1812 *Bemerkungen auf einer Reise um die Welt in den Jahren 1803 bis 1807*. 2 vols. Frankfurt am Main: Friedrich Wilmans.

1813–1814 *Voyages and Travels in Various Parts of the World, During ... 1803, 1804, 1805, 1806, and 1807*. 2 vols. London: Henry Colburn. [Reprinted: New York, NY 1968: Da Capo Press. 2 vols. (Biblioteca Australiana 41).]

Laybourne, R. S. Olson, and J. P. Angle

[1975] [Feather identification for California feather blanket No. 2119, 10 October 1975.] Catalog card for Ethnology, National Museum of Natural History, Smithsonian Institution.

Liapunova. R. G.

1967 Ekspeditsiia I. G. Voznesenskogo i ee enachenie dlia etnografii Russkoi Ameriki. *Sbornik Muzeia Antropologii i Etnografii* 24: 5–33.

Lichtenstein, Hinrich

1839 Beitrag zur ornithologischen Fauna von Californien ... *Abhandlungen der königlichen Akademie der Wissenschaften* 1838: 417–451.

Linduska, Joseph P.

1964 (ed.) *Waterfowl Tomorrow*. U.S. Department of the Interior, Bureau of Sport Fisheries and Wildlife, Fish and Wildlife Service. Washington, DC: G.P.O.

López Uraga, José

[1844–1883] Correspondencia y Documentos. Ms. Coll. 71/94, Bancroft Library, University of California, Berkeley, CA.

McGowan, Joseph A.

1961 *History of the Sacramento Valley*. New York, NY: Lewis Historical Publishing Company.

McKern, W. C.

1922 Functional Families of the Patwin. *University of California Publications in American Archaeology and Ethnology* 13(7): 235–258.

McLendon, Sally

1981 Preparing Museum Collections for Use as Primary Data in Ethnographic Research. In: Anne-Marie Cantwell, James B. Griffin, and Nan Rothschild (eds.), The *Research Potential of Anthropological Museum Collections* (Transactions of the New York Academy of Sciences 73), 201–227.

[1991] Ferdinand Deppe, Mysterious Collector on the California Coast. Paper read at the 12th American Indian Workshop, 30 May–1 June, at University of Rome.

1995 Rare California Feather Blanket. *Terra* 32(5): 4–5.

Maloney, Alice Bay

1945 (ed.) *Fur Brigade to the Bonaventure: John Work's California Expedition, 1832–1833, for the Hudson's Bay Company*. San Francisco, CA: California Historical Society.

Merriam, C. Hart

1967 Ethnographic Notes on California Indian Tribes, Part III. *Reports of the University of California Archaeology Research Facility*, 68. Berkeley, CA.

Milliken, Randall

1995 *A Time of Little Choice: The Disintegration of Tribal Culture in the San Francisco Bay Area, 1769–1810*. Menlo Park, CA: Ballena Press.

Nuttall, Zelia

1924 Two Remarkable California Baskets. *California Historical Society Quarterly* 2(4): 341–343.

Ogden, Adele

1944 Business Letters of Alfred Robinson. *California Historical Society Quarterly* 23: 301–334.

Okladnikova, Lena

1985 Kaliforniiskie kollektsii MAE. *Sbornik Muzeia Antropologii i Etnografii* 40: 111–165.

[Phelps, William Dane]

1871 *Fore and Aft; or, Leaves from the Life of an Old Sailor. By "Webfoot."* Boston, MA: Nichols & Hall.

Pickering, Charles

1848 *The Races of Man, and their Geographical Distribution*. United States Exploring Expedition, vol. 9. Philadelphia, PA: C. Sherman.

Robinson, Alfred

1846 *Life in California: During a Residence of Several Years in that Territory*. New York, NY: Wiley and Putnam.

Rozina, L. G.

1978 The James Cook Collection in the Museum of Anthropology and Ethnography, Leningrad. [1966] In Kaeppler 1978: 3–17.

Shur, Leonid A. and James R. Gibson

1973 Russian Travel Notes and Journals as Sources for the History of California, 1800–1850. *Quarterly of the California Historical Society* 52(1): 37–63.

Uhle, Max

1886 Über einige seltene Federarbeiten von Californien. *Mitteilungen der Anthropologischen Gesellschaft in Wien* 16: 15–20.

Vallejo, Mariano Guadalupe

n.d. Historia de California, Vol. 3. Ms. in Bancroft Library, University of California, Berkeley, CA.

Vatter, Ernst

1925 Ein bemaltes Büffelfell und andere seltene amerikanische Ethnographica im Städt. Völkermuseum zu Frankfurt am Main. *Abhandlungen zur Anthropologie, Ethnologie und Urgeschichte* 2: 75–112.

Wilkes, Charles

1845 *Narrative of the United States Exploring Expedition During the Years 1838, 1839, 1840, 1841, 1842*. 5 vols. Philadelphia, PA: Lea and Blanchard.

Willoughby, Charles C.

1922 Feather Mantles of California. *American Anthropologist* 24: 432–437.

Wilson, Norman L. and Arlean H. Towne

1978 Nisenan. In: Robert F. Heizer (ed.), *California* (William C. Sturtevant, gen. ed., Handbook of North American Indians 8. Washington, DC: Smithsonian Institution), 387–397.

Documenting the Speyer Collection

William C. Sturtevant

The original source of objects in collections—their ultimate provenience (this form is a shibboleth for anthropologists; art historians say "provenance")—is increasingly recognized as important for both anthropology and art history. The value of an object as cultural and historical evidence on a specific society depends to a great extent on the reliability of data as to where and when it was collected and by whom. Although "the uncertainty of an attribution increases with the square of the distance from the collector's statements" (Feest 1968a: 145), it is sometimes possible to shorten that distance by a detailed investigation of museum records and of associated evidence on the activities of the original collector.

Anthropologists usually focus on the original source of an object—where (and when) it was first collected, what its culture of origin was, and when it was made and used. Because ethnographic and archaeological objects are unsigned and usually not attributable to an individual artist or maker, detailed provenience is even more important than it is for fine art paintings. For fine art it seems to be at least as important to trace the subsequent owners, particularly the well-known collections through which an object has passed. Such information may also be important for anthropological collections, especially for discovering the ultimate source of the object and the subsequent deterioration or improvement of provenience data. Thus the provenience needed includes both the original source of an object and its pedigree through subsequent owners. The usual beginning is a search for evidence as to the earliest collections through which the object passed.

In the 1950s and 1960s the need for reliable provenience data was rarely recognized for anthropological artifacts. For example, in auctions at Parke Bernet in New York and Sotheby's and Christie's in London some forty or fifty years ago the provenience of objects of "primitive art" was rarely given and seemingly had little or no effect on the prices they made. Norman Feder was one of those responsible for the shift to the modern situation, where detailed provenience is usually as important for "ethnographica" as it is for "fine art."

In 1964, while he was on the staff of the Museum of the American Indian, Heye Foundation (where provenience was not considered to be very interesting in the tradition of George Heye, who founded and ran the museum), Feder conducted and published an important, carefully-researched study of the Jarvis collection in the Brooklyn Museum, consisting of early, well-documented eastern Plains materials (Feder 1964). This was one of the earliest such studies of an anthropological collection in a museum, and it had considerable influence in both anthropology and art history and is still cited in auction and other catalogs.

Feder's background as an Indian-hobbyist, and his continuing relations with the hobbyist network (and with dealers and collectors), made him sensitive to artifakery—a term I learned from him—in evaluating American Indian objects on the market and in museum and private collections. Artifakery increases as the market value rises, as do invented or exaggerated provenience data; and now, the greater the market value of an object, the more suspicious one should be of prove-

William C. Sturtevant has been Curator of North American Ethnology in the National Museum of Natural History, Smithsonian Institution, since 1965. From 1956 to 1965 he was on the staff of the Bureau of American Ethnology. In addition to ethnographic field work among American Indians and in Burma (including making museum collections), he has since 1960 studied the collections in many museums in North America and Europe. He is General Editor of the *Handbook of North American Indians*.
Author's address: Department of Anthropology, Smithsonian Institution, Washington, DC 20560, U.S.A.

{At the request of the author, the editor has added from his own files information on the documentation of the Speyer collection. Braces are used throughout this paper to indicate such editorial additions.}

nience data that cannot be traced back to a time before market values escalated.[1]

One of the most important collections of early North American materials was put together by Arthur Speyer and his son of the same name. It contained a remarkable number of objects from the Plains, Subarctic, and East collected between about 1760 and about 1860.

{The story of the Speyer collection begins with Arthur Speyer (I) (1858–1923), an entomologist and mineralogist, who followed a dual career as an academic and natural history dealer, and who added ethnography to his interests early enough to be commissioned to install a Museum for Natural History and Ethnology near Ostende in 1898. Moving from Hamburg to Strasbourg to Berlin, he also began to supply other museums with ethnographic objects, especially from Africa, Oceania, and the Americas; North America was apparently hardly represented in his offerings to museums. His own collection was strong on Cameroon and New Guinea, areas of German colonial activity, which meant relatively easy access to artifacts through civil servants and officers in the colonies.

His son, Arthur Speyer, Sr. (II) (1894–1958), continued his father's business in Berlin. Beginning in 1926 and under the influence of Patty Frank, the circus artist and collector who was to become the first director of the Karl-May-Museum in Radebeul, he increasingly focused on acquiring North American Indian materials,

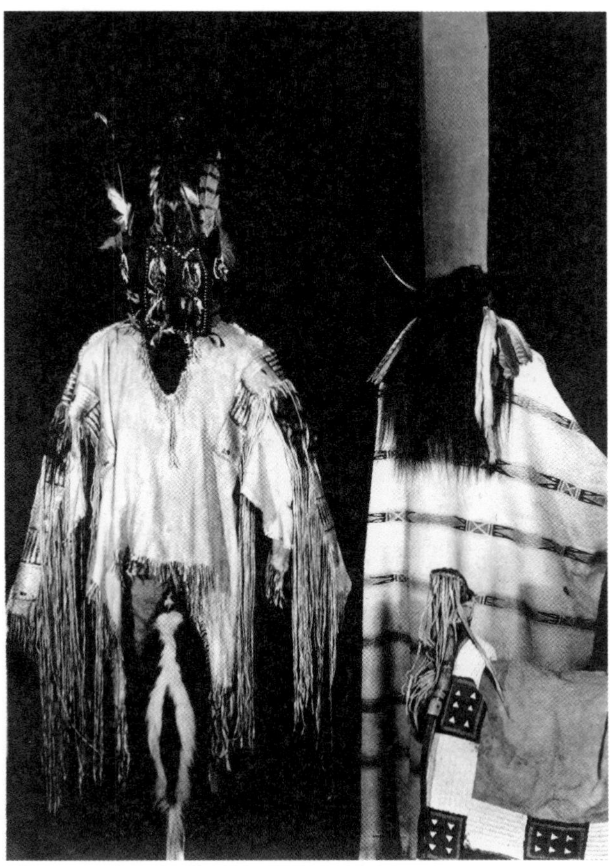

Fig. 1 Some of the earliest North American acquisitions of Arthur Speyer, Sr. in a photograph taken in his apartment in Berlin-Wilmersdorf in the late 1920s. Left: Headdress (cp. LVII 168 below), shirt (LVII 239), and skunk skin bag (LVII ba), all from the ethnographic collection of the Duke of Gotha; right: woman's robe (XXXIV af) from the Maximilian Prince of Wied collection, saddle with saddle blanket (LVII aw) and horned headdress (above robe) of unknown pedigree. Photograph courtesy of Arthur Speyer, Jr.

especially from the Plains, by purchase and by exchanging non-American artifacts. His business contacts (not necessarily as sources for North American materials) included Ratton, Carre, Ascher, Guillaume, and Roudillon in Paris, Oldman and Ohley, Sr. in London, Lemaire in Den Haag and Amsterdam, Umlauff, Sr. in Hamburg, and Krenz, Fritsche, and Bohlken in Berlin.} Many of his acquisitions came from museums, especially in Germany, others from private collections. A special search was made for objects preserved by descendants of the Hessian mercenaries who served in the American Revolution.[2] {In some cases, at least, objects were thus saved for posterity which may not have survived in museums for lack of adequate care.[3]}

After his father's death, Arthur Speyer, Jr. (III) (1922–) took over the collection {(then 180 objects, of which thirty-eight of post-1860 origin were later traded)} and

1. {Feest (1993: 4, 6) dates the shift from associating objects with notable events or previous owners to associating them with famous collectors to a paradigmatic change in the collecting of ethnographic material in the wake of James Cook's circumnavigations and the emergence of "ethnology" as a separate field of scholarly inquiry during the late 18th century. But it was only with the rapid rise of market values of ethnographic material from North America since the early 1970s, which was caused in part by the purchase of the Speyer collection in particular and concerted Canadian efforts to "repatriate" the country's Native heritage in general, that the focus on documented provenance championed by Feder came to influence sales prices. Feest (1998) provides a case study of the role of real and imagined collection histories for the scholarly and market values of artifacts.}

2. {Hans Plischke, who was professor of anthropology at the University of Göttingen, reportedly told his students after World War II how before the war he had made a special effort to visit estates in those German provinces, such as Brunswick or Hesse, which during the American Revolution had supplied mercenaries to the King of England (Meinhard Schuster, pers. comm. to Christian Feest, 1997). Since none of this material has ended up in the university collection in Göttingen, it must be assumed that Plischke merely accompanied his friend Arthur Speyer, Sr. on the latter's quest to enlarge his North American collection. Some of this material was apparently traded by Speyer to his mentor Patty Frank.}

3. {In at least one case, A. Speyer, Sr. was unable to prevent the official destruction of objects which had been infested with insects.}

enlarged it, acquiring fine quality objects, broadening the coverage beyond the Plains to include Northeastern and Subarctic groups, and limiting the collection to objects made in the century following 1760. Many of the objects in the collection came from eighteenth-century aristocrats' cabinets of curiosities and from collections made by members of the German and British nobility in the nineteenth century, {but others were obtained from dealers, fellow collectors, or at flea markets. Acquisitions from museums were generally made on an exchange basis, often with African or Pacific material supplied in order to obtain North American artifacts.}

The younger Speyer was interested in improving the documentation of the objects in the collection by research in the published literature and by consultation with other collectors and with museums. He investigated the functions and construction of the artifacts and their ultimate tribal origins and dates. He was less interested in gathering and preserving a record of the routes the objects had traveled through collectors and museums until he had acquired them. When most of his collection was shown in a fine temporary exhibit in the Deutsches Ledermuseum in Offenbach during the summer of 1968, Speyer published an excellent, well-illustrated catalog (Benndorf and Speyer 1968) to accompany the exhibition. He included detailed descriptions of the construction and materials of all the 270 objects that were exhibited. He indicated the culture and sometimes the date of origin of each piece, distinguishing between provenience that came with the object and provenience determined by himself.

Speyer did not state in the catalog his source for the data on provenience that accompanied the object, and he was not very precise in indicating the sources for his own determinations of the cultures of origin. He never included information on the original or subsequent collections through which an object had passed, although he did have some records of these matters and remembered much relevant information.[4] He concealed his sources partly, no doubt, to avoid competition, and because most museums and some private collectors would have been embarrassed to have it known that they were divesting themselves of fine objects.[5]

Presumably enough time has now elapsed so that these reasons no longer apply. The purpose of this paper is to provide information on the sources of objects in the Speyer collection, pointing the way toward future research that should further document these important objects.

After 1968 the Speyer collection was dispersed. The National Museum of Man (now the Canadian Museum of Civilization) acquired 259 items from Speyer in the early 1970s (Brasser 1976: 11), and some were acquired from him then and later by other museums and collectors.[6] On 16–17 August 1968 I went with my friend Ted J. Brasser (then on the staff of the Museum voor Volkenkunde, Leiden) to see the collection of Arthur Speyer in the temporary loan exhibit at the Ledermuseum in Offenbach, Germany, and to visit Mr. Speyer in his nearby home in Wiesbaden. We discussed with him (hardly interviewed him about) the provenience and the tribal attributions of objects in his collection. I took notes in a copy of the catalog of the exhibition, which I had purchased for DM8 ($2.50). I also made some quick sketches in the margins of the catalog, especially of objects that were not illustrated in the book. I added information that Brasser conveyed to me from his several earlier visits to Mr. Speyer. My copy of the catalog also includes information from Feest's 1968 review of it, of which he had sent me a pre-publication copy before I visited Offenbach. It also contains notes on a conversation on 26 July 1969 with Colin Taylor (the collector and hobbyist in Hastings, England, who later obtained a degree and a teaching position in anthropology), who knew Speyer and his collection and had exchanged items with him.

4. {An obstacle for the reconstruction of the documentation of the Speyer collection is the fact that Arthur Speyer, Sr. had intended to save his son from the collecting mania. Arthur Speyer, Jr. thus began to work in the silk trade and took only peripheral interest in his father's collection. It was only one year before his death that the father began to initiate his son into the field of collecting North American Indian artifacts. While the son now took every opportunity to question the father about the provenance of the objects, the father had never kept records of his acquisitions and thus had to rely on his already failing memory. The father's untimely death prematurely ended the son's attempts in this direction.}

5. This information on the history of the collection is based on Benndorf and Speyer (1968: [iii–iv], 1–2), especially Speyer's essay "Problematik der Herkunftsbestimmung"; Brasser (1976: 11–13); and my memory of conversations with Speyer in 1968. {The best account of the collecting activities of three generations of Arthur Speyers is found in Gerlach (1995: 156–161), which is based in part upon recollections and personal records supplied by Arthur Speyer, Jr. Boden (1995) cites an unpublished manuscript on "One hundred years of ethnological collections Arthur Speyer" (Speyer 1993), now also available to Feest. Data from these sources and from interviews with Arthur Speyer, Jr. conducted by Christian Feest on 27 July and 18 August 2000 have been added to the account given herein.}

6. {Spurred by the envious interest for this outstanding collection in the German museum world after the 1968 exhibition and by the criticism that the Speyer family had established their collection largely at the expense of museums in Germany, Speyer disposed of some of the material included in the catalog to a number of German museums (especially Berlin, Offenbach, Freiburg, and Frankfurt).}

Feder visited Speyer in 1969, and we exchanged lists of attributions. He wrote to me (9 September 1969) that:

"The following list was prepared in an effort to document the Speyer collection at least as to source in an effort to substantiate tribal identification and date of collection, etc. It was prepared largely on the basis of information supplied by Mr Speyer; with additions from Ted Brasser and Christian Feest. Mr Speyer was somewhat reluctant to supply this information, and does not want it published—his feeling seems to be that it will embarrass the various museums who gave up some of their treasures. Many pieces collected by Speyer Sr. are not positively identified as to source —this includes many of the items from Darmstadt."

Feder's list includes a good many more pieces than does mine. A few days after I sent a copy of my notes to Feder, he responded (17 September 1969) that:

"With everyone working together we might be able to piece the entire thing together. I did not have the Taylor material and [was] glad to get this (Speyer never even mentioned Taylor). With more time and effort we could do more—for example a check of accession records of all the European museums for items exchanged to Speyer (but he traded so wildly that many of the items he once had, he no longer owns).[7] It's a darn shame that Speyer did not just publish all this information himself."[8]

In 1970 Brasser moved from Leiden to the National Museum of Man in Ottawa (now the Canadian Museum of Civilization in Hull) where he persuaded the museum to purchase the Speyer collection (or most of it) as part of the repatriation project then under way among Canadian national museums. In 1976 his exhibition entitled "Bo'jou, Neejee!" displayed many of the Speyer materials—and I was invited to speak briefly at the opening, where I was politely requested not to mention the fact that many of the Speyer objects "repatriated" to Canada had been collected from tribes within the present United States.

Not all the Speyer items in the Canadian Museum of Civilization are included in the *Bo'jou, Neejee!* catalog, for Ruth Phillips (1998; cp. also 1984) has recently illustrated and described three dolls illustrated in Benndorf and Speyer 1968 (numbers 69, 70, 71), but not in *Bo'jou, Neejee!*, that are in the Canadian Museum. In addition, the collector John W. Painter acquired a knife sheath from Speyer on 21 October 1982 and several pieces of Sir John Caldwell's collection from Speyer on 3 December 1983 (Painter [1991]: numbers 20, 211—a source referred to me by Ted Brasser, pers. comm., 13 October 1998).[9]

Here I list the objects in the Benndorf and Speyer catalog (1968) for which Feder and I collected provenience information from the above mentioned sources. Also included are all the Speyer pieces in the *Bo'jou, Neejee!* catalog (Brasser 1976), which illustrates all the objects exhibited and gives their catalog numbers in the Canadian Museum of Civilization. By my count, there are 100 pieces in Benndorf and Speyer (1968) that are not in *Bo'jou, Neejee!*, fourteen Speyer pieces in *Bo'jou, Neejee!* but not in Benndorf and Speyer (1968), and I list twenty-five Speyer pieces that are in neither of these two catalogs.[10] Omitted in the listing that follows are the pieces in Benndorf and Speyer (1968) for which no further information is available.

7. {In hindsight it would appear that for a number of reasons Feder was overly optimistic in his belief a re-documentation of the Speyer collection could be pieced together in a co-operative effort: (1) It appears that pre-World War II accession (and more especially deaccessioning) records in some museums leave much to be desired; (2) such a procedure is impossible in the case of private collections or of material obtained from dealers; (3) the number of North American Indian objects (including regions not represented in his 1968 catalog, such as the Southwest) that passed through the collection of two generations of Arthur Speyers is staggering; cp. note 10, below. (For an incomplete listing of Southwestern specimens supplied by Arthur Speyer, Sr. and Jr. to museums in Berlin, Bremen, Frankfurt, Göttingen, Offenbach, and Stuttgart, cp. Kaemlein [1967: 110, 112, 116, 118, 123, 128].)}

8. Feder added: "Regarding George Catlin: Speyer purchased two painted coats somewhere in England ([he] would not give me specific data) which were without doubt a part of the Catlin collection. They bear painting in pictographic form identical to Catlin material at [the] Smithsonian. Speyer, completely on his own, realized that these were not original Indian workmanship, and he assumed that the coats were painted by Catlin himself—so he traded both. One is now on display at the Ledermuseum in Offenbach {XVIII t}; the other he traded to Edinburgh {XVIII u}. [I] still can't understand why Ewers refuses to recognize the fact that Catlin was an artifaker." Later, John C. Ewers did, somewhat reluctantly, recognize that Catlin had "improved" some of his artifacts when he exhibited them—see Holm (1992).

9. {Additional data on Speyer material in the CMC were added from other published sources and in a few cases from CMC catalog cards. No attempt, however, has been made to identify all of the CMC's Speyer collection.}

10. {The editor's far from systematic notes taken in European museums over the past thirty-five years contain references to North American Indian material supplied by Arthur Speyer, Jr.—and sometimes on objects exchanged by his father with museums—that would probably be at least equal in number to the artifacts here included; the editor has added just a few items to this list which seemed to be of particular interest or had been previously published. As a rule, only objects from the area and period covered by the 1968 catalog have been included. Complete coverage has not been attempted and would go far beyond the scope of the present contribution. The editor is grateful to the curators of various museums credited in notes below for supplying additional information on very short notice.}

The nine drawings reproduced below are based on my quick sketches in my copy of the catalog, adjoining objects not illustrated there (nor in *Bo'jou, Neejee!*). These drawings should assist in identifying these objects, for which the present location is unknown.[11]

The items are arranged according to Speyer's (or his father's) sources, starting with the largest source collection and concluding with a list of items for which I have data not in Benndorf and Speyer (1968), but for which the sources are as yet unknown.

Of course this is not the end of research on the provenience of Speyer pieces. An important source is the records of museums which exchanged pieces with the Speyers (or sold to them). One hopes that such museum records indicate which pieces once in their collections they exchanged with the Speyers, and what was received from them (as Feder said to me).

For most collectors the important question is, "Is it genuine?" For anthropologists what matters is "Where and when was it made and first used?" Furthermore, the details of the transmission of artifacts through collectors, museums, dealers, and auction houses give us interesting information on the nature and history of collecting. Many important collections, private and museum, would show complex histories of exchange, purchase, and other (de)-accessioning if careful work were done. Research on these topics is important for the development of accurate data on material culture and on the trade in such material.

Experience (including my own in this study and elsewhere) shows that copying records often introduces errors. What one hopes for are photographs or accurate drawings, detailed descriptions (especially measurements), and a record of the sources of information, including who made changes or additions to the catalog data, and on what basis and when. For the Speyer collection we have photographs and good descriptions, including measurements. What is needed is information on the provenience and the current location of the items so well described by Speyer.

Sources of the Speyer Collection

The following key indicates the source of the information about each object:

B&S: Information from Benndorf and Speyer (1968). Tribal attributions and dates in italics (from B&S) indicate Speyer's personal opinion, sometimes based on comparative material seen by Speyer. Benndorf and Speyer (1968) includes a bibliography, but this is often not referred to in Speyer's attributions, nor are specific items in museum collections indicated when museums are referred to as the source for his attributions. Tribal attributions and dates in roman (from B&S) indicate information that came with the material (but did not necessarily come directly from the source of the object). Further research in the indicated sources is almost always advisable.

F: Source of object or other information from Feder (1969).

S: Source of object or other information by Sturtevant from 1968 visit to A. Speyer, Jr.

B: Information from Ted Brasser gathered during 1968 visit to A. Speyer, Jr.

CF: Information from Feest (1968a).

CFF: Information from Feest's files and from conversations with A. Speyer, Jr., 27 July and 18 August 2000.

T: Information from Colin Taylor (conversation 26 July 1969).

BN: Information from Brasser in his *Bo'jou, Neejee!* (1976).

P: Information from Painter [1991].

The italic headings that indicate the collections from which Speyer acquired the objects are from information provided by Feder (often confirmed by S and B), unless some other source is stated.

The number in the margin by the description of each object indicates the catalog number in Benndorf and Speyer (1968), or if within parentheses the catalog number in *Bo'jou, Neejee!* (Brasser 1976) or if in parentheses with "P" the catalog number in Painter [1991]. An asterisk, *, indicates that there is no illustration of this object in Benndorf and Speyer (1968). All the Speyer objects in *Bo'jou, Neejee!* are illustrated there.[12]

11. {A few photographs of pieces once in the Speyer collection were added from Feest's files and by courtesy of Arthur Speyer, Jr.}

12. The following abbreviations will be used for museum collections referred to in the text:

AMF	Adelhauser-Museum [formerly: Museum für Völkerkunde] (Freiburg im Breisgau, Germany)
BHM	Bernisches Historisches Museum (Berne, Switzerland)
CMC	Canadian Museum of Civilization (Hull, QC, Canada)
DLO	Deutsches Ledermuseum (Offenbach am Main, Germany)
EMB	Ethnologisches Museum [formerly: Museum für Völkerkunde] (Berlin, Germany)
HMV	Hamburgisches Museum für Völkerkunde (Germany)
ISZ	Indianermuseum der Stadt Zürich (Switzerland)
LMS	Linden-Museum (Stuttgart, Germany)
MAI-HF	Museum of the American Indian—Heye Foundation (New York, NY, U.S.A.)
MEN	Musée d'Ethnographie (Neuchâtel, Switzerland)
MVF	Museum für Völkerkunde (Frankfurt am Main, Germany)
MVW	Museum für Völkerkunde (Vienna, Austria)
NLH	Niedersächsisches Landesmuseum (Hannover, Germany)
NMS	National Museum of Scotland (Edinburgh, Scotland)
RJMK	Rautenstrauch-Joest-Museum (Cologne, Germany)
SEUG	Sammlung für Ethnologie [formerly: Völkerkunde], University of Göttingen (Germany)
SMVM	Staatliches Museum für Völkerkunde (Munich, Germany)
VSMRM	Völkerkundliche Sammlungen der Stadt Mannheim im Reiß-Museum (Mannheim, Germany)
VUZ	Völkerkundemuseum der Universität Zürich (Switzerland)

I. Sir John Caldwell Collection

Feder provided some notes on this collection, and he and Brasser (1976: 72) cite Oswald (1961) on Sir John Caldwell, who was fifth baronet, Castle Caldwell, County Fermanagh, Ireland. Speyer acquired the collection in 1968 (S) from Caldwell's heirs at Sniterton Hall, Derbyshire. Caldwell was in the Eighth Regiment of Foot during the American Revolution, 1774–1780, briefly at Niagara and then at Fort Detroit. He had close associations with the Ojibwa and Potawatomi and "supposedly councilled with Munsee, Delaware, Iroquois, Shawnee, Huron, Illinois" (F). According to Feder, "a few pieces from his collection are in the Liverpool Museum and they also have a complete set of color slides of the entire collection, as does the Horniman Museum [in London]." There is a full-length oil portrait of Caldwell dressed in Indian clothing, including many pieces that survive from his collection, in the King's Regiment Collection, Merseyside County Museum, Liverpool (reproduced in color on the cover of Brasser [1976]), with copies of this portrait in the Royal Regiment's quarters and in Sniterton Hall. Feder wrote that "Speyer has a tendency to identify most of this collection as Ojibwa, with a few pieces labeled as Huron, Potawatomi, Cree. Since none of the pieces are marked with identifications, it is just a guess in each case. Collections of comparable material are as follows: a collection at the Liverpool Museum made by the Commander at Ft. Detroit (not seen); a collection made by a Capt. Malcolm and now in the Bernisches Historisches Museum; the Foster collection now at the [Museum of the American Indian,] Heye Foundation; and parts of the Fuller collection in [the Field Museum in] Chicago. All are lacking in tribal identification. It is my personal feeling that much of the collections mentioned are of Huron origin. The loom quill work on moccasins and moose hair embroidery; the burden straps with false embroidery in moose hair; the wampum belts; etc. all appear to me to be Huron. Other items I would guess to be Ottawa or possibly Potawatomi. A pipe tomahawk at Bern in the Capt. Malcolm collection has the word "Ottawa" inlaid in brass. Plus of course, that the Huron and Ottawa were known to be in the Ft. Detroit area during the Revolution."

27 (63) Man's coat. F. B&S: Ojibwa, ca. 1780; *Lake Winnipeg Cree*. Now CMC, cat.no. III-X-229; BN: northern Ontario, ca. 1780; cp. Burnham (1992: 6).

29 Knee band or arm band. F. B&S: Ojibwa, ca. 1780; *Lake Winnipeg Cree*.

58 (77) Pair of moccasins. F; S. B&S: Ojibwa, ca. 1780; *old Huron style*. Now CMC, cat.no. III-H-432; BN: Huron type, ca. 1780.

59 Pair of moccasins. F: perhaps Caldwell; by 1969 no longer owned by Speyer;[13] S: not Caldwell. B&S: Ojibwa, ca. 1780; *old Huron style*.

76 Chief's cloak. F; S. B&S: Ojibwa, ca. 1780; *Iroquois*.

99 (147) Wampum belt. F: no information. B&S: Iroquois, before 1780. Now CMC, cat.no. III-X-253; BN: Eastern Great Lakes, ca. 1780.

123* (103) Shirt (worn by Caldwell in his portrait). F; S. B&S: Ojibwa, ca. 1780. Now CMC, cat.no. III-X-244; BN: Eastern Great Lakes, ca. 1780.

13. {Reported by Ewing (1982: 255) as being part of the Wellington collection; probably the pair worn by Caldwell in the painting.}

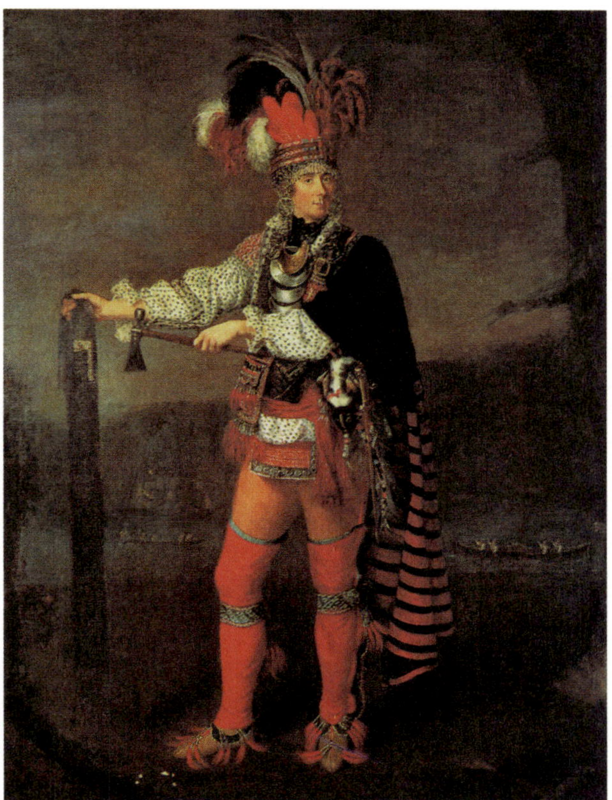

Fig. 2 Unknown artist, "Sir John Caldwell, Lieutenant-Colonel of the 8th Foot, in the dress of an Indian Chief," ca. 1780. Oil on canvas, 128.3 x 102.9 cm. Courtesy Major F. E. G. Bagshawe, Sniterton Hall, nr. Matlock, Derbyshire.

124 (118) Breechclout (worn by Caldwell in his portrait). F; S. B&S: Ojibwa, ca. 1780. Now CMC, cat.no. III-X-248; BN: Eastern Great Lakes, ca. 1780.

125* Pair of man's leggings. F; S; description in Benndorf and Speyer 1968 agrees with the leggings worn by Caldwell in his portrait. B&S: Ojibwa, ca. 1780.

126* Pair of man's leggings. F; S. B&S: Ojibwa, ca. 1780.

127 Pair of moccasins. F; S. B&S: Ojibwa, ca. 1780.

132 Pair of knee bands. F; S. B&S: Ojibwa, ca. 1780.

133 Pair of knee bands. F; S. B&S: Ojibwa, ca. 1780. {Now CMC, cat.no. III-G-849ab; Phillips (1984: 50, #79): "Ojibwa?, c. 1780."}

134 (173) Knee band (perhaps worn by Caldwell in his portrait). F; S. B&S: Ojibwa, ca. 1780. Now CMC, cat.no. III-X-255; BN: Eastern Great Lakes, ca. 1780.

138 (21) Fingerwoven sash. F; S. B&S: Ojibwa, ca. 1780. Now CMC, cat.no. III-X-230; BN: Eastern Great Lakes, ca. 1780.

139 (102) Fingerwoven sash. F; S. B&S: Ojibwa, ca. 1780. Now CMC, cat.no. III-X-243; BN: Eastern Great Lakes, ca. 1780.

140 (130) Network sash. F; S. B&S: Ojibwa, ca. 1780. Now CMC, cat.no. III-X-250; BN: Eastern Great Lakes, ca. 1780.

143 (114) Three silver gorgets (worn by Caldwell in his portrait). F; S. B&S: Ojibwa, ca. 1780. Now CMC, cat.no. III-X-247; BN: Eastern Great Lakes, ca. 1780.

144* (P211) Ball and cone silver nose ornament (sketch of this by Sturtevant matches the one worn by Caldwell in his portrait). F; S. B&S: Ojibwa, ca. 1780.
145 (113) Five silver ear pendants (two? worn by Caldwell in his portrait). F; S. B&S: Ojibwa, ca. 1780. Now CMC, cat.no. III-X-246; BN: Eastern Great Lakes, ca. 1780.
146 (32) Pouch. F; S. B&S: Ojibwa, ca. 1780. Now CMC, cat.no. III-G-824; BN: Eastern Ojibwa type, ca. 1780.
149 (78) Pouch and strap. F; S. B&S: Ojibwa, ca. 1780. Now CMC, cat.no. III-G-828; BN: Eastern Ojibwa type, ca. 1780.
151 Pouch and strap. F; S. B&S: Ojibwa, ca. 1780.
153 Pouch and strap. F; S. B&S: Ojibwa, ca. 1780.
157 (100) Belt. F; S. B&S: Ojibwa, ca. 1780. Now CMC, cat.no. III-X-242; BN: Eastern Great Lakes, ca. 1780.
158 (P211) Knife and sheath. F; S. F: knife marked with a trident [or flower—F sent a small sketch]. B&S: Ojibwa, ca. 1780.
160 (64) Burden strap. F; S. B&S: Ojibwa, ca. 1780. Now CMC, cat.no. III-X-237; BN: Eastern Great Lakes, ca. 1780.
166 Feather headband. F; S. B&S: Ojibwa, ca. 1780.
167 (112) Scarf headdress. F; S. B&S: Ojibwa, ca. 1780. Now CMC, cat.no. III-X-245; BN: Eastern Great Lakes, ca. 1780.
169 Fingerwoven head ornament. F; S. B&S: Ojibwa, ca. 1780.
171 Pipe with catlinite bowl. F. B&S: Ojibwa, ca. 1780.
174 Wampum belt. F; S. B&S: from an Ojibwa collection, ca. 1780.
176 (117) Fingerwoven sash. F; S. B&S: Ojibwa, ca. 1780; *Potawatomi*. Now CMC, cat.no. III-X-261; BN: Great Lakes Algonquians, ca. 1780.
177 (140) Powderhorn with sash. F; S. B&S: Ojibwa, ca. 1780 (strap); *Potawatomi*. Now CMC, cat.no. III-X-262; BN: Great Lakes Algonquians, ca. 1780.
(P211) Silver gorget inscribed with Caldwell's and royal coats of arms. S.
(P211) Two silver epaulettes. S.
(P211) Twist of green wool thread. S.
a Brass or copper gorget inscribed "Loyal Erne Rangers." S.
b Silver rings. S.
c Sword(?) strap of metal threads. S.
d Sash, network. S; F: not in B&S.[14]
e Two cloth breechclouts. F: not in B&S.
f Birchbark pouch or purse. S: small, with silk ends; F: not in B&S.
g Club (for wild rice?). S: ca. 18" long; F: not in B&S.
h Scabbard (with quilled trim, tab at bottom; with European knife). S; F: not in B&S.
i Woven sash. S: yellow or green, with white beads; not in B&S.

II. Earl of Warwick Collection, Warwick Castle

The following seven items are given in Brasser (1976) as from the Speyer collection, but do not appear in Benndorf and Speyer (1968).[15]
(33) Wampum belt. Eastern Great Lakes, 18th c. Now CMC, cat.no. III-X-234.
(69) Knife and sheath. Mohawk-Iroquois type, late 18th c. Now CMC, cat.no. III-I-1323.
(87) Headdress. Great Lakes, 18th c. Now CMC, cat.no. III-X-241.
(105) Knife. Iroquois type, late 18th c. Now CMC, cat.no. III-I-1325.
(126) Knife and sheath. Swampy Cree type, 18th c. Now CMC, cat.no. III-D-568.
(148) Garters. Central Algonquian or Eastern Plains, 1820. Now CMC, cat.no. III-X-240.
(177) Pouch. Great Lakes, 18th c. Now CMC, cat.no. III-X-256.
j {Quilled pouch. Now CMC, cat.no. III-G-841: "Eastern Great Lakes (Eastern Ojibwa type), late 18th c." Cp. Phillips (1984: 49, #73).}
k {Quilled knife and sheath. Sheath is now DLO, cat.no. 12150, acquired from A. Speyer, Jr. in 1971: "Mohawk, ca. 1790." Cp. Völger (1976: 4.50.20). Knife originally with this sheath was sold to CMC together with XXXII 83 below.}

III. Greatorex Collection, Whitechapel Museum, London[16]

{All of the Greatorex material was acquired by A. Speyer, Jr. via the Hooper collection [see VI below].}
62 {Moccasins. B&S: *Huron, pre-1825*. Now EMB, cat.no. IV B 12824, acquired from A. Speyer, Jr. in 1968: "Huron."}
63 {Pouch with strap. B&S: Huron, pre-1825. Now EMB, cat.no. IV B 12825, acquired from A. Speyer, Jr. in 1968: "ex Greatorex collection."}
90 (29) Burden strap. F; {now said by A. Speyer, Jr. to have come from the Fred North collection, cp. XV}. B&S: *Iroquois*, pre-1770. Now CMC, cat.no. III-I-1330; BN: Iroquois type, pre-1770.
142 (178) Sash. F; BN: Greatorex collection, Whitechapel Museum, later in the James Hooper collection. B&S: Ojibwa, pre-1800. Now CMC, cat.no. III-X-257; BN: Eastern Great Lakes, 18th c.
148 (80) Pouch. F; BN: later in the James Hooper collection. B&S: *Ojibwa, pre-1800*. Now CMC, cat.no. III-G-829; BN: Eastern Ojibwa or Ottawa type, 1800.
150 (19) Pouch. F; BN: later in the James Hooper collection. B&S: Ojibwa, pre-1780. Now CMC, cat.no. III-G-822; BN: Ojibwa, pre-1780.
152 Pouch and strap. F. B&S: Ojibwa, *Mississauga, pre-1800*. {Now DLO, cat.no. 11999, acquired from A. Speyer, Jr. in 1968; cp. Völger (1976: 4.20.29).}
154 Pouch and strap. F. B&S: Ojibwa, pre-1800.
156 (149) Pouch and strap. F; BN: later in the James Hooper collection. B&S: *Ojibwa, ca. 1800*. Now CMC, cat.no. III-X-263; BN: Great Lakes, late 18th c.
179 Pouch. F. B&S: Menomini, pre-1850. {Now CMC, cat.no. III-N-33.}

14. {Reported by Ewing (1982: 219) as part of the Wellington collection.}
15. {The collection was only acquired by A. Speyer, Jr. at a Sotheby's sale in December 1969. Another item from the same collection has been added after Phillips (1984).}
16. {Rev. Dan Greatorex was vicar of St. Paul's Church in the London Docks between 1862 and 1867 and assembled his ethnographic collection, which became part of the now defunct Whitechapel Museum in London, largely by attending to the spiritual needs of sailors, who rewarded him with exotic artifacts. This account, however, does not explain the presence of eighteenth- and early nineteenth-century North American material; cp. Feest (1997: 43).}

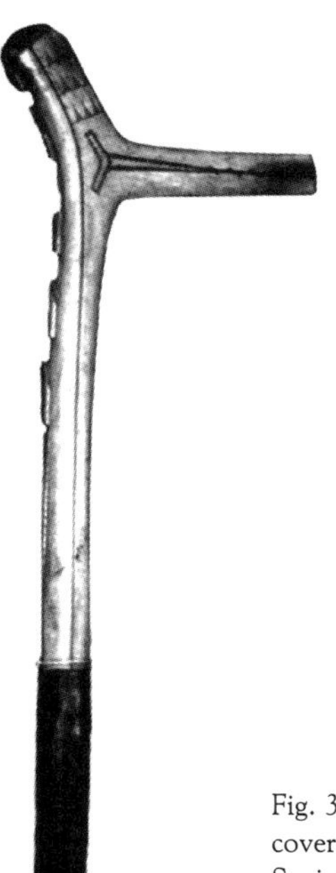

Fig. 3 Caribou antler club (IV 1), handle covered with leather. Ex London Missionary Society. "Ingalik, pre-1830." EMB, cat.no. IV A 9475. Photograph: C. F. Feest.

182 (127) Gunstock club. F; S: obtained in England. B&S: *Menomini*, pre-1840. Now CMC, cat.no. III-G-834; BN: Central Ojibwa type, 1800;

189 Ball-headed club. F. B&S: Sauk, *pre-1825*.

198 Ball-headed club. F. B&S: Oto, pre-1800.

IV. Methodist Missionary Society, London

{Acquired by A. Speyer, Jr. from James Hooper; cp. VI below.}

216* Lance. F. B&S: Dakota, ca. 1860.

218 Quiver and thirteen arrows. F. B&S: Eastern Dakota, pre-1840.

222 Pipe. F. B&S: Missouri; *Dakota, pre-1850*.

224 (138) Pipe bowl. F. B&S: *Dakota, pre-1835*. Now CMC, cat.no. III-G-840; BN: Minnesota Ojibwa type, early 19th c.

264* Stick rattle. F. B&S: Blackfoot, ca. 1860.

265 (135) Pipe bowl. F; BN: later in the James Hooper collection. B&S: Blackfoot or neighbors. Now CMC, cat. no. V-B-422; BN: Blackfoot type, early 19th c.

270 Ring-and-pin game. F. B&S: Assiniboin, *pre-1850*.

1 Club, of caribou antler (Fig. 3). Said to be from the "London Missionary Society, pre-1830." Now EMB {cat. no. IV A 9475}, acquired from A. Speyer, Jr. in 1963; Ingalik or perhaps Ahtna (Bolz and Sanner 1999: 197).

{*V. Missionary Loan Society* [i.e., *Exhibition*] (Phillips 1984: 50)}

{Acquired in 1960s by A. Speyer, Jr.}

36 {Quilled pouch. B&S: Red River Ojibwa, pre-1840. Label attached identifies Rev. Brass as lender to the exhibition. Now CMC, cat.no. V-Z-6; cp. Phillips (1984: 50, #76): "Red River Metis."}

17. {On James T. Hooper and his collection, cp. Phelps (1976).}

18. {On Alfred Walter Francis Fuller (1882–1961), cp. Force and Force (1971).}

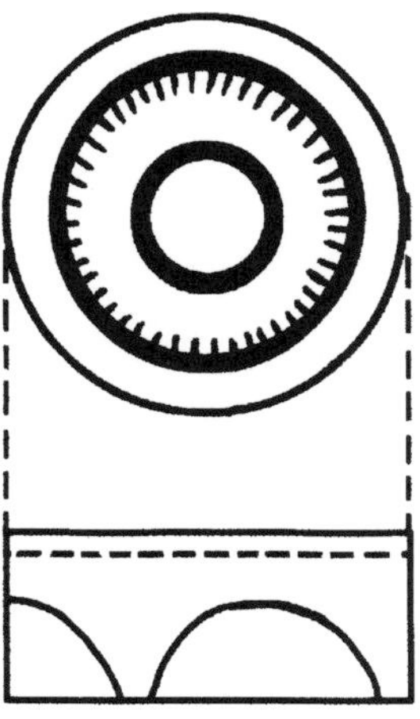

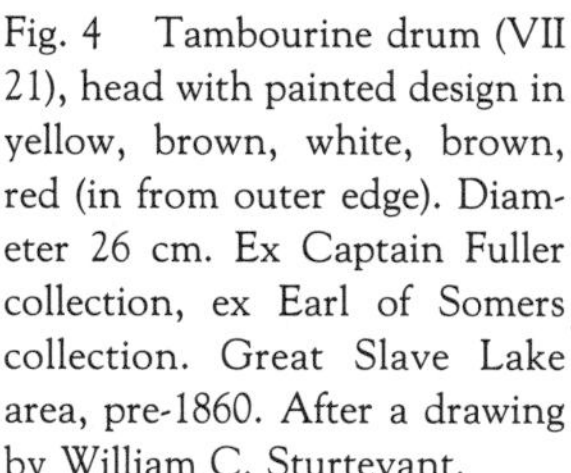

Fig. 4 Tambourine drum (VII 21), head with painted design in yellow, brown, white, brown, red (in from outer edge). Diameter 26 cm. Ex Captain Fuller collection, ex Earl of Somers collection. Great Slave Lake area, pre-1860. After a drawing by William C. Sturtevant.

VI. James Hooper Collection, England[17]

{Acquired in the 1960s by A. Speyer, Jr. Hooper was also the source for all the material formerly in the Greatorex collection (III) and the Methodist Missionary Society (IV).}

5 Pouch with strap. F: no information on source; S: Herzog v. Leuchtenberg collection (see XXXVII below); {CFF: Hooper collection}. B&S: *Cook Inlet, Alaska*, pre-1830.

18 Beadwork band. F: no information; T: perhaps from Hooper, London. B&S: Slave, pre-1840.

19 {Pouch. B&S: Slave, pre-1840. Said to have been collected in or by 1855 by Lt. W. C. Gordon, R. N. Now CMC, cat.no. VI-N-118; cp. Thompson (1994: 25): "Group unknown, circa 1850, formerly James Hooper collection."}

25 (68) Pouch. F: no information; BN: formerly in the James Hooper collection. B&S: Chipewyan, pre-1840. Now CMC, cat.no. III-D-566; BN: Cree type, before 1840.

89 (70) Burden strap. F: no information; BN: formerly in the James Hooper collection. B&S: Iroquois, pre-1775; *Mohawk*. Now CMC, cat.no. III-I-1230; BN: Iroquois, pre-1775.

94 (8) Ball-headed club. F: no information; BN: formerly in the James Hooper collection. B&S: *Iroquois, pre-1800*. Now CMC, cat.no. III-I-1312; BN: Iroquois type, 18th c.

114 (60) Pouch. F: no information; BN: formerly in the James Hooper collection. B&S, BN: Ottawa, pre-1800. Now CMC, cat.no. III-M-1.

159 (66) Knife sheath. F: from a private collection in England; BN: formerly in the James Hooper collection. B&S: *Ojibwa, ca. 1800*. Now CMC, cat.no. III-X-239; BN: Eastern Great Lakes, pre-1800. [For the knife of 159 (66), see under XXV below.]

201 (30) Whip. F: no information; BN: formerly in the James Hooper collection. B&S: Iowa, pre-1860. Now CMC, cat.no. V-X-394; BN: Eastern Plains Siouan type, 1800.

223 (179) Pipe. F: no information; BN: formerly in the James Hooper collection. B&S: Dakota, ca. 1860. Now CMC, cat.no. V-E-276; BN: Sioux, ca. 1860.

(P20) Knife sheath. P: James Hooper coll., then Christie's London, 1976, item #79, then Arthur Speyer, then Painter, 21 October 1982. P: Red River Cree.

VII. Capt. Fuller Collection

F: "Part of the Fuller collection is now at the Field Museum."[18]

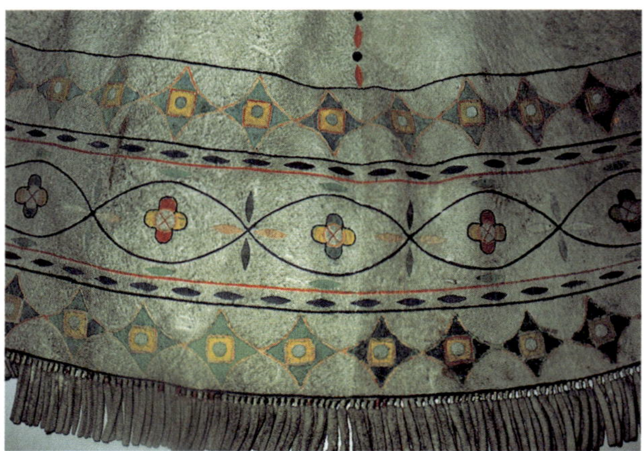

Fig. 5 Detail of painted coat (VIII m). Ex Sir C. Lyell collection. VSMRM, cat.no. V Am 3106. "Cree, 1843." Photograph: C. F. Feest.

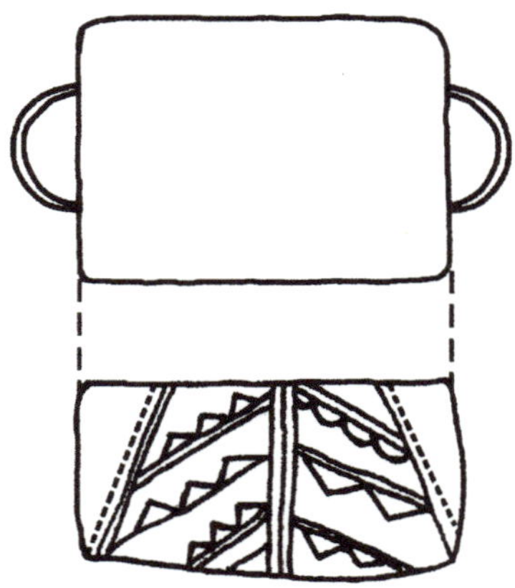

Fig. 6 Bark container (XIII 48), stitched together, with scraped design, leather loop handles. 21.5 x 26 cm. Bought at Berkeley Galleries, London, no previous history. After a drawing by William C. Sturtevant.

{Acquired by A. Speyer, Jr. via Earnest Ohley (cp. XIII).}

12 Gun case. F: "Obtained by Fuller from Earl of Somers at Reigate Priory"; T: probably from Capt. Fuller; sold in a London saleroom and acquired by Keggie, who had a stall in the Portobello Road, London, who sold it to Speyer. B&S: Loucheux (Kutchin), ca. 1860; *Nakotcho Kutchin, lower Mackenzie River.* {Now DLO, cat.no. 12079, acquired from Speyer in 1969; cp. Völger (1976: 4.20.36).}

21* Tambourine drum (Fig. 4). F: Fuller collection, from Earl of Reigate. B&S: Great Slave Lake area, pre-1860.

26 Hood. F: now in Berlin museum. B&S: *Swampy Cree, ca. 1860.* {Now EMB, cat.no. IV B 12827 (Bolz and Sanner 1999: 200, fig. 186).}

80 Pair of moccasins. F. B&S: *Lorette, pre-1830 (Iroquois).*

269 (190) Sewing bag. F; BN: old label says "A Cree Indian's Woman Sinew Pouch, ... Plains on the Banks of Saskatchewan River." B&S: Saskatchewan River Cree, ca. 1850. Now CMC, cat.no. V-A-408; BN: Plains Cree, 1830–1840.

VIII. Sir Charles Lyell Collection

BN: "Lyell, 1797–1875, was in Nova Scotia in 1841, and again in North America in 1845."

F: "Lyell was a British geologist, born in Kinnordy and buried at Westminster Abbey; was in Nova Scotia in 1841; in N. Amer. 1845."

{Acquired by A. Speyer, Jr. via Earnest Ohley (cp. XIII); the objects are said to have come from the Grierson Museum in Thornhill, Scotland.[19]}

20* Birchbark bowl. F: purchased from a dealer; from Sir Charles Lyell collection. B&S: Great Slave Lake area, pre-1841; *Slave.*

66* (155) Pair of moccasins. BN; F: Lyell, noting that CF disagrees; CF: from MVW, cat.no. 12020 {see XXV and note 29 below}. B&S: *Huron*, pre-1840. Now CMC, cat. no. III-H-427; BN: Huron type, 1840s.

263* Bearclaw necklace. F. B&S: *Blackfoot*, pre-1841. {Now VUZ, cat.no. 13669, acquired from A. Speyer, Jr. in 1969.}

267 Woman's robe. F: Lyell collection, "Old label marked Saskatchewan." B&S: Saskatchewan River Cree, pre-1845. {Now CMC.}

m {Man's painted coat (Fig. 5). Now VSMRM, cat.no. V Am 3106, acquired from A. Speyer, Jr. in 1966: "Cree, 1843."}

IX. H. B. Bompas Family Collection[20]

{Acquired by A. Speyer, Jr. via Earnest Ohley (cp. XIII).}

10 Necklace. F; S: Leuchtenberg (see XXXVII below). B&S: Koyukon, Alaska, pre-1840. F: "Labelled Yukon."

23 Net bag. F. B&S: Dogrib, ca. 1860. F: "Labelled Dogrib in pencil."

190* Ball-headed club. F. B&S: *Sauk, pre-1850.*

199* Ball-headed club. F: "Originally labelled Oto, but cleaned by Speyer to remove shellac"; S: on club in old hand: "Indians Child's Club Lord [? word uncertain] J. J. .E[rest of word unclear] with F[rest of word unclear]." B&S: Oto, pre-1840.[21]

X. Miss Halifax at Hudson's Bay

{Acquired by A. Speyer, Jr. via Earnest Ohley (cp. XIII).}

30 (26) Pouch. F; BN: from a Miss Halifax at Hudson's Bay; S: not part of Caldwell collection. B&S: *Lake Winnipeg Cree*, pre-1840. Now CMC, cat.no. III-D-565; BN: Cree, pre-1840.

19. {Much of Dr. Grierson's Museum at Thornhill, collected between 1861 and 1889, was later transferred to the Dumfries Museum, Dumfries, Scotland, where Grierson's manuscript catalog and an 1894 "Catalogue of Dr. Grierson's Museum ... written by Black of The National Museum of Antiquities" may be found (Gathercole and Clarke 1979).}

20. {At least the first two items appear to be related to William Carpenter Bompas (1834–1906), who was first Anglican bishop of Athabaska, 1874–1884, first bishop of Mackenzie River, 1884–1891, and first bishop of Selkirk (Yukon), 1891–1906, and the author of a Slavey prayer book (Bompas 1889); cp. Cody (1908).}

21. {Ewing (1982: 93) describes and illustrates this club as part of the Wellington collection, identifies it as "Southern Great Lakes, tribe unknown, c. 1820," and notes inscription on handle reading "Lord G. G. Leveson (?) with Fit's Love."}

XI. Beasley Collection, London[22]

{Acquired by A. Speyer, Jr. via Earnest Ohley (see XIII) between 1962 and 1967.}

98 Wampum belt. F: no information; S: records of EMB, seen by Sturtevant in 1986, say this item, their cat.no. IV B 12836, was acquired from Speyer who acquired it from Beasley collection. See also Bolz and Sanner (1999: 68). B&S: *Delaware, pre-1790.*

n {Wampum belt. "Beasley N. America 4.9.37." Now MVF, cat.no. 47389, acquired from A. Speyer, Jr. in 1969: "Ottawa"; cp. Völger (1976: 4.40.54).}

o {Chilkat blanket. Now NLH, cat.no. 10612: "Tlingit, c. 1860," ex Beasley collection, acquired from A. Speyer, Jr. in 1961; cp. Dohrmann and Deimel (2000: 56–57).}

p {Chilkat blanket, Tlingit. Now Rietberg-Museum, Zürich, cat.no. RNA 18; cp. Haberland (1971: 78–82).}

XII. Olde Curiosity Shop, Seattle[23]

{Acquired between 1962 and 1967 by A. Speyer, Jr., probably from Earnest Ohley; cp. XIII.}

9* Bone pick. F: head of pick used to dig roots. [See also XXXVII 9 below.] B&S: Koyukon, Alaska, before 1850.

XIII. Berkeley Galleries {Earnest Ohley}, London

{From 1962 onward, Arthur Speyer, Jr. regularly acquired material from London dealer Earnest Ohley (the owner of Berkeley Galleries), who sought to obtain material to fit Speyer's collecting program. In addition to the material listed below, for which information about previous ownership is lacking, Ohley provided Speyer with items listed under VII (Capt. Fuller), VIII (Sir Charles Lyell), IX (H. B. Bompas Family), XI (Beasley), and perhaps also X (Miss Halifax) and XII (Olde Curiosity Shop).}

35 (142) {Knife and sheath. BN: acquired from a London dealer. B&S: *Red River Ojibwa, pre-1840.* Now CMC, cat.no. III-G-835; BN: Northern Ojibwa type, ca. 1800.}

48* Bark box (Fig. 6). F: no information. B&S: *Montagnais, ca. 1840.*

68 (139) {Finger-woven sash. BN: acquired from a London dealer. B&S: *Huron, pre-1820.* Now CMC, cat.no. III-H-428; BN: Huron type, 1800.}

109 (123) Canoe model with four dolls and equipment. F: no information; BN: acquired from a London dealer. B&S: *River Desert Indians (Maniwaki), ca. 1780.* Now CMC, cat.no. III-E-311; BN: Malecite type, ca. 1800.

194 {Belt bag. S: old label says Shawnee, pre-1840; F: old label says "Shawnee given by Mr. George Bogne, N.A. 27." B&S: Shawnee, pre-1840. Now at CMC.}

22. {H. G. Beasley was one of the major English private collectors of American Indian artifacts in the first half of the twentieth century. A substantial portion of his collection is now at the Pitt Rivers Museum, Oxford, and at the British Museum, London.}

23. {On Ye Olde Curiosity Shop, cp. Duncan (2000).}

24. {Daniel Wilson (1816–1892), a pioneer Scottish archaeologist, moved to Canada in 1853 and became a friend of the painter Paul Kane, who contributed to Wilson's interest in pipes by providing drawings and perhaps specimens. Cp. Wilson (1857).}

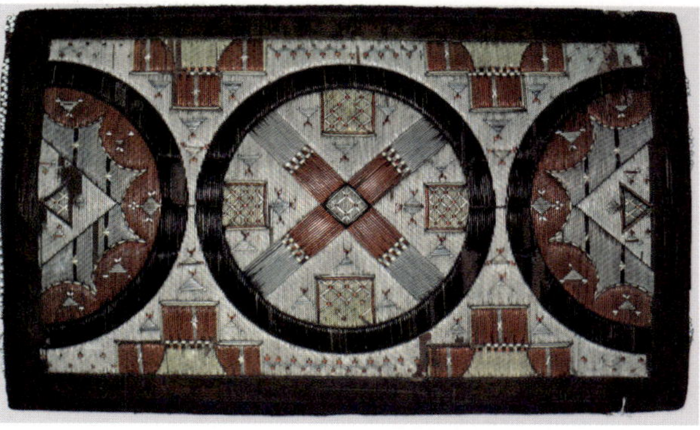

Fig. 7 Panel (XVI r), quillwork on birchbark. Collected by Captain Campbell. EMB, cat.no. IV B 12855. "Micmac, 1840–1850." Photograph: C. F. Feest.

202 (38) Headdress. F: no information; BN: from Berkeley Galleries, London, ca. 1952–1953. {Obtained via Lemaire (cp. XLIX) from Berkeley Galleries by A. Speyer, Sr.} B&S, BN: "previously acquired by Capt. J. C. Phillips, of Gateshead, England, at Wounded Knee, South Dakota, in 1892, with the information that it originally belonged to Chief Little Crow (1803–1863), Chief of the Kaposia-Mdewakanton Sioux, who added the trailer and feathers after his father's death in 1828. In the battle of the Little Bighorn in 1876, the headdress was said to have been worn by Chief Rain-in-the-Face (1835–1905), a Teton. The beadworked brow band apparently dates from that period"; T: from Berkeley Galleries, London, about 1952–1953, in an exhibit opened by C. A. Burland, who referred to this piece as attributed to Little Crow. Taylor told Speyer that the bead type is later than 1828, and T supposed that Speyer then added his comment about the brow band. B&S: Santee Dakota. Now CMC, cat.no. V-E-257; BN: Eastern Sioux, 1820s.

q {Man's coat. Obtained from Ohley in the 1960s. Now RJMK, cat.no. 49717, acquired from A. Speyer, Jr. in 1967: "Hudson Bay Cree," later changed to "Red River Métis type, ca. 1840" (Boden 1995: 195, color pl. I).}

XIV. Sir Daniel Wilson Collection,[24] *Toronto (BN)*

{Acquired by A. Speyer, Jr., possibly from the Fred North collection; cp. XV. Attribution to Wilson by Brasser in BN.}

(39) Pipe bowl. Now CMC, cat.no. III-G-823; BN: Ojibwa type, ca. 1845.

XV. Fred North Collection, London

{In addition to the specimens listed below, obtained in the 1960s by A. Speyer, Jr., other pieces (possibly) coming from this source are listed as XIV (39) and XLIX aj.}

28 (76) Belt. BN: formerly in the collection of Fred North, London. B&S: Cree, pre-1840; *Lake Winnipeg Cree.* Now CMC, cat.no. III-D-567; BN: Swampy Cree, before 1840.

75* (84) Pipe bowl. F: no information; BN: formerly in the collection of Fred North, London; S: sketch agrees with BN 84 photograph. B&S: Wyandot, *pre-1850.* Now CMC, cat.no. III-G-832; BN: Eastern Ojibwa type, 1840.

79* (23) Pair of moccasins. F: no information; BN: formerly in the Fred North collection, London. B&S: Iroquois, before 1830. Now CMC, cat.no. III-I-1310; BN: Iroquois (Seneca), before 1830.

84 {Sash. B&S: *Iroquois*, pre-1840. Acquired by A. Speyer, Jr., perhaps from F. North. In 1982 reported as part of the Wellington collection (Ewing 1982: 214): "Western Great Lakes, ... 18th century."}

90 {Burdenstrap. B&S: *Iroquois*, pre-1770. Ex Fred North collection; cp. III above.}

{*XVI. Captain Campbell (CFF)*}

{Acquired by Arthur Speyer, Jr. from a London dealer.}

r {Quilled bark panel (Fig. 7). Now EMB, cat.no. IV B 12855, acquired from A. Speyer, Jr.: "Micmac, ca. 1840–1850."}

{*XVII. Sir Henry Lefroy*[25] *(CFF)*}

{Acquired by Arthur Speyer, Jr. from a London dealer.}

s {Man's leggings. Now VSMRM, cat.no. V Am 3106ab, acquired from A. Speyer, Jr. in 1966: cataloged as "Cree" and as having been collected in 1843. Cp. Harrison (1987: #W26: "Eastern Cree, early 1840s").}

XVIII. Undisclosed English Source

{Acquired by A. Speyer, Sr.}

t {Man's shirt; painted decorations probably by or after George Catlin [see note 8]. Now LMO, cat.no. 11343: "Eastern Dakota," acquired from A. Speyer, Jr. in 1962; cp. Völger (1976: 4.42.29).}

u {Man's shirt; painted decorations probably by or after George Catlin [see note 8]. Now NMS, cat.no. 1963.56: "Shaman's painted shirt, N. Dakota," acquired from A. Speyer, Jr. in 1963.}

XIX. Sir Walter Scott (1771–1832) Collection (BN)

{Obtained in the 1960s via Ralph Nash; ultimately from W. Scott Museum, Abbotsford, Scotland.}

118 {Ball-headed club. B&S: *Ottawa, pre-1840.*}

(90) Pipe bowl. Now CMC, cat.no. III-G-833; BN: Ojibwa type, late 18th c.

v {Crupper. Traded by A. Speyer, Jr. to E. Zielinski collection, Berlin; cp. Zielinski (1971: cat.no. 1): "Plains-Cree, ca. 1840."}

w {Quilled pouch. Now CMC, cat.no. III-M-6. Cp. Phillips (1984: 49, #72): "Eastern Great Lakes."}

XX. Commodore Walzer, Salisbury, England

F: "Family tradition places all three as Blackfeet according to Speyer. The dress No. 253 is certainly Cree, and perhaps the shirt and leggings as well."

{Acquired by A. Speyer, Jr. from the daughter of Commodore Walzer in the 1960s.}

251 (97) Shirt. F; T: acquired by Speyer about 1964–1965, who would not tell Taylor where he got it. Taylor suspected it might be from the Nationalmuseum, Copenhagen, where he remembered seeing it or one nearly identical; BN: acquired from Commodore Walzer, Salisbury, England. B&S: Blackfoot, pre-1845. Now CMC, cat.no. V-B-413; BN: Blackfoot, 1840.[26]

252 (65) Leggings. F. B&S: Blackfoot, pre-1845. Now CMC, cat.no. V-B-415; BN: Blackfoot, 1840.

253 (96) Dress. F. B&S: Blackfoot, pre-1840. Now CMC, cat.no. V-A-439; BN: Plains Cree type, 1840.

XXI. Collection of Capt. Alexander Hood, R.N.

{Acquired by A. Speyer, Jr. in England.}

141 (151) Sash. F: collection of Capt. Alexander Hood of English Royal Navy, who died in a French battle in 1796. Originally thought to be South Seas; BN: formerly in the collection of Capt. Alexander Hood, Royal Navy (d. 1796), a lieutenant under Capt. James Cook; S (entry for 142, surely should be 141): from Alexander Hood, lieutenant under Capt Cook (later a Capt.); was described as from South Seas; thus (B&S) Ojibwa is not the original documentation. Speyer showed us the original label, with this data, which adds that Hood died in action in 179_[7?]. B&S: *Ojibwa*, pre-1792. Now CMC, cat.no. III-X-254; BN: Eastern Great Lakes, late 18th c.

XXII. Colin Taylor, Hastings

{Acquired by A. Speyer, Jr.}

236* Single legging. F: no information; T: acquired about 1960 from Taylor, accompanied by no data. According to Taylor, probably Nez Perce, or possibly Crow, rather than Hidatsa. B&S: *Hidatsa, pre-1840.*

247 (99) Halter trimming. F: no information; BN: acquired from a London dealer in 1963; T: acquired from Taylor, in exchange, who acquired it about 1963 from a London dealer accompanied by absolutely no data. B&S: *Plains Cree, ca. 1840.* Now CMC, cat.no. V-A-440; BN: Plains Cree type, 1840.

XXIII. Private Collection in Scotland (BN)

(129) Ball-headed club. Now CMC, cat.no. V-X-395; BN: Eastern Plains Siouans, said to be of Omaha origin, 1800.

XXIV. Royal Scottish Museum [now: National Museum of Scotland], Edinburgh[27]

161 (157) Cradleboard. F: in museum in 1860, called Chip-

25. {Captain John Henry (later General Sir Henry) Lefroy (1817–1890) traveled to Hudson Bay and the Mackenzie River valley in 1843–44 and published *Magnetical and Meteorological Observations at Lake Athabasca and Fort Simpson* (1855); cp. Stanley (1955).}

26. {The shirt and leggings appear in two paintings, "Scouts on the Rocky Mountains" (1851) and "Indian Medicine Men" (1851) by G. P. Manley, an artist who apparently never left England. Both paintings were in the collection of the Hudson's Bay Archives in the late 1960s; the first of the two was illustrated in the Winter 1970 issue of *The Beaver*.}

27. {Additional information kindly supplied by Dale Idiens, 8 August 2000.}

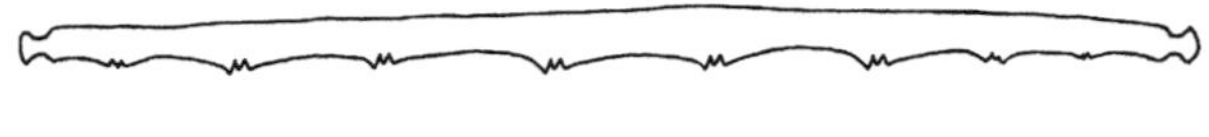

Fig. 8 Bow (XXV 119), rectangular cross section, with twisted bast (?) bowstring. Accompanied by crude arrow with stone point, sinew lashing. Length 65.5 cm. Ex Museum für Völkerkunde, Vienna, cat.no. 131725 (Martin Pitzer coll.), Ottawa, 1851–1853. After a drawing by William C. Sturtevant.

pewa. B&S: Ojibwa, pre-1850; *Michipicoten, Lake Superior.* {NMS, cat.no. 1904.131: "Cradle (*teknauken*), Le Bole tribe, Ojibeways, Lower Canada, 1867, from Richmond Museum, Yorks.," exchanged by A. Speyer, Jr. in 1963.} Now CMC, cat.no. III-I-1328; BN: Iroquois (Mohawk?) type, before 1860.

x Boy's coat. {NMS, cat.no. 1881.37.43: "Nascappie, ... 'Wood Indians,' interior of Labrador, bought for 5s. 6d from Chapman & Son, Edinburgh," exchanged by A. Speyer, Jr. in 1963.} Now MVW, cat.no. 145506, acquired from Speyer in 1964. "Montagnais-Naskapi, Quebec-Labrador, probably about 1800" (Burnham 1992: 177).

y Skin coat. Evidently not in B&S. {NMS, cat.no. U.C. 278 [transferred ca. 1850 from University collection, Edinburgh]: "Indian of Algonquin family, Hudson Bay territory," exchanged by A. Speyer, Jr. in 1962.} Now EMB, cat.no. IV B 12823, acquired from A. Speyer, Jr. in 1968, who said it "was received in exchange ... with the Museum in Edinburgh" and was from Barren Ground Cree, about 1800 (Bolz and Sanner 1999: 199).

XXV. *Museum für Völkerkunde, Vienna*[28]

{The items listed below were part of an exchange with A. Speyer, Jr. in 1964 for the Naskapi coat, XXIV x above.}

66* (155) Pair of moccasins. F; BN: Sir Charles Lyell collection [see VIII above]; according to Brasser, MVW, cat. no. 12028 {i.e., 12020}; CF (in pre-publication manuscript of Feest 1968a): MVW, cat.no. 12020, J. G. Schwarz collection, collected 1820–1867, probably pre-1848 {no provenience recorded}. B&S: *Huron,* pre-1840. Now CMC, cat.no. III-H-427; BN: Huron type, 1840s.[29]

28. {On the history of the North American collections in Vienna, including the Klinger, Schwarz, Pitzer, Kormann, Ward, Müller collections, cp. Feest (1968b: 26–29), Feest and Kasprycki (1993: 16–19); on Schwarz, see also Kasprycki (i.p.), on Müller see Feest (1999: 83).}

29. {Identification of B&S 66 with MVW, cat.no. 12020 by CF, based on verbal description only, was erroneous; the pair had already been traded in 1967 to the RJMK (cat.no. 49718); cp. Boden (1995: 196; illustration in color plate IV is laterally reversed).}

30. {In 1931 A. Speyer, Sr. received in an exchange with the Neuchâtel museum a pipe tomahawk, a scalp, and a knife sheath; there are no records of other exchanges involving North American material, and even for 1931 the documentation is insufficient. Since no museum inventory exists prior to 1921, the documentation of earlier items is problematic (Roland Kaehr, pers. comm. to CFF, 21 July 2000, on which also additional data in the entries are based).}

31. {Lt.-Col. Frédéric Matthey (1777–1850) had been a member of the Swiss colony at Lord Selkirk's settlement on the Red River from 1816 to 1824. His collection came to MEN in 1841.}

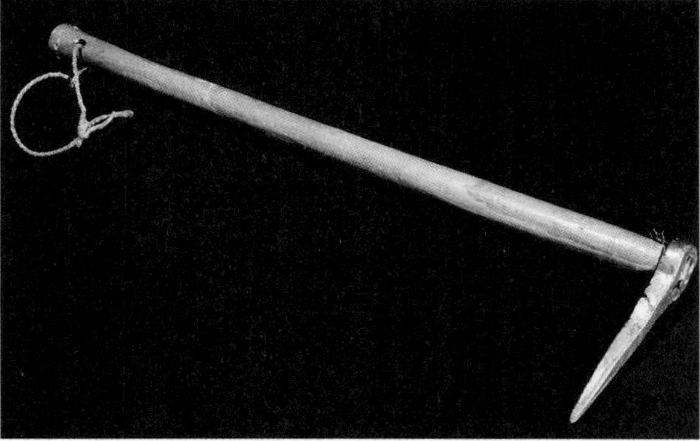

Fig. 9 Tomahawk (XXV 261), wooden handle, wrought iron head. Length 60 cm. Ex Museum für Völkerkunde, Vienna, cat.no. 21564 (Hugo Müller coll.), "Blackfoot," before 1885. Photograph: Edeltraut Mandl.

103* Lacrosse racquet. F; CF: MVW, cat.no. 7957, Ignatz Korman collection, in museum by 1879 {original attribution: "Canada."}. B&S: Iroquois, ca. 1860.

119* Bow and arrow (Fig. 8). F; CF: MVW, cat.nos. 131725, 131702, M. Pitzer collection, collected 1851–1853 {Pitzer (1854: 14): "Ottawa"}; F: on display at Kloster Herzogenburg. B&S: Ottawa, pre-1850.

129 (88) Pair of moccasins. F; CF: MVW, cat.no. 11976, J. G. Schwarz collection, collected 1820–1867, probably pre-1848 {original attribution: "Ojibway"}. B&S: Ojibwa, *pre-1850.* Now CMC, cat.no. III-G-831; BN: Ojibwa, 1830.

159 (66) Knife. F; CF: MVW, cat.no. 11965b, J. G. Schwarz collection, collected 1820–1821 {original attribution: "Alegonk" [i.e., Algonquin]}. F; BN: blade marked "A. Hatfield." B&S: *Ojibwa, ca. 1800.* Now CMC, cat.no. III-X-238; BN: Eastern Great Lakes, pre-1800. [For the sheath of 159 (66), see under VI above.]

221 (40) Chest ornament. F: purchased from Ward's Science, Rochester 1879, labeled Dakota; museum has another obtained at the same time; CF: MVW, cat.no. 9189; BN: MVW, Ward collection, received 1879. B&S: *Eastern* Dakota, *ca. 1860.* Now CMC, cat.no. V-E-282; BN: Eastern Sioux, 1860.

230* Quiver and three arrows. F; CF: MVW, cat.no. 397, J. Klinger collection, received 1825. B&S: Plains Ojibwa, pre-1850.

261 Tomahawk (Fig. 9). F; CF: MVW, cat.no. 21564, Hugo Müller collection, received 1885. B&S: Blackfoot, *ca. 1860.*

XXVI. *Musée d'Ethnographie, Neuchâtel*[30]

{Acquired by A. Speyer, Sr. in the 1930s.}

208 (108) Pipe tomahawk. F: from Neuchâtel museum, "inscription in French says: Red Cloud's Brule"; BN: "An attached label reads "'Tomahawk' ... de la tribu des Brules Sioux dans le Wyoming Territory. Le chef de cette tribu est le célèbre 'Red Cloud' ..." {Exchanged in 1931, original MEN cat.no. and collector unknown.} B&S: Oglala Teton Sioux, ca. 1850. Now CMC, cat.no. V-E-272; BN: Teton Sioux, ca. 1850.

213 Pipe. F: from Neuchâtel, "from Lt. Col. Matte?"[31]

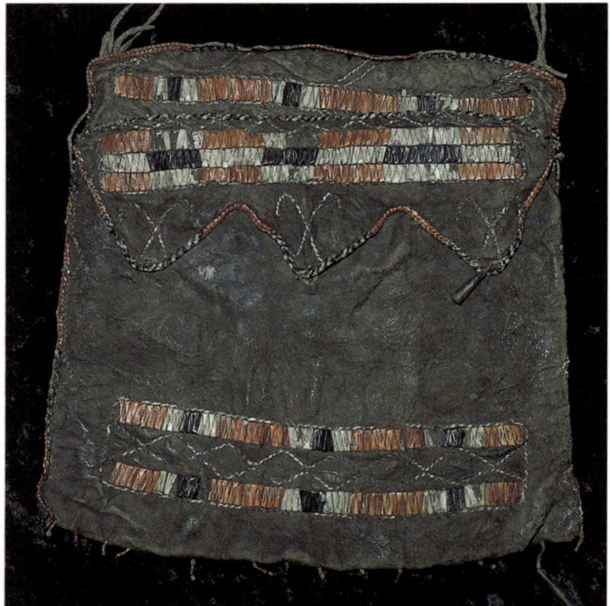

Fig. 10 Pouch (XXIX ab), quill appliqué on black-dyed buckskin. MVW, cat.no. 148707, said to be from the Duke of Coburg-Gotha collection. Photograph: Fritz Mandl.

{MEN, cat.no. IV.A.183 (no. 3 on Matthey's 1840 list): "pipe de guerre des Sioux-Yanktons donnée par le chef Oua-natan." Pipe no longer at MEN; no deaccession records.} B&S: Yanktonai Dakota, pre-1830.

215 Knife and sheath. F: "Neuchâtel No. 269. Old label: 'M. H. Guye, Sioux'." {Henri Guye donated several pieces, some of them with the original numbers 206, 272, and 278, to MEN in 1865–66; some of them are missing; no deaccession records.} B&S: Sioux, pre-1840.

{*XXVII. Bernisches Historisches Museum (CFF)*}

266 {Man's tailored, quilled coat. BHM cat.no. NA 16, Lorenz Alphons Schoch[32] collection: "travel or hunting costume of Mr. A. L. Schoch (not on his original list)"; acquired ca. 1935 by A. Speyer, Sr. B&S: no provenience; *Saskatchewan River Cree, before 1840*. Now CMC.}

XXVIII. Duke of Hessen Collection, Hessisches Landesmuseum, Darmstadt[33]

F: All were acquired by Arthur Speyer, Sr., although the last four are questionably from Darmstadt. {Cp. also LVII 97.}

88 (2) {Slit pouch. BN: "previously in the collection of the Duke of Hessen-Darmstadt." B&S, BN: Iroquois, pre-1800. Now CMC, cat.no. III-I-1314.}

110 Pair of moccasins. B&S: Algonkin, pre-1825; *Ottawa*.

111* Pair of moccasins. B&S: Canada, pre-1829; *Ottawa*.

113 (93) Pouch. BN: no previous collection history. B&S: Iroquois, pre-1790; *Ottawa*. Now CMC, cat.no. III-I-1324; BN: Iroquois, before 1790.[34]

155 Pouch and sash. B&S: Ojibwa, pre-1790.

192 Pouch. B&S: Miami, pre-1790; *Ojibwa*.

193 Pouch. B&S: *Southern Great Lakes*, pre-1790.

XXIX. Duke of Gotha, Chinese Cabinet in East Germany[35] *(F)*

{Acquired in or before 1928 by A. Speyer, Sr.; cp. also XXX 170; XLVIII 238; LVII 93, 97, 168, 239, am below.}

41 Man's coat. F. B&S: *SW Labrador*, pre-1770. Now AMF, cat.no. III-2103, "acquired from the Speyer collection {in 1969} and has no known history" (Burnham 1992: 306).

56 {Pipe, quill-wrapped stem. Note in A. Speyer, Jr.'s records suggests that this comes from Coburg-Gotha collection. B&S: Penobscot, pre-1790.}

64 (164) Pair of moccasins. F. B&S: Canadian Indian, pre-1829; *Huron*. Now CMC, cat.no. III-H-425; BN: Huron type, before 1829.

65 (82) Pouch. F. B&S, BN: Huron, pre-1829. Now CMC, cat.no. III-H-426.

82 Pouch. F. B&S: Mohawk, pre-1790.

83 Sheath and knife. F. B&S: Mohawk, pre-1790. F: "Knife has 'ROX' mark with inverted heart."[36]

95 (107) Pipe-tomahawk. F; {Schlossmuseum Gotha, cat.no. Americanische Gegenstände 5, accessioned before 1830, no provenience}. B&S: Seneca, ca. 1850. Now CMC, cat.no. III-I-1315; BN: Seneca, 1800.

170 (55) Calumet. F: no information; BN: "Formerly in the collection of the Duke von Coburg-Gotha." B&S, BN: Ojibwa, pre-1830. Now CMC, cat.no. III-G-826. [See *XXX* below.]

178 (171) Pair of moccasins. F. B&S: Menomini, pre-1790. Now CMC, cat.no. III-N-32; BN: Menomini(?), late 18th c.

180 (59) Pouch. F. B&S: Menomini, pre-1780. F: "Marked 'From Canadian Indians, Michigan'." Now CMC, cat. no. III-M-2; BN: Ottawa, late 18th c.

181 Knife sheath. F. B&S: Menomini, 1772. {Now CMC, cat.no. III-N-35.}

184 {Pouch with quilled fringe. B&S: Winnebago, pre-1800. Now CMC, cat.no. III-O-1 (Phillips 1984: 49).}

32. {On Schoch (1810–1866), see Thompson (1977: 147). Thanks to Thomas Psota for information from accession book.}

33. {All inventories of the Hessisches Landesmuseum, Darmstadt, were lost during World War II, which makes it impossible to verify the possible previous presence in this museum of the items noted below. What remains of the collection includes eighteenth-century material from the eastern Great Lakes region presumably collected by Hessian mercenaries in the American Revolution and probably from the collection of the Grand Duke of Hessen-Darmstadt.}

34. {Kasprycki (1997: 68) reports that in 1995 Arthur Speyer remembered only that "the pouch had been obtained by his father, presumably from a German museum." On the basis of comparative evidence she suggests that "the Speyer pouch may have also been collected by a German mercenary in the southern Quebec and Lake Champlain area" (Kasprycki 1997: 74), which fits well with a possible history in the collection of the Grand Duke of Hessen.}

35. {The Ducal Museum's ethnographic collections, whose earliest North American specimens were acquired in the eighteenth century, were attached to the Chinese Cabinet. Some of the museum's catalogs and surviving material from North America were briefly studied by CFF in 1984; the catalogs were not available for restudy at the time of this writing.}

36. {Like probably others of the items listed here, this sheath and knife are not from the Duke of Gotha's collection. The original catalog numbers clearly identify the sheath as coming from VSMRM; see XXXII 83 below. For the sheath, cp. II k.}

z {Moccasins. Now AMF, cat.no. III-1949, acquired from Speyer in 1968: said to have come from the collection of the Duke von Coburg-Gotha; "Huron, ca. 1845."}

aa {Moosehair-appliqué pouch. Now AMF, cat.no. III-1950, acquired from Speyer in 1968: said to have come from the collection of the Duke von Coburg-Gotha; "Huron, ca. 1845," probably based on information supplied by Speyer.}

ab {Quilled pouch (Fig. 10). Now MVW, cat.no. 148707, acquired from Speyer in 1969: said to have been collected in 1776, probably from the Ojibwa, and to have come from the collection of the Duke von Coburg-Gotha.}

ac {Small drum, no provenience. MVF, cat.no. NS 26369, acquired in 1928 from A. Speyer, Sr. as having formerly been in the "collection of the Grand Duke of Jena [clearly a mistake for Gotha]"; destroyed during World War II.}

XXX. *Duke of Sachsen-Weimar Collection*[37]

{Acquired before World War II by A. Speyer, Sr.}

170 (55) Calumet. F: no information; BN: "Formerly in the collection of the Duke von Coburg-Gotha." {Cp. XXIX above. Inventory of Schlossmuseum Gotha, cat.no. Americanische Gegenstände 4: "Eine nordamerikanische Pfeife, eine sogenannte Freundschaftspfeife," collected by Duke Bernhard von Sachsen-Weimar on his trip to North America in 1825, donated to "Herr von Lindenau," who donated it to the cabinet in Gotha before 1830.} B&S, BN: Ojibwa, pre-1830. Now CMC, cat.no. III-G-826.

211 Pair of leggings. F: no information other than source. B&S: *Yankton Dakota*, pre-1836.

XXXI. *Großherzog von Baden Collection*[38]

F: "No information on how Speyer obtained this collection." {Obtained by A. Speyer, Sr. in the early 1930s from the Badisches Landesmuseum, Karlsruhe. Cp. XXXII below.}

32 Sash. F. B&S: Cree, pre-1795; *Saulteaux*. F: called Cree.

38 (48) Painted skin. F. B&S: Nenenot (Naskapi), pre-1770; F: "marked Nenonot." Now CMC, cat.no. III-B-588; BN: Naskapi, ca. 1740.

39 (92) Man's coat. F. B&S: Nenenot (Naskapi), pre-1770; F: "marked Nenonot." Now CMC, cat.no. III-B-589; BN: Naskapi, pre-1770; Burnham (1992:130): "Montagnais-Naskapi, Quebec, probably early 18th century."

43 (17) Leggings. F. B&S: Nenenot (Naskapi), pre-1780. Now CMC, cat.no. III-B-591; BN: Naskapi, pre-1770.

44 (45) Pair of moccasins. F. B&S: Nenenot (Naskapi), pre-1780. Now CMC, cat.no. III-B-592; BN: Naskapi, pre-1780.

46 (49) Pouch. F. {Not from Grand Duke of Baden collection; see XXXII 46 below.} B&S: Nenenot (Naskapi), pre-1780. Now CMC, cat.no. III-B-594; BN: Naskapi, pre-1780.

203 Feather fan. F. B&S: Santee Dakota, ca. 1860; F: "labeled Santee Sioux."

204 (136) Calumet. F: "From Frankfurt Mus. Lichtenberger Coll."; BN: formerly in the collection of the Grand Duke of Baden {this attribution probably correct; see XXXIX 204 and note 55 below}. B&S: Santee Dakota, pre-1860. Now CMC, cat.no. V-E-290; BN: Yankton Sioux, pre-1843.

212 (89) Pipe. F: Grand Duke of Baden {this attribution probably incorrect; see XXXIX 212 and note 55 below}; BN: Lichtenberger. B&S: Yankton Dakota, pre-1843. Now CMC, cat.no. V-E-289; BN: Eastern Sioux, 1860s.

228 Flute. F. B&S: Dakota, *pre-1850*.

237* Scalp. F. B&S: Missouri, pre-1842.

ad Beaded sash. Now EMB, cat.no. IV B 12755, sold by Speyer in 1964: Choctaw, before 1850 (Bolz and Sanner 1999: 66, fig. 46).

{XXXII. *Völkerkundliche Sammlungen der Stadt Mannheim im Reiß-Museum*[39] *(CFF)*}

{Acquired by Arthur Speyer, Sr. Cp. also XXXI and note 38 above.}

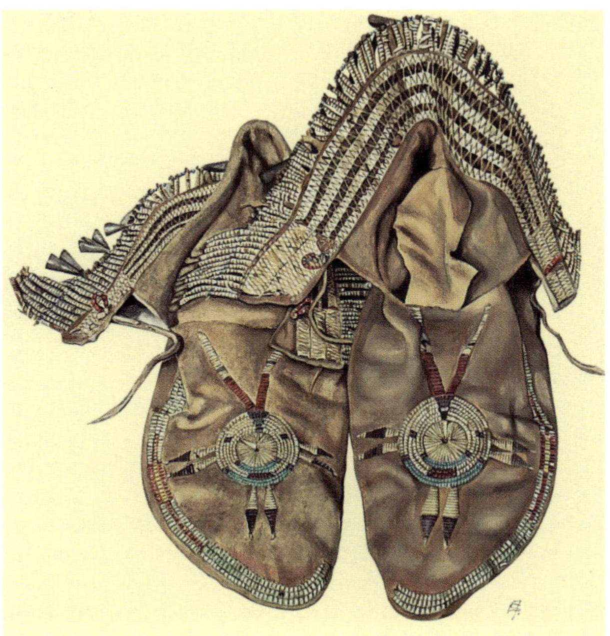

Fig. 11 "Moccasins of the Mandan. From the former collection of the Grand Duke of Baden" (XXXII 241). Crayon drawing by Arthur Speyer, Jr., ca. 1947–1949.

37. {Duke Bernhard of Saxe-Weimar (1792–1862) traveled to North America in 1825–1826. His travel account (Luden 1828) describes his visit to Clark's Museum in St. Louis, but contains no reference to his own ethnographic collecting.}

38. {The various collections of the Grand Duke of Baden, which in the 1760s and 1770s were combined into a new Kunstkammer in Karlsruhe, are known to have included "artificialia exotica atque varia" since at least 1720. The ethnographic material was transferred to the later Badisches Landesmuseum (Karlsruhe) in 1872 and ultimately to VSMRM in the 1930s. The long-lost catalog of the ethnographic collection has only recently resurfaced and was not available for inspection at the time of this writing.}

39. {All of the items listed below were originally part of the collection of the Altertumsverein [Antiquarian Society], Mannheim, which had formerly been part of the Großherzogliches Antiquarium [Grand Ducal Antiquarium], of which apparently no early records exist. The four items are documented on photographs taken in 1938; no records exist to document their deaccessioning (Henning Bischof, pers. comm. to CFF, 28 July 2000, in which he also provided the Mannheim catalog numbers).}

46 (49) Pouch. F: Großherzog von Baden collection. {VSMRM, cat.no. V Am 1793, ex Altertumsverein Mannheim, cat.no. Fe. 11.} B&S: Nenenot (Naskapi), pre-1780. Now CMC, cat.no. III-B-594; BN: Naskapi, pre-1780.

83 Sheath and knife. F. B&S: Mohawk, pre-1790. F: "Knife has 'ROX' mark with inverted heart." {Erroneously attributed in F's notes to Duke of Gotha collection. Sheath now in CMC, cat.no. III-I-1313, is marked "Am 1785" and "1074a, N64 A.S.P." on tag. The knife, which in B&S is still shown together with the knifecase, was traded to the Wellington collection, where Ewing (1982: 150) also reports the number "Am 1785" as well as "A.U. [i.e., A.V.] Fd. 72." VSMRM, cat.no. V Am 1785, ex Altertumsverein Mannheim cat.no. Fd. 72. The knife now with CMC, cat.no. III-1-1313 formerly belonged to the knife case II k, above.}

154 {Strap of quilled pouch. Strap only VSMRM, cat.no. V Am 1805, ex Altertumsverein Mannheim, cat.no. Fd. 71. B&S: Ojibwa, pre-1800.}

241 (98) {Quilled moccasins. B&S: Crow, pre-1840. Identified on drawing by A. Speyer, Jr. (Fig. 11) as "Mandan" and as having been part of the collection of Grand Duke of Baden. VSMRM, cat.no. V Am 1796, ex Altertumsverein Mannheim, cat.no. Fd. 63. Now CMC, cat.no. V-H-1; BN: Mandan, pre-1840.}

XXXIII. Herzog Paul von Württemberg Collection[40]

196 Pipe. F. B&S: Kansa, pre-1830. {Anonymous (n.d.: 3): "15. Friedenspfeife (Calumet) von Oua-kantie (*le chef americain*), einem Oberhaupt der Kanza erhalten." LMS, cat.no. 12574; exchange with Arthur Speyer, Sr. in 1957; now CMC, cat.no. III-G-845. Cp. Klann (1999: 59.)}

ae {Pair of leggings. Anonymous (n.d.: 7): "100. Zwei Paar Mitassen (lederne Strümpfe) von Cabri-Leder, getragen von Ua-Tschi-mi-ka, einem Otto-Indianer." Ex Patty Frank collection; Arthur Speyer, Sr. collection; now AMF, cat. no. III 1945b, acquired in 1967. Cp. Klann (1999: 70).}

XXXIV. Collected by Prinz Maximilian zu Wied-Neuwied

191 (109) Gunstock club. F: from Linden Museum [LMS], No. 35982;[41] collected by Wied (Wied catalog no. 12); S: from Maximilian; old no. 35982; BN: "Written on handle in black ink: 'Missouri, M. Z. Wied'." {Acquired in 1956 by A. Speyer, Sr.} B&S: Missouri, pre-1832; *Sauk or Fox*. Now CMC, cat.no. V-N-3; BN: Missouri, 1833.

232 Pair of leggings. F: from Wied collection (perhaps from Berlin?) {in fact acquired by A. Speyer, Sr. from LMS, cat.no. 36112: "Mandan"}. B&S: Mandan, pre-1832.

(18) Boy's robe [see under XXXV below]. Not in B&S. BN: acquired from EMB {cat.no. IV B 207; no. 16 on Prince Maximilian's original list: "Piekan"}. Formerly in the collection of Prince Maximilian of Wied. BN: Piegan, before 1833. {This piece was never part of the Speyer collection, but was directly exchanged with CMC in 1939.}

af Woman's robe. Not in B&S or BN. Acquired in 1920s by Arthur Speyer, Sr. (cp. Fig. 1) from EMB (cat.no. IV B 104; no. 23 on Prince Maximilian's original list: "Blackfoot"), described and illustrated in Krickeberg (1954: 73, Abb. 15, Taf. 9b: "Piegan") and Völger (1976: 4.44.09). {Now DLO, cat.no. 9378, acquired from A. Speyer, Sr. in 1950 (Eberhard 1956: 77, no. 1214: "Crow").[42]}

XXXV. Museum für Völkerkunde [now: Ethnologisches Museum], Berlin

For material collected by Maximilian Prince of Wied formerly at the Ethnologisches Museum, Berlin, see XXXIV.

8a Mask. F: "From Berlin Mus. Collected by Jacobson. No longer in Speyer collection"; S: from Herzog von Leuchtenberg [see XXXVII below]; {EMB, cat.no. IV A 6587, Jacobsen coll.}. B&S: Copper River, southern Alaska, ca. 1860.

220 Medicine pouch. F: "From Berlin Mus. Collection of Baron von Rönne;[43] Dakota 1839." {EMB, cat.no. IV B 215; acquired by A. Speyer, Jr.} B&S: Eastern Dakota, pre-1839.

(18) Boy's robe. [See under XXXIV above.] BN: Piegan, before 1833. {Was never part of the Speyer collection, but was directly exchanged with CMC in 1939.}

XXXVI. Linden-Museum, Stuttgart

{For material collected by Duke Paul of Württemberg and Maximilian Prince of Wied formerly at the LMS, see XXXIII and XXXIV.[44]}

(137) Pipe bowl. Not in B&S. {Perhaps ex LMS, cat.no. 36137: "Dakota." Acquired by A. Speyer, Sr.[45]} Now CMC, cat.no. V-E-291; BN: Eastern Sioux type, early 19th c.

XXXVII. Herzog von Leuchtenberg Collection[46]

F: "Herzog v. Leuchtenberg (Eugene de Beauharnais) was 2nd King of Italy in 1805; adopted by Napoleon I in 1807; received his title in 1817 from his father-in-law in Bavaria. Re-

40. {An overview of Duke Paul's ethnographic collections from North America, now mainly at EMB, LMS, and British Museum, London, is provided by Klann (1999), who partly draws upon an early published list of the collection before its dispersal, i.e., at least prior to 1867 (Anonymous n.d.).}

41. {Recorded in the catalog of the LMS as "Punca, Ob. Missouri"; illustrated in Wied (1839–1841, Atlas: Tafel 48, no. 4; identified in 1: 239 as "Saki und Foxes").}

42. {The account given by Bolz (1995: 203, 211) of the history of this piece is misleading; a correction is offered in Bolz and Sanner (1999: 78).}

43. {The material associated with Rönne was actually from the collection of Thomas L. McKenney (Feest and Kasprycki 1999: 44, 304–305n45; Bolz and Sanner 1999: 53–54).}

44. {In addition to these items, the Speyer collection acquired from the Linden-Museum a Blackfoot cradleboard (now at NMS, cat.no. 1963.473) and a Cheyenne quiver/bowcase.}

45. {Cataloged together with the Wied material, but does not appear on the original transfer list of 1904. No record of deaccessioning exists in the files of the Linden-Museum (Sonja Schierle, pers. comm., 9 August 2000).}

46. {In 1839 Maximilian Eugen Joseph Napoleon (–1852), the second Duke of Leuchtenberg and son of Eugène de Beauharnais, married the Russian Grand Duchess Maria and moved to Russia, where he must have acquired the material from Russian Alaska in the Leuchtenberg collection. Wrangell, who had served as Governor of

lated in some way to Wrangell and may have secured his collection from Wrangell. Possibly a part of the same collection [was] given to Senckenberg Mus. in Frankfurt by Baron v. Rossil[l]ion."

S: Nos. 4–11 below from collection of Herzog v. Leuchtenberg, who had relations with Russia through Wrangell.

{Acquired by A. Speyer, Sr. before World War II.}

3 Trousers. F: "Now in Ledermuseum, Offenbach to match a shirt they owned which was from the Wrangell Collection. Speyer now has a pair from Leuchtenberg [not in B&S], which matches a shirt in Mannheim and he plans to trade them to Mannheim so they will have a complete matched outfit." B&S: Tanaina, Alaska, pre-1821.[47]

4 Glove. F: from Herzog v. Leuchtenberg, marked "Kisipak." B&S: Tanaina, Alaska, pre-1821. {SMVM, cat.no. L 789: "Aglechmuten." Acquired by A. Speyer, Sr. in 1951.}

6 Strap. F. B&S: Tanaina, Alaska pre-1821. F: "called Bering St."

7 Quiver and two arrows. F. {SMVM, cat.no. L 788: "Aglechmuten." Acquired by A. Speyer, Sr. in 1951.} B&S: Tanaina, Alaska, pre-1821. F: "Called Kisipak River."

8 Club. F. {Old number 16.} B&S: Tanaina, Alaska, pre-1821. F: "Called Kalaushan {Kalauschen} [i.e., Tlingit] from Tomeihouska Town."

8a Mask. F: from Berlin Mus. [see XXXV above], collected by Jacobsen; no longer in Speyer collection; S: Leuchtenberg; {CFF: definitely from Berlin, cp. XXXV 8a}. B&S: Copper River, southern Alaska, ca. 1860.

Alaska between 1829 and 1835, may be a less likely source than his successor Ivan A. Kupreanov. In 1858 the Leuchtenberg collection became property of the Bavarian state and is now part of the SMVM. Cp. Müller (1980: 24–25). Thanks to Jean-Loup Rousselot for checking some of the records on Leuchtenberg and other material in Munich.}

47. {The trousers were substituted in 1968 for the pair cataloged earlier as cat.no. 11245, "Kutchin, pre 1821, ex Wrangell collection." The pair they replaced was moved in 1968 to VSMRM with the number 11245 still clearly legible (now cat.no. V Am 3219b, "Alaska, 1830, ex Wrangell collection"). According to A. Speyer, Jr., the sets are not correctly matched, with the LMO set coming from the Leuchtenberg collection (which may be correct), and the VSMRM set from the Wrangell/Rosillon collection in Frankfurt (which is incorrect). Cp. XXXVII ag, LVII aq, ar below.}

48. {The North American collection of Princess Therese of Bavaria at the SMVM includes exclusively material collected by herself in 1891. The mittens are more likely to have come from the older collections of the royal family known as "Hausgut" and "VIII. Abteiung." On Princess Therese, cp. Rousselot (1997).}

49. {Obtained by the King of Bavaria in 1825 from Captain Samuel Hadlock, whose collection list published in 1823 refers to it as "15. North American Indian's belt, singularly wrought with Porcupine's quills"; a German list published in 1824 establishes the identity beyond reasonable doubt: "Ein künstlich gearbeitetes, nordamerikanischen Indianers Degengehenk, mit Stachelschweins-Borsten verziert" (Feest in Wright [1987: 231n3], quotation after 1823 English copy of the collection list added). On Johnson's collection, see Burch (1990).}

50. {On Augustin Lamare-Picquot (1785–1873), see Müller (1980: 24) and Feest and Kasprycki (1999: 22–23, 296n12).}

51. {Thanks to Mona Suhrbier for access to the museum's catalogs. In addition to the objects listed below, the Speyer collection traded since 1928 at least nine other North American objects from the Cronau and Lotichius collections at the MVF.}

9* Bone pick. F: from Olde Curiosity Shop, Seattle [see XII above]; head of pick used to dig roots; S: Leuchtenberg. B&S: Koyukon, Alaska, pre-1850.

10 Necklace. F: "From H. B. Bompas family. [See IX above.] Labelled Yukon"; S: Leuchtenberg. B&S: Koyukon, Alaska, pre-1840. {Now DLO, cat.no. 12149, acquired from Speyer in 1971; cp. Völger (1976: 4.20.40).}

11 Mitten. F: "No information; now in Berlin Museum"; S: Leuchtenberg. B&S: *Kutchin, ca. 1860.* {Now in AMF.}

ag {Man's shirt. Now DLO, cat.no. 11244, acquired from A. Speyer, Jr. in 1962: "Kutchin, pre-1821" (cp. Völger 1976: 4.20.18), said to have been from the Wrangell/Rossillon collection at MVF, which is incorrect. Cp. XXXVII 3 and note 47 above.}

XXXVIII. Staatliches Museum für Völkerkunde, Munich

For material from the Leuchtenberg collection in the SMVM, see XXXVII.

45 (81) Pair of mittens. B: Otto Zerries [the curator at the SMVM] said that Speyer obtained them from the SMVM, which got them from a Herzogin; F; BN: formerly in collection of Princess Thérèse of Bavaria.[48] {Acquired by A. Speyer, Jr.} B&S: Labrador, *Naskapi*, pre-1840. Now CMC, cat.no. III-B-593; BN: Naskapi, pre-1840.

92 (141) Sword belt. F: from Munich museum, collection of Bavarian king in 1913; BN: formerly in collection of a king of Bavaria, acquired in 1913 by SMVM; bears partly illegible label in Latin [translation by Sturtevant and Ives Goddard: "Belt for sword made from porcupine quills by an Iroquois Indian woman [...] gave as a gift to(?) William Johnson, Bart. [...] New York province administrator"].[49] {SMVM, cat.no. Y59, Hg. 1049, acquired by A. Speyer, Sr. in 1951.} B&S: *Mohawk* Iroquois, pre-1774. Now CMC, cat.no. III-I-1327; BN: Iroquois (Mohawk?), 1760–1770 .

115 (28) Sash. F: "Collected by Lamarepiquet [sic],[50] a French biologist. Marked 'Mandana or Mandam', perhaps by Munich"; BN: "formerly in the Lamarepiquet Collection, ... Munich. (Lamarepiquet was a French biologist.)" {SMVM, cat.no. L 978; acquired by A. Speyer, Sr.} B&S: Iroquois, pre-1800, *Ottawa*. Now CMC, cat.no. III-X-233; BN: Eastern Great Lakes, 18th c.

147 Pouch and strap. F: "Collected by Lamarepiquet, a French biologist." {SMVM, cat.no. L 977; acquired by A. Speyer, Sr. in 1951.} B&S: Iroquois; *Ojibwa, pre-1800.*

205 {Quilled and painted shirt. B&S: Brulé Sioux, Teton Dakota, ca. 1860. SMVM, cat.no. 94367: "Dakota?," Buchner coll., ex H. A. Ward's Natural Science, Rochester, NY; acquired by A. Speyer, Sr. in 1951.}

206 {Single quilled and painted legging. B&S: Brulé Sioux, Teton Dakota, ca. 1860. SMVM, cat.no. 94366: "Dakota?," Buchner coll., ex H. A. Ward's Natural Science, Rochester, NY; acquired by A. Speyer, Sr. in 1951.}

XXXIX. [Städtisches] Museum für Völkerkunde, Frankfurt am Main[51]

{Acquired by A. Speyer, Sr. before World War II.}

78 (94) Pair of moccasins. F: Frankfurt museum #E162ab, marked Lorette; B: published by Vatter (1925: 95, Taf.

18); BN: note glued on sole says acquired from Indians in Buffalo, and in 1836 given to Senckenbergische Gesellschaft Frankfurt, by Mrs. Sophie Kraus, née Rüppell. B&S: Indians of Buffalo on Lake Erie, pre-1836, *Seneca*. Now CMC, cat.no. III-I-1309; BN: Seneca type, ca. 1830.[52]

185 Whip. F: from Frankfurt; collected by Lichtenberger[53] 1867, marked "Minnesota"; {MVF, cat.no. E. 483, "Minnesota"}. B&S: Winnebago, pre-1842. S: according to Speyer, should read Minnesota, pre-1842.

195* Calumet. F: from Frankfurt, J. B. Klein[54] collection. {MVF, cat.no. E. 152, no provenience; other material in the Klein collection is identified as Minnesota "Sioux" and "Menomini."} B&S: *Osage or neighbors*, pre-1825.

204 (136) Calumet. F: "From Frankfurt Mus. Lichtenberger Coll."; BN: formerly in the collection of the Grand Duke of Baden [see XXXI above].[55] B&S: Santee Dakota, pre-1860. Now CMC, cat.no. V-E-290; BN: Yankton Sioux, pre-1843.

210 (36) Painted robe. F: from Frankfurt Museum (see Vatter); BN: "Collected by Gabriel André[56] on the upper Missouri River in 1843"; B: formerly in Senckenberg collection, Frankfurt; published by Vatter (1925: 87–88, Abb. 5); {MVF, cat.no. E. 460, "Upper Missouri"}. B&S: Yankton or Yanktonai Dakota, pre-1842. Now CMC, cat.no. V-E-281; BN: Sioux type, 1843.

212 (89) Pipe. F: Grand Duke of Baden [see XXXI above]; BN: from H. A. Lichtenberger, who acquired it from the Minn. Sioux before 1867. {MVF, cat.no. E. 475, "Minnesota"; cp. note 55.} B&S: Yankton Dakota, before 1843. Now CMC, cat.no. V-E-289; BN: Eastern Sioux, 1860s.

235 Shirt. F: from Frankfurt, collection Gabriel André (see Vatter [but this shirt is not specifically mentioned in Vatter 1925]). {MVF, cat.no. E. 463, "Upper Missouri."} B&S: *Hidatsa*, pre-1841.

XL. Sammlung für Völkerkunde [now: *Ethnologie*], *Georg-August-Universität, Göttingen*[57]

1 {Shirt. "Blumenbach coll.," acquired by A. Speyer, Sr., probably before 1935. B&S: Kenai, Alaska, ca. 1800. Now CMC, cat.no. VI-Y-5 (Harrison 1987: 91, #S2: "Tanaina type, c. 1800").[58]}

121 (185) Man's hood. F: collected by Hermann Domeier,[59] in Europe by 1852; BN: "Previously owned by Hermann Domeier, who acquired it in Europe in about 1852." {SEUG, cat.no. 3141, deaccessioned to A. Speyer, Sr. in 1951.} B&S: Chippewa Territory, Minn., pre-1852. Now CMC, cat.no. III-G-838; BN: Minnesota Ojibwa, pre-1850.

122 Leggings. F: same information as for 121. {SEUG, cat.no. 3131, no record of deccessioning. Now CMC.[60]} B&S: Chippewa Territory, Minn., pre-1852.

162 (35) Ball-headed club. F: from Göttingen, see Stolpe; B: ex collection Göttingen University; perhaps published by Dietschy [not in Dietschy 1939; Stolpe (1897: 90–91, fig. 10) gives its SEUG cat.no. as 393]. {"Blumenbach coll.," acquired by A. Speyer, Sr., probably before 1935; cp. note 58.} B&S: *Chippewa, pre-1800*. Now CMC, cat.no. III-X-236; BN: Great Lakes, 18th c.

ah {Bird skin parka. "Blumenbach coll.," acquired by A. Speyer, Sr., probably before 1935; cp. note 58. Now DLO,[61] cp. Völger (1976: 4.10.30): "Kodiak."}

XLI. Collected by Ehrentraut, in a museum by 1852 (F)

{A collection of seven items from northeastern and central North America was acquired from "Hofrat Ehrentraut"[62] in 1852 by the King of Hanover and is presently at NLH (Abteilung für Völkerkunde).}

209 Shirt. F. {NLH, cat.no. 87, acquired by Arthur Speyer, Jr. in 1959.} B&S: *Sisseton Sioux*, pre-1841.

255 Pad saddle. F. {NLH, cat.no. 84, acquired by Arthur Speyer, Jr. in 1961.} B&S: *Blackfoot*, pre-1842.

256 (145) Crupper. F; BN: originally collected by Ehrentraut, but in a museum by 1852 {No NLH cat.no., probably thought to be part of the saddle.[63]}. B&S:

52. {Sophie Kraus donated to the Senckenbergische Naturforschende Gesellschaft *two* pairs of moccasins, one from "Buffalo on Lake Erie" (E. 161ab) and one from Lorette (E. 162ab). The catalog of the MVF records that E. 162ab was traded to Arthur Speyer, Sr., but the label quoted in BN clearly indicates that E. 161ab was exchanged.}

53. {On Lichtenberger, cp. Feest and Kasprycki (1999: 43, 304n43). His collection was accessioned by the Senckenbergische Naturforschende Gesellschaft in Frankfurt in 1867.}

54. {On Johann Baptist Klein (1778–1831), cp. Feest and Kasprycki (1999: 43, 304n44). His collection was accessioned by the Senckenbergische Naturforschende Gesellschaft in Frankfurt in 1825–1826.}

55. {The two very similar pipes 204 and 212 are alternately attributed to the Grand Duke of Baden and Lichtenberger collections. Measurements for the Lichtenberger pipe (ex MVF, cat.no. E. 475, "Minnesota") agree more closely with 212 (89). 204 may thus possibly be from the Grand Duke of Baden collection.}

56. {The Senckenberg catalog reports that the Andreae material was donated to the museum in 1843 by Beronus du Fay. Andreae is said to have been a native of Lorraine and to have lived in St. Louis from 1827 to 1843; most of his collection, including the two items in the Speyer collection, had originally been collected by (Honoré) Picotte of the American Fur Company.}

57. {In addition to the five pieces listed below, A. Speyer, Sr. obtained at least eight more North American pieces from SEUG in 1953, including an Iroquois headband (Am 1081), Sioux quiver and sash (Am 452, 453).}

58. {XL 1, 162, and ah are thought to be from the late eighteenth/early nineteenth-century collection at Göttingen University curated by J. G. Blumenbach. No records of these pieces have, however, been found in either old or new (post-1935) catalogs of the collection, nor are there any records of deaccessioning. Cp. note 2 above.}

59. {Domeier settled around 1855 at Chengwatana on the Snake River, Cross Lake, MN, and befriended the local Chippewa chief Ogema Geshik. He returned to Germany before 1862; his collection was sold to SEUG in 1940 and 1950. Cp. Feest and Kasprycki (1999: 42–43), who report that two other Domeier pieces (Am 3139 and Am 3140, both beaded cloth bags) were also traded to A. Speyer, Sr. in 1953.}

60. {A pair of plain buckskin leggings now cataloged in SEUG under this number (cp. Feest and Kasprycki 1999: 259) appears to be a substitute for the woman's leggings now at CMC, which match the hood in material and decorative style.}

61. {In trades with and purchases from the DLO since 1933, the Speyer collection acquired at least eighteen North American objects from the Elk Eber collection—and material DLO had received from A. Speyer, Sr.}

62. {Heinrich Georg Ehrentraut (–1866) is best known as a collector of material on the local history and language of the Frisians near Jever, Lower Saxony. His American connections are unknown.}

Blackfoot, influenced by Cree, pre-1842. Now CMC, cat.no. V-X-393; BN: Northeastern Plains type, ca. 1840.

{*XLII. Staatliches Museum für Naturkunde und Vorgeschichte, Oldenburg (CFF)*}

245 (153) {Tobacco pouch with pipe tamper. B&S: *Interior Salish*, pre-1840. According to attached label acquired in San Francisco, 1840; accessioned by museum in 1887 from C. D. Carstens; cat.no. 334 (old no. 135). Now CMC, cat.no. V-B-423; BN: Blackfoot type, early 19th c.}

XLIII. Hamburgisches Museum für Völkerkunde

2 Shirt. F: 69th Infantry Regiment 'Harburg'; perhaps a gift from a soldier; S: from Hamburg. {HMV, cat.no. 37.35: 3: "Tanaina."[64] Acquired by A. Speyer, Jr. in 1965 in exchange for LVII ay. Now in MVF, cat.no. NS 47390, acquired from A. Speyer, Jr. in 1969: "Tanaina, 1830."} B&S: Tanaina, Alaska, *pre-1825*.

XLIV. A German Museum

40 (143) Man's coat. F: no information; S: received by Arthur Speyer, Sr. in 1938 from a German museum with a Nazi director who was burning all "savage" items; Burnham (1992: 126): "Herr Speyer, Sr. collected it from a German Museum, where it was about to be discarded. There is no record identifying the museum";[65] BN: "Formerly in a German museum." B&S: Naskapi, pre-1780. Now CMC, cat.no. III-B-590; BN: Naskapi, early 19th c.

XLV. Collection of Harding, a German Privy Councillor {Hofrat}, *who acquired it in July 1825 (BN)*

{Acquired from a German museum by A. Speyer, Sr.}

(1) Pouch. Now CMC, cat.no. III-X-231; BN: Eastern Canada, before 1825.

63. {Thanks to Claus Deimel for searching the catalog and other documents for information about this piece.}

64. {Received in 1937 as part of a collection of 114 American objects, with no indication how they came to to be owned by the 69th Infantry Regiment (Corinna Raddatz, pers. comm., 9 August 2000).}

65. {According to Arthur Speyer, Jr. (pers. comm. to CFF in July 2000), he was misunderstood when he told the story to his visitors in the late 1960s. The museum director, who was indeed a Nazi, was burning old North American Indian artifacts which were badly motheaten. A. Speyer, Sr. obtained the coat before the incineration took place.}

66. {According to Speyer family tradition, the Erbach collection was acquired by Patty Frank, much to the chagrin of A. Speyer, Sr., who considered Erbach im Odenwald his "home territory." Contrary to Hotz (1975), the ISZ catalog identifies the piece as an acquisition from P. Frank. Hotz did obtain, however, other material both from A. Speyer, Sr. in 1936 and Jr. in 1973, and indirectly via C. Taylor—the latter a Sioux cradle bag said to have been traded by Speyer from the Linden-Museum. Thanks to Denise Daenzer and Tina Wodiunig for data from the catalog.}

67. {On the Umlauff family business, cp. Gerlach (1995: 46–153).}

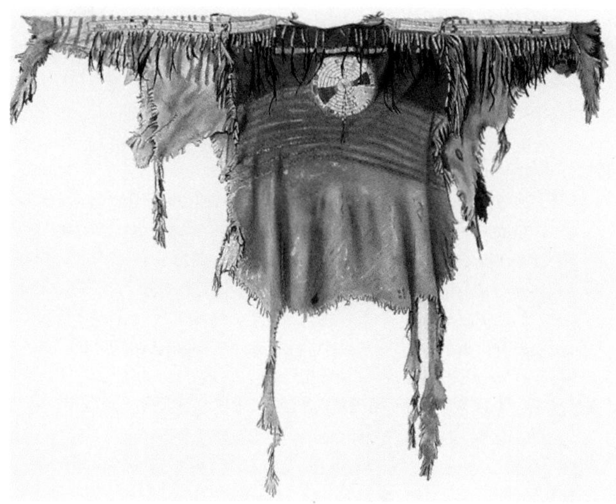

Fig. 12 "War shirt with quilled decoration, scalplocks. Blackfoot before 1850" (XLIX aj). Crayon drawing by Arthur Speyer, Jr., ca. 1947–1949.

{*XLVI. Graf Erbach-Erbach (CFF)*}

ai {Quilled sash or carrying strap. Said to have been acquired by A. Speyer, Sr. from Graf Ehbach-Ehbach [sic] collection,[66] later traded to Gottfried Hotz. Now ISZ, cat. no. 7.1,3; cp. Hotz (1975: 43): "Iroquois, perhaps pre-1800."}

XLVII. Acquired from Umlauff, a Hamburg dealer[67]

{Acquired by A. Speyer, Sr.}

42 Dress. F: "Purchased from Umlauff, a Hamburg dealer; labelled Montagnais 1830." B&S: Montagnais, pre-1830. Now EMB {cat.no. IV B 12853}, acquired from A. Speyer, Jr. in 1971 (Bolz and Sanner 1999: 199).

231 (37) Man's shirt. F: "Purchased from Umlauff in Hamburg; old no. 432 (D.III S. Mandan Coll. 1832)." B&S, BN: Mandan, pre-1832. Now CMC, cat.no. V-H-2.

{*XLVIII. From a Private Collection, Berlin (CFF)*}

{Acquired by A. Speyer, Sr. before World War II.}

238 Robe, bison skin. F: no information. B&S: Crow, before 1845. Now EMB, cat.no. IV B 12835, acquired from A. Speyer, Jr. in 1969 (Hartmann 1973: 304–305); also said to be from Duke of Gotha collection (XXIX above) (Bolz and Sanner 1999: 100–101).

{*XLIX. M. L. J. Lemaire, Amsterdam (CFF)*}

{Acquired probably before World War II by A. Speyer, Sr. from the well-known dealer Lemaire.}

246 (24) Pair of moccasins. F: no information; BN: from an Amsterdam dealer {Lemaire}, who acquired it in England. B&S: Plains Cree, pre-1840. Now CMC, cat.no. V-H-3; BN: Mandan-Hidatsa type, early 19th c.

aj {Man's shirt and leggings (Fig. 12). Obtained from Lemaire, who probably had it from Fred North (cp. XV above). Now VSMRM, cat.no. V Am 2651ab, acquired from A. Speyer, Jr. in 1965; said to have been collected in 1827 by "Lord Elvenstone [i.e., Elphinstone[68]]" among the "Teton of the Burnt Woods." Cp. Feest (1999: 51).}

L. Heyink, collector in Rotterdam[69]

{Acquired by A. Speyer, Jr.}
112 Pouch. F: bought at auction in Holland; B: gotten by exchange about 1966 from Heyink, collector in Rotterdam, who got it at auction in Holland. Brasser helped arrange the exchange. B&S: *Ottawa, ca. 1800.*

{*LI. Musée Royal de l'Afrique Centrale, Tervuren (CFF)*}

{Acquired by A. Speyer, Jr.}
101 {Husk face. B&S: *Iroquois, c. 1860.* Originally collected in 1929 among the Onondaga by Frans Olbrechts.[70] Now VUZ, cat.no. 13598, acquired from Speyer in 1970.}

LII. Dealer(s) in Brussels (BN)

{Acquired in 1960s by A. Speyer, Jr. from two different non-specialized dealers in Brussels.}
(156) Birchbark container. Now CMC, cat.no. III-H-436; BN: Huron type, ca. 1850.
ak {Double knifecase. Now CMC, cat.no. III-N-36; cataloged as "Menominee type, 1800." Cp. Feest and Kasprycki, this volume, fig. 5. According to A. Speyer, Jr., the dealer thought the piece to be North African.}

{*LIII. Charles Ratton, Paris (CFF)*}

{Acquired by A. Speyer, Sr.}
69–71 Three dolls (man, woman, baby in cradleboard). F: no information; S: the man has an old number, 2507.1, on his head. The cradleboard has written on the back "1788/18 Jeun lorete" and "1054c" ["18" probably for "le", influenced by the Jesuit "8"="ou"]. B&S: Jeune Lorette Huron, Quebec, 1788. Phillips (1984: 51; 1998: 86): Now CMC, cat.nos III-H-429, -430, -431.
105–108 {Three dolls and miniature cradleboard model. B&S: River Desert Algonquin, pre-1779; *Maniwaki.* Acquired by A. Speyer, Sr. Now CMC.}
120 (54) Cradleboard decoration. F; BN: from a French collection, marked "Georgian Bay" on an old label. B&S: *Ottawa, pre-1800.* Now CMC, cat.no. III-G-848; BN: Ojibwa type, 18th c.

LIV. An old French mission in the St. Augustine area of Quebec (Burnham 1992: 197; Bolz and Sanner 1999: 199)

{Acquired in the 1960s by A. Speyer, Jr.}
al Man's coat. Now EMB, cat.no. 12822, acquired from A. Speyer, Jr. in 1967. Montagnais-Naskapi, Quebec-Labrador, probably about 1800.

LV. Museum of the American Indian, Heye Foundation, New York

{Acquired in the 1960s from Stolper Galleries by A. Speyer, Jr.[71]}
57 (154) Sealskin coat. F: Speyer purchased it from Stolper; came from MAI-HF, cat.no. 3/4669; BN: "Acquired from

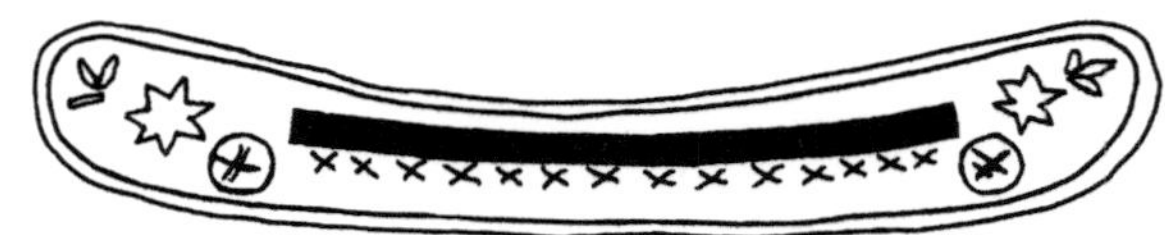

Fig. 13 Model canoe (LVII 55), birchbark, quill decorated, no thwarts. Length 50.5 cm. "Indians from the St. Lawrence River, 1795"; Micmac, 1850–1865. After a drawing by William C. Sturtevant.

a dealer." B&S: Huron, *ca. 1845.* Now CMC, cat.no. III-H-424; BN: Huron, ca. 1845.

LVI. Floyd Schulz Collection of Kansas Potawatomi material (BN)

197 (34) Prescription stick. F: with illegible scratched inscription (MAYSK?); BN: acquired from a dealer in Munich, formerly part of Schulz collection. {Acquired in the 1960s by A. Speyer, Jr. not directly from dealer but from Munich collector, probably Hermann Vonbank.} B&S: Pawnee, 1835; F: not Pawnee, more likely Potawatomi or related tribe. Now CMC, cat.no. III-Q-1; BN: Prairie Potawatomi, ca. 1800.

LVII. Source Unknown

There are 113 items listed in B&S for which no source is known to me. Below are listed the items in this category for which more information is at hand than appears in B&S.
13 {Belt, quill-decorated. B&S: Slave, pre-1830. Acquired by A. Speyer, Sr. Now CMC, cat.no. VI-N-114 (Thompson 1994: 18): "Slavey type, pre-1850."}
15 Knee bands, quill-decorated. F: no information. B&S: *Slave, before 1840.* {Acquired by A. Speyer, Sr.} Now EMB {cat.no. 12826}, acquired from Speyer in 1969 (Bolz and Sanner 1999: 199).
22 {Knee band, quill-decorated. B&S: Great Slave Lake, pre-1840; *Dogrib.* Acquired by A. Speyer, Jr. Now CMC, cat.no. VI-E-110 (Thompson 1994: 34): "Dogrib, Slavey, or Chipewyan type, circa 1850."}
37* {Burdenstrap with woven quillwork. B&S: *Red River Ojibwa, pre-1840.* Now EMB, cat.no. IV B 12828, acquired from A. Speyer, Jr. in 1969.}
49 {Quilled chair seat. B&S: Indians from St. Lawrence River, 1792, *Micmac.* Acquired by A. Speyer, Jr. Now DLO, cat.no. 12161, obtained from A. Speyer, Jr. in 1971; cp. Völger (1976: 4.50.21).}
53* {Oval box, quill-decorated. B&S: Micmac, St. Lawrence, pre-1820. Acquired by A. Speyer, Jr. Now VUZ,

68. {Lord Elphinstone, after whom Elphinstone, MB, was named, visited western Canada only in 1879–80—an unlikely place and time to acquire a Lakota dress from the 1820s. Lord Mountstuart Elphinstone (1779–1875), the former governor of Bombay left his post for Europe in 1827. It is not known whether he visited North America in the same year.}
69. {On Jacobus Heijink (1906–1997), cp. Wojciechowski (1997).}
70. {The Belgian anthropologist Frans M. Olbrechts collected forty-two False Faces and Husk Faces among the Onondaga in 1929, most of which are today in Belgian museums. Cp. Holsbeke (1996: 92).}
71. {Acquired together with several Plains shirts, one of which was later traded to the Hermann Vonbank collection.}

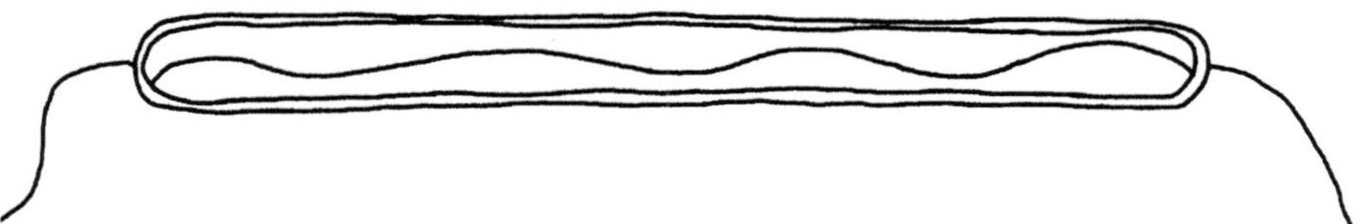

Fig. 14 Cloth sash (LVII 85), white cloth with embroidered design in red wool, edged with 0.5 cm wide blue cloth appliqued band with large white beads on each side. Length without ties 142 cm, width 6.5 cm. "Iroquois, before 1850." After a drawing by William C. Sturtevant.

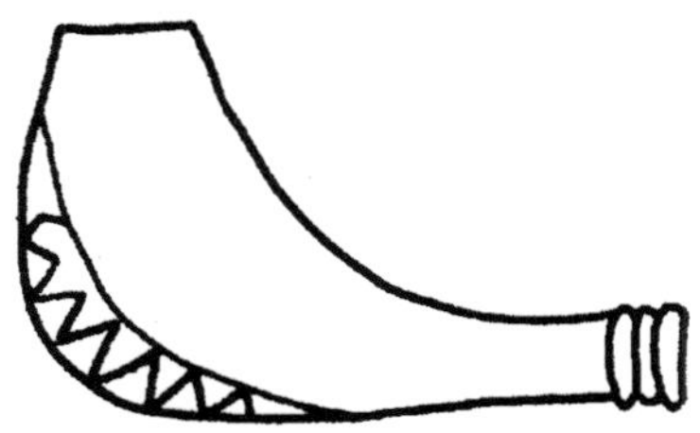

Fig. 15 Catlinite pipe bowl (LVII 96), thin blade with incised design. "Seneca, *pre-1800*." Length 7.7 cm. After a drawing by William C. Sturtevant.

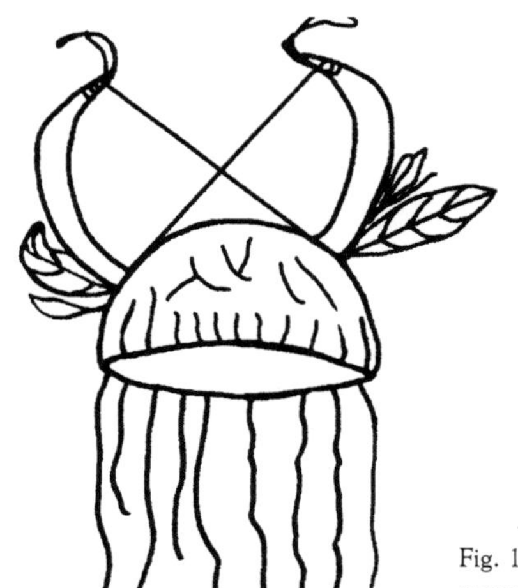

Fig. 16 Headdress (LVII 207), leather, with two thinned buffalo horns. "Teton Dakota, *pre-1860*." Height 33 cm. After a drawing by William C. Sturtevant.

Fig. 17 Ball stick (LVII 187), curved head lashed to shaft. Length 75.5 cm. "Great Lakes, 1849." After a drawing by William C. Sturtevant.

cat.no. 13339, acquired from Speyer in 1969. Ruth Whitehead, in VUZ files: "c. 1860."}

55* Canoe model (Fig. 13). F: no information. {Acquired by A. Speyer, Jr. Now VUZ, cat.no. 13340, obtained from Speyer in 1969; Ruth Whitehead, in VUZ files: "c. 1850–65."} B&S: Indians from the St. Lawrence River, 1795; *Micmac*.

60 {Pair of moccasins. B&S: Huron, pre-1810. Acquired by A. Speyer, Jr., perhaps from L. Bretschneider (cp. LVII 67). Now VUZ, cat.no. 13341, acquired from Speyer in 1969.}

61 {Moosehair-appliqué purse. B&S: Huron, pre-1810. Acquired by A. Speyer, Jr. at Frankfurt flea market. Now DLO, cat.no. 14086, gift from A. Speyer, Jr. in 1986.}

67* {Pair of children's moccasins. B&S: Huron, pre-1850. Acquired by Arthur Speyer, Jr. from Ludwig Bretschneider, a dealer in Munich, as part of a lot of various moccasins Bretschneider had obtained from a collection in Sweden, including perhaps also LVII 60.}

72 (165) {Caribou leg pouch. B&S: Lorette Huron, 1843. Now CMC III-H-437; BN: Huron type, 1843.}

85 Sash (Fig. 14). F: no information. {Acquired by A. Speyer, Sr.} B&S: Iroquois, before 1840; *Seneca*.

93 {Four arrows, one of them a blunt bird arrow. B&S: *Iroquois and Southeastern tribes, pre-1860*. Acquired by A. Speyer, Sr. before 1928.}[72]

96* Pipe bowl (Fig. 15). F: no information. B&S: Seneca, *pre-1800*.

97 Wampum belt. F: no information. B&S: Has several old inscriptions, in German, Dutch, French, and Latin. Dutch and French wording not given. German (Sturtevant translation): "Belt of white and purple Turkish [turquoise] shells, called wampum, of the five tribes in North America, which they use in public affairs"; Latin (reading of B&S improved by Sturtevant and Feest, translation by Sturtevant and Ives Goddard): "A belt. Or belt from little pieces of shell called Wampum, here joined together. From this the inhabitants of the Carolinas and elsewhere often, like money dedicated to saints, in holy public conferences [illegible] show (good) faith. D. W. Bell. About such a belt see Lawson Hist. Catal. [i.e., Carol.] 194." [This is a reference to *A New Voyage to Carolina*, by John Lawson, London, 1709, which contains a good description of wampum beads used as money and on a string as a necklace, but does not mention wampum belts.] {Third label is in German, Dutch, and French: "[German only: Bone Belt of the Iroquois."]} B&S: Iroquois, before 1760; *Tuscarora*.[73] {Now CMC.}

100 (62) {Falseface mask. B&S: Iroquois, 1850; *Cayuga or Onondaga*. Now CMC III-I-1317; BN: Iroquois, ca. 1850.}

72. {Almost certainly from the Ducal cabinet in Gotha (XXIX above), where the catalog lists "four arrows of various kinds, one to shoot birds, one to shoot fish," donated prior to 1869 (and after 1830) by Mr. Fleischmann, whose son had collected them in North America. Said to have been collected among the Comanche.}

73. {Identified by A. Speyer, Jr. in August 2000 on the basis of notes accompanying a photograph as from the collection of the Grand Duke of Hessen-Darmstadt (XXVIII above). A knife case from the Darmstadt collection has a similar Latin label glued to its back (Feest in press), in a handwriting that is similar, but may not be identical to the one on the belt. Alternately, the belt may be from the Ducal cabinet in Gotha (XXIX above), where the catalog lists a wampum belt acquired before 1830, which is no longer in the collection.}

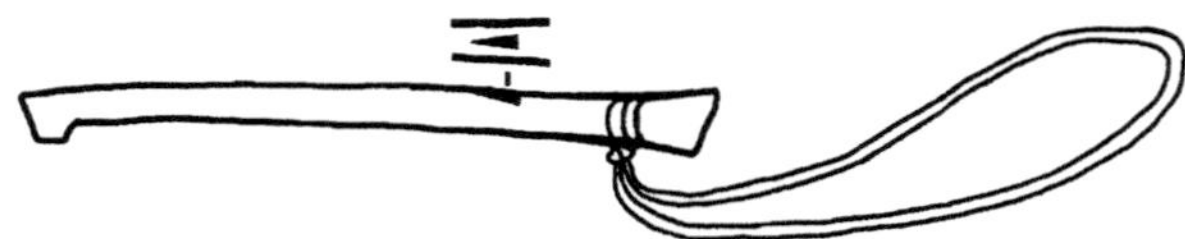

Fig. 18 Bone whistle (LVII 234), undecorated bone with single whistle hole, with white, tanned leather loop. Length 21.5 cm. "Mandan, before 1841." After a drawing by William C. Sturtevant.

116 {Knife sheath. B&S: *Ottawa or Ojibwa, pre-1830.* Published in 1982 as part of the Wellington collection (Ewing 1982: 150), marked "1102."}

118 (51) {Ball-headed club. B&S: *Ottawa, pre-1840.* Acquired by A. Speyer, Jr. between 1959 und 1967. Now CMC III-X-235; BN: Great Lakes, pre-1840.}

128 (20) {Moccasins. B&S: *Ojibwa,* pre-1790. Now CMC III-X-232; BN: Eastern Great Lakes, late 18th c.}

163 {Ball-headed club. B&S: Ojibwa, pre-1792. Acquired by A. Speyer, Sr. Reported by Ewing (1982: 141) as part of the Wellington collection.}

164 {Gunstock club. B&S: *Chippewa,* pre-1832. Acquired by A. Speyer, Sr.}

168 (58) Headdress. F: no information; {CFF: acquired by A. Speyer, Sr. before 1928 (cp. Fig. 1)}. B&S, BN: Ojibwa, pre-1845. Now CMC, cat.no. III-G-827.[74]

186 (128) {Gunstock club. B&S, BN: Winnebago, pre-1835. Acquired by A. Speyer, Sr. Now CMC III-O-3.}

187* Ball stick (Fig. 17). F: no information. {Acquired by A. Speyer, Sr.} B&S: Great Lakes, 1849; *Winnebago.*

188* {Quilled bark box. B&S: Menomini, pre-1840. Now CMC III-N-37. Cp. Phillips, this volume, fig. 6.}

200* (31) {Roach. B&S, BN: Omaha, pre-1850. Now CMC V-Q-2.}

207* Headdress (Fig. 16). F: no information. B&S: Teton Dakota, *pre-1860.* {Acquired by A. Speyer, Sr.}

217 {Bow. B&S: Dakota, *pre-1850.* Note in A. Speyer, Jr.'s records says: "2.1488, Slg. Scheurlen."}

219* Lasso. F: no information. S: A simple cord, multiple strand round braid, elements slightly S-twisted. B&S: *Northern Plains,* pre-1840. {Acquired by A. Speyer, Sr.}

234* Bone whistle (Fig. 18). F: no information. B&S: Mandan, pre-1841. {Acquired by A. Speyer, Sr.}

239 Man's shirt. F: no information; T: he saw it in Speyer's house in 1963–1964; at that time Speyer had no tribal attribution, and Taylor told him probably Crow. B&S: Crow, pre-1840. F: More likely Yanktonai, not Crow (compare with the Clark collection, ca. 1865, at Minnesota Historical Society). {Acquired by A. Speyer, Sr. before 1928 (cp. Fig. 1).}[75]

242 (42) {Shield and shield cover. B&S, BN: Crow, pre-1842. Acquired by A. Speyer, Sr. before 1928. Now CMC V-L-28.}

244 (47) {Rock medicine. B&S, BN: Crow, ca. 1860. Now CMC V-L-26.}

248 {Steatite pipe bowl with lead and catlinite inlays. B&S: Cree Indians, North-West; *Plains Cree, pre-1840.* Now in Bründl collection (Bründl 1999: 81).}

258* (4) {Skin scaper. B&S, BN: Blackfoot (type), ca. 1860. Now CMC V-B-416.}

260a* (10) {Mountain sheep horn ladle. B&S, BN: Blackfoot (type), ca. 1860. Now CMC V-B-421.}

(3) {Snowshoes. BN: Ojibwa type, 19th c. Now CMC III-G-821.}

(115) {Silver armband. BN: Iroquois, pre-1792. Now CMC III-1-1326.}

(132) {Cloth leggings with ribbon appliqué. A. Speyer, Jr. believes that this piece came from the J. G. Schwarz collection at MVW, but no such item was ever traded. Now CMC, cat.no. III-X-251; BN: Great Lakes, 19th c..}

(134) {Pipe bowl. BN: Eastern Canada, early 19th c. Now CMC, cat.no. III-X-252.}

(150) {Garter pendant. BN: Eastern Great Lakes, late 18th c. Now CMC III-X-258.}

(166) {Birchbark box. BN: Huron type, ca. 1850. Now CMC, cat.no. III-H-438.}

(191) {Mittens. BN: Eastern Sioux type, ca. 1840. Now CMC, cat.no. V-E-293.}

am Mirror. For signalling. {Acquired by A. Speyer, Sr. before 1928.} Now EMB, cat.no. IV B 12808, acquired from A. Speyer, Jr. in 1966. "Attributed to Plains Ojibwa, after 1870" (Hartmann 1973: 343).[76]

an Effigy pipe. Listed as from Arthur Speyer in Vincent et al. (2000: 32). No information on Speyer's source. From Speyer it passed to Ralph Nash (London), then to Walter Randel Works of Art (New York), then to Alice Kaplan (New York), then to Jean K. Davidson (New York), then to Thaw collection, Cooperstown, NY, where it is catalog number T718. Middle Woodland period, TN-AL border.

ao Man's coat. Now EMB, cat.no. IV B 12730, acquired from A. Speyer, Jr. in 1961 (Bolz and Sanner 1999: 199; Burnham 1992: 165). "Montagnais-Naskapi, Quebec-Labrador, probably about 1800" (Burnham 1992: 165).

ap Man's coat. Now DLO, cat.no. 11569 {acquired from A. Speyer, Jr. in 1964}: "Montagnais-Naskapi, Quebec-Labrador, probably about 1800" (Burnham 1992: 194).

aq {Trousers. Before 1967 at DLO, cat.no. 11245, acquired from A. Speyer, Jr. in 1962: "Kutchin, pre-1821," said to have been from the Wrangell/Rossillon collection at MVF, which is incorrect. Exchanged in 1968 via A. Speyer, Jr. to VSMRM, cat.no. Am 3219b: "Alaska, 1830, ex Wrangell collection."}

ar {Man's shirt. Now VSMRM, cat.no. 3219a, acquired from Speyer in 1968: "Alaska, 1830, ex Wrangell collection." Attribution to Wrangell/Rossillon collection at MVF is incorrect.}

as {Knife sheath. Now CMC, cat.no.VI-Y-1: formerly Arthur Speyer collection: "Tanaina, Alaska, pre-1821" (Harrison 1987: 93, #S8).}

at {Man's coat. Now VSMRM, cat.no. 3105, acquired from Speyer in 1966: "Naskapi."}

74. {Almost certainly from the Ducal cabinet in Gotha (XXIX above), where the catalog lists a "cap with eagle feathers and [deleted: squirrel] fur." Documentation as in note 72 above.}

75. {Almost certainly from the Ducal cabinet in Gotha (XXIX above), where the catalog lists a "coat of deerskin, decorated with scalps." Documentation as in note 72 above.}

76. {Almost certainly from the Ducal cabinet in Gotha (XXIX above), where the catalog lists "a small round mirror." Documentation as in note 72 above.}

au {Quilled pouch. Now RJMK, cat.no. 49719, acquired from A. Speyer, Jr. in 1967: "Athabaska Lake," later changed to "Cree or Chipewyan, late 18th c." (Boden 1995: 201, color pl. XXV).}

av {Man's shirt. Now AMF, cat.no. III-1944, acquired from A. Speyer, Jr. in 1967: "Crow."}

aw {Saddle blanket. Acquired by A. Speyer, Sr. before 1928 (cp. Fig. 1). Now DLO, cat.no. 9379, acquired from A. Speyer, Sr. in 1950: "Crow, ca. 1870." Cp. Völger (1976: 4.41.01).}

ax {Quilled pouch. Now DLO, cat.no. 12174, acquired from A. Speyer. Jr. in 1971: "[Lake Winnipeg] Cree, ca. 1850." Cp. Völger (1976: 4.20.30).}

ay Club with stone head. Now EMB, cat.no. IV B 12750, acquired from A. Speyer, Jr. in 1963. "Probably southern Plains" (Hartmann 1973: 342).

az {Man's coat, Naskapi. Now HMV, cat.no. 65.41:1, acquired from A. Speyer, Jr. in 1965.}

ba {Skunk skin bag (cp. Fig. 1). Now Bründl collection (Bründl 1999: 77): "Winnebago, before 1850."}[77]

bb {Heart-shaped pin cushion, moosehair on birchbark. "Huron style," collected between 1851 and 1853 by Martin Pitzer, presumably among the Ottawa of Michigan. Cp. Pitzer (1854: 23, no. 40): *"jabonigan-mashkibodens."* Acquired by A. Speyer, Sr., perhaps from monastery in Herzogenburg, before the Pitzer collection came to MVW in 1948 (cp. XXV 119). Now CMC.}

Index by tribe (culture) or region

References are to the source collection (the roman numeral) and the object (by the marginal number or letter). Provenience given in the paragraph describing the source is indicated as, for example, I intro.

77. {Almost certainly from the Ducal cabinet in Gotha (XXIX above), where the catalog lists "a tobacco pouch of the fur of a skunk." Documentation as in note 72 above.}

References Cited

{Anonymous
n.d. *Ethnographische Sammlung. Gesammelt von Sr. königl. Hoheit Herzog Paul von Würtemberg.* n.p.: August Kranzbühler.}

Benndorf, Helga and Arthur Speyer
1968 *Indianer Nordamerikas 1760–1860. Aus der Sammlung Speyer.* Offenbach am Main: Deutsches Ledermuseum.

{Boden, Gertrud
1995 *Nordamerika. Die Sammlung des Rautenstrauch-Joest-Museums.* Ethnologica, NF 20. Köln: Rautenstrauch-Joest-Museum.}

Bolz, Peter
1995 "Ethnographische Gegenstände aus Nord-America": Die Sammlung des Prinzen zu Wied im Museum für Völkerkunde Berlin. In: Volker Heidt and Andreas Bitz (eds.), *Maximilian Prinz zu Wied: Jäger, Reisender, Naturforscher* (Fauna und Flora in Rheinland-Pfalz, Zeitschrift für Naturschutz, Beiheft 17, Landau), 191–214.

Bolz, Peter and Hans-Ulrich Sanner
1999 *Native American Art: The Collections of the Ethnological Museum Berlin.* Ann Leslie Davis, transl. Berlin: Staatliche Museen zu Berlin—Preußischer Kulturbesitz.

{Bompas, William Carpenter
1889 *Lessons and Prayers in the Tenni or Slavi Language of the Indians of MacKenzie River, in the North-West Territory of Canada.* [London]: Society for Promoting Christian Knowledge.}

Brasser, Ted J.
1976 *"Bo'jou, Neejee!" Profiles of Canadian Indian Art.* Ottawa, ON: National Museum of Man, [and] Montreal, QC—Kingston, ON: McGill-Queen's University Press.

{Bründl, Heinz J.
1999 *Mythos Wild West. Die Sammlung Bründl—The Bründl Collection.* Zell: Winona GmbH.}

{Burch, Wanda
1990 Sir William Johnson's Cabinet of Curiosities. *New York History* 71(3): 261–282.}

Burnham, Dorothy K.
1992 *To Please the Caribou: Painted Caribou-Skin Coats Worn by the Naskapi, Montagnais, and Cree Hunters of the Quebec-Labrador Peninsula.* Toronto, ON: Royal Ontario Museum.

{Cody, H. A.
1908 *An Apostle of the North. Memoirs of the Right Reverend William Carpenter Bompas.* New York, NY: E. P. Dutton.}

Dietschy, Hans
1939 Die amerikanischen Keulen und Holzschwerter. *Internationales Archiv für Ethnographie* 37: 87–205.

{Dohrmann, Alke and Claus Deimel
2000 *Kunstwerke der Indianer Nordamerikas. Arktische Regionen und Nordwestküste.* Hannover: Niedersächsisches Landesmuseum Hannover.}

Duncan, Kate
2000 *1001 Curious Things: Ye Olde Curiosity Shop and Native American Art*. Seattle, WA: University of Washington Press.
{Eberhard, Hugo
1956 (ed.) *Deutsches Ledermuseum, angeschlossen Deutsches Schuhmuseum*. Offenbach a.M.: Graphische Werkstätte.}
{Ewing, Douglas C.
1982 *Pleasing the Spirits. A Catalogue of a Collection of American Indian Art*. New York, NY: Ghylen Press.}
Feder, Norman
1964 *Art of the Eastern Plains Indians*. New York, NY: Brooklyn Museum.
1969 Letters to William C. Sturtevant, 9 September and 17 September. Manuscripts, in Sturtevant's possession.
Feest, Christian F.
1968a [Review of Benndorf and Speyer 1968]. *Archiv für Völkerkunde* 22: 144–147.
{1968b *Indianer Nordamerikas*. Wien: Museum für Völkerkunde.}
{1993 European Collecting of American Indian Artefacts and Art. *Journal of the History of Collections* 5(1): 1–11.}
{1997 Tab Pouches of Northeastern North America. *American Indian Art Magazine* 22(4): 34–47, 120.}
{1998 Transformations of a Mask: Confidential Intelligence from the Lifeway of Things. *Baessler-Archiv*, N.F. 46(2): 255–293.}
{1999 (ed.) *Sitting Bull. "Der letzte Indianer."* Darmstadt: Hessisches Landesmuseum.}
{in press Quilled Knifecases from Northeastern North America.}
{Feest, Christian F. and Sylvia S. Kasprycki
1993 *Über/Lebenskunst nordamerikanischer Indianer*. Wien: Museum für Völkerkunde.}
1999 *Peoples of the Twilight. European Views of Native Minnesota, 1823 to 1862*. Afton, MN: Afton Historical Society Press.}
{Force, Roland W. and Maryanne Force
1971 *The Fuller Collection of Pacific Artifacts*. New York, NY: Praeger.}
{Gathercole, Peter and Alison Clarke
1979 *Survey of Oceanian Collections in the United Kingdom and the Irish Republic*. n.p.: UNESCO.}
{Gerlach, Heike
1995 Der gezielte Aufbau der Sammlungen: Ankäufe von Sammlern und Händlern. In: Eva Gerhards (ed.), *Als Freiburg die Welt entdeckte. 100 Jahre Museum für Völkerkunde* (Freiburg: Promo Verlag), 146–163.}
{Haberland, Wolfgang
1971 *Die Kunst des indianischen Amerika*. Zürich: Museum Rietberg.}
Harrison, Julia D.
1987 (intr.) *The Spirit Sings: Artistic Traditions of Canada's First Peoples: A Catalogue of the Exhibition*. Toronto, ON [—Calgary, AB]: McClelland and Stewart—Glenbow Museum.
Hartmann, Horst
1973 *Die Plains- und Prärie Indianer Nordamerikas*. Veröffentlichungen des Museums für Völkerkunde Berlin, N.F. 22, Abteilung Amerikanische Naturvölker 2. Berlin.
Holm, Bill
1992 Four Bear's Shirt: Some Problems with the Smithsonian Catlin Collection. In: George P. Horse Capture and Suzanne G. Tyler (eds.), *Artifacts/Artifakes: The Proceedings of the 1984 Plains Indian Seminar* (Cody, WY: Buffalo Bill Historical Center), 43–59.
{Holsbeke, Mireille
1996 Frans M. Olbrechts and his Ethnographical Research in North America. In: M. Holsbeke, *The Object as Mediator* (Antwerp: Etnografisch Museum Antwerp), 92.}
{Hotz, Gottfried
1975 *Indianer Nordamerikas. Katalog zur Sammlung Hotz der Stadt Zürich*. Zürich: Schulamt.}
{Kaemlein, Wilma R.
1967 *An Inventory of Southwestern American Indian Specimens in European Museums*. Tucson, AZ: Arizona State Museum.}
{Kasprycki, Sylvia S.
1997 Quilled Drawstring Pouches of the Northeastern Woodands. *American Indian Art Magazine* 22(3): 64–75.
in press A Devout Collector: Johann Georg Schwarz and Nineteenth-Century Menominee Art. In: J. C. H. King and H. Lidchi (eds.), *Woodlands Indian Art* (London: British Museum Press).}
{Klann, Kilian
1999 *Die Sammlung indianischer Ethnographica aus Nordamerika des Herzog Friedrich Paul Wilhelm von Württemberg*. Wyk auf Foehr: Verlag für Amerikanistik.}
Krickeberg, Walter
1954 Ältere Ethnographica aus Nordamerika im Berliner Museum für Völkerkunde. *Baessler-Archiv*, N.F. 2.
{Luden, Heinrich
1828 (ed.) *Reise Sr. Hoheit des Herzogs Bernhard zu Sachsen-Weimar-Eisenach durch Nord-Amerika in den Jahren 1825 und 1826*. Weimar: Wilhelm Hoffmann.}
{Müller, Claudius C.
1980 400 Jahre Sammeln und Reisen der Wittelsbacher. In: C. C. Müller (ed.), *Wittelsbach und Bayern. 400 Jahre Sammeln und Reisen. Außereuropäische Kulturen* (München: Hirmer Verlag), 11–33.}
Oswald, Arthur
1961 Sniterton Hall, Derbyshire: the Home of Mr. and Mrs. Bagshawe. *Country Life* 2 February 1961: 228–231.
Painter, John W.
[1991] *American Indian Artifacts: The John Painter Collection*. Cincinnati, OH: George Tassian Organization, Inc.
{Phelps, Steven
1976 *Art and Artefacts of the Pacific, Africa and the Americas: The James Hooper Collection*. London: Hutchinson.}
Phillips, Ruth B.
{1984 *Patterns of Power. The Jasper Grant Collection and*

Great Lakes Indian Art of the Early Nineteenth Century. Kleinburg, ON: The McMichael Canadian Collection.}

1998 *Trading Identities: The Souvenir in Native North American Art from the Northeast, 1700–1900.* Seattle, WA—London: University of Washington Press [and] Montreal, QC—Kingston, ON: McGill-Queen's University Press.

{Pitzer, Martin

1854 *Verzeichniß der Gegenstände und Arbeiten eines Indianer-Stammes im nördlichsten Amerika.* München: J. G. Weiß'sche Universitäts-Buchdruckerei.}

{Rousselot, Jean-Loup

1997 Weltausstellung, Eisenbahn und Indianer: Prinzessin Therese in Nordamerika. In: H. Bußmann and E. Neukum-Fichtner (eds.), *"Ich bleibe ein Wesen eigener Art." Prinzessin Therese von Bayern* (München: Ludwig Maximilians Universität), 72–81.}

{Speyer, Arthur

1993 Hundert Jahre völkerkundliche Sammlungen Arthur Speyer (1893–1993). Unpublished manuscript in its author's possession.}

{Stanley, George F. G.

1955 (ed.) *In Search of the Magnetic North: A Soldier-Surveyor's Letters from the North-west, 1843–1844.* Toronto, ON: Macmillan.}

Stolpe, Hjalmar

1897 Studies in American Ornamental Art. *Proceedings of the Tenth International Congress of Americanists*: 79–112. Stockholm.

{Thompson, Judy

1977 *The North American Indian Collection. A Catalogue.* Berne: Historical Museum.

1994 *From the Land. Two Hundred Years of Dene Clothing.* Hull, QC: Canadian Museum of Civilization.}

Vatter, Ernst

1925 Ein bemaltes Büffelfell und andere seltene amerikanische Ethnographica im Städt. Völkermuseum zu Frankfurt a. M. In: *Festschrift zur Feier des 25jährigen Bestehens der Frankfurter Gesellschaft für Anthropologie, Ethnologie und Urgeschichte* (Abhandlungen zur Anthropologie, Ethnologie und Urgeschichte 2, Frankfurt am Main), 75–112.

Vincent, Gilbert et al.

2000 *Art of the North American Indians: The Thaw Collection.* Cooperstown, NY: Fenimore Art Museum [—Seattle, WA]: University of Washington Press.

[Völger, Gisela]

1976 *Indianer Nordamerikas, Zirkumpolare Völker.* Deutsches Ledermuseum Katalog 4. Offenbach am Main.

{Wied, Maximilian Prinz zu

1839–1841 *Reise in das Innere Nord-America 1832–34.* 2 vols. and atlas. Koblenz: J. Hoelscher.}

{Wilson, Daniel

1857 *Pipes and Tobacco. An Ethnological Sketch.* Toronto, ON.}

{Wojciechowski, Frans L.

1997 In Memoriam Jacobus Heijink (1906–1997). *De Kiva* 34(4): 110–117.}

{Wright, Robin C.

1987 The Traveling Exhibition of Captain Samuel Hadlock, Jr.: Eskimos in Europe, 1822–1826. In: C. F. Feest (ed.), *Indians and Europe. An Interdisciplinary Collection of Essays* (Aachen: Rader; reprinted Lincoln, NE 1999: University of Nebraska Press), 215–233.}

{Zielinski, Erich

1971 *Die Prärie-Indianer Nordamerikas 1840–1890.* Berlin: Amerika Haus Berlin.}

Comparative Evidence, Critical Reasoning, and the Identification of Styles
A (Knife)Case in Point

Christian F. Feest and Sylvia S. Kasprycki

Artifacts—things made by people to serve both functional and emotional needs according to learned and socially accepted standards—are our only immediate (literally: unmediated) sources for the study of most of the historic and prehistoric cultures of the world. In the case of prehistoric cultures, they are virtually our only source, but even many aspects of historic cultures, for which we generally also have (mediated) written and pictorial information, are accessible today exclusively through the study of artifacts. Due to the peculiar nature of objects, the only information that can be derived from them directly relates to their physical properties, such as shape, color, or mass; broadly based analogy allows inferences on the technologies used in their manufacture and to some extent also on their functions. Culturally specific meaning encoded in artifacts is generally inaccessible by visual inspection alone, because the decoding (even of inherently ambiguous and polysemic symbolic codes) can ultimately be based only on an independently transmitted knowledge of the system. Western scholarship's propensity for meaning is one of the reasons for its frequent disenchantment with artifactual sources, although the study of prehistoric archaeology has often been cited as an example for what may be learned from the inspection of man-made objects. Art history provides another prominent case.

The main reason for the gross neglect of the study of artifacts historically collected from Native America, however, lies in another peculiar feature of objects. The collecting of artifacts always entails their alienation from the cultural context which defines their significance. Any attempt to use as cultural documents those objects now artificially preserved in Western museums must therefore rest upon an interpretive process aimed at restoring as much of the original context as possible. Since cultures are known to be in a state of perpetual adaptation to their changing natural and social environments, any reasonably successful attempt to recontextualize artifacts has to be based on a profound knowledge of the historical ethnography of the makers and users of the artifacts to be studied. The reconstruction of historical ethnographies of Native American cultures is still in its infancy, because the standard descriptive accounts assembled by anthropologists on the basis of fieldwork mostly done between the 1880s and the 1920s were somewhat naively assumed to depict a largely static "traditional" culture before its degeneration caused by the evil forces of acculturation.

Objects from periods significantly predating the standard ethnographic accounts may make no sense when viewed in the context of the latter. Knifecases, for example, suspended from the neck to hold hunting and scalping knives, were no longer used by the Iroquois when Lewis Henry Morgan published his classic account of Iroquois culture in 1851, because scalping had ceased with the end of armed conflicts, hunting had lost much of its former importance for the reservation communities, and styles of dress had changed.

Christian F. Feest is Professor of Anthropology at the Johann Wolfgang Goethe-Universität in Frankfurt am Main. His published work on Native American history, anthropology, and art includes *Native Arts of North America* ([2]1992), *Indians and Europe* (ed., [2]1999), *Beseelte Welten. Die Religionen der Indianer Nordamerikas* (1998), *Sitting Bull. "Der letzte Indianer"* (ed., 1999), and *Die Kulturen der nordamerikanischen Indianer* (ed., 2000).
Author's address: Institut für Historische Ethnologie, Liebigstraße 41, D-60323 Frankfurt am Main, Germany.
Sylvia S. Kasprycki has studied anthropology at the University of Vienna and has published on various aspects of the material culture, visual arts, and ethnohistory of the Great Lakes region in particular. She has been Editorial Assistant of the *European Review of Native American Studies* since its first appearance in 1987.
Author's address: Fasanenweg 4a, D-63674 Altenstadt, Germany.
An earlier version of this paper was read at the Symposium on American Indian Art at the Fenimore Art Museum, Cooperstown, NY, 12 July 1995. The authors gratefully acknowledge the help extended to them over the years by the curators of the various museums whose objects are discussed herein.

Morgan was able to collect for the New York State Cabinet of Natural History (today's New York State Museum) two "scalping" knives, which were listed among the museum's acquisitions but not noted in Morgan's accompanying report (1850a: 61; 1850b; cp. Tooker 1994: 102, 279), yet no examples of knifecases were collected or described by him. Quillwork, which is found on all knifecases from northeastern North America, is only mentioned by Morgan (1851: 384, cp. 360) as having given way to beadwork; similarly, Morgan describes and illustrates needle books and women's beaded work bags of cloth, but quilled tobacco pouches or men's hunting bags of leather are not even noted; a partly quilled moccasin is the only such article shown (Morgan 1850b: 68, pls. 1, 11, 12). It was only in 1852 that Morgan, based on his 1850 fieldnotes taken among the Tonawanda Seneca, briefly described the Iroquois technique of work in porcupine quills (Morgan 1852: 96–97, pls. 10–12; cp. Tooker 1994: 152, 240–241). While Morgan realized that Iroquois material culture had changed since the days of Henry Hudson, his suggestion that George Catlin's "Scenes at the skirts of the Rocky Mountains" provided an adequate substitute for a historical ethnography of the Iroquois because "Indian life is essentially the same" (Morgan 1850b: 94), would hardly be found acceptable by contemporary scholars.

While the lack of good historical ethnographies presents a problem for any interpretation of historically collected artifacts, an even greater obstacle is found in the lack of documentation accompanying most of the early collections: Without reliable clues as to the place and time of an artifact's manufacture and/or use, recontextualization is impossible, even if historical ethnographies were generally available. In the old *Kunstkammer* tradition of ethnographic collecting, which prevailed until the contextual collecting strategies initiated by James Cook's Pacific voyages of exploration, and which persisted alongside the new paradigm in the collecting of non-scientific travelers, objects were valued for their age, remote origin, unusual material, or remarkable craftsmanship, rather than as documents of specific cultures (cp. Feest 1993, 1995). Lack or inadequacy of record-keeping, changes of ownership, and the inadvertent destruction of documents have led to a further loss of crucial information that would help us place the artifacts in time and space and thus ultimately into an appropriate cultural context.

Provenance and Attribution

Of the two variables just mentioned, dating poses the lesser problem. Even if it is unknown where a traveler might have obtained an artifact, it is often known when he made the trip (especially if it was to a faraway place). Even if the name of the field collector is unknown, we usually have a museum accession date providing a terminus ante quem, which sometimes may be fairly close to the collecting date. Trade goods, such as silk ribbons or specific types of glass beads, often provide useful and reliable markers of certain time periods (cp. Feder 1965: [7]–[8]). Nevertheless, it should be obvious that a documented date is always preferable to one established by inference and that every reliable date will further increase our ability to speak with certainty about the temporal distribution of artifact types or styles, which in turn may be used to date undocumented objects.

Linking an artifact to a specific group of people is incomparably more difficult. Even if we knew (as we rarely do in the case of pre-1850 objects) who had obtained an artifact when and where, we often cannot be certain of its ultimate origin. Many early pieces of Native American origin were obtained not from their makers or users, but through middlemen such as traders, who may or may not have passed along to the buyer all the collection data known to them (Feder 1971: 28–30). Just as the collecting value of an artifact might be raised by associating it correctly or not with the name of a famous person (e.g., Sitting Bull's daughter's dress), the attribution of an artifact to a specific people might be based on the latter's notoriety. Many early specimens were attributed to the Iroquois simply because they were better known than the Nipissing, the Stockbridge, or the Piankashaw.

Many early artifacts, however, are not at all associated with any cultural provenance, right or wrong, and attributions of origin are habitually made by museum curators, auction houses, and private collectors alike on the basis of comparisons with other, similar items and on the assumption of the existence of distinctive "tribal styles" (Feder 1971: 28). The reliability of such secondary attributions obviously decreases greatly if they are based on material that has no documented provenance of its own. This happens more frequently than is generally assumed, but anyone who has been around museums knows how some curators in the past have used their own ethnic labels to reduce undocumented material under their care to the needs of well-kept storage areas and meaningful displays (cp. Sturtevant 1973: 44–45, citing "Feest's Law of Museum Documentation ...: The uncertainty of an attribution increases with the square of the distance from the collector's statements").

All of this highlights the importance of the small number of reasonably well documented artifacts, which should serve the purpose that type specimens serve in natural history (cp. Feder 1965). All too many of these ethnographic type specimens, however, have never been properly identified and described; some that have been published in languages other than English have been neglected by the majority of the profession.

In his catalog *"Bo'jou Neejee!" Profiles of Canadian Indian Art*, Brasser (1976: 50) has attempted to introduce the concept of "type" to the question of the provenance of artifacts in a sense and manner that is slightly different from what has just been suggested. By "type" Brasser refers to an attribution based on comparative evidence ("arrived at through research"), which is not made explicit and thus is sometimes based on secondary attributions.[1]

More importantly, it may be asked what the label attached to such "types" really means: Can the makers (or users) of an artifact be identified beyond reasonable doubt from a comparison of its formal features? Does the distribution of certain technical or stylistic elements really coincide with the distribution of groups defined on the basis of language, kinship, territorial organization, or "ethnicity," and if so, with which of the various group characteristics mentioned? In other words: Is the "one tribe—one style" assumption tenable? Studies of ethnicity have shown that the factors by which a group of people define themselves and by which they mark their difference from one another varies widely from case to case (and sometimes also from situation to situation). Dress, for example, is generally considered a very common visual marker of identity, but whether it is the shape of the hats, the pattern on the shirts, the color of the pants, or the presence or absence of footwear can neither be predicted, nor conclusively deduced without a documented account of the symbolic codes employed. In the case of historically collected ethnographic material, such information is generally not available, and we are thus often unable to make the important distinction between "characteristic" and "distinctive" features of artifacts.

In the past, "culture" has sometimes been mechanically defined as the sum of a trait list. Current definitions favor its conceptualization as a symbolic system: Identical or closely related forms may thus be part of different cultures which impart different meaning to them. But culture is also learned behavior and thus depends upon a process of transmission largely based upon imitation, which often favors the limited distribution of formal features: The pots made by a woman are likely to be more similar to those made by her mother or sisters than to pots made in a neighboring household; yet all the pots made within a village may share elements distinguishing them from the products of another village. This hierarchy of formal relationships, allowing the identification of individual, local, regional, and pandemic styles, can alternately be seen as a network of graded distinctions, in which every point can be perceived as a center. Only when such continuous gradations abruptly terminate at clearly demarcated boundaries, can peripheries (and by implication also centers) be objectively defined. The prevalence of continuities or discontinuities will certainly be influenced by the permeability of a group, depending upon the importance of interethnic marriages, the frequency of adoptions of strangers (such as prisoners of war), or the susceptibility to exogenous cultural influences through trade, intercultural socializing, or the spread of religious movements or of fashions. As these factors may change over time, so will the gradations and boundaries.

Our goal should always be to identify the symbolic system imparting meaning to visual forms—a system commonly associated with an "ethnic" label—but our analysis of styles may lead us only to stylistic networks,

1. Following the notions championed by Norman Feder (1964, 1965), Brasser's catalog was one of a new generation of Native American art(ifact) catalogs which gave greater attention to the question of documentation and the difference between documented and attributed dates and provenances. It also followed in the footsteps of the Benndorf and Speyer (1968) catalog of the Speyer collection, of which Brasser (1976) included a major part; Benndorf and Speyer also distinguished between documentation (or rather previous attribution) and Mr. Speyer's attributions of date and provenance; it also seems to have been the first catalog of its kind making reference to comparative material, some of it unpublished. The senior author's own contemporaneous catalog of the Vienna collection (Feest 1968) likewise clearly identified provenance as either based on catalog information or secondary attribution, and qualified dates as either those of manufacture, collecting, acquisition by the museum, or other earliest documented date.

whose boundaries are often not congruent with ethnic or cultural boundaries.

An additional problem that must be taken into account in the interpretation of historically collected artifacts is that of quantitative representation. Obviously, the size of our sample will influence our ability to distinguish between the various levels in the hierarchy of styles. According to statistical expectations, a small sample will preclude the recognition of any but regional stylistic differences; yet accidental factors, such as the proximity (in the widest sense) of individual makers to the collectors' market may well favor the representation of individual rather than more generalized characteristics. Although there is no easy solution to the problem, it does help to recognize its presence.

In 1989 the junior author visited the major museums in the United States, Canada, and Europe (as well as many minor museums in Wisconsin) in order to identify and document artifacts made by or collected from the Menominee. An illuminating example drawn from this study is, for instance, provided by Menominee moccasins. Of thirty-three pairs identified, twenty-eight are beaded, four quilled, and one decorated with silk embroidery. Only three have documented dates earlier than 1860, and only four were probably made earlier than 1850. Given the unlikely assumption that in the second half of the nineteenth century every Menominee had only one pair of moccasins in his or her lifetime, the present sample would amount to less than a half percent of the Menominee moccasins once existing. For the early part of the nineteenth century, higher population figures, more extensive use of moccasins, and fewer surviving examples combine to reduce the survival rate of Menominee moccasins to less than one tenth of one percent.

The preceding discussion has suggested that the attribution of "ethnic" labels to discrete stylistic types may not be entirely meaningful—quite apart from the questionable usefulness of terms such as "Ojibwa" or "Cree" which relate to widely scattered populations representing considerable cultural variation. For purposes of conceptualization, it will always be necessary to construct hierarchically organized typologies largely based on analytical distinctions established by the viewer. It is important to remind oneself on occasion that such types are tools and not necessarily a reflection of a historical or ethnographic reality. An alternative model of representation should be based on the notion of styles as graded networks, in which horizontal relationships are stressed; by allowing a more realistic demarcation of stylistic boundaries, it may ultimately aid in the identification of stylistic cores and—with some luck—even of canons as stylistic conventions used in the encoding of meaning (cp. Kaufmann 1992: 77).

Knifecases of Northeastern North America[2]

Our major case in point illustrating the problems and possibilities encountered in applying comparative evidence and critical reasoning to the question of the attribution of styles is a rather unusual type of quilled knifecase.

Various types of quilled knifecases occur all over an area ranging from the northeastern United States to the western Canadian Subarctic. Based upon the manner in which they were worn, an often asymmetrical variety attached to the belt can be distinguished from a symmetrically shaped form suspended from the neck. Examples of the latter kind, which has its widest distribution east of the Plains, were made in several shapes and prior to the introduction of glass beads were generally decorated with porcupine quills. In northeastern North America south of the Subarctic, the manufacture of knife sheaths was abandoned about the same time as quillwork faded from general use.

The lack of written, pictorial, or artifactual evidence for knifecases in the Northeast prior to the second third of the eighteenth century suggests a post-European origin of knifecases or at least an adaptation of earlier forms to the increasing use of sharp metal knives. To some extent this suggestion is supported by linguistic evidence, which indicates the lack of common root terms for this artifact in related languages, in whose stead apparent neologisms were used. In general, written and pictorial material illustrative of shapes, decoration, and uses of knifecases is extremely wanting. Without the evidence from artifacts, little could be said about the variety of forms that once existed. But without written or pictorial documentation, the meaning of the differences observable in the material remains highly dubious.

While the written and pictorial evidence for North-

2. For a discussion of the written and pictorial sources and the material evidence on knifecases in northeastern North America, see Feest (in press).

eastern knifecases in the period between 1750 and 1800 focuses on the Iroquois and the Fox, most of our sources in the nineteenth century relate to the Menominee (cp. Kasprycki 1990: 67–71, 79–80, 94, 103–104, figs. 1–7, 21, 50, 64, 65). Much as the profusion of documentary evidence for Menominee knifecases may be gratifying, the nearly total absence of any pictorial (and apparently also written) evidence for other Native groups in the western Great Lakes region during the same period is nevertheless highly surprising.

The exception to the apparent Menominee monopoly on neck-worn knifecases in nineteenth-century illustrations is provided by an 1852 drawing by the German artist Adolf Hoeffler, who shows a double knifecase worn by the Mdewakanton Dakota leader Bad Hail (Andreas 1998: 38–39; Feest and Kasprycki 1999: 224–225; cp. Fig. 1). The knifecase clearly carries a stylized floral decoration, which we would not instantly recognize as typical for the Dakota. So the possibility remains that even this knifecase had ultimately been obtained from some of the Dakota's eastern neighbors such as the Menominee.

Quilled knifecases from northeastern North America preserved in European and American collections generally appear to date from the middle of the eighteenth to the middle of the nineteenth century. Of more than seventy knifecases from this region and period, published and unpublished, that we have studied, less than a third have a documented history before 1850, and less than ten percent of them have reasonably well documented provenances, including the Iroquois, Ottawa, Menominee, and Winnebago.

Of the symmetrical neck-worn knifecases used south of the Subarctic and east of the Plains most were decorated with appliqué quillwork. The type most commonly encountered in collections, however, is characterized by a decorative unit consisting of two narrow quill-wrapped slats of wood, bark, or rawhide(?) with additional quills interwoven to form plaited patterns. It is also the only type for which a comparative study exists, which was based upon eleven specimens (Feest 1987: 292–296).[3]

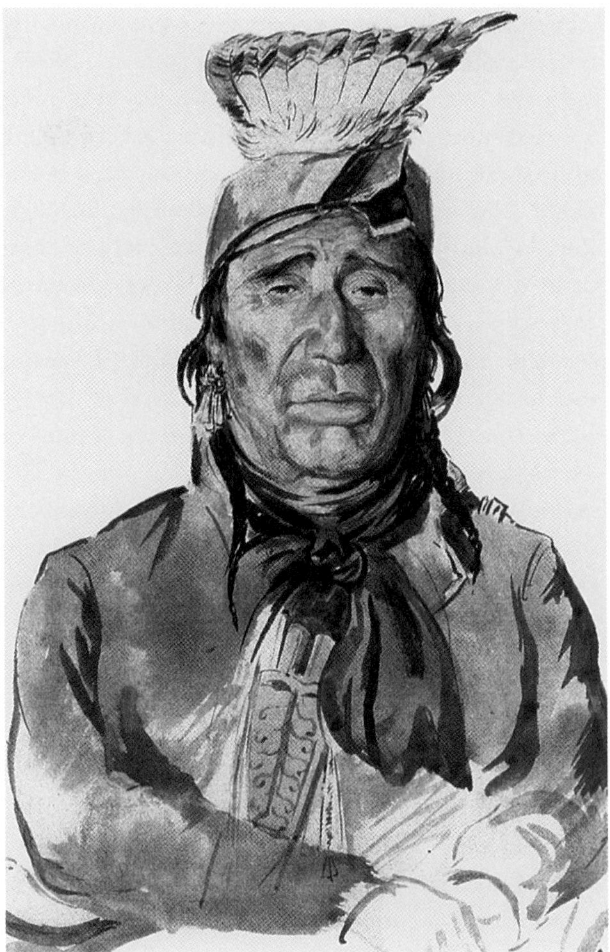

Fig. 1 Adolf Hoeffler, "Bad Hail. Chief of the Sioux Nation. Minnesota Territory October 1852." Pencil and watercolor. Privately owned. Photograph: Kunsthandlung J. P. Schneider, Jr. (Frankfurt am Main).

This "two-lane quill-wrapped"-type has commonly been attributed to the Iroquois in general or the Mohawk in particular, but the "evidence" for this attribution turns out to be very poor. The use of birchbark slats may on the contrary be seen as a fairly strong indication of an Algonquian origin. Quill-plaiting, the central design technique employed on this type, has a wide distribution from the Canadian Maritimes to the western Subarctic and cannot be regarded as especially characteristic of Iroquois work; the technique also occurs on two pairs of moccasins without provenance or known collection history (cp. Feest 1987: 293–295); the fact that the designs are different on the inside and outside flaps, respectively, may again be suggestive of a western rather than eastern Great Lakes origin.

3. Three of these have since been published for the first time or in better illustrations than were available in 1987: Dräger, Krusche, Hoffmann 1992: 30–31, 64 ("Radebeul I, II"); Phillips in Harrison et al. 1987: 50, no. W62 ("Winterthur"). Five additional examples (including a sufficiently detailed eighteenth-century drawing) can now be added (Sotheby's 1988: no. 68; Turner 1992: fig. 22; Phillips and Idiens 1994: 29, fig. 6; unpublished example in the University of British Columbia Museum of Anthropology, Vancouver, BC; drawing by Sarah Stone, ca. 1780, of a specimen then in Museum of Sir Ashton Lever in King 1993: 33, fig. 1).

In addition to the "two-lane quill-wrapped"-type, our sample includes thirty-six knifecases from the Northeast with appliqué quillwork (including two nineteenth-century drawings based on actual specimens), of which nine have documented collection dates before 1850. Almost all of their provenances (Iroquois, Huron, "Huron or Cherokee," Delaware, Menominee, Ottawa, Chippewa/Ojibwa, Cree, Dakota) are based on secondary attribution, but one Ottawa, one Menominee, and one Iroquois case are reliably documented. Most of the subtypes that may be discerned are represented by just a few examples, and about a third of the knifecases studied may be considered unique. The most common design pattern (with variations) consists of one patterned triangle band flanked by wavy lines, with either a piece of netted fringe or horizontal triangle bands along the upper edge of the front panel.

Double Knifecases

Thanks to their unusual form, double knifecases clearly stand apart from all the other knifecases so far discussed. As the name indicates, they are distinguished by combining two sheaths in one knifecase. In order to accomodate two knives, the front and back panels have to be substantially wider than those of the other types. In addition to the side seams, there is also a central seam extending along the whole length of the front panel. In most examples known, the two tips give the lower end a bilobed appearance. All of the back panels are likewise bilobed with either pointed or rounded ears. Only three of the knifecases currently have a carrying strap (consisting of a simple, undecorated string of leather and cloth, respectively), but several others show evidence of some sort of strap formerly attached to the ears. With a range from 18.9 to 29.2 cm (mean length 26.6 cm, median length 27.5 cm) this type exceeds the others not only in terms of width, but also in length.

Sixteen examples (including two early depictions of actual specimens) form the corpus on which our analysis is based. By a streak of good luck, this group includes six objects with documented dates ranging from 1823 to 1849, two of which also have reasonably reliable documentation of their provenance. In view of what was said above about other types of knifecases, it may be significant that eight of the fourteen surviving objects in this group have no European collection history, which may be taken as an indication of a more western

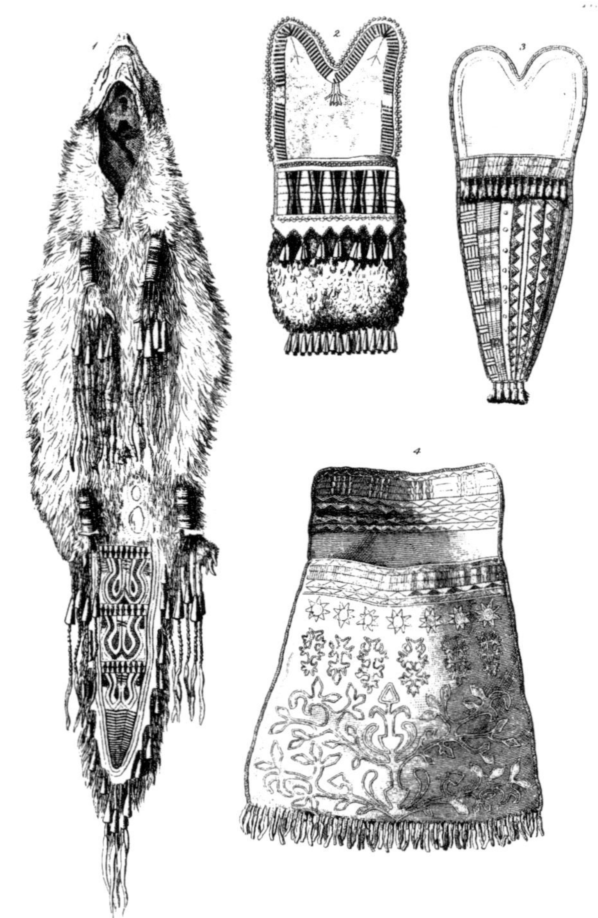

Fig. 2 T. B., "Plates of Indian Ornaments, &c I." Engraving in Beltrami (1962, 2: pl. 1). 1 is identified as "A Medicine Sack, made of the coat of an animal," 2 as "A Pouch (Sioux)," 3 as "A Knife-sheath (Cypowais)," and 4 as "A Woman's Apron-pouch."

origin and thus a longer survival of the artifact type. It is likewise typical that of these fourteen objects only five have been published so far.

The earliest published record appears on one of the lithographs in the 1828 English edition of the travel account of Giacomo Costantino Beltrami, who claimed to have discovered the sources of the Mississippi River in 1823 (Fig. 2). The plate depicts a knifecase which by its very width may be identified as a double knifecase, despite the fact that the lower end is not bilobed. Further proof for this assumption may be found by comparing its asymmetric design to that of the very similar specimens to be discussed next. It is also distinguished by a row of tin cones filled with (presumably dyed) deer hair, both below the upper edge of the front panel and at the squarely cut off lower end.

Beltrami's identification of this item as from the (southwestern) Chippewa ("Cypowais") is interesting, but should be regarded in the light of his depiction of a

Mississippian-period tobacco pipe from the collections of the New-York Historical Society as from the Sauk and of a Maori architectural ornament as from the Chippewa (Fiorentino 1990: 32, fig. 2; Feest 1996). The plates include artifacts never owned by Beltrami (such as the pipe just noted) or no longer surviving in the two Beltrami collections preserved in Italy (cp. Laurencich-Minelli 1990, Marino 1986, 1987, Vigorelli 1987a, 1987b). It is of interest, however, that plate I shows next to the double knifecase and a Dakota tobacco pouch two unprovenanced artifacts (presently not in any of the Beltrami collections) for which a Menominee attribution may be suggested. One is a trapezoidal pouch with band- and linework, a type of which several other examples are either documented as or have been attributed to the Menominee (e.g., Feest and Kasprycki 1993: 62, no. 46; Penney 1992: 70–71, pl. 4). The other is an otterskin medicine bag with a quilled tail, whose unusual design strikingly resembles a motif on a pair of quilled moccasins attributed to the Menominee (Penney 1992: 72–73, pl. 8). In May of 1823 Beltrami (1962: 172–174) encountered a group of Menominees and Winnebagos at Prairie du Chien, and it is possible that he obtained some of the objects at that point.

The earliest documented surviving double knifecase was donated in 1825–1826 by J. B. Klein to the Senckenbergische Naturforschende Gesellschaft in Frankfurt (now in the Museum für Völkerkunde, Frankfurt; Fig. 3). The old Senckenberg catalog identifies it as a "dagger with sheath" from the "Menomenos" on the "upper Mississippi." The knife, whose grooved wooden handle is visible on two older illustrations of the piece (Vatter 1925: pl. XVIII; Burland 1965: 58), has been missing since World War II. Johann Baptist August Klein (1778–1831) was a school teacher in Coblenz, a city at the confluence of the Rhine and Mosel. He was a collector of locally found Roman antiquities, a collection of which he donated to the Prussian king in Berlin. He is not known to have left his native region, let alone to have visited America (B. 1831). Given the specific nature of the documentation (which at that time would not have been available to the uninitiated), we assume that Klein had received the artifacts from someone who had the opportunity to visit a rather remote part of North America in the early 1820s, such as an explorer or a fur trader. "Upper Mississippi" refers to the region around Prairie du Chien, Wisconsin, which had been frequented by groups of Menominees since the late eighteenth century. Klein's small collection also features material attributed to the Dakota on the St. Peters River and, more importantly, a Menominee quilled slit pouch with designs matching those of the knifecase (cp. Vatter 1925: 77, pl. XVIII). The fact that the St. Peters River (today's Minnesota River) is called "St. Pierre" in the Senckenberg catalog may indicate that the original collector who supplied this information was a Frenchman. This makes sense in view of the fact that Klein's native region had been under French rule for more than twenty years.

Like the slit pouch, the front panel of the knifecase is decorated with three bands of quilled triangle bandwork with black, white, and blue patterns on an orange background, flanked by white quilled lines; the central band features sections of overlay triangle bandwork producing slanted bars and W-shapes. The bands enclose chains of alternating diamonds and circles in solid linework of the same colors. Except for the colors of the circles, the pattern is symmetrical. The upper edge of the front panel is decorated in a variety of quillwork techniques,[4] including a single wavy line, triangle bandwork, and overlay bandwork producing a white and orange sawtooth pattern. All edges are decorated by means of one-quill edging in white, white and orange, and white and black. The back panel has white and red lines and a double line linking circles in solid linework running parallel to the edges.

Solid linework, prominently included on the Frankfurt knifecase, must be regarded as a characteristic feature of Menominee quillwork. Despite some technical differences, it resembles moosehair appliqué in general appearance, the most spectacular examples of which are known to have been produced by the Huron, who on their semi-circular pouches and their moccasins also combined it with quilled triangle bandwork. The lack of a filled-in background as well as "graceful openwork" made up of quilled lines is regarded by Skinner (1921: 267) as a typical feature of Menominee quillwork.

A double knifecase with a design fairly similar to the one illustrated by Beltrami was purchased in 1919 for two Swiss francs by the ethnographic museum of the city of St. Gallen (Fig. 4). Like the one on Beltrami's plate, it has a row of tin cones filled with white and red-dyed deer hair below the triangle bandwork at the

4. For illustrations of the quillwork terminology employed in this essay, see Fig. 18 below.

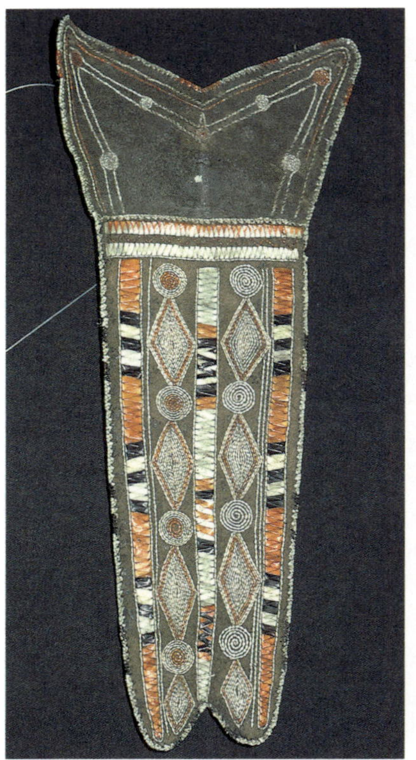

Fig. 3 Double knifecase, Menominee, before 1825. Length 28 cm. Museum für Völkerkunde (Frankfurt am Main), cat.no. E.156 (J. B. Klein coll.). Photograph: Christian F. Feest with the permission of the Museum für Völkerkunde, Frankfurt am Main.

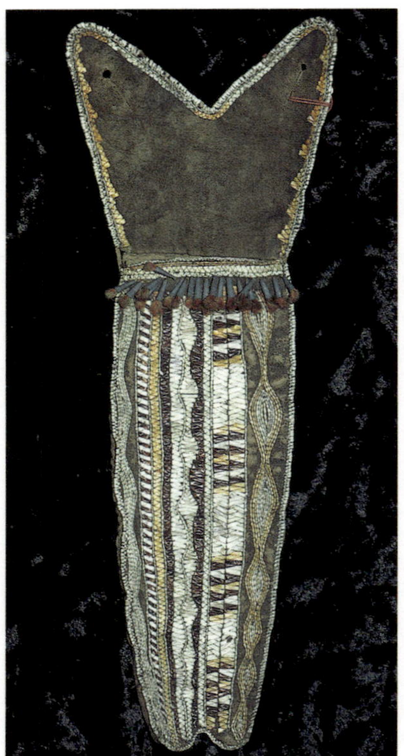

Fig. 4 Double knifecase, no collection history before 1919. Length 28 cm. Sammlung für Völkerkunde (St. Gallen), cat.no. D 1446. Photograph: Christian F. Feest with the permission of the Sammlung für Völkerkunde, St. Gallen.

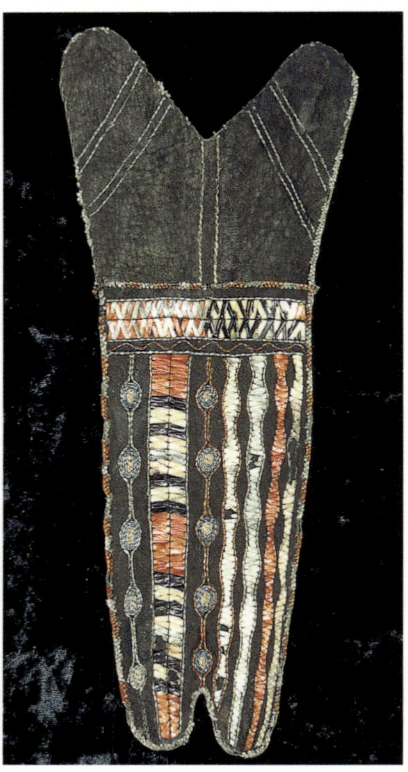

Fig. 5 Double knifecase, no collection history before 1950s. Length 28.5 cm. Canadian Museum of Civilization (Hull, QC), cat.no. III-N-36 (ex A. Speyer coll.). Photograph: Sylvia S. Kasprycki with the permission of the Canadian Museum of Civilization.

upper edge of the front panel. The asymmetric design consists of two groups of triangle bandwork, one with patterns of brown and orange on white background, the other with diagonal bar bands. These bands enclose a solid section of shaped triangle bandwork (in which the width of the folded quills varies) producing a chain of ovoid diamonds; they are flanked by solid linework producing another chain of diamonds and a wavy band. In addition to the simple quilled edging found on all edges, the back panel features a narrow triangle band which along the sides of the pointed ears is shaped to produce a serrated effect.

Unfortunately, the seller of the St. Gallen knifecase remains as unknown as the time and place where it had been obtained. Well-meaning visiting experts have left guesses ranging from "Iroquois—St. Lawrence" to "Great Lakes Region" on the catalog card for the knifecase. What we do know, however, is that the piece was sold to the museum together with a late nineteenth-century Plateau cradleboard—and another one of those trapezoidal pouches illustrated by Beltrami.

Even less is known about the double knifecase in the Canadian Museum of Civilization (Fig. 5), which had been part of the collection of Arthur Speyer, Jr., who in turn had acquired it from a dealer in Brussels, probably not long before the sale of his collection to Ottawa (now Hull). The attribution "Menominee, 1800" found on the catalog card may have been Speyer's.

Its asymmetric design is made up on the left of triangle bandwork with black, yellow, and blue patterns on an orange background, flanked by double lines linking circles in solid linework (with color asymmetry reminiscent of the Frankfurt piece), and on the right of a series of shaped, pulsating triangle bands without a filled-in background. Below the upper edge of the front panel are bands with W-forms and with color asymmetry; the wavy single line below the bands will recur on some of the following examples. The edging is in alternate sections of blue and orange quillwork on the front panel, and in white quillwork on the ears, whose simple pattern of double lines is symmetric.

Asymmetry both of the main design and of the bands below the upper front edge is also encountered in the second piece for which we have specific collec-

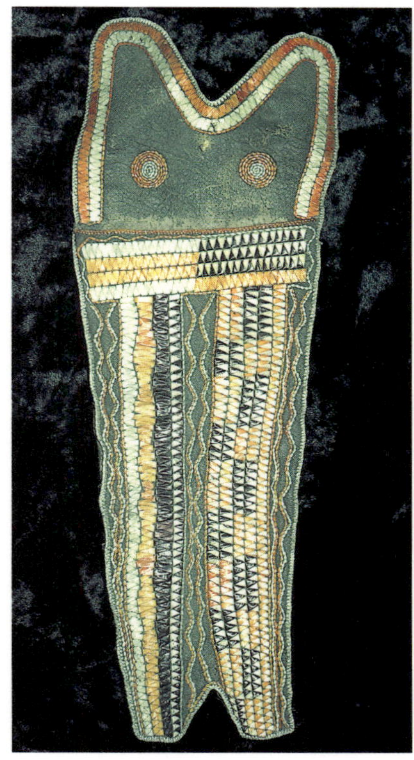

Fig. 6 Double knifecase, Winnebago, Green Bay, Wisconsin, before 1842. Length 27.5 cm. Nationalmuseet (Copenhagen), cat.no. e.H.c. 84 (C. C. Rafn coll.). Photograph: Christian F. Feest with the permission of the Nationalmuseet, Copenhagen.

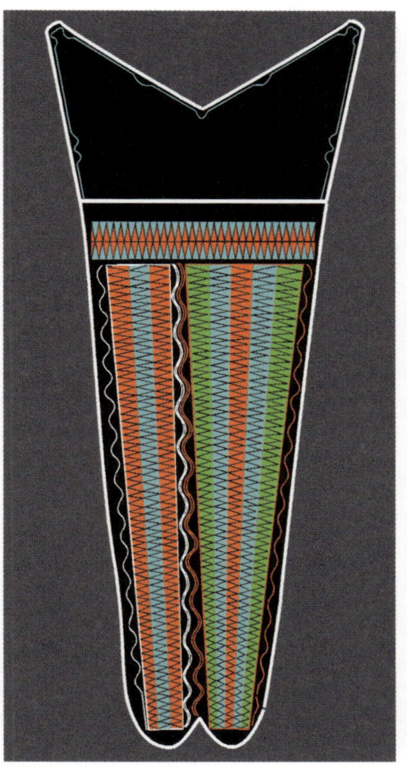

Fig. 7 Design pattern of double knifecase, no collection history before 1960. Length 26.4 cm. Denver Art Museum (Denver, CO), cat.no. 1968.370 (VMen-2-Ex). Drawing by the senior author.[6]

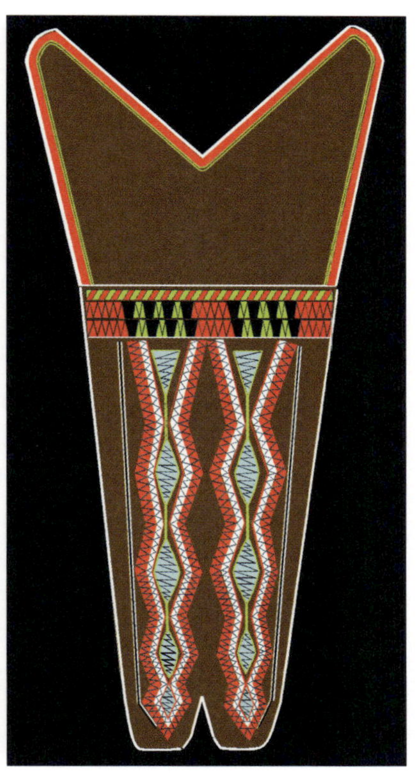

Fig. 8 Design pattern of double knifecase, no collection history. Length 29 cm. Richard Manoogian collection (ex Richard A. Pohrt collection). Drawing after Penney (1992: 71, pl. 5) by the senior author.

tion data (Fig. 6). Given in 1842 to the ethnographic collection of the National Museum of Denmark in Copenhagen by Carl Christian Rafn, its provenance is recorded in the museum's catalog as "Winnebago, Green Bay." Rafn, a Danish antiquary, was the author of *Antiquitates Americanae* (1837), a book on the Norse discovery of North America, but had never been to the United States (C. S. Petersen in Engelstoft and Dahl 1933–1944, 19: 50–54). Yet the designation is so specific and non-stereotypical that it must have been based on information received with the item. There is nothing that would speak against the Menominee's generally friendly neighbors, the Winnebago, having a knifecase stylistically very close to the ones we have considered so far. By 1842, however, the Winnebago had ceded all of their lands in Wisconsin, and most had moved to the west of the Mississippi, which makes a Winnebago presence in Green Bay after the early 1830s less likely.[5]

In addition to the features already noted, the Copenhagen knifecase prominently displays sawtooth bandwork with black/white and orange/white patterns (some of them arranged in checkerboard fashion), a solid area of shaped, pulsating triangle bands, and pairs of wavy lines producing an openwork pattern. Edging is in white quillwork (red on the upper front edge), and the rounded ears feature triangle bands and single lines along the edges and two circles in solid linework.

A somewhat simpler version of the style of the Copenhagen example is found in the collections of the Denver Art Museum (Fig. 7). This double knifecase also has the sawtooth pattern in the panel below the upper front edge, but there is no color asymmetry; it has the groups of triangle bands flanked by wavy lines, but there are no overlay and only very simple, symmetric color patterns; there is white quill edging, but along the edges of the ears there is only a single, slightly undulating blue line.

5. It is at least a curious coincidence that Rafn's "General Chart exhibiting the Discoveries of the Northmen in the Arctic Regions and America," which accompanied *Antiquitates Americanae* (1837), shows a single location in all of present-day Wisconsin: "Menomenie," a village at the southwestern end of Green Bay.

6. Permission to reproduce a photograph of this piece taken by the junior author was denied by the Denver Art Museum.

According to the museum's records, this piece was once "part of the Schultz Coll. from a small private museum in Portersville, Penna. Prior to 1960 the museum was in Pittsburgh. Sold about 1966 to R. Arrowsmith, who purchased the entire museum collection," and from whom the Denver Art Museum purchased the knifecase in 1968. The same source states that the attribution "Menominee?, ca. 1800" had been provided by Norman Feder, the museum's curator, on the basis of "several specimens of comparable age at the Neville Public Museum which are Menominee." If such specimens ever existed at the Neville Public Museum, no trace of their existence (or that of any other Great Lakes knifecase) can be found there today. It is more likely that Feder had the Frankfurt case in mind, which he had seen in Europe in 1968.

An "Ottawa" attribution is suggested for a double knifecase which was recently sold at auction (Sotheby's 1994: no. 151; Fig. 9). It shares the panel with W-forms in overlay bandwork (but not its asymmetry) with the case from the Canadian Museum of Civilization; like the Copenhagen and Denver cases it displays vertical bandwork alternating with wavy lines, but here the bands are single and feature W-forms in overlay. A new kind of asymmetry is introduced by the left side being made up exclusively of free-standing patterns (here: crescents) in solid linework.

The same type of asymmetry is found on an undocumented double knifecase from the Alfred Corning Clark collection in the Fenimore Art Museum in Cooperstown, New York, which also features a panel of complex overlay bandwork on the upper edge of the front panel (Fig. 10). The solid linework on the left side consists of two chains of linked diamonds and circles (strongly reminiscent of the Frankfurt case) and wedges somewhat resembling the crescents on the Sotheby's item. The vertical two-lane strip of patterned triangle bandwork is comparable to the Speyer collection case now in Hull. Like the item sold at Sotheby's and the Copenhagen piece, the Cooperstown case has simple designs (bunches of leaves or feathers) in the ears, which are edged like the Copenhagen case and the one in Milwaukee to be discussed later. The undocumented Cooperstown case has been attributed on the collection's object worksheet to the "Menominee" and to a much too early "1750" date.

Closely similar to the Sotheby's and Cooperstown specimens is a single knifecase collected prior to 1838

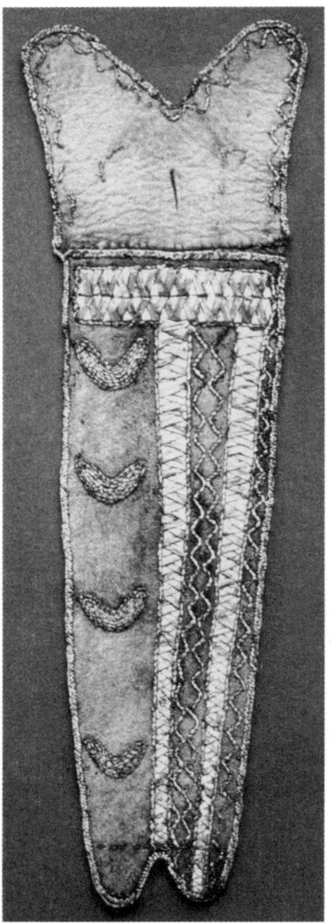

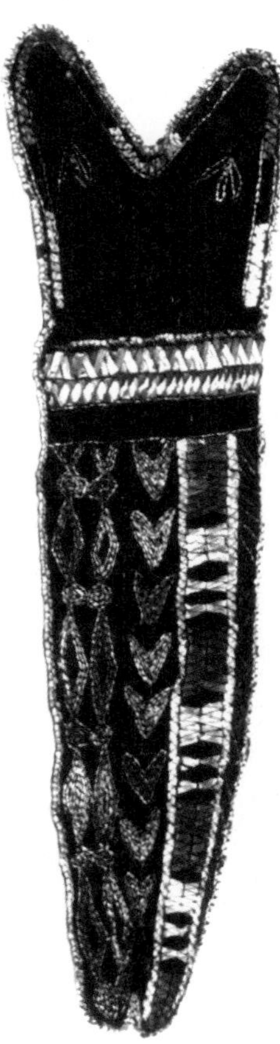

Fig. 9 Double knifecase, no collection history before 1994; attributed to the Ottawa. Length 29.2 cm. After Sotheby's (1994: no. 151).
Fig. 10 Double knifecase, no collection history before 1892; attributed to the Menominee. Length 28.5 cm. Fenimore Art Museum (Cooperstown, NY), cat.no. N-252.92 (A. C. Clark coll.). Photograph: Fenimore Art Museum.

among the Ottawa—one of only two such knifecases presently known with an asymmetric design (Fig. 11; cp. Feest 1968: 44, no. 20, pl. 2a; Graham et al. 1984: 44, no. 61).[7] Similarities include the type of asymmetry, wedge-shaped solid linework motifs, two-lane patterned triangle bandwork, two-lane overlay bandwork along the upper edge of the front panel, and triangle band edging of the ears. This item helps to illustrate the existing ties between Menominee and Ottawa styles of quillwork.

The earliest evidence for the existence of the type of knife sheath under discussion is a watercolor drawing made in 1816–1817 by Charles Hamilton Smith, a British officer, during a visit to North America. His draw-

7. The other one has been attributed to the Dakota (Acevedo et al. 1983: 29, fig. 26). Another feature of double knifecases, which also appears on two single knifecases, is shaped bands (Orchard 1971: pl. Va; Völger 1976: 4.20.34, not illustrated; both items carry somewhat dubious attributions).

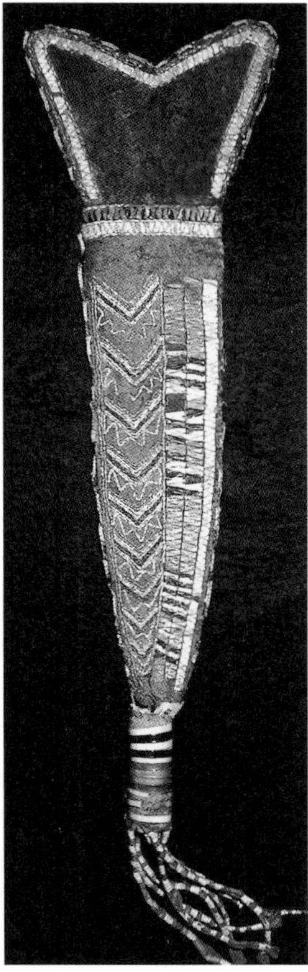

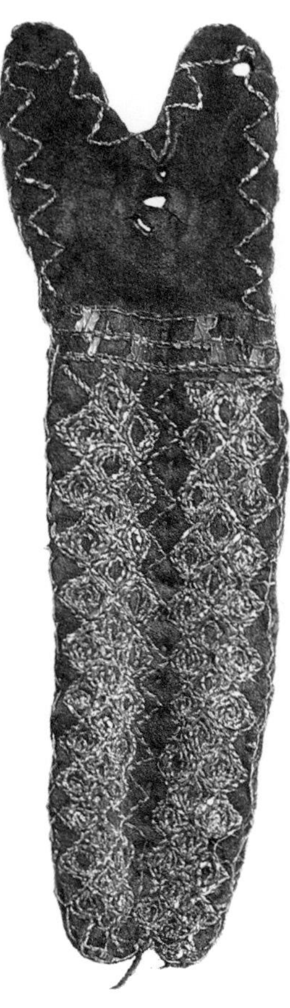

Fig. 11 Single knifecase, Ottawa, before 1838. Length 26.5 (without fringes). Museum für Völkerkunde (Vienna), cat.no. 11,966 (J. G. Schwarz coll., probably ex F. Rese coll.). Photograph: C. F. Feest.
Fig. 12 Double knifecase, collected in Wisconsin or Minnesota in 1823. Length 23 cm. Museo Civico "E. Caffi" (Bergamo), no cat.no. (G. C. Beltrami coll.). After Vigorelli (1987a: 12).

ings, now at the Victoria and Albert Museum, include a number of items from the western Great Lakes and eastern Plains region which have survived in European and American collections (King 1994). One of the sketches shows a double knifecase immediately next to a trapezoidal pouch, already twice noted above in association with double knifecases. The caption provides no attribution, but simply reads: "Knifecase worn round the neck" (King 1994: 59, fig. 1).

The knifecase shown by Smith has a simple band (here of leather) for suspension from the neck and displays an asymmetrical design consisting of patterned bandwork on one side and interlocked chains of diamonds on the other. The latter may have been produced by solid linework or by shaped triangle bandwork framed with linework—both techniques employed for similar patterns on the tails of Menominee otterskin medicine bags (e.g., National Museum of the American Indian, cat.no. 9/1885). The shared presence of the interlocked chains of diamonds provides further proof for the relationship between the knifecase and pouch in the same drawing. The row of tin cones below the triangle bands at the upper front edge recalls the St. Gallen knifecase and the Beltrami lithograph. A V-shaped openwork pattern of lines and solid linework is featured on the back panel, which appears to be edged with red silk ribbon appliqué and glass beads.

The latter interpretation is supported by a specimen from the Richard Manoogian collection (ex Richard A. Pohrt coll.; Penney 1992: 71, pl. 5; cp. Fig. 8), which also shows the combination of ribbon appliqué and bead edging, perhaps imitating the similar quillwork pattern on the Copenhagen example. (The Beltrami lithograph might possibly also show a ribbon and bead edging—if it does not illustrate a fine quilled line running parallel to the quilled edge.) With this fairly simple piece, we return to a symmetric form of decoration, with chains of diamonds of shaped bands flanked by straight double lines. The triangle bandwork along the upper front edge has one overlay triangle band with slanted bars and two triangle bands with black and white patterns on red. This double knifecase, whose previous history is unknown, was attributed to the "Menominee (?), 1800–1830."

The symmetric pattern based on two groups of interlocked chains of diamonds in solid linework on another double knifecase from the 1823 collection of Giacomo Costantino Beltrami (Fig. 12) is at least reminiscent of the immediately preceding example. Two badly damaged triangle bands below the upper front edge and a zigzag line along the edge of the back panel (similar to the Sotheby's case described above) cannot dispel the evidence provided by this artifact that not all the works produced by Native Americans in the western Great Lakes area before 1850 were masterpieces.

One of the many unheralded treasures of the National Museum of the American Indian, which for many years had been hidden on display at the Washington Heights permanent exhibition is a double knifecase (Fig. 13) purchased in 1924 from an undisclosed source and identified as "Menominee" in the card catalog.[8] It is possible that the Frankfurt knifecase, published in

8. Another (presumably double) knifecase from the Menominee in the National Museum of the American Indian, cataloged as cat.no. 13/5889 immediately following the specimen just discussed, could not be located in the museum's storage facility in 1995.

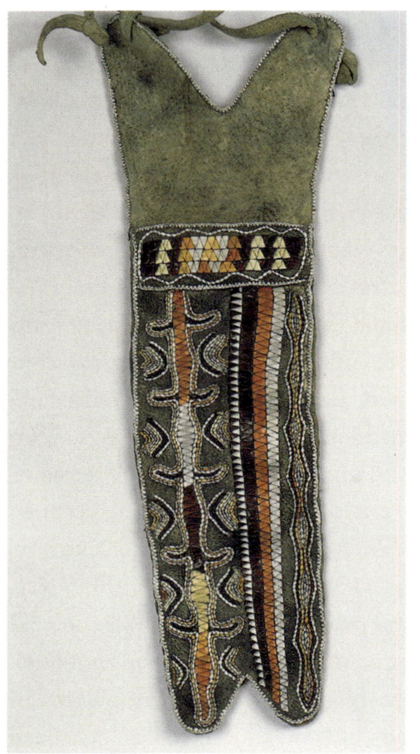

Fig. 13 Double knifecase, no collection history before 1924; attributed to the Menominee. No measurements available. Courtesy of the National Museum of the American Indian, Smithsonian Institution (Washington, DC), cat.no. 13/5888. Photograph: Pam Dewey.

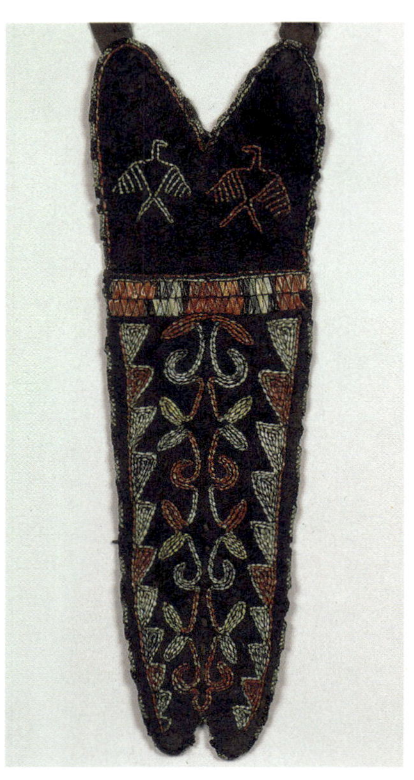

Fig. 14 Double knifecase, no collection history before 1968; attributed to the Iroquois. No measurements available. Courtesy of the National Museum of the American Indian, Smithsonian Institution (Washington, DC), cat.no. 24/1952. Photograph: Janine Jones.

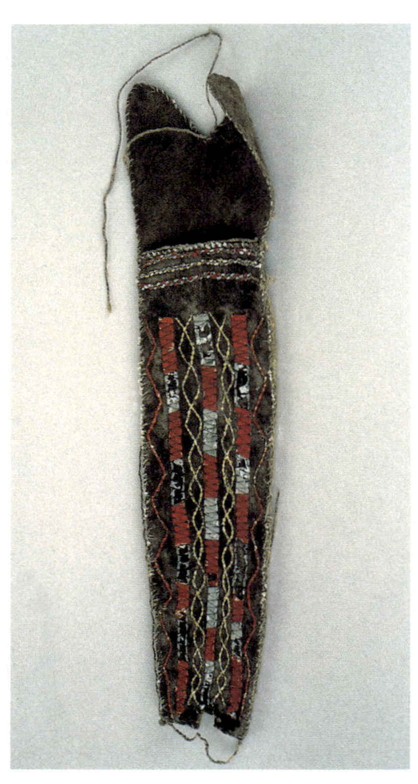

Fig. 15 Double knifecase, probably collected in Wisconsin in 1849. Length 26 cm. Haffenreffer Museum of Anthropology, Brown University (Bristol, RI), cat.no. 79-83 (Francis W. Greene coll.). Photograph: Haffenreffer Museum of Anthropology.

1925, may have guided the attribution, but it is also possible that the information came together with the item itself.

There can be little doubt of its Menominee origin, since the left side provides an exquisite illustration of the "delicate openwork" noted by Skinner, which here consists of a central shaped, pulsating triangle band of alternating sections of orange, black, blue, and yellow, flanked by ornamental linework in the same colors plus white. The right side features four triangle bands (one of them with an overlay sawtooth pattern) and a chain of diamonds in solid linework. The asymmetric triangle bands below the upper front edge are placed on a false flap sewn to the upper and side edges. All edging is done in white quillwork. The type of asymmetry links this case to the Sotheby's and Cooperstown examples discussed above.

Its openwork design, on the other hand, is only a somewhat stylized version of a design encountered on a mostly symmetrical double knifecase also at the National Museum of the American Indian (Fig. 14). The piece was acquired in 1968 as a gift of the Mattatuck Historical Society, Waterbury, Connecticut; its attribution to the Iroquois of New York, whether already part of the knifecase's heritage in 1968 or added upon receipt in its new home, is unconvincing. The central design is now of a rather obvious floral derivation.[9] It is flanked by a serrated border of solid linework, reminiscent of a similar border edging the ears of the St. Gallen case. The most unusual feature is the depiction on the ears of two thunderbirds, whose colors (red and yellow) provide the only claim to asymmetry of this specimen.

If one accepts the view that the openwork design on the first NMAI example is a stylized version of that on the second one, the next step would be to view the linked chains of diamonds, of circles, and of diamonds and circles appearing on other examples here discussed

9. The motif occurs in a similar form and technique on a single knifecase in the Canadian Museum of Civilization (cat.no. III-X-309), obtained in 1975 without documentation from Douglas C. Ewing and identified in the CMC catalog as "Great Lakes, possibly Ojibwa." The suggested provenance is based upon a remotely similar design found on a pair of leggings attributed to the Ojibwa.

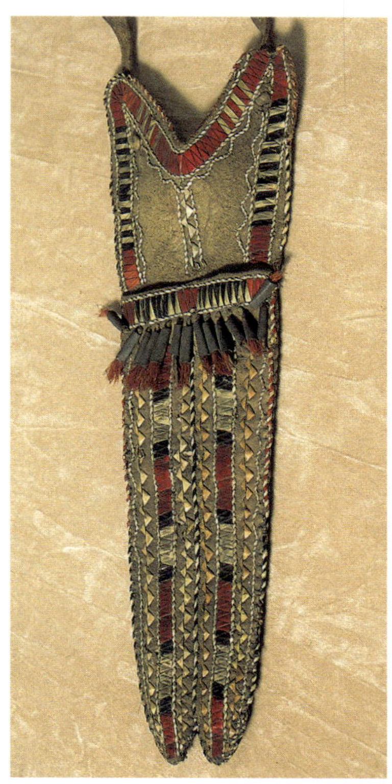

Fig. 16 Double knifecase, no collection history before 1931. Length 18.9 cm. Pitt Rivers Museum, University of Oxford (Oxford), cat.no. 1954.9.46 (H. G. Beasley coll., ex Blackmore Museum). Photograph: Pitt Rivers Museum.

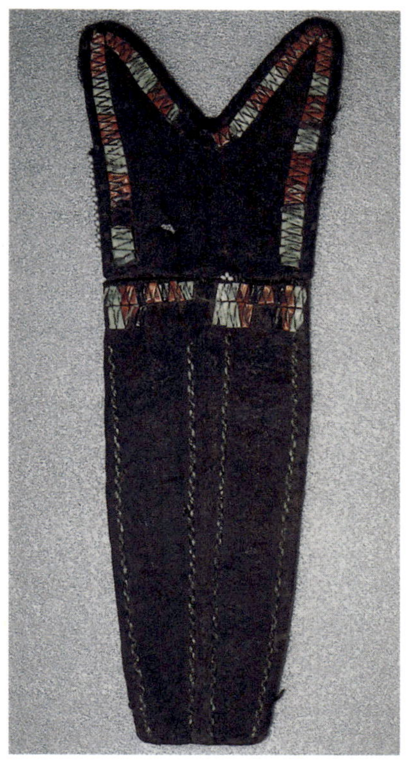

Fig. 17 Double knifecase, no collection history before 1965; attributed to the Menominee. Length 26 cm. Milwaukee Public Museum (Milwaukee, WI), cat.no. 59147/19851. Photograph: Christian F. Feest with the permission of the Milwaukee Public Museum.

as further stylizations of the central spine of the same design.

Yet another example of this type is a somewhat better conserved double knifecase in the Haffenreffer Museum of Anthropology (Fig. 15). Like the Copenhagen and Denver examples, this one has a design of patterned triangle bandwork flanked by wavy lines. But instead of the complex execution of the basic design, especially on the Copenhagen knifecase, the three single bands on the Haffenreffer piece are very simply patterned (cp. also the Sotheby's case). Instead of bandwork, there are only three sawtooth lines below the upper front edge.

Hail (1980: 204, no. 272) identifies this piece as an "Eastern Dakota type, 1830–1850," which is clearly erroneous. The catalog card notes "Woodland to Ottawa" as the attribution offered in February 1984 by Richard Conn, which is much preferable. An even closer guess may be ventured on the basis of the documentation available at the Haffenreffer Museum, which indicates that the knifecase was part of a collection "brought back from the West by Job Greene Warriner ... previous to 1849." This collection was made up of five pieces: a pair of Menominee garters, one pair of women's moccasins of probable Menominee origin, two Chippewa belts, and the knifecase in question. The knifecase was thus most likely obtained in Wisconsin and probably either from the Menominee or from the Chippewa. The closest parallels for its design pattern may indeed be found among single knifecases, such as an item in the National Museum of the American Indian (cat.no. 19/6534; Orchard 1971: pl. XXIX far left), in all likelihood also erroneously attributed to the Delaware, which has three patterned triangle bands flanking two wavy lines. A much larger number of single knifecases conform to a pattern of one or a block of three patterned triangle bands flanked by wavy lines (e.g., Orchard 1971: pl. XXIX; King 1982: 18, fig. 7a; 1991: 39, fig. 8; Acevedo et al. 1983: 28, fig. 24), none of which is documented, but all of which appear to be of eastern rather than western origin.

A double knifecase preserved in the Pitt Rivers Museum in Oxford (Fig. 16) differs in many respects from the others so far discussed. It is by far the shortest specimen, and it features two unusual quilling techniques. The rare type of edging with two quills of different colors is reminiscent of (but not identical with) the decoration along the upper edge of the front panel of the Haffenreffer case; the zigzag lines framing the two panels of triangular bandwork and running down the center of the back panel is found on at least two of the trapezoidal pouches, which are related to or associated with some of the other double knifecases (Museum der Kulturen [Basle], cat.no. IVa38; National Museum of Natural History [Washington, DC], cat.no. 5425). The sawtooth pattern is found on the Denver, Copenhagen, and second NMAI knifecases; the diagonal bars reappear on the examples in St. Gallen and in the Pohrt collection; St. Gallen, the Smith drawing, and the Beltrami lithograph also feature the tin cones below the upper edge of the front panel. The wavy fine lines are shared by the Denver, Haffenreffer, Copenhagen, Bergamo, Sotheby's, and second NMAI pieces.

Once again, there is no documented provenance. The Pitt Rivers knifecase was formerly in the Beasley collection and had previously been part of the Blackmore Museum in Salisbury, England. It may be assumed that it was collected by the museum's founder, William Blackmore (1827–1878), who had frequently visited the United States between 1863 and 1874, decades after the knifecase in his collection had been made.

The last item in our series was found in 1965 without any documentation in the storeroom of the Milwaukee Public Museum (now cat.no. 59.147/19.851 and attributed to the "Menominee"; Fig. 17). In the *Art of the Great Lakes Indians* catalog (Hodge et al. 1973: 4, no. 5) this badly damaged specimen is dated "c. 1780" (which may be about 50 years too early) and said to be of "buffalo hide." In its present condition, only the triangle bands with orange patterns on blue along the edges of the back and front panels are clearly discernible. There are also traces of an edging with white glass beads and some indication that the main design was made up of two pairs of triangle bands. It cannot be ascertained whether the overall design of this case was symmetric or asymmetric. One of the most notable features is the squarely cut off lower end, which parallels the item on the Beltrami lithograph.

Conclusions

Despite their strikingly unusual form, double knifecases are nowhere mentioned in the written ethnographic sources. There are apparently only two images depicting double knifecases in actual use: An engraving based on a lost daguerreotype portrait of the Menominee chief Oshkosh published in 1856 suggests the use of this type, although only a single knife handle is visible; this is also true of a surviving daguerreotype of the same series, on which, however, the knifecase is less easily recognized as a double one (Kasprycki 1990: 103–105, Figs. 64–65). The 1852 drawing by Adolf Hoeffler illustrated above (Fig. 1) depicts two identical handles sticking from the double knifecase, but we still have no recorded explanation why anyone would want to have a knifecase for two knives, or whether these were really two knives. Hodge et al. (1973: 4) suggest that the two pockets may have been intended for the use of a knife and file. The Beltrami double knifecase presently contains two "wooden utensils" (Vigorelli 1987a: 13, 64, no. 51), one of which is a "brave stick" recording war honors, while the other looks like a foreshaft of an arrow probably not from the Great Lakes region. Only one of the examples examined here had been accompanied by a knife—and one knife only. It is therefore difficult to say whether the two pockets were indeed intended to hold two knives, or whether the duplication was largely symbolic, like the two bowls on some Plains catlinite pipe heads. If that was the case, the symbolism has to our knowledge never been recorded.

Available documentary, stylistic, and inferential evidence indicates that double knifecases were popular in Wisconsin during the period between ca. 1810 and 1860, and that most of them were made by the Menominee, probably including the example documented in 1842 for the Winnebago and the one shown by Hoeffler as worn by a Dakota man.

A statistical analysis of the available corpus supports the view that the known specimens form a closely-knit group which cannot be subdivided on the basis of the correlation of distinctive features. The analysis was based on twenty-six formal, technical, and stylistic properties, whose range and significance will be briefly discussed before presenting the final results.[10]

Of the examples for which measurements of *size* are available, all except two range between 26 and 29.2 cm in length; only MCC (23 cm) and PRM (18.9 cm) are significantly smaller. There is some variation in the *overall shape* of double knifecases, with pointed or rounded "ears" of the back panel combining freely with pointed, rounded, or squared-off lower ends. As far as the *color* of the leather is concerned, there is wide range of hues, but the majority appear to be black or faded to grey from a previous black; a minority (including NMAI 1, PRM, RP, SNY) have a light, brownish appearance. Most of the double knifecases make use of five *quill colors*: white, red/orange, yellow, blue/green,

10. The following abbreviations will be used to the refer to the knifecases presented in this essay: CHS (Charles Hamilton Smith; not illustrated); CMC (Canadian Museum of Civilization; Fig. 5); DAM (Denver Art Museum, Fig. 7); FAM (Fenimore Art Museum; Fig. 10); GCB (Beltrami 1862; Fig. 2); HMA (Haffenreffer Museum of Anthropology; Fig. 15); MCC (Museo Civico "E. Caffi"; Fig. 12); MPM (Milwaukee Public Museum; Fig. 17); MVF (Museum für Völkerkunde, Frankfurt; Fig. 3); NMAI 1 (National Museum of the American Indian; Fig. 13); NMAI 2 (Fig. 14); NMD (Nationalmuseet [National Museum of Denmark], Copenhagen; Fig. 6); PRM (Pitt Rivers Museum; Fig. 16); RP (Richard Pohrt coll., Fig. 8); SNY (Sotheby's, New York; Fig. 9); SVSG (Sammlung für Völkerkunde, St. Gallen; Fig. 4).

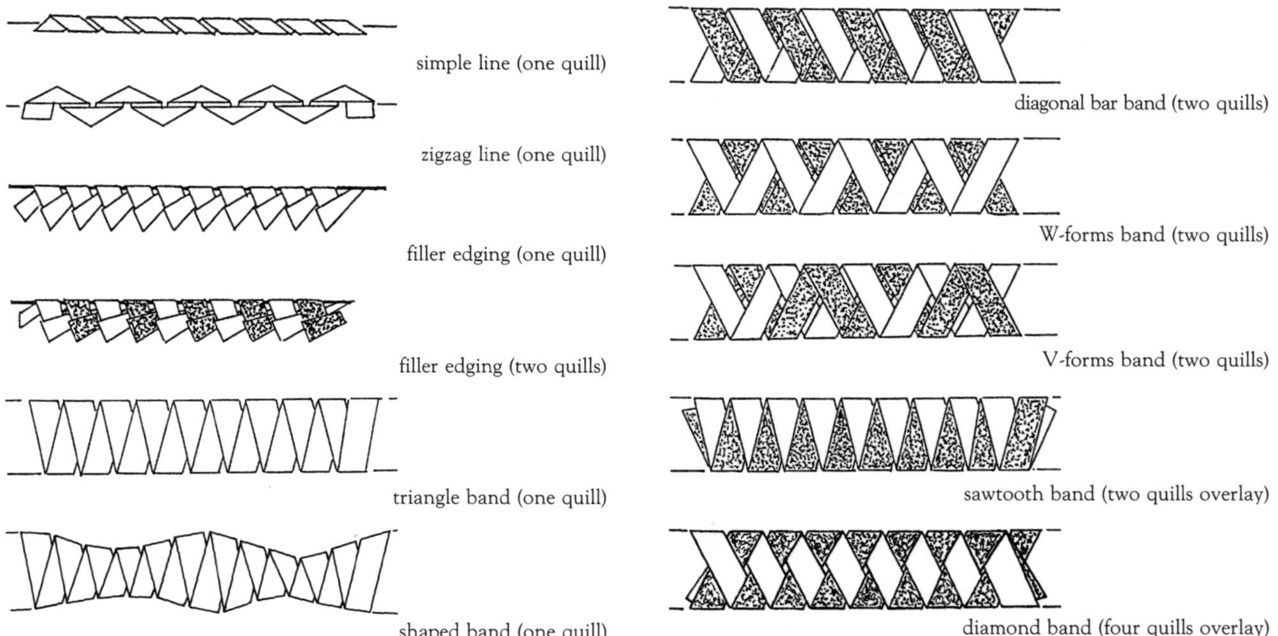

Fig. 18 Quilling techniques found on double knifecases. Drawings by the senior author.

brown/black; MVF differs in having both red and orange instead of yellow, PRM has red and orange instead of blue. DAM and HMA lack black (four colors), MCC and SNY lack black and yellow (three colors). In addition to the ubiquitous quillwork, (white) *glass beads* appear only on RP and MPM, (red) *silk ribbons* on RP (and perhaps on CHS), and *metal cones* on GCB, CHS, PRM, and SVSG.

Figure 18 shows the quillwork techniques found on double knifecases. *Simple linework* is a feature shared by all specimens except MPM (which is badly damaged and may once also have had it); *solid linework*, in which solid shapes are built up with lines, is widespread, but is missing on DAM, HMA, MPM, PRM, and RP. PRM is unique in its use of *zigzag lines* and possibly in its use of the *two-quills edging* technique. Simple *triangle bandwork* is only absent on MCC and SNY, but whereas MCC has no bandwork at all, SNY shares bands with *W-forms* with CMC, FAM, and MVF. Equally or even more common among the techniques using two or more quills are *diagonal bar* bands (MVF, PRM, RP, SVSG) and *sawtooth* bands (DAM, MVF, NMD, PRM, NMAI 1); *V-form* and *diamond* bands each occur only once on SVSG and FAM, respectively. *Shaped bands*, a distinctive variant of triangle bands, are found on CMC, NMAI 1, NMD, SVSG, and in a transitory form on RP.

Quillwork patterns (as distinguished from quillwork techniques) include both iconography and basic structure, such as *symmetry*. Closer inspection reveals that double knifecases cannot be distinguished according to a simple distinction between "symmetric" and "asymmetric" forms, because symmetry may independently occur with regard to three variables: main pattern or front panel, pattern at top of front panel, and use of color (back panel patterns are universally symmetric). Combinations result in four symmetry patterns: completely symmetric (HMA, MCC, MPM), symmetric design pattern with color asymmetry (MVF, NMAI 2, PRM, RP), asymmetric main pattern (and thus color asymmetry) with symmetric top of front panel (DAM, FAM, GCB, CHS, SNY, SVSG), and completely asymmetric (CMC, NMAI 1, NMD).

Among the conspicuous iconographic elements of the front panel are *linked chains of circles and/or diamonds* (circles: CMC; diamonds: RP; circles and diamonds: FAM, MVF), to which are related *interlocked chains of diamonds* (CHS, MCC) and *comlex openwork designs arranged around a linked-diamond spine* (NMAI 1 and 2), as well as *pulsating shaped bands* (CMC, NMD, SVSG). These patterns have a more distant relationship with *pairs of facing wavy lines* (HMA, NMD, SNY, SVSG), which are equally related to *simple wavy lines* in the main pattern (DAM, PRM, SNY) or along the edges of the back panel (DAM, MCC, PRM, SNY).

Another form element that occurs more than once on double knifecases are *chevrons* (FAH, SNY).

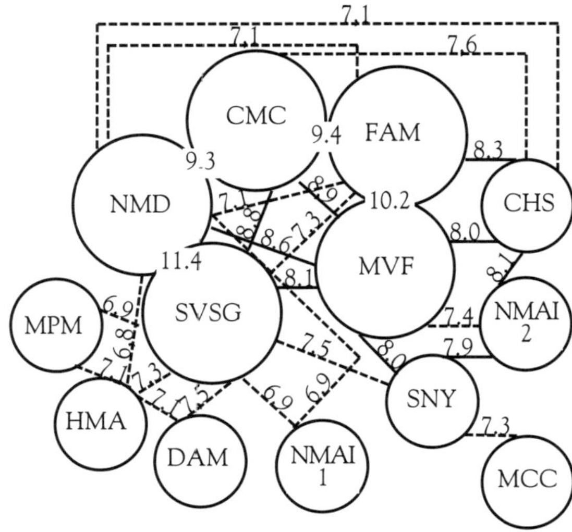

Fig. 19 Field diagram of formal relationships between double knifecases. GCB, PRM, and RP are excluded, because their closest relationship with any other specimen is below 6.8. Stylistic proximity in the diagram is not to scale, but relationships above 10.0 are shown by overlapping circles, between 9.0 and 9.9 by contiguous circles, between 7.9 and 8.9 by unbroken lines, and between 6.8 and 7.8 by dotted lines.

SVSG	**NMD**	**CMC**	**MVF**	**FAM**	**CHS**	**NMAI2**	**SNY**
NMD 11.4	SVSG 11.4	FAM 9.4	FAM 10.2	MVF 10.2			
CMC 8.8	CMC 9.8	NMD 9.3	CMC 8.9	CMC 9.4			
MVF 8.1	MVF 8.6	MVF 8.9	NMD 8.6	CHS 8.3	FAM 8.3	CHS 8.1	MVF 8.0
SNY 7.5	FAM 7.1	SVSG 8.8	SVSG 8.1	SVSG 7.3	NMAI2 8.1	SNY 7.9	NMAI2 7.9
DAM 7.5	CHS 7.1	CHS 7.6	CHS 8.0	NMD 7.1	MVF 8.0	MVF 7.4	SVSG 7.5
FAM 7.3	NMAI1 6.9				CMC 7.6		MCC 7.3
HMA 7.3	HMA 6.8				NMD 7.1		
NMAI1 6.9							
MPM 6.9							
6.8	**6.5**	**6.0**	**6.3**	**5.7**	**5.2**	**5.0**	**5.7**

Fig. 20 Partial tabulation of formal relationships between double knifecases of the central cluster and the linked group. Arrangement is by degree of similarity. Bold figure in lowest line indicates the average relationship of the head of the respective column to all others.

Triangle bands patterned by *repeated blocks of different quill colors* are widely distributed and are also found on double knifecases, either in the main panel (CMC, FAM, CHS, HMA, MVF, PRM, SVSG), or along the top of the front panel (CHS, MPM, RP), and even on bands running alongside the top of the back panel (MPM). Since these blocks are of different pattern and complexity, they should probably be seen as a structural, rather than an iconographic feature.

The top of the back panel of double knifecases is always bordered with quill or bead edging and often also with triangle bands (FAM, MPM, NMD, PRM), shaped bands (SVSG), wavy lines (DAM, MCC, PRM, SNY), complex line pattern (MVF), or ribbon (CHS, RP), but is otherwise often undecorated (DAM, GCB, MCC, MPM, NMAI 1, NMD, RP, SNY). When designs occur, they are generally unique; only *stylized floral patterns* (FAM, CHS) and *vertical dividing lines* (NMD, PRM) occur more than once.

A tabulation of the distribution of these features permits a quantification of the formal relationships between the fourteen actual specimens and two early depictions of double knifecases. Although like in all such statistics the coding necessarily tends to be to some extent subjective, the results (expressed in diagrammatic form in Fig. 19 and in tabular form in Fig. 20) are interesting enough. The detailed analysis shows that it is impossible to subdivide the group into types with distinctive features that are exclusive to such types. What emerges is rather a network of relationships, which form clusters more or less closely or distantly related to one another.

The tabulation shows a relatively closely related cluster (SVSG, NMD, CMC, FAM, MVF), of which CMC forms the center, because its relationship to the other four varies less than those of the others, while SVSG and NMD on one side and FAM and MVF on the other side are the closest relatives of one another. CHS, NMAI 2, and SNY are rather a peripheral part of the cluster, whose relationships among themselves are not stronger than to members of the central cluster; MCC is on the periphery of this side. The same is true of MPM, HMA, and DAM on the other side of the diagram, and of NMAI 1, whose closest relatives (however distant) are SVSG and NMD. (Some of the spatial arrangements on the diagram follow figures not shown here; thus the next relatives of NMAI 1 are in fact CMC, SNY, and DAM.)

It is also obvious that variation between the specimens is substantial. Out of a possible maximum of 25 points, the maximum actually encountered is 11.4, the minimum 2.1. The average for the specimen with the closest relationships to the others (SVSG) is only 6.8—just about a quarter of a full match. One of the results of this situation is that the proximity of the relationships is not necessarily apparent to the naked eye.

While the five core members of the cluster obviously share some features, none of them is exclusive and distinctive: All are made of black-smoked buckskin and have slightly pointed ears and rather rounded lower ends; their lengths range from 27.5 to 28.5 cm; all use quills of five colors, and all have an asymmetric color pattern; all make use of solid linework and use at least two of the more complex techniques of bandwork.

It appears that the MPM, HMA, and DAM periphery is characterized by a four-color pattern, the absence of solid linework and of linked chains of diamonds and/or circles or pulsating bands, and a length ranging from 26 to 26.5 cm.

Combined with the documentary, stylistic, and inferential evidence on provenance, the analysis supports the idea that the cluster may be the work of members of one cultural tradition, presumably Menominee. Deviant specimens, such as PRM, may either reflect influence from or represent manufacture by other groups. Applying the analysis to the single knifecase documented to have been collected among the Ottawa (Fig. 11), we find relatively high values of relationship with MVF (9.4) and SVSG (9.1) and an average in the range of the SNY, NMAI 2, and CHS periphery (5.2). While a Menominee manufacture of this piece cannot be ruled out, this example nevertheless reminds us how little we know about the relationship between cultural affiliation and stylistic properties in northeastern North America throughout the historic period.

References Cited

Acevedo, Alexander et al.
1983 *Akicita. Early Plains and Woodlands Indian Art from the Collection of Alexander Acevedo.* Los Angeles, CA: The Southwest Museum.

Andreas, Christoph
1998 *Adolf Hoeffler.* Frankfurt am Main: Verlag von J. P. Schneider Jr.

B., D.
1831 Johann Baptist August Klein. *Neuer Nekrolog der Deutschen* 9.

Beltrami, Giacomo Costantino
1962 *A Pilgrimage in America.* [London 1828.] Chicago, IL: Quadrangle Books.

Benndorf, Helga and Arthur Speyer
1968 *Indianer Nordamerikas.* Offenbach a.M.: Deutsches Ledermuseum.

Brasser, Ted J.
1976 *"Bo'jou Neejee!" Profiles of Canadian Indian Art.* Ottawa, ON: National Museum of Man.

Burland, Cottie
1965 *North American Indian Mythology.* London: Hamlyn.

Dräger, Lothar, Rolf Krusche, Klaus Hoffmann
1992 *Indianer Nordamerikas. Ausstellung im Blockhaus "Villa Bärenfett" des Karl-May-Museums.* München: Karl M. Lipp Verlag.

Engelstoft, Povl and Svend Dahl
1933–1944 (eds.) *Dansk Biografisk Leksikon.* 27 vols. København: J. H. Schultz.

Feder, Norman
1964 *Art of the Eastern Plains Indians. The Nathan Sturges Jarvis Collection.* Brooklyn, NY: The Brooklyn Museum.
1965 *American Indian Art Before 1850.* Denver, CO: Denver Art Museum.
1971 *American Indian Art.* New York, NY: Harry N. Abrams.

Feest, Christian F.
1968 *Indianer Nordamerikas.* Wien: Museum für Völkerkunde.
1987 Some 18th Century Specimens from Eastern North America in Collections in the German Democratic Republic. *Jahrbuch des Museums für Völkerkunde zu Leipzig* 37: 281–301.
1993 European Collecting of American Indian Artefacts and Art. *Journal of the History of Collections* 5(1): 1–11.
1995 The Collecting of American Indian Artifacts in Europe, 1493–1750. In: Karen O. Kupperman (ed.), *America in European Consciousness, 1493–1750* (Chapel Hill, NC: University of North Carolina Press for Institute of Early American History and Culture), 324–360.
1996 Early Views of an Early Pipe. *European Review of Native American Studies* 10(1): 63–64.
in press Quilled Knifecases from Northeastern North America.

Feest, Christian F. and Sylvia S. Kasprycki
1993 *Über/Lebenskunst nordamerikanischer Indianer.* Wien: Museum für Völkerkunde.
1999 *Peoples of the Twilight. European Views of Native Minnesota, 1823 to 1862.* Afton, MN: Afton Historical Society Press.

Fiorentino, Daniele
1990 Accidental Ethnographers: Italian Travelers and Scholars and the American Indians (1750–1900). *European Review of Native American Studies* 4(2): 31–36.

Graham, Stephen B. et al.
1984 *Beadwork & Textiles of the Ottawa.* Harbor Springs, MI: Harbor Springs Historical Commission.

Hail, Barbara
1980 *Hau, Kóla! The Plains Indian Collection of the Haffenreffer Museum of Anthropology.* Bristol, RI: Haffenreffer Museum of Anthropology.

Harrison, Julia et al.
1987 *The Spirit Sings. Artistic Traditions of Canada's First Peoples. A Catalogue of the Exhibition.* Toronto, ON: McClelland and Stewart.

Hodge, G. Stuart et al.
1973 *Art of the Great Lakes Indians.* Flint, MI: Flint Institute of Arts.

Kasprycki, Sylvia S.
1990 Image and Imagination: Menominee Portraits, 1825–1860. *Archiv für Völkerkunde* 44: 65–131.

Kaufmann, Christian
1992 Stil und Kanon. Zum Stilbegriff in der Ethnologie der Kunst—Versuch einer Standortbestimmung. *Ethnologica Helvetica* 16: 31–89.

King, J. C. H.
1982 *Thunderbird and Lightning. Indian Life in Northeastern North America 1600–1900.* London: British Museum Publications.
1991 Woodlands Artifacts from the Studio of Benjamin West, 1738–1820. *American Indian Art Magazine* 17(1): 34–47.
1993 Woodlands Art as Depicted by Sarah Stone in the Collection of Sir Ashton Lever. *American Indian Art Magazine* 18(2): 32–45.
1994 Native Art as Depicted by Charles Hamilton Smith, a British Intelligence Officer in the United States, 1816–1817. *American Indian Art Magazine* 19(2): 58–67.

Laurencich-Minelli, Laura
1990 G. C. Beltrami (1779–1855) and His Filottrano North American Indian Collection (Filottrano, Ancona). *Museologia Scientifica* 6: 237–254.

Marino, Cesare
1986 A Preview of the Beltrami Collection with a Note on North American Ethnographic Material in Italian Museums. *Council for Museum Anthropology Newsletter* 10(2): 1–13.
1987 A Preview of the Beltrami Collection with a Note on North American Ethnographic Material in Italian Museums. *Archivio per l'Antropologia e la Etnologia* 117: 183–196.

Morgan, Lewis H.
1850a Schedule of Articles Obtained from Indians Residing in Western New York. *Third Annual Report of the Regents of the University on the Condition of the State Cabinet of Natural History* (Revised edition, Albany, NY), 59–62.
1850b Report to the Regents of the University, Upon the Articles Furnished to the Indian Collection. *Third Annual Report of the Regents of the University on the Condition of the State Cabinet of Natural History* (Revised edition, Albany, NY), 63–95.
1851 *League of the Ho-de'-no-sau-nee, or Iroquois.* Rochester, NY: Sage & Brother. (Reprint: Secaucus, NJ 1972: Citadel Press.)
1852 Report on the Fabrics, Inventions, Implements and Utensils of the Iroquois. *Fifth Annual Report of the Regents of the University on the Condition of the State Cabinet of Natural History* (Albany, NY), 63–117.

Orchard, William C.
1971 *The Technique of Porcupine Quill Decoration among the Indians of North America.* 2nd ed. Contributions from the Museum of the American Indian Heye Foundation 4(1). New York, NY.

Penney, David W.
1992 *Art of the American Indian Frontier: The Chandler-Pohrt Collection.* Seattle, WA: University of Washington Press.

Phillips, Ruth B. and Dale Idiens
1994 "A Casket of Savage Curiosities": Eighteenth-Century Objects from North-Eastern North America in the Farquharson Collection. *Journal of the History of Collections* 6(1): 21–33.

Skinner, Alanson B.
1921 *Material Culture of the Menomini.* Indian Notes and Monographs 20. New York, NY.

Sotheby's
1988 *Important American Indian Art Including Property from the Collection of Mr. and Mrs. Fred Boschan.* Sale number 5785 "MARIA." New York, NY.
1994 *Fine American Indian Art.* Sale number 6567 "ACOMA." New York, NY.

Sturtevant, William C.
1973 Museums as Anthropological Data Banks. In: A. Redfield (ed.), *Anthropology Beyond the University* (Southern Anthropological Society Proceedings 7, Athens, GA), 40–55.

Tooker, Elizabeth
1994 *Lewis H. Morgan on Iroquois Material Culture.* Tucson, AZ—London: The University of Arizona Press.

Turner, Geoffrey
1992 *Indians of North America.* [1979] New York, NY: Sterling.

Vatter, Ernst
1925 Ein bemaltes Büffelfell und andere seltene amerikanische Ethnographica im Städtischen Völkerkundemuseum zu Frankfurt a.M. *Abhandlungen zur Anthropologie, Ethnologie und Urgeschichte* 2: 75–112.

Vigorelli, Leonardo
1987a *Gli Oggetti Indiani Raccolti da G. Costantino Beltrami.* Bergamo: Civico Museo E. Caffi.
1987b Gli Oggetti Indiani della Raccolta Beltrami. Un Catalogo. *Rivista del Museo Civico di Scienze Naturali "Enrico Caffi"* 11: 9–133.

Völger, Gisela
1976 *Indianer Nordamerikas, Zirkumpolare Völker.* Kataloge des Deutschen Ledermuseums 4. Offenbach: Deutsches Ledermuseum.

Index